Small Business

AN ENTREPRENEUR'S PLAN

Second Edition

Small Business

AN ENTREPRENEUR'S PLAN

Second Edition

J. D. RYAN

Irvine Valley College

LEE A. ECKERT

Saddleback College

ROBERT J. RAY

Chapman College

HARCOURT BRACE JOVANOVICH, PUBLISHERS

San Diego   New York   Chicago   Austin   Washington, D.C.
London   Sydney   Tokyo   Toronto

Preface

This book—with its 78 "action steps"—is your personal roadmap to success in small business. Beginning with Action Step 1, the book will guide you through the bustling marketplace—through trends, target customers, and promotion; through shopping malls, spreadsheets, and hushed, gray bank buildings; through independent businesses that are up for sale and through franchise opportunities—all the way to your own small business. Along the way you'll meet fascinating people, you'll have fantastic adventures, and you'll have some fun. Furthermore, by completing the action steps, you will be writing your own ticket for small business success: a complete Business Plan that clearly evaluates and illuminates your opportunity for entrepreneurial success.

ON THE WAY

You will start your journey by taking a careful look at yourself and your skills. What work pleases you? How secure is your present job? How long does it take you to get organized? What internal drives make you an entrepreneur?

Next, you'll step back and look at the marketplace. What's hot? What's cooling down? Where are the long lines forming? What are people buying at the supermarket? How is it packaged? What distinguishes the up-and-comers from the down-and-outers?

Then you will brainstorm a business that will fit into an industry niche. You toss numbers around—to get a feel for how they turn into money—and you keep having fun.

Then it will be time to profile your target customer, assess the competition, figure out some clever promotional strategies, and scout locations. By that time you will be almost halfway through this book, and you will know where you're going and feel that you're in control of your own destiny.

That's when you can get serious. **Chapter 8** will help you to look ahead to the day you open the doors of your own business. It will help you anticipate trouble spots and problems that could slow you down, or even cripple your effort. **Chapter 9** continues this line of probing by helping you pull some numbers together. Using spreadsheets, you'll get the figures out of the shoebox and onto a computer so that you can really crunch them.

By then, you will have completed more than forty action steps and it'll be time to leave academia for a little while to see what's out there in the real world of small business. The easiest way to learn about the real world is to investigate some businesses that are on the market. Find out why the sellers are selling. What are they asking? How much are they asking for the goodwill they've established? A business up for sale is like a laboratory in which you can investigate for free. We will remind you often to take along a notebook but to leave your emotions and your checkbook at home.

Chapter 10, "Buying a Business," may be a splash of cold water on your face; it will make you aware of what's ahead. Remember, however, that this is only one doorway to small business. The other two—franchising and starting up a new business—are discussed later, after you've taken the time to think about raising money, the best legal form for your business, building a winning team, and the contents of your "entrepreneurial toolkit."

By now you have probably gathered that the twin thrusts of this approach to entrepreneurship are *planning* and *momentum*. Without a plan, you are doomed to failure; without momentum, you are doomed to boredom. The plan will give you direction, and momentum will keep you moving.

After you have pulled your toolkit together, you need to consider the other door-ways to small business: franchises and engineering your own start-up. If you are a neophyte entrepreneur just testing the waters of small business for the first time, you will certainly want to examine franchises—several of them—to see what they offer. **Chapter 15** will help you do this. For the first-time entrepreneur who is accustomed to the power, image, and "family" feeling of a large corporation, franchising can provide a helpful security blanket. On the other hand, if you are an entrepreneur with more experience, you should consider the option of Doorway Three: your own start-up, built from the stuff of your dreams and your personal strengths.

Your Complete Business Plan

By the time you reach **Chapter 16** you will have gathered enough material to write a complete Business Plan for showcasing your business to the world—that is, to bankers, vendors and lenders, venture capitalists, credit managers, key employees, your family, and your friends. Your finished plan will be a blueprint for your business. It will provide a walk-through of your industry, generate excitement in potential lenders, demonstrate your competence as a thoughtful planner, and underline the reasons customers are going to clamor for your product or service. Your plan will also serve you as a means of channeling your creative energies.

Let's think about that for a moment.

One reason you're reading this book is that you're creative. You like to build, to pull things together, to plant seeds and watch things grow, to develop projects, to produce. When your mind is cooking, you probably come up with more ideas than you can handle. *That* is when you need a plan. A plan will help you keep your entrepreneurial energies on track while the creative steam rises. Perhaps you've always dreamed of working for yourself—being your own boss. Well, you can have that dream if you're *prepared*.

Read this book and put yourself through the paces of the action steps. The action steps will help you produce a Business Plan that will get you where you want to go. Starting with your dreams of success, move through the book at your own pace. You will wind up at the end with a street-smart Business Plan and some great memories.

Visualize Your Business Plan

Figures A, B, and C portray a complete Business Plan as a pie chart, with each piece of the "pie" representing a part of the plan. Each chapter of this book is designed to help you complete one or more of the parts of your Business Plan. You will notice that a pie illustration appears at the beginning of each chapter. Those pies show which part (or parts) of the plan is addressed by the action steps in each chapter. The pies will also help you to track your progress as an entrepreneur; when all the pieces of the pie are in place, your Business Plan will be completed and you'll be ready to open your doors.

ABOUT THE ACTION STEPS

Our roadmap to success in small business is comprised of 78 action steps. Completing these steps should *quadruple* your chances of reaching your business goals. You see,

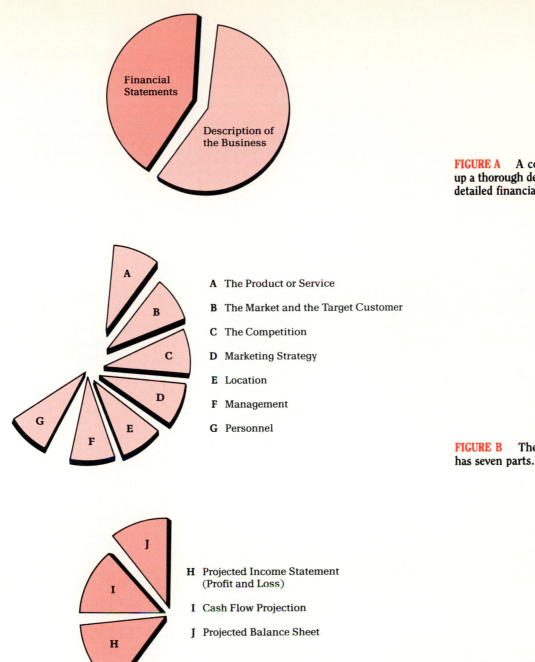

FIGURE A A complete Business Plan backs up a thorough description of the business with detailed financial statements.

A The Product or Service

B The Market and the Target Customer

C The Competition

D Marketing Strategy

E Location

F Management

G Personnel

FIGURE B The description of the business has seven parts.

H Projected Income Statement (Profit and Loss)

I Cash Flow Projection

J Projected Balance Sheet

FIGURE C Three financial statements show that the business will succeed.

the world of business is like a maze—a series of twisting corridors and paths—and the action steps are designed to thread you through the maze, from A to B, to C, and so on.

Each action step is an exercise that accompanies our explanation of a particular portion of the "maze." In fact, the steps grew naturally out of the material of this book. For example, in Chapter 1 we profile Nancy Tremaine, a literature major who became successful in small business because she dug into her skills repertoire to find out what she was good at. Nancy's case is tied to Action Step 8, "Inventory Your Personal Skills."

Model Action Steps

To help you visualize some of the action steps, we have reprinted model action steps at the ends of Chapters 1 through 8. These eight action steps were completed by a student named Pete Craigmoe. When he took our entrepreneurship course, Pete was working for the Santa Fe Railroad and dreaming of taking early retirement so that he could work on his novel. Pete used the steps to focus on a small business that would create corporate newsletters. He now spends thirty percent of his time making money with desktop publishing and the other seventy percent writing his novel.

Some Advice

If you are a beginning entrepreneur, you'll probably need to complete most of the action steps. Since searching for a winning business idea is a mind game, a hefty percentage of the early steps ask you to brainstorm. These steps will teach you to trust yourself and to see things with "new eyes." Some of the steps involve library research. Others ask you to hit the streets, look around, ask questions, find out what's going on in the world.

If you are an experienced entrepreneur with one or more small business enterprises behind you, you're probably in a hurry. In that case, you might want to check the **List of Action Steps** on page 335 and focus on those steps that will complete the picture for you.

Whether you are a beginner or not, we suggest that you take the time to write a complete Business Plan. We cover that, from start to finish, in Chapter 16, "Pulling the Plan Together."

THIS BOOK IS FOR *YOU*

The book can be used on at least two levels. One level is fast-track. That's for the action-oriented entrepreneur who wants to get on with the start-up. The other level is slower, and it's for the creative dreamer who can afford to take the time to savor the atmosphere of the business arena.

As you're reading the book, keep pencil and paper close by so that you can jot down ideas. Get used to brainstorming. Also, it's not a bad idea to carry a cassette recorder in your car so that you can record ideas that occur to you while you're driving. The inspiration that you get from a freeway billboard four hundred miles from home might be the seed from which your winning business will grow.

Our point is that this is *your* book. Use it in whatever way suits your needs. Make notes in the margins; use a "high-lighting" pen. Chuckle your way through some **case studies**. Complete some or all of the **Study Guide** exercises. Check out the materials in the **Appendixes**. Use the **margin definitions** to build your business vocabulary. If you need more information about the topics we discuss, the **References** section at the end of each chapter will direct you to it. Use the book as a handbook or as a textbook, or as both. It's designed for a wide range of creative, energetic people who want to own their own business, and someplace in that range of people is *you*. Good luck!

ACKNOWLEDGMENTS

We couldn't have written this book without a lot of help from a lot of people. The book is built on a foundation of case studies, and the action steps are taken from real-life tactics in the marketplace. Many entrepreneurs have succeeded out there in the real world, and we've just tried to tell you how they've done it.

Our thanks go to:
Professor Paul Menges, *Cumberland College*;
Professor James Moreau, *Rock Valley College*;
Professor John Seely, *Tulsa Junior College*;
Greg Beck, *president of the UCI/Orange County Venture Forum*;
Professor Mort Meiers *of Lake Tahoe Community College*;
Professor Carol Holcomb *of Spokane Falls Community College*;
Cheryl Moore, *president of "Something Moore"*;
Terri Baas, *president of Candela Corporation*;
Steve Waddell *of the U.S. Small Business Administration*;
Clare Thain, *publisher of* Entrepreneur *magazine*;
John Connors *of Plante, Strauss, Vanderburgh & Connors*;
Al Slattery, *president of ASA/Advertising*;
Chuck Goodson and Tom Herndon *of Dana Niguel Bank*;
Rosemary Utesch and Jeanette Cox *of Mega Travel*; and
Bill Webster, *president of Star Software Systems.*

We are grateful to Mickey Cox, Carole Reagle, and Bill Teague of Harcourt Brace Jovanovich for their help in shaping this work into a book that we are proud of. We also thank the other members of our HBJ bookteam. They are Don Fujimoto, Leslie Leland, Paulette Russo, Diane Southworth, Linda Wild, Cheryl Solheid, and Jan Duffala.

Last but not least, we thank Barbara, Priscilla, and Margo for their constant support and understanding.

J. D. RYAN
LEE A. ECKERT
ROBERT J. RAY

Contents

1
Doorways to Small Business
3

2
The Big Picture: Charting Trends for Your Small Business
25

3
Power Marketing
53

Profiling the Target Customer

71

Reading the Competition

95

Promotion: Connecting with the Customer

111

Location

131

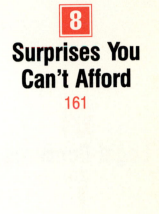

Surprises You Can't Afford
161

Numbers and Shoebox Accounting
175

Buying a Business
195

Buying a Franchise
275

16

Pulling the Plan Together
289

STUDY GUIDE

Small Business

AN ENTREPRENEUR'S PLAN

Second Edition

FIGURE 1.1   Before you begin to write your Business Plan, investigate the doorways to small business.

1

Doorways to Small Business

LEARNING OBJECTIVES

■ To understand where business is headed in the next 5–10 years. ■ To learn how you can fit in, survive, and prosper in business. ■ To brainstorm a clear picture of success in small business. ■ To be able to identify successful and unsuccessful businesses in your community. ■ To discover your personal strengths. ■ To improve your information-gathering skills. ■ To expand your knowledge of small business through interviewing small business owners.

ACTION STEP PREVIEW

1   Assess your job security.

2   Look into your business future by drawing a "future wheel."

3   Brainstorm three new businesses capitalizing on the "cocooning" trend.

4   Assess your interests and abilities.

5   Assess your accomplishments.

6   Organize your information.

7   Survey your friends about success.

8   Inventory your skills.

9   Investigate the marketplace for opportunities with "new eyes."

Life is short, and you only go around once. So you want to make sure you're getting what you want, having fun, making money, and being the best person you can be.

How do you do that?

Some people do it by going into business for themselves. If *you* are thinking about owning your own business, this book is written for you.

Try this line of thought: What do you want to be doing in 1994? In 2001? What's the best course of action for you right now? What might be the best business for you? What are your strengths? This chapter will address these questions.

This is the age of the entrepreneur. There are almost 17 million small businesses out there. Each year, more than 600,000 new corporations are started. Most new jobs in the private sector are being created by firms with fewer than twenty employees. Yes, it's a great time for the entrepreneur. You could have the time of your life. Come along with us!

KNOCKING AT THE ENTREPRENEURIAL DOORS

There are three doorways to small business ownership (Figure 1.2). Doorway one is buying an ongoing business: you look around, find a business you like, and buy it. Sounds pretty easy, doesn't it? A business broker will make it sound even easier, so beware.

Doorway two is buying a franchise: you find a logo you like, one with national visibility, and you buy it. In exchange for your money, the franchisor supplies you with inventory, advice, and a product or service that is well known in the marketplace. Sounds pretty easy, doesn't it? A slick franchisor will make it sound even easier.

Doorway three, our favorite, is starting a new business—a business that is compatible with your interests and skills, one that is backed up by careful research that shows strong customer need. Entering the world of small business by *any* of these doorways demands a carefully designed **Business Plan**—words and numbers on paper that will guide you through the gaps, the competition, the bureaucracies, the products, the services. The 78 action steps presented in this book will show you exactly how to write a Business Plan and how to have fun as an entrepreneur!

Business Plan
a blueprint for your business start-up or expansion

What about These Three Doorways?

Sixty-seven percent of all entrepreneurs enter the world of small business by buying an existing business or a franchise operation. When these people have gained some experience and confidence, many of them decide to start a totally new business from scratch. However, few entrepreneurs are happy with just one business. They start up. They sell. They start up again. And they become experts at writing Business Plans.

No matter which doorway you choose, you're going to need a Business Plan. If you buy an ongoing business, you may inherit the seller's Business Plan. It's still smart to write one of your own, however. Ask the seller (again and again, if necessary) for the data you need for writing your own plan. That way, before you commit to purchase, you can check out those claims of huge potential profit and endless goodwill for yourself.

If you buy a franchise, you'll be buying a Business Plan from the franchisor. Until you see it, however, you won't know for certain if you'll need to prepare one of your own as well. If you don't understand the franchisor's plan, by all means write your

FIGURE 1.2   There are three doorways to owning a small business. Doorway One is buying an ongoing business. Doorway Two is buying a franchise. Doorway Three is starting up a brand-new business.

own. Writing a Business Plan is a lot cheaper than plunking money down on a franchise that may not work.

If you start your own business, a Business Plan is a must, an *absolute must.* That plan stands between you and failure.

What's Happened to the Forty-Hour Week, the Golden Parachute, and the Gold Watch?

Good question. Just how serious are you about entering the bustling arena of small business? Can't you get a job—executive recruiters call it a "position"—in "big business"? How much pressure is there on you to travel the entrepreneurial road through one of these small business doorways?

Let's say that you decide not to go into small business after all. Let's say you discover some things about yourself as you read this book, perhaps that you don't thrive on competition; that you think a sixty-hour work week is madness; that you get edgy when you think about mortgaging your house for start-up money. And so you decide entrepreneurship is too much work for too little gain. You read the book— enough of it, anyway, to get the picture about entrepreneuring. You try some Action Steps—you find them stimulating, and fun, but they take time away from your weekend, the beach, the movies. You have this dream of wearing a suit to work and driving a snappy sports car. You see yourself working a forty-hour week and when Friday comes you hop into your snappy car and peel off for a great weekend and not—repeat, not—taking work home with you.

So you close the book on small business planning with a snap and snatch up the classifieds and start hunting for a *real job,* a job with a corporation, a job with a future. And in your mind is this scenario: "Okay, enough of entrepreneuring. It's too hard to pronounce. It's impossible to spell. I'm going to work for a big company, something visible, something with clout and prestige and a logo and great perks."

Good thinking, but is that scenario still realistic? Or is it a misty dream out of the distant fifties?

What's Happening to Big Business?

Big business, once the backbone of America, is in trouble. Takeovers continue. Mergers loom. Hostile suitors, wearing three-piece suits and Italian shoes, lurk in the underbrush at the edge of the marketplace. John Naisbitt predicted most of what's happening today in *Megatrends* (published in 1982 and still a good read). He noted that:

labor unions are shrinking, both in size and in power. At the same time, they are becoming more security-conscious. In their negotiations with General Motors, the United Auto Workers opted for a job-security package rather than the wage hike offered by GM.

manufacturing that used to be done on U.S. soil is now being handled offshore. Steel, once an American staple, is being produced in Korea and Brazil.

foreign goods dominate U.S. markets. Look around in your own house, your own garage. Is your television a Sony, a Hitachi, or an RCA? (RCA's are made offshore. RCA Records is owned by a German communications conglomerate.) Is your car a Toyota, Honda, Volkswagen, Volvo, BMW, or Mercedes?

foreign capital is pouring into the U.S. When the dollar began to drop in value, the stream of capital widened. For example, in 1985, Nippon Kokan paid just under 300 million dollars for 50 percent of National Steel. Alcan of Canada owns Atlantic Richfield's aluminum operations in Kentucky and Indiana. In 1984 Nestlé of Switzerland took over Carnation for 3 billion dollars. Foreign companies are buying U.S. banks and financial services firms, and according to the *Wall Street Journal,* the hottest U.S. export is our expertise in mergers and acquisitions—that is, how to load, fire, aim, and shoot yourself in the foot.

The world is changing, and you must assess the changes and act accordingly. You want to survive. You want to have fun. You want your life to have meaning. You want substance and honesty and security and success. So, in order to decide which road to take, do some research and you keep your eyes open. You will come up with some insights on the direction of big business. To get you started, read the list of trends found by researcher and author John Naisbitt in Box 1.1.

The Direction of Big Business

In some respects the direction of big business is obvious. In other respects we can only speculate. Consider these things:

> In the seventies, big business did not create new jobs; the new jobs were created by small business.

BOX 1.1   Naisbitt's Megashifts

In his best-selling book *Megatrends,* John Naisbitt identified ten major trends, which he calls transformations or "megashifts." According to Naisbitt, we are moving:

1. from an industrial society to an information society.
2. from forced technology to a balance between high tech and "high touch."
3. from a national economy to a world economy. [Consider the mergers and joint ventures of U.S. car makers with those of Europe and Japan.]
4. from short-term cover-ups to long-term planning.
5. from centralized control to more local control via states, counties, cities, neighborhoods, and private associations.
6. from institutional help to self-help (health, wellness, education, the entrepreneurial explosion in business, and so on).
7. from representative democracy to participatory democracy (independent voters, new political parties, tax initiatives, referenda, consumerism as marketplace control).
8. from hierarchies (corporate and government pyramids) to networking (clustering together, sharing, "the horizontal link.")
9. from North (the Frost Belt) to South (the Sunbelt), especially to the West, Southwest, and Florida. [See the *Wall Street Journal's* weekly Section-II columns on regions and real estate for up-dates and refinements in the North–South megashift.]
10. from either/or to multiple-option choices. Doing your own thing is now not only possible, but also feasible and profitable. [Consider the 19 million singles, more than 750 models of cars and trucks available in the U.S., the rise in births to women over 30, the explosions in art and religion, designer fruits and vegetables. All of these spell opportunity for the eager entrepreneur.]

Naisbitt gives some advice on what to do with a trend once you see it. He writes, "Trends, like horses, are easier to ride in the direction they are going."

In the eighties, big business began to shrink. The business media called it "downsizing."

In the mid-eighties, services (banking, insurance, real estate, airlines and travel, etc.) accounted for 70 percent of the jobs in the U.S. and 60 percent of the gross national product.

The Information Age, almost unimaginable ten years ago, is upon us as communication networks span the globe. Marvin Cetron, author of *The Future of American Business,* predicts that by the year 2000 half of all service jobs will be in information processing.

Robots are doing more and more work in factories and offices. Computers are everywhere. Need we wonder what will happen to middle management when top managers learn to operate desktop computers?

Retraining is in everyone's future, whether he or she is a people-person or a thing-person. Cetron predicts that engineers and technicians will have to be retrained every five to ten years, depending on how quickly things become obsolete.

Much of the burden for this retraining will be on the educational establishment. Think about where your state taxes now go—roads, parks, state police, legislators, *education.* Will education be the next big business?

Crystal-Ball Gazing into the Past

Each year, *Fortune* magazine publishes a list of the 500 largest firms in the nation. As early as April 1984, *Fortune* came to Naisbitt's conclusion that the giants no longer create new jobs. In fact, during the decade of the seventies, the word among the *Fortune* 500 was *retrenchment*—cutting back—and that's what they did. They cut employment 10%, from 15.5 million jobs to 14 million. At the same time, sales per employee rose 11.5% during the seventies.

Impressive? Yes; survival always is. But while the 500 were laying off employees, the nation's small businesses created 6 million new jobs. This, also, is impressive.

There are now more than 16 million small businesses in the United States, which make up 97% of all nonfarm businesses. Approximately 58% of all new inventions come from small business.

Why do these new firms survive and thrive? Because they are founded by people who are not afraid of risk. Because they can effect changes quickly, without going through umpteen layers of managers and vice-presidents. Because they are in touch with their customers. Because they are not huge.

THE AGE OF THE ENTREPRENEUR

The business world is changing faster and faster so what do you do? Life is not what you thought it would be, so what do you do? The big firm you wanted to work for is now closed. The job you trained for is obsolete. What do you do?

Hang in there! You live in a great country. And that greatness is not a matter of size alone. Smaller companies, those with fewer than 500 employees, employ almost half the workers in the U.S. New start-ups create the new jobs. These jobs are created by an absolutely unique partnership—the marriage of money and work. The money comes from our unique system of venture-capital financing. The work comes from the driving force of the **entrepreneur**.

entrepreneur
a visionary self-starter who loves the adventure of a new enterprise

Pioneering is alive and well in America. In 1988, 700,000 new corporations were founded. If you add partnerships and sole proprietorships, experts estimate that 1.3 million new enterprises were added to the U.S. economy *each year.* In the last decade of the twentieth century, entrepreneurship should blossom and grow. The fields— biotechnology, semiconductors, computers, telecomputing—are ripe and ready for harvest, so plant early. The nineties will certainly be the Age of the Entrepreneur.

To hammer home our point, we want you to complete Action Step 1.

Do you really have job security? Are you sure? Scan the last three or four issues of *Business Week* or two to three weeks of the *Wall Street Journal.* Did you notice any companies announcing a layoff or plant closing? Did you read of a company president being fired? What would happen to your job if the head of your company died?

You may have had a good job for twenty years. You may belong to a union. But if the managers of your company are not doing a good job, you could be out of work tomorrow. Ask around. Talk to other workers in other jobs. Think about the deal the UAW made with GM.

How secure is a job in big business? Derek Campbell's experience is not uncommon.

> "After five years of faithful service as a pilot, I was furloughed by the airline that employed me, so I had time to look around and think about my future. One of the books I read was *Megatrends.* It was like seeing a lighthouse beacon after a long, dark sea voyage."

When Derek Campbell got furloughed the third time from his pilot's job with a major airline, he was frustrated and angry at the world. He had done his work and loved flying the big planes, but the airline industry was in chaos. Size didn't make any difference. Even the giants were in trouble.

"Three furloughs and you're out," Derek said. "For me, that was the handwriting on the wall. I was fed up with working for someone else, tired of being a puppet on someone else's string. It was time to call a few tunes of my own."

Like a lot of entrepreneurs, Derek was a workaholic. His first move was to make a list of his past accomplishments, his strengths, his skills. He had a bachelor's degree in engineering, an MBA, and several years' experience as an instructor in the Marines. And he'd always been interested in computers.

Derek hired himself out as a computer consultant. His work was largely on the phone, making contacts, locating prospects. Then he'd go out for a location visit and size up the problems.

"Literally everyone on my list could have used some kind of computer," Derek recalls. "And that's what gave me the idea for a computer school. There was, on the one hand, a crying need for more efficiency. And on the other hand, there was a lot of fear and misunderstanding about computers in general and about small computers in particular."

So Derek kept his consulting business going while he organized a founder's team to help him brainstorm strategies for opening a computer school. It was an interesting mix of people: two lawyers, another expilot, a woman banker, a marketeer from big business, a numbers wizard, an expert in corporate mergers.

Derek used his microcomputer to create a stunning eighty-five-page Business Plan. The plan helped him get a line of credit from a local bank for $40,000. And nine months after the idea had first hit him, Derek and his team began offering their first class, Computer Fundamentals.

"Planning makes all the difference," Derek says. "The minute we opened the doors, we had business. That told us we had targeted our industry, and our particular segment, accurately. Of course, if you don't stay in there punching, don't keep your image right out there, business tends to fall off. But gap-analysis helped us find our foothold in the marketplace—computer education—and it's paying off fast. We're in the information business to stay. We're not pushing hardware or software. We're here to teach people how to help themselves by learning the vast capabilities of the microcomputer."

Derek leans back, clasps his hands behind his head, smiles, and adds, "And the best part of all, it's great fun!"

ACTION STEP 1

Assess your job security.

On a sheet of paper write down your present job title, the firm or organization you work for, how long you've worked there, how many hours a week you work, and the three tasks that take up most of your time.

Are you on the phone a lot? Do you shuffle paper? Do you spend time in meetings? Does your job put you on the road more than once a week? How do the three tasks you listed square with your job title?

Now, rank your job security on a 1–10 scale. How easily could you be replaced? If you currently are not working, rank the job security of your mother or father, brother or sister, friend or relative.

Why did Derek Campbell succeed? He was successful because he:

1. was able to turn adversity into opportunity.
2. knew his strengths—engineering, teaching, computers.
3. saw a gap in the marketplace.
4. knew where to go for information to develop a Business Plan. (The plan proved on paper that his computer school would earn him a handsome return on his investment.)
5. was ready for self-employment.

Derek Campbell became a beneficiary of the Information Age.

Plotting Your Future

What Derek Campbell had to reckon with was change. Although change is occurring at a much faster rate than it was a generation ago, projecting future needs is easier than you might image. There are clues that point the way.

Two thinkers who can help guide you into the future are John Naisbitt (see Box 1.1) and Faith Popcorn, the founder of BrainReserve, a trend-analysis firm based in Manhattan. Box 1.2 summarizes some of the trends Faith Popcorn has noted. See also Box 1.3. The "future wheel" in Figure 1.3 illustrates an imaginary combination of Naisbitt's idea of "the electronic cottage" with Faith Popcorn's concept of "cocooning." We call this combination "the enchanted fortress."

Briefly, the "enchanted fortress" is where an imaginary family of the future lives, works, and plays. It is a world within the world. The family eats here, bathes, exercises, gets tanned, watches movies, does their banking electronically, and is protected from

---

BOX 1.2   **Faith Popcorn's Predictions**

Faith Popcorn is the founder of BrainReserve, a trend-analysis firm based in Manhattan. Her job is forecasting the tastes and whims of American shoppers for such clients as Campbell's Soup, Eastman Kodak, and Pilsbury. Popcorn coined the term *cocooning* for the recent trend of people to retreat to the safety of their homes. The trend is the result of our collective desire to insulate the home from impending danger.

Here are some of BrainReserve's predictions for the 1990s:

"Mom foods"—such home-style foods as mashed potatoes, meatloaf, chicken potpie

nostalgia, led by the older population

desire for fitness and health that recognizes that a person can be too thin

walking, rather than jogging, for exercise

attractive aging

personalized products

"we-ness"—The extreme interest in the self of the "Me Decade" will be replaced by a concern for the environment and a return to old-fashioned virtues and values.

"cocooning"—smaller, nestlike living areas; spa bathrooms; more home deliveries of take-out food; catalog shopping; home media centers; the search for the perfect environment with small, efficient, and multifunctional equipment

quality—willingness to pay more for premium brands

gardening—will become the number-one leisure activity

BOX 1.3   The "Cocooning" of Magazine Readers

The fastest-growing consumer magazines according to the February 1988 issue of *Adweek:*

Better Homes and Gardens
Metropolitan Home
1001 Home Ideas
Country Living
Country Home
Gourmet

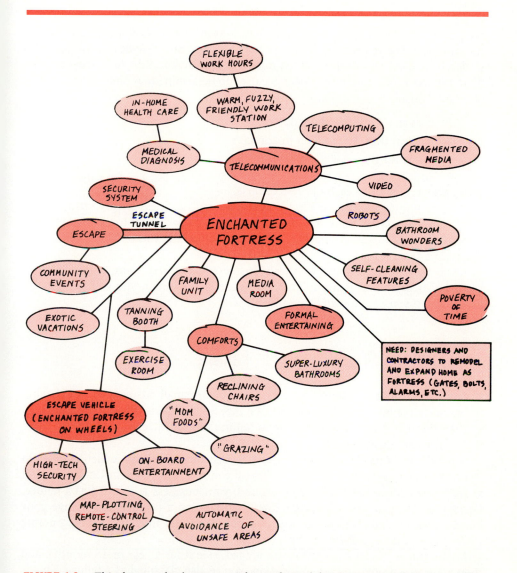

FIGURE 1.3   This future wheel portrays "the enchanted fortress"—a combination of "the electronic cottage" and a "cocoon." It was developed through brainstorming. Refer to it as you brainstorm in Action Step 3.

ACTION STEP 2

Look into your business future by drawing a future wheel.

Get a pencil and paper and spend ten minutes modifying our future wheel (Figure 1.3) into your own enchanted fortress. There is no such thing as a wrong idea or a wrong direction. Just close your eyes for a moment and allow your imagination to take over. See how many additional lines and balloons you can connect. This will also introduce you to brainstorming. You can predict the future as well as anyone else; all you need to do is mesh information with your imagination and go for it!

ACTION STEP 3

Brainstorm three new businesses capitalizing on the "cocooning" trend.

Open your eyes.

Get a pencil and paper. Write the word *cocoon* in the center of the page and draw a mind map using the trends that radiate out from it. Repeat the same mind mapping process you used in Action Step 2. Allow yourself to get a little far out; release your creativity. Refer to Figures 1.3 and 2.4 for inspiration.

Mind mapping allows you to plot a chain of ideas graphically without losing your train of thought. If you are mind mapping with a group, use a large writing board or poster board to encourage participation.

intruders by an invisible wall. The enchanted fortress is a personal "warm fuzzy." It reunites the family after two decades of fragmentation.

There are only two problems with this fantasy life: how to afford it, and cabin fever. Both these problems are handled by leaving the enchanted fortress and returning to the world outside. How do you leave? Well, you go out through an escape tunnel to your car. And what is your car? It's a cocoon on wheels, packed with electronic gadgets, and designed to be as warm and fuzzy as your home.

Action Step 2 gives you the opportunity to stretch your imagination—to fantasize your own "enchanted fortress." After you've designed your dream home, go on to Action Step 3 and explore the small-business implications of "cocooning."

What Is a Small Business?

Businesses are classified by a coding system known as *Standard Industrial Classification Codes.* You've probably heard the abbreviation: SIC. (We deal with SIC codes in depth in the next chapter.) When a person goes to the SBA to borrow money, three criteria linked to the SIC codes are used to determine how small is small; that is, a *small* business is one that

1. does not dominate the industry,
2. has less than $10 million in annual sales, and
3. has fewer than 1,000 employees.

There are exceptions to each of these criteria.

For the purposes of this book, we define a small business as any venture with spirit, any business you want to start, any idea you want to chase into the marketplace. It may be part-time, something you do at home, something you try alone, something you need a team for.

If you prove it out on paper—in your Business Plan—first, there's a good chance you'll be successful. This means that if you are going to fail, you will fail only on paper. And if you *plan* to *win,* you probably will.

The Myth of Small Business Failure

It seems you can't talk to anyone on the street about small business without having the subject of failure come up. After all, the U.S. Small Business Administration tells us that 55 percent of all small businesses fail in their first five years. Actually, these SBA figures are misleading.

The SBA bases its conclusions on the U.S. Census of Business, which is taken in years that end in a 2 or a 7. This means that if you start a business in 1987 you aren't *at the same address* when 1992 rolls around, your business is counted as a failure. Or, if you start out as a sole proprietor, then take on a partner and change your business name, and then merge with a corporation and move into the corporate GHQ, you will also go down on the charts as a failure.

Furthermore, if you latch onto a trendy fad, ride it for a year or 18 months, and then take your profits and go on vacation, you're also classified as a failure. This is how the SBA statistics report the business success of Mr. Dahl, the man who created the Pet Rock back in the seventies. He identified a fad and produced a product to take advantage of it. When the fad wound down, Mr. Dahl took his profits and left the marketplace. That's not failure. That's smart marketing!

If You Fail to Plan, You're Planning to Fail!

To get the maximum benefit from this book, you'll need to go beyond the classroom walls and experience the risks and joys of entrepreneurship. You'll also read a lot, of course, and you'll construct your own Business Plan.

The action steps will help you with your Plan. They'll also give you energy boosts that will help you maintain momentum. If you'd like to see some examples of how action steps have been handled by one student, turn to the appendixes at the end of some of the chapters of this book.

You've looked at job security, and you've tried a future wheel. Now do Action Step 4, a sort of a self-assessment guide to the world of entrepreneuring. It'll help you learn some things about yourself.

Then, we'd like you to meet Judd O'Herlihy.

At forty, Judd O'Herlihy was unhappy with his dead-end job as branch manager of a major electrical manufacturer. He was making good money, but that did not make his job more bearable. Judd needed change.

Seeking a fresh direction for his life, he registered for a career guidance class at a local community college. At the second session the instructor–counselor gave the class some aptitude tests. Then the instructor asked them to list every accomplishment in their entire lives that gave them a good feeling.

Judd hated writing, and he resisted the process at first. However, his list soon began shaping up:

1. ball monitor, third grade
2. 2nd prize, paper drive, fourth grade
3. pole vault, new high school record, age 16
4. organized Lion's Club pancake breakfast, 5,000 served, senior in high school

He was playing with the idea, making fun of it, when he remembered something else from his high school years. He'd bought old cars and fixed them up. The first car was an Alfa Romeo 916. He'd bought it for $800 and resold it, after the fix-up, for $1500. Remembering the cars made him think of other accomplishments. He'd been an Eagle Scout, a decorated war hero, a carpenter and cabinetmaker, and a fair trumpet player. After he and his wife bought a house, he'd designed and contracted to build their swimming pool. After catching the spirit of the exercise, he filled up three pages. But only one thing on his list held his attention—building that swimming pool.

The instructor asked Judd to explain why this was so high on his list.

"Well," Judd said, thinking back. "We wanted a pool for the kids, so I asked several pool contractors for bids. I have five kids. I wanted a bigger-than-average pool so they wouldn't be fighting over territory. My specs were simple. I wanted a 40-foot pool, 30 feet wide, with 12 feet under the diving board. My pool didn't fit the specs of any of the contractors. They had standard plans, with only eight and a half feet under the diving board. One contractor even told me that to go deeper would violate the city code. So since their plans didn't fit my yard, and since they had knocked each other pretty hard trying to get my business, I lost confidence in the whole crowd. Only one contractor offered to do the pool. It would cost double, he said, and he was certain I wouldn't like it."

The instructor asked Judd what he did then.

"I was discouraged, but summer was coming and my kids kept pressing me. So I said, 'What's the big deal with a swimming pool? It's just a concrete hole in the ground attached to some plumbing.' So I looked in the yellow pages and located a civil engineer who considered himself a pool specialist who got turned on by out-of-the-ordinary designs. For less than $300, the engineer pulled all the permits and showed me how to find the best subcontractors.

"My friends and neighbors tried to dissuade me," Judd went on, "but I collected bids anyway. I got bids from diggers, steel riggers, electricians, tile people, gunnite and

ACTION STEP 4

Assess your interests and abilities.

Do you have what it takes to make it in small business? To find out, profile yourself as an entrepreneur. You won't be a perfect fit, because there is no such thing. Nonetheless, you will get much more out of this book if you will mentally immerse yourself in the role of the successful entrepreneur. Fantasize yourself in a new and exciting venture. Entrepreneurship isn't for everyone, and you will probably need some help along the way. Keep your mind open and your pencil sharp. The opportunities are unlimited.

This action step will help you to assess your abilities and interests and get your creative juices flowing. Complete as much as you can in the spaces provided, and feel free to write things in the margins. You will probably come back to this action step several times.

How would your best friend describe you? _____

How would your worst enemy describe you? _____

How would you describe yourself? _____

How much money do you need to survive for six months? _____

For twelve months? _____

How much money can you earn in your present position in three years? _____ Five years? _____

What is the maximum potential of your earning power? _____

Are you comfortable taking moderate risks? _____

Are you constantly looking for newer and better ways to do things? _____

What can you do better than most people? _____

Where do you live now? (Describe your home, residential area, geographical area, amenities, etc.) _____

In what way would you like to change any of the above? _____

Do you enjoy being in control? _____

How do you spend your leisure time? _____

Do you look forward more often than backward? _____

How important is winning to you? _____

Who do you know whose strengths might complement some of your weaknesses? _____

concrete contractors. When I tallied them up, I discovered I could get my pool—with the 12-foot depth I wanted—at about half the cost of the lowest bid from the big-time pool firms.

"So I built the pool myself. Along the way, every subcontractor showed me how to save money. I photographed the process and kept detailed notes. In less than a month, the pool was finished. It was perfect. The neighbors came around asking questions, and I helped them subcontract their pools. I even wrote a 16-page booklet, 'How to Contract Your Own Concrete Pool and Save 50%.' I advertised the booklet in the pool sections of some newspapers and sold 2,000 copies for $9.95 each. My cost, including mailing, was 96 cents. We got the pool we wanted, and the profit from the booklet paid for it twice."

"A great story, Mr. O'Herlihy!" said the instructor. "But tell me. If this was so rewarding, why didn't you go on building?"

"Too busy," Judd said.

"That's too bad," said the instructor. "With talent like *that,* you should *make* time."

Later that night when Judd was about to fall asleep, he was still glowing with the memory of his pool-building. He woke up his wife. "Honey!" he said. "Wake up. I'm going to build us a *house*!"

"Yes, dear," said Linda O'Herlihy. "Now go to sleep."

The memory of a single past accomplishment changed Judd's life. With new confidence, he quit his job and started building rental units. Today, Judd O'Herlihy has his own company and is financially independent. He'll never work for someone else again.

Action Step 5 focuses on some of your past accomplishments. The purpose of this is to give you confidence. After all, you've come *this* far, right?

Action Step 5 should trigger your imagination and give you confidence that will get you rolling. Small business is your dream, your venture. When you get going on it, you'll learn more about yourself than you'd learn through group therapy or from several years with a psychiatrist.

Joe Talmadge gained a lot of confidence when he inventoried his skills and interests. Although he'd once felt the thrill of bringing a new product into the marketplace, he was working for someone else and feeling frustrated. And frustration made Joe even more inventive.

The autumn that Bailey's Irish Cream® hit the marketplace, Joe Talmadge was working as a specialty liqueur marketing expert for a major distillery. The figures for that fall speak for themselves. The suppliers had 100,000 cases of Bailey's out in the marketplace and they thought it would last through Christmas, which was two months away. Market surprise. The Bailey's sold out in four days. And Joe Talmadge saw an opportunity: a gap in cream-based liqueurs.

In their kitchen at home, Joe and Ann Talmadge got creative with some old family recipes until they came up with a smooth taste. Joe wanted to position his product against Ireland, the home of Bailey's, so he found a family of wine makers in Italy. They'd been in business for 300 years, which gave Joe the depth of history he wanted, and they had a fantastic supply of old bottle molds embossed with their regal family logo. This was just the image Joe was after. Gambling a little, Joe named his liqueur "Creme de Napoli."

There were problems—manufacturing, distribution, the basic instability of cream, the Italian government and its endless red tape—but Joe persevered and selectively spent money in his test market. It took several months, but he gradually expanded his market area, proving he had a winner. And two years after he and Ann had concocted the recipe for Creme de Napoli at their kitchen table, Joe Talmadge sold the product to a major international liquor maker.

How much did his product bring? Creme de Napoli sold for more than a million dollars. As part of the deal, Joe worked for the purchasers for one year at a very good salary.

ACTION STEP 5

Assess your accomplishments.

Begin by listing all the things in your life that have made you proud. What, for example, has given you the most satisfaction? What is your sweetest memory? How old were you? What were you doing at the time? Were you alone, or with someone? How did it feel to be victorious? How did it feel to be in control?

Then move to the present. Where are you now with your accomplishments? What have you done lately that you're proud of? What about the future? Where do you want to be in three years? In five years? In ten? In twenty?

Also, list things that you *don't* like to do or that you don't do *well*. All entrepreneurs have their weaknesses. What you want is a business that takes advantage of your strengths. If you can identify your likes and dislikes, then you can direct yourself toward things that you enjoy and avoid the things you hate. You may find some surprises when you review your lists.

But Joe is an entrepreneur; he loves risk and he likes being in control. Working for someone else frustrates him. Thus, six months after selling Creme de Napoli, he left the international liquor giant to start his own marketing-consulting business.

Joe understands the market and is good at helping businesses solve problems. He travels a lot and loves his work. And he is financially secure so that he doesn't have to work unless he chooses to.

When Joe thinks back, he remembers how it all started at the kitchen table, being creative, working with his wife, taste-testing, trying to come up with a product to position against Bailey's.

How can *you* operate like Joe Talmadge? First, you need to get organized. Action Step 6 will help you to do that.

Some people have the feeling that getting organized will stifle their creativity. Marci Reid was like that until she saw the value of her Adventure Notebook.

Marci Reid loved to travel, so when she graduated from high school, she got herself a job with a travel agency. For fourteen months she worked as a secretary, learning the business. From her first week, Marci kept a diary form of notebook, listing what seemed to be important elements of the travel business.

Over the next dozen years Marci worked for three different travel agencies, and her diary/notebook grew. She spent four years in Europe—France, the Greek Islands, Spain—and when she returned home she knew it was time to strike out on her own. By then her diary/notebook filled four volumes.

"I know the travel business," Marci said to a friend. "All I need are a few more business skills. Then I can have my own agency."

Marci read and reread her notebooks. She spent time boiling down the information. Then she consulted with her family and with a friend she'd been considering for a partner. Everyone she talked to was excited. Marci's friend also was tired of working for other people and enthusiastically agreed to be her partner. So, for three months, the two friends hunted for a location for their new business. When they'd found three they thought would work, Marci enrolled in a course in entrepreneurship. She knew she needed help in refining her voluminous notes into a workable Business Plan.

In the first class, it was made really clear that you've got to plan every move," said Marci. "I admit I fought the idea at first, mostly because I was so eager to get started, but also because I thought that too much planning would throttle my creativity. But then as I examined each step of building the Business Plan, the patterns began to appear and I saw how things would work out in the long run. Then I didn't feel cramped at all. My travel industry diary became my Adventure Notebook.

"It was high anxiety once we opened up for business. Our contractor was four months behind, so we had to rent temporary space almost ten miles away from our target customers. And since we couldn't get our location right away, our banker chopped our line of credit in half. Luckily, we had followed the advice of our instructors and we had a back-up bank. Then an airline strike forced us to stay up three nights rerouting customers. Without a plan, we'd have gone under.

"Adventures in Travel is three years old now, and my partner and I are thinking about another start-up. The other evening, I brought out my Adventure Notebook—the one I'd used to plan our travel agency—and read through it. I was amazed at its accuracy. I think that shows that you can do a lot in life if you get organized.

"On this next start-up, believe me, we'll do even more planning. You can dream yourself silly, but when you go into business for yourself, you need to put those dreams behind you and get down to the nitty-gritty—customers, sales, profit, winning."

Most people begin a new business with less planning than they give a family vacation. Marci's Adventure Notebook was the incubator for ideas that helped her prepare her Business Plan, which proved, on paper, that she could be successful. As Marci and her partner continue in business, they continue to up-date their plan. Now we'll show you how to select a business idea and how to start planning for its success.

ACTION STEP 6

Organize your information.

If you're the typical entrepreneur, you probably write 90% of your important data on the back of an envelope. That's fine, but now that you're doing this for real, get yourself an organizer, some kind of container (a shoebox, a briefcase, a folder) to put those envelopes in. Even better, compile an **Adventure Notebook**, something with pockets so that you can keep track of small items like ticket stubs.

Your Adventure Notebook should have:

a twelve-month calendar

an appointment calendar

a priority list of things you need to do

your name, company address, and phone number (at the front, in case you leave it somewhere)

an idea list

a "new eyes" list, for keeping track of successful and not-so-successful businesses you come across, plus notes about the reasons for their success or failure

list of possible team members (Who impresses you and why? What are their key attributes?)

list of possible "taxi squad" members—experts who serve as resource people when you need them, such as a lawyer, a CPA, some bankers, successful businesspeople, and so on.

Adventure Notebook
storage place for valuable business information

WHAT IS SUCCESS?

Success is how you define it.

Action Step 7 is optional, but it's fun. Thinking about success can be stimulating and enlightening. What makes a business successful? Unsuccessful? How do *you* measure success? How do your friends measure it?

You and your friends can only speculate about what businesses are doing well. Only a detailed examination of their books would give the whole picture, but we still urge you to exercise your marketplace intuition. Personal observation is a good way to become more aware of what is happening to small firms in your community. For example, next time you eat out, try this:

Estimate the number of customers in the restaurant.

Estimate the total number of customers the restaurant serves each day.

Estimate the average price per meal.

Multiply that average by the total number of daily customers.

Do this for other businesses you patronize as well. Pretty soon you'll begin to get the feel for which businesses are losing and which are winning. Observe small businesses with **new eyes**, and success factors will begin to emerge.

Success is a personal, subjective thing. Whereas income and return-on-investment are measurable, success wears many faces. You need to think about this as you start your adventure. This success checklist will help you. At the end of it, add other items that might signify success to you.

Do you measure success in dollars? How many?

_____ $50K a year?

_____ $100K?

_____ $250K?

_____ $1,000,000?

_____ return-on-investment? How much? _____

Or do you measure success in other ways?

_____ being able to enjoy a certain lifestyle

_____ friendly customers who appreciate the service

_____ power (You know how things should be done. When they're done your way, you feel terrific.)

_____ being able to live where you want

_____ providing employment for others

_____ being the best business in your area

_____ looking out the door and seeing long lines waiting for your service

_____ time to do what you enjoy doing

_____ teamwork (a smooth operation with lots of key employees reporting to you)

_____ fame (your face on TV, your name a household word)

_____ being in control (You like things done your way. You feel uncomfortable giving up control.)

Do you measure success by concrete achievements—like the car you drive or the location of your dream house?

_____ in the heart of a lavish up-scale residential area

_____ a penthouse atop a tall building, in the poshest metropolitan area

_____ anywhere that's safe

ACTION STEP 7

Survey your friends about success.

The next time you're at a party and there's a lull in the conversation, pass out paper and pencils and ask people to list three to five small businesses (IBM does not count!) they perceive as successful. Then ask them to list the signs of those firms' success and the reasons for their success.

Group the negative thinkers together in a Devil's Advocate Group and have them list unsuccessful businesses and point out the reasons those firms are losing out.

After the party look at the two lists together and attempt to come up with insights about the way *you* feel about success.

new eyes
observation with intuition

_____ a place where your kids can play

_____ a cozy cabin on a quiet lake

_____ a fancy, beautifully decorated city apartment

_____ a tropical island, isolated, quiet

_____ your name on a building

_____ hanging loose, doing what makes you happy

_____ _____

_____ _____

_____ _____

After you have thought about what success means to you, complete Action Step 8 to see how equipped you are to achieve it.

CONDUCTING RESEARCH

Research opens doors to the Information Society. There are three approaches to research. You'll need a combination of all three to make it big in small business.

Primary Research

Primary research is carried out by interacting with the world directly by talking to people—perhaps interviewing them. You might ask small business owners questions like: Where were you when the entrepreneurial bug bit? Who do you bank with? How did you choose your lawyer? Your accountant? What would you do if you started up tomorrow, knowing what you know today? Customers can be asked questions like: Is there something we don't carry that you need? How else can we be of help to you? How did you learn about our business? Vendors and suppliers are asked questions like: What advertising works best in businesses like ours? What products are hot? What services are being offered?

Secondary Research

When you read, second-hand, what someone else has discovered you're carrying out **secondary research**. You go to the library and look up "small business" in the Business Index. You locate and read magazine and newspaper articles that contain information you think will be helpful.

Or you write to trade associations in your industry. You find data on sales that will help you project how much money you can make in small business. Good techniques here will save you lots of footwork.

"New-Eyes" Research

New-eyes research provides a variety of fresh ways to look at a business. You play detective. You might become "mystery shopper" to check out your competition. You might sit in your car and take telephoto pictures of a business you're thinking about buying; when **target customers** appear, you photograph them so that you can profile them later. You may stand in a supermarket and, trying not to look nosy, observe what's in people's shopping carts. For example:

personal skills
your strengths, where you shine, the tools that will help you be successful in business

primary research
interacting with the world through interviews, observation, etc.

secondary research
reading about someone else's primary research

new eyes research
the use of intuition and observation to learn things about the marketplace

target customer
a customer with the highest probability of buying your product or service

Steak + Scotch + Cigarettes + Twelve-pack of 7-Up = Party time

Cereal + Dog food + Diapers + Baby food = Family with children

psychographic profile
analysis of the descriptive features of people's lifestyles

Doing this allows you to develop a **psychographic profile** of your target customer. See Figure 1.4.

New-eyes research is fun. Combined with books, magazines, trade journals, publications like the *Wall Street Journal,* and talking to people, it will get you all the

FIGURE 1.4 How would your target customer spend $100,000? Developing a psychographic profile of that person will give you clues.

way to your Business Plan. And the Business Plan will either make you a success or show you that your idea isn't worth any more of your time.

It's time to start filling your Adventure Notebook. Action Step 9 will get you going.

How to Develop a Business's Profit Profile

When you're interviewing a business owner, attempt to develop the business's profit profile. Here's how you do it. In the course of your interview, find out a few key numbers. These include such figures as gross sales, cost of goods sold, rent, salaries (owner, management), and how much they spend on marketing (advertising, commissions, promotions, and so on). You can estimate the other expenses and come up with a range that will give you perspective when it comes time to work with your own numbers.

For example, let's take a business with $500,000 in sales. The cost of goods sold (C of GS) averages 53%. Rent is $2,000. Total salaries are 15% of gross sales. They spend 6% of their gross on marketing. Those are the only numbers you learned from your interview. Based on them, you can estimate benefits, including FICA costs, at 20%–30% of salaries, and other expenses (supplies, utilities, phone, accounting, legal, auto, entertainment, and so on) at 8%–12%. Combining what you were given with your estimates yields this profit profile:

	High Side	Low Side
Sales	$500,000	$500,000
C of GS (53%)	− 265,000	− 265,000
Gross Profit	235,000	235,000
Less: Marketing (6%)	30,000	30,000
Salaries (15%)	75,000	75,000
FICA/Benefits	15,000	22,500
Rent (2,000/mo.)	24,000	24,000
Other Expenses	40,000	60,000
Net Profit	51,000	23,500

On the high side, the profit profile is slightly better than 10%, or $51,000. On the low side, it's slightly below 5%, or $23,500. (That $23,500 is not as low as it looks; the owner has already taken out a salary and most likely auto and entertainment expenses.)

BLACK MONDAY

Back in 1929, October 29th was the important date. The stock market crashed and changed history. We thought that could never happen again. "Too many controls," we said. "Lots of government regulations and safeguards. Too many lessons learned."

Well, on October 19, 1987, the Dow Jones Industrial Average crashed over 500 points—the biggest point-drop in history—and investors lost billions of dollars.

ACTION STEP 9

Investigate the marketplace for opportunities with "new eyes."

Interview at least three people who are self-employed. One of them should be in your own area of interest. (If you're a potential competitor, you may need to travel 50 miles or more to get real help.)

Successful entrepreneurs love to tell the story of how they made it. Being up front about what kind of information you want from these people and why you want it, make appointments with them at times and places convenient to *them.* You may be amazed at how much help you get.

Open-ended questions are best, because they leave room for embellishment. Here are some suggestions to start you off:

When did you decide to start your own business?

What was your first step?

Do you remember how you felt?

If you had it to do all over again, what would you do differently?

How large a part does creativity play in your particular business?

Are your rewards tangible or intangible?

What was your best advertisement or promotion?

What makes your business unique?

How important is price in your business? Would a price war increase your customer base?

Depending on how you hit it off, you might be able to think of these first interviewees as sources of marketplace experience. They may be able to help a lot when you start to assemble your "taxi squad"—your lawyer, accountant, banker, and so on.

It's helpful to take some notes during the interviews. If you want to use a cassette recorder, however, be sure to ask permission.

Don't worry about evaluation at this stage. The information will fall into patterns sooner than you think.

Since then, in spite of reports from the Securities and Exchange Commission and the Fed and a mountain of investment newsletters, we're *still* trying to figure out what happened.

A popular TV program for stock investors is "Wall Street Week." Each week a panel of guest experts discusses the market and the direction the market is going. And each week the experts disagree. Maybe that should be a clue. If the *experts* can't agree, what are *we* doing playing the game? As far as we are concerned, *playing* is the key word. We are strong believers in the old saying, "There ain't no free lunch." If you're going to invest in the stock market, you had better not only do your homework, you'd also better be sitting in front of your TV and PC with modem connected when the market is open. As we learned on October 19, 1987, the market moves at electronic speeds, and you must be prepared to move just as rapidly. October 20 was too late.

If you had money in the stock market, you know what happened to it. But what happened to the deal makers who were at the controls that fateful day? Well, money got tight and they left their jobs. And on March 14, 1988, a lead story in the *Wall Street Journal* reported on a dozen top executives from prestigious New York financial firms. Five of the dozen had taken the entrepreneurial route and formed their own businesses.

If you enjoy sitting in a dimly lit room watching numbers roll across a TV screen, and you like the 2001 feeling of sitting in front of a green screen and talking with HAL, well, investing in the market may be for you. But if you like to be in control, to be a mover and a shaker, to be one who makes things happen instead of having them happen to you, then invest in yourself, in your own business, in something that is fun and exciting. Put your dollars into something that can grow and expand as a direct result of your efforts. Many entrepreneurs find investors who believe in them and decide to share their dream. People like to be a part of something new and exciting.

Anyway, have fun, keep your new eyes peeled, and talk with customers, suppliers, and competitors. Don't be a ticker-tape watcher and develop ulcers because all you can do is watch.

SUMMARY

Ten years ago, the big story in the business world was the end of smokestack America and the rise of the Information Society. Today, we are living in the Information Age, and half of us are doing information jobs. By the early 1980s, less than four decades after the United States moved from an industrial economy to a service economy, the information industry was doing $800 billion a year—almost half of the gross national product. Changes are afoot for the entrepreneur: big business is downsizing; foreign investors are buying up America; Megatrends loom even larger on the horizon. And we are entering the Age of the Entrepreneur.

THINK POINTS FOR SUCCESS

◣ Change is accelerating everywhere, and that includes the world of business. Change creates problems. Entrepreneurs are problem solvers.

◣ The Information Society, the big news of the eighties, is well upon us. To see what's next, scan the environment with new eyes.

◣ To find your doorway into small business, gather data and keep asking questions.

◣ Get reckless on paper before you get reckless in the marketplace. Brainstorm. Draw a future wheel. Confirm your venture with numbers and words before you enter the arena.

◣ Even though you may not be in business yet, you can intensify your focus by writing down your thoughts about the business you think you want to try. Stay flexible.

◣ Remember: We are entrepreneurs. Work is our fun. We never sleep.

REFERENCES

Birch, David L. "The Hidden Economy." *Small Business, The Wall Street Journal Reports,* June 10, 1988.

Brown, Buck. "Small Business: Business Failure Rates Aren't So Bad After All." *Wall Street Journal,* May 20, 1988. [Another myth dispelled. Common knowledge says four out of five start-ups fail during the first five years. Wrong, say two researchers from the SBA and Babson College in Massachusetts. For eight years, the researchers tracked all companies formed between 1976 and 1978 who had ratings from Dun & Bradstreet. The findings: only three out of five failed during the first six years. Companies that added employees had a better chance of surviving. Only 49 percent of service companies added employees, compared to 69 percent in manufacturing.]

Brabec, Barbara. *Homemade Money: The Definitive Guide to Success in a Home Business,* second edition. White Hall, Va.: Betterway, 1986.

Bulkeley, William M. "Lotus, after 1-2-3 Delay, Moves to Quell Client, Market Fears; Stock Drops 11%." *Wall Street Journal,* March 24, 1988, sec. 2, p. 30. [Lotus started as a small business, grew to a giant on one product, Lotus 1-2-3, and now causes shakes in the stock market when it's late on an upgrade; a keen testament to the absolute power of the Information Age. At this writing, Lotus had 45,720,000 shares out there at about $25 a share. Check your financial pages for current values.]

Buzan, Tony. *Use Both Sides of Your Brain.* New York: Dutton, 1976. [Teaches the fine art of mind mapping, which helps the fine art of brainstorming.]

Carrington, Tim, "Military's Dependence on Foreign Suppliers Causes Rising Concern." *Wall Street Journal,* March 24, 1988, sec. 1, p. 1. [Sobering evidence of the extent of offshore manufacturing; 100,000 subcontractors are making defense equipment, most of them being supplied by small foreign firms, like the small German plant 30 miles from the border of Czechoslovakia that makes the high-purity silicon used for chips for guided missiles.]

Chipelo, Christopher J. "Foreign Rivals Imperil U.S. Firm's Leadership in the Service Sector." *Wall Street Journal,* March 14, 1988, sec. 1, p. 1. [Who owns *your* bank?]

Duke, Paul, and Ronald Alsop. "Advertisers Beginning to Play Off Worker Concern over Job Security." *Wall Street Journal,* April 1, 1988. [Since Black Monday, the business world has not been a safe, convivial place.]

Home-Based Business: The Basics of Doing Business from Your Home. Washington, D.C.: U.S. Small Business Administration, Office of Management Assistance. Small Business Management Training Instructors' Guide, No. 109, 1984. [Produced by the American Association of Community and Junior Colleges under contract to the SBA, Contract No. SBA 4873-MA 80.]

Kimura, Doreen. "Male Brain, Female Brain: The Hidden Difference: Gender Does Affect How Our Brains Work—But in Surprising Ways." *Psychology Today,* November 1985, pp. 26–30.

Kishel, Gregory. *Dollars on Your Doorstep: The Complete Guide to Home-Based Businesses.* New York: Wiley, 1984.

Naisbitt, John. *Megatrends: Ten Directions Transforming Our Lives.* New York: Warner Books, 1982. [A must read for entrepreneurs.]

Naisbitt, John. *Reinventing the Corporation: Transforming Your Job and Your Company for the New Information Society.* New York: Warner Books, 1985.

Nulty, Peter. "The Princes of Productivity." *Fortune,* April 30, 1984, pp. 253–56. [Backs up what Naisbitt is talking about with numbers that define the retrenchment of the *Fortune 500.*]

O'Boyle, Thomas F. "Other Steel Firms Consider Merging in Wake of LTV Offer for Republic." *Wall Street Journal,* November 9, 1983, sec. 2, p. 1. [A story of the Industrial Age in which mergers are likened to marriages. Good picture of a smokestack industry.]

Rickles, Roger, and Amanda Bennett. "Market's Crash Continues to Take Psychological Toll." *Wall Street Journal,* March 31, 1988. [Since Black Monday, more than 15,000 Wall Street workers have lost their jobs. Brokers are into booze and drugs. Brokers, once flush with cash, have experienced an 80% drop in income.]

Rico, Gabriele. *Writing the Natural Way: Using Right-Brain Techniques to Release Your Expressive Powers.* Los Angeles: J. P. Tarcher, 1982. [Introduces a form of mind mapping called "clustering." Good stuff for the entrepreneur in a hurry.]

Ries, Al, and Jack Trout. *Positioning: The Battle for Your Mind.* New York: Warner Books, 1982. [Two NYC ad men offer advice on how you can **position** yourself in the minds of prospects and stay there.]

Solomon, Caleb. "As U.S. Wells Go Dry, Reliance on Oil Imports Is Sure to Keep Rising." *Wall Street Journal,* March 30, 1988, sec. 1, p. 1. [A gloomy picture: the U.S. imports four of every ten barrels of oil. We're edging toward imports of 50%. In January 1988, the 214 million barrels of imported crude accounted for a whopping 29% of the trade deficit. The move toward a plastic world is costing a bundle.]

Swartz, Steve. "Bickering, Infighting Beset Securities Firms as Money Gets Tight." *Wall Street Journal,* March 8, 1988, sec. 1, p. 1. [In the continuing aftermath of Black Monday, heavy hitters in the money game move to new jobs. Out of a dozen men tracked, five are bitten by the entrepreneurial bug and form their own firms. Let's hear it for small business!]

Toffler, Alvin. *Previews and Premises.* New York: William Morrow, 1983.

Toffler, Alvin. *The Third Wave.* New York: William Morrow, 1981.

Tolchin, Martin, and Susan Tolchin. *Buying into America: How Foreign Money Is Changing the Face of Our Nation.* New York: Times Books, 1988.

Wayman, Lynn. *Starting and Managing a Business from Your Home.* Washington, D.C.: U.S. Small Business Administration, Starting and Managing Series, Vol. 2, 1986.

Weaver, Paul H. *The Suicidal Corporation: How Big Business Has Failed America.* New York: Simon and Schuster, 1988.

Wright, Richard W., and Gunther A. Pauli. *The Second Wave: Japan's Global Assault on Financial Services.* New York: St. Martin's Press, 1988.

position
establish your image in the eyes of the target customer

APPENDIX 1.1 • Model Action Step 8: Inventory your skills.

1. What kind of work do you do?
Writer–editor, primarily in journalism, secondarily in advertising. Also more than moderately skilled in brochure production.

2. What kind do you really enjoy?
Working as a writer and/or editor in a highly competitive atmosphere, where spot news is breaking or where there is plenty of action.

3. What are your hobbies?
Writing, editing, furniture building and refinishing. I spend all my weekends doing these things. Formerly was active in camping, astronomy, wildflower photography, shell collecting. Often I took up a hobby merely to become proficient as a writer in that area.

4. What really excites you?
The thrill of discovery during competitive research. Thoroughly trouncing the competition.

5. Do you like to work alone?
It's all right. I do a lot of it these days, although most of my career has involved working with others, usually as an editor/mentor.

6. Are you a self-starter?
Definitely. Always have been.

7. What would three people say about your three major skills?

1. He's a top-notch editor, with a special eye for tasteful, appealing layout in a publication. He knows how to work with top-drawer art directors and the finest printers. He knows a great deal about professional-quality desktop publishing.

2. He's a good writer on spot news, on people features, and in explaining complex things like science and chemistry for the lay reader. Because of his age, he is not a good advertising copywriter for the following VALS: Sustainers, Emulators, I-Am Mes, and probably is marginal with Experimental audiences. His greatest affinity is with these VALS audiences: Achievers, Belongers, Societally Conscious, and Integrated. (Note that the graphic arts industry today is probably dominated by people in the Experimentals and Achievers VALS lifestyles.)

3. From lack of practice, he's long over the hill as a working photographer, but he is a good photo editor because of his lengthy experience and training as a photographer.

8. Boldface your skills in this list.
Sell, **write**, negotiate, soothe, counsel, **synthesize**, **coordinate**, **create**, **analyze**, compile, teach, persuade, tend, plant, **nurture**, **supervise**, help out, copy, add and subtract, follow instructions, **delegate**, **lead**.

Your top five skills:

1. Write
2. Nurture
3. Analyze/Synthesize
4. Create
5. Lead/Supervise/Delegate

Five that are impossible for you:

1. Personal selling on a sustained and effective basis
2. Getting excited over bookkeeping: adding and subtracting (My wife complements me here; she is outstanding in this field.)
3. Negotiating from a tough stance. I'm too much of a patsy. (But once again my wife has excellent skills in this area.)
4. Teaching large groups or persuading large audiences. I'm best with small groups of half a dozen. I was not effective over a period of time with a class of 30 students.
5. Tending, copying, or doing routine, repetitive work

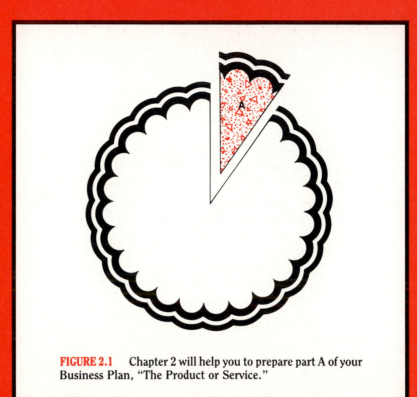

FIGURE 2.1   Chapter 2 will help you to prepare part A of your Business Plan, "The Product or Service."

The Big Picture—Charting Trends for Your Small Business

LEARNING OBJECTIVES

■ To understand how to analyze the potential for small business success by applying the life-cycle yardstick to industries, products, services, and locations. ■ To determine what business you're really in. ■ To become excited about the techniques of brainstorming. ■ To use diagrams and mind maps to explore market segmentation. ■ To discover market signals that indicate trends and opportunities. ■ To discover market forces that underlie the trends. ■ To be able to deduce a person's lifestyle from the contents of his or her shopping cart. ■ To select information sources that are efficient. ■ To begin your search for the business that best fits your aptitudes. ■ To increase your ability to read market signals that forecast future needs.

ACTION STEP PREVIEW

10 Travel back in time and observe a marketplace of the past.

11 Define your business and test your definition.

12 What's new? What's hot? What's cooling down?

13 Assess the lifestyle of your potential target customer by walking its neighborhood.

14 Have some fun with segmentation and gap analysis.

15 Decode the secrets of the shopping cart.

A Business Plan begins with the "big picture"—the industry overview. Industries go through life cycles. Products and services within industries also progress through the process—birth, growth, maturity, and decline. The industry overview helps you gain perspective on your "niche" and helps the reader (lender or investor) understand why you have chosen to pursue this segment of the market.

WHY LOOK AT THE BIG PICTURE?

To be successful in small business you need to know two things: what business you are really in, and where your business is on the great lifecycle yardstick. Entrepreneurs tend to be in a big hurry. They want to push on, to get on with it, to throw open the doors to customers, and to read the bottom line, and that's not all bad. But before *you* charge into the arena, step back and examine what's going on in your industry **segment**. Where are the lines? The crowds? What are people buying? In what part of your community do you see "Going Out of Business" signs? Where are the start-ups? What's hot? What's cooling down? What business segments will still be thriving five years from now? If you opened the doors of your new business today, how long would it be before your product or service was no longer valuable?

So look before you leap. Brainstorm with your family and friends and interview your potential customers. Study the marketplace. Read industry journals. Use your new eyes. And use this chapter to help you define the **trends** and **gaps** in your industry—in other words, to see the big picture.

segment
an identifiable slice of an industry

trends
pathways to your future

gap
an area of the market where needs are not being met

Recognizing Opportunities

What are the best business ventures to pursue today? Where can you find a business that will really pay off? One that will make you rich? One that will make you famous?

Only you can answer the question, because the best business for you is one that you enjoy. The best business for you uses those experiences, skills, and aptitudes that are unique to *you*. The early action steps in this book are designed to help you discover what is unique about you. Who are you? What are your skills? What turns you on? What do you already know that distinguishes you from other people?

As a consumer you know, for example, that restaurants have a high failure rate. One week you're having dinner at The Hound and Glove; the next week it's locked up with a CLOSED sign on the door. You don't want that to happen to your business. That's why *you* do **market research**. That's why you're going to make sure your business serves a *need*. This means that you will automatically enter the marketplace from a position of strength.

market research
collection and analysis of data pertinent to your current or potential market

Let's back up and get the big picture. Before the Industrial Revolution, most people were self-employed. Farmers and sheepherders were risk-takers because they had to be; there were few other options. The family functioned as an entrepreneurial unit.

The growth of the megacorporations in the twentieth century should not be seen as a threat to the small entrepreneur, but as an opportunity. First, most large corporations are dependent on small business to produce support products and support services. Second, bigger isn't better, and many small businesses—even those whose markets are expanding rapidly—are barely noticed by the large corporations. And there lies the opportunity.

The exploding need for specialized products and services is mind-boggling. You may see as much change in the next ten years as your parents have seen in their lifetime, and change creates opportunities for fast and flexible firms. If you stay in touch with change and the exploding market niches that change creates, you will always see more opportunities than you can pursue. Action Step 10 will give you some perspective on change.

KNOW YOUR REAL BUSINESS

The Importance of Stepping Back

Watch a painter at work at an easel. She works close to the canvas, layering the paint with brush and spatula. But at regular intervals, the painter will step back for a long view of the work. Up close, the artist can see only brushstrokes and colors. From a few feet back, the entire painting can be seen. From a few more feet back, the landscape being painted becomes apparent.

What business is the painter in?

Watch a carpenter framing a new house. He works close to the wood, nailing with quick strokes of his hammer. But to get a view of the total house, the structure that will become someone's home, he must walk across the street. He has to step back, away from his detailed work, to see the shape of the whole.

What business is the carpenter in? Is he in the nail-driving business? The framing business? The home-building business? Or is he in the business of satisfying the age-old "nesting" need?

Only by stepping back can you answer the question of what business you are in. This is a very important question.

If you went far enough back in time in Action Step 10, you probably saw pictures of trains. Railroads used to be big business in America. Rail lines eventually linked the east and west coasts, and if you remember your American history, you probably remember the historic linkage at Promontory Point, Utah, in 1869, when the Union Pacific met the Central Pacific.

What has happened to the railroads since then? Well, the same thing that happens to lots of large business organizations. They downsized and lost their focus. And much of the track has been taken over by the government and run by Amtrak.

Why did this happen? Why was a huge, powerful industry forced to downsize?

The Railroads Forgot What Business They Were In

Okay, let's look back. Half a century ago, rail lines criss-crossed the continent. You could step onto a train in New York City and ride in safety, ease, and splendor all the way to California. Trains were the great movers of products and people. They owned timber, grazing land, mineral rights, country. Their names—*Chief, Super Chief, California Zephyr, Commodore Vanderbilt, New York Express, Texas Special*—had the aura of confidence, empire building, power, the grand strategy of efficient transportation. It was a magnificent era.

define your business
develop a clear picture of what business you are really in

Yet, somewhere along the line, railroad magnates committed a grave error: they failed to **define their business.**

THE RR's SAID:	THE RR's MIGHT HAVE SAID:
"We're in the railroad business."	"We're in the transportation business."

life cycle
four stages, from birth to death, of a product, business, service, industry, location, etc.

That, coupled with the automobile, jumbo jets, interstate highways, and the general fickleness of consumers, was the beginning of the end for them. They entered the decline stage of their **life cycle.** Can they come back? As this book goes to press, America's major cities, caught in traffic gridlock, are asking the federal government for billions to build people-movers. There is talk of bullet-trains like those in France and Japan. There is nostalgia about people-movers like the once-popular Los Angeles "Red Cars."

The lesson here is to know what business you are in—to know who your customers are and what satisfies their needs. Mary Clark's experience illustrates the importance of understanding what business you are really in.

Mary Clark was a forty-year-old teacher who had always been more interested in riding her prize-winning saddle horses than in teaching school. When her grandmother died and left her $200,000, Mary made a down payment on a boarding stable and left teaching forever, she thought.

The boarding stable was run down. It had stalls for 100 horses, but only forty of them were occupied. Mary did everything she could think of to make the place better for horses. She spent $57,000 rebuilding, painting, grading. She made Clark's Stables a very attractive place. She bought the highest quality of feed and gave the horses the best care money could buy.

When the owners began to move their horses to other stables, Mary couldn't understand. She had not increased her fees, and she treated the horses like friends. In six months, only three customers remained. In nine months, she was behind on her mortgage payments. In her tenth month, Mary had to sell the stables.

Mary made the simple mistake of thinking horses were her target customers. Her real target customers were young girls between the ages of seven and fourteen. Mary thought she was in the business of stabling horses. The business she should have seen she was in was providing services for girls who rode horses. The girls wanted recreation, training, and social activities. Mary's customers left because other stables were providing lessons, trail rides, barbeques, and pony and horse shows. Today, Mary is back in the classroom wondering why people don't care more about their horses.

Define Your Real Business

What business are *you* really in? What business do you want to be in? Naming anything is a game of words, and a small business is no exception. The following examples can help you define your business. If you're hesitant about defining at this early stage, remember what happened to the railroads—and to Mary Clark's stable.

IF YOU'RE IN:	TRY SAYING:
Software sales	"I'm in the problem-solving business."
Pie baking	"I'm in the reward and satisfaction business."
College teaching	"I'm in the information business."
Medicine	"I'm in the healing business."
Auto sales	"I'm in the ego-gratification business."
Mattresses	"I'm in the sound sleep business."
Cameras	"I'm in the happy memory business."
Gourmet cookware	"I bring fun back into the kitchen."
Locksmithing	"I'm in the security business."
Badge manufacturing	"I'm in the recognition business."
Renters' guide publishing	"I help landlords find tenants."

Now complete this sentence:

I'm in the business of _____.

Explain why you chose this definition and how it relates to your target customer.

_____

_____

Keep honing your definition of your business. Once a month is not too often to redefine it, especially before the start-up. Check your definition against the signals you get from your potential target customers, since they may perceive your business differently. You may have new letterhead stationery printed after you talk to them, but as business expenses go, that's a small price to pay to overcome customer confusion.

Now you're ready to do Action Step 11.

HOW TO MINIMIZE MARKETPLACE HEARTACHE—WATCH TRENDS

Let's say you've tried a small business and failed. Let's say you followed in the footsteps of Mary Clark, the teacher who loved horses; you opened a business out of love, and it fell apart. Your customers left you, and your creditors scared you to death. Okay, you failed once. Worse, you're still unhappy in your job. So, after licking your wounds, you've decided you'd like to try it again. After all, this is the Age of the Entrepreneur, right? So what's the next step?

Well, you look around with those new eyes. Study that list you made of products from twenty-five years ago and try to make some generalizations about how things have changed. Here's a quick overview.

The Splintering of the Mass Market

Today's consumers are informed, individualistic, and demanding. Their buying habits are often difficult to isolate because they tend to buy at several levels of the market. For instance, many purchasing agents buy the office copier from Xerox but the paper

---

ACTION STEP 11

Define your business and test your definition. Follow these steps:

1. Brainstorm what business you're really in. Let your mind play at this. Try to keep negative statements to a minimum.

2. Once you've decided what business you're in, visit your printer and order some one-color business letterhead stationery. (One-color is cheaper, so you save money right from the start.)

3. Next, go to the library and look for a thick publication called the *Encyclopedia of Associations.* Locate the name of a trade association your business would be a part of. Write down the address, phone number, and name of a contact person.

4. Before you leave the library, check the *Gale Directory of Publications* for a trade journal that covers your industry. Try to find one that's not connected to the association you found listed in the *Encyclopedia of Associations.* Write down the name of the publication; the publisher's name, address, and phone number; and the cost (if any) of a subscription.

5. Look in the *Thomas Register of American Manufacturers* for a company that manufactures a part or a product that you will need in your business. Note the specific name of the part or product and the manufacturer's, name, address, and phone number.

6. Finally, write letters to or telephone the publications and trade associations that are in your area of interest. Ask them for a "rate card" and for demographic studies. It's free because you are a prospective advertiser. The trade association will tell you about themselves and provide membership details.

You will soon be buried with useful information.

from a discount office supply warehouse. High-fashion, high-income consumers patronize the up-scale boutiques and yet buy their household appliances at K-Mart.

For the consumer, three key factors have splintered the mass market: (1) a shrinking middle class—there are both more high-end, affluent consumers and more consumers who live at or near the poverty level; (2) shifting sizes of age groups; (3) new living arrangements—including smaller houses, smaller furniture, enclosed patios, and twin master suites for working roommates. If you look around with new eyes, you can see major market segments emerging that were not here a decade ago: **Baby Boomers;** newly liberated women; vigorous, healthy over-50-year-olds; teens, especially females; and singles.

To get a better view of today's trends, contrast consumer values of the two decades between 1960 and 1980 with those we can project for the 1990s. Here's what you have:

Baby Boom
the increase in the U.S. birthrate between 1946 and 1963

Changing Consumer Values

1960–1980	1990–2000
Quantity	Quality
Things	Experiences
Initial cost	Total use cost
High expectations	Modified expectations
Liberal credit	Tightened credit
Conformity	Individuality
Impulse shopping	Planned expenditures
Experimental lifestyles	Return to old values
Video games	Home entertainment
Car status	Home status
Stable middle class	Shrinking middle class
Child-oriented homes	Adult orientation
Throw away	Reuse

Action Step 12 will take you out into your community to conduct some trend research. (See Appendix 2.1.)

A List of Trends to Start You Off

Let's say you like taking care of people and you have worked for ten years in an infant day-care center. However the neighborhood is aging, affluent families have moved away, and the day-care center has closed due to lack of business. You decide to go into business for yourself. What business do you choose? How about a care center for elderly people?

Let's think about where other opportunities exist.

There is a trend toward dual-income families. That means no one is at home during the day. Obvious business opportunities are child care and home security systems.

With both adults working to pay the bills, no one has enough time (the "poverty of time" trend). Obvious business opportunities are easy-to-fix meals, fast food, teleconferences.

People are exercising for fitness and they want to look good while sweating. Opportunity: attractive sports clothes.

People must change jobs and they need retraining. Opportunity: education.

Continue the list here.

TREND	OPPORTUNITY

Some people make a business of trend watching. See Box 2.1.

THE LIFE-CYCLE STAGES

When you have produced a long list of trends, divide them into four groups according to the stage of their life cycle. See Figure 2.2. If a trend is just beginning, is in its formative stage, label it *Embryo.* If it's exploding, label it *Growth.* If it's no longer growing and is starting to cool, label it *Mature.* If it's beyond maturity and is feeling chilly, label it *Decline.* Think about these life-cycle stages often. Everything changes—products, needs, technology, neighborhoods.

Looking at the life-cycle diagram, you can see that the auto industry as a whole is very mature. Nonetheless, some of its segments are promising; for example, minivans, sports models, and upscale imports. Convertibles are back, and in the suburbs, you see young mothers driving around in Jeep 4×4s. Despite traffic jams, people are still driving. But the cars they drive reflect changing lifestyles.

How do consumer habits determine trends? Well, people are keeping their cars longer, so one growth segment in the auto industry would be the **aftermarket.** Examples of businesses in that segment would be paint, detailing, electronic accessories, engine rebuilding. If you're interested in the auto industry, consider the aftermarket.

In the computer business, competition and the microchip have brought down the price of computer hardware. A personal computer system that sold for $5,000 three

BOX 2.1   *Megatrends* Started a Trend

John Naisbitt's book, published in 1982, established the bedrock for futurists. His company, the Naisbitt Group, is still in business. Each year they produce a book that peers into the future.

When *Megatrends* was published, Naisbitt was all alone in the duck pond. Today, entrepreneurs with crystal balls under their arms are scrambling to nudge him aside. These other futurists want their share of the pond. Some of the new businesses are Inferential Focus (New York), Alternative Futures Associates (Alexandria, Virginia), Forecasting International, Limited (Arlington, Virginia), SRI International (Menlo Park, California), the Futures Group (Glastonbury, Connecticut), and BrainReserve (New York).

ACTION STEP 12

What's new? What's hot? What's cooling down?

1. Take your new eyes out into the marketplace and observe what's happening at the local (or regional) level. Your community is a marketing lab. To discover what this means for you and your business, prowl around a supermarket and analyze what's going on. A locally owned store will give you a clearer picture than a chain will, because it serves the needs of your area. Chains only show you what the country is buying, and that's not much help for an entrepreneur.

What's on sale? What's dusty? What's wilted? What is the store promoting? What conclusions can you draw about the store's marketing strategy? Which department has the most space? Which has the longest lines? Which has the most workers? Which has the highest prices? What products must move fast? Can you guesstimate the shelf velocities in the various departments?

Move on to other locally owned stores—hardware stores, drugstores, restaurants, gift shops, and others.

2. Give your new-eyes research a data base by checking with the local newspaper. Visit the display advertising department and ask to see research they've compiled on the area.

3. Go to the public library and study last year's *Survey of Buying Power,* published by *Sales and Marketing Management* magazine. For your city or county, note:

the total dollars spent, autos, related products

the percentage of households with incomes above the national average

the total city/county population.

How do your new-eyes research findings correlate with what you found in the secondary sources?

shelf velocity
the speed at which a product moves from storage to shelf to customer

aftermarket
the marketplace where replacement items can be purchased. Auto tires and sewing machine belts are examples.

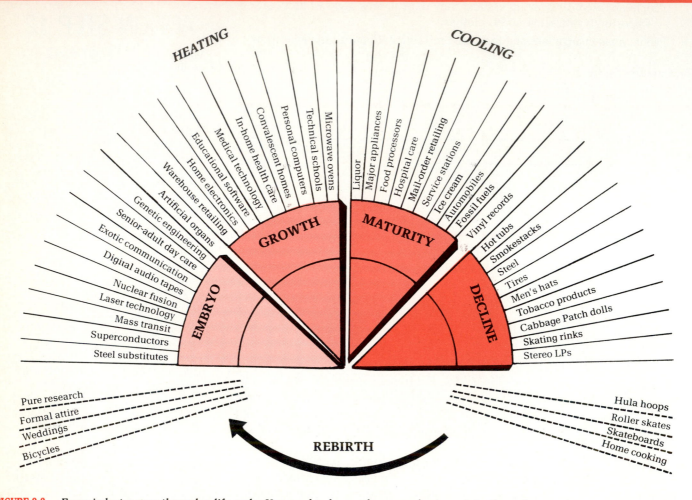

FIGURE 2.2 Every industry goes through a life cycle. You need to know where your business is in the cycle.

years ago can be purchased for one-third of that today. And that same $5,000 buys a system with more speed, more power, more bells and whistles. With the gain in power comes more sophisticated software. Some of the software, despite claims of being "user-friendly," has a long learning curve. So one opportunity in the computer field is computer instruction. In chapter 3 you'll read a case study about a group of entrepreneurs who found a niche in computer instruction.

Where can you find gaps in the life-cycle diagram? Where is your business in its four-stage cycle?

Watch for Market Signals

Market signals are everywhere—in the newspaper (classified ads, display ads), in the lines at the theatre, in the price-slashing after Christmas, in discount coupons, rebates, closings, grand openings. With practice, you can follow a product right through its life cycle.

For example, consider designer jeans. In the early 1980s, massive ad campaigns convinced otherwise-sane Americans they should pay $40 and up for jeans carrying designer labels. The jeans were available only in the posh stores. A year later, designer jeans had reached the discount stores. Jeans that had sold for $55 were now selling at **deep discount**—for $9.99. A bargain? Yes, and also a trend.

What items have you seen go through their life cycle, from upscale out of sight to deep discount?

deep discount
cutting a price to near cost, cost, or below cost

_____

_____

Now go back to the life-cycle diagram and see if you can add some products and industries to it.

How Deep Is Deep?

When merchandise slides into deep discount, the profit party is over. The air is chilly. The market is flooded; sinking is likely, and drowning is possible. If that's happened to your job—or to your business—it's time for you to find a **growth segment** of a **growth industry**.

Experts tell us that the average working American will have at least five kinds of jobs in his or her lifetime. No one's job is completely secure. Rhonda Van Warden thought hers was, until her company eliminated her position. When that happened she started to look at the trends in her community and in the nation. Rhonda has some great assets, including intelligence and being a good listener, and she has the flexibility to see herself in a totally new role when opportunity knocks.

growth segment
an identifiable slice of an industry that is expanding more rapidly than the industry as a whole

growth industry
an industry whose annual sales increase is well above average

Rhonda was a great teacher. She had a warm personality, a terrific smile, and an intuitive understanding of what kids needed from a world of adults. When she was offered a job as a counselor in the school where she'd been teaching, she didn't hesitate. As a counselor, she knew she could reach more kids.

Then the district cutbacks started. Due to forces beyond her control, Rhonda was furloughed. Naturally, she was very upset. Here she'd been working overtime, supporting the system, counseling her heart out, and what did she have to show for it? Not much.

But Rhonda's a fighter who doesn't give up easily. She attended seminars, read books about job-hunting, and networked her friends for leads. One day she was talking to a couple of friends, and their conversation turned to lingerie.

"What I wish," said Kary, "is that I could buy some of that semisexy stuff without having to go into Le Sex Shoppe to buy it."

"There're always the catalogs," Marsha pointed out, "and there are ads in the back of every magazine I subscribe to."

"I don't trust those catalogs," Kary replied. "When I pay that much money for something so small, I want to see what I'm getting!"

Marsha turned to Rhonda. "You're sitting there not saying a word, Rhonda. What're you thinking about?"

"I think," Rhonda said, smiling, "I've just discovered the business I want to be in."

Rhonda's idea was to network her women friends for potential target customers who would like to come to her home for a private showing of women's intimate undergarments. Rhonda came up with the name for her business, "Private Screenings," and had letterhead stationery printed. Then she began to contact suppliers and manufacturer's reps. They were interested in her idea.

Her first "private screening" was well-attended. Only women were present, and Rhonda sold almost a thousand dollars' worth of merchandise. The women loved what they saw and they had fun. Ten years earlier they probably wouldn't have considered buying the things they bought that night, but times and people change.

Rhonda went on from her success in selling to develop a line of products that she sells through her own catalog. Her husband has joined her in the business, and she has hired a woman to present her intimate merchandise through seminars. (The seminars also are held in private homes.) Rhonda spends most of her time recruiting personnel and developing new products.

"When I started in this business," Rhonda admits, "I thought it might help to supplement my husband's income. But it's expanded so much that we have to scramble to keep up with orders. We travel a lot, talking to manufacturers about trends, picking up ideas. This business is a full-time job for *both* of us."

Rhonda was a sharp reader of market signals—the trends that reflect changes in how people think. What trends have helped to make Rhonda's business successful?

1. Specialized consumer tastes. Rhonda's target customers are discreet middle-class women in their forties and fifties, many of whom would be uncomfortable walking into a specialty shop to see intimate lingerie. When Rhonda brings the merchandise to them, they feel comfortable, special, and adventurous.

2. High-tech/high-touch. We can't stop the approach of computers and the Information Age. But we all try to balance the electronic effects of whirring machinery with human responses—Rolfing, EST, dance, the arts, feeding our fantasies. Private Screenings capitalizes on the desire for softness in these high-tech times.

3. Relaxing attitudes about sex. Private Screenings was founded in the early eighties, a time when attitudes toward sex were becoming more relaxed.

What other trends do you see contributing to the success of Private Screenings?

_____

_____

_____

CONDUCT YOUR OWN RESEARCH

This is a good time to take a walk. Action Step 13 will get you out into the neighborhood of your target customers. Take along your new eyes.

Rich Cameron is a very precise and careful person and he understands research *and* trends. If you're considering a venture you know very little about, you should work in that kind of business for awhile to get experience. If you can't do that, then do what Rich did.

When Rich Cameron celebrated his thirty-fifth birthday, he was in the marketing end of the computer industry. The industry was doing all right, but Rich was frustrated with his job.

"I was your typical workaholic," Rich said. "I'd do overtime at the office, put out a lot of energy for the company, and then wonder why I didn't feel terrific. If someone had told me I was experiencing corporate burnout, I'd have laughed in his face."

Rich had been in the habit of changing jobs when he got frustrated. He started working as a grocery bagger when he was twelve, and since then he'd worked in sales, management, real estate, insurance, finance, research, and computer programming. Now he started to look around for something else to do. He arranged to work a four-day work week—ten hours a day—and spent the three other days exploring.

"When I was a kid in high school, my dad took me aside and gave me some valuable advice. 'Son,' he said. 'Remember this. You are your greatest resource.' So one of the first things I did—before I checked out the marketplace—was take some aptitude tests. They told me three things: I'm good with spatial problems, I like being creative, and I like to play. The last one—play—is the one that threw me. I grew up in a family where we learned to work hard, and *play* is a word we didn't use much. It took me more than a year to accept the fact that I like to play."

While Rich was digesting this news about himself, he attended some seminars, mostly in small business, and kept to his work schedule of four days for his boss and three days for himself. He walked more than a hundred neighborhoods and interviewed more than a hundred small business owners. He studied **traffic patterns**, shopping habits, and trends. After a year, he knew that he wanted to combine work and play by opening a toy store. He was about to settle on a location in a major shopping center when he happened to interview the owner of an antique store.

Rich asked the antique store owner why he'd chosen this location.

"We did research," the man said. "My wife is the mathematician of the family. She worked the whole thing out on paper."

"Great," Rich said. "I've been at it for more than a year, myself. What kinds of things did she do?"

"We counted the cars in the parking lot," the owner said. "We counted them every day for two weeks. This lot was packed solid from dawn to dark."

Rich looked out. Today, the parking lot was packed. "What about weekends?" he asked.

The antique store owner looked at the floor. "Now there," he admitted, "we've been having problems—ever since we lost our anchor tenant."

"How long ago was that?" Rich asked.

"Six months ago tomorrow," the man said.

Rich thanked the owner and kept on exploring. He had liked this center. It was close to a perfect target neighborhood. Yet, something was wrong. He could feel it.

Rich was still talking to store owners when evening rolled around and the parking lot began to empty, fast. He stopped his interviewing to do some "new-eyes" observing. Cars full of people kept pulling into the lot and stopping. Everyone except the drivers got out of the cars and walked to parked cars. None of the people went into the stores. Rich quickly deduced that this shopping center parking lot was being used by car-pooling commuters.

"I'd been interviewing store owners all afternoon," Rich says, "and not one of them told me about this "park and ride" situation. Maybe they didn't know it. Maybe they were hiding something. Either way, it was a signal for me to keep on looking."

It took Rich Cameron two years to find what he was looking for—a location close to a target neighborhood packed with kids, young parents, station wagons, and toys. He named his store "Toys from Middle Earth." He now works seventy hours a week until the Christmas Season, and then he works one hundred hours a week. He's not frustrated any more.

"The main thing you've got to watch in the toy business," Rich says, "is how fast a trend can end. One week, you're selling hula hoops like crazy. The next week, hula hoops won't even move at deep discount and the kids are coming in the store asking for gear they've seen on a new TV show or in some movie. To make it in toys these days, you need to keep one eye on the kids, the other on the future." He grins. "If you'd told me this a couple years back, I wouldn't have believed you. But you learn to read the customers in this business, or you go under."

Rich Cameron won't go under. He likes to win too much.

Rich took a hard look "inside" and then spent two years researching the toy industry. Today, his toy business is growing steadily because he planned well and because he matched his skills with his business. Rich is a researcher to model yourself after. He integrated new-eyes research with hard data from secondary sources.

ACTION STEP 13

Assess the lifestyle of your potential target customer by walking its neighborhood.

The best time to **walk a target neighborhood** is on the weekend, when the people are home and the garage doors are open. What you're looking for are clues to lifestyle.

How many cars? What makes and models? How old? What condition? Sports cars and low-slung two-door hatchbacks indicate owners who are young, or trying to be. Station wagons suggest families. Trucks, four-wheel drives, and luxury cars tell you other things.

Do you see any sports or recreation equipment? Any tools? Any pets, doghouses, stables?

What's the maintenance level of the homes? Are they patio homes, condos, townhouses, or single-family? Estimate the number of bedrooms, bathrooms, square feet, and so on.

Visit a real estate office and get a ballpark figure on housing costs in the neighborhood. Use these costs to estimate household income. (If the average price for a home in your target neighborhood is $200,000 and buyers can finance $160,000, the household income is probably $60,000–$90,000.)

If you don't have time to walk the neighborhood, bike it or drive it.

Commonly available secondary information can help you confirm your observations. See what data your community newspaper or cable station has already gathered. Also, review information from this census track. It's all free!

Study your target customer from all angles. You can't afford to make any blind guesses.

walk the neighborhood
tramp through the dust and gold of the marketplace

clues to lifestyle
things that indicate what's important to people

traffic pattern
pathway of frequent travel

Secondary Sources

Now we're going to introduce you to some valuable secondary sources that you can use for gathering hard data.

Newspapers John Naisbitt's Trend staff monitors 6,000 regional and daily newspapers. *Megatrends* grew in part out of that research. Faith Popcorn's BrainReserve staff also does heavy research. Study the local newspaper, starting with the classifieds and display ads. For a bigger picture, read the *Wall Street Journal.*

Magazines Faith Popcorn herself watches sitcoms and devours *People* magazine. The ads tell you what's hot and where the money is flowing. If you haven't looked at it already, check out *Sales and Marketing Management* magazine. *S & MM* also publishes two annual supplements of interest to small business pioneers: the *Survey of Buying Power* (lists results by counties all across the U.S.) and the *Survey of Industrial and Commercial Buying Power* (gives a dramatic big-picture look at regions, counties, industries, and metro areas). These *S & MM* supplements are definite must-reads.

trade journal
publication directed to the specific needs of an industry

Trade Journals These are a valuable source once you know what industry you're in. Use your new business letterhead to write trade associations. You can find these listed with their addresses in the *Encyclopedia of Associations* and in the *Gale Directory of Publications.*

Banks Banks are in the business of renting money, and any bank above medium size has a staff of economists, marketing experts, and so on, who research and write forecasts and reports of economic trends. Ask to see those reports.

Planning Offices Cities and counties employ planners to chart the future and plan for growth. Check the city and county offices listings in the phone book to find out where these offices are. For the best service, however, you'll need to visit the office, make friends with the staff, and be pleasant and patient. Many counties use federal data to develop annual reports.

Reports from Colleges and Universities State universities publish annual and semiannual reports on economic conditions in the state. You can probably get copies of these by writing to the university public relations office. Reports are also published by private institutions of higher learning with special interests in business. Inquire in your area.

Real Estate Firms Large commercial and industrial real estate firms have access to developers' site research. The more specific you can be on your requirement, the easier it will be for them to help you. Familiarize yourself with the dynamics of the area. What firms are going into business? What firms are leaving business? (For more details on this, see chapter 7.)

The SBA The Small Business Administration of the U.S. government has tons of booklets. Call the nearest office or write to U.S. Small Business Administration, P.O. Box 15434, Fort Worth, TX 76119. Put tax dollars to work for yourself.

Federal Depositories Scattered across the U.S. are special libraries that contain sources of census information on Consolidated Metropolitan Statistical Areas (CMSAs; for example, the New York–Long Island–Southwestern Connecticut–Northern New Jersey area, which has 17 million people), Primary Metropolitan Statistical Areas

(PMSAs; for example, New York City), and Metropolitan Statistical Areas (MSAs; for example, Peoria, Fresno, and so on). These three were formerly grouped all together as Standard Metropolitan Statistical Areas (SMSAs), a category that will linger in the minds of marketeers for another decade or so. No matter what you call it, you can find census information in these Federal Depositories, where the 1980 SMSA for your area is probably still intact. Also look for a booklet called County Business Patterns. For the whereabouts of the nearest Depository, ask the friendly reference librarian at your public library.

SIC Codes

While you're scanning the big picture for trends, you might want to develop a feel for what you can do with SIC Codes. Starting with your own code will help you define your industry. It will give perspective to the big picture.

SIC stands for *Standard Industrial Classification.* It's a numerical system that assigns a number to almost every identifiable industry. SIC numbers come in three groups:

> 2-digit (for example, 36)—Major Group
> 3-digit (for example, 366)—Industry Group
> 4-digit (for example, 3662)—Specific Industry Group

SIC codes are contained in a government publication called *The Standard Industrial Classification Manual,* which is available at most libraries. To use it, first find the industry you think you're in in the alphabetical index. Then go to Major Group, Industry Group, and Specific Industry.

For example, let's say you're a creative entrepreneur who's just invented a device you can manufacture for $4.22 per unit that will make radio transmission easier. Your primary market will be manufacturers of radio equipment, and a secondary market might be telephone equipment makers. Before you start production, however, you want to assess the size of the market.

So you find your SIC classification in the alphabetical index under number 3662, "radio and TV communication equipment." That's you, all right. This number refers you to Major Group 36, "electrical, electronics," and then to Specific Industries under 3662. You notice that 3661 is "telephone and telegraph supplies," which is another industry category you need to explore.

You will notice that the manual will lead you only so far and no further. That's because the government does not release the sources of its data. So, where do you go from here? To private enterprise. Figure 2.3 shows three different tracks you can follow with your SIC code, depending on what you want to learn.

Track I   Track I leads to *S & MM's Survey of Industrial and Commercial Buying Power,* an annual study of markets that is available at most libraries. The *Survey* gives you a big-picture look at business trends at the national level. It reports:

> the major industry groups
> the top 50 manufacturing counties
> the 50 leading industrial metropolitan markets
> regional and state summaries of manufacturing markets
> profiles of the 50 largest manufacturing industries

Tables 2.1 through 2.6 illustrate the value of the data in the *Surveys.* They are drawn from the 1988 *Survey* (published August 15, 1988).

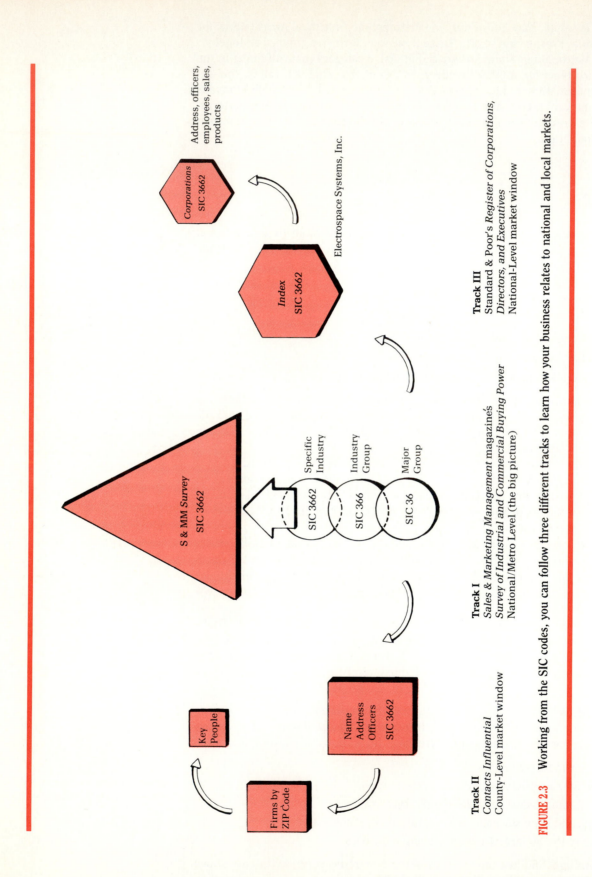

FIGURE 2.3 Working from the SIC codes, you can follow three different tracks to learn how your business relates to national and local markets.

TABLE 2.1 Regional and State Summaries of Population as of December 31, 1987*

REGION/STATE	POPULATION — NUMBER (Thousands)	POPULATION — % OF U.S.	POPULATION — MEDIAN AGE	POPULATION BY AGE GROUP (Thousands) — 0–17 YEARS	18–24 YEARS	25–34 YEARS	35–49 YEARS	50 & OVER	HOUSEHOLDS — NUMBER (Thousands)	HOUSEHOLDS — % OF U.S.
NEW ENGLAND	12,918.8	5.2597	33.5	3,091.4	1,448.7	2,245.9	2,527.0	3,605.8	4,795.8	5.2788
Connecticut	3,242.5	1.3201	34.2	769.4	342.6	551.5	671.3	907.7	1,187.3	1.3068
Maine	1,191.8	.4852	32.9	307.7	126.4	203.7	228.2	325.8	443.3	.4880
Massachusetts	5,884.1	2.3956	33.6	1,375.3	681.2	1,029.8	1,127.0	1,670.8	2,201.1	2.4228
New Hampshire	1,060.1	.4316	32.4	268.4	117.9	195.1	212.0	266.7	394.7	.4344
Rhode Island	990.0	.4031	34.1	228.9	115.9	164.8	182.3	298.1	363.3	.3999
Vermont	550.3	.2241	31.8	141.7	64.7	101.0	106.2	136.7	206.1	.2269
MIDDLE ATLANTIC	37,666.0	15.3348	34.3	9,061.5	3,907.8	6,284.2	7,583.3	10,829.2	14,083.8	15.5024
New Jersey	7,728.6	3.1465	34.5	1,881.7	768.9	1,284.1	1,619.2	2,174.7	2,828.6	3.1135
New York	17,964.0	7.3136	34.2	4,326.1	1,853.7	3,053.3	3,664.9	5,066.0	6,736.4	7.4149
Pennsylvania	11,973.4	4.8747	34.5	2,853.7	1,285.2	1,946.8	2,299.2	3,588.5	4,518.8	4.9740
EAST NORTH CENTRAL	42,162.8	17.1656	32.1	11,108.6	4,764.3	7,320.9	8,227.5	10,741.5	15,558.0	17.1250
Illinois	11,657.6	4.7461	32.4	3,007.2	1,304.4	2,036.7	2,302.8	3,006.5	4,292.7	4.7251
Indiana	5,570.8	2.2680	31.9	1,497.3	632.5	956.5	1,090.2	1,394.3	2,023.6	2.2274
Michigan	9,262.9	3.7712	31.5	2,507.0	1,067.0	1,635.0	1,803.4	2,250.5	3,372.1	3.7118
Ohio	10,834.9	4.4112	32.5	2,827.4	1,201.7	1,862.9	2,126.0	2,816.9	4,064.3	4.4736
Wisconsin	4,836.6	1.9691	32.1	1,269.7	558.7	829.8	905.1	1,273.3	1,805.3	1.9871
WEST NORTH CENTRAL	17,854.6	7.2692	32.6	4,596.0	2,034.6	3,036.9	3,357.4	4,829.7	6,679.0	7.3517
Iowa	2,860.7	1.1647	32.7	736.7	327.7	474.5	522.6	799.2	1,102.9	1.2140
Kansas	2,495.0	1.0158	32.7	626.1	291.4	427.7	466.7	683.1	946.4	1.0417
Minnesota	4,292.3	1.7475	31.8	1,126.0	494.8	769.5	821.6	1,080.4	1,592.2	1.7525
Missouri	5,173.6	2.1063	33.5	1,302.7	561.5	851.3	1,004.2	1,453.9	1,910.9	2.1034
Nebraska	1,616.8	.6583	32.3	420.2	185.2	276.8	297.5	437.1	609.7	.6711
North Dakota	694.3	.2827	30.9	186.7	89.0	120.4	119.9	178.3	249.0	.2741
South Dakota	721.9	.2939	31.7	197.6	85.0	116.7	124.9	197.7	267.9	.2949
SOUTH ATLANTIC	42,087.3	17.1349	33.2	10,402.6	4,655.2	7,326.0	8,438.7	11,264.8	15,772.9	17.3617
Delaware	642.5	.2616	32.4	163.7	75.7	110.7	130.8	161.6	231.1	.2544
District of Columbia	623.3	.2537	33.3	125.8	79.9	127.9	123.9	165.8	254.5	.2802
Florida	12,163.9	4.9523	37.3	2,648.8	1,185.2	1,875.1	2,270.0	4,184.8	4,904.1	5.3980
Georgia	6,295.2	2.5629	31.1	1,730.0	703.9	1,164.6	1,298.8	1,397.9	2,258.7	2.4862
Maryland	4,562.6	1.8576	32.5	1,139.2	502.7	847.1	989.7	1,083.9	1,653.8	1.8204
North Carolina	6,463.6	2.6315	32.1	1,651.6	767.5	1,143.3	1,311.8	1,589.4	2,393.0	2.6341
South Carolina	3,458.4	1.4080	30.7	953.7	422.1	619.5	679.6	783.5	1,238.7	1.3634
Virginia	5,943.2	2.4196	32.0	1,483.2	714.6	1,111.9	1,271.1	1,362.4	2,111.1	2.3237
West Virginia	1,934.6	.7877	32.9	506.6	203.6	325.9	363.0	535.5	727.9	.8013
EAST SOUTH CENTRAL	15,484.3	6.3040	31.9	4,194.2	1,734.5	2,615.6	3,017.6	3,922.4	5,642.0	6.2103
Alabama	4,137.1	1.6843	32.0	1,125.2	461.2	686.2	807.5	1,057.0	1,522.4	1.6757
Kentucky	3,771.5	1.5355	31.8	1,018.5	428.1	649.9	727.8	947.2	1,361.3	1.4984
Mississippi	2,676.2	1.0895	30.6	792.0	305.6	425.8	488.0	664.8	930.7	1.0245
Tennessee	4,899.5	1.9947	32.6	1,258.5	539.6	853.7	994.3	1,253.4	1,827.6	2.0117
WEST SOUTH CENTRAL	27,170.2	11.0617	31.0	7,505.8	3,151.5	4,851.5	5,280.5	6,380.9	9,744.5	10.7262
Arkansas	2,420.0	.9852	33.4	644.2	246.7	381.4	457.5	690.2	890.3	.9800
Louisiana	4,517.8	1.8393	30.1	1,310.9	545.1	790.0	847.6	1,024.2	1,587.4	1.7473
Oklahoma	3,344.4	1.3616	32.7	863.1	373.2	565.8	654.3	888.0	1,265.9	1.3935
Texas	16,888.0	6.8756	30.7	4,687.6	1,986.5	3,114.3	3,321.1	3,778.5	6,000.9	6.6054
MOUNTAIN	13,417.9	5.4629	30.5	3,737.7	1,572.9	2,525.7	2,611.1	2,968.5	4,979.5	5.4811
Arizona	3,441.1	1.4010	31.9	910.7	391.2	604.6	653.8	880.8	1,312.2	1.444
Colorado	3,346.3	1.3624	30.8	854.4	409.7	708.5	689.7	684.0	1,301.2	1.4323
Idaho	1,033.9	.4210	30.1	309.0	113.9	183.8	194.8	232.4	360.4	.3967
Montana	832.1	.3388	31.5	223.9	92.9	151.7	161.0	202.6	321.6	.3540
Nevada	1,026.7	.4180	32.5	251.0	112.6	199.4	231.4	232.3	420.8	.4632
New Mexico	1,525.0	.6209	30.0	449.2	175.8	273.9	296.8	329.3	546.7	.6018
Utah	1,712.4	.6971	26.5	596.0	214.4	303.9	287.9	310.2	530.9	.5843
Wyoming	500.4	.2037	29.3	143.5	62.4	101.9	95.7	96.9	185.7	.2044
PACIFIC	36,860.8	15.0072	32.1	9,133.8	4,235.1	7,124.0	7,474.9	8,893.0	13,593.5	14.9628
Alaska	545.7	.2222	28.2	163.2	67.6	132.0	120.8	62.1	186.5	.2053
California	27,939.0	11.3748	32.2	6,863.4	3,230.9	5,360.3	5,690.7	6,793.7	10,223.6	11.2534
Hawaii	1,088.8	.4433	30.6	285.1	136.0	218.3	215.5	233.9	343.8	.3785
Oregon	2,738.4	1.1149	32.5	683.4	287.6	534.3	535.4	697.7	1,060.7	1.1675
Washington	4,548.9	1.8520	32.1	1,138.7	513.0	879.1	912.5	1,105.6	1,778.9	1.9581
TOTAL UNITED STATES	245,622.7	100.0000	32.5	62,831.6	27,504.6	43,332.7	48,518.0	63,435.8	90,849.0	100.0000

SOURCE: *Sales & Marketing Management; 1988 Survey of Buying Power.*

*S & MM estimates

TABLE 2.2 State and Regional Population Growth 1980–1987

REGION/STATE	POPULATION (thousands)			PERCENT OF U.S. POPULATION		
	1987	1980	% CHANGE 1980–87	1970	1980	1987
NEW ENGLAND	12,918.8	12,386.1	+ 4.3%	5.78%	5.42%	5.26%
Connecticut	3,242.5	3,109.0	+ 4.3	1.49	1.36	1.32
Maine	1,191.8	1,134.3	+ 5.1	.48	.50	.49
Massachusetts	5,884.1	5,741.1	+ 2.5	2.77	2.51	2.40
New Hampshire	1,060.1	935.5	+13.3	.35	.41	.43
Rhode Island	990.0	949.6	+ 4.3	.47	.42	.40
Vermont	550.3	516.6	+ 6.5	.22	.23	.22
MIDDLE ATLANTIC	37,666.0	36,779.6	+ 2.4%	18.19%	16.10%	15.33%
New Jersey	7,728.6	7,380.2	+ 4.7	3.54	3.23	3.15
New York	17,964.0	17,526.3	+ 2.5	8.91	7.67	7.31
Pennsylvania	11,973.4	11,873.1	+ 0.8	5.74	5.20	4.87
EAST NORTH CENTRAL	42,162.8	41,800.9	+ 0.9%	19.76%	18.29%	17.17%
Illinois	11,657.6	11,452.7	+ 1.8	5.45	5.01	4.75
Indiana	5,570.8	5,512.9	+ 1.1	2.55	2.41	2.27
Michigan	9,262.9	9,287.9	− 0.3	4.38	4.06	3.77
Ohio	10,834.9	10,813.3	+ 0.2	5.23	4.73	4.41
Wisconsin	4,836.6	4,734.1	+ 2.2	2.15	2.07	1.97
WEST NORTH CENTRAL	17,854.6	17,281.8	+ 3.3%	8.02%	7.56%	7.27%
Iowa	2,860.7	2,942.8	− 2.9	1.38	1.28	1.16
Kansas	2,495.0	2,374.9	+ 5.0	1.11	1.04	1.02
Minnesota	4,292.3	4,103.6	+ 4.6	1.86	1.80	1.75
Missouri	5,173.6	4,947.9	+ 4.6	2.31	2.17	2.11
Nebraska	1,616.8	1,579.6	+ 2.4	.73	.69	.66
North Dakota	694.3	657.1	+ 5.7	.30	.29	.28
South Dakota	721.9	694.2	+ 3.9	.32	.30	.29
SOUTH ATLANTIC	42,087.3	37,481.6	+12.3%	15.14%	16.40%	17.13%
Delaware	642.5	599.4	+ 7.1	.27	.26	.26
District of Columbia	623.3	628.5	− 0.8	.37	.28	.25
Florida	12,163.9	10,026.0	+21.3	3.40	4.39	4.95
Georgia	6,295.2	5,536.4	+13.7	2.27	2.42	2.56
Maryland	4,562.6	4,236.8	+ 7.7	1.93	1.85	1.86
North Carolina	6,463.6	5,930.6	+ 9.0	2.50	2.60	2.63
South Carolina	3,458.4	3,157.7	+ 9.5	1.28	1.38	1.41
Virginia	5,943.2	5,399.0	+10.1	2.28	2.36	2.42
West Virginia	1,934.6	1,967.2	− 1.7	.84	.86	.79
EAST SOUTH CENTRAL	15,484.3	14,801.0	+ 4.6%	6.30%	6.48%	6.30%
Alabama	4,137.1	3,921.9	+ 5.5	1.69	1.72	1.68
Kentucky	3,771.5	3,698.4	+ 2.0	1.58	1.62	1.54
Mississippi	2,676.2	2,540.2	+ 5.4	1.10	1.11	1.09
Tennessee	4,899.5	4,640.5	+ 5.6	1.94	2.03	1.99

(continued)

TABLE 2.2   *Continued*

REGION/STATE	POPULATION (thousands)			PERCENT OF U.S. POPULATION		
	1987	1980	% CHANGE 1980–87	1970	1980	1987
WEST SOUTH CENTRAL	27,170.2	24,096.8	+ 12.8%	9.58%	10.55%	11.06%
Arkansas	2,420.0	2,311.3	+ 4.7	.95	1.01	.99
Louisiana	4,517.8	4,251.2	+ 6.3	1.80	1.86	1.84
Oklahoma	3,344.4	3,059.5	+ 9.3	1.26	1.34	1.36
Texas	16,888.0	14,474.8	+ 16.7	5.56	6.33	6.88
MOUNTAIN	13,417.9	11,692.5	+ 14.8%	4.11%	5.09%	5.46%
Arizona	3,441.1	2,805.6	+ 22.7	.88	1.23	1.40
Colorado	3,346.3	2,940.4	+ 15.2	1.10	1.29	1.36
Idaho	1,033.9	963.9	+ 7.3	.35	.42	.42
Montana	832.1	795.3	+ 4.6	.34	.35	.34
Nevada	1,026.7	822.0	+ 24.9	.24	.36	.42
New Mexico	1,525.0	1,323.1	+ 15.3	.54	.58	.62
Utah	1,712.4	1,497.1	+ 14.4	.52	.66	.70
Wyoming	500.4	482.1	+ 3.8	.16	.21	.20
PACIFIC	36,860.8	32,239.8	+ 14.3%	13.13%	14.11%	15.00%
Alaska	545.7	410.2	+ 33.0	.15	.18	.22
California	27,939.0	23,979.8	+ 16.5	9.87	10.49	11.37
Hawaii	1,088.8	979.1	+ 11.2	.39	.43	.44
Oregon	2,738.4	2,678.4	+ 2.2	1.04	1.17	1.11
Washington	4,548.9	4,192.3	+ 8.5	1.68	1.83	1.85
TOTAL U.S.	245,622.7	228,497.1	+ 7.5%	100.00%	100.00%	100.00%

SOURCE: *Sales & Marketing Management; 1988 Survey of Buying Power.*

TABLE 2.3   Metro Population Growth Leaders, 1980–1991

1980–86		1986–91, PROJECTION	
METRO	GAIN	METRO	GAIN
Naples, FL	43.7%	Anchorage, AK	17.7%
Ocala, FL	40.9	Naples, FL	17.7
Midland, TX	38.9	Midland, TX	17.6
Anchorage, AK	37.3	Austin, TX	17.4
Fort Pierce, FL	37.0	Ocala, FL	17.3
Austin, TX	36.6	Fort Myers–Cape Coral, FL	16.9
Fort Myers–Cape Coral, FL	35.9	Fort Pierce, FL	16.9
Melbourne–Titusville–Palm Bay, FL	32.5	Melbourne–Titusville–Palm Bay, FL	16.5
West Palm Beach–Boca Raton–Delray Beach, FL	31.9	West Palm Beach–Boca Raton–Delray Beach, FL	16.4
Fort Walton Beach, FL	29.7	Bryan–College Station, TX	16.0

SOURCE: *Sales & Marketing Management; 1988 Survey of Buying Power.*

If you're still following that SIC number 3662, you can get a breakdown, by employment totals, total shipments, percentages of SIC classifications, and so on, of the top seventy-one counties in the country. The *Survey* reports, for example, that Los Angeles County has eighty-three plants that make radio and TV equipment. Up above, in 3662, you'll notice that Cook County, Illinois, has eight companies that make telephone/telegraph gear.

Now, depending on your business and how wide you want to fling your marketing net, you take one or two more tracks. Track II leads to *Contacts Influential,* and Track III leads to Standard & Poor's *Register of Corporations, Directors, and Executives.*

Track II   *Contacts Influential* gives information at the county level. Follow your SIC number (3662 in our example) to the first *Contacts* book, which gives you the name of a particular corporation, its address and phone number, and the names of the key officers. Next you double-check your data in the section where 3662 firms are listed by zip code. Finally, you look up the list of the key officers in their own section.

SIC 3662 has led you to some possible contacts in a specific county of interest. If you believe your device might be marketable at the national level, go on to Track III.

Track III   SIC 3662 will lead you first to Standard & Poor's *Index,* where you locate the company you want, Electrospace Systems, Inc., located in Richardson, Texas. Then you move to another S&P volume, entitled *Corporations,* where you look up Electrospace Systems. Here you'll find the company's address and phone number, a list of its officers, the number of employees, regional contacts, its sales for the previous year, a list of its products, and your old friend SIC 3662.

Since the listings in *Corporations* are alphabetical, you'll find other interesting corporations beginning with *electro*——Electronics Corporation of America, Elec-

TABLE 2.4   Metros with the Highest and Lowest Median Household Effective Buying Income, 1987

HIGHEST		LOWEST	
METRO	**MEDIAN EBI**	**METRO**	**MEDIAN EBI**
Nassau–Suffolk, NY	$45,412	Alexandria, LA	$18,624
Bridgeport–Stamford–Norwalk–Danbury, CT	42,751	Monroe, LA	18,566
San Jose, CA	41,748	Panama City, FL	18,130
Middlesex–Somerset–Hunterdon, NJ	41,378	Brownsville–Harlingen, TX	17,588
Washington, DC	39,355	Ocala, FL	17,553
Lake County, IL	38,254	Gadsden, AL	17,546
Oxnard–Ventura, CA	38,157	Las Cruces, NM	17,214
Bergen–Passaic, NJ	38,147	Jacksonville, NC	16,506
Anaheim–Santa Ana, CA	37,532	McAllen–Edinburg–Mission, TX	15,460
Trenton, NJ	36,457	Laredo, TX	15,390

SOURCE: *Sales & Marketing Management;* 1988 *Survey of Buying Power.*

TABLE 2.5 Metros with the Highest Percentage of Households with Incomes of $50,000 or More, 1987

METRO	% OF HOUSEHOLDS WITH EBIs OF $50,000+	MEDIAN HOUSEHOLD EBI
Nassau–Suffolk, NY	44.0%	$45,412
Bridgeport–Stamford–Norwalk–Danbury, CT	42.6	42,751
San Jose, CA	39.9	41,748
Middlesex–Somerset–Hunterdon, NJ	38.3	41,378
Washington, DC	36.9	39,355
Bergen-Passaic, NJ	35.5	38,147
Oxnard–Ventura, CA	34.5	38,157
Anaheim–Santa Ana, CA	33.7	37,532
Trenton, NJ	33.7	36,457
Lake County, IL	33.4	38,254
Newark, NJ	32.2	35,056
San Francisco, CA	31.7	34,648
Oakland, CA	31.3	34,920
Manchester–Nashua, NH	30.5	35,668
Hartford–New Britain–Middletown–Bristol, CT	30.3	35,784
Poughkeepsie, NY	30.0	35,920
Monmouth–Ocean, NJ	29.4	33,725
Anchorage, AK	29.4	34,008
Boston–Lawrence–Salem–Lowell–Brockton, MA	29.3	33,895
New Haven–Waterbury–Meriden, CT	29.2	34,288
Honolulu, HI	28.3	32,848
Seattle, WA	27.5	33,476
Kenosha, WI	27.1	34,483
Richland–Kennewick–Pasco, WA	26.5	34,398
Los Angeles–Long Beach, CA	26.2	30,059
U.S. Total	18.1%	$25,888

SOURCE: *Sales & Marketing Management; 1988 Survey of Buying Power.*

TABLE 2.6 Metros with the Highest and Lowest Median Age, 1988

	HIGHEST			LOWEST	
RANK	METRO	MEDIAN AGE	RANK	METRO	MEDIAN AGE
1.	Sarasota, FL	51.1	309.	Grand Forks, ND	26.7
2.	Bradenton, FL	45.4	310.	Champaign–Urbana–Rantoul, IL	26.6
3.	Fort Myers–Cape Coral, FL	42.8	311.	Lawton, OK	26.6
4.	Daytona Beach, FL	41.8	312.	Kileen–Temple, TX	26.5
5.	West Palm Beach–Boca Raton–Delray Beach, FL	41.7	313.	Laredo, TX	26.4
			314.	Lawrence, KS	26.2
6.	Fort Lauderdale–Hollywood–Pompano Beach, FL	40.7	315.	Fayetteville, NC	26.1
			316.	Bryan–College Station, TX	24.5
7.	Tampa–St. Petersburg–Clearwater, FL	40.5	317.	Jacksonville, NC	23.7
			318.	Provo–Orem, UT	23.1
8.	Naples, FL	40.1			
9.	Fort Pierce, FL	39.5			
10.	Ocala, FL	38.3			

SOURCE: *Sales & Marketing Management;* 1988 *Survey of Buying Power.*

tronics Corporation of Texas, Electronics Research, Inc. (which you learn makes FM broadcasting antennas—perhaps another market tie-in), and so on.

In summary, SIC codes can help you to:

1. discover what industry you're in,
2. define the boundaries of that industry,
3. locate customers and suppliers within that industry, and
4. reach out to other industries thoughtfully and systematically.

SEGMENTATION AND GAP ANALYSIS

The idea of market segmentation is to keep breaking down potential markets into as many "digestible" subsegments as possible. The more you learn about an industry, the farther you'll be able to go. This procedure will help you to isolate opportunity gaps and to see combinations of gaps that may constitute markets. Figure 2.4 illustrates a mind map that "explodes" one segment of the health-care industry into subsegments. This is the kind of thinking we want you to do in Action Step 14. It's another brainstorming type of activity, so have fun with it.

Entrepreneur Fred Hayes searched for gaps and opportunities by taking a long look at a major, far-reaching trend—the Baby Boom. Fred explains:

"I got into baby bedding by studying the home. What did it need? What would it be like in five years? Then I targeted the last wave of Baby Boomers—they were in their late twenties when I founded Sweet Dreams Bedding. My market research showed me that these people were having fewer kids but were spending more money

---

ACTION STEP 14

Have some fun with segmentation and gap analysis.

Form some of your friends into a focus group and poll them about gaps in the marketplace. Ask them to respond to such questions as:

What products do they need that they can't get?

What services?

How could they increase their productivity without working more hours?

What products or services would enhance their quality of life?

Make a list of the gaps that the group identifies. Then project the list out as far as you can, and follow the wants and frustrations of your friends into the marketplace. Are any of the needs they mentioned national in scope?

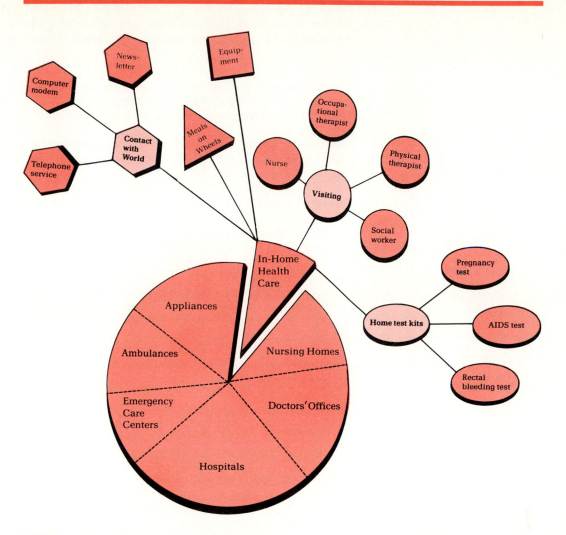

FIGURE 2.4   A mind-map analysis of just one segment of the health care industry. Use mind maps to explore *your* industry.

on the ones they did have. That info told me to position my products in what we called "the New Nursery." My first year, sales were spotty. My second year, I grossed over a million dollars. I listen to my customers, and they tell me what they want me to produce. That nursery is my marketplace."

Fred Hayes is a big man, six-two, 210 pounds. He served in the Air Force, where he learned to sew on industrial machines and do construction work, and after that he made good money in commercial construction. An on-the-job accident put an end to that career, however.

Fred was in the hospital three weeks recuperating, and when he got out, the pain in his back told him he wouldn't be able to continue in construction work. Fred was bitter, but he was willing and able to shift careers.

"Okay, I was forty-one years old. I had two great kids and a good marriage. I started collecting workmen's comp and looking around for a job, but it soon became clear that no one wanted to hire me.

"That meant I was going to have to work for *myself.*

"I signed up for a seminar in small business. I was a stand-up student, because it hurt to sit for more than twenty minutes at a stretch. But I got the message of small business loud and clear. . . .

" 'Know what business you're in,' the prof said. 'Scrounge up some customers who agree with you. Ask them what products they need and want. Find out what they can pay. Make the product. Ship it. Always pay your bills. And make sure you're pals with your banker before you run short of cash.' "

It was good advice, and Fred took it. Market research told him there was room in the baby bedding business, and he found a job sewing for a mattress manufacturer—to learn the business from the inside. In his spare time he designed a nursery set for some neighbors who had a new baby, and they were impressed. That's how Sweet Dreams Bedding began.

Fred worked out of his home the first year. When orders came in, he hired some help and moved into a small warehouse. As someone else took over the sewing, Fred went into sales. He kept an accurate customer file and was always careful to ask the customers what they liked about his product.

"When you're in the baby business," Fred says, "and especially in the bedding segment, you study birthrates. I spent half my life in the library, looking at SIC codes and census tracts. I knew the Baby Boomers wouldn't have babies forever."

But business is funny. The second year Fred discovered that although young couples were having fewer children, they were spending a lot more money outfitting the children they did have. This gave Fred the clue that he should expand into coordinated nursery items—pillowcases, dust ruffles, and coverlets that go together.

" 'Trends are like customers,' my small business prof used to say. 'You can spot some of them by standing outside and staring through the window. But others don't show up until you're in business, working and sweating away, wondering whether or not you'll make it.' "

shopping-cart analysis
a process of primary research in which you observe purchases in a supermarket, drugstore, or other mass-market arena

Action Step 15 can help you make some informal judgments about the marketplace. **Shopping cart analysis** is another window through which you can view the market.

SUMMARY

A trend is a direction of movement. For example, the trend of our present civilization is away from the smokestacks of the Industrial Age toward the computers of the Information Age. An easy way to start studying trends is to see what is happening in big business—since it is highly visible—and then move on to your own arena—the neighborhood, nearby shopping malls, Main Street, your trade association, your supermarket.

Two tools will help you chart trends: looking around with "new eyes" (that is, playing marketplace detective), and applying the life-cycle yardstick to products, industries, and so on. A life cycle has four phases: embryo, growth, maturity, and decline. Before you open the doors of your small business, you need to be aware of what phase your product is in. For example, if you think there's easy money in selling microcomputers, you need to know that this industry is now maturing. If you want to install security products, you need to know that this industry is between the embryonic stage and the growth stage. If you're thinking about opening a toy store, you need to know that the toy industry is mature and seems to be on the decline (see news articles on what happened at Mattel), and that you'll have to steal customers from other people.

Just for fun, select three to six businesses at random—for example, a foreign auto repair business, a restaurant–bar, a flower shop, a bedding manufacturer, a travel agent, and a computer school—and determine their life-cycle stages. While you're doing that, remember what happened to the railroad industry in the U.S. Is the same thing happening to some of the smaller firms you know because they're failing to see what business they're really in?

Information on trends is all around you—on the freeways, in the stores in mid December and after Christmas, in the headlines and classifieds, at government agencies, in the many trade associations. This information can give you the big picture if you know how to seek it out.

ACTION STEP REVIEW

10 Travel back in time and observe a marketplace of the past. How has it changed?

11 Define your business and test your definition by reaching out beyond the classroom.

12 What's new? What's hot? What's cooling down?

13 Assess the lifestyle of your potential target customer by walking its neighborhood.

14 Have some fun with segmentation and gap analysis.

15 Decode the secrets of the shopping cart using your new eyes.

THINK POINTS FOR SUCCESS

◤ The most valuable tool you can use for charting trends is the four-stage life-cycle yardstick.

◤ The life-cycle yardstick helps you find a growth industry, decide what business you're really in, and discover gaps and segments that are promising.

◤ Once you know what segment you're in, you can focus on market research with new eyes.

◤ Try to latch onto a trend that will help you survive (in style) for the next 10–15 years.

◤ Trends don't develop overnight. The signs are out for all to read months, and sometimes years, in advance.

REFERENCES

Agins, Teri. "Murjani and Its Former President Will Relaunch Gloria Vanderbilt Jeans." *Wall Street Journal,* May 18, 1988. [An old story in market trends: too many brands slapped onto too many products fuzzied the Gloria Vanderbilt image and confused customers, chopping profits out of a market that raked in $500 in 1980. Marketeers, beware.]

Akey, Denise, ed. *Encyclopedia of Associations,* 17th Edition. Vol. 1, National Organizations of the U.S.; Vol. 2, Geographic and Executive Index; Vol. 3, New Associations and Projects. Detroit: Gale Research Co., 1982.

Bohigian, Valerie. *How to Make Your Home-Based Business Grow: Turning Products into Profits.* New York: New American Library, 1984.

Brademus, J. "Making America Work Again—Report of a National Commission on Jobs and Small Business," *Financial World,* June 2, 1987.

Buss, Dale, D. "GM Weighing More Big Cuts in Work Force." *Wall Street Journal,* February 21, 1984. [Predicts a cut in the GM work force up to 120,000 people by mid 1986. An internal company document talks about wage increases based on corporate performance, robotics, and "aggressive productivity." The essay reads like a chapter out of *Megatrends.*]

"Chrysler, Having Cut Muscle as Well as Fat, Is Still in a Weak State." *Wall Street Journal,* July 15, 1983. [Summarizes the Chrysler saga from bail out through repayment of the first $400 million to the federal government. Excellent piece on a segment of the auto industry.]

Contacts Influential, 13132 Magnolia Street, Suite B, Garden Grove, CA 92644; 714-539-2032. [Publishes metropolitan-area business directories that takes off from SIC codes and lists firms by zip code. It names key individuals and gives telephone numbers. Currently covers the following metropolitan areas: Los Angeles County, Orange County (Ca.), San Diego County, San Francisco Bay Area, Denver, Kansas City, Minneapolis/St. Paul, Seattle/Tacoma, Tampa/Orlando, Vancouver, and Calgary. Plans to expand into many other metropolitan areas.]

Encyclopedia of Associations, 22nd Edition. Vol. 1, National Organizations of the U.S.; Vol. 2, Geographic and Executive Indexes; Vol. 3, New Associations and Projects; Vol. 4, International Organizations, Associations Periodicals. Detroit: Gale Research Co., 1988 (annual).

Engelmayer, Paul A. "Worker-Owned and -Operated Supermarket Yields Financial Success, Personal Rewards." *Wall Street Journal,* August 18, 1983. [Heartwarming piece about the union and union-member purchase of a going-out-of-business A&P supermarket in Philadelphia. It reads like a page from Naisbitt's book—the end of the pyramid, the demise of the large corporation, the move to local control and local ownership. Along with *Megatrends,* the *Journal* can keep you up on what's happening in the world and in business. This is not an advertisement.]

Entrepreneur, monthly magazine. 2392 Morse Avenue, Irvine, CA 92714-6234.

Furlong, Tom. "Japanese Investors Raise Profile, Eyebrows in U.S." *Los Angeles Times,* April 7, 1988. [As the dollar dropped in 1987 and 1988, foreign investors were buying up U.S. real estate. California was the prime target. Experts say the Japanese held ownership to more than twelve billion dollars' worth of American real estate not including office buildings. The trend is toward buying country clubs.]

Gale Directory of Publications, 120th Edition. Detroit: Gale Research Co., 1988. [Good starting point for running down trade associations.]

Gibson, Richard. "Electronic Price Labels Tested in Supermarkets." *Wall Street Journal,* March 31, 1988. [If you thought you could find work at your local supermarket, think again. The big guys are retrofitting their stores with electronic price changers. The cost is $100,000 per store, but it takes one person about nine hours to change 600 labels. The benefits: supermarkets not only save labor, they are better able to keep up with price changes. What's next, shelves stocked by robots?]

Inc., monthly magazine. 38 Commercial Wharf, Boston, MA 02110.

Journal of Small Business Management, quarterly magazine. Bureau of Business Research, West Virginia University, P.O. Box 6025, Morgantown, WVa 26505-6025.

Kamm, Thomas. "Midnight Madness: French Pay Francs to See Commercials." *Wall Street Journal,* May 11, 1988. [The latest trend in trend-conscious Paris is *Nuit des Publivores,* "Night of the Ad-Eaters." The ads feature movie stars such as Romy Schneider and Catherine Deneuve and push such products as Woolite®, Perrier®, Fiats, and Hamlet® cigars. Think they can export that?]

Lieberoff, Allen. *Climb Your Own Ladder: 101 Home Businesses that Can Make You Wealthy.* New York: Simon and Schuster, 1982.

Market Guide. New York: Editor and Publisher (annual). [Provides market data for more than 1,500 U.S. and Canadian cities where a daily newspaper is published. Gives info on location, transportation, population, banks, climate, shopping centers, retail stores, etc.]

Merriam, John E., and Joel Makower. *Trend Watching: How the Media Create Trends and How to be the First to Uncover Them.* New York: The Tilden Press, 1988. [An elaborate system for tracking media decisions to cover news. Uses Naisbitt as a whipping boy. Might be helpful to investors.]

Naisbitt, John. *Megatrends: Ten New Directions Transforming Our Lives.* New York: Warner Books, 1982. [Naisbitt's book makes trend-charting easy. The book is well-written, positive, and farsighted. We've said it before: this book is a must-read for entrepreneurs.]

National Trade and Professional Associations of the United States, 23rd Edition. Washington, D.C.: Columbia Books, 1988 (annual).

1986 Sourcebook of Demographics and Buying Power for Every Zip Code in the USA. Fairfax, Va.: CACI, Inc., 1986. [For more information, call 800-292-2224.]

Plawin, Paul. "Your Home Business: Starting It Right." *Changing Times,* August 1987.

Rand McNally Commercial Atlas and Marketing Guide. Chicago: Rand McNally (annual).

Slocum, Ken. "The Sun Belt Gains Manufacturing Jobs as Nation Loses Them." *Wall Street Journal,* April 1, 1988. [The Sun Belt has more manufacturing jobs—over five million since the slump of 1984–1987; the Rust Belt has fewer—down 392,000 to 7,701,700. Across the nation, we've lost 382,000 manufacturing jobs, mostly because of foreign inroads. It's a grim picture, because manufacturing creates other kinds of jobs. North Carolina now has 30% of its jobs in manufacturing.]

Standard and Poor's Register of Corporations, Directors, and Executives. New York: Standard and Poor's Corporation (annual).

Survey of Buying Power. New York: Sales and Marketing Management Magazine, 1983. [S & MM publishes supplements to its magazine that are extremely helpful to the small business owner. We like the *Annual Survey of Buying Power* and the *Annual Survey of Commercial and Industrial Buying Power.* If your library doesn't carry these, you can inquire at the S & MM office, 633 Third Ave., New York, NY 10164-0563.]

Tepper, Terri, and Nona Dawe Tepper. *The New Entrepreneurs: Women Working from Home.* New York: Universe Books, 1980.

Thomas Register of American Manufacturers. New York: Thomas Publishing Co., 1984. [If you're wondering whether your invention has already been invented, check the Thomas catalogs of manufacturers—complete with product descriptions, photos, and so on.]

"Turn Your Play into Pay." *Changing Times,* November 1986.

Venture, the Magazine for Entrepreneurs, monthly magazine. 521 Fifth Avenue, New York, NY 10175.

APPENDIX 2.1 • Model Action Step 12: What's new? What's hot? What's cooling down?

What's New?

What is new is the adoption of PostScript as a *de facto* standard as a programming language for the graphic arts industry. An in-depth report on PostScript is contained in Action Step 25, which relates to editorial and advertising research that I undertook for that assignment. PostScript arrived on the scene in January 1985 with the introduction of the Apple LaserWriter. The product was mismatched with the equipment (Apple Macintosh), and the inventor, Adobe Systems, made little progress in an Information Age Revolution until March 1985. That's when

Allied Linotype, the big professional typesetting company, adopted PostScript as the page description language for two of its professional typesetting systems.

Since then, IBM and Hewlett-Packard have fallen in line behind PostScript, and Xerox Corporation has bowed to the inevitability of PostScript's supremacy by incorporating PostScript (instead of Xerox's own Interpress) as a printer driver in Ventura Publisher. Aldus Systems Pagemaker for the PC, a PostScript-compatible program, quickly won IBM's endorsement. Now we learn that Morisawa, the Mergenthaler of Japan, has entered a joint venture with Adobe Systems to create a PostScript driver for 7,000 Kanji characters in the Japanese syllabary. Since PostScript is already available in all the Romance languages, we have only Chinese, Arabic, Hebrew and a few other alphabets and syllabaries to make PostScript the world standard.

What's Hot?

PostScript printing devices are hot, hot, hot. Thirty months ago, there was only the Apple LaserWriter. Mergenthaler provided a major thrust forward. As recently as a year ago, the jury was still out on whether PostScript or another document-description language would become the standard for laser printers. Action Step 25 documents a 272 percent increase in advertising for PostScript hardware and software in the 1987 desktop publishing trade journals compared with a similar issue in 1986. Ads for all competing systems, notably Hewlett-Packard and Tall Tree Systems, recorded a 36 percent decrease from 1986 in 1987. In addition, the editorial copy is all enamored of PostScript in news and feature articles alike.

Projection of Dollars to Be Spent

The market research firm CAP International reports that in-plant graphic arts desktop publishing was a $65 million business in 1985, with 33 percent of the desktop publishing market. (Low-level office automation accounts for more than 55 percent of the market. Office automation, while a large market, is a low-technology support group for professional desktop publishing, where the big bucks are.)

CAP International estimates that by 1990, desktop publishing will account for a $2.5 billion market, up from less than $200 million in 1985. The in-plant graphic arts portion of this market will grow from $65 million to $630 million by 1990. In-plant technical publishing using desktop devices (a medium-level technology) will nearly equal the graphics portion. Office automation will level off with half of the market, the low-technology word processing half.

My own intuition, yet to be confirmed by research, is that the following value and lifestyle groups will be the pioneers in professional desktop publishing: Achievers and Experimental groups will lead the pack. The Societally Conscious will lead the Belongers. (The I-Am-Mes and Emulators will remain stuck in amateur desktop graphics, a la the Macintosh.) The Survivors, Sustainers, and Integrated audiences will never represent a viable market for advanced desktop publishing.

What's hot in page-composition software are the programs that support PostScript: Ventura Publisher for lengthy documents and Aldus PageMaker PC for short documents where a high degree of control is required. (It is instructive for the technically oriented to know that the PostScript printer drive in Ventura Publisher requires one megabyte of memory on the computer's hard disk. The Ventura printer driver for the Hewlett-Packard LaserJet Plus requires three megabytes of hard-disk memory. That is a sure indication of the elegance of the PostScript language.)

The *Wall Street Journal* charges about $42,000 for a full-page ad in all editions nationally. Glancing through a week's issues of this national newspaper aimed at businesspeople readily indicates that PostScript-compatible hardware and software is winning the lion's share of the ad space in desktop publishing. The competing technologies typically take quarter-page space, or less. That's a solid indicator of what is happening at the national level in advanced desktop publishing.

What's Cooling Fast?

What is cooling fast are the competing technologies from Xerox, Hewlett-Packard, and a score of other manufacturers of non-PostScript laser printers. As one example, the $6,000 Xerox 4045 laser printer (which does double duty as a photocopier) is being discounted into the

$2,000 range. That's a 66 percent discount, indicative of a mature or declining market. Even Hewlett-Packard's new Series II successors to the LaserJet Plus are being discounted by up to 28 percent, with published prices of $1,800 for the $2,300 printers. For a machine that is absolutely brand new to the marketplace, that news is devastating—to Hewlett-Packard.

The graphic arts people also want color, and the laser printers based on the Canon LPB-CX engine can easily provide toner cartridges of different colors. Those like Xerox, Ricoh, and Kyocera use toner bins, which means that different colors cannot be provided without emptying the bin and changing to another color of toner. Letters to the editor in the desktop publishing magazines are bewailing these after-purchase discoveries.

Correlation with Research Sources

The big market for advanced desktop publishing is just now beginning to emerge as an infant technology. For those who are prepared to capitalize on it, there are dollars to be earned.

FIGURE 3.1   Chapter 3 will help you prepare part B of your Business Plan, "The Market and the Target Customer."

Power Marketing

LEARNING OBJECTIVES

■ To mesh your personal business objectives with one of the many opportunities in the marketplace. ■ To understand that your business objectives provide a positive and unique thrust to your business. ■ To narrow your industry research until viable gaps appear. ■ To gain insight into hidden pockets of the life-cycle by using an industry chronology. ■ To understand how problems can be turned into opportunities. ■ To combine demographic (population) data with psychographic (picture of a lifestyle) data to produce a customer profile. ■ To identify heavy users of your product or service. ■ To brainstorm creatively. ■ To use a matrix grid for blending your objectives with your research findings to produce a portrait of a business. ■ To explore the fun of power pricing.

power marketing
seven-step process by which you select a market opportunity corresponding to your strengths and objectives.

As you head for one of the doorways to small business, you may notice that you feel weighted down with information. That's part of life in this Age of Information. Opportunities exist that were unheard of five years ago, and the speed of change is awesome. If you've done the research suggested in chapter 2, you're probably experiencing information overload. That's understandable. In spite of the fact that you're a creative person and wound up and ready to charge, unless you live—vigorously—for two hundred years, you'll never be able to follow up on all the ideas you have.

What you need is a filter system, something like a wine press or a Moulie Mill, that kitchen machine that turns apples into applesauce. You have all this wonderful information and all these super ideas. To turn them into a business, you need a sifter. You need power marketing.

WELCOME TO POWER MARKETING

Power marketing is a tool that will help you exploit gaps—market segments—in the marketplace. It connects your skills to your research. It shows you what new skills you need to develop. It aims the power of your mind at a particular segment of small business.

Power marketing has seven steps (Figure 3.2). If you've been doing each action step as you move through the book, you're ahead of the game now. Here's a quick preview of the steps in power marketing:

1. Identify your business and personal objectives.
2. Learn more about your favorite industry.
3. Identify three to five promising industry segments.
4. Identify problems that need solutions.
5. Brainstorm for solutions.
6. Mesh possible solutions with your objectives.
7. Concentrate on the most promising opportunity.

At this point, you have just begun to plan. The marketplace lies open in all its excitement and confusion. The most important thing is not to lose your momentum. Momentum is related to confidence, and confidence helps you to win.

Power marketing is like a huge funnel equipped with a series of idea filters (Figure 3.3). You pour everything into this funnel—your goals, personality, problems, hopes, fears, industry data—and a viable business idea drains out at the bottom. Carrying out this process gives you the knowledge of where you're going. And that is *power*.

To illustrate how power marketing works, we've developed a case study that will lead you through the seven steps. The case study also introduces an important concept—teamwork.

Meet the Info Team

Five principals teamed together to explore opportunities in some segment of the information industry. They chose the information industry because they saw it as the wave of the future and because it accounts for a major share of the Gross National Product. It was obvious to them that the information industry held many opportunities. However, because anything that huge is hard to define, they needed a systematic process for locating gaps.

1. LIST YOUR BUSINESS AND PERSONAL OBJECTIVES.
2. RESEARCH YOUR FAVORITE INDUSTRY.
3. IDENTIFY 3-5 PROMISING SEGMENTS.
4. LIST PROBLEMS THAT NEED SOLUTIONS.
5. BRAINSTORM FOR SOLUTIONS.
6. MESH POSSIBLE SOLUTIONS WITH YOUR OBJECTIVES BY USING A MATRIX GRID.
7. CONCENTRATE ON THE MOST PROMISING OPPORTUNITY.

FIGURE 3.2   The seven steps of power marketing.

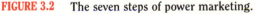

Before we describe the process they used, however, we'd better introduce the principals:

Principal A—an organizer with experience in small business consulting. His background was in engineering and commercial flying. He was fascinated with the power of computers long before they became popular.

Principal B—a manager, marketeer, and teacher. Her background was in big business and psychology.

Principal C—an attorney.

Principal D—a teacher, seminar leader, consultant to small business. His background was corporate, and his expertise was in the marketing of industrial products.

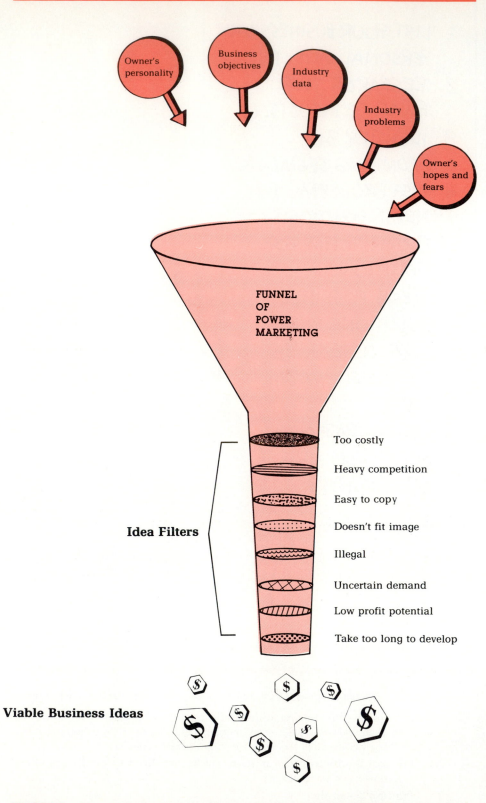

Owner's personality

Business objectives

Industry data

Industry problems

Owner's hopes and fears

FUNNEL OF POWER MARKETING

Idea Filters

Too costly

Heavy competition

Easy to copy

Doesn't fit image

Illegal

Uncertain demand

Low profit potential

Take too long to develop

Viable Business Ideas

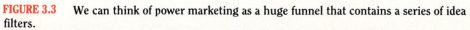

FIGURE 3.3 We can think of power marketing as a huge funnel that contains a series of idea filters.

Principal E—a teacher, seminar leader, inventor, engineer, programmer. He had worked with the mass transit industry in Japan, where he had done some work with robotics. His expertise was in the creation of products.

IDENTIFYING OBJECTIVES

All five members had extensive experience in owning and operating small businesses. Because of this, they knew very well that their first task was to list their **business objectives.**

business objectives
measurable goals a business is trying to reach

The team argued a long time, but they finally agreed on nine objectives that sounded like heaven:

1. **Psychological rewards**   They wanted to build something, to plant a seed, to watch it grow.
2. **Teamwork**   They wanted to be a part of something bigger than they could accomplish as individuals. Each member of the team had strengths and weaknesses. With luck, blending, and balancing, the team could be greater than the sum of its parts.
3. **Money**   They wanted to see a respectable return on their investment (ROI), a minimum of 25% per year.
4. **Safety**   They did not want to lose money.
5. **Growth industry**   The members of the team had a combined business experience of 163 years. They had known both failure and success. They wanted to find a booming segment of a growth industry.
6. **Time**   They knew that getting a business up and running takes a year at the very least. They decided they wanted a business that would make money in three years or one they could sell in five years for $20 million or more.
7. **Key people**   They wanted to attract the best people in the field.
8. **Fun, adventure, excitement**   From experience, they knew that starting a small business, even in a growth or glamour industry, would involve hassles, problems, and expensive surprises. So they decided to make sure their business would be one with which they would also have some fun.

growth industry
an industry whose annual sales growth is considerably above average

That's why they chose the information industry. What industry will *you* choose? Action Step 16 will help prepare you for this decision.

INDUSTRY RESEARCH

As you searched for trends in chapter 2 you probably found a dozen industries that seemed interesting. Now it's time to explore one of those industries in more depth. The industry that interests you the most might be genetics, robotics, entertainment, food service, travel, education, publishing, retailing, construction, small manufacturing, or information; it should be something that looks interesting to *you*.

As you move into your favorite industry, collect information from your previous action steps. For secondary data, visit the library for a look at periodicals like the *Wall Street Journal, Venture, Inc.,* and *Entrepreneur* and at other, general business or news sources. Most libraries are equipped with computer data bases that will help you with your search. In addition, you can check through the *Reader's Guide to Periodical Literature* or the more specific *Business Periodicals Index.* What you're looking for is an accurate picture of trends in the industry that interests you. You need to learn what's breaking, what's cresting, and what's cooling down.

To focus on your industry, break down your search into categories such as life cycle, speed of change, history, competition, recent industry breakthroughs, costs of positioning yourself, target customers, and so on. Later, after you have gathered the

ACTION STEP 16

List your business objectives.

What do you want from small business? Money? Fame? Job security? To be your own boss? Freedom to explore the marketplace? Control of your own destiny? Or maybe you just want to be a president.

Think back to the forces that made you interested in small business in the first place. What were those forces? Where were you when you first thought about owning the store? How have circumstances changed your goals?

You probably won't have trouble writing down objectives, but if you do, flip back to the notes you made for Action Step 4 and to your skills analysis (Action Step 8).

List everything you want, even if it seems unreasonable or is embarrassing to you. This is your personal list, after all, and you will sift through the ideas later.

data, you can use these categories as idea filters for sifting information through the power marketing funnel.

For example, using the life-cycle yardstick will sharpen a first look at any industry. When you're reading a newspaper and you see a headline that says CBS TRIES TO SHED STODGY IMAGE IN PRIME TIME—BUT CAN IT BE HIP?, you make three fast-reflex judgments. First, the industry is entertainment. Second, the segment is network television. Third, the shows are in the mature phase, on their way to decline.

And when you're driving down the street and you see a shopping mall being renovated, you know that the facelift is an attempt to shove the mall back from a mature or decline phase into a growth phase. The point of all this is to find an industry segment where there is room for growth.

A second helpful category is **competition**, which we'll be analyzing in detail in chapter 5. Competition varies with each stage of the life cycle. Using competition as an idea filter can save you years of grief.

A third category that might be helpful is the concept of the industry **breakthrough**. What is there in your industry or segment that really hums? Remember the first computers? They filled large rooms and ran on punch cards. The first industry breakthrough was the printed circuit. The second one was the microchip. And the third? Or picture yourself as a film director during the era of silent movies. What would have been your reaction to hearing Al Jolson in *The Jazz Singer*?

What breakthroughs are occurring in your industry? Does your business idea capitalize on the latest advances in technology and imagination? Put this kind of thinking into Action Step 17.

competition
a contestant in your arena who is fighting you for business

breakthrough
a new way through, over, under, or around an obstacle

ACTION STEP 17

Research your favorite industry.

What industry really attracts you? What's out there that has a magnetic pull that you cannot resist? To help you get started, recall what you discovered in Action Steps 12 (What's New? What's Hot?) and 14 (segmentation, gap analysis) and dive in. Also, think about what you discovered when you interviewed small business owners in Action Step 11.

A good idea at this stage is to remember the American railroads and stay wide-angle in your views. Look at genetics, robotics, entertainment, food service, travel, education, publishing, the auto industry, retailing, construction, small manufacturing, information—anything that looks interesting.

After you've decided on "your" industry, research it like crazy. It might help to organize your research into categories like life cycle, speed of change, history, competition, recent industry breakthroughs, costs of positioning yourself, customer base, and so on. One thing the Info Team did was develop an industry chronology, parts of which you will see later. A chronology helps you take a longer view of a particular industry.

IDENTIFYING MARKET GAPS

Now let's get back to our Info Team. Let's follow them through the process of industry research and see how they analyzed their data.

After gathering their research, the Info Team decided to focus on the changing role of the microcomputer within the information industry and to attempt to list some problems that need solutions. Here's what they found:

Life Cycle   Computer hardware is locked at the mature stage, with occasional lunges back to the growth stage when new innovations appear. The hardware battle is between IBM, which introduced PC/2 in 1988, and Apple, which is upgrading its Macintosh, adding more bells and whistles. At least a dozen companies have "cloned" the IBM personal computer, known in the industry as the "PC." The continuing innovation is in the laptop area, making compatibles smaller. The market for laptops consists of executives, salespeople, and programmers who travel a lot.

In 1983 the life of a piece of a typical personal computer hardware was eighteen months. Today, by adding circuit boards and microchips, PC users can upgrade their machines, extending the useful life by expanding its power and increasing its speed.

Software programs are hanging in there. Wordstar, the first word-processing program with power, is still being used but it is being jostled by programs like WordPerfect, a favorite among female office users, and Microsoft Word. The original spreadsheet programs (Supercalc, Visicalc) have been integrated into multi-taskers like Jazz, Lotus, and Symphony. The fun area of software is computer graphics. At the low end of the graphics market is clip art. At the high end is the color slide presentation for corporations.

(Problem: finding a gap that has a longer life cycle.)

Competition   Heaviest competition is in the manufacture and retailing of hardware. The only gap, cloning IBM, is filled with competitors even before the machines hit the market. The next-heaviest is in the creation, manufacture, and retailing of software. Dozens of word-processing programs compete for users. Accounting packages abound. Everyone seems to be writing software.

Industry Breakthroughs   In the computer industry, breakthroughs occur with breathtaking speed. The printed circuit pulled the hardware away from vacuum tubes. Microchips have poured power into smaller units. If you bought a PC back in the early eighties, you bought a component system—a computer (they called it a CPU), display terminal, detachable keyboard, cables—that bore a marked resemblance to a home stereo system—turntable, tape deck, speakers, and so on. Hooking up a system, if it worked, was fun, a do-it-yourself activity that made some consumers feel creative. Other major consumer breakthroughs were the portables, introduced by Adam Osborne in July 1981, and the lap models, which came in 1982.

(Problem: if you enter the information industry, which hardware do you aim at? Which software do you use?)

Quickie Conclusion   The speed of change in the computer industry continues to be overwhelming. Innovations appear every day.

(Opportunity: Take advantage of this speed.)

Industry research will give you an overview of what's happening in the segment you have chosen. As you write down what you learn, do not be overly concerned with reaching final decisions. Nevertheless, you will probably feel yourself drawing closer.

Industry Chronology

The Info Team kept things fluid, collecting information and reserving judgment. Then Principal E pulled together an **industry chronology** that gave the team a quick historical look at things. Here's what it looked like:

1977   Apple introduces the micro.

1981   One million computer systems shipped by U.S. manufacturers.

1982   Adam Osborne launches sewing-machine-size portable. IBM sells two million computers. Apple still in first place with 33% of market. According to Naisbitt's "Trend Letter," personal computers in homes increase from 340,000 to 2.4 million. At Comdex, the microcomputer industry's giant show in Las Vegas, the new "wrinkle" is that more people are developing more software for the IBM PC than for any other 16-bit machine.

1983   Pacific Stereo decides to explore computer retailing. Computerland of Connecticut drops six-year-old Apple contract. Softmart, Inc., launches network of stores devoted entirely to IBM PC software. Kaypro, the other producer of portables, goes public. Six-month sales were $26.1 million, up from previous $1.9 million. To date, Kaypro has sold 47,500 units. Analysts think Kaypro may not survive. Adam Osborne, the creator of the first portable computer, seeks bankruptcy protection. Suffering from low sales for Lisa, Apple computer counts heavily on Macintosh to keep company afloat.

1984   IBM drops prices and adds features to PCjr.

1985   IBM discontinues production of PCjr due to lackluster market performance.

1986   Burroughs and Sperry unite to form Unisys. Less costly PC clones manufactured in Korea and Japan begin to invade the U.S. market. Computer-aided medical diagnosis becomes a reality. Computer graphics on the rise. First hints of desktop publishing.

1987   Desktop publishing grows. IBM introduces the PS/2 in the minicomputer market. Compaq named by *Business Month* as among the five best-managed companies. Hewlett-Packard ships long-awaited top-line Spectrum.

1988   Once-bankrupt Franklin Computer Corporation announces software company purchase. PS/2 prototype clones announced by Tandy and Compaq—to be available by summer. Desktop publishing in growth phase.

industry chronology
the time sequence of major developments in an industry

What can you learn from an industry chronology? Well, first, it gives you a feel for time and tradition. If you're a printer, you know that the big event in your industry occurred in the fifteenth century: Gutenberg's invention of movable type. Suddenly, books moved out of the monasteries into the world, and the world changed. A quick comparison of the printing industry with the computer industry indicates how much faster breakthroughs occur in the late twentieth century.

Second, you see how long it took the industry to spread beyond the core market. The price of books fell rapidly after Gutenberg's invention, but the market remained low. This was because of the literacy problem. Education being the province of the nobility, relatively few people could read. The same thing happened with computers. (Remember the phrase *user-friendly*?) The hardware hummed impressively; computer salespeople told customers that computers could solve many problems; but the software was tricky to use and the manuals were unreadable. In the early days of personal computers, the core market was engineers, computer techies, and a few professional writers. It took awhile for the computer makers to realize they weren't going to sell to the household market without a major change in the industry.

Third, an industry chronology will help you see things that you wouldn't notice otherwise, as it did for the Info Team. Some of these relate to market gaps and industry segments.

Follow That Customer

When you write your Business Plan, you'll need to explain why you have chosen a particular market segment (gap). If you have chosen a promising segment and have communicated your excitement about it, you'll have developed a "hook" for the banker or venture capitalist who will read your plan.

The secret to focusing on gaps is to find a target customer, a person who needs a particular product or service that you could provide. Then you profile your target customer (we do this in detail in the next chapter), and that profile becomes one of your idea filters.

The Info Team made a few quick decisions that helped them to focus on a particular segment of the information industry.

> "Okay," Principal A said, "we've done our research. Tons of the stuff. But what we haven't looked at is *people*. Who's using computers today? What are they using them for? Where do they work? How old are they? What are their problems, their needs?"

These questions helped the Info Team to develop their first customer profile, and doing that led them to a different market.

> After looking hard at the information industry, the team drew some conclusions (see Figure 3.4):
>
> Hardware production was out; too much competition.
>
> Software writing/creation was possible, especially in the graphics segment, which was still in the growth phase.
>
> Software users complained about the difficulty of getting up and running on applications software.
>
> The hot growth area was desktop publishing, which combines graphics with text.
>
> The biggest gap seemed to be in education and training.
>
> Brainstorming began. Words flew around the room as the team identified computer users: "Businesspeople!" "Students!" "Educators!" "How about engineers and the CadCam?" "Secretaries!"

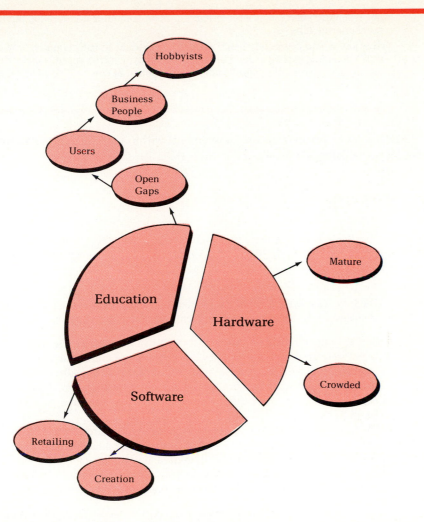

FIGURE 3.4   By segmenting the information industry, the team was able to identify the biggest gap with the greatest growth potential.

The next step was to rough out some customer profiles. One obvious problem was computerphobia—the fear of computers that many people feel. Another was the learning curve—it takes several days to get going on a piece of complex software. So the team did some primary research. They attempted to learn who's afraid of computers and who needs to get going. By doing this, they identified two target customers: Customer A and Customer B. Here are their profiles.

computerphobia
fear of the tools of the Information Age

software
the information base that tells computer hardware what to do

CUSTOMER A	CUSTOMER B
Where employed: in an office; clerical or analytical position	Where employed: at home or in a small office
Sex: female	Sex: male, 55%; female, 45%
Age: 20–55	Age: 30–60
Education: high school, limited college	Education: some college
Uses computer: at work	Uses computer: at home; small office situation
Income: $22,000	Income: $30,000 plus

(continued)

problems
opportunities

short life cycle
very rapid movement from birth to death of a product/service

Main computer use: word-processing, number-crunching

Motivation to use computer: helps with workload; status symbol; in order to keep job or get a promotion; professional development

Main computer use: desktop publishing

Motivation to use computer: joy of creativity; control; speed; superior reports; potential competitive advantage

Now it's your turn to focus on the segments within your industry and spot some that look promising. Complete Action Step 18.

IDENTIFYING INDUSTRY PROBLEMS

After you have identified at least two major target customers, you need to identify **problems** that exist in the industry. *Turning problems into opportunities* is the key to small business success.

The Info Team made a list of the problems they identified in their industry. It soon became obvious to them that some problems are common to many industries.

1. Buried computerphobia   User frustration had ebbed since the early days of the PC, when secretaries were frustrated by the technical computerese in the word-processing manuals. Problems still existed here, but the gaps were smaller because software companies had found ways to move beyond the core market. The clearest case of a user-friendly system was the Macintosh, which uses icons (symbols) instead of words to tell the user what's going on.

The real problem was a buried computerphobia. When hardware and software prices dropped, many businesses and government agencies had bought computer systems, and many of those systems were being underutilized. A year after computers were installed at a large insurance company, it was still taking thirty-nine people to produce a policy update. The people weren't *afraid* of the computers; they were *ignoring* them.

2. Speed of change   A software product can be here today and updated tomorrow. If you were using Easy Writer, the company, in its zeal to stay competitive, would bring out Easy Plus. Meanwhile, the original manufacturer had been absorbed in a leveraged buyout, and the technical support people had vanished. Calls to manufacturers about problem software were met with the words: "We no longer support that product."

3. Minimal support from software manufacturers   Because of the short life cycle of their product, software companies were putting the bulk of their energies into creating new products so they could compete in the marketplace. A few software makers had established 800-number hotlines to answer the questions of frustrated users.

4. Minimal support from retailers   Retail merchants who sold hardware and software had little time to provide service after the sale. Salespeople, trained to sell and close deals with all the energy of the fast track, were unavailable following the sale.

5. Mounting buyer exasperation   After the computer purchase, the average buyer made ten trips back to the retailer for information, help, trouble-shooting, explanations, and hand-holding.

6. Clumsiness in the marketplace   The few retailers that did attempt to provide training used ineffective teaching techniques—dull lectures, blackboard, rote memorization, do-as-I-say instruction—and the instructors tended to be as frustrated by it all as the students. The instruction was not cost-effective for the retailer or pleasing to the neophyte computer user.

Action Step 19 will help you to see opportunities in *your* industry segment.

BRAINSTORMING FOR POSSIBLE SOLUTIONS

It was clear to the Info Team that a human need was not being met. They had found a widening gap in the marketplace. This was the problem they would transform into an opportunity through the process of brainstorming. Brainstorming is a process used by many large corporations to generate fresh ideas. The goal is to come up with lots of ideas, some that may seem far out or even erroneous, and then, as momentum grows, to see concepts develop. The key to brainstorming is to reserve judgment initially so that creativity is not stifled.

What follows is a recap of a brainstorming session held by the Info Team as they began to turn problems into opportunities. You'll be able to see how personality and motivation mesh with business objectives at this stage.

Principal A took the lead. "All right," he said, "what we've got is a going business or an educational institution like a college or university. They put out a lot of paper. Their data base is growing steadily. They spend $400,000 on a networked system of IBMs, IBM clones, and Macintoshes. Their two major tasks are word processing and accounting tabulation. Then a manager reads an article about desktop publishing and asks two employees to publish a monthly newsletter. However, the word-processing people can't handle the graphics software, and the accounting people are bogged down."

"So," D asked, "what's his first move?"

"Easy," E said, "the employees go to the documentation. The first newsletter never gets out. More employees pitch in to help. Meanwhile, data backs up in the old In box. The documentation is now easy to read, but the manuals are complicated and so are the steps."

"So hire a techie," suggested B.

"There's a hiring freeze," C broke in, "and they were counting on this desktop stuff to help them through a publicity campaign."

[They had defined the problem; the time was right for brainstorming.]

"So what do we do about it?" A asked.

"I've got it!" D said. "Let's invent a *robot*! The robot could take the place of the office staff. We could program it to run the computer. . . . All it would take is some regular WD-40 and the electricity to run its battery."

"I know this guy in Hong Kong," D said, grinning. "He'd love to have a contract for a robot that does computer graphics. And he's got the Japanese contacts to make it fly."

"Let's run seminars," E said. "We could train people to care for their computerized robots."

"Let's push that seminar idea," A said.

"Yes," B said, "*seminars*."

"Push it all the way to Tahiti?" C asked. "Or Armonk?" C was tired.

"What about a school?" A asked.

"School? What *kind* of school?" E asked.

"A *computer* school. One that teaches software."

"My Uncle Charley's a farmer, back in Dubuque," D said. "He just bought a PC. Uncle Charley could be our first student."

"It's not a bad idea, you know," B said. "We could focus on the more difficult software and do desktop publishing on the side."

"Why not just do desktop publishing?" C said.

"You may not believe this," D said, "but we've got data that shows there are still people out there who haven't learned to love computers. There's still a need for a basic course. Have you tried to use WordPerfect linked with a page set-up program?"

"Sure," E said, "I even built a *better* system."

"But you're a super-techie," A said. "*I* think we've got a direction here. What's the next step?"

B said, "Our school would have to be fast . . . one-day classes . . . no quarters or semesters . . . and *no grades*. And it would have to be well-organized."

"She's right," D said. "These people are *busy*."

"And it would have to be user-friendly," A said, beginning to write on the board. "That would solve one huge problem."

"It would have to be *comfortable*," E said. "I always learn faster when I'm comfortable."

B smiled, warming to the idea. "We could *guarantee learning*," she suggested.

"How?" C asked.

"There won't be any grades in our school, so if they don't get it the first time through, they can come back for another try."

"Like mail order," E said. "We give them a guarantee."

"Right," B said.

"I like it," A said.

"So do I," E said.

"I hate to admit it, guys," C said, "but I kind of like it, too."

"How do we promote it?" B asked.

"Better yet," A said, "how much do we *charge*?"

"How about seminars?" E said. "We could work the colleges and universities."

"Have classroom, will travel!" B said.

"Yeah, yeah."

It's helpful to summarize after a brainstorming session so that you can identify the most useful ideas. Let's summarize what happened in this session:

1. The team identified problems and possible solutions.
2. All ideas were good ideas.

TABLE 3.1   Matrix Grid for Proposed Information Business

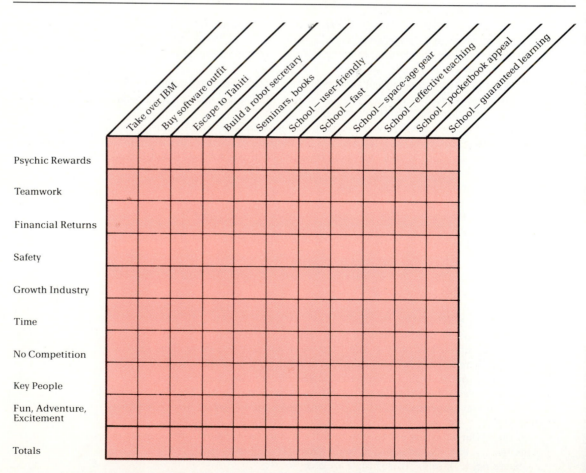

3. Graphics was the most exciting area, but the gap being created as more and more institutions purchase personal computers seemed most promising to the team.
4. The learning to be offered would have to be fast and fun.

Now that you understand what brainstorming is and what it can accomplish for a business, give it a try with your own business. Assemble your partners or some friends and go to it. Action Step 20 gives you some directions.

MATRIX ANALYSIS

Whereas some people like to use lists or mind maps for arriving at conclusions, others prefer a more systematic method. A **matrix grid** can provide the desired structure. After you have brainstormed some possible solutions, you need to improve your focus on them and evaluate them. The matrix grid in Table 3.1 helped the Info Team do this. At their next meeting they took a vote on each possible solution they'd brainstormed earlier.

When the numbers were tallied, the team saw that:

Four of the five members wanted to take over IBM. It would be great fun, they said. They could move the GHQ from Armonk to Orlando. They believed IBM was overconfident, and that a takeover would provide them with psychic rewards equalled only by the conquest of the Holy Land by the Crusaders.

The dissenting team member wanted to escape to Tahiti. Tahiti was his psychic reward, and his friend who worked for the Bank of Tahiti had guaranteed him 15% on his money. This team member had always been fascinated by off-shore banking.

Three members thought the Hong Kong robot was a great idea. When the robot wasn't programming with dBASE II, it could serve as janitor/maid/butler in the homes of the founders.

Two team members knew of software companies for sale. They urged the others to pool their money for a buyout. Buying companies held great fascination for those two.

The school to teach software emerged as the most viable option, and the plan for teaching seminars at nearby colleges and universities as a reasonable backup. The team decided that the school would:

Solve problems. People with computer systems have problems. Businesspeople have problems to solve and tasks to perform. The computer can take the load off. All you need is an open mind and the right software.

Provide clarity. Software documentation can be confusing. The school would devise a super-clear, streamlined, space-age teaching system.

Offer speed. Businesspeople are in a hurry, and time is money. Could the school teach software in a month? A week? A day? A half-day?

Build a psychological cushion. The founders would start a club. Once the students had taken a course, they'd be a club member for life and entitled to take the course over again at no charge.

Charge reasonable fees. Studies showed that businesspeople would pay $100 a day to learn software.

Be fun. If clients have fun learning, they'll relax and learn more. If they learn more, they'll spread the word about the school.

Now prepare a matrix grid to help you focus on the best course of action. Action Step 21 tells you how to do it.

ACTION STEP 20

Brainstorm for solutions.

Okay, here's where you need to get creative. Dig out the list of problems in your industry that you made in Action Step 19. Every problem can be turned into an opportunity.

You'll generate better ideas in the long run if you just let your imagination roll. Don't be concerned with a lot of logic and reason—not at this stage; just let your mind run and leap. You might begin with a quick overview of what you know so far and then slide into possible (and impossible?) solutions. A cassette recorder can be useful.

Have fun.

matrix grid
a screen through which ideas are passed in order to find solutions

psychological cushion
a unique, untouchable rung on the ladder in your target customer's mind

ACTION STEP 21

Mesh possible solutions with your objectives using a matrix grid.

A matrix analysis will help you focus, especially if you're working with a group and you have diverse objectives to satisfy. If you prepare a large grid and put it on the wall, all members of the team can participate.

Down the left side, list the objectives you brainstormed in Action Step 16. Along the top, list the possible solutions you came up with in Action Step 20. Select a rating system to use for evaluating the match of each possible solution with each of your objectives. It could be a ten-point scale or a plus-zero-minus system:

plus (+) = 3
zero (0) = 2
minus (−) = 1

When you've rated all of the combinations, find the total for each column. The totals will indicate your best prospects. The rest is up to you.

Taking Stock

What have you learned about power marketing? Before you answer this, take a minute out to rethink what you want to achieve in small business. If you feel a little uneasy about how fast you've run the last couple of laps, perhaps it's because you haven't yet identified your industry. It's time to take stock.

What is your industry?

_____

What is your segment?

_____

What are some opportunities for you?

_____

_____

Now, before you lose the feel for the process of power marketing, try sketching out a rough picture of your journey through your favorite industry. If it doesn't feel like home, you should sense it now. Action Step 22 will help you to do this.

POWER PRICING

Think of the costs of producing a heart valve. The valve may contain only twenty dollars' worth of parts, but the amounts spent for developing and marketing it are staggering. But how much is it worth to the patient?

If you own a computer and you need a piece of software to solve a particular problem, how much are you willing to pay to solve the problem fast? How much did you pay for the cup of coffee or the soda you had with your lunch yesterday? How much did it cost to produce that beverage and get it to the cafe?

Look at the history of American business in the last fifty years. How many firms made it big by cutting prices? How many made it big because they offered benefits?

The power pricing way is to think of user benefits.

> The Info Team realized that the seats in their school were "perishable." Each unsold seat would represent unsold inventory that could never again be sold. Therefore it was important that they fill as many seats as possible and give the early impression of a big, successful operation. This philosophy had direct implications for their decisions about pricing.
>
> All pricing decisions hinge on the answer to the question "What is it worth to the customer?" A business or institution that has just invested $5,000 to $500,000 for computers might be willing to pay $100, per class, or even $1,000 per class, to get its employees trained as quickly as possible. A market survey showed that prices in the competition ranged from $59.00 per day—for classes in an old-fashioned classroom situation—to $500 for on-site training at the workplace. Because their equipment and training tools would be state-of-the-art, the team felt that they could test the market at $99 per day. This would make their break even point 3.5 students. To fill the classroom, however, they decided to offer two classes for the price of one.
>
> The strategy worked. Their classes filled. Many customers commented, "You people are too cheap!"
>
> Within nine months, they had moved the daily price to $199 and had dropped the two-for-one deal. In the slow seasons—summer and the month of December—they again offered the two-for-one special when attendance slacked off. They tested some classes at $299 and others at $399. Those prices worked for special programs that were not yet being offered by competitors.

ACTION STEP 22

Narrow the gaps and see your target customer emerge.

All right, you've found your segment and you've tested parts of it. Now you need to stay with this segment until you know whether or not it will work for you.

One way to keep concentrating is to make a simple sketch or list that sums up what you've learned so far. Figures 3.2 and 3.5 may help guide you. Use a large sheet of paper, because you need to consider all the important things you've learned here. Begin with your objectives and move on through a review of what has happened.

After you've done your sketch, identify the gap in your industry that looks most promising for you.

Because most classes at the new school were booked a month or more in advance, the team knew when it was time to offer a special to keep the classroom full—so as to minimize their "perishables."

Power pricing decisions are not easy. Action Step 23 will help you begin testing the market for your own power pricing.

SUMMARY

You've found the industry that interests you. You've applied the life-cycle yardstick to learn what stage the industry is in and how long you've got to make your business go. If your skills don't exactly guarantee success, you're sure of at least three things: you know where to acquire the skills you need, you know how long it will take to get them, and you're having fun exploring the marketplace.

To illustrate the seven steps of the power marketing process, we've followed the progress of a five-person team that founded a successful software school—a training facility that teaches people how to use complex computer programs in one day.

Step 1 The team held a group brainstorming session to develop a list of their business objectives. All members had read *Megatrends* and were interested in the massive changes occurring in society because of the computer. Their brainstorming was very creative, and it helped weld them together as a team.

Step 2 Using the life-cycle yardstick and an industry chronology for historical perspective, the team researched the industry. The entire information industry proved too big a bite, so they focused on the segment that was forming around the micro-computer. Their quickie chronology began in 1977, with the introduction of the Apple computer into the marketplace. A major breakthrough was the "component" computer, a system composed of movable parts that resembled a home stereo system and made repair easier. In 1982, entrepreneur Adam Osborne introduced the portable computer. In 1983, Osborne filed for bankruptcy protection, throwing the industry into a "shakeout." His company had grown too fast. (The team recognized speed as an integral aspect of the industry.) In late 1983, Apple sales were down and IBM was emerging as the industry standard, the yardstick by which all other computer systems would be measured.

Step 3 Despite the apparent chaos in the industry, the team saw some promising segments. They eliminated hardware (both production and retailing) from their consideration because of too much competition. They recognized software creation as a possibility. The real gap they found was in software education; many people are afraid of computers but yet they need to use them to keep up with the information flow. Their target customer would be the small service business whose major output was paper—reports.

Step 4 The team listed industry problems—user frustration, poor documentation, minimal support from manufacturers, minimal support from retailers, and so on.

Step 5 Then they brainstormed for possible solutions—take over IBM, write software that explained itself, rewrite documentation, build a robot to replace office staff, and finally, found a software school.

Step 6 The team built a matrix grid that helped them evaluate the match of each of their objectives with each possible solution. Thus they discovered which solutions would satisfy which objectives. They could see that a software school would satisfy the most objectives.

ACTION STEP 23

Try your hand at power pricing.

Review the pricing policies of other people who sell your product or service. Do their customers respond to freebies? Discounts? Guarantees of outstanding service? Doing business with a firm they trust?

Call or visit three firms that offer products or services similar to yours. Attempt to learn which factors affect their pricing policies.

Then define *your* product and its benefits to the user. Check your prices against the competition's. Make every attempt to measure the value of your particular product or service. Is it faster, cleaner, more compact? How much more might the customer pay for such benefits? Ask for feedback on your product or service. Study all of your production and marketing costs. What margins do the resellers need? What is it worth to the customers?

Consider all of these things and establish a powerful price.

ACTION STEP REVIEW

Power marketing is the tool that pulls everything together. Eight action steps outlined the process in this chapter:

16 List your business and personal objectives—fame, money, being your own boss, planting yourself in a growth industry, no competition, and so on.

17 Research your favorite industry. Two very helpful tools for this are the life-cycle yardstick and the industry chronology.

18 Identify promising gaps or segments within the industry. You are hunting for your market niche.

19 List industry problems in need of solutions—in other words, opportunities.

20 Let yourself be creative; brainstorm solutions to the problems.

21 Use a matrix grid to mesh your possible solutions with your business objectives.

22 Narrow down the gaps into a solid business idea and watch your target customer emerge.

23 Explore the connection between user benefits and pricing as you try to price for power. Determine what your product or service is worth to the customer.

Step 7 With the project firmly in mind, they began to define the chief element of their survival—the target customer.

As the customer profiles emerged, the team was able to do some market testing with power pricing. That's what you should do, too.

THINK POINTS FOR SUCCESS

▲ Be bold about brainstorming your business objectives. Who knows, some of them may take you through a doorway you didn't know existed.

▲ Build your business around your likes and your strengths.

▲ Power marketing aims the power of your mind at a particular segment of small business.

▲ The customer is always right.

▲ The target customer can always be profiled.

▲ Looking at businesses for sale is a great educational experience, but leave your checkbook at home. (We'll cover the tactics of this in chapter 10.)

▲ Price according to the value as perceived by the buyer.

REFERENCES

Barrier, Michael. "Walton's Mountain." *Nation's Business,* April 1988, pp. 18–26. [Wal-Mart's Buy American Program helps small businesses.]

Baty, Gordon. *Entrepreneurship in the Eighties.* Reston, Va.: Reston Publishing Co., 1981.

Cohen, William A. *The Entrepreneur and Small Business Problem Solver: An Encyclopedic Reference and Guide.* New York: Wiley, 1983.

Jennings, Diane. *Self-Made Women: Twelve of America's Leading Entrepreneurs Talk about Success, Self-Image, and the Superwoman.* Dallas: Taylor Publishing Co., 1987.

Laumer, J. Ford, et al. *Researching Your Market.* Washington, D.C.: U.S. Small Business Administration, Office of Business Development, Management Aids No. 4.019, 1988.

"Presidential Praise for Economic Expansion." *Nation's Business,* January 1988, p. 22. Highlights successful entrepreneurs.

Ries, Al, and Jack Trout. *Positioning: The Battle for Your Mind.* New York: McGraw-Hill, 1980. [The best book around on the power of positive positioning. Warner Books published this in paperback in 1986.]

Sobel, Robert. *The Entrepreneurs: An American Adventure.* Boston: Houghton Mifflin, 1986.

White, Richard M. *The Entrepreneur's Manual: Business Start-Ups, Spin-Offs, and Innovative Management.* Radnor, Pa.: Chilton Book Co., 1977. [Excellent discussion of gap analysis, a larger, corporate version of power marketing.]

APPENDIX 3.1 · Model Action Step 17: Research your favorite industry.

Professional desktop publishing for the graphics arts industry has magnetic attraction for me. From Action Step 17, I know it is emerging as a hot new technology, one that makes present typesetting equipment wholly obsolete.

For my own part, I have been involved in some portion of the graphics arts industry for the past 25 to 30 years. (Having successfully installed my own choice of type faces on a daily newspaper in 1958 gives me some qualification in choosing type. Working with highly gifted designers like Ken Parkhurst and Rick Runyan further polishes this qualification.)

In March 1982, I became computer literate with the purchase of a Xerox 820-II computer and Diablo 630 letter-quality printer. In 1984, I upgraded to an AT&T PC 6300 computer. In 1986, I purchased a QMS-PS 800 PostScript laser printer and entered the desktop publishing business. At present, I have three state-of-the-art page composition programs:

1. Front Page Plus, a program for precision control over one- and two-page documents that need careful layout and typography. (Studio Software, which distributed Front Page Plus, went out of business in February 1987, largely as a result of the introduction of Ventura Publisher by Xerox Corp.)

2. To supplement Front Page Plus, for which there no longer is support, I purchased Aldus Corporation's PageMaker PC program. It provides more precision control over single-page documents than Ventura Publisher.

3. Ventura Publisher, a fast generator of large documents, which offers good control over layout but lacks some of the finer points of typography.

All three page composition programs support PostScript, as does Microsoft Word 3.1, my choice of word processors. At the office, I have an IBM PC and HP LaserJet Plus. Using Microsoft Word 3.1, I have become proficient on this "brain damaged" configuration, producing business documents that are superior to those produced on a Penta-Mergenthaler configuration and a Berthold forms production system.

Graphics Capabilities

At this stage, I am just beginning to become proficient in the graphics programs. Until 1987, these programs were so rudimentary that I preferred to use clip art or custom art from a commercial designer or artist. My plans call for acquiring a Dest Scanner later on, perhaps this year if cash flow will support the $4,000 purchase.

Life Cycle

This is definitely the embryo stage of desktop publishing's life cycle. Until early 1987, there were not enough elements in place to sustain it on an advanced or professional level. We are still awaiting major refinements in graphics programs. They are coming. So are scanners with better capabilities in reproducing halftones (photos).

Speed of Change

The speed of change is so rapid that it is almost physically impossible to keep up with the state of the art. Every week brings startling new announcements. Most of my weekends are devoted to incorporating significant developments in my *1987 Graphic Arts Guide to Professional Desktop Publishing.* My present goal is not to publish this comprehensive report as a book, but rather, to sell it as an up-to-date report as of the week that I print out the document in Ventura Publisher. The list price will have to be at least $100, perhaps $250. That will be a small price to pay when planning the investment in a $20,000 basic desktop publishing system. My greatest known competitors in this arena—employees of Epsilon Graphics Systems, Santa Ana—readily concede that my knowledge of page composition software is superior to theirs. I know from seeing their printed output that my talents in typesetting and page design are superior to theirs, also.

History

There wasn't much change in the graphic arts industry from the time of invention of movable type by Gutenberg in the 1400s until the mechanical Mergenthaler typesetter appeared in the late 1800s—which made the Montgomery Ward catalog possible. Cold type (early forms of phototypesetting) began to appear on the commercial market in the 1960s. As editor of *Seventy-Six* magazine, I researched it then, found it wanting, and returned to hot type. By the middle 1970s, cold type was rapidly phasing out hot type. Minicomputer typesetters began appearing about 1980. Now, in the mid 1980s, it is possible to set type from a microcomputer. Change is increasing in velocity and will continue to do so.

FIGURE 4.1 Chapter 4 will help you complete parts B and C of your Business Plan, "The Market and the Target Customer" and "The Competition."

Profiling the
Target Customer

LEARNING OBJECTIVES

■ To understand that your key to survival in small business is the target customer. ■ To develop your customer profiling ability into a reflex. ■ To use your intuition to forecast what will happen in your industry. ■ To use simple observation techniques to gain insight into consumer behavior. ■ To simplify the messages you communicate through your business. ■ To discover how popular magazines aim at the target customer. ■ To match your target customer with what he or she reads, watches, and listens to. ■ To know the heavy users of your product or service. ■ To recognize the market, the target customer, and competitors who are about to surface. ■ To gather critical market input from target customers through field interviews.

ACTION STEP PREVIEW

24 Use your new eyes on some magazines.

25 Do some secondary research on specific magazines.

26 Profile your target customer and try to identify the heavy users in your industry.

27 Interview prospective target customers.

target customer
a person or type of person that has the highest probability of buying your product/service

Flashback: Hefner sights his target customer and builds an empire.

It's the fifties. Americans in crew cuts are listening to a Senator named Joe McCarthy. Ike is in the White House. Actress Rita Hayworth has astounded the world by marrying an Arabian prince. A young woman named Marilyn Monroe is about to become an important sex symbol. The movie houses are showing newsreels of a costly "police action" on a remote Asian peninsula called Korea. The Soviets are getting ready to launch Sputnik. Color TV is only a rumor on Madison Avenue.

And in snowy Chicago, a frustrated young writer named Hugh Hefner is sitting at his kitchen table, probing the future with the **new eyes** of an entrepreneur.

What did Hefner see when he looked out his kitchen window? He saw his **target customers**, lots of them, who would make him rich, famous, and envied around the world. Hefner believed his target customers would build him an empire.

And they did.

The entrepreneur with a dream can learn a lesson from Hugh Hefner's story. Your product will, no doubt, be much different from his, but study how he learned about his target customer, and use that knowledge to help *you* own the store.

THE POWER OF PROFILING

Hugh Hefner's message hasn't changed since the fifties. "Play," he says. "Play your ears off. You owe it to yourself to play. Play hard and never grow old, and find a playmate to keep you young."

Of course, anyone could say that, man or woman, a person of any age. But Hefner was careful to aim his message at a target audience that was super-receptive. Here's a quick profile of his target customer:

HEFNER'S TARGET CUSTOMER*

SEX: male

AGE: 18–34 (75%)

EDUCATION: some college (52%)

BACKGROUND: upper middle class

INCOME: $37,500 annually [adjusted to 1990]

MARRIED: 50%

RESIDENCE: urban/suburban (64%)

PURCHASING HABITS:

consume more than 7 drinks per week	25%
consume more than 10 drinks per week	18%
consume more than 15 drinks per week	12%
own 3 or more cars	17%
heavy smokers	21%
purchased car new	54%
purchased 7 or more dress shirts	17%
purchased 4 or more pairs of shoes	16%

*Material on the Playboy target reader has been adapted from *Subliminal Seduction: Ad Media's Seduction of a Not-So-Innocent America*, by Wilson Brian Key. Prentice Hall, Inc., 1972, pp. 118–119. Used by permission.

Hefner didn't pull these **demographics** out of thin air. He knew how to use secondary sources to help him complete his profile. You can do the same thing to learn about your target customer.

An easy way to understand the power of profiling is to analyze media sources that are aimed at different target markets. For example, what would you find if you contrasted *McCall's* magazine with *Playboy* magazine?

Often, we walk past magazines without giving them a sideways glance. That's unfortunate, because magazines hold the key to many questions about marketing. One way to regard a magazine is as a glossy cover wrapped around some pages of ads and editorial copy. With new eyes, however, you can see that a mass-market magazine exists because it is a channel to the subconscious of a certain type of reader.

That knowledge is power.

What can you learn about target markets, consumption patterns, and buying power from the advertisements in a magazine? Put yourself in an analytical frame of mind. Begin by counting the ads. Then notice the types of products that dominate the ads; these ads are probably aimed at the heavy users of those products. Next, study the models; they are fantasy images with which the target customer is expected to identify, connect, remember. The activities pictured in the ads enlarge the fantasy, and the words link it to real life. A good ad becomes a slice of life, a picture that beckons the customer inside, toward the product.

We took an issue of *Playboy* (it has a carefully profiled reader) and one of *McCall's* (a strikingly different target market) and did a new-eyes analysis. After we looked at the data, we drew a few conclusions. We developed categories as we went along (One of the nice things about **new-eyes research** is that you can expand the model as you collect data.) Here are what we looked for:

- total number of ads one-third page or larger
- ads aimed at heavy users (type of products that are advertised the most)
- large ads (two pages or more)
- demographics of models (estimated age, income, and occupation; race)
- male
- female
- main activities depicted
- objects depicted (including mail order ads, if any)

Using the Model—An Analysis of *McCall's*

The total number of ads of one-third page or more was 80. Thirty-six of those were devoted to food, dieting, or eating, which suggests that the heavy users who read *McCall's* not only enjoy food, but they also cook and probably regard cooking as a way to express themselves creatively. Dieting is the escape hatch that attempts to balance any indiscretionary overindulgence in food. Five diet-food ads ran two pages; 21 ran a full page.

The next major product grouping was clothes; there were 2 double-page ads and 8 full page for clothes. After clothes came cigarettes, with 3 double-page ads and 5 full pagers. There were 6 ads for beauty/skin/hair care products, 3 for "intimate" products (bras, pantyliners), 5 for children's products (shoes, cereal, baby food, toothpaste), and 2 for headache pills.

A two-page ad for Kools cigarettes was dominated by a Porsche 928S equipped with a super-dooper Blaupunkt audio system. Liquor was not advertised in this issue, nor were cars.

Female models seemed to range in age from their late teens to a couple of women in their late forties or early fifties. All models seemed to be comfortably middle class; none were portrayed as ostentatiously wealthy. All were white.

demographics
key characteristics of a group of people—age, sex, income, where they live

new-eyes research
marketplace detective work; it's observation with intuition

The major activity depicted was people smiling into the camera. One ad showed the lower three-fourths of a woman talking on the phone in an office as she advertised L'Eggs panty hose. Another showed a slender, slightly perspiring woman drinking Sprite with a background of weights and chrome barbells. In general, the ads with models pictured a world of charm and order, of women in control of themselves. Models were either young and famous, like Brooke Shields and Christie Brinkley, or they were aging gracefully.

Eight men, including Superman, made it into the *McCall's* ad stable: the Marlboro Man, the Barclay's Man, a Mazola Man, three musicians touting Kools, and Bill Cosby, advertising Jello. The median age of the men would be somewhere between 35 and 50. The Marlboro Man rides a spirited horse across an autumn landscape. The Barclay's Man lights his own cigarette while he cuts his eyes to the left, where an elegant female hand holds a glass of bubbly. The Mazola man—a husband archetype—is pictured with some apparatus to test blood pressure, suggesting a connection between eating Mazola and living longer. Bill Cosby—the only nonwhite adult in the magazine's ads—is surrounded by children munching Jello. (One of the six children is black.)

Conclusions   The objects depicted in these *McCall's* ads relate to the home, the hearth, the happy homemaker. A clean floor tied with a huge red ribbon extols the virtues of Brite. The glory of food is lauded with a plate of fancy spaghetti, cake mixes, frozen pie crust dough, a set of china, a perfect chocolate cream pie, and so on. Mail-order items were scarce. Most items advertised for mail order carried the magazine logo—for example, a *McCall's* pastry cloth set and a *McCall's* tart pan. What does this data tell us?

1. *McCall's* readers are predominantly female, age 19–55, with household incomes around $27,000. They live in metro-suburban areas. A high percentage are married, with children under 18. A high percentage are employed. The percentage of white readers far outweighs other racial groups.

2. The focus of *McCall's* readers is the home. Their adventures occur in the kitchen, when they get creative with food.

3. *McCall's* readers make decisions on lots of small purchases—Moisture Whip Maybelline foundation, Shaklee's Instant Protein, cigarettes, Sizzlelean.

4. *McCall's* readers are object-centered, private about bedrooms and intimate wear. If they dream about escape, they do so briefly, with lots of control. If they use alcohol, they use it sparingly or in secret.

We're on target. These conclusions have been confirmed by material we received from the *McCall's* **display ad department**. The point of our doing this new eyes-analysis is to show you how you can arrive at some exciting conclusions on your own. Let's apply the same kind of analysis to *Playboy* now.

display ad department
department of a magazine or newspaper publisher that can provide market data; it sells and produces "nonclassified" ads

Using the Model—An Analysis of *Playboy*

The issue of *Playboy* we studied contained 292 pages (the *McCall's* we studied had 158), with 79 ads one-third of a page or over, 33 of which were for hard liquor (Scotch, gin, brandy). This corroborates the findings reported in *Subliminal Seduction* about *Playboy* readers being heavy users of alcohol. Twenty-six of the liquor ads were full-page, 2 of them covered two pages, and 5 were half-pagers. The next cluster came with 22 for electronic entertainment gear—video, audio, camera, stereo, phones, fuzzbusters. There were 8 ads for cigarettes, which ties the *Playboy* smoker with the controlled smokers for *McCall's*. We found 8 ads for clothes and 4 each for perfume, cologne, and diamonds.

The largest ad was a five-page superspread for the newest Nissan "Z" model, a hummer of a car that would seem to guarantee to prolong the buyer's playing life, and suggesting that enough *Playboy* readers can afford a Nissan 300ZX to make advertising it this way worthwhile.

In contrast to *McCall's, Playboy* carried no food ads. The *Playboy* reader's attention is on a world beyond the hearth and family.

Except for a wry, satiric Santa Claus (advertising Crown Royal), the male models appeared to range in age from 25 to 45. Several were portrayed as indoorsy muscle-types working out on expensive exercise equipment. Most of the outdoorsy types wore work clothes, uniforms, heavy boots, and so on and had mustaches. Female models appeared to range in age from 21 to 30; some were portrayed as girlish flirts and others as elegant, worldly women. In several of the ads, a man appeared between two women, suggesting an abundance of female companionship.

The only product strong enough to cross over from *McCall's* to *Playboy* was Marlboro. In *Playboy,* the Marlboro Man seems closer to us, less romantic, more rugged. He has replaced his *McCall's* horse with a macho calf-rope, symbolic of dexterity and control.

Playboy ads portray more action than *McCall's* ads. Examples include romantic settings at the top of the world (Hennessy cognac), adventure settings in the wilds (Camel), and rescue settings on isolated Arctic ice (Winston). The Gordon's gin ad portray two black models (male pianist, female dancer in white tights) in a tastefully austere, mirrored studio.

Many of the objects depicted in the *Playboy* ads are machines for grown-up play— Toyota trucks, a fire-engine red Nissan, radar detectors, videos, stereos, cameras. They project images of the indoor Good Life at night and the outdoor Rugged Life during the day. Night and day, the *Playboy* reader who can afford it can have the best of all possible worlds.

This issue contained one mail-order ad (800-number included) for Karess sheets. The other mail-order ads offered various products from the magazine—the "Playmate" calendar, "Playmate" and adventure videos, and so on.

Conclusions   We presented demographic data on the *Playboy* reader earlier in the chapter. Our new-eyes research supports the data; it tells us that:

1. The Good Life costs, but it's worth every penny. Female companionship is available if the "playboy" has the bucks. If he can't handle the fire-engine red Nissan right now, he'll have to settle for the toney grey VW Quantum until he can.

2. The *Playboy* reader makes big-purchase decisions—cars, stereos, phone systems, cameras, VCRs. He's a heavy user of hard liquor.

3. The *Playboy* reader spends hefty amounts of money on entertainment— some in his apartment, a lot more out in the playgrounds of the world. (In this issue, snow-covered mountains called to the winter sports nut: Come and ski. Come and ski.)

4. *Playboy* readers are filled with hopes of achieving the Good Life permanently. Until they do, *Playboy* will line their dreams with products from the Playboy Information Empire.

Lesson from an Information Empire

Play is serious business, and it doesn't come cheap. If a *Playboy* advertiser spends $50,000+ for a full-page ad, the ad needs to generate a million dollars in gross sales—20 times the cost of the ad—for the advertiser to break even. What that means for you as a user of secondary research is that expensive ads are highly targeted. They must hit the target. If they do not, the advertiser takes his or her business elsewhere.

ACTION STEP 24

Use your new eyes on some magazines.

Study some magazines and their target readers. Then do a comparative analysis, following the example of our analyses of *Playboy* and *McCall's*. Glance quickly at each magazine's cover. What qualities does it project? Flip through the magazine. What strikes your eye? Are the ads aimed at men? At women? At teens? At seniors? At everyone? What appears to be the age range of the target customer? The income range? Is the marketing effort national or regional?

You're just beginning to look at magazines as marketing tools, so you can start anywhere. Begin with magazines in your home, or buy a couple at a newsstand or drugstore. Ask the above questions about each one.

The next time you're in a store where magazines are sold, observe shoppers at the magazine rack. Note what magazines they buy. How many of these purchases could you have predicted? Record your observations in your Adventure Notebook. If you have a chance, interview a couple of these magazine buyers. Ask them why they bought what they did. Use what they say to build reader profiles in your mind. Without being too obvious, collect as much demographic data as you can on these shoppers. Could any of them be your target customers?

You can benefit from big business's advertising through new-eyes secondary research. Use it often; make it a habit.

You will certainly want to analyze the advertising in a magazine that your target customer reads soon. But first, get a feel for magazine advertising in general. Action Step 24 will help you do this. Have fun with this action step.

MOVING TARGETS: CONSUMERS ON THE LIFE-CYCLE YARDSTICK

What's become of the *Playboy* reader of the fifties? What is he reading today? Where does he live? Does he work, or is he retired? We can be pretty sure that his tastes have changed and that his income has quadrupled. He's probably changed jobs a couple of times. If he plays tennis, he's having trouble with tennis elbow, or maybe a trick knee. He travels more now. The world has changed, and his horizons have shifted dramatically.

What does this mean? It illustrates the fact that the target customer is always moving. There's a lesson in what happened to the *Playboy* empire; the lesson is *change:* watch the target customer.

The age range of *Playboy's* target customer has always been 18 to 34 years. That hasn't changed. The first *Playboy* readers started in the fifties, read the magazine for fifteen years, and then moved on to other magazines. Meanwhile, using the magazine as his cornerstone, Hefner built a diversified empire. What happened to the empire? Troubles developed after 15 or 20 years.

The fifties "playboy," Hefner's original target customer, grew up, perhaps still reading the magazine occasionally, but leaving the empire behind. The magazine, still the cornerstone, has not changed much in the thirty-five years.

In thirty-five years, tastes change and competitors emerge. As the life-cycle diagram in Figure 4.2 shows, *Playboy* magazine has moved from its embryo stage in the fifties to its maturity in the eighties. It's almost as if the Playboy empire has accompanied its target customer through those stages. The Playboy Clubs, which once symbolized male fun and male freedom, have closed their doors. Like much of corporate America, the Playboy empire is downsizing. Along those same lines, the young male reader of the fifties now has more money and more time. He now seeks fitness, a more realistic good life, and life extension.

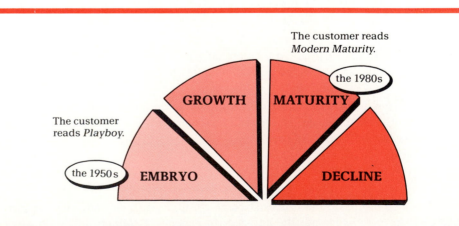

FIGURE 4.2   Life-cycle diagram of the moving target customer.

People who began reading *Playboy* in 1953 at the age of 20 are in their mid fifties today and their magazine is likely to be *Modern Maturity*. With a present circulation of 17 million readers, *Modern Maturity* should soon have the largest circulation in the U.S.

Now *there's* a market.

Lessons from the Magazines

Display ad departments spend lots of money digging into the segment of their marketing pie. By tapping into their data base, you can save yourself months of market research. You can find new customers and glean hot ideas.

Just for fun, let's move the magazine life-cycle diagram into the eighties and use the *Playboy* strategy to gather new data in the marketplace. If you check your local newsstand or bookstore, you'll see that several flashy magazines are competing for the same readers. *Savvy* competes with *Executive Female. Sassy* competes with *Elle* and *Seventeen. M* competes with *Playboy* and *Esquire.* (See Figure 4.3.)

Let's look for a moment at *M.* This magazine reaches the upscale male, average age 37.4 years, a decade older (and a decade richer) than the *Playboy* reader. The *M* reader is better educated: 92% attended college; 30% have master's degrees or more. The house owned by the *M* reader is twice as valuable as *Playboy's* condo. He spends lots of money on collectibles: 32% buy one or more paintings a year; 24% buy antiques. He likes his plastic: 94% of *M* readers use credit cards. As you might expect, *M* readers are part of the core market for yachts, classical music concerts, live theater, and memberships in tennis and boating clubs. They are users of catering services, tailors, specialty clothing stores, upscale travel agencies, auto detailers, fine restaurants, and the best wines.

For a Fun Profile, Find a Fun Magazine

By now, you've discovered the secret of profiling. What do *Playboy, M,* and *Esquire* have in common? What do *Vogue* and *McCall's,* and *Savvy* and *Sassy* have in common? Answering these questions call for analytical judgment. Marketeers call it *segmentation.* You start with large classifications like sex (for example, *Esquire* for men and *McCall's* for women). You go on to age (*Modern Maturity* for seniors). And then you combine sex and age (*Sassy* for young women; *Lear's* for mature women). Then you keep adding layers of classification that lead you to numbers that allow you to make judgments. For example, here's a quick customer profile of *Sassy* readers:

SASSY'S TARGET CUSTOMER

AGE: 13–19

SEX: female

EMPLOYMENT: 42.9% are employed

INCOME: $30.7 billion from employment and allowances

WHERE THEY SPEND IT: apparel, $19 billion; food for the family, $16 billion

---

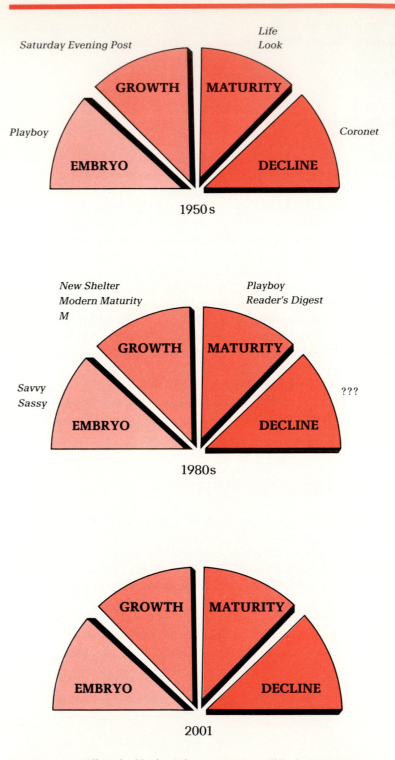

FIGURE 4.3   Fill in the blanks. What magazines will be hot in 2001?

The *Sassy* Strategy

The publishers of *Sassy* have found a big pie. They estimate total teen spending in 1986 was $52 billion. (Marketing data is always a couple of years out of date.) In 1985, for comparative purposes, it was $49.8 billion. Between 1970 and 1986, the number of teens owning cars tripled. There is a huge market here, and it's growing. *Sassy* competes with *Teen* and *Seventeen,* and its publishers have targeted their market very carefully.

Once you get some data together, it's interesting to look at it in chart form. Figures 4.4 and 4.5 were done originally on a Macintosh computer, using a program called "Microsoft Chart." The bar graph, Figure 4.4, compares spending in dollars by teenage girls aged 16 to 19 and 13 to 15—a further example of segmentation. The circle graph, Figure 4.5, gives a quick visual breakdown of where girls aged 16 to 19 spend their money. (Teens buy jeans.)

Use Action Step 25 to conduct some secondary research on your target customers at no cost.

Customer profiles are also available from newspapers and radio stations. For other specific data, you can contact trade associations through the Gale directory, which can be found in most libraries. Get into the habit of profiling. It's your key to success in small business. Box 4.1 gives you some guidelines.

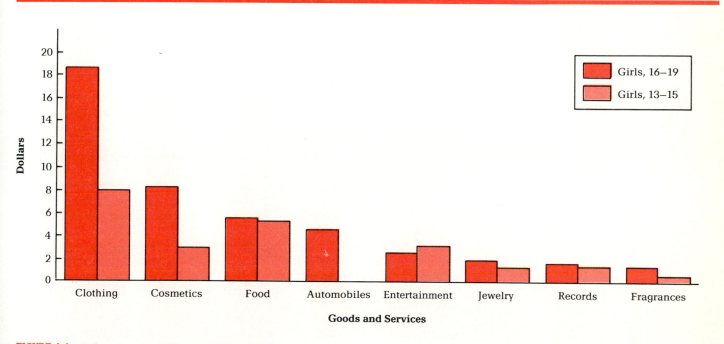

FIGURE 4.4   Where teenage girls spend their money.

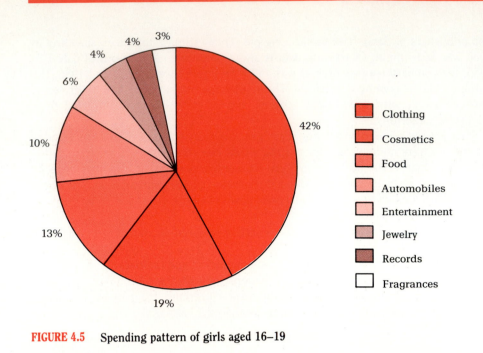

FIGURE 4.5 Spending pattern of girls aged 16–19

BOX 4.1 Getting a Handle on Profiling*

You can't profile your target customer too much. Here's a model to follow, from chapter 8 of *Subliminal Seduction* by Wilson Brian Key.

The average age of *Vogue* readers is in the early thirties, and 72 percent are married. Some, at least the younger ones with high-upward-mobility husbands, work. The majority are married to men with managerial or executive responsibilities who are likely to be older than them. Men tend to hit their earnings peak in their mid to late forties.

A significant portion of *Vogue* readers are in their second marriages; their husbands, in their second, third, or fourth marriages.

The place of children in the life of the *Vogue* reader is curious. Two-thirds of *Vogue* families have no children under 18. This would not seem so surprising if the average age of the readers was over 40. At any rate, children do not play an important role in the typical *Vogue* reader's life.

Vogue readers are well-educated: 78 percent attended college; 41 percent graduated. Of their husbands, 83 percent attended college, 64 percent graduated. As to their occupations (which tend to determine lifestyle, fashions, clubs, travel, sport, and amusements), 35 percent are professionals and 32 percent are executives, proprietors, managers, or officials.

Ninety-seven percent of *Vogue* readers belong to one or more clubs. They entertain frequently with dinner parties, buffets, and luncheons, and they are entertained by others as well; they average 6.4 social engagements monthly.

Adapted from *Subliminal Seduction: Ad Media's Manipulation of a Not-So Innocent America* by Wilson Brian Key, published by Prentice-Hall, Inc.

MAGAZINE SURVEY REVISITED

How many **general-interest magazines** did you spot on the racks you checked out? How many do you read? How many do you subscribe to? *Life, Look, Colliers, Coronet, Saturday Evening Post*—these were all general-interest magazines: they all aimed at the "general" reader. As you may suspect, they seem to have gone the way of the railroads. Table 4.1 shows you who's surviving in the magazine game these days. As you can see, segmentation means "money grooves."

No one can say if the phenomenon of the highly specialized audience is here to stay. *Saturday Evening Post* and *Life* have been revived, as monthlies. The new *Post*'s circulation is around 700,000—slightly more than *EasyRider*'s—and *Life*'s is 1.5 million. Think about what this means for advertisers.

New magazine titles of the past decade include the likes of *New Age Journal, Lefthander, Slimmer, Bestways,* and *Lear's. Lefthander* has a circulation of 22,000; *Slimmer,* of 250,000; and *Bestways,* of 300,000. *Lear's* was a start-up in 1988, so solid figures are not yet available.

Modern Maturity data indicates that seniors over fifty control half of the disposable income in the United States. What does this tell you about surviving in the marketplace?

general-interest magazine
publication directed at a mass audience that crosses demographic lines

A Different Kind of Target Reader

"Our readers," a publisher of romance novels wrote, "are starved for the good life. Most of them will never see Europe, never eat in an elegant restaurant, never meet anyone famous or important. Their days are spent scrimping, watching the budget,

TABLE 4.1 Magazines, Target Readers, and Circulation

MAGAZINE	TARGET READER	CIRCULATION
D&B Reports	owners/top managers of small businesses with $9 million annual sales	71,000
Car & Driver	male; 34–35; college-educated professional	900,000
Money	middle-upper income bracket; sophisticated	1,100,000
Penthouse	male; 18–34; upper income brackets; college	5,300,000
Cosmopolitan	female; 18–34; middle-income bracket; career-minded	2,500,000
Sassy	99% female; 13–19; fun-loving, sophisticated young women seeking self-image	500,000
Esquire	64% male; 30–49; upper-middle income bracket; fashion, social issues	705,000
M	94% male; 33–49; top executives; 43% single; investments, collectibles, fine food, fine wine	200,000
Modern Maturity	male/female over 50; median age 63.4; family-oriented; socially active; 35% attended college; brand-loyal	17,000,000

doing dishes and the laundry. Their husbands are indifferent. If our readers work, they have jobs that are dull. They are going nowhere, and they want to read about women who have made it, who don't think twice about what something costs. Our readers live vicariously—they want to have the confidence of someone who has everything!"

Sarah was fifty-two when her husband died. They'd been married thirty years, and she missed him terribly. Her children lived three thousand miles away in California. They flew in for the funeral, looking fit, tanned, rushed, and happy with their lives. They both invited Sarah to come to visit them soon, which she did. However, after three days in her son's house in a smoggy southern California suburb, she went back home. She decided she belonged in New England.

Sarah grieved for her husband. To stay busy, she began to bake fine home-made pies for the Old New England restaurant down the road. The money helped to pay the bills, which were scary for Sarah. Her husband had always handled the money, and there had always been enough, even with the children, but now it seemed as if the insurance checks wouldn't quite stretch from month to month.

So Sarah baked more pies.

In the tourist season, business was brisk, so Sarah hired a teenage neighbor girl to help her. In a year, she had made enough money to pay all the bills, expand her kitchen, and hire another assistant. Sarah had some extra time now, so she went back to college. Since she'd always loved to read, she decided to take the course, How to Write a Mystery Novel.

Sarah's stories were set locally—old houses, dense forests, small New England towns— and they were pretty good stories. She did eight revisions of her final project before her professor was satisfied. When she was about to give up, the professor said she'd like to send it to a friend of hers in the publishing business in New York.

Sarah was nervous. She's always held publishers in high esteem. She didn't want to be hurt or disappointed.

Surprise—the publisher liked her story! They wanted to publish it, and they wanted to see more.

Sarah sold five mysteries in the next three years. She turned out to be a super storyteller, and she loved sitting at her desk with a fire in the fireplace, spinning out mysteries. She was paid an average of $3,000 for each book—not much, unless you're thrifty, which Sarah was.

Then one wintry November, Sarah's New York publisher broke her heart when he turned down her sixth novel. "The market's terrible for mysteries," he wrote. "Try me again when this has blown over."

Sarah was confused. She didn't understand. Market? What market? The only market she knew was Eldredge's, down the road, where she sold extra pies. Of course, she'd always heard people grousing about the *stock* market, but she'd never paid much attention. Markets were not her cup of tea.

A year passed, and she kept on writing. Two more mysteries were turned down, for the same vague reasons. Now Sarah was nervous. Her expenses in the pie business had increased, and she had a competitor now, a young woman who had just moved there from Boston. She'd come to rely on the money from her books, and that was now drying up.

Fighting back discouragement, Sarah began to study what goes on in the world of publishing. She read *Publisher's Weekly,* a trade journal. She read biographies, books by agents, books by publishers. She did not unearth any secrets.

Then, one day Sarah ran into a woman at the public library. Younger than Sarah, and heavier, she was carrying a stack of paperback romances. With gentle probing, Sarah learned from her that she read as many as ten romances a week and that she belonged to two romance book clubs and a romance readers' group.

"What organization," Sarah thought. Then she began to wonder how many romance readers there might be in New England, on the East Coast, and across the country.

That question was a turning point for Sarah. It directed her to a new set of target readers.

Working with New England diligence, Sarah did some research on the leisure activities of the American housewife. In an obscure marketing journal, she found a 1970 study that said housewives spend almost 70% of their leisure time reading. Not mysteries, Sarah thought. A *Publisher's Weekly* study reported that 37% of the fiction sold was romance fiction.

This helped to explain what her publisher had been talking about: market means *people.* In publishing, the market is *readers.* She wondered why he hadn't said that in the first place.

Sarah quickly wrote to romance publishers, requesting information on the mechanics of writing romance fiction. Practically immediately she received detailed reader profiles, plot suggestions, and length suggestions for each type of romance—in other words, blueprints for books.

"Our readers," one publisher wrote, "are starved for the Good Life. Most of them will never see Europe, never eat in an elegant restaurant, never meet anyone famous or important. . . ."

Sarah read through all of the material carefully. None of her friends read romances, and she wondered what they'd think if they learned she was writing them. She decided to use a pseudonym. Two days later she began to write her first romance novel, *Amelia Thorn.* A publisher snapped it up. It sold 300,000 copies and made more money in its first print run than all of Sarah's mysteries combined. Her second romance, *Rachel Duncan,* outsold *Amelia Thorn,* and forced her to find an honest lawyer who would help her incorporate.

Sarah's been a **corporation** for two years now. Six young women work for her, baking pies, and she's planning to start her own publishing operation—to do a cookbook called *Sarah's Pies.* One thing she learned from her research on publishing was that the bigger publishers don't like to do small print runs because they're not profitable for them. She regarded that as a market gap.

corporation
a legal entity that stands separate from its owners

Before Sarah finished the pie book, she hired a young man from one of the business schools to do some market research for her. He determined that there would be 25,000 readers for *Sarah's Pies.*

Sarah Routledge had discovered the key to small business.

"I think what helped me the most," she now says, "was discovering that I was in *business.* Because when you're in business, you think about *customers.* All I'd thought about before was pies and books. Customers are the key."

"Finding the right customers is like slicing a pie," Sarah goes on. "You take out only what you need for yourself. You leave the rest for somebody else. If someone comes along and wants the whole pie, then you have a choice—either you move on, or you dig in your heels and fight. The key to business, whether it's baking pies or writing books, is to know who's going to eat 'em or read 'em."

MAKE CUSTOMER PROFILING A REFLEX

We're trying to help you make customer profiling a reflex. If you keep at it, it will continually adjust your focus on the all-important marketplace.

Box 4.2 presents two contrasting profiles from *Nine American Lifestyles,* Arnold Mitchell's book about psychographics in America. For illustration purposes, we've selected just two of Mitchell's lifestyles, "Belongers" and "Experientials." Belongers are outer-directed, whereas Experientials are inner-directed. It might help you to do a comparative chart that will highlight the differences in the two groups' consumption patterns. Read the profiles and then profile your own target customer by doing Action Step 26.

ACTION STEP 26

Profile your target customer and try to identify the heavy users in your industry.

Prepare a checklist that will help you identify your target customer. Include *demographic* factors—age, sex, income level, household size, residence, and so on—and *psychographic* factors such as those described by Arnold Mitchell in *Nine American Lifestyles.* Psychographic factors include such considerations as what a person reads, eats, drinks, drives (What do cars tell you about people's self-images?), does in his or her leisure time, and so on. The more factors you include on your checklist, the better your profile will be—the clearer your picture of the person whose needs you want to serve. Add to your checklist as you continue to think about your TC. (You may want to look ahead to page 85; the VALS onion provides another way to classify lifestyles.)

Now that you're deeper into your venture adventure, you'll have more information about the kinds of people you should aim your product or service at. Entrepreneurs we have known tell us you should watch for at least three TCs:

1. **Primary.** That's the one you just profiled with your checklist. It's the perfect target customer for your business, and he or she could be a heavy user. (The woman Sarah Routledge talked with at the public library was a heavy user of romance novels.)

2. **Secondary.** This one is not a heavy user, and may not be apparent at first, but is nonetheless "bread and butter." (The word processors in chapter 2 were the Info Team's secondary TCs.) Sometimes the secondary TC will lead you to the "invisible" customer.

3. **Invisible.** This customer appears after you open the doors, after you've mustered up the courage to go ahead and start up.

Think about your TC often. Dream about it. Your target customer is the key to your survival in small business. And you cannot do too many of these profiles.

BOX 4.2   Two Contrasting Target Customer Groups

While you're training your new eyes to zoom in on the marketplace, study these profiles of two very different target customers. *Nine American Lifestyles* analyzes the consumption patterns of nine distinctive customer groups. These descriptions will introduce you to two of those groups.

Belongers. Belonger households are major buyers of both large and compact American-made autos. Important purchase considerations for them are convenience of dealer location, cost of repairs and servicing, and safety features—the last probably reflecting concerns for the family. Exterior styling is relatively unimportant. They prefer American-made cars to imports.

In appliances, Belongers show a higher-than-average level of ownership of freezers and lower ownership levels for dishwashers, garbage disposals, food processors, and microwave ovens. These patterns possibly reflect their preference for doing things in the traditional way, as well as their tendency to live in older homes and rural areas.

Belonger women frequently wear slacks. Slacks appear to be sufficiently ingrained in their lifestyles that it shows little relationship with employment status.

Belongers are substantially below average in consumption of all types of alcoholic beverages and regular carbonated soft drinks. A higher-than-average percentage consume fruit juices, as well as regular and decaffeinated coffee.

Experientials. Experiential households have among the highest incidence of ownership of compact, subcompact, and small specialty cars. They are the highest in ownership of, and preference for, foreign cars, and they show the highest ownership of European cars of all VALS types. (Box 4.3 gives short descriptions of the nine VALS types.)

Ownership of dishwashers and garbage disposals is high among this group, as is ownership of recreational equipment. Experiential households are substantially above average in owning camping and backpacking equipment and racing bicycles. In-home electronic products higher-than-average ownership levels prevail for photo games and prerecorded and blank recording tapes.

Experiential women show an interesting pattern in their clothing preferences. Disproportionately more of them wear jeans, skirts, and dresses. They wear bras less frequently than the other VALS types, perhaps reflecting their "free spirits." Experiential men are among the most frequent wearers of jeans and sport and casual shirts, but they also wear suits more often than average.

Wines, including champagnes, and domestic and imported beers are the favored alcoholic beverages.

Source: Reprinted (with changes) by permission of Macmillan Publishing Company from *Nine American Lifestyles: Who We Are and Where We Are Going* by Arnold Mitchell, pp. 91–92, 132–133. Copyright © 1983 by Arnold Mitchell.

Invisible Customers

Some people go into business for themselves because they can't work for someone else. Some of them are mavericks who don't like to take orders. Others are dreamers who love their own ideas. Still others, like Fred Bowers, have some handicap that keeps them from getting a job with a large firm.

Fred's experience illustrates that customers sometimes "come out of the woodwork."

> Fred Bowers had planned to be a career Marine until he was injured in a fall from a training helicopter. He could still walk, painfully, but his military career was over. With a medical discharge in his pocket, Fred looked around for work.

"I'd always loved soccer," Fred said. "I'd been a pretty fair player, and my coaching experience had given me a good understanding of kids. I thought there might be a place for a soccer specialty shop in our community, but before I went for financing I spent a year checking it out."

Fred found eighteen sporting good shops in the area he was interested in. None of them carried a full line of soccer products. When he began profiling his target customers, Fred came up with two easy targets:

> Primary target: boys, age 6–17
>
> Secondary target: girls, age 6–12
>
> Household income (both targets): $28,000–$32,000
>
> Socioeconomic level: middle, upper middle
>
> Interest: sports

Then Fred segmented the youngsters into two groups: members of school teams, and members of American Youth Soccer Organization (AYSO) teams.

His description of his target customers was so good that when he showed his fifty-two-page Business Plan to a couple investors, they put up all the money he needed to start up Soccer City. Because of Fred's knowledge of the game, his store prospered. Schools counted on him for an honest deal, and parents of players counted on him for advice on equipment.

"I had thought I'd just be selling," Fred said. "What I was really doing was providing a service."

After he'd been in business a year, a third market began to emerge. The customers in this third group were adults, mostly foreign-born, from places like Great Britain, Germany, Mexico, and South America. They had grown up playing soccer and they loved the game. To them, it was a fiercely fought national sport, and they still liked to play. These heretofore invisible customers would drive 50–75 miles to Fred's shop for equipment they couldn't find anywhere else.

"They didn't show up in my research," Fred said. "If I hadn't opened up, I wouldn't have known about them. Now they make up at least 30% of my business. One day they weren't there; the next day, they were. I like that. I like it a *lot.* It makes this whole adventure more interesting."

Placing Target Customers on the VALS Onion

VALS is an acronym for *v*alues *a*nd *l*ifestyles, a profiling system developed by SRI International, a Menlo Park, California, firm that specializes in market research. Arnold Mitchell, the author of *Nine American Lifestyles,* has developed an onion diagram that graphically relates the nine VALS lifestyles; see Figure 4.6.

Note in the figure that the "Survivors" are at the bottom and "Integrateds" are at the top. Where are Fred's customers on the onion? To answer, study the figure for a moment and then read Box 4.3. After you find Fred's target customers, look for your own. Which part of the VALS onion will buy *your* product or service?

Portrait of an Integrated   The VALS onion is actually an updated version of Abraham Maslow's "needs pyramid," which tops off with self-actualization. The VALS onion tops off with an individual called an "Integrated." There aren't a lot of Integrateds around—only three million or so, according to Mitchell. This is because it takes a lot of climbing to get there. You can find them on magazine covers, behind CEO desks, and heading up large organizations. Lee Iacocca is an Integrated, and so is Norman Cousins.

One clear portrait appeared in a 1988 issue of the *Wall Street Journal,* which profiled writer–producer–activist Norman Lear, creator of the controversial television show, "All in the Family," which gave us Archie Bunker. In 1985, he and cofounder Bud Yorkin sold Tandem Productions to Coca-Cola for $485 million.

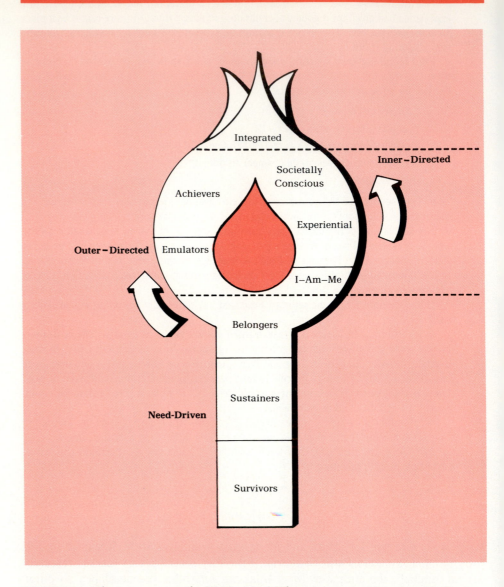

FIGURE 4.6 Where are you on the VALS onion? Where is your target customer? (Source: Adapted by permission of Macmillan Publishing Company from *Nine American Lifestyles: Who We Are and Where We Are Going* by Arnold Mitchell. © 1983 by Arnold Mitchell.)

At 65, Lear has become what the *Journal* calls "a savvy and unabashed capitalist." He is buying up movie theaters, magazines, and television stations. His business is called "Act III," for Act III of his life. Among his other media acquisitions are two movie theater chains in Texas for which he paid $47 million. Act III will not release figures, but experts estimate annual revenues of more than one hundred million dollars.

Norman Lear is a picture of intelligence, sharp taste, wit, and power. He's looking for gaps and buying up properties far away from the glitz of Hollywood and other media centers.

Doesn't it make you want to shinny up that onion?

BOX 4.3   **Find Your Target Customers Here**

Nine American Lifestyles is almost as helpful to the entrepreneur as *Megatrends.* Author Arnold Mitchell, director of the VALS Program at SRI International, gathered data for twenty years before writing the book. Locate your target customer in Mitchell's nine lifestyle groups.

Survivors   Old, very poor, fearful, depressed and despairing, far removed from the cultural mainstream; misfits. There are 6 million Survivors, most of whom are over 65; 77% are female, incomes are below $7,500, and the education median is 8th–9th grade.

Sustainers   Living on the edge of poverty, angry and resentful, streetwise, involved in an underground economy. There are 11 million Sustainers, 58% of whom are under 35; 55% are female; the median income is $11,000, and the education median is 11th grade.

Belongers   Aging, traditional and conventional, contented, intensely patriotic, sentimental, and very stable. There are 54 million Belongers, whose median age is 52; 65% are female; the median income is $17,500, and about 50% graduated from high school.

Emulators   Youthful and ambitious, macho, show-off, trying to break into the system and make it big. There are 16 million Emulators, whose median age is 27; 53% are male, the median income is $18,000, and many of them have some education beyond high school.

Achievers   Middle-aged, prosperous, self-assured, materialistic, able leaders, builders of the "American Dream." There are 37 million Achievers, whose median age is 37; 60% are male; the median income is $31,400, and 32% have graduated from college.

I-Am-Me   Transition state; exhibitionistic, narcissistic, young, impulsive, experimental, active, and inventive. There are 8 million I-Am-Mes, 91% of whom are under 25; 64% are male; the median income is $8,800, and most of them have some college.

Experiential   Youthful, person-centered, artistic, seek direct experience and inner growth. There are 11 million Experientials, whose median age is 27; 55% are female; the median income is $23,800, and 38% have graduated from college.

Societally Conscious   Mission-oriented, mature, successful, leaders of single-issue groups; some of them live lives of voluntary simplicity. There are 14 million SCs, whose median age is 39; 52% are male; the median income is $27,200, 58% are college graduates, and 39% have some graduate school.

Integrated   Psychologically mature, tolerant, and understanding, they have a large field of vision and a sense of fittingness. There are only 3.2 million Integrateds.

Source: Reprinted (with changes) by permission of Macmillan Publishing Company from *Nine American Lifestyles: Who We Are and Where We Are Going* by Arnold Mitchell, pp. 98–99, 176–179. Copyright © 1983 by Arnold Mitchell.

Field Interviewing Target Customers

A lot of people go into small business because they don't have much choice. Many of them have to learn new skills and learn them fast. Fortunately, entrepreneurs tend to be bright, creative, and hard-working. Julia Gonzales is a good example.

It's no secret that I was distressed when my husband was transferred. I didn't blame him wanting the transfer; I would have wanted it, too. But I had a terrific job, as manager

ACTION STEP 27

Interview prospective target customers.

Now that you've profiled several target customers, it's time for you to take a big step. It's time to move from the tidy world inside your head to the arena of the marketplace. It's time to rub elbows with the people who'll be buying your product or service.

You know where your TC hangs out, and you know its habits, income, sex, personality, and buying patterns. You can guess at this customer's dreams and aspirations, and you've identified the heavy users of your product or service. Now you're going to check out these things by interviewing your potential TCs—yes, through primary research.

Make up some questions in advance. Some of them should be open-ended questions, which call for more than just a simple yes or no. Here are some questions to help get you started:

Do you like to shop at this store?

What products did you buy today?

Are the salespeople helpful and courteous?

How did you learn about this store?

Is this your first visit? How often do you shop here?

What are you looking for that you didn't find in the store today?

Where do you live?

What do you read?

Remember, no one is totally happy with a particular store or business, and your questions may unearth some gaps that you didn't know of before.

interview
a planned conversation with another person or group of persons for the purpose of eliciting specific information

of a full-line baby furniture and bedding store, and to keep both job and husband I'd have had to commute over a hundred miles a day five days a week. So, I quit my job.

But I missed the store, and it was hard living on one salary when we'd gotten used to two. When I started to look for work, I found that my reputation had preceded me. Store owners knew of the store where I'd worked, and they were pretty sure that all I wanted to do was work for them to get a feel for the area so that I could open a store of my own and compete with them.

This gave me an idea. I hadn't *considered* doing that. So when I couldn't find work, I decided to go for it, to go ahead and compete with them. Their fear gave me confidence!

One thing I learned on my way up from stock clerk to store manager is that it pays to know your customer. So in the mornings I'd get the kids off to school, pick up the house a bit, and drive to a baby store. I'd park my car a block away and when customers came out of the store I'd strike up conversations with them.

"Hi!" I'd say. "My name's Julia Gonzales, and I'm doing market research for a major manufacturer who's interested in this area. I'm wondering if you might have a minute to answer a few questions about babies."

My enthusiasm must have helped. I like people and babies, and I guess it shows. Being a mother helps me understand other mothers, too. I always dressed up a little bit and carried a clipboard. I'd ask the obvious questions like:

What do you like about this store?

What things did you buy?

Were the people helpful and courteous?

And so on.

Sometimes, I parked in the alley, to research the delivery trucks. At the beach and the shopping malls, I would stop every pregnant woman I saw. I developed a separate list of questions for pregnant women:

Have you had a baby shower?

Which gifts did you like best?

Which gifts seemed most useful?

What things are you buying before your baby comes?

What things are you waiting to buy?

How are you going to decorate the baby's room?

What do you really need the most?

The research was time-consuming, but after thirty interviews I had enough information to make some very sound decisions. I also knew the weaknesses of my competition. And I located my new store right in the middle of a coming baby boom.

When Julia Gonzales discovered that she would have to work for herself, she quickly began to research her target customers. The method she chose was **interviewing.** You can do the same thing for your business. Action Step 27 tells you how to do it. Why not get out there and try a couple!

KNOWLEDGE IS POWER

When Hugh Hefner had the vision about *Playboy,* he was alone in that market. His target customers were 17–34 years old. That was more than thirty years ago. Those same people are now 47–64 years old, and recent surveys suggest that *Playboy*'s readership is declining. Any product's life cycle is affected by the age of the customers. What is the life cycle of a magazine?

In autumn 1982 *Penthouse* magazine ran ads in major newspapers suggesting that it would run *Playboy* out of the arena. There is a word for the phenomenon of someone going after your target customers; it's *competition*. Competition is the topic of the next chapter.

SUMMARY

Your target customer is your key to your survival in small business. Constructing a customer profile is like drawing a circle around that customer in order to turn the circle into a target at which you can aim your product or service. Before you open your doors, you should profile your target customer at least five times. After your doors are open, it's a good idea to gather data through surveys, interviews, and so on, and refine the profile monthly.

A profile combines demographic data (age, sex, income, education, residence, cultural roots, and so on) with psychographic insight (observations of lifestyle, buying habits, consumption patterns, attitudes, and so on). The magazines read by your target customer will reveal a well-drawn profile of your TC; this is because the purchasers of this very expensive advertising have already researched the customer very thoroughly.

Profiling your target customer is important because it shows you:

1. how to communicate your message with a minimum of confusion
2. what additional service your TC wants, such as delivery, credit, gift wrapping, installation, post-sale service, and so on
3. how much the TC can pay
4. what quality the TC wants
5. where large groups of TCs live
6. who else is after your TC

ACTION STEP REVIEW

Action Steps 24–27 help you zero in on your target customers.

24 Use your new eyes on some mass-market magazines to develop your profiling reflexes.

25 Do some secondary research on specific magazines.

26 Profile your target customer and try to identify the heavy users in your industry.

27 Back up your profile with primary data you collect by interviewing prospective target customers.

THINK POINTS FOR SUCCESS

◄ *Psychographics* is derived from *psyche* and *graphos,* Greek words for "life" or "soul" and for "written," respectively. Thus, psychographics is the charting of your customer's life, mind, soul, or spirit.

◄ Profiling draws a "magic" circle around your target customer. Placing the customer in the center of that circle transforms the whole arena into a bullseye.

◄ Segmenting is like slicing pie; it allows you to help yourself to a piece of the pie.

◄ You can save a lot of steps by using market research that has been done by others.

◄ Contact magazines and newspapers. They employ market researchers.

REFERENCES

Akst, Daniel. "Hollywood Liberal Norman Lear Returns for Act III of His Life as Capitalist, Activist." *Wall Street Journal,* April 8, 1988. [A portrait of a VALS "Integrated." Lear created Archie Bunker.]

Alsop, Ronald. "Advertisers Put Consumers on the Couch." *Wall Street Journal,* May 13, 1988. [Right brain/left brain moved into the world of advertising as the McCann–Erickson ad agency probed the reasons for an aerosol-spray roach killer's success. Researchers found that the women in the study identified roaches with men who had abandoned them. Spraying the roaches, the researchers concluded, was like spraying the men. What would Dr. Freud say?]

Bernstein, Peter W. "Psychographics Still an Issue on Madison Avenue." *Fortune,* January 1978, pp. 77–80, 84. [Early Pinto advertisements linked the car with a frisky pony. Market probes by a research firm showed that buyers wanted a dependable car. The next run of ads showed the Pinto on a split screen with the Ford Model A—whose reliability was legendary. This is a good example of a response to the wishes, dreams, mythic desires, etc., of the market.]

Brady, Frank. *Hefner.* New York, Macmillan, 1974. [Easy-to-read book about the man who founded an empire on an image—the rabbit, "playboy" of the animal world.]

Byer, Stephen. *Hefner's Gonna Kill Me when He Reads This.* Chicago: Allen–Bennet, Inc., 1972.

Falk, Kathryn. *How to Write a Romance and Get It Published.* New York: NAL, 1984.

Hawkins, Del, et al. *Consumer Behavior: Implications for Marketing Strategy.* Dallas: Business Publications, Inc., 1980.

Iacocca, Lee A. *Iacocca, An Autobiography.* New York: Bantam Books, 1984.

Key, Wilson Brian. *Subliminal Seduction: Ad Media's Seduction of a Not-So-Innocent America.* Englewood Cliffs, N. J.: Prentice-Hall, 1972. [Fascinating study of methods used by the media to persuade us to buy things. Chapter 7, on *Playboy,* and Chapter 8, on *Cosmo* and *Vogue,* are especially valuable for helping you zero in on target markets.]

Kiam, Victor. *Going for It!: How to Succeed as an Entrepreneur.* New York: William Morrow, 1986.

King, Florence. "Ripping Clio's Bodice—The Chronicles of a Sweet Savage Hack." *New York Times Book Review,* May 3, 1987, p. 27.

Kotler, Philip. "Prosumers; A New Type of Consumer." *Futurist,* September–October 1986, pp. 24–28.

Lauder, Estée. *Estée: A Success Story.* New York: Random House, 1985.

Lofflin, John. "Help from the 'Hidden Persuaders': What's New in Subliminal Messages." *New York Times,* March 20, 1988, p. 17.

Meyers, William. *The Image-Makers: Power and Persuasion on Madison Avenue.* New York: Times Books, 1984.

Mitchell, Arnold. *Nine American Lifestyles: Who We Are and Where We're Going.* New York: Macmillan Publishing Co., 1983. [A comprehensive, data-based study of psychographic patterns in America. Contains an illuminating chapter on Europe. Projects the future. Excellent to read in combination with *Megatrends.*]

Mitchell, Constance. "Some Blacks Plunge into the Mainstream in Creating Business." *Wall Street Journal,* May 11, 1988. [Black-owned businesses are moving beyond the traditional markets, crossing over into the mainstream.]

Packard, Vance. *The Hidden Persuaders.* New York: Pocket Books, 1958.

Publishers Weekly. *Publishers Weekly Yearbook: News, Analyses, and Trends in the Book Industry.* New York: R. R. Bowker and Co., 1983.

Rice, Berkely. "The Selling of Life-Styles: Are You What You Buy? Madison Avenue Wants to Know." *Psychology Today,* March 1988.

Schlesinger, Jacob M. "GM Seeks Revival of Buick and Olds; New Models, Marketing Unveiled in Bid to Redefine Units' Image." *Wall Street Journal,* April 13, 1988. [Remember the Old Days? You started with a Chevy; if you had dash and flare, you moved up to a Pontiac; if you were fussy, to an Olds. As your wealth demanded more status, you moved up to a Buick, then a Caddy. All this changed in the eighties, the age of downsizing and sharing of parts among the GM divisions. People who once bought a Buick for its classy look started buying foreign—BMW, Mercedes, Saab, Volvo. GM is now aiming the Olds at the American middle-class, while Buick, in an attempt to gain luxury share, has added wire wheels to the Regal. Might corporate-giant GM have forgotten to watch its target customer?]

Townsend, Bickley. "Psychographic Glitter." *Across the Board,* March 1986, p. 41.

Van der Merwe, Sandra. "Grampies: A New Breed of Consumers Comes of Age." *Business Horizons,* November–December 1987, pp. 14–19.

APPENDIX 4.1 • Self-Assigned In-Depth Research of Magazines in My Industry*

Part A: New-Eyes Primary Research

The magazines I buy and read are generally not available on supermarket racks; they are available only by subscription. These magazines are specifically related to computers and desktop publishing, and their publishers find me through mailing lists. In order of usefulness, they are:

1. *Publish*
2. *Personal Publishing*
3. *PC Magazine*
4. *PC World*
5. *InfoWorld*

These publications are aimed directly at me, and I subscribe to all of them, as do many of my friends. They present state-of-the-art information that can be gained nowhere else. One insight I have noted is that few people understand or appreciate what *Publish* and *Personal Publishing* contain. Graphic arts people seem to have a computer phobia that they need to overcome. This is a challenge, but challenge also spells opportunity.

Part of my new-eyes research was done on the TV tube. Look at any TV station in our area and you will see lavish (and highly competitive) use of computer-generated graphics on the screen. (Even Channels 5, 9, 11, and 13 are active.) These effects are not primarily optical; many of them are entirely computer generated, on a mainframe or minicomputer. Such graphics capabilities have not been available on PCs, even the Macintosh. ISSCO, a San Diego–based graphics software company for mainframes and minis, recently was purchased by Computer Automation, the SuperCalc company. Last January, the guru of mainframe graphics, Allen Paller, told a small group of graphic arts specialists from the aerospace industry that ISSCO-type mini graphics will be available for PCs by mid 1987. For the most part, the computer industry is still unaware of this development. Hardly anyone in the graphic arts industry knows it.

As for the graphic arts industry, events of vital, even crucial, importance have taken place in the last year or two. When Apple Computer came out with the LaserWriter in January 1985, even Apple's management was not thinking of desktop publishing. Their ads praised the ability of the LaserWriter to "write a flashy memo." Apple management was thinking of office automation.

The Apple LaserWriter contained inside its workings a software program of profound significance to the graphic arts industry. It is called PostScript. It is the program that prints the amazing graphics on the LaserWriter and any other PostScript printing device. PostScript has two tremendous advantages over the competing technology, as represented by Hewlett-Packard and Tall Tree Systems:

1. PostScript is device-independent, meaning any computer with a PostScript printer driver can drive any printer containing the PostScript language. A Mac can drive a professional Mergenthaler phototypesetter.

---

*Student Peter Craigmoe conducted this research in 1987.

2. PostScript has not only typesetting capabilities, but also fantastic graphics capabilities. So far, only Adobe Systems, the inventor of the PostScript language, has written a program that takes advantage of more than five percent of PostScript's native capabilities. Very soon a mountain of advanced PostScript graphics programs will hit the marketplace. (The PostScript language is something like the Forth computer language; it is not at all difficult to learn. One problem is that it is so comprehensive. It has about 200 commands, and it takes time for programmers to learn to use all of PostScript's capabilities.)

The Apple LaserWriter came out in January 1985 and soon it was a hit with the computer-literate public. It produced a resolution of 300 dots per inch (dpi). Two months later, Allied Linotype introduced two PostScript phototypesetting machines: the Mergenthaler 101 and 303. The 101 outputs at a resolution of 1,450 dpi; the 303, at 2,540 dpi. These are industrial- and professional-quality typesetting machines costing $30,000 and $50,000 each. Since then, CompuGraphics, a competing phototypesetting company, has introduced a 400-dpi laser printer using PostScript and a full-scale PostScript phototypesetter. Others are quickly following and there are at least a score of laser printer manufacturers who now support PostScript.

For most professionals in graphic arts, the Apple Macintosh system was flawed in the design stage back in 1984. Apple's people were enamored of the 72-dpi resolution on the screen of the new Macintosh and married it to the Apple Imagewriter, then the printer of choice. Adobe Systems provided character-width tables for the Apple LaserWriter printer and character-width tables for the Macintosh monitor, so the screen would show up as What You See Is What You Get (WYSIWYG). But Apple chose not to implement Adobe's width tables for the Macintosh screen, substituting instead simple mathematical formulas to account for differing widths of characters on the computer screen. Boldface type was made 1.3 times as wide as regular type, which produced a flawed display on the screen—a flaw that is carried over to the Mergenthaler when PostScript files are output to that device. On the other hand, the programmers who wrote typesetting software for the MS-DOS PC computers generally chose not to use the WYSIWYG format. (Professional typesetting machines do not project WYSIWYG, so the graphics professionals readily accept the PC format.)

Hewlett-Packard muddied the waters in 1986 by announcing support for a page-description language for laser printers that went counter to PostScript. It was called document description language (DDL). Because six low-cost HP LaserJets were sold for every high-cost Apple LaserWriter, the computer-literate public believed PostScript was dead, or had met its match. Early 1987 brought clear waters. IBM opted for PostScript, and a *de facto* standard was soon set. Hewlett-Packard, after waffling for months, came out with a PostScript version for its LaserJet Plus machines and the new Series II laser printers. Perhaps one reason for this fast shuffle is that Quality Micro Systems of Mobile, Alabama, announced the PS-Jet upgrade kit that would convert the "brain-damaged" LaserJet into a PostScript device.

How did these startling developments affect the market for desktop publishing? Well, for one thing, graphics professionals now knew there was a clear standard. If they didn't, at least they were beginning to become aware that something drastic had happened to the market. They knew that a Penta-Mergenthaler phototypesetting system that sold for $188,000 late in 1984 was now worth less than $25,000. At the 1987 Gutenburg Festival in Long Beach, a 1983 Berthold forms production system, which had cost $58,000, drew offers of $1,250 and less. PostScript made all pre-1985 phototypesetting systems obsolete. This means there is a huge market out there just waiting to be converted to the new PostScript technology. Not all of it will be converted in a year, but the industry must convert over the next six to ten years or be left out in the cold.

A comparison of ads in the desktop publishing magazines proved to be an illuminating endorsement of my intuition. I believe I have struck paydirt in aiming at a market for one-on-one training and support in the area of professional desktop publishing using the PostScript programming language. I counted the number of pages of ads devoted to PostScript hardware and software in single issues of each *Personal Publishing* and *Publish* magazines in 1986 and in 1987. (A near-majority of the editorial copy was devoted to PostScript hardware and software.) The figures below show that PostScript is emerging as the winner.

PostScript Systems: 1986, 18.5 pages; 1987, 50.5 pages, a 272 percent increase.

All competing (HP and other) systems: 1986, 17 pages; 1987, 12.5 pages, a 36 percent decrease.

Scanners: 1986, 1 page (One issue was devoted almost entirely to scanners but carried no ads for them.); 1987, 9.5 pages, a 950 percent increase.

Part B: Write for Media Kits

There hasn't been enough time yet for the five magazines' display advertising departments to respond to my requests. But writing for them was a good idea, and I followed up on it pronto. Also, I plan to ask them how many subscribers they have in Orange and southern Los Angeles counties.

Part C: Comparative Analysis

Upcoming, when the media kits arrive.

FIGURE 5.1 Chapter 5 will help you prepare part C of your Business Plan, "The Competition."

Reading the Competition

LEARNING OBJECTIVES

■ To relate the four-phase life cycle to competition. ■ To define the competitive arena in terms of size, growth, profitability, innovation, market leaders, market losers, and potential competitors. ■ To understand the value of positive positioning. ■ To view competition as a struggle inside the mind of the target customer. ■ To evaluate competitors by all three kinds of research (primary, secondary, and new eyes). ■ To develop skill as a marketplace detective. ■ To use a competitor test matrix to determine the intensity of competition. ■ To learn ways to disarm competitors. ■ To see ways of changing the arena to your advantage.

ACTION STEP PREVIEW

28 Find your position in the marketplace.

29 Disguise yourself as a shopper and construct a competitor test matrix.

30 Use networking to learn about your competitors.

31 Formulate a plan for disarming competitors.

penetration of the arena
a calculated thrust into the marketplace

conglomerate
an organization involved in several diverse businesses

ike everything else in life and business, competition has a life cycle of four stages: embryo growth, maturity, and decline. In this chapter we will examine these stages and look at ways you can meet and beat your competition. Briefly, we can describe the four stages of the competition life cycle as follows:

1. In the *embryonic* stage, the arena's empty. There's just you and your idea for a product or service and a tiny core market.

2. As your industry *grows*, competitors smell money and attempt to **penetrate the arena** to take up positions they hope will turn to profit. Curious target customers come from all directions. You have visions of great success.

3. As the industry *matures*, competition gets fierce and you are forced to steal customers to survive. Shelf velocity slows. Production runs get longer. Prices begin to slide.

4. As the industry goes into *decline*, competition becomes desperate. Many businesses fail; weary competitors leave the arena, which is now silent except for the echoes of battle.

Figure 5.2 summarizes these stages.

A LIFE-CYCLE SCENARIO

The following scenario will help you understand the life cycle of a product. As a product progresses through the cycle, businesspeople vary their strategies to meet changing circumstances in the marketplace. This scenario, like the one in chapter 3, emphasizes the importance of teamwork in small business. It shows you how a manufacturing team brainstormed its way to a brilliant success.

THE SETTING: *The lunchroom at XRD, the giant telecommunications* **conglomerate**.
THE PLAYERS:

BETTY, an energetic woman with an M.B.A. from Wharton, who worked in marketing and sales. Before coming on board at XRD, she had worked for Exxon, IBM, and TRW. Even though she had just received a promotion and a good raise, Betty was getting tired of having her marketing strategies shot down. She was ready to try entrepreneurship on her own.

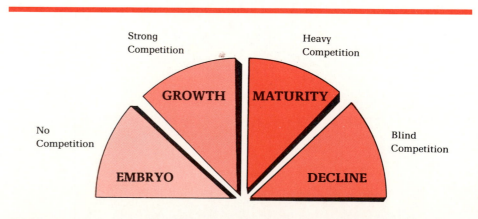

FIGURE 5.2   The product life cycle defines four stages in the intensity of competition.

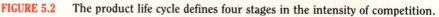

BRUCE, a junior vice-president. His favorite saying seemed to be "Let's have the bottom line, here." His dream was to be president of XRD, then Chairman of the Board, then U.S. Senator, and then President of the United States. His hero was John DeLorean. "John was framed on the drug thing," Bruce was fond of saying. "It was an obvious case of entrapment. The company was his family. He was just trying to save his family." Bruce's desk was a paper jungle, and he was known for being impatient with subordinates. Though barely thirty-five, his hair was turning grey, and he suffered from a stomach ulcer.

HUGH, a designer who worked a flex-time schedule in the XRD "creative dungeon" and came to work in jeans, blue work shirts, and running shoes. Hugh could program a computer in his sleep. Because shaving took time away from his creative endeavors, he wore a beard. You could drive by his home any night or weekend and find him tinkering away. Hugh devoured books on art, computers, architecture, self-hypnosis, investing, and right-hemisphere power.

DAN, in Public Relations. He had a B.A. in journalism from Columbia University, and he'd worked for an ad agency for ten years before coming to XRD. He dressed in three-piece suits from Brooks Brothers and drove a red convertible. He was always looking for a party; if someone else wasn't throwing one, Dan would throw one himself.

ACT I

"Listen, fellow inmates," Hugh said, finishing his cola, "last night, I came up with an idea that could make us all rich."

Bruce's ulcer was bothering him. He glared at Hugh. "Spare us the details, Hughie. Let's just have the bottom line, okay?"

"Skates for ducks!" Hugh said, smiling like a mad inventor.

Betty's marketing intuition told her some exciting changes were about to take place. "Don't jump on him, Bruce," Betty said. "Go ahead, Hugh."

"*Ice skates?*" Dan asked. "Or *roller?*" Dan was already thinking of promotional angles.

"You're off the deep end, Hugh-Boy," Bruce said, looking around the table. "Why ruin another good lunch with your holistic nightmares?"

"Take the afternoon off, Bruce," Betty said. "Play some racquetball. They're working you too hard up there in the Executive Tower."

"I've got tennis elbow," Bruce said, "or I'd be on the court right now."

"You ever watch a duck?" Hugh asked. "They can stand on one foot. Their leg muscles are rock solid. And their feathers keep them warm, even when it's *really* cold."

"The **core market** is pretty thin," Betty said, "but I like the idea. It has an innovative touch that's almost sexy. Can we have something for the December Show?"

"I'm testing the prototype Saturday at Dorman's Pond. It's a tame duck, of course, but you're all welcome to observe."

"The real market's in *wild* ducks," Betty said.

"The real promo angle is too," Dan said.

"You're all crazy," Bruce said, and he left the table.

So on Saturday, only Dan and Betty showed up for the test. They were amazed. Hugh's duck skated across the ice of Dorman's Pond serenely, like something out of a Walt Disney film. A gaggle of Mallards gathered to watch the performance, and a young Mallard came up afterward to try on the skates.

The Mallard was a natural. He swirled out onto the ice, did ripostes and pirouettes. Betty was thrilled with what she saw. The ducks on the sidelines applauded. Betty sensed widespread customer interest.

"This is *exciting*!" Betty said.

"The PR possibilities are *endless,*" Dan said. "We'll start with an autograph party this spring, as they fly north out of Mexico and South America."

The three friends had been in business before, so they started on a small scale. Hugh found a manufacturer in the next town who would make a hundred pairs of duck skates. They promoted the skates with a direct mail piece to duck owners in the local area.

core market
customers whose perceived needs best fit a product's characteristics

"Win a free pair of skates for your duck," the promo said. "Enter your duck in the Dorman's Pond Regional."

They developed an essay contest at the local high school. The topic was "Should American Ducks Have Access to Jet-Powered Ice Skates?" (The jet-powered models were still on Hugh's drawing board, but this was the moment to test the market for **product innovation**.)

product innovation
improvement in the utility or design of a product

The response from the students was an overwhelming *yes.*

Their skate manufacturer thought he had enough inventory to last until Christmas. Surprise. All one-hundred pairs were sold within a week. Catalog houses were calling, wanting the skates. The core market had emerged.

The three friends were excited. They hadn't lost a dime, and there was still no competition in sight.

One problem surfaced. At the duck races in West Ossipee, New Hampshire, three Fleet Mallards sustained severe injuries when they achieved speeds in excess of 237 m.p.h. and their skates flew off.

ACT II

Working late one night in his garage, Hugh developed an innovation: a Velcro heel strap that solved the flying skate problem. Endorsements by famous ducks quickly followed. Television networks began selling time for events featuring ducks on skates. As soon as Betty and Dan came up with a suitable company name—The Fire and Ice Skate Company—Bruce resigned from XRD and came on board as president.

distribution
the physical movement of the product from manufacturer to ultimate consumer

There was one ugly occurrence during **distribution**. A railroad car loaded with the all-new Luke Skywalker rocket-powered skates was hijacked by a gang of masked coots. Several coots were blown away when the skates they were wearing exploded. Editorials across the land carried the same message: Technology kills.

In Hollywood, celebrities that had never given a thought to ice-skating ducks were now sponsoring duck races, skate regattas, and skate ballets.

On New York's Publishers Row, major publishing houses entered a race to see who could bring out the definitive study of duck behavior. Would skating change the face of duckhood over the planet?

An entrepreneur at Texas A&M in College Station developed an "arctic refractor" that could freeze over a medium-sized lake in three hours flat. DuPont and GE put their plants into 24-hour R&D to show the world who would build the first arctic refractor. Meanwhile, the U.S. Government hired biologists to train ducks to stop migrating.

"We don't want them skating in Mexico," said one government spokesman. "We need them up here—at home on our glorious lakes. It'll boost the national morale." All over the duck world, ducks were entering the work force. Parallax, Inc., the noted motivation research firm, stated that the major reason for this was that the ducks wanted to increase their income so that they could afford upgraded skates.

Wary of being exploited, ducks began to demand higher wages. They wanted their own show. In Pittsburgh, duck skaters' unions were founded, and they spread south and west.

Fire and Ice Skate Company had been in business only eighteen months when it declared an astronomical dividend. Hugh's new developments, coupled with aggressive management from Bruce, marketing expertise from Betty, and superpromotions from Dan, enabled the four friends to pay themselves two million dollars each in combined salary and executive perks. Bruce decided to fire their small accounting firm and sign with one of the Big Eight. Dan decided to throw a party.

With three scotches in him, Bruce slapped Hugh on the back and admitted he had been hasty in calling him crazy.

"*Time* wants me on their cover," Bruce said. "What's on the drawing board, anyway? Anything cooking?"

"Yes," Hugh said. "I'm off to Tibet."

"Tibet?" Bruce was shocked. "What for?"

"Ideas," Hugh said, pointing to his right brain. "Ideas."

ACT III

Price wars plagued the industry. Mallard Eski-Skates made cuts of 25%. Canadian Goose, Ltd., makers of the luxury Ugly Duckling model, slashed their prices by 40%. At Fire and Ice GHQ in Manhattan, Bruce took a look at the balance sheet and called down to Design with orders for seventeen new variations of the Fire and Ice turbo skate.

Betty came up with an idea for saving the firm—a duck skate palace in Armonk, New York—but the bank said Fire and Ice was already overextended as it was. Up in PR, Dan hadn't had an idea for media sizzle in days. The Fire and Ice computer told the story: the end was near.

"Where is Hugh when we need him?" Bruce asked at the group's regular Friday meeting. "We're in a trough. He could bail us out."

"Our marketing data says we've peaked, dear," Betty said. "The Armonk skate palace was our last stand for this product."

"Show me that on the bottom line," Bruce said aggressively.

"I'm thinking about moving to Florida," Dan said. "According to this guy Naisbitt, that's where the action is."

The executive group meeting disintegrated into wild schemes and bickering. After the meeting broke up, Bruce kept the accounting department working through the night. "You people will stay here," Bruce said, "until you produce me a spreadsheet that does not forecast the end of my world."

But the numbers would not lie.

ACT IV

That year, Fire and Ice Skate Company tripled production to more than seventeen million pairs of duck skates. Prices were slashed. New colors were added. Velcro straps were striped with silver and gold. Five million pairs had to be sold at deep discount.

On December 26, Mallard Eski-Skates, the major competition, filed for Chapter Eleven. In January Fire and Ice closed its plants in California, Texas, Alabama, and southern New Hampshire.

DuPont's prototype arctic refractor blew up at a lake site in Louisiana, killing several hundred ducks and splattering more than a million fish across northern New Orleans. Ducks reacted by dropping their skates onto city streets at rush hour. The knife-sharp blades cut into the very heart of city traffic.

"How awful," Betty said.

"I'm off to Florida," Dan announced. "What will you give me for my stock?"

"Great news, men," Bruce said. "We just killed Canadian Goose, Ltd. They closed all their plants."

"We must do something," Betty said.

"I'm selling my car," Dan said. "Any takers?"

In the midst of chaos and depression, Hugh arrived from Tibet with an idea—a ten-speed turbo skate for people on the go.

As he was leaving, Dan met Hugh in the hall outside Executive Tower. Hugh had the sketches for the turbo skate in his shirt pocket. Dan noticed that Hugh's beard could use some immediate barbering.

"Great idea, Hugh!" Dan said. "Why didn't you think of this before?"

"It came to me on a mountaintop in Tibet," Hugh said, smiling peacefully. "How are things in the corporate universe?"

"I think," Dan said, "that we are back in business."

Dan promoted the turbo skate with a full-page four-color magazine ad. There was a photo of a young man in sweater and scarf sitting at the edge of a frozen pond. The ad copy read: "Romance fading? Dazzle her with the new F & I Turbo. With ten speeds, you can skate uphill, skate to work, or write her name in ice!"

Production geared up to make the Turbo. Bruce became F & I CEO and brought in a new man—a hotshot manager from the soft-drink industry—as president. Dan got busy making a documentary on the history of the skating duck movement. It would make great PR, he said, and enhance the company image. The documentary was set to air on network TV. Betty spent most of her time at trade shows, promoting the new ten-speed skates. She got an endorsement from a retired Olympic figure skater, which led to the idea to have a Turbo Skate Power Championship at the next Winter Olympics. Bruce the competitor fell in love with the idea and joined Betty on the road as they networked their way into the highest skating circles in the land. On their last joint report to the executive group, Betty and Bruce announced their engagement.

When last seen, a bearded, glassy-eyed Hugh was locked in the lab at Fire and Ice, working on an idea for two computer games—Skates in Space and The Duck in the Dungeon—and finalizing the sketches for his Hobby Skate model kit, which should be available in a toy store near you by Thanksgiving.

The Lessons to Be Learned

The moral of this scenario is that, to survive, you must know what stage of the life cycle you are in and compete accordingly. Figure 5.3 will help you to visualize this, and Box 5.1 will help you to *feel* each stage.

Life cycles exist for everything—industries, segments, products, locations, and so on; thus the life-cycle yardstick could be the most useful tool in your entrepreneur's toolkit. In chapter 4 you saw the effect of the life cycle on Hugh Hefner's information empire. *Playboy* readers got older (the moving target concept), and the kingdom became a dukedom. It took Hefner and *Playboy* thirty years to move through the cycle, and that arc is smooth and even. Contrast the life-cycle arc of the hula hoop

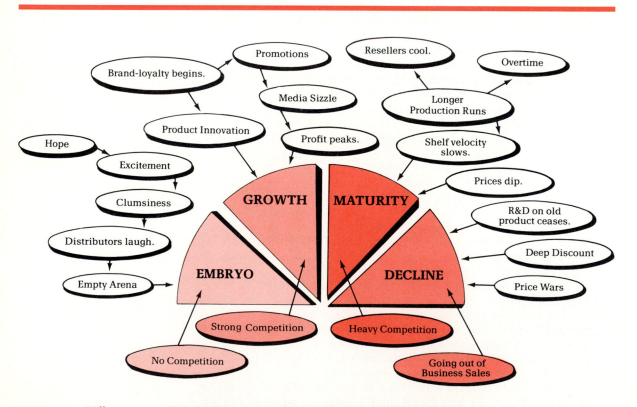

FIGURE 5.3   Different competitive strategies are needed at each stage of the product life cycle.

or the Pet Rock. They illustrate shorter life cycles, in which the movement from one phase to another is electric.

The other lesson in the Fire and Ice scenario is the value of teamwork. We'll cover teamwork in detail in chapter 13, and we'll discuss the need for a balance of personalities and skills on a team. The "DISC scale" is used there to describe the ideal balance. According to the DISC theory of balance, the ideal team would have a Dominant member, an Influencing member, a Compliant one, and a Steady one. Fire and Ice had this combination:

Bruce is a no-nonsense hard driver; he's impatient and wants to be president of everything. Bruce is a *Dominant.*

Dan is a flashy, outgoing person who loves the spotlight and is good with words. Dan is an *Influencing.*

Betty is the manager/negotiator; she smooths feathers. She's a *Compliant.*

Hugh is the individualistic inventor who can be counted on to come up with good new ideas. Furthermore, he's good with detail. Hugh is a *Steady.*

BOX 5.1   The Competition Life Cycle

THE EMBRYONIC STAGE

The embryonic stage is marked by excitement, naive euphoric thrust, clumsiness, a high failure rate, and much brainstorming. Pricing is experimental. Sales volume is low—because the market is very small and production and marketing costs are high. It's difficult to find distributors, and resellers demand huge gross margins. Profit is chancy and speculative. Shrewd entrepreneurs, however, can close their eyes and divine the presence of a core market. Competition has not yet appeared.

THE GROWTH STAGE

The growth stage is marked by product innovation, strong product acceptance, the beginnings of brand loyalty, promotion by media sizzle, and ballpark pricing. Product innovation occurs. Distribution becomes all-important. Resellers who laughed during the embryonic stage now clamor to distribute the product. Strong competitors, excited by the smell of money, enter the arena of the marketplace, as do new target customer groups. Profit shows signs of peaking.

THE MATURE STAGE

The mature stage is marked by peak customer numbers and zero product modifications. Design concentrates on product differentiation instead of product improvement. Competitors are going at it blindly now, running on momentum even as shelf velocity slows. Production runs get longer, so firms can take full advantage of capital equipment and experienced management. Resellers, sensing doom, are cool on the product. Advertising investments increase, in step with competition. Some firms go out of business. Prices are on a swift slide down. Any competitor who enters the market now is either dumb or overconfident or both. In the once-hot marketplace, there's a pervasive air of depression.

THE DECLINE STAGE

The decline stage is marked by extreme depression in the marketplace. Competition becomes desperate. A few firms still hang on. R&D ceases. Promotion vanishes. Price wars continue. Opportunities emerge for entrepreneurs in service and repair. Diehards fight for what remains of the core market. Resellers cannot be found; they've moved on.

So Fire and Ice worked for two reasons: it found a segment that wasn't crowded, and it was a balanced team.

Where are your industry and your segment on the life cycle? What does this mean to you if you're a start-up venture? What are the implications for your survival? When your industry enters its maturity and decline, will you be ready with Plan B?

competitor test matrix
a grid used to get a clear picture of the strengths, weaknesses, and sales volume of your competitors

mature industry
growth has slowed here, few new competitors, strong competition, little real new product innovation

COMPETITION AND POSITIONING

Basically, competition is a mind game played out in the customers' minds, since that is where buying decisions are made. Inside customers' minds are many "ladders"—ladders for products, ladders for services, ladders for sports figures, TV programs, banks, wines, and rental cars. To compete for a position at the top of one of these ladders, a business must first of all get a foothold and then wrestle with other businesses to improve its position. It's that simple. Looking at competition from this perspective helps you focus on the mind of the target customer. To explore this idea, read *Positioning: The Battle for the Mind* by Al Ries and Jack Trout. Action Step 28 can help you get a foothold and improve your position on your ladder.

Competition in a Mature Industry

If you're in a mature industry, you're going to have to win customers away from competitors in order to survive. One way of doing this is by giving better service. That's what Roy Modell did.

Roy Modell grew up in Arkansas. After he graduated from high school he took off to see the world. Ultimately, he wound up in Detroit. He was an independent kind of guy, and after working for someone else for awhile, he opened his own business—a gas station.

"I did like a lot of guys in Motown," Roy says. "I just sort of jumped into something. It went along okay for a while, but one day I realized the business was broke."

It took Roy five years to pay off his debts, but those years paid off. He built a solid reputation with three oil companies, and when he moved to the West Coast, that reputation followed him; oil company reps would come to him to give him first bid on station sites.

He was in Orange County, running two stations near where a planned community was being developed. An oil company rep was pushing him to open a station there. Here's how Roy checked it out.

Around 7:30 in the morning, he parked across the street from the only other station within three miles. He counted the cars buying gas for an hour. He developed a **competitor test matrix** to rate the station. For example, he noted the make of each car and correlated that with time at the pump. He had industry figures on tank capacity for all vehicles, and he knew from long experience the average amount of gas sold for each type of car. Roy had an insider's knowledge.

He came back around noon, and then again during the evening rush hour. He compared weekday business with business on the weekends, just before people went out for some distance driving.

In the employee sector, Roy saw a lot of opportunity for competition. "They were 'pump jockeys,'" Roy says. "They could have been a lot more courteous. They made five moves when one should have done. And there wasn't much attempt at selling tires, accessories, and batteries. That could have been because the owner wasn't around much."

In any **mature industry**, Roy knew, you have to be ready to steal customers from your competition. He was prepared to do that with service.

Roy put in his bid, and opened his station—at a great location: a busy corner in a medium-sized shopping center. Furthermore, his station had a good, efficient layout. The three service bays were always full, with two cars parked on the driveway outside, waiting to get in. After taking a good long look at the tire dealers in his area, Roy began running ads in the Sunday paper. In less than a year, he was outselling most of them.

Roy succeeded because he knew what business he was in and he knew how to compete. He knew how to wrestle his way to the top of the ladder.

layout
physical arrangement of a business

Scouting the Competition

The better you understand your competition, the more clearly you will see how you can position yourself for success. Table 5.1 is a sample competitor test matrix that will help you evaluate your potential competitors. Follow Roy Modell's example and study your competition. Action Step 29 will help you. Remember, work from your strengths, and strength is built on knowledge. Knowing your competitors will increase your confidence. Then you can win.

TABLE 5.1   Competitor Test Matrix

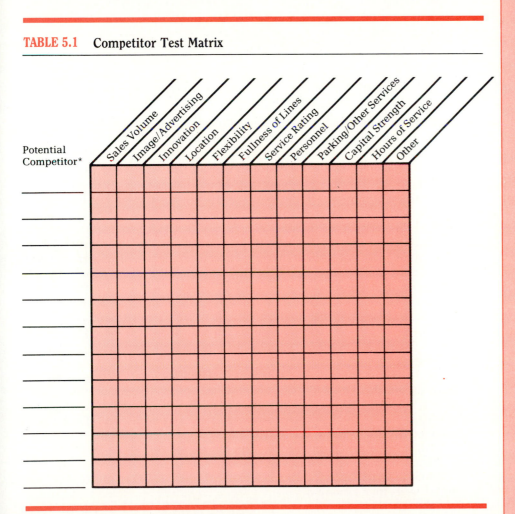

*Rating System: 1 = Good; 2 = Average; 3 = Weak.

DISARMING THE COMPETITION

disarm the competition
cancel out competitors' strengths

Plan B
the counterattack blueprint that you have ready to implement in the event of shifts in the marketplace

The two case studies that follow illustrate two tactics for **disarming the competition**. In the first case, Ben Jones grabs an exclusive rung on his target customer's ladder by being unique. In the second case, Ford Johnson is always one step ahead of the competition because he is ready with a **Plan B**.

Establishing Image and Presence

image
the way a business is perceived

presence
a heightened awareness in the mind of the target customer

Every business projects an **image**. Some businesses are so concerned about theirs that they employ image consultants and store image designers. Image and **presence** help to establish a business in the minds of customers.

> Ben Jones believes in keeping his image right up there. When he ships his expensive camera lenses (some wholesale for $2,000), he makes sure people who work in the shipping room will remember him—he packs the lenses in bags of popcorn or Virginia peanuts. And the bags are stamped with his company logo.
>
> The people who work in the shipping room are Ben's target customers.
>
> In addition, Ben sends out cards on April Fool's Day (instead of at Christmas), and when he visits clients he wears a Superman suit. He definitely maintains a presence. His clients remember him.

Being Ready for Change

Change is the most predictable element of competition. Because of this, the entrepreneur needs to keep one eye on the market and the other eye on Plan B.

inferior product
a product that is lower in utility than the product it's being compared to

> Ford Johnson has been in the mail order business for a dozen years now. He says it gives him a lot of freedom to be creative. Ford was trained as an electrical engineer, and he spent twenty years in the aerospace industry before going into business for himself.
>
> Ford has developed and marketed more than two hundred products—from a Mylar heat sheet (for pets) to Engine Coat (a motor lubricant using Teflon) to space monkeys (dried shrimp eggs that hatch when dropped into water). He's also developed a hundred strategies for handling his competitors. The best one is how he competes with himself. Here's the way it works:
>
> He introduces a quality product in the marketplace. It retails for $12, which nets him a reasonable profit after overhead. Because he deals with established mail order houses (they ship to thousands and thousands of customers), Ford knows someone out there will copy his idea and try to ace him by bringing out a lower-quality product for less money.
>
> So for the first couple of runs, Ford manufactures a quality product, using the best materials available. He charges full price for it, and waits for the phone to ring. When it does, he knows it's the buyer from the catalog house, telling him there's a competitor waiting in the wings with an **inferior product** that will retail for $6—half of what Ford's costs. So Ford has a cheaper one ready to roll.
>
> "When do you need them, and how many can you handle?" Ford asks.
>
> "Wait," the buyer says. "What kind of numbers are we looking at?"
>
> "Mine will retail for $5.75," Ford says. "And I can have 10,000 on your loading dock by two weeks from tomorrow."
>
> "You're kidding," the buyer says. (He's new on the block. Other buyers have watched Ford work before.)
>
> "Can you move 20,000?" Ford asks.

"Ten for sure," the buyer says. "And if we need more I'll get back to you in two weeks."

"Over and out," Ford says. "It's great doing business with you."

Now, let's really get an in-depth understanding of your competitors. When you understand your competitors, you'll be better able to visualize the position of your new company in the grand arena of the marketplace. Action Step 30 will help you dig.

If you're a potential buyer, everybody will compete for your dollar. If you change positions and become the store owner, you'll want to move fast to locate the ladder inside your TC's mind. If you can't locate the ladder or run into other difficulties, be ready to look for a different ladder.

CHANGING THE ARENA

Sometimes it becomes clear to a lone entrepreneur or a Big Business think tank that making a **change in the arena** can spell opportunity. The change may be very small— a slight change in some aspect of the product or service—but the effect on the market can be very large indeed. The world of business, large and small, is filled with stories of such breakthroughs, and the common thread of these stories is the discovery of an **area of vulnerability** in the existing product or service. Entrepreneurs love to hear these stories, and it's no wonder; the stories contain lessons and inspiration. That's why we include three of them here.

Bob and Ted Did It

IBM Corporation seems to have forgotten what made it one of the top ten largest corporations in America: customer service. Until it introduced the personal computer, IBM always dealt directly with customers. IBM employees sold and serviced IBM equipment. The customer could reach out and touch "Big Blue" through its employees.

Since the advent of the PC, however, IBM has effectively insulated itself from the customer. For example, IBM now sells its PCs through Sears, Businessland, Computerland, and other retail outlets. Then these computer retailers sell and service the IBM products along with the other products they handle. This represents a big change in the way IBM deals with the business community. And two sharp entrepreneurs believed it created a gap in the marketplace.

In the fall of 1983, Bob Ward and Ted Sundstrom got together and started brainstorming about the problems and opportunities in the computer industry. Bob had a degree in electronics from Cal Tech. Ted held a master's degree in computer science from the University of California at Irvine. While checking the ladder in the arena of business computers, they spotted the gap in the market abandoned by Big Blue— customer service. Checking around, they noted increased frustration when busy businesspeople dealt with retail employees.

They thought the opportunity was too good to pass up. But could they do it? Could they take the same approach IBM had used to score with the business community? Could a professional approach to service overcome their small size?

The partners each purchased a couple of "sincere" business suits. They incorporated, leased some office space, and had business cards and stationery printed. They named their firm Serich Computers: Professional Solutions to Business Problems.

Bob explains that they leased office space rather than retail space because their target customer likes to buy in a professional way. "We bring the prospect into a conference room and we sit down to discuss the problems they need to solve. After discussing the problems, we move to a demonstration room where we show them the equipment we

---

ACTION STEP 30

Use networking to learn about your competitors.

Leave your mystery shopper disguise at home and really dig into this competitor research. Some of it will be easy: yellow pages, newspapers, trade advertising, signs, former and present customers, and vendors/suppliers.

Interview everyone who will talk to you about them.

If your competitors have stock that is publicly traded, ask your stock broker about them or look them up yourself in Moody's or Standard and Poor's. Another neat trick is to ask your librarian to get you a 10K corporate report. (A 10K is required of public companies by the IRS and the Securities and Exchange Commission.) In addition, most firms are listed and rated by Dun & Bradstreet. Ask your friendly banker for a peek at the D&B reports.

Keep expanding your competitor test matrix. Use a 1–10 scale on everything you can see, hear about, touch (image, location, advertising, their signs, the way the employees dress, parking, target customers, product mix, pricing, hours of service, and so on). Whenever you unearth some hard data, compare it with industry averages.

Keep looking for those areas of vulnerability.

---

change the arena
transform a product or service by adding a simple benefit that has immediate customer appeal

area of vulnerability
your competitor's soft underbelly or Achilles' Heel—a weakness ready for you to exploit

believe will serve their needs. We wanted to distance ourselves from the "used car sales" image—an evolving image in the computer field—because we're in this for the long haul; we've not interested merely in moving a hunk of iron."

Serich follows the same track with its employees. All the salespeople have degrees in computer science. Each employee has his or her own personal computer, and all of the PCs are networked.

In just six years, Serich has grown to $2.75 million in sales and has increased its staff every year. They now employ nineteen people.

The moral here is don't insulate yourself from your customers. Reach out and touch them. Listen to their problems, and then offer them solutions that are logical and effective.

ABC Did It

Several years back, ABC televised only college football. The other major networks, NBC and CBS, had pro football covered, and pro football had captured most of the viewers—by which we mean advertising dollars.

What did ABC do? It changed the arena by introducing Monday Night Football.

ABC could change the arena because it knew what business it was in—the entertainment business. And a larger market was available to be entertained on Monday night than on Sunday afternoon.

"Manufacturer B" Did It

"Manufacturer B," a very large electrical manufacturer, wanted to penetrate the market for movie projector lamps. The problem was that "Manufacturer A," another large company, had the market sewn up.

Manufacturer B's creative, entrepreneurial-type people went to work on the problem and discovered an area of vulnerability in Manufacturer A's bulbs. They then designed a new bulb with a four-prong locking flange pin. The new bulb was easy to install, it was safe, and the new design provided better focusing.

To promote the new bulb, Manufacturer B gave away the quarter-size sockets that were fitted to it and the bases into which to set the sockets. It was the system approach.

Because Manufacturer B's new system worked better and more smoothly than the piecemeal approach provided by Manufacturer A, the customers (Kodak, Bell and Howell, and other big companies) went for it. By the time Manufacturer A woke up to the change in the arena, it was almost too late, and when they started making bulbs with locking flange pins, they had to pay Manufacturer B, the owner of the patent, to produce them.

You Can Do It, Too

These are just three of many stories we could tell you about innovators who disarmed the competitors and brought about big changes in the marketplace. It's altogether possible that we may someday be telling such a story about *you*. Yes, you, too, can do it. You just need to:

know what business you're in,

know your target customer,

know your competition,

know your product, and then

give rein to your creativity and your entrepreneurial spirit.

Go for it. Surprise us! Action Step 31 shows you how.

ACTION STEP 31

Formulate a plan for disarming your competitors.

Make this a brainstorming session with family or friends. Start with a novel idea (such as packing expensive gear in popcorn or competing with yourself) and let go with the wild ideas.

Keep your mind on the industry ladder as you brainstorm. What's unique about your product or service? Are you supplying something your target customer wants and/or needs? What tactics of your competitors can you utilize? Where are your competitors' areas of vulnerability? What might you do to establish presence? What image would be good for your business? Is there some way that you could become so unique that you would build your own little monopoly?

Consider what you might do if you start out in an embryonic industry and the arena soon becomes filled with competitors. Come up with a Plan B.

Think. Imagine. Create. Surprise. And have fun.

SUMMARY

This chapter describes the competition life cycle and its implications for the entrepreneur.

In the *embryonic stage,* the arena is empty. Competitors are nonexistent. Your target customer is a dim profile on yellow paper. Potential customers ignore you. Suppliers and distributors laugh at you.

In the *growth stage,* competitors enter the arena and target customers surface. They have been waiting for your product for years! Smart distributors sign you up.

In the *mature stage,* competition makes shelf space scarce and you are forced to steal customers to survive.

In the *decline stage,* a few competitors hang on tenaciously. By then the sharp entrepreneur has moved to a new arena and a new enterprise.

Competition is a mind game, because buying decisions are made in the customers' minds. A number of case studies in the chapter show how successful entrepreneurs have disarmed the competition—by stealing customers, by scouting the competition for strengths and weaknesses, by establishing customer recognition with their image and presence, by being ready for changing conditions with a Plan B, and by changing the arena of competition.

THINK POINTS FOR SUCCESS

- ◣ Do it smarter.
- ◣ Do it faster.
- ◣ Do it with more style.
- ◣ Provide more features.
- ◣ Provide more service.
- ◣ Treat your target customers like family; consider their needs.
- ◣ Be unique.
- ◣ Change the arena through innovation.
- ◣ Keep your image in the prospect's mind.
- ◣ Compete with yourself if necessary.
- ◣ Disarm the competition by being better, faster, safer, and easier to use.
- ◣ A new firm cannot win a price war.
- ◣ Old habits are hard to break; give your TC *several* reasons to switch over to you.
- ◣ Develop a monopoly.

REFERENCES

Allen, Gordon. "Tiny SolarCare Seeks Place in the Sun as a Start-up in a Competitive Market." *Wall Street Journal,* May 13, 1988. [Question: How many new nonfood products were tossed into the U.S. marketplace in 1987? Answer: 2,316. Question: How many of them were in the health and beauty-aid segment? Answer: eighty-eight percent. Crowded? Yeah. Still, with the ozone layer growing and new data about skin cancer appearing every day, sunscreen products count for more than forty percent of the suncare market. Retail sales in 1987 were $265 million—a juicy pie. So SolarCare entered the jammed arena with a sunscreen towelette aimed at tennis players, golfers, and spectators of both sports who don't want to carry around a bottle of greasy goo. (Are you inspired yet?)]

Baty, Gordon B. *Entrepreneurship: Playing to Win.* Reston, Virginia: Reston Publishing Co., 1974.

Carroll, Paul B. "IBM Models Likely to Fare Better in Round Two of PC Clone Wars." *Wall Street Journal,* April 29, 1988. [An interesting long look at what happened when rival firms began cloning the IBM personal computer. That was round one. Now IBM has brought forth a new product, the PS/2. The writer predicts that IBM will weigh in heavily but will not be able to avenge its honor in round two. Competing clones, he says, are firmly fixed in the arena of the personal computer.]

De Cordoba, Jose. "Hollywood Finds Hispanic Audiences Are a Hot Ticket at the Movie Theater." *Wall Street Journal,* April 6, 1988. [Film-makers discover that the simulreleases of a film in both English and Spanish can bump the gross up five to ten percent. The new pie is the Hispanic audience—they go to movies more often than other customer groups. There's some distance to go, however, as advertisers try to sell ads in English to Spanish-language stations.]

Ingrassia, Lawrence. "Day-Care Business Lures Entrepreneurs: Market Growth, Fragmentation, Spur Ventures." *Wall Street Journal,* June 2, 1988. [A hot segment of a hot growth market, day-care centers are springing up across the country. The main competition is nonprofit centers that charge lower fees, so start-ups are claiming to offer high quality for the high price. Chains like Kinder-Care and La Petite Academy are entering the low end of the arena, which leaves to the entrepreneur the markets for the children of Yuppies, "New Homesteaders," "Towns and Gowns," "Young Suburbia," "Blue-Chip Blues," and "Baby Boom Again." For some explanation of these terms, see chapter 7.]

Kahn, Joseph P. "800-356-9377," *Inc.,* July 1983, pp. 51–62. [Someone's after your 800-number, your key to telemarketing in the Age of Information. Across the nation, 356-9377 spells *FLOWERS.* Who got the number? A trucking firm.]

Kneale, Dennis. "CBS Tries to Shed Stodgy Image in Prime Time—But Can It Be Hip?" *Wall Street Journal,* April 7, 1988. [Audiences of CBS's mainstay shows ("Murder, She Wrote," "Dallas," et al.) are 50 years and over and are moving from the mature stage to the decline stage. Attempts to create shows for the 18 to 34 market have not worked. CBS is way behind on grabbing younger viewers. Furthermore, all three major networks are suffering from attacks by cable, independents, and video cassette recorders.]

Ries, Al, and Jack Trout. *Marketing Warfare.* New York: New American Library, 1986. [This is a follow-up book by the clever authors of *Positioning.* Examples: "Only the market leader should consider playing defense;" and "Find a weakness in the leader's strength and attack that point." They write well. If you're in business, read Ries and Trout.]

Ries, Al, and Jack Trout. *Positioning: The Battle for the Mind,* first edition revised. New York: Warner Books, 1988. [Update of the 1981 classic. Gives behind-the-scenes look at the details of many stunning business successes and failures.]

Ruffinach, Glenn. "Murdoch to Sell Boston TV Station, Ending a Battle." *Wall Street Journal,* April 22, 1988. [Arena battler Rupert Murdoch finally loses a round in his buyup of communications companies. To savor the spiciness of competition, research the world of mergers and takeovers.]

Sansweet, Stephen J. "As Toy Industry Changes, Mattel Cuts Product Line and Marketing." *Wall Street Journal,* April 6, 1988. [Downsizing continues at Mattel as the industry shifts: from 800 toys down to 650; 500 headquarters positions eliminated; 10 manufacturing facilities shuttered.]

APPENDIX 5.1 · Model Action Step 28: Find your position in the marketplace.

Competition

The hottest competition is already appearing in the hardware, followed by the software market. Most of the competition in the field of software support and training is in the office-automation segment of the market, the low-technology area. I must further research the competition in the advanced arena. I have already referred to Epsilon Graphics as being a specialist in desktop publishing. This tiny, storefront operation will do little to win the confidence of Fortune 1000 companies.

Cost of Positioning

At the present time, I have an open invitation from Nadek Computer Systems of Tustin, California, to enter a limited partnership in the sale, support, and training of in-plant employees for professional desktop publishing systems. Richard Sudek and Steve Natsuhara, principals at Nadek, wish to enter this potentially lucrative market. They know the hardware side and are proficient in local area network systems. But they readily acknowledge a complete lack of know-how in the area of typesetting, page composition, and graphics as they apply to desktop publishing. They are hesitant to enter this market unless they have instant access to in-depth desktop publishing know-how.

As for the cost of positioning ourselves, this should not be too expensive. A direct-mail program would suffice to get things started. Both Nadek and The Saddleback Scribe could embark on similar direct-mail programs, using computer-generated materials and mailing lists. Direct costs should not exceed $1,000, primarily for printing self-generated sales literature.

The only significant competition in desktop publishing that I am aware of at this point is Epsilon Graphics of Santa Ana. Dan Fili, the president, recently hired a typesetter, Dave Knoch, as a desktop publishing specialist. But Epsilon is targeting on the low-technology end of the market: its system is priced at $4,995. That's office automation in disguise.

Since its founding, Nadek has depended on word-of-mouth advertising for new business referrals. That marketing effort has been highly successful. The technical proficiency of the Nadek employees is generally laudatory. The marketing proficiency still leaves something to be desired. Perhaps my capabilities would complement theirs to produce a successful combination. Later this year, Nadek will be moving to larger offices. That is one tribute to their success in expanding their penetration of the market.

Customer Spread

Desktop publishing is entering in-house graphic arts departments and spreading to the technical documentation departments of medium-size and large corporations. There are many of these in Orange County and southern Los Angeles County. I still have to complete my detailed research on this market. Other related markets include commercial typesetting houses, printing companies, advertising agencies, and art production houses.

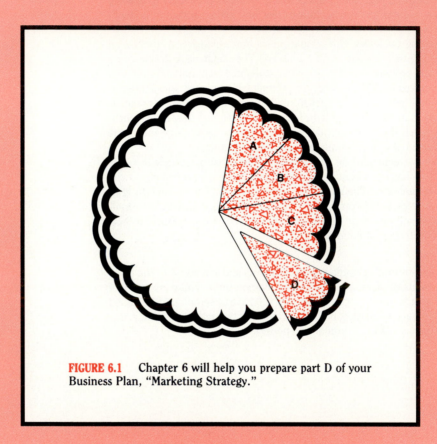

FIGURE 6.1   Chapter 6 will help you prepare part D of your Business Plan, "Marketing Strategy."

Promotion: Connecting with the Customer

LEARNING OBJECTIVES

■ To learn how to communicate with target customers using both conventional and creative promotional methods. ■ To use research to determine a promotional strategy. ■ To get free publicity. ■ To maximize economy in advertising and promotion. ■ To understand the value of personal selling. ■ To use brainstorming techniques to arrive at the right promotional mix. ■ To develop a customer list. ■ To promote through networking. ■ To build your own network.

ow that you have profiled your target customer and gained a sense of competition and market niche, it's time to plan a promotional strategy. But each business is unique, and you don't want to throw away money on promotional schemes that don't work.

For example, if your target customer is college-educated, suburban female age 45–55, who makes over $100,000, owns three cars, rides horseback ten hours a week, and reads *Practical Horseman* and *Performance Horseman,* your best chance of reaching her is with direct mail.

If, on the other hand, your target customers are male and female, age 24–57, with a high-school education, and income of $17,000, you'll have to resort to some form of mass-market advertising or rethink your target market.

Promotion is the art or science of moving the image of your business into the prospect's mind. *Promotion* comes from the Latin verb, *movere,* which means "to advance," "to move forward." It's an aggressive word, so learn to say it with a smile!

PROMOTIONAL STRATEGIES

The Promotional Mix

promotional mix
all the elements that you blend to maximize communication with your TC

The key to connecting with customers is to consider a wide variety of promotional strategies and then to pick the right **promotional mix.** Here's a list of some of the potential elements of that mix:

Paid media advertising
Point-of-purchase displays
Catalog sales
Direct mail
Money-back guarantees
Free ink/free air
Personal selling
Trade shows
Industry literature
Working visibility

All of these elements together make for a rich promotional mix. You may use some at one time or with one product, and others at another time or with a different product. For a closer look at each of these strategies, read on.

Potential Strategies

Paid Media Advertising   A surefire way to reach out is by ads in radio, newspaper, television, magazines, and trade journals. Advertising tickles the target customer's mind. With a good ad, you can reach right into your TC's mind and create the desire to buy from you.

preferred placements
best locations within a publication, a store, or a business area; or the best time slots on TV or radio.

Advertising has some obvious drawbacks: 1) it can cost plenty to create; 2) if you don't spend even more money, your ad won't get exposure; and 3) **preferred placements** go to big spenders.

Advice:

> Make sure that a large percentage of the listeners, viewers, or readers are in one of your TC groups. Otherwise your message is wasted.
>
> Your best ad is yourself. Stay visible.
>
> Check with vendors. Ask for tear sheets, copy, cooperative advertising money, and help on layouts.
>
> Check with marketing departments of newspapers. Ask for help, advice, information.
>
> Newspapers often offer advertising in special supplements at reduced cost. The offer often includes free editorial copy.
>
> Explore creative **co-op advertising**, in which suppliers share the cost.
>
> Don't be afraid to **piggyback**. Let Madison Avenue build the market. Then use your promotional mix to tell the TC to buy at your place.
>
> Start small, and test, test, test.

co-op advertising
when manufacturers co-sponsor or contribute to the retailer's cost of advertising

piggyback
a technique that allows you to coordinate your local ad campaign with the hoopla generated by national advertising

Point-of-Purchase Displays   These encourage impulse purchases of last-minute stuff like paperbacks, pantyhose, candy, magazines, and gum. A sharp P-O-P can improve your image and it serves as a tireless silent salesperson, always on duty. A good P-O-P can be used for customer education. If it is hard to understand how to use your product or the benefits aren't clear to the TC, your silent salespeople can deliver the message.

There are problems with these displays: 1) you can't sell large items because they crowd customers at the cash register, and 2) the display must sell itself as well as the product. (A tacky P-O-P will turn prospective customers *off* instead of *on*.)

Advice:

> Do weekly evaluations of all P-O-Ps. Make certain your silent salespeople are doing their work.

P-O-P (point-of-purchase) display
a display that acts as a silent sales clerk for a specific product

Catalogs   This sales tool is just right for isolated shoppers and shoppers in a hurry. Because we are becoming so "time poor," even general items are now being purchased via catalogs. A customer can shop at their convenience and not have to worry about store hours, parking, or traffic. **Catalog houses** such as Spiegel don't usually manufacture anything, so they are always looking for good products. Use catalogs as another kind of silent salesperson to reach smaller customers.

If you try printing your own catalogs, you'll run into at least two problems: 1) cost (they are expensive to print and to mail); 2) size limitations (it's tough to sell anything by catalog that's big, bulky, or inconvenient to ship).

Advice:

> Be prepared to take advantage of video catalogs. They are growing in number.
>
> Let major catalog houses do your promotion, but make sure you can deliver if your product takes off.
>
> Before you get in too deep, try a few major houses with a **product description** plus photographs. If they don't like your product, they may help you locate a catalog house that will. The feedback will be invaluable.

catalog house
business that buys products and resells them via catalogs

product description
a list of the features and benefits of a product

Direct Mail   This promotional tool lets you aim your brochures and flyers where they will do the most good. **Direct mail** is very important for small business, because it can go to the heart of your target market.

The success of direct mail depends on your ability to define the target market. If the market is too fragmented for you to do this, direct mail is not for you.

direct mail
advertisement or sales pitch that is mailed directly to TCs

Advice:

Stay up nights if you have to, but define the target market.

Develop customer lists. (Action Step 34 will help you do this later on in the chapter.)

Money-Back Guarantees   You may not have thought of a guarantee as a form of promotion, but it is. You can reach security-minded customers by emphasizing the no-risk features of your product.

The problem is that you must back up your guarantee with time and money.
Advice:

Figure 5% into your pricing to cover returned goods. If the product is fragile or easily misused—and people have been known to misuse just about everything—build in a higher figure.

Free Ink and Free Air   Reviews, features, interview shows, **press releases**, and newspaper columns cost you nothing, and they are tremendously effective. **Free ink/ free air** is an excellent way to promote because it establishes your company in a believable way. The target customer is likely to attach more credence to words that are not paid advertising.

The obstacle here is getting media people to think your business is newsworthy.
Advice:

Every business is newsworthy in some way. Dig until you find something.

Know the media people. Aim your release at *their* target readers, viewers, or listeners.

Make your press kit visual. Send accompanying photos of your principals, your facility, and your product or service in use.

Present your press kit in an attractive folder to influential representatives of the media.

Personal Selling   It doesn't matter if you've never sold before; no one is a better salesperson than you are. You are the business. If you listen carefully, your target customers will *tell* you how to sell them your product or service. That's why a good salesperson is a creative listener, not a fast talker. Most customers like to talk with the owner of the business. Use that to your advantage.

Unfortunately, **personal selling** is expensive, especially if you have to pay others to do it, and it will boost your overhead unless you pay your salespeople only by earned commission. And if you try to do it all yourself, you won't have the time and energy for other things that only *you* can do.
Advice:

Make everyone in your business a salesperson. It's security for them, because if they don't help and nothing sells, they don't have a job. Remind them that your TC needs a lot of TLC.

Consider developing a **network of sales reps** who will work on a percentage of sales. Keep cheerleading. Reps need encouragement, too.

Increase your personal visibility. Join **lead clubs** in your area. Join service clubs and trade associations. Write a newspaper column. Be bold. (See Box 6.1.)

Don't ever get so big that you don't spend some time selling and talking with your customers. If you lose touch with your customer, you may lose your business.

press release
a news item written by a business about itself and sent to the media as an attempt to get free ink

free ink/free air
information about your business that is published or broadcasted free of charge

personal selling
selling and taking orders by an individual salesperson

network of sales reps
independent businesspeople who sell a number of noncompeting products and services in a specific geographic area on a commission-only basis

lead club
a group of business and professional people who meet regularly to exchange sales prospects and tips

BOX 6.1   Bite a Lion on the Tail

For whatever reason, many people are afraid of personal selling. You can make that fear your challenge. Ever hear of the surefire cure for fear of lions? You just bite a lion on the tail.

It's the same way with fear of elevators. The best cure is to ride in lots of elevators.

If you're afraid of selling, go out and become your own best salesperson. *You can do it*—not only because you know the business better than anyone else, but because your very hesitancy indicates that you will be sensitive to your customers' needs.

But don't just go out there and be sensitive. Go out and bite a lion on the tail.

Trade Shows   These shows display your product or service in a high-intensity way. Trade shows develop a carnival, county-fair atmosphere, which can be so necessary in business. Besides, your appearance at a trade show asserts your position in your industry.

However, if the show is not in your area, you'll have transportation costs, and the booths are expensive. Furthermore, unless you're careful and make a study of the layout, you may rent a space that is thin on **traffic**. See Figure 6.2.

Advice:

Share booth space with another small business owner.

Combine functions by doing some market research while you're promoting.

Study the floor plan. Position yourself in a high-traffic area.

traffic
movement of vehicles and pedestrians

Industry Literature   Become a source of information in your industry by producing brochures, newsletters, handbooks, product documentation, annual reports, newspaper columns for the layman, or even the "bible" for your industry. (How would you like to be recognized as an expert in your field?) We think this is one of the best promotional devices around.

You may balk if you're not handy with words, and that *can* be an obstacle, but it's not an insurmountable obstacle. Remember that expertise is admired and sought out by others. As you grow in expertise, you'll also grow in confidence and the ability to communicate with words.

Advice:

Hire a writer.

Talk is cheap. If you get your thoughts down on paper, you're two steps ahead of the talkers.

Don't be afraid of audacity; it stirs the blood.

Working Visibility   In chapter 5, our case study on Ben Jones painted a picture of an entrepreneur who knew how to maintain a presence. You can do the same thing even on a small budget. Most service firms display their presence as they work. In other words, they put signs on everything: their business, their trucks, and their work sites. Wherever they're busy, they let people know it. They make themselves visible.

The drawback here is similar to one of the drawbacks with P-O-P displays. If the presence you maintain doesn't sell itself—if it is unattractive, or if it calls attention to an unsavory part of your business—you will lose potential customers rather than gain them.

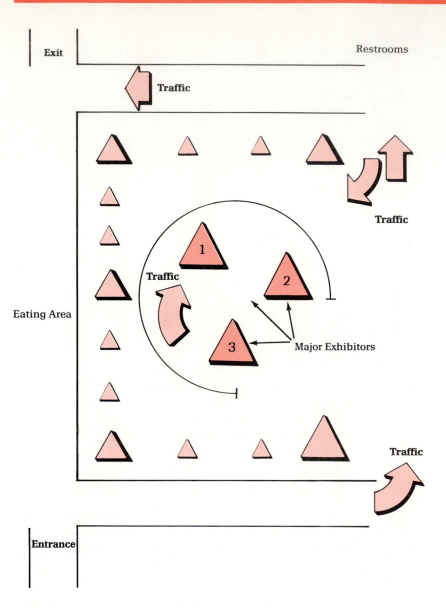

FIGURE 6.2 If you can preview the layout of a trade show for where the heaviest traffic flows will be, you can position your booth to take advantage of it.

Advice:

Exploit your public activities with signs that tell people who you are.

Review your displays weekly. Make sure the message is working.

How to Make the Right Decision

Any promotion or promotional mix that advances the image of your business is worth considering. You've just surveyed some of the most common and traditional means of promotion. Before you decide on your promotional strategy, make sure you're open to all options. That's why we ask you to keep an open mind throughout this chapter, as you brainstorm for strategies, examine promotion campaigns, and come to understand the importance of planning ahead. Then you will truly be able to make good decisions on how to connect with the customer.

SALES REPS AS CONNECTORS

Suppose you have a new product that has immediate sales potential across the country. How can you connect with the whole United States? Should you hire your younger brother to take care of it for you, or should you seek out some professional sales reps?

An army of sales reps awaits your call. However, a rep is not a rep is not a rep; select your reps carefully. Exercise caution because the reputation of your sales reps will become *your* reputation.

The best way to find good reps is to interview potential buyers of your goods. Ask them to recommend some reps who have impressed them. When the same name surfaces several times, you will know where to start your contacts.

Aggressive reps may contact you. Prepare yourself to ask them the right kinds of questions:

Who are your customers?

How many salespeople do you have?

What geographic areas do you cover?

What lines have you carried?

What help can you offer in collecting overdue accounts?

What ideas do you have for trade show presentations?

Do you have a showroom?

Could you work with us on a regional roll out, while we get ready for national coverage?

What percentage commission do you expect?

Can I participate in your sales meeting?

Do you handle competitive lines?

What kind of reports on your sales calls can I expect?

What kind of performance guarantees do you offer?

How can our agreement be terminated?

Can I pay you after I have collected from customers?

Provide all the encouragement and support to your reps that you can, and never stop being a cheerleader. Nonetheless, insist on sales call reports that will keep you informed on what is going on in the field, and pack your bags and make some calls with the reps. Write monthly sales letters and encourage feedback from both your reps and their customers. You *could* learn the worst—that a new line has taken your place or that the reps have been sleeping. This feedback will help you to evaluate your product line and your reps.

COURTESY AS PROMOTION

A luxury imported auto dealer mailed five thousand postcards to prospects selected demographically according to high income. The message on the postcard read something like: "Come in and test-drive this road warrior and receive a nice gift."

ACTION STEP 32

Brainstorm a winning promotional campaign for your business.

Disregard all budgetary restraints. Pretend that money is no object. Close your eyes, sit back, and develop the ideal campaign for connecting with your target customers. It's okay to "get crazy" with this, because excellent, workable solutions often develop out of such bizarre mental activity!

If your product or service needs a multimillion-dollar advertising promotion with endorsements by your favorite movie star, fantasize that it's happening now.

If you need a customer list created in marketing heaven, specify exactly what you need and it is yours.

If you are looking for the services of a first-class catalog house, just whisper the name three times and you are in business.

If your business at its peak could use a thousand delivery trucks with smiling drivers who make your TC feel terrific, write down "1,000 smiling delivery people."

If your product is small, brainstorm the perfect point-of-purchase device, perhaps one with slot machines whose money-tubes are connected to your private bank vault.

Watch the money roll in.

This chance to ignore costs won't come around again. (Reality is right around the corner.) But for now, have fun.

promotional campaign
a sales program designed to sell a specific product or service, or to establish an image/benefit/point

One potential customer came from forty miles away for his test drive. The gift was a good incentive, but he'd been looking at cars for a year and was about ready to make a decision, so he wanted the test drive. That morning he had transferred funds to his checking account. "Honey," he said to his wife as he left the house, "I'll be home with a car." His pink slip on his trade-in smoldered in the glove compartment.

Mr. Serious Prospect entered the dealer's showroom wearing old clothes and clutching his postcard. Four dapper salesmen in three-piece suits had seen him coming and had left the showroom quickly.

Without a salesperson in sight, the prospect spent ten minutes waiting, reading the literature. The demos were locked, so he couldn't even sit behind the wheel for a fantasy drive. At last, a secretary entered the showroom, asked him for his postcard, and gave him the premium gift. About this time, one of the salesmen returned, hands in his pockets and looking bored. The prospect took the opportunity to ask some questions about the car, to which the salesman responded without enthusiasm in monosyllables—and with a yawn.

(Would *you* feel like doing business with such a place?)

Mr. Prospect took his business elsewhere that morning. He found the car he wanted and wrote a check for $25,000.

The objective was to bring in customers for a test drive—not to give away premiums. Everything worked except the last person in the chain. How many other deals did that dealer lose during the promotion?

Be dramatic. Impress your employees with the fact that you mean business about customer courtesy. Close down your business for a day and have all employees attend a sales retreat that stresses the importance of potential customers to your remaining in business. Follow up the retreat with incentive programs that reward employees for acts of exceptional courtesy to customers.

PLANNING AHEAD

You need to make a lot of intelligent noise before you open your doors for business. When you open, open with a bang. Start-ups are ironic—you need to spend bushels of money to overcome buyer inertia, yet you don't have those dollars to spend. What're you to do? Use your head instead of your checkbook.

Plan for your opening now. Few businesses are profitable at first, so yours probably will not be either. Many of the promotional tools we've just discussed cost very little. You will need to use those to lure customers and build confidence that you are in this game to win. Yes, use your head instead of your checkbook. And keep your target customers clearly in mind so that you'll be able to tell them how your product or service will benefit them.

Don't Keep Your Business a Secret

Earlier we said that if you fail to plan, you're planning to fail. When it comes to promotion, if you fail to plan you're planning to keep your business a secret.

One way to avoid keeping your business a secret is to brainstorm an ideal **promotional campaign** with no holds barred and with no worries about costs. Action Step 32 makes sure you consider all of your creative ideas before you discard them because you think they are unrealistic. Save the ideas you come up with in this action step, because we'll use them later. Box 6.2 shows how two entrepreneurs applied ingenious—and cost-effective—solutions to their promotional needs. Later in the chapter we share four case studies from our own file on creative promotions. As you'll

BOX 6.2   Creative Promotional Ideas from *Streetfighter*

Don't be afraid of being different. What's hot? What's cool? What's melting in your arms?

Problem: Salespeople at Wisman's Trusted Appliances & TV, Inc., feared that they were losing business when customers left the store to comparison-shop. *Solution:* The owner packed a freezer with ice cream. Every customer who looked at a freezer got a half-gallon carton, free. Instead of comparison shopping, the customers raced home to their refrigerators. That gimmick kept Wisman's in the mind of the prospect and helped increase sales by 11%.

Contest? Fat prize? Insure yourself with Lloyd's.

The owner of a small print shop was tapped for $750 by the organizers of a charity golf tournament. Wanting as much mileage as possible for his promotional dollar, he offered a hole-in-one contest prize of $10,000, to be split between the first golfer to ace the ninth hole and the charity. The owner's picture was taken with an oversize check, and the media kept cameras trained on the ninth hole. And if the golfer had sunk one? No problem. The shop owner was insured with Lloyd's of London against business loss with a premium of $450—$300 less than his name on the donors' board would have cost.

Source: Adapted by permission from *Streetfighter,* a newsletter published by RMI, P.O. Box 15719, Fort Wayne, IN 46885. Telephone (219) 485-7037. The *Streetfighter* motto is "Don't outspend the competition; out-think 'em."

see throughout this chapter, the entrepreneurs who succeed are the entrepreneurs who have the best fix on their target customers. They are also the entrepreneurs who understand the importance of market research.

PROMOTIONS AND MARKET RESEARCH

As you gain experience in promoting your small business, you'll see for yourself just how much promotional strategy and the target customer are interlocked. That's why you can't plan your promotional mix without dipping back into market research. The pros do both at the same time. But don't take our word for it—ask entrepreneur Frank Williams. He combined his research with promotion—a smart recipe. And he used a freebie for a come-on.

> Frank Williams was really happy with his microcomputer until the switch went out two days after the 90-day warranty was up. Frank put the micro into his car and drove to the repair shop.
> "You turn it on and off a lot?" the repairman asked.
> "Of course," Frank said. "Several times a day. Why?"
> "That's what wore it out," the repairman said. "The switch is the only moving part. The rest of this baby will last ten years, at least."
> The repair bill was $150, and when Frank got back home he gave the situation some thought. The reason he had to keep turning the machine off was so his youngest child wouldn't mess up his files. The easiest way to handle it was to turn the machine off.
> The lock box idea came to Frank as he was dropping off to sleep that night. The next weekend he designed a prototype of wood. His model had a hinged lid, a brass lock, and a space-age look. Frank took it to a friend of his who was a manufacturer. The friend thought it would fly. They consulted their wives on colors, and the group came up with eight colors—red, orange, yellow, black, beige, blue, white, and avocado.

"That's a lot of paint," the manufacturer said. "How can we narrow it down?"

"Market research," Frank said.

Frank took a prototype Lock Box to a computer trade show. He put up a large sign that said: **Register for a Free Micro Lock Box.** People crowded into Frank's booth to sign up for his drawing. The card had a place for their name, address, phone number, type of computer, and—what color they would like.

It worked. Frank's market research was cheap and fast. In a day and a half, he got 1,400 people to tell him what color Lock Box they wanted. The overwhelming favorite was beige. Furthermore, he had a good start on a customer mailing list.

By being curious and thorough, Frank Williams had discovered one of the secrets of the marketplace: You can promote and do market research at the same time. He also learned that if you don't know what your target customers want, all you have to do is ask them.

Ask the Customers Questions

When you're trying to brainstorm your promotional campaign, ask your customers how they perceive your business. Then ask them questions:

Is there anything they couldn't find?

Is this their first visit to your store? (or some other greeting that you can use instead of "Can I help you?")

What do they want?

Where are they from?

How did they find you?

How else might your company be of service?

Listen to the answers they give you, and value the information for what it is: primary market research data. Write down the customers' exact words in your Adventure Notebook.

Freebies in General

Freebies are a tremendously effective promotional gimmick. You can use them to get your customer's attention, to create interest in a new product, or (like Frank Williams) to gather market research. Freebies don't have to be expensive to help you connect with customers. Box 6.3 describes some inexpensive freebies that entrepreneurs have used to grab the mind of the target customer. (Note that many of the freebies are purely informational. Could you boost sales by offering free advice?)

Discount Coupons

Discount coupons are a special form of freebie because they give you positive feedback on your promotion. They should have an expiration date and multiple-use disclaimers (as, for example, a disclaimer that the coupon cannot be used in conjunction with other promotions or discounts). They should be coded to identify the source so that you can find out where your advertising is paying off, and they should be tested in small quantities before major use.

Everyone seems to like coupons. Even if your product or service is "upscale," consider trying coupons as an introduction or at your slow times of the year.

BOX 6.3   How Street-Smart Are Your Freebies?

Every business has a "freebie" that will help grab the mind of its target customer. This book is full of examples: the toy store retailer who gave away a large jar of pennies in exchange for a start on a customer mailing list; the appliance store that gave away ice cream so that potential customers wouldn't have time to price freezers elsewhere; the inventor who gave away one computer lock box in exchange for a mailing list of 1,400 names. Here are some more examples of effective, street-smart freebies.

Orange Juice. A manufacturer of a new juice squeezer served freshly squeezed orange juice at a trade show.

Hot Dogs. A retailer obtained hot dogs and buns from a local hot dog maker, then advertised with promotions that read "Bring your buns to our August Sale at noon." At noon, the line of hot dog lovers stretched around the block. Curious customers, lured by free food and the carnival atmosphere, walked into the store to check out the sale. The cost of this promotion was $66.

Health Drink. The distributor of an expensive food blender gave away cups of a health drink and a booklet of recipes at a trade show. Salespeople were on hand to take orders for the blender.

Advice. A men's clothing store employed a woman fashion consultant during the month of December to give advice to women who came in to shop for presents for men.

A flower shop passed out "Green Thumb" information leaflets on plant care.

A hardware store expanded into the parking lot for a "home improvement weekend." Professionals were on hand to give tips and instruction on laying tile, repairing garden hoses, fixing leaky faucets, and installing dead-bolt locks.

Source: Adapted in part from *How to Get Free Press* by Toni Delacorte, Judy Kimsey, and Susan Halas (San Francisco: Harbor Publishing, 1981) pp. 120–21, 125, 127, 131–32.

MAKING DECISIONS

By now you should be ready to make a few decisions about your promotional mix. Let's begin with price.

Attach Price Tags to Your Promotion Strategies

A freebie, like other promotional strategy, costs money. Look at the ideal promotional strategies you came up with in Action Step 32 and pick the top four or five elements. Then determine the price of each. (For example consider the difference in cost between a magazine ad and a press release.) Action Step 33 walks you through the process.

Don't be discouraged if price knocks out part of your ideal promotional mix. That's why we've filled this chapter with so many inexpensive promotional ideas. And in the meantime, you have used the powers of your imagination to brainstorm the best possible promotional effort for your business.

Even as you make decisions, keep thinking of that best possible effort—and of your target customer—and you can't go wrong.

Concentrate Your Efforts

One promotional strategy may prove to be a big winner for your business. The examples that follow show how several entrepreneurs discovered their winning strategies. While reading what these entrepreneurs have to say, you may discover your own winning strategy. Look for inspiration.

ACTION STEP 33

Attach a price tag to each item of your promotion package.

What will your Customer Connection cost? To get some idea, go back to Action Step 32 and list the top four or five connections you want with your customers. Then research what they cost.

Let's imagine that you have chosen this promotional mix:

1. **Magazine Ads.** This choice assumes you know what your TC reads. Good. Contact the display ad department of the magazines. Ask for their media kit and a reader profile. At the same time, ask for the rates for their mailing lists for the geographic areas you want to reach. Many magazines will sell lists by zip code.

2. **Direct Mail.** Look up mailing list brokers in the yellow pages under *Direct Mail.* Tell them what business you are in and ask for information and strategy tips. Ask for sample names so you can check mailing list accuracy against your TC profiles. Compare the cost of buying the lists from brokers with the cost of buying them from magazines.

3. **Press Releases.** Visit the marketing department of your local newspaper for information on targeting its readers. Use this information to angle your release. Type the release double-spaced. Make sure you catch the reader's attention. Keep the message simple. Be sure to wield the five W's (who, what, where, when, why) and the noble H (how) of journalism.

4. **Personal Selling.** If you cannot reach customers this way yourself, you will need to budget for someone who can. If you are planning on selling yourself, locate lead clubs in your area and start building a network of contacts. Figure your salary and expenses as a promotional cost. (For tips on how to profile your personality and how it can be balanced by others, see chapter 13.)

Once you know what each item of your promotional package will cost, you can decide which of them you can afford.

EARTH-TO-AIR TRAVEL, INC.—NEWSLETTER

Two years ago we missed the ironclad deadline for getting our ad in the phone book yellow pages, so we tried to make up for that by placing fun-type ads in community newsletters within a two-mile radius of our agency. The ads didn't cost much, and we hoped they would help to keep our visibility high. Our best response came from a mobile home park less than a mile away. It's a gold mine of retirees with steady incomes who dearly love to travel.

By studying the community newsletters, we came up with our own format, and now we send out our own agency newsletter every couple of months. On the front page we feature a catchy travel theme, along with a picture of our employees. The picture helps us connect, especially with first-time customers. They see our smiling faces, and most of them feel they know us when they walk through our door.

We're already on the way to being friends.

THE SOFTWARE SCHOOL—DIRECT MAIL

When we started The Software School, we quickly discovered that the major local newspaper covered the northern half of the county, while the market we'd targeted—executives and small business microcomputer owners—lived in the southern half. The one sure way to reach the center of the market was with a direct mail piece. Our strategy was to buy a list from a magazine whose readers matched our customer profile—in this case, *Personal Computing*—and then we sent out our brochure.

The response was terrific. We generated enough business for a healthy start-up, and satisfied customers sold for us after that by talking up our one-day teaching system.

Direct mail allowed us to go right to the heart of our market. When you're just starting out in a new venture, that kind of accuracy is worth every penny it costs.

sign on car
a simple promotional technique—you park your car or truck in a high-traffic area—the sign points the way to your business

ARGOSY AUTO PARTS—A SIGN ON YOUR CAR

The main reason we chose Argosy was because we thought it was a good name. My husband had thirty-two years of experience in the auto parts trade—in retailing and also in distribution—and when we opened our store in South Coast we felt it was a guaranteed money-maker.

We opened our new store in midsummer, but by September we were ready to call it quits. Sales had averaged only $2,000 a month, and that wasn't even enough to pay the rent.

Fortunately, we got help from a small business seminar. It was made clear to us that although everyone was familiar with the name Argosy, very few people knew we were Argosy in South Coast.

Our first step was simple—we parked our car on the main street near our store. On the back we placed a large sign, with an arrow pointing to our store. The sign read ARGOSY AUTO PARTS. Business picked up right away, and that gave us the confidence to make contact with service stations in the area.

Gradually, we built up our own network. I joined some local service clubs, and that led me to a sales lead club. We meet once a week, for breakfast, and if you don't bring someone a lead, you have to put a dollar into the kitty.

Things are all right now, but when I look back, I know that without that sign on the car we'd have been out of business in no time.

GARMENT GUIDE—FREE INK

When my partner and I got the idea for guiding shoppers through the L.A. garment district, we thought it would be so exciting we wouldn't have to do much except stop off once a week to make bank deposits.

Were we ever wrong.

We ran a good-sized ad in the local paper. It filled a couple of buses, but then our market ran out, because those customers didn't need a return trip on the bus. We had some flyers printed up and we covered every car in every parking lot in our community. Two thousand flyers netted us half a bus.

Then I just happened to read a feature story in the View section of the *L.A. Times* about a tour to Hollywood and Universal Studios. On an impulse I called the reporter up and told her about Garment Guide. It worked.

On the next trip, the reporter came along, and brought a staff photographer. Two weeks later, *our* story was on the *front page* of the View section—a beautiful third of a page—and customers began calling us! Our local papers followed a month or so later with features about the service, and after we got bigger, a TV reporter profiled us for one of the evening news magazines on television.

Now business is great. We haven't had to advertise for eighteen months. When people ask me what kind of promotion I believe in, I tell them free ink!

We hope you found inspiration by reading about these entrepreneurs, who, through planning or perseverance, found successful promotional strategies. Now let's go on to two of the most useful promotional tools for *every* small business, mailing lists and networking.

MAILING LISTS

Sometimes the winning component of a promotional mix is a **mailing list** that goes to the heart of your target market. An accurate and up-to-date mailing list can mean money in the bank. Entrepreneur Mel Cartwright developed a database on his target customers in a fun and painless manner—in the midst of his Christmas promotion.

Mel Cartwright had worked for three large corporations before he decided to start a business of his own. He used some money of his own and founded Mel's Toys on the East Coast.

For the first six months, business was fair, and Mel broke even. Sales picked up dramatically the day after Thanksgiving. The parking lot in the shopping center was crammed with cars, and Christmas-conscious people came in hunting for gifts for their children. That Friday Mel made more money than he had in all of September.

"The toy business is seasonal," Mel said. "And with all those people coming through the door, I wanted to make sure I developed a solid customer base."

So for three weeks, Mel hired a Rent-a-Santa and a professional photographer. Every child that came into Mel's Toys was photographed, free, on Santa's knee. While the children were being photographed, the parents filled out information cards with their child's name, age, toy preferences, and date of birth.

At the end of the three weeks, Mel had developed a fine customer list. He also had one valuable piece of information—the birthday of every child who had been photographed.

So, every time a birthday rolled around, Mel mailed a small inexpensive toy along with some copies of the Santa photograph. As an added bonus, he made the negatives available to parents, many of whom ordered Christmas cards picturing their child talking to Santa.

As his mailing list grew, Mel came up with another idea.

"I was at the cash register one day when one of my employees was sick with the flu, and I noticed five customers in a row who spent more than $50. I kept those checks and credit card slips separate, and at the end of the day I photocopied them and started a Big Spender list. Today, my Big Spender list has grown to several hundred customers, and I've developed a special mailer aimed just at them."

I wish someone would have told me how important a mailing list would be in this business before I got into it. With what I know now, I think I could branch off into at least a dozen industries and do very well."

Mel smiles. "And to think it all began with a Rent-a-Santa."

You may not need a Rent-a-Santa, but you do need well-organized information. Action Step 33 asks you to organize the information you already have. See how the concept of a mailing list may begin with a **customer file**, but expands to include your other contacts as well. You can't help but gather information as you operate your small business. With good files, that information becomes useful. Organized information is power. Action Step 34 shows you how to get that power.

mailing list
names and addresses of potential customers

customer file
a list of persons or firms that have purchased from you

ACTION STEP 34

Organize your files.

Begin with a study of what your target customer reads. Move from there to a reader profile and a mailing list, to find out where your TCs are concentrated.

For every customer you contact, make up a file card. Use your handy demographic set-up (sex, age, income, education, and residence—or size of company, type of industry, what department did the buying, and so forth) and launch yourself early into analyses of lifestyle or business style. If you have a microcomputer, this is a great time to use it.

Try to segment the big spenders and develop a special strategy for them. (Every industry has its heavy users. Who are the heavies in your industry?)

Start a media file by contacting all potential advertising media in your area. Ask for rate cards and demographics.

If you have not done it yet, start a file on your competitors and how they promote. Try to learn what is working. What ideas can you borrow?

Start a How-Can-They-Help-Me File on your vendors and suppliers. Action Step 53 in chapter 11 will help you create your own vendor statement. Most vendors have been in the industry awhile. Get to know them, ask for advice, listen carefully. You may not buy from them, but the information you obtain could save your neck.

networking
communicating through person-to-person channels in an attempt to sell or gain information

ACTION STEP 35

Build your network.

Visualize yourself as being in the center of a web of interpersonal contacts and associations. This web connects you with your family, friends, neighbors, acquaintances, business associates—everyone you know—and it is your potential network. Here's how to develop a functioning network for yourself.

Write down what you know about each person in your web—business, hobbies, residence, children, interests, and who they might know. Recall where you met the person. Does the meeting place tell you anything helpful? Are you members of the same group or club? What interests do you share? What, after all, is the connection between you and the person?

Now, from all these people, build a couple of core groups. Start with two or three people. Are they interested in networking? Are they diverse enough? (You'll need doers, stars, leaders, technicians, an organizer or two—people who will tend to "balance out" your own talents. See chapter 13 on Team Building.) Make sure the people you contact are not competing for the same target customers. The members of a core group must *not* be competitors; if they are, the group won't function as it should.

Set up a meeting. If you are working, breakfast usually works best. If the core group catches on, you can share phone duties and arrange further meetings.

Before you know it, you will be networking your way through the channels of your community, business to business.

pyramid hierarchy
a form of bureaucratic organization with the Pharoah, Chief, King, President, Chairman, Chancellor, CEO, or Boss at the top, all others below

core groups
clusters of influential, key individuals that share a common area of interest

NETWORKING

Another source of promotional power is the technique of **networking** (Figure 6.3). Networking carries the image of your business to a support group of noncompetitive helpers. It is the wave of the future in small business. Gena D'Angelo speaks for many when she gives this testimonial for networking.

When Rob and I decided to go into business for ourselves, we looked around for more than a year. I had some training in graphics and Rob's good with numbers, and what we finally decided on was a franchised mail-box operation. We paid the franchisor a flat fee and agreed to pay them a percentage of our gross. They gave us aid and assistance and a well-developed business plan.

What they didn't tell us about was networking.

When you're in the mail-box business, giving good service is how you forge ahead. We knew we had to promote our image and we tried everything—brochures, leaflets, flyers, and full-page display ads in the local newspapers. But the business didn't start rolling in until I joined my first network.

It's a sales lead club, and the membership is varied. We have a real estate broker, an insurance agent, the president of a small bank, the owner of a coffee service, a printer, a sign manufacturer, the owner of a chain of service stations, a sporting goods store owner, a travel agent, two small manufacturers, and a contractor. We meet once a week for breakfast. If you don't bring at least one sales lead for another club member, you have to put a dollar into the kitty. I've gotten more business from that club than from all my other promotional efforts combined.

So I joined another one, and I used the contacts I made to build my own network.

Business has been good ever since. We opened our second shop last April, put in a word processor to keep up with the typing, and added an answering service. That first year, we networked our way to even more business, and we're planning to open a third shop ten miles south of here by this time next year.

Networking gives you confidence, and it allows you to pass on helpful information to people who aren't competing with you—as well as receive that kind of information.

Why You Should Network

Look around you. The days of the **pyramid hierarchy** are drawing to a close, and it is sunset in the industrial desert. Church, state, corporation, and neighborhood—the old structures are crumbling, wheezing, and breaking apart.

One reason is what has come to be called "Toffler's trough." The old structures are wallowing in the cultural trough between the Industrial Age and the Information Age. As the engines of the industrial society slow down and break apart, they lose their efficiency. When that happens, people begin to ask questions and to cluster together for all kinds of reasons—to trade information, to solve problems, to nurture each other, to help each other survive. Networking is an example of this clustering.

You've probably been networking all your life. In school, you networked for information about teachers and courses. When you moved into a new community, you networked for information about doctors, dentists, car service, babysitters, and bargains—all the life-supporting details that make up existence. On the job, you networked your way to sales leads, brainstormed your way to better designs, or got in a huddle with some fellow managers or co-workers to solve problems.

As a small business entrepreneur, you can network your way to a surprising number of new customer connections, which can spell success in big letters. If you don't have a network, use Action Step 35 to build one. Develop your network and build **core groups** of people within it. Because a network grows naturally from the loose association of people you already know, and because you are at the *center* of the net, it has to help you.

NETWORKERS' BALL
DON'T FORGET TO EXCHANGE BUSINESS CARDS

FIGURE 6.3 Networking friends and acquaintances can produce a creative, vital flow of information; it can be used to gather sales leads and to carry the image of your business into the community.

SUMMARY

Promotion is the art or science of moving the image of your business into the prospect's mind. Anything that will advance that image is a good tactic to consider. We recommend that you survey the whole range of promotional strategies available to you and then choose the promotional mix that will work best for your unique business. Potential strategies include paid media advertising, point-of-purchase displays, catalog sales, direct mail, money-back guarantees, free ink and free air, personal selling, trade shows, industry literature, and working visibility.

We also recommend that you seek creative solutions to the problem of promoting within a small budget, and we give examples of how other entrepreneurs have responded to that challenge. Other topics covered include the proper place of freebies, the reasons why an accurate and up-to-date mailing list is a must for survival, and the importance of networking for sales leads and other information.

Throughout the chapter, we stress the relationship between market research—your strategy for locating target customers and learning their needs—and promotion—letting your customers know your business can serve their needs and make them happy in the process. The overall message of the chapter is to use your head as well as your checkbook in connecting with the customer.

THINK POINTS FOR SUCCESS

◄ Be unique with your promotions. Instead of Christmas cards, send Thanksgiving cards or April Fools' Day cards.

◄ Stand in your target customer's shoes. Think like your TC. Find the need. Find the "ladder" in the TC's mind.

◄ Maintain a visual presence.

◄ A world in transition means opportunities for entrepreneurship. Fast footwork can keep you in the game.

◄ To start your own mailing list, give away something for free. In return, potential customers will give you their names.

◄ Rent a Santa. Rent a robot. Rent a hot-air balloon. Rent a talking dolphin. Create some excitement, because excitement sells.

◄ When you think you have it made, keep connecting with that customer anyway. You will never be so big that you can afford to disconnect. Remember this and it will make you rich.

◄ Remember to promote the *benefits* of your product or service.

REFERENCES

Advertising Your Small Business. Washington, D.C.: U.S. Small Business Administration, Office of Management Assistance, Small Business Management Training Instructors' Guide, No. 112, 1984. [Produced by the American Association of Community and Junior Colleges under contract to the U.S. Small Business Association, Contract No. SBA 4873-MA 89.]

Bennett, Steven J. *Playing Hardball with Soft Skills: How to Prosper with Nontechnical Skills in a High-Tech World.* New York: Bantam, 1986.

Blake, Gary, and Robert W. Bly. *How to Promote Your Own Business.* New York: New American Library/Plume Books, 1983. [A nicely written paperback. Good tips on trade shows and writing good ad copy and press releases.]

Boe, Ann. "Networking: Management's New Contact Sport." *Manage,* July 1986, p. 15.

Canape, Charlene. *How to Capitalize on the Video Revolution: A Guide to New Business Enterprises.* New York: Holt, Rinehart and Winston, 1984.

Cook, James. *The Start-Up Entrepreneur: How You Can Succeed at Building Your Own Company or Enterprise Starting from Scratch.* New York: E. P. Dutton, 1985.

Croft, Nancy L. "Marketing with a Twist." *Nation's Business,* April 1988, p. 88.

Delacorte, Toni, Judy Kimsey, and Susan Halas. *How to Get Free Press: A Do It Yourself Guide to Promote Your Interests, Organization, or Business.* New York: Avon, 1984. [Contains an excellent chapter called "PR for Small Businesses," which has many solid ideas for promotions.]

Delano, Sara. "How to Get a Fix on Free Ad Dollars." *Inc.,* July 1983, pp. 94–96. [Cooperation among noncompeting retailers—a clothing store, a computer store, and a car dealership—creates snappy ads and allows the costs to be split.]

Deutsch, Mitchell F. *Doing Business with the Japanese.* New York: New American Library, 1984.

Donnelly Demographics, 1986. Los Angeles County/Orange County. File 575 of the Dialog Database System.

Guiles, Melinda Greiner. "Why Melinda S. Gets Ads for Panty Hose, Melinda F. for Porsches." *Wall Street Journal,* May 6, 1988. [Fascinating study of the mailing list game by a veteran reporter. Guiles managed to get on various mailing lists by changing her middle initial. Melinda F. subscribed to *Fortune* and got an invitation to test-drive a Porsche. Melinda S. subscribed to *Savvy* and was barraged with ads for classes in upgrading her communications skills. Melinda O. subscribed to *Organic Gardening* and received ads for garden tillers.]

Harrell, Wilson. "Entrepreneurial Terror: Starting a Company? Get Ready for the Most Terrifying Experience of Your Life." *Inc.,* February 1987, p. 74.

Hawken, Paul. *Growing a Business.* New York: Simon and Schuster, 1987.

"The Hot 100 Growth Companies: Small Companies That Took Big Chances—and Are Finding Big Rewards." *Business Week,* May 23, 1988, p. 120.

Husch, Tony. *That's a Great Idea!: The New Product Handbook: How to Get, Evaluate, Protect, Develop and Sell New Product Ideas.* Oakland, Calif.: Gravity Publishing, 1986.

Jacobs, Sanford L. "Split Yellow Pages Highlights Problems in Phone-Book Ads." *Wall Street Journal,* December 8, 1983. [You've probably seen those business-to-business yellow pages floating around. It's a tactic devised by the local phone company to give you an incentive for knowing who your target customer is so you won't run ads in the business-to-business YPs and the ones for ultimate consumers. Straight talk in this essay about what you get when you buy any old ad in the YPs.]

Kleiman, Carol. *Women's Networks: The Great New Way for Women to Support, Advise, and Help Each Other Get Ahead.* New York: Ballantine Books, 1981.

Laumer, J. Ford, Jr., et al. *Researching Your Market.* Washington, D.C.: U.S. Small Business Administration, Office of Business Development, Management Aids No. 4.019, 1988.

Levinson, Jay Conrad. *Guerilla Marketing.* New York: Houghton Mifflin, 1984.

Naisbitt, John. *Megatrends: Ten New Directions Transforming Our Lives.* New York: Warner Books, 1982. [Naisbitt devotes most of chapter 8 to networking for the future. As we've said, this is must reading for any entrepreneur.]

The 1986 Sourcebook of Demographics and Buying Power for Every Zip Code in the USA. Fairfax, Va.: CACI, Inc., 1986. [For further information call 1-800-292-2224.]

Ouchi, William. *Theory Z: How American Business Can Meet the Japanese Challenge.* New York: Addison–Wesley, 1981.

Siropolis, Nicholas C. *Small Business Management,* third edition. New York: Houghton Mifflin, 1986.

Slutsky, Jeffrey, and Woody Woodruff. *Streetfighting.* Englewood Cliffs, N.J.: Prentice-Hall, 1984. [Slutsky is the owner/creator of Retail Marketing Institute. This entertaining newsletter is tailored to small businesses. You can subscribe by writing to RMI, Box 15719, Fort Wayne, IN 46885.]

Smith, Leslie. "Back to Basics: Networking." *Executive Female.* January–February 1988, p. 69.

U.S. Department of Commerce, Bureau of the Census. *County Business Patterns, 1985* (state), 1987.

Weber, Fred I. *Locating or Relocating Your Business.* Washington, D.C.: U.S. Small Business Administration, Office of Business Development, Management Aids No. 2.002, 1988.

Welch, Mary S. *Networking: The Great New Way for Women to Get Ahead.* New York: Warner Books, 1981. [Contains lists of networks already in process.]

APPENDIX 6.1 · Action Step 32: Brainstorm a winning promotional campaign for your business.

The Business Niche

For this action step, the proposed business is a limited-partnership joint venture with Nadek Computer Systems, Inc., of Tustin, California. The business niche is the sale, support, and training of desktop publishing systems to in-house graphic arts and public relations departments of medium to large corporations in Orange County, later expanding into southern Los Angeles and western Riverside counties.

Nadek Computers will sell the hardware and software. Jointly, we will determine the needs of the client and recommend the hardware and software configuration. Nadek will burn-in and install the hardware, which may include a large array of PCs on a Novell network. The Saddleback Scribe will install the software, get it running, and support the client with start-up training, customized style sheets, and printed instructions that supplement the tutorial materials supplied by the software maker. During a period that may last one to six months, The Saddleback Scribe will provide training and support to the client, with the work being billed directly to the client.

Rationale for the Business Niche

For the record, this is a proven business niche for Nadek Computers. The principals at Nadek have demonstrated expertise in hardware and networking systems. They readily acknowledge their lack of expertise in specialized software support, such as desktop publishing and accounting systems. To offer that expertise, they work with limited joint ventures. Kreisler Systems of Irvine provides a similar service in the area of business accounting systems.

The Perfect Promotion

The target customer group consists largely of people with VALS in the Achievers and Experimental segments, whose employees are in the Experimental and Societally Conscious segments. They will be highly responsive to direct mail.

The 1987 Guide to Desktop Publishing for Graphics Professionals

The Saddleback Scribe has nearly completed a comprehensive study of desktop publishing for graphic arts professionals (designers, artists, writers, publishers, typesetters, and printers) entitled *The 1987 Guide to Desktop Publishers for Graphics Professionals*. A working subtitle is "What Bove and Rhodes Failed to Tell You." (Even the second edition of their rapidly mass-produced book *Desktop Publishing* contains glaring errors and even more glaring omissions. And it is really targeted at nonprofessionals.) This guide will be offered to professionals for $100. It will be constantly updated—each copy being directly produced on a PostScript laser printer. It will launch The Saddleback Scribe as an expert in desktop publishing for professionals.

Direct Mail

From a list of Orange County's largest employers, we will develop a direct mail list, aiming for the in-plant graphic arts, public relations, or publications departments. The promotional package will include a letter, a flyer, and several samples comparing printed materials produced by professional typesetting equipment with those produced by desktop publishing. Most important, these samples will be accompanied by time sheets that show how much time was required to produce the similar documents by conventional and desktop methods. The time figures will be translated into dollar figures. The package will contain an offer for a larger kit of materials that can be obtained by returning a post-paid business reply card or by calling Nadek Computers directly. The promotional materials also will offer *The 1987 Guide to Desktop Publishing for Graphics Professionals* at a special price of $75. The goal is a joint sales call by Nadek and The Saddleback Scribe. (Nadek recently hired a very competent sales manager.) After a prudent time interval, a follow-up promotional package will be mailed.

Trade Association Memberships

The Saddleback Scribe will become active in the Orange County chapters of the business marketing and promotion trade association, the advertising association, the public relations association, and the editors' association. The Scribe will take copies of the promotional materials to the monthly meetings of these groups for distribution on a one-on-one basis to target customers. The Scribe also will offer *The 1987 Guide to Desktop Publishing for Graphics Professionals* at a reduced rate of $75. The joint venture also will buy ad space in the newsletters of those trade associations that publish them. This is a highly selective but highly effective medium.

Networking and Leads Clubs
The Saddleback Scribe will become active in several networking and leads clubs in the Irvine area with a goal of promoting this joint effort with Nadek.

Radio
Radio spots reach a large audience for a cost-effective investment. Our spots will run at varying times between 5:30 A.M. and 7:30 A.M., and 4:30 P.M. and 6:30 P.M. on radio stations that carry freeway Sig-Alert and traffic announcements.

Magazine Ads
During special promotions such as Printing Week, the joint venture will buy ad space in local and regional trade journals such as *Adweek* to promote their unique capabilities. The radio spots will be tailored in support of these special promotions.

Word of Mouth
Present heavy-user customers of Nadek will be polled directly for leads. Nadek has grown at a rapid rate in recent years strictly on the basis of word-of-mouth referrals.

Free Ink
To gain free ink for *The 1987 Guide to Desktop Publishing for Graphics Professionals,* The Saddleback Scribe will attempt to get the book reviewed, or get an interview into print in the business section of a daily newspaper or in one of the local business magazines.

P-O-P Display at Nadek Computers
Nadek Computer Systems will be moving to larger quarters soon. There will be an open house to announce the grand opening at the new location. Nadek will be mailing invitations to former, present, and potential clients. News of the desktop joint venture will be included in a special flyer inserted in the invitations. At the open house, a new point-of-purchase display that announces Nadek's new desktop publishing capabilities will be unveiled.

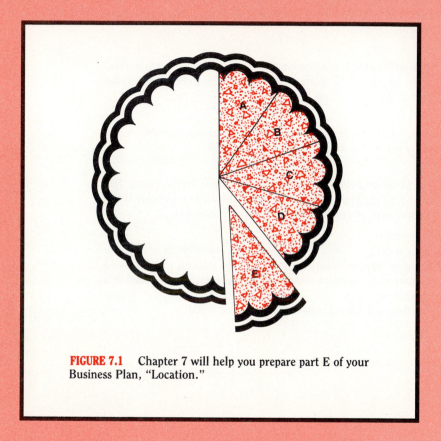

FIGURE 7.1 Chapter 7 will help you prepare part E of your Business Plan, "Location."

Location

LEARNING OBJECTIVES

■ To understand the contribution of location to small business success. ■ To understand the uniqueness of your business location needs. ■ To develop skill in analyzing location dynamics. ■ To develop a checklist for evaluating potential sites for your business. ■ To use media demographic resources to refine your customer profile. ■ To consult commercial real estate brokers in your search for a location. ■ To negotiate a lease contract. ■ To know when you need to consult an independent market research firm.

One of the most important decisions the entrepreneur makes is where to locate the business. Location is particularly important in retailing, and retail leases reflect that importance in their length and complexity; thirty to fifty pages is not unusual. This chapter will lead you through the processes of finding a good location for your business and negotiating a lease that will serve you well.

THE IMPORTANCE OF LOCATION

What Is the Perfect Location?

perfect location
the optimum physical site for a business firm; its 100% location

The **perfect location** is different for every enterprise. If you're in the housecleaning business, you can work out of a station wagon equipped with a cellular telephone. If you're in the mail-order business, you can work out of a "cocoon" or a post office box. Action Step 36 asks you to brainstorm the perfect location for *your* business.

A good location can make everything easier for a new business. A highly visible building that's easy for your customers to reach will save you advertising dollars. Once you've been discovered and your customer base is well established, however, location is less important. Nonetheless, for a retailing firm, a good location is absolutely essential.

For what kind of business would location be a secondary consideration? While you're thinking about this, work through Action Step 37. It will help you analyze the effect of location on your shopping habits. Use new eyes to examine your own consumer behavior.

ACTION STEP 36

Fantasize your 100% location.

Sit down where you won't be disturbed and brainstorm the ideal location for your small business. Get a pencil and paper and let yourself dream. Draw a mind map, or use a list format; the idea is to get your thinking on paper.

For example, if you were going to open a candy/cigarette/cigar stand, you might want to locate in the center of New York's Grand Central Station, where 10,000 people pass by every hour. Of if you were opening an extremely upscale boutique, you might visualize a location on Rodeo Drive in Beverly Hills.

Once you have the general idea of the type of neighborhood you have in mind, write down what else is terrific about this location. Writing everything down will give you a starting point as you move out to explore the world.

A LOCATION FILTER

Before you charge out to scout possible locations for your business, you need to decide what you really need. This checklist will help you zero in on that. Use a scale of 1 to 10 to rate the relative importance of each item on this list. When you finish scoring, go back and note the high numbers, anything, say, above 5. Then after you've read the rest of the chapter, come back to this list to see if your priorities have changed.

_____ **Target Market.** How far will your customers be willing to travel to get you? Can your business travel/deliver to the customers (flowers, dry cleaning, plumbing, pizza, etc.) If so, how far can you travel and still make a profit?

_____ **Transportation Lines.** How much will your business depend on trucks, rail, buses, airports, shipping by water? If you're in manufacturing or distribution, you'll need to determine your major transportation channel. It's also a good idea to have a backup system. A good technique here is to make a diagram of the location and all the lines of transportation your business will use. (Common-carrier rate listings may help you.)

neighbor mix
the industrial/commercial makeup of nearby businesses

_____ **Neighbor Mix.** Who's next door? Who's down the street? Who's going to help pull your target customers to the area? Which nearby business pulls the most customers? If you're considering a shopping center, who's the anchor tenant (the big department store or supermarket that acts as a magnet for the center)?

BOX 7.1   Summary of Site-Selection Concerns

Ask these questions about a potential location:

How close is the target market?

How accessible is it to the transportation lines you will use?

What's the neighbor mix?

How close is it to competitors? (How close do you *want* to be?)

How safe is this location?

If you need labor, where's the nearest pool?

What ordinances will affect you?

What services are free (paid for by taxes), and what services would you have to pay for?

How much would it cost to rent (or buy)?

Who owns the property?

Would your customers be able to find you easily?

Could you expand here if you needed to?

Is there sufficient parking area?

_____ **Competition.** Do you want competitors miles away or right next door? Think about this one. If you're in the restaurant business, it can help you to be on "restaurant row." (A good example of a working "competitor cluster" is San Diego's well-known Miles of Cars; having Nissans, Dodges, Chevrolets, Toyotas, and others all in one area cuts down customer driving time and allows for easy comparison shopping.)

_____ **Security, Safety.** How safe is the neighborhood? Is it as safe as a nursery at noon but an urban jungle at midnight? Is there anything you can do to increase the security?

_____ **Labor Pool.** Who's working for you, and how far will they have to commute? Does your business require more help at certain peak periods of the year? How easy will it be to find that kind of help? Will you need skilled labor? If so, where's the nearest pool of it? Is the site near a bus (train, subway) Will you need technical people? How far will they travel? Don't overlook the potential of part-timers, teens, seniors, and homemakers.

_____ **Restrictions.** What local rules (state, county, city, merchants' association, and so on) will affect your location? For example, what are the restrictions on signage? Hours of business? Parking assignments? Deed restrictions? Zoning restrictions? Covenants and other conditions?

_____ **Services.** Police and fire protection, security, trash pick-up, sewage, maintenance. What is included in the rent, and who pays for those services that are not?

_____ **Costs.** The purchase price if you're buying; otherwise, the rent or lease costs. (We advise against buying property and starting a business at the same time, because it diverts your precious energies and capital that you need for the business.) Taxes, insurance, utilities, improvements, association dues, routine maintenance. You need to know who pays for what. Can you negotiate a few months' free rent?

_____ **Ownership.** If you're still planning to buy the property, who will you get to advise you on real estate? Consider a lease with option to buy, but have the contract reviewed by a real estate attorney.

ACTION STEP 37

Use your new eyes to evaluate business locations.

Think about how location affects your spending habits. For example, where do you buy gas for your car? Do you buy it on your way to work or school, or on your way home? Why?

Now, with your Adventure Notebook in hand, look through your home. How important was the location of the retailer from which you purchased the items you see? For example,

cigarettes, candy, sodas
washing machine
paintings, wallhangings
carpeting, paint
dry-cleaning service
mail-order items such as books, magazines, clothing, CDs
custom-made golf clubs
eyeglasses
prescription drugs
designer clothes
wristwatch, jewelry
power tools, lawn and garden equipment
TV set, VCR
car, motorcycle
collectibles
your home itself

A random look through your checkbook might trigger your memory. Feel free to add to this list.

How far did you travel, for example, for your last dinner out with a friend? For a carton of milk? A magazine? A lounge chair? A video cassette rental? How far would you travel to use the services of a brain surgeon?

What conclusions can you draw about the importance of location in making a purchase?

You can expand upon this action step by interviewing purchasing agents and buyers of commercial and industrial goods. Ask them what impact location has on their choice of vendors or on their recruitment of employees

labor pool
qualified people who are available for employment near your business location

restrictions
city/county laws governing business locations

_____ **Accessibility to customers.** Will your target customers—lured by your terrific promotions—find you easily and then have a place to park when they get there? Consider highway access, and potential obstacles that could make coming to your place of business inconvenient or unpleasant.

_____ **Space.** If you need to expand, can you do it there, or will you have to move to a new site?

_____ **History of the Property.** How long has the landlord owned this property? Is it likely to be sold while you're a tenant? If the property is sold, what will happen to your business? What will happen to your tax obligations? If the property goes on the market, do you want the first right to meet an offer?

_____ **Physical Visibility.** Does your business need to be seen? If so, is this location visible? Can you make alterations to increase its visibility?

_____ **Life-Cycle Stage of the Area.** Is the site in an area that's embryonic (vacant lots, open space, emptiness), growing (high-rises, new schools, lots of construction), mature (building conversions, cracked streets, sluggish traffic), or declining (vacant buildings, emptiness)? What will the area be like in five years? What effect would that have on your business? What do the municipal planners have in mind for the area? When will the highway department tear up the street? (See Figure 7.2.)

_____ **Image.** Is the location consistent with your firm's image? How will nearby businesses affect your image? Is this an area where your customers would expect to find a business like yours? (Look for a place that reinforces your customers' perception of your business.)

location life cycle
the stages of a commercial/industrial area from birth to death

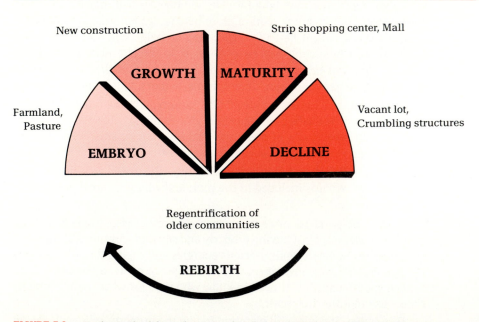

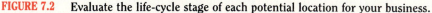

FIGURE 7.2 Evaluate the life-cycle stage of each potential location for your business.

Marcia Meadows's Own Story

Michael, my husband, had worked in the automotive industry for seventeen years—the last dozen in California—when his company decided to transfer him back to Buffalo. The new job would be a nice promotion, and for awhile we were happily making plans. Then one day, coming back from the beach with the kids asleep in the back seat, I realized that I really didn't want to leave California. We had a lovely home, the children had good friends, and Michael and I both dreaded Buffalo's long winters.

So we decided to start our own Saab and Volvo repair business, since Michael knew a lot about servicing those makes of cars. I got busy and took a course in small business at the local community college.

The first thing we did was locate our competitors. We found three. The largest was in the north part of the county. The next-largest was west of here, a couple miles from the beach, and the other one was south of here. If you drew lines connecting them on a map, you'd have a wide-spread triangle. No one was in the middle, and Michael knew from experience that those three couldn't handle all the repair business in our area.

Our next step was to get a list of all the Volvo owners in the area. We contacted the Department of Motor Vehicles about this, and they were very helpful. For several days, we stuck little colored pins into our area map—one pin for each Volvo owner—and as the number of pins grew we noticed a growing cluster right in the middle of the three existing repair businesses. That's where we located *our* business.

Our research and planning worked. Now, when we hear of all that winter they're getting in Buffalo on television, we're very glad we're where we are.

Location was important to Marcia and Michael Meadows for a couple of reasons:

1. Convenience. Customers will drive only so many miles to have their cars repaired.
2. Equipment. A major expense in car repair service is equipment, and you don't want to have to move that from one location to another if a location doesn't work out.

An SBA booklet entitled "Starting and Managing a Small Business" tells how many people are needed to support particular businesses. A men's and boys' clothing store, for example, needs just under 12,000 people. A record shop needs 112,000; a toy store, 61,000. How many people does *your* business need to support it?

WHERE TO GO FOR LOCATION INFORMATION

Businesspeople tend to stay in a location for awhile because it's expensive to pack up and move. Selection of a location is a *very* important decision. You need to make sure you're in the heart of your target market. So where do you go for information?

1. **Census tracts.** The most obvious place is a federal depository, where you look at census data from the federal government. Every ten years, census takers walk through neighborhoods gathering data on household size, income, occupation, housing costs, and so on—things you need to know to start a small business. Your taxes pay for this service, so use it. It's readily available to you. The census data is a profile of the U.S.
2. **Zip codes.** Research firms—such as Claritas based in Alexandria, Virginia—have developed customer data based on zip codes. This data is similar to census-tract data but is more up to date. You can also request zip-code data from the research department of your local newspaper and from the public relations department of your local utility.

3. **Neighborhood clusters.** Claritas, just mentioned, and National Decision Systems, based in Encinitas, California, have extended their market research into smaller segments. Each firm has identified a dozen main groups and several subgroups. NDS and Claritas are private research firms, which charge fees for their services. Claritas, whose product is called "Prizm," provided data for the book *The Clustering of America* by Michael J. Weiss. (See the Claritas and Weiss entries in the section at the end of this chapter.)

Targeting by Census Tract

Every ten years the government pulls together some valuable data. Until 1982, it was compiled for large population blocks known as Standard Metropolitan Statistical Areas (SMSAs) in statistical form broken down along demographic lines (age, income, roots, and so on.) The data to come in the 1990 census, not in time for this edition of this book, will be divided into three subdivisions: Consolidated MSAs, Primary MSAs, and Metropolitan MSAs. (Chapter 2 contains a more detailed explanation of the reorganization.) The data for the 1980 census are still contained in SMSAs. Your first step is to locate a Federal Depository. Check the phone book or ask your friendly reference librarian.

Your second step is to find your general area on the SMSA Index Map and learn your tract number. Census information comes in different sizes, you see, and tract data provides the kind of information most useful to small businesses. Once you know your tract number you can use the census tables to learn those familiar demographic indicators—income, occupation, education, and so on—which predict buying power, consumption patterns, and lifestyles. Figure 7.3 summarizes this process.

To provide you with some experience with census data, we've developed an analysis of the 1980 census for the SMSA Anaheim–Santa Ana–Garden Grove area of northern Orange County, California. This is a general analysis, a model you can use for a starting point. Here's how we started:

To find income, we check Table P-11, Income and Poverty Status in 1979 (Table 7.1 in this book).

To find occupation, we checked Table P-10, Labor Force and Disability Characteristics of Persons (Table 7.2).

To find education, we checked Table P-9, Social Characteristics of Persons (Table 7.3).

The tables are vast; we've only summarized them here. You can see the complete tables at your nearest Federal Depository.

A fourth table we found helpful was H-1, Occupancy, Utilization, and Financial Characteristics of Housing Units (Table 7.4). This table reports the value of households in your tract, the median rents charged, the number of rented households, and the race and origin of the residents.

For comparison purposes, we chose two tracts from the Anaheim–Santa Ana–Garden Grove SMSA. The tracts each have between 2,700 and 3,000 persons, a good number for a target market. Tract 740.06 is in the city of Santa Ana; we'll call it Tract SA. Tract 630.07 is in the city of Newport Beach; we'll call it Tract NB.

Analyzing Census Tract Data

Your goal is to find a good location for your business. If you're in the mail-order business, you want to be near a post office. But if you're in retailing—a bookstore, for example, or a men's clothing store—you want to be near your target customers.

SMSA Index Map

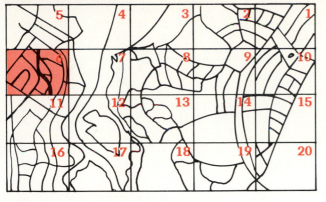

1. Use the index map to locate the detailed sheet map showing the area you want to investigate.

Detailed Sheet Map

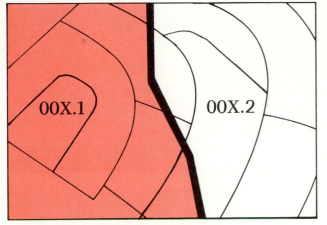

2. Use the detailed sheet map to determine the number of the tract you want to research.

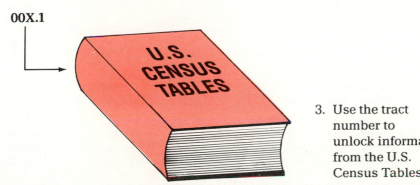

3. Use the tract number to unlock information from the U.S. Census Tables.

FIGURE 7.3   Unlock the information in census tables by following three steps.

In chapter 4 you learned to profile your target customer's lifestyle by using demographic and psychographic data. As you do your various walkthroughs, you will want to gather information quickly and efficiently. After all, life is short, and you're eager

TABLE 7.1 Census Table P-11, Income and Poverty Status

	TRACT SA (0740.06)	TRACT NB (0630.07)
INCOME IN 1979		
Households	1 384	1 057
Less than $5,000	88	38
$5,000 to $7,499	99	19
$7,500 to $9,999	83	—
$10,000 to $14,999	279	52
$15,000 to $19,999	227	63
$20,000 to $24,999	218	81
$25,000 to $34,999	258	107
$35,000 to $49,999	107	152
$50,000 or more	25	545
Median	$18 264	$51 061
Mean	$19 319	$69 568
Owner-occupied households	335	912
Median income	$22 476	$53 545
Mean income	$24 748	$72 180
Renter-occupied households	1 049	145
Median income	$16 696	$30 494
Mean income	$17 585	$53 137
Families	563	888
Median income	$21 696	$55 965
Mean income	$22 170	$77 461
Unrelated individuals 15 years and over	1 291	197
Median income	$10 861	$19 712
Mean income	$11 242	$23 815
Per capita income	$ 9 667	$24 373
INCOME TYPE IN 1979		
Households	1 384	1 057
With earnings	1 337	925
Mean earnings	$19 019	$60 068
With Social Security income	75	117
Mean Social Security income	$ 2 686	$ 4 662
With public assistance income	7	—
Mean public assistance income	$ 1 405	$ —
MEAN FAMILY INCOME IN 1979 BY FAMILY TYPE		
Families	$22 170	$77 461
With own children under 18 years	$22 657	$68 252
Without own children under 18 years	$21 799	$85 652
Married-couple families	$23 944	$82 604
With own children under 18 years	$28 104	$74 619
Without own children under 18 years	$21 647	$89 433
Female householder, no husband present	$17 120	$23 569
With own children under 18 years	$13 613	$18 957
Without own children under 18 years	$23 625	$31 374

SOURCE: Adapted from 1980 U.S. Census.

Note: Data are estimates based on a sample.

to get going. Thus, you need to select some categories of data that are absolutely basic to your location decision. Income, occupation, education, and home ownership are some of these categories.

TABLE 7.2   Census Table P-10, Labor Force and Disability Characteristics of Persons

	TRACT SA	TRACT NB
LABOR FORCE STATUS	(0740.06)	(0630.07)
Persons 16 years and over	2 426	2 361
Labor force	2 134	1 494
Percent of persons 16 years and over	88.0	63.3
Civilian labor force	2 125	1 485
Employed	2 081	1 433
Unemployed	44	52
Percent of civilian labor force	2.1	3.5
Female, 16 years and over	1 253	1 208
Labor force	1 043	554
Percent of female, 16 years and over	83.2	45.9
Civilian labor force	1 043	554
Employed	1 037	542
Unemployed	6	12
Percent of civilian labor force	0.6	2.2
With own children under 6 years	131	60
In labor force	58	24
Married, husband present	384	775
In labor force	254	285
Civilian persons 116 to 19 years	126	289
Not enrolled in school	69	25
Not high school graduate	7	18
Employed	7	12
Unemployed	—	—
Not in labor force	—	6

OCCUPATION AND SELECTED INDUSTRIES

	TRACT SA	TRACT NB
Employed persons 16 years and over	2 081	1 433
Managerial and professional specialty occupations	781	632
Executive, administrative, and managerial occupations	413	384
Professional specialty occupations	368	248
Technical sales, and administrative support occupations	850	592
Technicians and related support occupations	118	36
Sales occupations	250	360
Administrative support occupations, including clerical	482	196
Service occupations	162	69
Private household occupations	7	6
Protective service occupations	4	13
Service occupations, except protective and household	151	50
Farming, forestry, and fishing occupations	—	7
Precision production, craft, and repair occupations	122	97
Operators, fabricators, and laborers	166	36
Machine operators, assemblers, and inspectors	93	14
Transportation and material moving occupations	23	—
Handlers, equipment cleaners, helpers, and laborers	50	22
Manufacturing	589	243
Wholesale and retail trade	480	348
Professional and related services	390	315

SOURCE: Adapted from 1980 U.S. Census.

Note: Data are estimates based on a sample.

Income   Small business depends on accurate targeting, so one clue you're looking for is discretionary income. If two households have incomes of $20,000 each, but

TABLE 7.3   Census Table P-9, Social Characteristics of Persons

	TRACT SA (0740.06)	TRACT NB (0630.07)
NATIVITY AND PLACE OF BIRTH		
Total persons	2 784	3 001
Native	2 504	2 831
Born in State of residence	1 098	1 416
Born in different State	1 386	1 400
Born abroad, at sea, etc.	20	15
Foreign born	280	170
LANGUAGE SPOKEN AT HOME AND ABILITY TO SPEAK ENGLISH		
Persons 5 to 17 years	260	719
Speak a language other than English at home	15	59
Percent who speak English not well or not at all	—	13.6
Persons 18 years and over	2 390	2 189
Speak a language other than English at home	323	233
Percent who speak English not well or not at all	10.2	2.6
SCHOOL ENROLLMENT AND TYPE OF SCHOOL		
Persons 3 years old and over enrolled in school	751	1 070
Nursery school	12	25
Private	12	18
Kindergarten	13	22
Private	5	7
Elementary (1 to 8 years)	185	367
Private	8	107
High school (1 to 4 years)	32	355
Private	—	35
College	509	301
YEARS OF SCHOOL COMPLETED		
Persons 25 years old and over	1 575	1 921
Elementary: 0 to 4 years	5	—
5 to 7 years	6	16
8 years	24	6
High school: 1 to 3 years	107	68
4 years	330	371
College: 1 to 3 years	587	549
4 or more years	516	911
Percent high school graduates	91.0	95.3

Source: Adapted from 1980 U.S. Census.

(Note: Data are estimates based on a sample.)

household A's income must support seven people and household B's must support only one, there's a good chance that household B has more discretionary dollars.

According to the census data, the median incomes for Tracts SA and NB, respectively, were $18,264 and $51,061 (see Table 7.1). The mean income for Tract SA was $19,319, while for Tract NB it was $69,568. The household income for families in Tract SA is just over $22,000; for Tract NB, it's more than $77,000. Incomes of married-couple families in Tract SA rise to almost $24,000, while married-couple families in Tract NB rise to $82,000 + . The highest income in Tract NB is recorded for married-couple families with no children under 18 years: $89,000 + . In Tract SA, that same category is just $21,000 + .

TABLE 7.4   Census Table H-1, Occupancy, Utilization, and Financial
Characteristics of Housing Units

	TRACT SA (0740.06)	TRACT NB (0630.07)
Total housing units	1 988	1 138
Vacant seasonal and migratory	3	8
Year-round housing units	1 985	1 130
YEAR-ROUND HOUSING UNITS		
Tenure by Race and Origin of Householder		
Owner-occupied housing units	302	911
Percent of occupied housing units	21.8	86.0
White	267	892
Black	9	…
American Indian, Eskimo, and Aleut	3	…
Asian and Pacific Islander	14	10
Spanish origin	12	11
Renter-occupied housing units	1 082	148
White	939	142
Black	39	…
American Indian, Eskimo, and Aleut	8	…
Asian and Pacific Islander	66	3
Spanish origin	74	3
Rooms		
1 room	68	—
2 rooms	220	4
3 rooms	471	12
4 rooms	739	57
5 rooms	348	154
6 rooms	74	203
7 rooms	43	257
8 or more rooms	22	443
Median, year-round housing units	3.8	7.0
Median, occupied housing units	3.9	7.0
Median, owner-occupied housing units	4.8	7.2
Median, renter-occupied housing units	3.7	5.1
VALUE		
Specified owner-occupied housing units	89	636
$50,000 to $59,999	1	—
$60,000 to $79,999	7	3
$80,000 to $99,999	34	4
$100,000 to $149,999	46	23
$150,000 to $199,999	—	125
$200,000 or more	1	481
Median	$101 700	$200000+
CONTRACT RENT		
Specified renter-occupied housing units	1 038	136
Median	$340	$500+

Source: Adapted from 1980 U.S. Census.

Note: Data are estimates based on a sample.

Income data never tells the whole story about an area, of course, but it's a very good starting point. It's clear in the income data that households in Tract NB have at least three times the income of households in Tract SA.

Occupation   A look at the labor force table (Table 7.2) shows that more people in Tract SA work, and the highest percentage of them (850, almost 41%) are in technical, sales, and administrative support. In Tract NB, the highest percentage of workers (632, 44%) are either managerial or professional. Tract NB has a higher percentage of people in sales occupations: 350, or 24%. In Tract SA only 250, or 12%, of the workers are in sales. (Keep in mind that many salespeople make good money.) For a sharper contrast, move across the page to Tract 645.01, where 2,451 persons work and only 95, or 3.8% of them, are managerial/professional.

Education   Education data is especially important if you're in entertainment, the arts, publishing, books, travel, recreation, or leisure-related fields. Table P-9 (Table 7.3 in this book) tells us that 91% of the residents of Tract SA and 95% of these in Tract NB are high school graduates—not much difference. When you compare years of college completed, however, the picture sharpens. Tract NB has 911 people who finished 4 or more years of college (47% of the people surveyed), and Tract SA has 516 (only 32%).

If you combine this census data with the consumption patterns predicted by the VALS lifestyles descriptions discussed in chapter 4 (Emulators, Achievers, Experientials, and so on), you can predict what the people in these two census tracts buy, what their dreams are, and so on. And all of this will help you with site selection.

Who Lives Where   Another helpful category is Table H-1, Occupancy, Utilization, and Financial Characteristics of Housing Units (Table 7.4). This table reports the number of owner-occupied units, the number of rentals, the value of real estate, and so on. In Tract SA, for example, there are more than 1,000 renter-occupied housing units out of a total of almost 2,000. In Tract NB, there are only 148 out of 1,138. Thus, rental units account for 53% of Tract-SA homes and just 13% of Tract-NB homes.

Also, the homes in Tract NB are larger; 443 of them have more than eight rooms. Not surprisingly, the median value of homes in NB is higher: $200,000, as opposed to $101,700 in SA. And the rents in Tract NB are higher: $500+ as opposed to $340 in Tract SA.

Think about it this way. What do renters need, and what do homeonwers need? Renters generally live in multiple dwellings (apartments, condos, and so on) where space is limited. Renters tend to buy portable things, smaller appliances they can carry with them when they move. (Limited space means renters will buy space-savers. Homeowners, on the other hand, will be a market for larger appliances and furniture—bigger-ticket items that are more difficult to move. Table 7.5 summarizes some of the most important data from Tables 7.1 through 7.4

An Example

This quick analysis has only scratched the surface of the vast census data bank. We've tried to show you what to look for first, and where it might lead. Other tables can help you if you have a specific business in mind. For example, let's say you just inherited seven oil-delivery trucks and you have a chance to get into a partnership in the energy field. You could sell utility gas or you could sell heating oil.

One of your problems is to determine where the users of these products live so that you can locate your holding tanks and your general headquarters near them. You live in Greenfield, Wisconsin, a suburb of Milwaukee, which your spouse says is no place for oil tanks. So you go to your nearest Federal Depository, on the campus

TABLE 7.5   Summary of Selected Data from Two Census-Tract Tables

FROM TABLE P-11:	TRACT SA	TRACT NB
Mean household income	19,319	69,568
Mean family income	22,170	77,461

FROM TABLE P-10:		
Employed persons	2,081	1,433
Managerial	781	632
Technical	850	592

FROM TABLE P-9:		
Persons 25 years old and over	1,575	1,921
Percent high school graduates	91	95.5
4 or more years of college	911	516

FROM TABLE H-1:		
Total housing units	1,988	1,138
Renter-occupied housing units	1,082	148
Value of owner-occupied housing units	$101,000	$200,000

of the University of Wisconsin. You find the Milwaukee SMSA and you look up Table H-7, Structural, Equipment, and Household Characteristics of Housing Units; see Table 7.6. You're a nuts-and-bolts person, so you start with Tract 1201 in the city of Greenfield. Tract 1202 is where you live. Under Tract 1201 you find a selection called House Heating Fuel:

HOUSE HEATING FUEL	
Utility gas	946
Bottled, tank, or LP gas	24
Electricity	203
Fuel oil, kerosene, etc.	313
Other	57

This data doesn't give you a lot of hope. But right next to Tract 1201 is Tract 1202, where the numbers for utility gas are higher—3,597. You feel a surge of hope, a sense of excitement. You don't have the total picture yet, but at least you're on your way. And all with the help of government statistics.

A Caveat

The government takes a census every ten years. The data-gathering job is immense, and after the gathering is completed it takes awhile for the information to be put into a usable form. Locations often change dramatically between censuses. A bustling shopping center (growth phase) could very easily stand in what was rolling farmland (embryonic phase) ten years earlier. Thus census data is most useful in mature industries like automobiles, service stations, and heating oil. Census data is thorough, and it's a good starting place, but local bureaus and private research firms might help you home in faster on your perfect location.

TABLE 7.6 Census Table H-7, Structural, Equipment, and Household Characteristics of Housing Units

	GREENFIELD CITY, MILWAUKEE COUNTY		
	TRACT 1201	TRACT 1202	TRACT 1203
Year-round housing units	1 586	4 525	884
SELECTED CHARACTERISTICS			
Complete kitchen facilities	1 586	4 491	877
1 complete bathroom plus half-bath(s)	473	1 355	399
2 or more complete bathrooms	356	497	70
Air conditioning	1 057	3 461	565
Central system	385	1 092	267
Source of water, public system or private company	1 276	4 475	856
Sewage disposal, public sewer	1 288	4 520	884
UNITS IN STRUCTURE			
1, detached or attached	1 071	2 147	668
2	45	175	141
3 and 4	—	100	—
5 to 9	10	604	40
10 to 49	440	1 161	35
50 or more	20	333	—
Mobile home or trailer, etc.	—	5	—
HEATING EQUIPMENT			
Steam or hot water system	316	1 667	92
Central warm-air furnace	1 058	2 605	782
Electric heat pump	35	39	—
Other built-in electric units	138	145	6
Other means	39	69	4
None	—	—	—
Occupied housing units	1 543	4 443	874
HOUSE HEATING FUEL			
Utility gas	946	3 597	728
Bottled, tank, or LP gas	24	13	—
Electricity	203	241	6
Fuel oil, kerosene, etc.	313	579	133
Other	57	13	7
No fuel used	—	—	—

Source: Adapted from 1980 U.S. Census.

Note: Data are estimates based on a sample.

Targeting by Zip Code

Let's stay with our Santa Ana–Newport Beach comparison as we move from census tract to zip code. These two suburban cities are less than two miles apart, but they are as diverse as two different worlds. The information in Tables 7.7 and 7.8 is from the research department of the *Orange County Register* and it is five years newer.

TABLE 7.7 Demographics by Zip Code: Corona Del Mar, Newport Beach (92625 and 92660)

	92625	92660
Population & Age		
Total Population	15,702	24,886
Age		
Under 18	18.9%	21.2%
18–34	28.5	25.1
35–54	27.8	29.9
55+	24.8	23.8
Median age	36.7	37.5
County median	29.5	29.5
Race/Ethnic Origin		
White	98.6%	96.3%
Black	0.1	1.5
American Ind.	0.2	0.4
Asian/Pac. Isl	1.1	1.8
Hispanic Origin	2.1	3.3
Median Years of School	15.7	15.1
Home Ownership Data		
Own	60.2%	57.1%
Rent	39.8	42.9
1985 median rent	$501	$501
Median home value	$200,100	$200,100
County Median	$136,427	$136,427
Single units	83.2%	77.9%
Multifamily	16.6	19.3
Mobile homes	0.2	2.8
Occupation		
Prof'l/mgr'l/tech'l	47.7%	49.9%
Sales	20.4	19.8
Clerical/support services	13.4	13.6
Precision crafts & prod.	10.0	7.7
Laborers	8.5	9.0
Households		
Total Households	7,175	10,476
Household size		
1–2 persons	67.7%	65.0%
3+ persons	32.3	35.0
Married w/children	19.5%	23.3%
Household income		
Less than $15,000	15.3%	15.3%
$15,000–$29,999	21.8	20.9
$30,000–$49,999	19.9	22.4
$50,000+	43.0	41.4
Median	$42,947	$41,227
County median	$31,092	$31,092

(continued)

TABLE 7.7   *Continued*

	92625	92660
Labor force		
Percent employed	97.8%	96.9%
Families with 2 + workers	45.2	49.5
Marital Status		
Married	52.7%	55.5%
Single, never married	28.6	26.3
Divorced/separated	13.2	12.9
Widowed	5.5	5.3

Source: *The Orange County Register,* based on information from *Rezide*™, *Zip Code Encyclopedia,* Claritas Corporation, 1986

Incomes in the Newport Beach zip codes are twice those in Santa Ana, and more than forty percent of the household incomes are $50,000 or more. In Santa Ana, only nine percent of the household incomes are above $50,000.

In occupation, Newport Beach is still heavily professional–managerial–technical and still heavy in sales. Santa Ana is heavy in precision crafts and production labor.

Targeting by City

The "pop facts" data in Table 7.9 come from National Decision Systems of Encinitas, California, which uses a system called "Vision." This kind of report is available for most of the United States. Vision divides the country into twelve demographic groups with designations like "Suburban Wealthy" and "Urban Affluence" at the top end of the scale, and "Rural Lower Income" and "Town Lower Income" at the bottom. The largest group is "Suburban Middle Class," which accounts for 23.1 percent of the households in the U.S. There are forty-eight subgroups in the Vision matrix. Subgroups within Suburban Middle Class (abbreviated *SM*) are

> Little League and Barbecues
> Baby Boom Again
> Industrial Upper Deck
> Porch Swings and Apple Pie
> Carports and Kids
> Declining Suburbia
> Ethnic Industrial

National Decision Systems prepared the material in Table 7.9 in response to information on a business site at the intersection of Baseline Road and Dobson Road in Phoenix, Arizona. The report was produced on a computer data base using nine information sources, which ranged from zip-code data to special Census Bureau data. As you can see in the table, the columns move out from the intersection in concentric circles—with radii of one mile, three miles, and five miles—to give a demographic profile of households surrounding it.

TABLE 7.8 Demographics by Zip Code: Santa Ana (92701, 92703, 92704)

	92701	92703	97204
Population & Age			
Total Population	40,878	45,619	59,569
Age			
Under 18	26.2%	35.2%	33.4%
18–34	38.9	34.2	35.8
35–54	18.6	17.6	19.4
55+	16.3	13.0	11.4
Median age	27.3	24.2	25.5
County median	29.5	29.5	29.5
Race/Ethnic Origin			
White	94.8%	89.0%	86.2%
Black	1.7	5.9	5.6
American Ind.	0.7	0.8	0.9
Asian/Pac. Isl	2.8	4.3	7.3
Hispanic Origin	47.4	63.8	38.5
Median Years of School	12.3	10.3	12.4
Home Ownership Data			
Own	32.9%	56.7%	59.8%
Rent	67.1	43.3	40.2
1985 median rent	$436	$455	$501
Median home value	$110,559	$ 90,096	$106,019
County Median	$136,427	$136,427	$136,427
Single units	53.0%	67.9%	67.7%
Multifamily	46.6	19.9	24.2
Mobile homes	0.4	12.2	8.1
Occupation			
Prof'l/mgr'l/tech'l	20.4%	11.9%	20.9%
Sales	7.7	4.8	8.5
Clerical/support services	15.3	12.1	16.2
Precision crafts & prod.	13.6	14.5	11.8
Laborers	43.0	56.7	42.6
Households			
Total Households	15,323	12,192	18,589
Household size			
1–2 persons	59.9%	37.5%	44.2%
3+ persons	40.1	62.5	55.8
Married w/children	25.7%	41.3%	38.1%
Household income			
Less than $15,000	34.6%	30.4%	22.6%
$15,000–$29,999	33.5	35.5	32.4
$30,000–$49,999	22.0	25.6	32.3
$50,000+	9.9	8.5	12.7
Median	$21,336	$22,753	$28,047
County median	$31,092	$31,092	$31,092
Labor force			
Percent employed	94.6%	92.7%	94.7%
Families with 2+ workers	60.1	59.2	63.5%

(continued)

TABLE 7.8   *Continued*

	92701	92703	97204
Marital Status			
Married	49.6%	52.9%	55.0%
Single, never married	30.5	32.3	29.9
Divorced/separated	12.5	9.1	10.6
Widowed	7.4	5.7	4.5

Source: *The Orange County Register,* based on information from *Rezide™, Zip Code Encyclopedia,* Claritas Corporation, 1986

Targeting by Neighborhood Cluster—An Example

If you were planning to open a bookstore and you had $300,000 to invest, where would you go? The answer might lie in the Prizm "clustering" system developed by Claritas, a marketing research firm. Prizm has identified forty-eight "clusters" among the 250,000 defined neighborhoods in the United States. Journalist Michael J. Weiss has related these clusters to four groups of book buyers:

> Self-Help Buyers
>
> Suburban Elite Business Buffs
>
> Gardening and Home Repair Fans
>
> Mature Mystery Mavens

Self-Help Buyers buy jazz records, drive convertibles, travel by cruise ship, enjoy sailing, drink imported beer, enjoy skiing, and belong to health clubs. They live in multiunit dwellings—usually in fringe areas—and are college educated. Some are single; others, divorced. They range in age from 25 to 34. They work at white-collar occupations, and there's a good chance they moved in last year.

They're buying business books and self-improvement books. They're young and eager, and have money to spend. So you scout those locations.

If you're interested in Prizm, you can contact Claritas using the information in the reference section at the end of the chapter.

The Commercial Real Estate Agent

The numbers are always changing, so whether you go for the big picture through census tracts or the narrow picture through Vision or Prizm, you must keep searching for the latest data. There is so much to know, and you make location decisions very infrequently. An experienced real estate agent can save you time and money. He or she can guide you through the maze of what is available and advise you on rents, prices, terms, tenant improvement costs, financing, zoning, public transportation, and the availability of workers.

Real estate agents are paid by the landlord or seller and earn their commissions only when a deal is final and money changes hands. Don't let yourself be rushed by these people, but bear in mind that they are probably the best sources of free market information you can find. You can save an agent a lot of time if you have already

TABLE 7.9   1980 Census Pop-Facts Profile Report for Baseline Road and Dobson
Road, Phoenix, Arizona; coordinates 33:22.70, 111:52.60

DESCRIPTION	1.0-MILE RADIUS	3.0-MILE RADIUS	5.0-MILE RADIUS
Population			
1992 projection	17,277	180,918	386,457
1987 estimate	14,142	145,920	313,629
1980 census	9,662	96,253	209,717
1970 census	620	31,185	112,013
Growth 70–80	1458.03%	208.65%	87.23%
Households			
1992 projection	6,153	67,542	144,686
1987 estimate	4,913	53,131	114,251
1980 census	3,200	32,966	71,950
1970 census	156	8,793	32,278
Growth 70–80	1946.20%	274.92%	122.91%
Population by race and Spanish origin	9,662	96,253	209,717
White	93.01%	92.12%	90.22%
Black	1.77%	1.60%	1.75%
American Indian	0.44%	0.57%	0.93%
Asian & Pacific Islander	1.73%	1.38%	1.19%
Other races	3.06%	4.33%	5.90%
Spanish origin (new category)	5.79%	8.34%	10.12%
Occupied Units	3,200	32,966	71,950
Owner-occupied	79.96%	70.16%	63.37%
Renter-occupied	20.04%	29.94%	36.63%
1980 persons per household	3.02	2.92	2.84
Year-round units at address	3,379	35,607	77,884
1	90.58%	76.76%	71.64%
2 to 9	2.49%	4.80%	7.31%
10 +	6.87%	14.94%	16.17%
Mobile home or trailer	0.06%	3.49%	4.88%
Single-multiple-unit ratio	9.67	3.89	3.05
1987 estimated households by income	4,913	53,131	114,251
$75,000 or more	4.78%	5.39%	4.80%
$50,000 to $74,999	21.09%	15.75%	13.69%
$35,000 to $49,999	30.92%	23.51%	20.47%
$25,000 to $34,999	21.36%	20.60%	18.81%
$15,000 to $24,999	13.71%	18.10%	19.59%
$7,500 to $14,999	5.41%	9.97%	12.89%
under $7,500	2.74%	6.69%	9.73%
Average	$38,266	$34,904	$32,264
Median	$38,224	$33,421	$30,079
Per capita income	$13,254	$12,757	$11,854
Population by age (years)	9,657	96,242	209,703
under 5	10.57%	8.49%	8.32%
5 to 9	9.50%	8.52%	7.84%
10 to 14	8.79%	8.81%	7.92%
15 to 19	6.39%	8.82%	10.07%
20 to 24	8.85%	11.48%	14.02%

(continued)

TABLE 7.9 *Continued*

DESCRIPTION	1.0-MILE RADIUS	3.0-MILE RADIUS	5.0-MILE RADIUS
25 to 29	14.30%	11.62%	10.93%
30 to 34	15.73%	11.24%	9.34%
35 to 44	13.60%	13.31%	11.41%
45 to 54	6.74%	8.06%	7.93%
55 to 59	2.41%	3.13%	3.52%
60 to 64	1.45%	2.25%	2.76%
65 to 74	1.20%	2.75%	3.67%
75 +	0.47%	1.50%	2.28%
Median age	27.29	27.14	26.67
Average age	26.55	28.65	29.46
Population 25 + by education level	5,375	51,938	108,868
Elementary (0–8)	1.88%	4.81%	7.73%
Some high school (9–11)	4.01%	7.11%	8.67%
High school graduate (12)	29.32%	31.38%	32.62%
Some college (13–15)	29.03%	26.12%	25.20%
College graduate (16 +)	35.75%	30.58%	25.78%
Population 16 + by occupation	5,020	49,049	102,510
Executive and managerial	16.48%	14.78%	12.61%
Professional specialty	21.20%	18.75%	16.63%
Technical support	4.33%	4.00%	3.80%
Sales	14.13%	13.90%	12.36%
Administrative support	17.51%	17.45%	16.94%
Service: private households	0.11%	0.35%	0.36%
Service: protective	1.75%	1.38%	1.47%
Service: other	6.38%	8.36%	10.25%
Farming, forestry, & fishing	0.55%	1.08%	1.45%
Precision production & craft	10.29%	10.55%	12.04%
Machine operator	3.59%	4.45%	5.82%
Trans. and material moving	1.32%	2.25%	2.74%
Laborers	2.37%	2.70%	3.54%
Females 16 + with children 0–18	1,625	14,637	28,955
Working, child under 6	23.20%	21.72%	21.84%
Not working, child under 6	29.97%	25.94%	26.03%
Working, child 6–18	34.12%	36.54%	35.54%
Not working, child 6–18	12.72%	15.79%	16.58%
Households by number of vehicles	3,187	32,996	71,941
none	0.46%	2.65%	4.43%
1	21.57%	29.35%	33.15%
2	49.67%	41.26%	37.69%
3 +	28.30%	26.74%	24.73%
Estimated total vehicles	6,740	65,146	135,012
Population by travel time to work (minutes)	4,993	48,035	100,670
under 5	0.79%	1.91%	2.58%
5 to 9	10.20%	12.54%	13.10%
10 to 14	18.20%	17.85%	19.02%
15 to 19	15.62%	17.00%	17.09%
20 to 29	23.06%	21.38%	21.05%
30 to 44	23.20%	20.96%	18.97%
45 to 59	5.71%	4.58%	4.52%
60 +	3.23%	3.77%	3.65%
average travel time	22.15	21.32	20.64

(continued)

TABLE 7.9

DESCRIPTION	1.0-MILE RADIUS	3.0-MILE RADIUS	5.0-MILE RADIUS
Population by transportation to work	5,011	48,700	101,764
Drive alone	71.16%	71.28%	68.70%
Carpool	21.57%	18.93%	18.86%
Public transportation	0.87%	1.29%	1.06%
Walk only	1.43%	2.31%	3.74%
Other means	3.83%	4.74%	6.16%
Work at home	1.14%	1.45%	1.48%
1980 Households by 1979 Income	3,200	32,966	71,950
$50,000+	4.68%	4.99%	4.00%
$35,000 to $49,999	16.30%	12.73%	10.13%
$25,000 to $34,999	32.36%	24.24%	19.80%
$15,000 to $24,999	30.79%	29.33%	28.85%
$7,500 to $14,999	12.03%	18.14%	21.91%
under $7,500	3.94%	10.56%	15.31%
1979 average household income	$26,793	$24,000	$21,504
1979 median household income	$25,829	$22,391	$19,607
Housing units by year built	3,372	35,837	78,295
1979 to March 1980	27.27%	15.60%	11.80%
1975 to 1978	52.67%	29.44%	20.65%
1970 to 1974	19.17%	31.51%	27.19%
1960 to 1969	0.81%	17.35%	24.30%
1950 to 1959	0.08%	4.31%	10.34%
1940 to 1949	0.00%	1.31%	3.53%
1939 or earlier	0.00%	0.49%	2.19%

Source: National Decision Systems, Encinitas, California.

defined your needs. If you compare each site against your ideal location, you will probably have several workable alternatives. Typically, on-site leasing people have different objectives because they are employees of the developer. They want to fill up the building. Most developers cooperate with real estate brokers, so a real estate agent can take you almost anywhere you want to go and, if asked, might help you negotiate more favorable terms.

Now you should be ready to complete Action Step 38.

SOME THINGS YOU MUST KNOW ABOUT LEASES

A **lease** document is drawn up by the property owner's lawyer. Although its language is very specific (see Box 7.2), the terms spelled out are *provisional;* that is, the terms are proposed as a starting point for negotiation. Nothing you see in the contract is cast in stone . . . unless you agree to it. Obviously, the terms proposed will probably favor the property owner. Consider the proposed lease seriously. Discuss it with your own lawyer and with others who have experience with leases, and determine how best to begin the negotiation. The following pages will guide you through this process.

ACTION STEP 38

Seek professional help in finding a location.

Visit to a commercial real estate office to gain information. Commercial real estate firms have access to planning reports and demographic information that will tell you a lot about growth in the community. Have your plan well in mind and make an appointment beforehand. Dress conservatively.

And leave your checkbook at home!

lease
contract for occupancy

BOX 7.2   The Language of Leases

Before signing on the dotted line, be certain you understand the language of the lease. These terms will get you started:

building gross area—The total square-foot area of the building when the enclosing walls are measured from outside wall to outside wall.

usable building area—The square-foot area within the building actually occupied by tenants measured from center partition to center partition.

common area—The square-foot area of the building servicing all tenants in common, such as lobby, corridors, lavatories, elevators, stairs, and mechanical equipment rooms. The building common area is usually between 10% and 12% of the gross building area.

rentable area—A combination of the tenants' usable building area plus each tenant's pro rata share of the common area.

gross rent—A rental per square foot, multiplied by the rentable area, to determine the annual rent due on a lease where the landlord provides all services and utilities including tenant janitorial services.

net rent—A rent per square foot multiplied by the rentable area to determine the annual rent due under a lease whereby the tenant also pays, in addition to the rent, its pro rata share of all utilities and services and real estate taxes.

loss factor—The proportion of usable building area to total rentable area. The usable area is that in which you may put furniture and equipment for actual office use. The rentable area often includes a proportionate share of ancillary building services. The lower the loss factor, the more usable space there is. Loss factors can vary from floor to floor in the same building. Rentable area may be calculated in a different manner for one building than it is for another, and this will affect your comparison of rental proposals.

Entrepreneur, Read Your Lease

landlord/landlady
a person/business you pay rent to

Entrepreneur Mick Beatty failed to read the terms of his lease. He thought he had a "gentlemen's agreement" with his **landlady**, but he was wrong. His story points up the importance of *assuming nothing* when it comes to leases.

I was on vacation when I discovered the perfect location for my business. It was in the sleepy tourist town of Laguna Beach, on the edge of the world in a fabulous part of Southern California. It was late summer, and I'd just spent a week driving down the coast from Washington State. When I saw Laguna I felt like I'd come home.

I discovered Eddie's Pub my first evening in town. It faced the beach, and sitting there sipping a cool one, I watched the sun reflect off the water. From time to time, people would drift in for a casual drink, and while I sat there feeling like a million, I must have talked to twenty different folks. Most of them looked very upscale, and they all said they loved the place, too.

Vacations don't last forever, and when I got back home I kept thinking about Laguna and Eddie's. I worked for a large corporation, making good money in a pressure cooker of a job, and even though I was enough of a culture-freak to appreciate New York City, I did not appreciate the winters and I wanted something more out of life. The first day it snowed, I sat in my office just staring out the window, thinking about the three days I'd spent on the beach in Laguna.

A business trip took me to Los Angeles the following spring, and I managed to get an extra day so I could stay overnight in Laguna and stop in at Eddie's.

I got the shock of my life when I got there. Eddie's Pub was for sale!

I called my banker in New York. He said I was crazy. I called two buddies—one from college, one from the Army. They thought it would be fun to be part of a new venture and they were ready to invest. I talked to Eddie, the owner, made a deal to pay him so much down and the rest out of profits, and there I was in business.

I phoned my boss, and he said I was crazy, too. "That whole beach is a dream," he said. "I was stationed there during the war, and I know. One day you'll wake up and it won't be there any more." Then he paused, and what he said next saved my life. "Tell you what, Mick. Don't pull the plug until you're absolutely sure. We'll give you six months. If you're still out there dreaming then, send me your resignation. Meanwhile, have fun. Every guy needs a fling before he settles down."

I said okay, and thanks, and that was that.

Eddie's Pub is only 450 square feet. The layout is long and narrow, and it has lots of mirrors and sort of a Gay Nineties atmosphere. The traffic is mostly walk-in—beach people, tourists—and the only promoting I did was to put up a sign that said HAPPY HOUR 4:00–6:30. I shook hands with the customers, gave some complimentary drinks, served the best espresso south of Los Angeles, and started making money my first day.

Then the trouble showed up. I'd been open a week when I got a call from my landlady. She was a crusty-voiced woman I'd barely talked to, and she told me there'd been some complaints about the music.

"Hey," I said, "I'm sorry. Who's complaining?"

"Your neighbors," she said. "They have rights, too, you know."

"Is it too loud?"

"No," she said, "it's not the volume. It's that rock stuff that's causing the trouble. It irritates the other tenants."

"Rock?" I said. "It's not rock, it's more like—"

"I don't know what you call it," she said, "but it's got to stop. And right now."

"My customers like it," I argued. "The music is part of the ambience of my place."

"Young man," she said, "What your customers like is neither here nor there. I own that property, and I have other tenants to think about. And if you have any questions, I'd advise you to read your lease." She hung up.

Well, I read the lease, carefully. And then I saw a lawyer. He confirmed what I'd read. According to the terms of the lease, my landlady had the power to tell me what kind of music I could play in my own small business. Incredible, but true.

So I turned off the music. Right away, my customers missed it. Drink orders fell off. I surveyed my neighbors and made a list of songs they didn't find offensive, but when I played that junk in the bar, my steady customers (who were becoming less steady) asked me to turn it off. As a last resort, I went to see my landlady and tried to renegotiate the lease. But she wouldn't budge.

There was only one thing to do. I sold the business and went back to my job on the East Coast. I still owe some money to my partners. When it snows I always think of the sun on the water at Laguna. Oh, I'll go back sometime, but right now I'm a little soured on the place. It's too bad. It's got a great beach . . . and a great little bar where you can sit and watch the sun go down. . . . My advice? Read the small print.

Anticipate the Unexpected

Bette Lindsay has always had a soft spot for books, and when she finally chose a business, it was a bookstore in a shopping center. She had researched everything— trends, census data, newspapers, reports from real estate firms, suppliers—but she failed to anticipate an important potential pitfall, dependency on an **anchor tenant**.

Few small businesses are themselves "destination locations." They must count on anchor tenants to draw traffic. Bette made an assumption that the anchor tenant in her center would be there forever. This case study shows the importance of having Plan B ready.

> My husband and I researched the small business field for almost two years, and my heart kept bringing me back to books. I've read voraciously since I was seven years old, and I love a well-written story. So when a new shopping center was opening a mile from our home, I told my husband, "This is it."

anchor tenant
a business firm in a commercial area that attracts customers

Everything looked perfect. They had a great anchor tenant coming in—a supermarket that would draw lots of traffic. The real estate agent we'd been working with during most of our search showed us the demographics of the area, which documented that we were smack in the middle of a well-educated market. According to statistics put out by the federal government, a book store needs a population of 27,000 people to support it. Our area had 62,000 people, and the closest bookstore was more than five miles away.

Everything else looked good, too. We had lots of parking. The neighbors (three hardy pioneers like ourselves) were serious about their business and pleasant to work with.

We wanted to be in for the Christmas season, because December is the peak season for bookstores, so we set a target date of mid October. The contractor was still working when we opened a month later.

We started off with an autograph party and we ran some best-seller specials. And even though construction work from our anchor tenant blocked our access, we had a very good Christmas that year. We started the new year feeling very optimistic.

One day in mid-January, construction work stopped on our anchor tenant's new building. The next day we read in the paper that the company had gone bankrupt.

Well, the first thing I did was call the landlord. He was out of town, and his answering service referred me to a property management company. They said they knew nothing about what was happening and that all they do is collect the rent. January was slow. So was February, and March. In April, two of our neighbors closed up. The construction debris was blocking customer access. It was a mess.

renegotiate a lease
obtaining a new/modified contract for occupancy

In May, I finally succeeded in getting in touch with the owner and tried to **renegotiate the lease**, but his story was sadder than mine.

Fourteen months after we moved in we finally got our anchor tenant. If I'd suspected it'd take anything like that long I could have built some provision for it into our lease. That expensive mistake does not bear repeating.

rewrite a lease
alter the wording of a lease to make it protect your interests

How to Rewrite a Lease

You live with a lease (and a landlord) for a long time. If you're successful in a retail business, your landlord may want a percentage of your gross sales receipts. If you're not successful or if problems develop, you're going to want several Plan Bs and a **location escape hatch**. For example, your lease should protect your interests:

location escape hatch
a way to cancel or modify your lease if the landlord fails to meet the specified terms

- if the furnace or air-conditioning system breaks down
- if the parking lot needs sweeping or resurfacing
- if the anchor tenant goes under
- if the building is sold
- if half the other tenants move out

The possibility of such grief-producing eventualities needs to be dealt with with precise words and precise numbers in the lease.

Read the lease slowly and carefully. When you see something you don't understand or don't like, draw a line through it. Feel free to rewrite the sentences if you need to. It's *your* lease, too, you see. If you need help from a lawyer, get it. And make sure that the owner (or the leasing agent) indicates his or her agreement with your changes by initialing each one.

Here's a checklist to start you on your rewrite.

1. Escape Clause If the building doesn't shape up or the area goes into eclipse, you will want to get out fast. Be specific. Write something like this into your lease: "If three or more vacancies occur in the center, tenant may terminate lease."

option to renew
a guaranteed opportunity at the end of your lease to extend for another specific period of time

2. Option to Renew Most businesses need at least six months to a year to get going. If your business does well, you will want to stay put. If it does not, you don't want to be saddled with a heavy lease payment every month. Get a lease for one year, with an **option to renew** for the next two or three.

BOX 7.3   Before You Sign . . .

Before you sign a lease, ask these questions:

Does the lease contain an escape clause?

Does it have an option to renew?

Can you "assign" the lease if you need to sublet?

Do you have a ceiling on rent increases?

Do you have a floating lease scale, according to how much of the center is occupied?

Have you tried to negotiate a period of free rent while you are preparing to open the doors?

Have you negotiated with the landlord to make the needed improvements and charge you for them over the total time of the lease?

3. Right to Transfer   Circumstances might force you to sublet. In the trade, this is called "assigning." Make sure the lease allows you to transfer your lease without a heap of hassle if such circumstances arise.

4. Cost-of-living Cap   Most leases allow the owner to increase rents along with inflation according to the Consumer Price Index. To protect yourself, insist on a **cost-of-living cap** so that your base rate won't increase faster than your landlord's costs. Try for half of the amount of the CPI increase, a standard measure. Thus if the CPI rises 10%, your rate will go up only 5%. It's fair, because the owner's costs won't change much. Major tenants in your center will insist on a cap, so you should be able to negotiate one also. Proceed with confidence.

cost-of-living cap
an agreement that the rent from one year to another cannot be increased by more than the CPI for the period

5. Percentage Lease   Percentage leases are common in larger retail centers. They specify that the tenant pays a base rate plus a percentage of the gross sales. An example: $3.00 per square foot per month plus 5% of gross sales over $500,000 per year.

6. Floating Rent Scale   If you're a pioneer tenant of a shopping center, negotiate a payment scale based on occupancy. For example, you may specify that you'll pay 50% of your lease payment when the center is 50% occupied, 70% when it's 70% occupied, and 100% when it's full. You can't build traffic to the center all by yourself, and motivation is healthy for everyone, including landlords.

7. Start-up Buffer   There's a good chance you'll be on location fixing up, remodeling, and so on, long before you open your doors and make your first sale. Make your landlord aware of this problem and negotiate a long period of free rent. The argument: if your business is successful, the landlord, who's taking a percentage, will make more money. If your business doesn't do well or if it fails, the landlord will have to find a new tenant. You need breathing space. You've signed on for the long haul. By not squeezing you to death for cash, the landlord allows you to put more money into inventory, equipment, service, atmosphere—the things that make a business go.

8. Improvements   Unless you're a super fixer-upper, you don't want to lease a place equipped with nothing but a dirt floor and a capped-off cold water pipe. You need a proper atmosphere for your business, but you don't want to use all your cash to pay for it before you open. Negotiate with the landlord to make the needed improvements and spread the cost of them over the total time of the lease. Otherwise, find a space that doesn't require heavy remodeling.

restrictive covenants
a list of things you can't do

9. Restrictive Covenants   If you're running a camera store and part of your income derives from developing film, you don't want a Fotomat booth to move into your center. If you're selling hearing aids, you don't want a stereo store next door. Build **restrictive covenants** into your lease to protect yourself.

10. Maintenance   When the parking lot needs sweeping, who pays for it? If the air-conditioner goes out, who pays? If the sewer stops up, who is responsible for the repairs? Get all of this written down in simple language. Your diligence with words and numbers will pay off.

A SUCCESS STORY

We close the chapter with Charlene Webb's success story because it illustrates very well the things we've discussed. You could almost use this case study as a checklist for small business success.

"My partner and I were both in education, so carrying out a lot of research for our gourmet cookware store didn't seem unnatural. We hoped to open in October in order to capitalize on the holidays, so we spent our week of spring vacation talking to owners of gourmet cookware shops in the Los Angeles area—where it seems there's one on every corner.

"We spent five days and visited an average of fifteen shops a day. The owners we talked to were helpful—since they knew our store would be sixty miles away.

"When spring vacation was over, we went back to our teaching jobs with our minds loaded with information and our hearts full of hope. Time pressures were heavy. If we were going to open in October, we knew we had to spend the summer on layout, image, and atmosphere. That meant we needed to find a good location very soon.

"Three days before the end of the school year we found a site—in a very safe and secure center near a convenient freeway off-ramp. Our nearest competition was six miles away, and a population study told us there were 55,000 people in the surrounding area to support us. It was perfect. All we had to do *now* was negotiate a lease we could live with.

"Perhaps it's because I was an English teacher, or because my dad's a lawyer, but whenever I came across a passage in the lease document I didn't like or didn't think was fair to us, I crossed it out. Several places I rewrote entire passages. When it was all over—after the landlord and I had discussed all my changes and we had both initialed the ones we agreed on—I had made four changes that really gave our business some flexibility and breathing space.

1. We got a one-year lease with option to renew for the next two. I knew if we were going to go under, it would be in the first year, and we certainly wouldn't want to have to continue paying a lease if our shop went under.

2. We got three months' free rent. I was very straightforward with the landlord on this. I said, "Look here, we can pay you three months' rent out of what cash we have left after fixing up the interior, or we can put that money into inventory that will help our start-up. I think it would be a benefit to both you and us if we put that money into inventory." The landlord agreed.

3. We got a 10% cost-of-living cap on the percentage the landlord can raise our rent each year. If I ever negotiate another lease, I'll go for 5%.

4. We refused to let the landlord or his representative look at our books."

grand opening
a splashy celebration announcing your entry
into the market arena

Charlene and her partner's shop started off nicely, with a **grand opening** party for 500 friends and friends of friends. To bring in business, she started a cooking school, and her students have become good customers. Once a week she holds a special class called "Lunch and Learn."

For $5.75 and fifty minutes of their time, students get a glass of wine, a quick cooking lesson, and lunch they've just prepared for themselves. The heavy users in Charlene's business are women. "Lunch and Learn" is targeted at getting men into the store—so that they will see what's there and then come back to buy gifts or items they've learned to use in the classes.

Charlene has developed a customer list of 4,500 names, and she stays visible in the community by being actively involved in music activities, the Chamber of Commerce, and the bank (she's now on the Board of Directors) and by writing a gossip column for the newspaper.

SUMMARY

Some short journeys will help you see how important location is to a business. First, walk up and down the main business street of your town. Walk it on different days (weekend, weekday) and at different times of the day (midmorning, noon, afternoon, evening rush hour). Take some notes on what you see happening.

Second, explore a local shopping center on weekends, weekdays, and at different hours. Where is the action at these various times? Observe both vehicle and foot traffic, and what the people are buying. Locate the dead traffic zones. A poor location can kill a new business. Location is probably the most important decision a retailer can make.

THINK POINTS FOR SUCCESS

◣ The irony of the search for a start-up location is that you need the best site when you can least afford it.

◣ Take your time selecting a location. If you lose out on a hot site, don't worry; another one will turn up shortly.

◣ Begin with a regional analysis that will allow you to compare neighborhoods.

◣ A site analysis should include everything that is unique to a specific building or space. Many successful centers have some dead traffic areas.

◣ Who are your neighbors? Are they attracting *your* type of customers or clients? What will happen if they move or go out of business?

◣ Know the terms and buzz words—*CCOR, net, gross, triple net, industrial gross,* and so on—and be aware that they may mean slightly different things in each contract or lease agreement.

◣ Everything is negotiable: free rent, sinage, improvement allowances, the rates, maintenance. Don't be afraid to ask; a dollar saved in rental expenses can be worth more than ten dollars in sales.

◣ Talk to former tenants; you may be amazed at what you learn.

REFERENCES

Black's Office Leasing Guide. New York: McGraw-Hill Publications, 1988. [These Guides are published annually for major metropolitan areas. They contain advertising by commercial and industrial developers and information on local rates and expenses. For information, contact McGraw-Hill Information Systems, P.O. Box 2090, Red Bank, NJ 07701.

ACTION STEP REVIEW

Three action steps help you select a good location for your business.

36 Brainstorm your 100% location. Leave all geographic and budgetary restraints behind, and have some fun dreaming up the perfect site for your business.

37 Focus for a moment on your own buying habits. How far do you travel for candy, cigarettes, beer, a movie, car repairs, eyeglasses, a doctor, a dentist, a new car, a microcomputer? How far did you travel the last time you had dinner with a friend? If you needed brain surgery, how far would you be willing to travel?

38 Get a commercial real estate broker to help you check out locations, but leave your checkbook at home for now.

Burstiner, Irving. *The Small Business Handbook: A Comprehensive Guide to Starting and Running Your Own Business.* Englewood Cliffs, N.J.: Prentice Hall, 1979. [Good, solid chapter on location.]

Claritas. *Prizm, The Standard in Geo-Demographic Targeting.* Alexandria, Va.: Claritas, 1988. [Claritas is a marketing company that develops target marketing plans for small business. (Their phone number is 800-368-2063.) You can read more about Prizm in the Weiss book listed below. The Prizm stuff looks like fun.]

Garreau, Joel. *The Nine Nations of North America.* New York: Avon Books, 1981. [This is a landmark study of America's population that divides the continent into comprehensible chunks. It anticipates the year 2000, which can be called "the year of demographics."]

Metcalf, Wendell O. *Starting and Managing a Small Business on Your Own.* Washington, D.C.: Small Business Administration, 1982. [Statistics always lag behind reality. You'll need to update these figures by contacting trade associations in your industry.]

National Decision Systems. *Vision.* Encinitas, Calif.: National Decision Systems, 1988. [NDS is a market consulting company that develops targeting plans for large and small business. You can phone them at 619-942-7000.]

Sullivan, Daniel J., and Joseph F. Lane. *Small Business Management: A Practical Approach.* Dubuque, Iowa: Wm. C. Brown, Co., Publishers, 1983. [Good chapter on location, which contains a model study of the South San Mateo County (California) Market. The study was prepared by the Redwood City *Tribune* and is an example of the kind of help you can get from local newspapers.]

Wiess, Michael J. *The Clustering of America.* New York: Harper and Row, 1988. [Weiss discusses Prizm, a target marketing technique that focuses on forty neighborhood clusters in the United States. His classifications and their names—"Blue-Blood Estates," "Furs and Station Wagons," "Sharecroppers," "Downtown Dixie-Style," and so on—are perceptive and memorable.]

APPENDIX 7.1 · Action Step 36: Fantasize your 100% location.

In the past, because my free-lance work as a writer has been service-oriented, location has been of little immediate concern. My telephone number has usually been more important than where my "shop" was located. I've never advertised, or even produced a brochure on my business. It has been all word-of-mouth, and I usually get as much work as I can handle on weekends. Now my new eyes are beginning to open and widen in anticipation of a business where image is an important perception to medium-to-big business clients.

My choice of location will be only a recommendation to Nadek Computer Systems, Inc., as they are the major partner in our joint-venture association. Based upon what I have learned in this class and from my own experience in shopping for computer equipment, I wholeheartedly endorse the Main and Red Hill location that Joe Ryan suggested.

Main and Red Hill Businesses

I have personally found the Main and Red Hill location to be convenient. Here are some companies I have called on in that vicinity since 1982.

The Learning Shack. This was a computer school and software sales business situated on Fitch, just off Main and south of Red Hill. The building was one of those all-glass-mirrored structures, quite impressive. Although I did not attend the school (no need to), I did buy my 1982 and 1983 federal income tax programs from the company. The cost was only $65, in a period when a typical word-processing program cost $700. Perhaps that's why the company went into Chapter 7 liquidation and I was unable to buy my 1984 income tax update program from them.

Studio Software. After considerable research and investigation, I concluded that the page-composition program called Do-It was the best answer for desktop publishing at my employer, Santa Fe International. When the company declined to buy it, I purchased the program myself.

The original cost of the software was $2,850. Through competition from Aldus PageMaker on the Macintosh, the cost of Do-It began dropping. When it got down to $1,295, I bought the program and a PostScript laser printer. Studio Software later renamed Do-It as Front Page ($695), Front Page Plus ($1,295), and Front Page to Type ($1,495). The latter contained a PostScript printer driver for the Mergenthaler 101 and 202. In February 1987, shortly after Xerox Corporation released Ventura Publisher, the backers of Studio Software closed the doors and dismissed the employees. After five years of effort, the company had never made a profit. Do-It and Front Page are difficult programs to learn and somewhat quirky to operate, but they are still my choices as the best page composition programs under $5,000. I wonder if the high rent in the Main and Red Hill area were contributing factors in the demise of Studio Software and The Learning Shack. In my own opinion, a wholly inept tutorial, poor after-sales support and downright terrible advertising and promotion were the major reasons for Studio Software's untimely expiration.

Priority 1 Electronics. The brains behind Priority 1 Electronics are in the Chatsworth area. They do have a knack for picking winning products, discounting them, and promoting them through catalogs and flyers. But how the store on McDurmott near Main and Red Hill remains open is a mystery to me. When I call there, I'm usually in the market to buy something. I have researched the product thoroughly and gone there because of a favorable price. Invariably, I must lasso and hog-tie a salesman to get waited on. I wanted a 20-megabyte hardcard disk there, but it was out of stock. Delivery was promised the following Monday. It did not arrive, though I was billed on my Visa card. I finally gave up on Priority 1 Electronics and bought a 21-megabyte HardCard by Plus Development from Inacomp. Location might be important, but so is service. At Priority 1 Electronics, all the salespeople seem to be on the telephone making pitches to heavy users. Because of that competition, I couldn't even get to be a heavy user!

Quality Micro Systems. Until recently, few people had heard of QMS, but they make one of the widest-range laser printers of all manufacturers. These are quality products. The QMS-PS 800 is a PostScript printer in the same market with the Apple LaserWriter. For reasons irrelevant to this Action Step, the QMS product is demonstrably superior to the Apple product. So is the service, as evidenced by the QMS Western Regional Service Center on McDurmott just a few feet from Priority 1 Electronics. The service manager, Gary Casper, is a superior person who projects a superior image for the QMS organization. His shop is small, but the employees are friendly and they remember their customers by name. I can't possibly say too much for the service. (They replace the defective motherboard on my PS-800 laser printer five days after the warranty had expired.)

Conclusions

Everything about the Main and Red Hill location bespeaks quality and positive image for someone in the microcomputer business. If space could be found at a reasonable price, I would highly recommend to Nadek Computer Systems, Inc., that they take space there, even if only for a sales office. Perhaps they could keep the present location on Myford Road near MAI/Basic Four as a service center, warehouse, and business office.

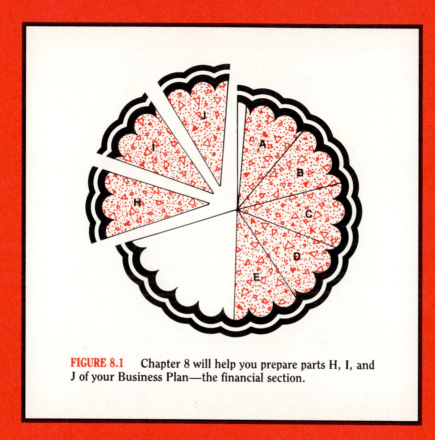

FIGURE 8.1   Chapter 8 will help you prepare parts H, I, and J of your Business Plan—the financial section.

Surprises You Can't Afford

LEARNING OBJECTIVES

■ To anticipate potential troublesome events that could occur in your business. ■ To develop Plan B (C, D, . . .) in order to minimize the ill effects of unfortunate surprises. ■ To learn the cost of each item you will need to do business, so that you know your total start-up expenses. ■ To develop a personal financial statement in order to know how much you will have to borrow to go into business. ■ To weigh the opportunity costs of going into business.

In earlier chapters, we've talked about the need for Plan B—an alternate strategy for bailing your business out of a tight spot created by some unforeseen, unfortunate occurrence. Having at least one Plan B is a must for every entrepreneur. Developing one can start with a list of potential problems and their solutions. We will help you develop such a list in this chapter. This kind of thinking can help you cut down your surprises by half.

EXPECT THE UNEXPECTED

Nonetheless, there's always something coming that you can't see, perhaps something like this case study illustrates.

Tommy Mankiewicz was in playing poker with a couple of his Army buddies when the idea of starting a small business came up.

"Dry cleaning," Rick said. "You can work out of the garage. All you need's a panel truck and a customer list. It's like coining money, right from the start."

"Sandwiches," George said. "And I know just the place. Traffic twenty-five hours a day—beach traffic, commercial, commuters, blue-collar workers, schoolkids. Gimme two cards." George had been in sandwiches in Florida. After a couple beers, Rick and Tommy often called him George the King of Sandwich. They assumed he knew a lot about Business.

"How much would it cost?" Tommy asked.

George whipped out a pencil and paper and pushed some numbers around. "Figure twenty grand apiece, tops," he said. "Plan to double your twenty in eighteen months, easy."

"Those are nice numbers at the end," Tommy said. "But which one of you big spenders can loan me the twenty at the beginning?"

"Hey," George said, "no problem! They don't call me the Sandwich King of Pampano Beach for nothing. Give me a handshake now and your name on a paper later, and we're in business."

So Tommy and Rick shook hands with George.

George was between jobs, so he handled lots of the details. He found the location, negotiated with the owner of the building, talked to equipment vendors, bought a great-looking sign. Tommy and Rick prepared financial statements to give to the banker George knew, and Tommy contacted relatives and friends to ask for start-up money.

Tommy and Rick and their wives spent some weekends fixing up the place. Tommy worked hard. He was handy with tools, and he built cabinets and shelves. But what really excited him was making interesting sandwiches.

"Hey!" Rick said. "This tastes great! Serve enough of these and we'll be famous!"

Everyone agreed that Tommy made the best sandwiches in the world. Tommy was encouraged by their support. He'd always been creative, and now he had a new arena in which to use his creativity. He bought books and researched the history of sandwiches. He dreamed about quitting his job with the state and teaching some seminars on the art of the sandwich. He began making notes for a book, a small book to start with, called *Cosmic Sandwiches: Secrets of the Universe,* although he didn't tell anyone about it.

Tommy was building one of his creations the day the city inspector dropped in at the shop to make his inspection. He was a heavy-set man with beady eyes and was carrying a clipboard. He walked around the place frowning and making notes. After awhile he asked Tommy, "Where's the restroom for the disabled?"

"What?" Tommy said, feeling a chill on the back of his neck.

"The disabled restroom. You know, wide enough for a wheelchair, regulation railing along the wall, special raised toilet facility. You gotta have one."

"Can you wait for my partner to come back?" Tommy asked. "He just stepped out. If you'll talk to him, I'm sure he—"

But the inspector just stood there, shaking his head. And Tommy knew that George hadn't taken care of it, and even when George did get there, all the inspector did was read them chapter and verse of the city code. *Every public place must have a restroom for the disabled.* They had to tear out a wall, put in a drain, move some machinery around in the kitchen, and replumb everything. It cost $12,000.

The inspector came back to check the work when they'd finished. He sat down at the counter, and Tommy brought him one of his finest creations. He told Tommy that they were lucky not to have been fined. The inspector paused and then said, "Your sandwiches are great. Once you guys get going, they'll make you famous."

The work on the new restroom delayed the opening of Tommy's shop more than a month.

Reading about these fellas' experience, it's all too easy to say "I told you so." It's easy to second-guess in such a situation and to say to yourself, "They should have known about that requirement. They just didn't do their homework."

But Tommy and his partners were experiencing the heady excitement of entrepreneurship. They were having fun and were caught up in the busy work of opening a business.

The same thing could happen to you. That's why you've got to plan for everything, even surprises.

A Plan B Checklist

Here's a checklist of some obvious start-up concerns. Add to this list as you think of things.

What's the anticipated cost of utilities for the first year?

What are the utility deposits?

Have you talked with a banker about a bank loan?

Have you used your personal credit to establish lines of credit?

Have you set up your inventory?

Have you devised your advertising campaign?

Have you trained your employees to be ready for opening day?

If the building is brand new, what kinds of permits do you need?

Have you had an inspection by the fire department?

If you are in a food-service business, have you checked on the needed inspections and permits?

Have you ordered telephone installation?

Have you checked out the prospects for zoning changes and growth in the neighborhood?

What is the life-cycle stage of your location?

Have you met your neighbors?

Do you know what the competition is doing?

Have you found a mentor? A coach? A guide?

Have you consulted with someone who knows more than you do about the big world of small business?

Have you set aside funds to cover possible surprises you haven't thought of?

If you get into the habit of making lists, doing mind maps, writing everything down, you'll improve your chances of surviving in small business. Action Step 39 will help you anticipate potential surprises.

ACTION STEP 39

Prepare your Plan B checklist.

Now that you've got your business well in mind, take a few minutes to brainstorm a list of surprises that could cost you money or time and thus threaten the survival of your business. Use our checklist to help you get started. Talk to businesspeople in your industry. Ask them to tell you how they handled unfortunate surprises. Once you select a site, ask the neighbors what has happened to them and how they're doing in this location. Talk to vendors, suppliers, customers, and insurance brokers. Ask. Probe.

When you finish your list, put a checkmark beside each item that will cost money.

Paying the Piper when the Purse Is Thin

Small businesses are especially vulnerable at start-up time, because that's when they're least able to afford surprises. If Ginny Henshaw had anticipated possible surprises, she'd have been better prepared for what happened to her.

> The reason I decided to start a day care center was because I really like kids. I talked it over with my husband, who said he'd help out if I got in over my head.
>
> I think we planned things pretty well. We found a good location—smack in the middle of a neighborhood of young families with an average 2.3 children—and then we spent weekends painting and fixing up. We worked hard, but it was fun, and it made us feel a part of something warm and cozy.
>
> Well, about three weeks before our opening, we called the Light and Power people to ask them to turn on the lights. "Sure thing," they said. "Just send us a check for $700, and the lights will be on in a jiffy."
>
> "What?" I asked. "Did you say $700?" We had around $800 in the kitty, but that was earmarked for emergencies.
>
> "That's right. You're a new commercial customer with a good credit rating. That's the reason the figure's so low."
>
> "You think $700 is low?" I asked. I was shocked.
>
> "For your tonnage," they said, "it's right on the money."
>
> "Tonnage? What tonnage?"
>
> "Your air conditioner," they said. "You have a five-ton unit on your roof. Figure you run it for a month, that's $310. The other $40 is for lights and gas."
>
> "But we're not planning to run it!" I said. "The breeze here is terrific. We don't need the air conditioner."
>
> "Sorry, ma'am. Our policy is pretty clear. As I said, sometimes we get three months' deposit, but for your business, we'll only require the two. Is there anything else I can help you with today?"
>
> "No," I said. "Nothing."

MANAGING THE UNEXPECTED

Risk management is old stuff. For example, how would you have protected yourself against unfortunate surprises if you were a fig trader in Damascus two thousand years ago and your main problem was brigands who robbed your caravan? You'd probably have hired guards to protect the merchandise.

How would you have protected yourself if you were a New Bedford whale oil dealer in 1845 whose underwriters were getting testy about financing another voyage because of your past losses due to shipwreck? You'd have hired better ship captains.

Most business surprises will cost you money, and your ability to cope with them will depend upon your ability to pay for them. The worksheet in Figure 8.2 and Action Step 40 will help you see how well prepared you are for the risks of doing business.

Getting Advice

Yes, you must be prepared, because there's a boatload of surprises awaiting every entrepreneur who enters the marketplace. We've talked about Plan B, formulating your strategy, checking and double-checking your market, and peering into the future to see what lies ahead. There's another angle to planning; it's called seeking advice.

Think for a moment about where you are right now on your road to the marketplace. You're halfway through this book. You've analyzed your skills and needs. You've

---

risk management
transferring risks to an underwriter and/or setting aside funds to meet deductible amounts

---

ACTION STEP 40

Attach price tags to your business.

Sit down at your desk and look around with new eyes.

A. List the items on your desk. Pencils, paper, telephone, typewriter, microcomputer, business cards, calendar, and so on. List the desk itself, the lamp, chair, bookcase, filing cabinet, coffee machine. Now go through the drawers, writing down every item you use to make your work run easier and smoother.

When you finish the list of things you can see and feel, make another list—a list of your expenditures for things you cannot see, some of which you might take for granted. These include such things as insurance protection, rent, utilities, taxes, legal services, accounting services, and so on.

B. Beside each tangible item and each intangible expense, write down how much it cost(s) you. If you don't know precisely, jot down a ballpark figure and move on. You can learn the exact amount later. Then add up those amounts.

C. Move all your items to the SBA data sheet (Figure 8.2). Note that the SBA differentiates costs as either start-up expenses or operating expenses. This is an easy way to think about costs.

As you gather more information, you'll be able to refine the numbers on this sheet.

ESTIMATED MONTHLY EXPENSES			
Item	Your estimate of monthly expenses based on sales of $ _____ per year	Your estimate of how much cash you need to start your business (See column 3.)	What to put in column 2 (These figures are typical for one kind of business. you will have to decide how many months to allow for in your business.)
	Column 1	Column 2	Column 3
Salary of owner-manager	$	$	2 times column 1
All other salaries and wages			3 times column 1
Rent			3 times column 1
Advertising			3 times column 1
Delivery expense			3 times column 1
Supplies			3 times column 1
Telephone and telegraph			3 times column 1
Other utilities			3 times column 1
Insurance			Payment required by insurance company
Taxes, including Social Security			4 times column 1
Interest			3 times column 1
Maintenance			3 times column 1
Legal and other professional fees			3 times column 1
Miscellaneous			3 times column 1
STARTING COSTS YOU ONLY HAVE TO PAY ONCE			Leave column 2 blank
Fixtures and equipment			Fill in worksheet 3 on page 12 and put the total here
Decorating and remodeling			Talk it over with a contractor
Installation of fixtures and equipment			Talk to suppliers from who you buy these
Starting inventory			Suppliers will probably help you estimate this
Deposits with public utilities			Find out from utilities companies
Legal and other professional fees			Lawyer, accountant, and so on
Licenses and permits			Find out from city offices what you have to have
Advertising and promotion for opening			Estimate what you'll use
Accounts receivable			What you need to buy more stock until credit customers pay
Cash			For unexpected expenses or losses, special purchases, etc.
Other			Make a separate list and enter total
TOTAL ESTIMATED CASH YOU NEED TO START WITH		$	Add up all the numbers in column 2

FIGURE 8.2   This SBA worksheet will help you estimate how much cash you need to open your business.

probed your past and surveyed your friends. You've discovered what success means to you, and you've plotted trends and found your industry segment. You've profiled your target customer, and studied the demographics, and developed a promotion campaign. You've examined the competition. You've used your new eyes to find a dynamite location. Now you need to find a **small business guru** and get some advice.

Where might you find a business guru? Well, what about your banker? Many people come to him or her for money—some of them carrying Business Plans, others not knowing a spreadsheet from bedsheet. What about your accountant? What about the real estate broker who helped you with your search for a location? What about your business insurance specialist? Have you contacted your local SBA office? Have you contacted SCORE?

You can use your network to find other people who may help you. Show them your list of potential surprises and ask for their advice. Ask them for their ideas about what other surprises might be in store for you. If one of those persons gives you wonderful advice, consider putting him or her on your board of directors.

small business guru
a wise person on the sidelines who can help you with advice and counsel

The Risk of Dishonest Employees

One of the nastiest surprises for a budding entrepreneur is employee dishonesty. You might think that because you're small, employees won't steal from you, but that is wrong. Small firms get hit more often than big ones. Here's a list of precautions that will help minimize the opportunities for employee theft and fraud.

Sign all the checks yourself.

Don't let any one employee handle all the aspects of bookkeeping.

Insist that all bookkeeping is done clearly and neatly.

Insist that your bookkeeper(s) take scheduled vacations.

Do regular physical inventories.

Open all mail containing payments yourself.

Track all cash transactions.

Use numbered order forms, and don't tolerate missing slips.

Insist on fidelity bonds for every employee who handles cash.

Triple-check references on resumes and employment applications.

If your business is a cash business, be there. Absentee owners, beware!

The Bottom Line

Although financial return may not be the number-one reason you want to start your own business, it should be high on your list. Money is a strong motivating factor; just thinking about it will help you keep your business on the success track. Here are some things to think about:

Income stream. What can you count on from your business? How much salary? How much profit? What benefits? Company car? Insurance? Travel? Retirement fund?

Profit from sale. What is the potential profit if the business is sold? What could you make if you took the company public via a stock offering?

Life cycle. How long will it take for your business to move from start-up to a profit position? Most businesses take at least two years, even three, to show a profit. What happens to your inventment if you project it two or three years down the road?

The rule: Every business should provide the owner with two sources of financial return: an income stream and growing equity. If you have income without equity, you're in trouble. If you have equity without income, you could starve to death.

THE PERSONAL FINANCIAL STATEMENT

How Much Money Do You Have Now?

The next question to ask yourself is Do you have enough **start-up money**? You can find out by getting a total for your assets (what you own), getting a total for your liabilities (what you owe), and then doing the easy arithmetic to determine your net worth—in other words, you need to see what you are worth right now by preparing a personal financial statement.

An easy way to do this is to ask your banker for a form for doing it. It will look something like the one in Figure 8.3. Pulling together a financial statement is important because it tells you where you are with money now, and it forces you to get organized.

Get some practice by doing Action Step 41.

financial statement
a list of assets and liabilities that will show your net worth

start-up money
all funds necessary to open the doors and to keep them open until you have a positive cash flow

Are You Prepared to Wait?

We've said before that it's going to be awhile before your business starts making money. In small business, you don't just rent a location, throw open the doors, and begin to show a profit. You need to be aware of **time-lags**.

What does this awareness mean? It means you've planned everything down to the doorknobs. It means you don't quit your job until you've finished your Business Plan and checked with your banker (and your backup banker) and know that you have enough money to withstand whatever surprises await you. It means you're not surprised when your business does not support you (right away) in the manner to which you've become accustomed.

A business is a living, breathing entity, and it takes time for the golden egg to hatch. Be prepared to wait awhile.

time-lags
periods of waiting—for mail deliveries, business cycles, and accounts receivable—that test the patience of an entrepreneur

OPPORTUNITY COSTS

Before You Take the Plunge

Before you jump into your own venture, make sure that you are being honest with yourself. What are the **opportunity costs**? What would your financial situation be if you kept working for someone else and did not go into business?

Any new business will take time—50–100 hours per week—so you will have to love what you're doing in order to succeed. Box 8.1 will help you measure the value of that time if you spent it elsewhere. It will also force you to consider the value of the fringe benefits you are probably earning while you work for someoned else.

Complete Action Step 42. The dollar **projection** you come up with should let you know precisely what you're getting into. If its hurts you to think about what you'll be giving up if you go into business, maybe you're not ready for the plunge.

opportunity cost
the cost of making an investment

projection
an intelligent forecast

ASSETS		LIABILITIES	
Cash in Wells Fargo	$	Notes Payable Banks—Schedule I	$
Cash in other—identify		Secured	
Stocks and Bonds—Schedule II		Unsecured	
Accounts Receivable		Accounts/Bills Payable—Schedule I	
Cash Surrender Value Life Insurance			
Face Value $			
Real Estate—Schedule III		Mortgages Payable on Real Estate—Schedule III	
Automobiles		Other debts—itemize	
Other Assets—Itemize			
		Total Liabilities	
		Net worth (total assets less total liabilities)	
TOTAL ASSETS	$	**TOTAL LIABILITIES PLUS NET WORTH**	$

SOURCES OF INCOME		SCHEDULE I—DEBTS AND CREDIT REFERENCES		
Salary	$	Notes Payable, Banks, Credit Cards, Dept. Stores, etc. itemized.		
Spouse's Salary—(if applicable)		(All debts are listed ☐ Yes ☐ No)		
Bonus and Commissions		**NAME AND ADDRESS OF CREDITOR**	**BALANCE**	**MO. PMT.**
Real Estate Income—Net				
Dividends				
Other Source (**Note:** you need not list income from alimony, child support or maintenance unless you wish it to be considered.)				
		Alimony, Child Support, Maintenance		
Total	$	Totals	$	$

SCHEDULE II—STOCKS AND BONDS					
DESCRIPTION	**WHERE QUOTED**	**COST OR MARKET**	**TITLE IN NAME OF**	**QUANTITY**	**VALUE**

SCHEDULE III—REAL ESTATE					MORTGAGE		
DESCRIPTION/ADDRESS	**DATE ACQUIRED**	**TITLE IN NAME OF**	**COST**	**MARKET VALUE**	**DUE TO**	**AMOUNT**	**MO. PMT.**

SCHEDULE IV—SEPARATE PROPERTY
Complete if married, and any assets listed above are separate property.

DESCRIPTION	**TITLE IN NAME OF**	**VALUE**

GENERAL INFORMATION—CONTINGENT LIABILITIES

Have you ever had a repossession? ☐ Yes ☐ No   Have you ever declared bankruptcy? ☐ Yes ☐ No

Are you an Endorser, Guarantor, Co-maker? ☐ Yes ☐ No

Are you a party to any Claims, or Suits? ☐ Yes ☐ No

Do you owe any taxes for years prior to the current year?
☐YES ☐NO   AMOUNT: $

FIGURE 8.3 A personal financial statement form—available at any bank—will help you construct an accurate picture of your net worth.

BOX 8.1 How to Project Opportunity Cost

Project your salary for the next 12 months.	_____
Add in benefits from your employer:	
Life insurance	_____
Disability insurance	_____
Health insurance	_____
Pension plan	_____
Company car	_____
Social Security (employer's contribution)	_____
Expense account	_____
Bonuses	_____
Other	_____
Total	_____

Calculate the interest you could earn in the 12 months on the capital you're planning to invest in your business. _Example:_ $25,000 × 7.75% = $1,937.50.   _____

Add in your time.

Hours per week you plan to work in your new business:	_____
Subtract the number of hours you now work.	_____
Hours available for moonlighting:	_____
Multiply moonlighting hours by hourly rate and then by 50 weeks.	_____

Total opportunity cost (your potential income for the next year)   _____

In weighing the opportunity costs of going into business, ask yourself questions such as these:

Can you afford to leave your job?

What are your gut feelings as you approach the point of no return?

How comfortable are those "golden handcuffs"?

Think Again about What Success Means to You

As we've pointed out before, money isn't the only measure of success. You need to keep your focus on what you really want. Make a list. Do a mind map. Dig deep into yourself and learn what makes you tick.

AN OUNCE OF PREVENTION

When survivors from any field or profession get together, they like to share horror stories. We have collected a few of these in the small-business surprise area and come up with some **preventive actions** for them. They're listed here. You can probably think of more.

ACTION STEP 41

Develop a personal financial statement.

Sit down with a pencil and paper and do some figuring.

1. List everything you own that has **cash value** and estimate its worth. Include: cash, securities, life insurance, accounts receivable, notes receivable, rebates/refunds, autos and other vehicles, real estate, vested pension, Keogh or IRA funds, and so on.

Don't stop now. Go on to list the market values of your home furnishings, household goods, major appliances, sports equipment, collectibles, jewelry, tools, livestock, trusts, patents, memberships, business interests, investment clubs, and so on.

Add up the amounts you've written down. The total represents your _assets_.

2. List every dime you owe to someone or something. Accounts payable. Contracts payable. Notes payable (such as car loans). Taxes. Insurance (life, health, car, liability, etc.). Mortgages/Real Estate Loans. Anything else you owe. These are your **liabilities**.

3. Subtract your liabilities from your assets to find your net worth. It's that simple.

Now you know how much you have and, thus, how much you need to raise so that you can start your business.

cash value
the value of tangible and intangible items when converted to cash

liabilities
a sum total of what you owe

preventive action
positive steps taken to minimize risk of potential adversities

ACTION STEP 42

Determine how much you can make if you do not go into business.

Calculate what will happen, money-wise, if you keep on with what you are doing and attach a value to the extra time you're going to have to spend in your new business. Box 8.1 can help you.

A. Project your salary for the next 12 months.

B. Add in the value of the fringe benefits you receive from your employer—insurance, pension plan, company car, expense account, bonuses, Social Security (employer's contribution), parking, free photocopying, complimentary paperclips, and so on.

C. Now figure in the capital you're planning to invest in the business. What would you make on this money if you invested it in a no-load family of money-market funds that allows you to switch from stocks to money markets and back to stocks when interest rates change?

D. Add in the value of your time. If you're planning to work 60 hours a week in your new business (many entrepreneurs work 100 during peak seasons), subtract 40 (your normal work week) from 60. That would leave you 20 hours a week available for **moonlighting**. Say you could make $7.50 per hour moonlighting. Then, 20 hours a week times 50 weeks a year times $7.50 equals $7,500.

E. Find the total.

moonlighting
holding down a second job

tickler file
a calendar-based reminder system

partner's remorse
backing out of a deal before the business gets rolling

escrow account
funds held by a neutral, state-regulated third party until the stated conditions are met

completion bond
an insurance policy that will pay for finishing a project

SURPRISE	PREVENTION
Your landlord decides to evict you and your business.	Get a lease. Rewrite the lease to favor your business. Keep in contact with the landlord. Make sure you have a renewal clause.
The newspaper does not run the ad for your grand opening.	Make connections with all media. Develop a **tickler file**. Make sure you see proof sheets. Withhold payment until they do it right.
An hour after you sign your name to guarantee the lease, your best friend and partner gets cold feet and pulls out. You do not have a thing in writing to protect you against **partner's remorse**.	Line up partnership commitments before the big day. Open a special **escrow account**. Everybody deposits. Everybody signs.
For eight weeks, during your peak season, the city has the sidewalk in front of your store torn up. The noise is deafening.	Network your way into city hall. Make sure you know your councilman. Try to rally media sympathy. Use the underdog angle.
Your general contractor goes bankrupt.	Get a **completion bond**. Ask the bonding agency to expedite.
Your bookkeeper disappears with $100,000, your books, two trade secrets from the company safe, and your spouse.	A fidelity bond would have protected you. Join a singles club.
Your best salesperson is hired away by the competition.	Woo **key employees**. Keep them involved and informed. Don't take them for granted. Think about giving them a piece of the business. Check the horizon for pirates.
Even though you're in a low-crime area, thieves broke into your store twice last month.	Set up a bunker in the back room. Get your Colt Commando. Wait for the thieves. Don't shoot them until they're inside the building.
Due to an administrative error, the bank calls your loan. It is payable in 30 days. If you would like to cash out, they will give you 25 cents on the dollar.	Take a banker to lunch. Take a **backup banker** to lunch. Back up the backup banker with a backup.
A new customer pays you by check, takes delivery of the goods, and then stops payment on the check before you get it to the bank. You were too busy to get check verification/authorization.	No matter how busy you are, take time for important survival tasks.
Your largest customer declares bankruptcy. The money owed you in receivables is 77% of your gross annual sales.	Don't keep all your eggs in one basket.
The bank where you have your checking account refuses to extend you a $3,300 line of credit to buy a piece of equipment that will double your business. The bank has a policy of not lending money to small firms.	Keep your banker in your information loop. Make sure you give your banker updates on your Business Plan. Get a backup bank. Discuss money long before you need it.
A new energy crisis makes 1974 look like child's play. Cars line up at the service station next door, blocking the traffic to your store.	Turn the lemon into lemonade.

Turn a Lemon into Lemonade

At some time in your business life, you're going to need to find a way to capitalize on one of those unfortunate surprises. When that time comes, we hope you will be as resourceful as Terry Adkins.

Terry and Susan Adkins' Donut Place got off to a slow start. They grossed only $275 a day the first month, when what they needed was closer to $700. But then things started picking up. They had weeks that averaged $310, $380, and then $475, and they could see that they were going to make it after all.

By Easter of the second year, they were pulling in $850 on weekdays and $600 on weekends, when trade naturally slowed down. They were beginning to look forward to taking their first vacation in six years when the Energy Crisis hit.

It didn't get as nasty in their community as it did in the big cities, but it was bad enough. Cars lined up for blocks to wait for available gas. Terry and Susan's business fell off dramatically because a major oil company station was on the nearby corner. Their customers were either waiting in line for gas, or they couldn't drive in for their morning donuts without having to break through the lines of waiting cars. If the shop took in $200 a day, they called it profit. It wasn't profit, of course; it didn't come anywhere near paying the bills. Needless to say, they were in despair.

After a week of no business, they had an idea. They borrowed a shopping cart from the supermarket and bought a fifty-cup coffee urn. They put the urn—full of steaming coffee—onto the grocery cart and stacked boxes of donuts, disposable cups, cream and sugar packets, and napkins around the urn. And then Terry took their donuts to the street.

While he sold donuts, Terry got to know the people in the cars. The second day he went out, he took along a paper and pencil. He wrote down the people's names and what kinds of donuts they liked. He didn't know that this is called "market research"; it just seemed like the smart thing to do.

Terry and Susan didn't make as much money as they had before the Energy Crisis, but they made enough to keep going until things got sorted out in the Persian Gulf. And when the Energy Crisis was over, they had more than a hundred new customers. And because of Terry's market research, they knew what kinds of donuts the new customers liked.

key employee
a worker whose loss would seriously affect the future of your business

backup banker
banker who would like to have your business and is ready to help

After Plan B

The reason for many small business successes is fast footwork. A small business can move more quickly than a big business. The idea is to keep informed, alert, and flexible. After you develop Plan B, work on Plans C and D.

SUMMARY

Start-up needs to go smoothly. What you don't need then is expensive surprises that knock you and your business for a loop. So before you open your doors, you need to have anticipated as many potential unpleasant surprises as possible and have a plan of action for each one of them. For example, what will you do if:

  your landlord decides to evict your business?

  your yellow pages ad stinks?

  the customer that accounts for 75% of your business declares bankruptcy?

Expecting and *planning for* the unexpected can make the difference between life and death in business. Looking closely at your present assets and liabilities—by developing a personal financial statement—and calculating the opportunity costs of going into business for yourself will help you eliminate some surprises and they may cause you to question whether you're truly ready to take the plunge. Just remember two things: no one can anticipate everything, and it will probably cost more and take longer than your planning indicates.

ACTION STEP REVIEW

Four action steps help you anticipate surprises:

39 Use your new eyes to develop strategies for dealing with unforeseen events that could cripple you.

40 Make a list of all your business needs and estimate their costs. List *everything,* the tangibles first and then the intangibles.

41 Develop a personal financial statement to learn your net worth. Look closely at your assets and your liabilities.

42 Assess the opportunity costs of going into business for yourself. Determine how much you will make if you do *not* go into business. If what you learn is painful, perhaps you're not ready to make the plunge into small business.

THINK POINTS FOR SUCCESS

◀ Be prepared for your competition to counterattack.

◀ Be aware of closing dates for yellow page advertising and other key media.

◀ Keep a time log that tells everyone (you, your founders, your key employees) how you are progressing on the Plan.

◀ Make sure your partners are as committed to the business as you are.

◀ Keep an ongoing list of unfortunate surprises that could hurt your business.

◀ Always have a Plan B. And a Plan C. And a Plan D.

◀ Let some key customers in on your planning; let them see it with their own eyes.

REFERENCES

Donoghue, William E., with Thomas Trilling. *No-Load Mutual Fund Guide: How to Take Advantage of the Investment Opportunity of the Eighties.* New York: Harper and Row, 1983. [An investment guide that can save you a lot of surprises. Donoghue's SLYC system (Safety, Liquidity, Yield, Catastrophe-proofing) is a smart alternative to small business start-ups. He predicts bank swallow-ups—two dozen superbanks by the end of the eighties. Thought-provoking book.]

Financial Management: How to Make a Go of Your Business. Washington, D.C.: U.S. Small Business Administration, Office of Management Assistance. Small Business Management Training Instructors' Guide No. 106, 1984.

Money Management Institute. *Your Savings and Investment Dollar.* Prospect Heights, Illinois: Household International, 1984. [One of a series of twelve booklets on money management available from Household Banks, or by writing: Money Management Institute, Household International, 2700 Sanders Road, Prospect Heights, IL 60070.]

Recordkeeping in Small Business. Washington, D.C.: U.S. Small Business Administration, Office of Business Development. Management Aid No. 1.017, 1987.

Van Caspel, Venita. *Money Dynamics for the New Economy.* New York: Simon and Schuster, 1986.

APPENDIX 8.1 • Action Step 40: Attach price tags to your business.

Saddleback Services has the advantage of being almost ten years old, though it was largely inactive from 1979 until 1982, the year I bought my first computer. In 1983, while I was re-registering Saddleback Services as a DBA firm, I also registered The Saddleback Scribe, which soon will be five years old. Since 1983, Saddleback Services has been a vehicle for my advertising copywriting and brochure production. The Saddleback Scribe is used for public relations and editorial work, such as writing and editing *NavCom World* magazine for Gould, Inc., in El Monte. (Saddleback Publications, a miserably failed attempt at selling books, is no longer active although I have a ton of stationery for it. To convert the stationery, I blank out the word *Publications* in black and overprint *The* and *Scribe* before and after the word *Saddleback.*

During the active period from 1982 to 1987, Saddleback Services and The Saddleback Scribe have invested and basically written off through Schedule 173 and ACRS depreciation about $25,000 worth of computers and office equipment, including: two computers, three printers (including a $5,000 PostScript laser printer), a suitable supply of stationery, lamps, fixtures, desks, tables, and office supplies, and a large assortment of software programs. I have the most important software programs for desktop publishing—Aldus PageMaker for the PC, Xerox

Ventura Publisher, Front Page Plus (also Do-It), and Microsoft Word 3.1 (investment of $3,600). I also have the usual spreadsheet programs, data-base management programs, project management programs, at least four accounting programs, and such popular word processors as WordPerfect 4.2 (not at all suitable for desktop publishing).

Because these investments are behind me and paid in full, and because I plan to enter what is essentially a consulting business, my start-up costs should be minimal. I can work out of my home, using Nadek Computer Systems, Inc., as my unpaid storefront. The main expense will be the salary I pay myself until cash flow can generate profits. All expenses itemized in the table are available to me at this time.

Estimated Expenses

MONTHLY ITEM	MONTHLY COST	AMOUNT NEEDED TO START
Salary of owner–manager	$3,000	$6,000
Other salaries/wages	none	none
Rent	none	none
Advertising	500	1,000
Delivery, supplies	none	none
Telephone	100	200
Other utilities	none	none
Insurance	50	100
Taxes, including FICA	360	720
Interest	none	none
Maintenance	none	none
Professional fees	100	200
Miscellaneous	500	1,000

START-UP ITEM		
Fixtures, equipment: scanner		$4,000*
Decorating, remodeling		none
Installation of fixtures		none
Starting inventory		none
Utilities deposits		none
Professional fees		none
Licenses, permits		none
Advertising for opening		1,000
Accounts receivable		1,000
Cash		1,000
Other: flyer, newsletter		1,000
TOTAL CASH NEEDED TO START		**$17,220**
Total if the scanner is leased		$14,020
Reserve for emergencies		$10,000

*I can lease a scanner on a lease–buy plan for 10% down and $150 a month.

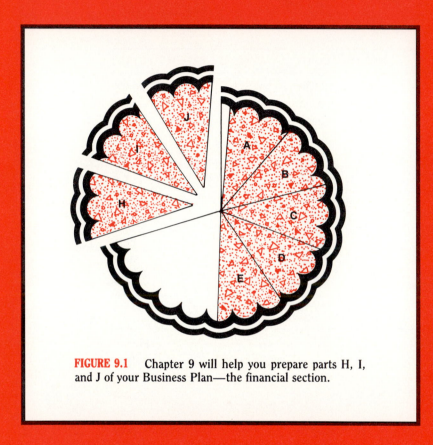

FIGURE 9.1 Chapter 9 will help you prepare parts H, I, and J of your Business Plan—the financial section.

Numbers and Shoebox Accounting

LEARNING OBJECTIVES

■ To be able to use numbers to project your business future. ■ To develop strategies for managing cash. ■ To project monthly sales. ■ To search your own financial history for creative ways to deal with shortfalls. ■ To understand that bills are paid with cash, not profit. ■ To understand that the government taxes *paper* profit. ■ To be able to use ratios as a cash management tool. ■ To create an income statement. ■ To create a cash flow projection. ■ To consider numerical projections in choosing a legal form for your business. ■ To know how to use shoebox accounting.

In this chapter, we urge you to move beyond your start-up plans and venture out into the uncertain future. It's time to set some numerical goals for your first year of operation. Running out of money in business is the end of the business. This chapter will show you how to avoid running out of money.

CHART YOUR BUSINESS FUTURE WITH NUMBERS

Which months will be strong in your particular business and which will be weak? What will be your gross sales the first year? The second? The third? How much profit will you make? Or how much will you lose? How can you project cash flow, bank loans, lines of credit, vendor credit? Can you add some people to the team who will bring in some cash? What will your cash picture look like when your start-up dollars are spread over a full year? How fast will your business grow? What would rapid growth do to your cash picture? Have any of your life experiences prepared you for handling money in business?

Start with the Past

Looking at your past can help you chart your business future. Money does indeed make the world go 'round, and up and down. Everyone has financial ups and downs. When were some of your "down" times? Action Step 43 directs your thinking to the past and to the future.

Collect Survival Information

In chapter 8 you worked out a personal financial statement. In Action Step 43 you recalled personal survival tactics—how you dealt with money problems in the past. Your next step is to begin building a business budget. There are four things you need to think about, generally, before you plunge into the numbers of business management: sales forecasting, seasonality, cash management, and profit and loss. We discuss each of these briefly here.

Sales Forecast   Before you jump into a business, you need to figure out how much it will produce in a given period of time. You can pull a first-year forecast together by combining information on sales from business owners and trade associations.

seasonality
the recognition that business, like life, flows in cycles connected to the four seasons

Seasonality Scenario   Almost every business experiences peaks and valleys. What will be your best month? Your worst? Attempt to develop a seasonality scenario for the first year of your particular business.

cash management
the tightrope balancing of liquid money resources to obtain maximum benefit from each dollar

Cash Management   Because of time lags (checks clearing, dating, credit sales, credit cards, bad risks, human factors, paperwork, weekends, and so on), you probably will not get paid the same day you make a sale. Meanwhile, you will have to pay out cash for labor, taxes, rent, utilities, inventory, and other expenses. If your business is to stay afloat in the interim, you're going to have to know where every dollar is. Long before the dollars stop trickling in, you must make arrangements for help.

Cash management involves knowing where the dollars are every month and maximizing the benefits of the money you are holding. The idea is to speed up the inflow and slow down the outflow. Remember, your expenses are someone else's sales.

Profit and Loss   Unless you are the exception to the rule, you are not going to make lots of money your first week in business, and if you do get rich, it will happen slowly. A projected profit and loss statement will tell you when you should start making a profit—which has to happen before you can start getting rich. If you're not going to make a profit for a while, you might want to structure your business so that your losses can be deducted from personal taxable income.

Forecast Sales

The following case study about a bookstore operation illustrates the value of planning. The owners, Patricia and Don French, carried out three important steps:

1. They developed a seasonal scenario so that they were not surprised by the Christmas crush and the February slump.
2. They gathered data from their trade association that gave them ballpark numbers.
3. They projected their sales by using ratios.

In any retail operation, you want to distinguish your product mix according to how fast it moves—that is, by its "shelf velocity." Industry data told Patricia and Don to separate paperbacks from hardbacks, because the shelf velocity for each category was different.

We planned every phase of our bookstore operation. My husband, Don, has always been a great reader, and my friends in college used to accuse me of being a bibliophile—but we quickly discovered when we did our research that a bookstore is a business. In business, you either grow fast or you die, so we needed to master a lot of new skills, fast.

Running a bookstore is not the same as being a happy-go-lucky English major in college.

We worked and saved for several years—in bookstores, teaching, advertising—and when we started our business we had over $30,000. In addition, we got our friends interested, and they contributed $50,000 more. With that in hand, we wrote up an eighty-page Business Plan and went to our banker, who extended us a line of credit for $25,000.

The location we found had about 2,500 square feet of floor space, and data from the ABA [American Booksellers' Association, the major trade association] indicated that sales for that size store in this demographic area would be around $130,000 annually. Our major competitor had done $150,000 the year before.

Our first question was how much to spend on inventory. To answer that, we used a ratio method of inventory projection. First, we found the annual **turn ratio** for hardbacks, which was 3. Then we found the annual turn ratio for paperbacks, which sell faster. That was 6.

To find the amount we needed for initial inventory, we first multiplied the annual sales figure by the percentage for gross sales. Industry figures told us hardbacks would account for 60% of sales and paperbacks, 40%. Thus,

60% × $130,000 = $78,000 annual hardback sales

Next, we figured cost of goods sold, which has gone up. It's now 65%. We multiplied $78,000 by 65%. That came to $50,700 for our annual cost of hardback goods sold.

To estimate what our start-up hardback inventory would cost us, we divided the cost of goods sold by the annual turn ratio, which for hardbacks was 3.

$$\frac{\$50,700}{3} = \$16,900$$

ACTION STEP 43

Recall hard times and look to the future.

A. Your Personal Money Past. Look back over your life, to times when you have been pressed for cash. List the times in your life when you ran out of money.

Where were you, and what were you doing? How old were you? How much job training and experience did you have? Who were you with? Did you have any dependents? How did you feel about running out of money? (Angry? Sick? Depressed? Victimized?)

How did you solve the problem? (Moonlight? Borrow money? Take out another mortgage? Tighten your belt and run leaner?)

B. Your Personal Money Future. Look ahead into the next year and list your expenses (shelter, food, medical expenses, transportation, insurance, phone, school, clothes, utilities, and so on). (If you need a form with blanks to fill in, ask your banker. Most banks have personal budget forms to give their customers.) Add up all the amounts and add 10% for a contingency fund.

Now, write down how you will handle these expenses. If it looks like you're not going to have enough money, what will you do?

turn ratio
a measurement obtained by dividing the average inventory into annual sales

So we knew our cost for the initial hardback inventory would be about $16,900.

We went through the same procedure for paperbacks—multiplying the annual sales by percentage of gross sales and by the cost of goods sold, and then dividing by the turn ratio:

$$\frac{40\% \times \$130,000 \times 65\%}{6}$$

or, simplified,

$$\frac{\$52,000 \times 65\%}{6} = \frac{\$33,800}{6} = \$5,630$$

Adding the two figures, we came up with $22,530, almost $23,000, that we needed for initial inventory. This seemed like a lot of money, but it was a relief to know where we were going.

After we'd been in business for a year, we did something we should have done before. We plotted out a **scenario for a year** and assigned percentages of sales to each month. This gave us a feel for the future, based on the past.

Before we opened, we knew that December would be our **peak time**, but we didn't realize the extent of the peak. The holiday season accounts for at least a third of our business. Here's our scenario:

scenario for a year
combining seasonality with sales percentages to produce a picture of the peaks and valleys of the business cycle

peak time
a high-volume period when maximum inventory and resources are needed

January (6.5%). "January is an anticlimax to Christmas, but it's still busy because of gift certificates and exchanges. Don and I run some good specials at the end of January, prior to taking our yearly inventory. Even though sales are slowing down, we have to order new titles, because publishers (our suppliers) are giving us advance notice on their lists for spring."

February (4.5%) and March (5%). "Very quiet. We take inventory, weed out stuff that didn't sell, send it back. We meet a lot of publishers' reps, who are out on the road pushing new titles. On March 15th we have an Ides of March sale. Next year we're planning a St. Patrick's Day tie-in."

April (5%). "Still slow. We get a slight jump in sales after the 15th, mostly because spring vacations give some people time to read."

May (8%) and June (8%). "Two holidays—Mother's Day and Father's Day—plus weddings and graduations give us our second-busiest season. Art books and gift editions do well, also encyclopedias and how-to's."

July (6%) and August (7%). "We're not in a tourist area, and summers for us are slow. We sell mostly easy-to-read paperbacks. Our minds are on ordering books for Christmas."

September (9%). "Saved by back-to-school purchases. We're interviewing people for Christmas jobs and making last-minute purchases of gift items."

October (10%) and November (12%). "The start of the busy season. Customers sense it, and we can feel the momentum. The rush is just around the corner. We usually hire more sales help at this time."

December (19%). "The crush. I work the front while Don stations himself in back, inputting our sales into the computer. We gather information daily so we can spot the direction holiday sales will take. It's different every year, but with two years of data gathering behind us, we're getting a feel for what really happens. And that helps us plan ahead for the next year."

Don and Patricia prepared Tables 9.1 and 9.2 before they opened their doors and Table 9.3 after their first year in business. These tables can serve as examples for you to follow.

After the first year of business, sales forecasting will become easier. Keep very careful records that first year, so that you'll know how your own peaks and valleys correlate with the seasonality of your industry.

Most businesses are seasonal, and you'll need to develop strong control systems to manage your financial resources. Start now to identify alternate sources of credit and find ways to collect cash from customers before all of your products or services are delivered.

TABLE 9.1   Bookstore Income and Expense Forecast, First Year*

	JULY	AUG	SEPT	OCT	NOV	DEC	JAN	FEB	MAR	APR	MAY	JUNE	TOTAL
Sales	7,800	9,100	11,700	13,000	15,600	24,700	8,450	5,850	6,500	6,500	10,400	10,400	130,000
Cost of Goods Sold	5,070	5,915	7,605	8,450	10,140	16,055	5,495	3,800	4,225	4,225	6,760	6,760	8,450
Gross Profit	2,730	3,185	4,095	4,550	5,460	8,645	2,955	2,050	2,275	2,275	3,640	3,640	45,500
Expenses													
Rent		1,875	1,875	1,875	1,875	1,875	1,875	1,875	1,875	1,875	1,875	1,875	20,625
Utilities	200	200	200	200	200	200	200	200	200	200	200	200	2,400
Adv./PR/4%	310	365	470	520	625	990	340	235	260	260	415	415	5,205
Insurance	75	75	75	75	75	75	75	75	75	75	75	75	900
Supplies/1%	80	90	115	130	155	245	85	60	65	65	105	105	1,300
Misc./5%	390	455	585	650	780	1235	425	295	325	325	520	520	6,505
Credit card fees	70	80	105	120	140	225	75	55	60	60	95	95	1,180
Loan interest				10									10
Total Expenses	1,125	3,140	3,425	3,580	3,850	4,845	3,075	2,795	2,860	2,860	3,285	3,285	38,125
Net Profit/Loss	1,605	45	670	970	1,610	3,800	−120	−745	−585	−585	355	355	7,375

*Sales: the first-year forecast of $130,000 is based on industry information gathered by the owners.
Cost of Goods Sold: Estimated at 65% of sales.
Rent: 75 cents per square foot × 2,500 square feet; no rent charged for the first two months; the owners used the first month to get ready for their opening.
Utilities: Figures are estimates from the local utility company.
Advertising and Promotion: Estimated at 4% of sales based on information from other bookstore owners.
Insurance: $900 per year is the rate quoted by owners' insurance agent.
Supplies: Estimated at 1% of sales based on interviews.
Miscellaneous: Estimated at 5% of sales based on interviews; added a fudge factor to cover unexpected expenses.
Loan Interest: This represents interest on the line of credit at 1% per month of the unpaid balance.
Credit Card Fees: Projected on the basis of 30% of sales being credit-card sales; the credit card company charges 3%.

TABLE 9.2   Bookstore Cash Flow Forecast, First Year

	JULY	AUG	SEPT	OCT	NOV	DEC	JAN	FEB	MAR	APR	MAY	JUNE
Cash on hand	1,900	3,945	100	145	610	5,715	21,070	20,990	20,360	22,030	21,200	20,950
Sales	7,800	9,100	11,700	13,000	15,600	24,700	8,450	5,850	6,500	6,500	10,400	10,400
Less: Credit fees	−70	−80	−105	−120	−140	−225	−75	−55	−60	−60	−95	−95
Loan			1,000									
Total	9,360	12,965	12,965	13,025	16,070	30,190	29,445	26,785	26,800	28,470	31,505	31,255
Disbursements												
Book purchases	4,255	9,880	9,305	8,030	6,720	4,575	5,080	3,760	2,045	4,545	7,440	8,420
Rent		1,875	1,875	1,875	1,875	1,875	1,875	1,875	1,875	1,875	1,875	1,875
Utilities	200	200	200	200	200	200	200	200	200	200	200	200
Adv./PR/4%	310	365	470	520	625	990	340	235	260	260	415	415
Insurance	450											
Supplies/1%	80	90	115	130	155	245	85	60	65	65	105	105
Misc./5%	390	455	585	650	780	1,235	425	295	325	325	520	520
Interest				10								
Loan payment				1,000								
Total	5,685	12,865	12,550	12,415	10,355	9,120	8,455	6,425	4,770	7,270	10,555	11,535
Net Cash Flow	3,945	100	145	610	5,715	21,070	20,990	20,360	22,030	21,200	20,950	19,720

TABLE 9.3   Bookstore Income and Expense Forecast, 2nd–5th Years*

			2ND YEAR			3RD YEAR	4TH YEAR	5TH YEAR
	1ST QTR	2ND QTR	3RD QTR	4TH QTR	TOTAL	TOTAL	TOTAL	TOTAL
Sales	34,320	63,960	24,960	32,760	156,000	201,175	210,800	237,200
Cost of Goods Sold	22,310	41,575	16,225	21,295	101,405	137,020	137,020	154,180
Gross Profit	12,010	22,385	8,735	11,465	54,595	64,155	73,780	83,020
Expenses								
Rent	5,905	5,905	5,905	5,910	23,625	24,805	26,045	27,350
Utilities	630	630	630	630	2,520	2,645	2,780	2,920
Adv./PR	1,375	2,545	1,000	1,310	6,230	7,330	8,430	9,490
Insurance	235	235	235	240	945	990	1,040	1,090
Supplies	345	640	250	330	1,565	1,835	2,110	2,370
Misc.	1,785	3,200	1,250	1,640	7,875	9,215	10,540	11,860
Credit card fees	310	575	225	295	1,405	1,650	1,900	2,135
Loan interest								
Total Expenses	10,585	13,730	9,495	10,355	44,165	48,470	52,845	57,215
Net Profit/Loss	1,425	8,655	−760	1,110	10,430	15,685	20,935	25,805

*2nd year: 20% growth
3rd year: 17.5% growth
4th year: 15% growth
5th year: 12.5% growth

Forecast Collections

If you're in the ice cream business, your sales will heat up in summer. The same is true of hardware (especially home improvement supplies) and auto parts, since people tend to drive more in the summer months. If you run a ski shop, you might have to order your skis at a summer trade show, pay for them when they arrive in September, and then wait until late March to sell the last of them.

If, on the other hand, you're in the bed-and-breakfast business, you can collect your money ahead of time—sometimes as far ahead as six months—and have it spent or invested long before you have to provide the bed and breakfast. The same is true for airlines, insurance companies, magazines, newspapers, advertising agencies, travel agents, universities that charge tuition, printers, and caterers. If you do business with such businesses as these, keep this in mind.

Develop an Income Scenario

Now it's time for you to project an income scenario. Action Step 44 takes you through the process. Note that more than just sales are involved; you also need to project times of collection and other time lags so you can get a feel for the way cash will flow through your business. The action step winds up by asking you a pointed question: Now that you have seen your sales percentages, what **management strategies** will you develop to get more control of your business? You need to tackle that question *before* you open your doors.

management strategies
making directional decisions

Think about that as you read the following case study. It tells the story of how Laserian, Ltd., a flashy company in a glamorous growth industry, got into money trouble because its CEO was too busy to attend to cash management.

Jerry Fiske's Laserian, Ltd., a manufacturer of laser optics, was entering its second year of operation when it started to run out of money.

Jerry was an engineer and an inventor, and he had fooled around with lasers for twenty years before he got some backers together to found Laserian, Ltd. He knew lasers, and every instinct told him it was the hottest growth industry going. So when he solved one of the tricky problems in the industry, he knew he would become rich and famous.

The problem Jerry solved was the problem of light leakage. Big communications companies were experimenting with sending messages through glass fiber tubes, which are a lot more efficient for carrying information than metal wires. The messages traveled without a hitch as long as the tubes were straight, but whenever there was a bend in the tube, some of the light would continue on in a straight line, resulting in light leakage and a garbled message.

Jerry's solution was to coat the inside of the tube with a substance that would bounce the light into a graceful curve, and thus help it to glide around corners.

At the moment he ran short of cash, Jerry was developing a dozen applications of his discovery, and other Laserian engineer–inventors were designing a scanner that would read labels for the food industry. Nonetheless, his research and development people told him the company needed a **cash injection.**

"We're out of money, Jerry. What's the story?"

Jerry didn't know. So he put on his coat and tie and went to see Phil Brill, his banker.

cash injection
infusion of dollars into a business, usually at a critical point to help meet cyclical needs

First Visit

"Jerry," Phil said, shaking hands. "Glad you called. Long time no see."

Jerry handed Phil a profit and loss statement he had roughed out on the back of an envelope. Phil took the envelope, glanced at the figures, then looked at Jerry.

"How's the laser business, anyway?"

"Booming," Jerry said. "We've got orders pouring in for our scanner. Every food chain in the country wants one the day before yesterday. We're starting up production of a holographic camera—one that will take pictures of automobile tires to check for defects. The Air Force has sent six guys out to see us about signing a contract to work on a new cryptographic device. The numbers speak for themselves, Phil. We did three hundred thousand dollars in sales this month and had a profit of more than fifty-two thousand."

The banker looked at the numbers on the envelope:

> Sales: $300K
>
> Cost of Goods Sold: $172K
>
> Gross Profit: $128K
>
> Expenses: $76K
>
> Profit: $52K plus

"How much do you need?"

"Thirty thou should do it, Phil. Just for odds and ends until our receivables start pouring in." (Jerry is a person who can pick up key words and use them right away. *Receivables* was one of those words.)

"From the look of these numbers," Phil said, "I'd say you'd be good for it."

Jerry smiled. This was easy street. "I never argue about money," he said.

Later that week, he had a check for $30,000. He turned the check over to his manager and got back into the lab, where he was happy.

A month later, Laserian ran short of cash again.

Second Visit

"Sorry to bother you again, Phil," Jerry said. "But we need another green transfusion." Jerry was smiling. He had received money before, and he knew this was a piece of cake.

"How much this time?" the banker said.

"What about ninety grand?" Jerry asked.

"Sounds steep," Phil said. "What's your cash picture?"

Jerry smiled. "We're in terrific shape, Phil." He handed Phil a sheet of graph paper that contained a short column of numbers. "Take a look at this month."

FEB	
Sales	$320,000
Cost of Goods Sold	184,000
Gross Profit	136,000
Expenses	87,000
Profit	49,000

The banker studied the figures without saying anything.

"Feast your eyes, Phil. Sales are up over last month. The total profit for the last two months is over a hundred grand. If things keep up at this rate, we'll have five million dollars in sales by the end of the year. And that means a million in profits."

The banker looked up at Jerry. "What's the money for?" he asked.

"Plastic," Jerry said. "Everything we build is housed in plastic, and my purchasing guy found a real deal. That stuff's made with oil, you know, and if the world runs short of oil, we've got to have enough plastic to get us through."

"A sound point," Phil said.

"I'm in kind of a hurry, Phil. When can I get the check?"

"Can you have your accountant get me a completed profit and loss statement?" Phil asked. "And do something on **cash flow**?"

"Can do," Jerry said. "I'll get my people right on it."

"Let us see the numbers," Phil said. "I'll get back to you."

Walking out of the bank, Jerry was disappointed in the banker's conservative attitude. He thought briefly of changing banks, then swung his mind back to the excitement of lasers.

Back at the plant, he told his manager to do up a profit and loss statement and a cash flow projection, and then he got back to his inventing.

This time, it took the bank almost three weeks to approve the loan, and two loan officers came out to have a look at Laserian, Ltd. Apparently they liked what they saw, because the check came through, just in time.

The $90,000 lasted a couple of months, and then Jerry had to go back to the bank a third time.

Third Visit

"I'll bet you know why I'm here," Jerry said.

"You'd better tell me, just the same," Phil said.

This time, Jerry had brought along computerized **spreadsheets**. He unrolled them for the banker. "Look at those numbers, Phil! Feast your eyes. That's over a million in sales you're looking at! It's also over $220,000 in profits, counting next month. The sales are already on the books, and we're showing a backlog that will carry us for two more months."

The banker studied the spreadsheets [see Table 9.4]. He noticed that they covered only the first four months.

Phil was a banker. Numbers were his business; he'd seen thousands of spreadsheets, and he knew that fast growth could kill a company that wasn't ready for it. "How much do you need this time, Jerry?"

Jerry smiled. He thought he'd found a money tree. "Thirteen thousand looks like what we need, but I thought we could double that, just to be on the safe side." Jerry paused. "Let's say $30,000."

cash flow
the lifeblood of any business

spreadsheets
displays of critical accounting data

TABLE 9.4 Laserian Income Statement

	JAN	FEB	MAR	APR	TOTAL
Sales	300,000	320,000	360,000	380,000	1,360,000
Cost of Goods Sold	172,500	184,000	207,000	218,500	782,000
Gross Profit	127,500	136,000	153,000	161,500	578,000
Expenses					
Sales/Commissions	27,000	28,800	32,400	34,100	
Advertising/Promotion	1,500	1,600	1,800	1,900	
Travel	500	5,000	2,000	5,000	
Equipment rental	800	800	800	800	
Auto/Truck	1,300	1,300	1,300	1,300	
Repair/Maintenance	800	800	900	900	
Rent	12,000	12,000	12,000	12,000	
Supplies	1,500	1,600	1,800	1,900	
Telephone	4,000	4,400	4,900	5,300	
Utilities	1,200	1,200	1,200	1,200	
Insurance	1,700	1,700	1,700	1,700	
Legal/Accounting	2,500	2,500	2,500	2,500	
Dues/Subscriptions	250	400	400	400	
Salary, management	15,000	16,000	17,000	18,000	
Salary, staff	3,000	5,000	7,000	9,000	
Miscellaneous	1,000	1,100	1,100	1,200	
Interest on bank loan		1,900	1,900	1,900	
Payroll taxes	1,300	1,500	1,700	1,900	
Total Expenses	75,350	87,600	92,400	101,000	356,350
Net before Taxes	52,150	48,400	60,600	60,500	221,650
Tax Reserve	23,450	21,800	27,300	27,300	99,850
Net Profit after Taxes	28,700	26,600	33,300	33,200	121,800

"You're already into us for $120,000," the banker said. "Before you get any more, I'd like to discuss how we're getting the one-twenty back."

"Hey," Jerry said. "I'm good for it. Look at those numbers!"

The room was silent. For a long time, the banker didn't say anything. When he finally said something, it was no.

What Went Wrong?

Bankers don't like surprises. The banker's job is to protect bank depositors, and bankers all over the world worry about small firms that don't plan in advance. Jerry Fiske's banker did not feel that the bank could afford to underwrite Laserian's prosperity, which was based on uncontrolled growth, regardless of Laserian's **gross profit**.

Therefore, Jerry Fiske did not get the money he needed to sustain the rapid growth of his company. The company was out of control, and Jerry didn't see it even when the numbers were down on paper.

gross profit
net sales minus cost of goods sold

What could Jerry have done differently? If he had prepared a cash flow projection ahead of time, his shortfall would have been predicted—and he could have applied for one big loan instead of a series of smaller, haphazard loans. Table 9.5 shows what that ideal cash flow would look like with an adequate loan of $200,000 in place. Note that the bottom line in Table 9.5 is "Cash Flow for Month."

What you need to aim for—over and above paper profits—is positive cash flow. Enough money should be available for you to buy what you need in order to stay in business.

Now let's revise Table 9.5 by taking away Jerry's one-time loan of $200,000 and see why Jerry had to run to the banker so often. January's cash flow becomes negative ($170,800 − $200,000 = −$29,200). No wonder Jerry needed to borrow $30,000 in a hurry! This negative cash flow carries on through. If we assume that Jerry wasn't able to borrow any money at all, our revised cash flows for each month would look like this:

	JAN	FEB	MAR	APR
Cash on Hand at Start of Month	$ 10,000	$(29,200)	$(117,600)	$(132,900)
Cash Received/ Accounts Receivable	210,000	280,000	316,000	352,000
Bank Loans	—	—	—	—
Total Cash Available	220,000	250,800	198,400	219,100
Total Disbursements	249,200	368,400	331,300	371,200
Cash Flow for Month	$(29,200)	$(117,600)	$(132,900)	$(152,100)

If you're figuring along, you'll notice that Total Disbursements now differ from the Total Disbursements in Table 9.5. This is because there won't be loan payments of $7,500 in February, March, and April if there is no loan. Note also that in spreadsheets, a negative amount like − $29,000 is often shown in parentheses, as $(29,000).

Fortunately, Jerry bagged a few loans, but another quick revision of the cash flow shows why $30,000 in January and $90,000 in February weren't enough:

	JAN	FEB	MAR	APR
Cash on Hand at Start of Month	$ 10,000	$ 800	$ 2,400	$(12,900)
Cash Received/ Accounts Receivable	210,000	280,000	316,000	352,000
Bank Loans	30,000	90,000	—	—
Total Cash Available	250,000	370,800	318,400	339,100
Total Disbursements	249,200	368,400	331,300	371,200
Cash Flow for Month	$ 800	$ 2,400	$(12,900)	$(32,100)

TABLE 9.5   Ideal Laserian Statement of Cash Flow

	JAN	FEB	MAR	APR
Cash on Hand at Start of Month	10,000	170,800	74,900	52,100
Cash Received/Accounts Receivable	210,000	280,000	316,000	352,000
Three-Year Bank Loan	200,000			
Total Cash Available	420,000	450,800	390,900	404,100
Cash Disbursements				
Manufacturing Disbursements				
Packing, etc.	18,000	19,000	21,000	23,000
Material	123,000	224,000	172,000	198,000
Outside labor	44,000	49,000	53,000	57,800
Other Disbursements				
Sales/Commissions	14,000	27,000	28,800	32,400
Salary, management	12,000	12,800	13,600	14,400
Salary, staff	2,700	4,500	6,000	7,600
Payroll taxes	4,500	4,500	5,300	6,000
Advertising/Promotion	1,400	1,500	1,600	1,800
Travel	500	500	5,000	2,000
Auto/Truck	1,300	1,300	1,300	1,300
Equipment rental	2,400			2,400
Repair/Maintenance	800	800	900	900
Rent	12,000	12,000	12,000	12,000
Supplies	1,400	1,500	1,600	1,800
Telephone	2,500	4,000	4,400	4,900
Utilities	1,200	1,200	1,200	1,200
Insurance	4,000			
Legal/Accounting	2,500	2,500	2,500	2,500
Dues/Subscriptions		1,200		
Miscellaneous	1,000	1,100	1,100	1,200
Interest on bank loan		7,500	7,500	7,500
Total Disbursements	249,200	375,900	338,800	378,700
Cash Flow for Month	170,800	74,900	52,100	25,400

And remember, Laserian showed $121,800 of net profit after taxes during these four months.

The Moral of the Story

Although Laserian was profitable on paper (as shown in Table 9.4), every month that sales increased, accounts receivable (money owed the company but not yet paid) also increased. Because the company was expanding, the money that came in had to go for inventory. Past sales could not generate enough cash to support the growth. Without outside sources of cash, the company could not keep up.

Project your income and cash flow before you open your doors—for at least a year in advance. If your Business Plan and numerical projections are sound, your banker is likely to loan you the amount needed to cover any negative cash flow.

INCOME STATEMENT AND CASH FLOW PROJECTION

A projected income statement tells you when you're going to make a profit on paper. A cash flow projection tells you whether or not you can pay the bills and when you'll have to visit the banker. Both of these projections are essential to the survival of your business.

Projected Income Statement

Projecting your income is like projecting a moving picture of your business. If you're careful in how you prepare your numbers, that movie will be reasonably accurate. Action Step 45 leads you through this projection step by step. You already have a head start because you forecasted your sales in Action Step 44. A worksheet from the SBA (Table 9.6) will help you, too.

If you discover that you won't show a profit for two years, you're going to need a very good plan, a team of terrific investors, and an understanding banker. A case

TABLE 9.6 Projected Sales and Expenses for One Year

	Total	JAN	FEB	MAR	APR	MAY	JUN	JUL	AUG	SEP	OCT	NOV	DEC
A. Net Sales													
B. Cost of Goods Sold													
1. Raw Materials													
2. Direct Labor													
3. Manufacturing Overhead													
Indirect Labor													
Heat, Light, and Power													
Insurance and Taxes													
Depreciation													
C. Gross Margin (A − B)													
D. Selling and Administrative Expenses													
4. Salaries and Commissions													
5. Advertising Expenses													
6. Miscellaneous Expenses													
E. Net Operating Profit (C − D)													
F. Interest Expense													
G. Net Profit before Taxes (E − F)													
H. Estimated Income Tax													
I. Net Profit after Income Tax (G − H)													

Source: Small Business Administration, *Business Plan for Small Manufacturers*, SBA Management Aid 2.007 (Small Business Administration: Washington, D.C., 1981), 8.

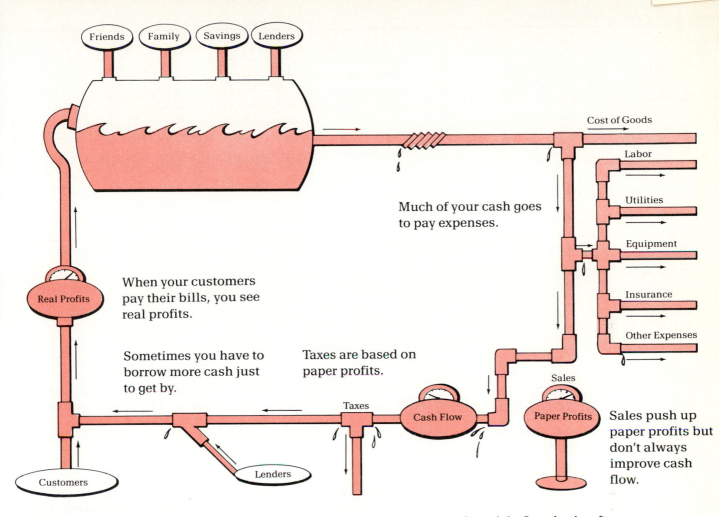

Friends   Family   Savings   Lenders

Cost of Goods

Labor

Utilities

Much of your cash goes
to pay expenses.

Equipment

Real Profits

When your customers
pay their bills, you see
real profits.

Insurance

Other Expenses

Sometimes you have to
borrow more cash just
to get by.

Taxes are based on
paper profits.

Sales

Taxes

Cash Flow

Paper Profits

Sales push up
paper profits but
don't always
improve cash
flow.

Lenders

Customers

FIGURE 9.2 This simple cash flow diagram shows the typical time lag between paper profits and the flow of real profits. Plan ahead for this lag.

study later in this chapter will suggest something you can do if your Business Plan forecasts losses for the first year or so of operation.

Cash Flow Projection

As Jerry Fiske's experience illustrates, an income statement doesn't tell the whole story. (Even a documentary movie is shot from only one angle at a time.) It's nice to watch paper profits, but you must be alert to what is happening to real cash. Figure 9.2 shows the typical pattern of cash flows.

Cash flow projection is a tool for helping you control money. Action Step 46 leads you through a monthly cash flow projection. An SBA worksheet, Table 9.7, will help you. When you have finished, show the results to an expert. Ask him or her if it looks accurate. It's better to know the truth now, while you're working on paper; paper truth is a lot easier on the pocketbook than real truth.

TABLE 9.7   Projected Cash Flow

	JAN	FEB	MAR	APR	MAY	JUN	JUL	AUG	SEP	OCT	NOV	DEC
1. Cash in Bank at Start of Month												
2. Petty Cash at Start of Month												
3. Total Cash (1 + 2)												
4. Expected Accounts Receivable												
5. Other Money Expected												
6. Total Receipts (4 + 5)												
7. Total Cash and Receipts (3 + 6)												
8. Disbursements (for month)												
9. Cash in Bank and Petty Cash at End of Month (7 − 8)*												

Source: Small Business Administration, *Business Plan for Small Manufacturers,* SBA Management Aid 2.007 (Small Business Administration: Washington, D.C., 1981), 9.

*This is your Total Cash balance for the start of the next month.

Break-Even Analysis

Knowing a few key numbers can help you avoid painful surprises. If you know your costs (variable and fixed) and your gross sales, you can use a couple of break-even formulas to tell you when you will start making money. Break-even analysis is useful at start-up time, when you have completed your income and expense projections, and when you are considering launching a new product or service.

A small manufacturing company was completing a plan for its second year of operation. Its first-year sales were $177,000, and a sales breakdown for the last three months of their first year looked like this:

October	$24,000
November	29,000
December	15,000
	$68,000

The owners took a look at the numbers and called in a consultant to help. The consultant gathered information from sales reps, owners, and customers and then projected that sales for the second year would be a whopping $562,000. The owners reacted with disbelief.

"You're crazy," they said. "That's more than three times what we did last year."

The consultant smiled. "Didn't you tell me you were going to add three new products?"

"Yes."

"And new reps in March, June, and September?"

"Yes, but—"

"And what about those big promotions you've got planned?"

"Well, sure, we've planned some promotions, but that doesn't get us anywhere near three times last year."

"All right," the accountant said. "Can you do $275,000?"

The owners got into a huddle. Based on the fourth quarter, they were sure they could stay even, and four times $68,000 (the fourth-quarter sales) was $272,000. They knew they had to do better than last year.

"Sure, no problem. We can do $272,000."

"All right," said the consultant, rolling out his break-even chart. "I've just projected $562,000 in sales for the year. To break even, you only need $275,000."

"Hey," the owners said, "we're projecting $90,000 the first quarter."

"I'm glad you're thinking my way," the consultant said. "Because if you don't believe you can reach a goal, you'll never get there." He paused, then said, "By the way, that $90,000 is three times what you did your first quarter last year!"

"Just tell us what to do," the owners said.

Based on a careful cash-flow analysis, the consultant determined that the company would need to borrow money. The owners knew their business—industry trends, product line, competitors, sales and promotion plans—but what banker would believe such growth? The key to getting the loan would be to convince the banker that the company could do better than break even. The consultant prepared a break-even chart on the $562,000 sales figure. [See Figure 9.3.] Note in the chart that after $280,000 in sales, the firm will have passed its break-even point and be making a profit.

The banker did grant them the loan, because he realized the company could pass the break-even point, and then some. The key, as usual in business, was a combination of numbers and human confidence.

PROJECTIONS HELP DECIDE YOUR BUSINESS FORM

Working with sales projections and cash flow numbers can help you decide the legal form your business takes. The three partners in the next case were smart. Numerical projections told them they would not make a profit for several months after they opened the doors. So they held onto their jobs and used the losses to offset their regular income.

Once they understood that their break-even point would not occur until the first eight months, they chose to form a subchapter S corporation—a legal form that gives you some protection while allowing you to write losses off on your personal income tax.

Herman, Terry, and Mitch were having some beers one night after a big win over the best team in their bowling league, and they started griping about their jobs.

"My boss hates my guts," Herman said. "I feed him great ideas and he just shoots them down. Boom!"

"Yeah," Terry said. "I came up with a boiler plate that would save my company 50K per annum, and they just smiled me out the door."

"Both of you should quit," Mitch said, "and go into the pizza business with me."

"Too risky," Terry said. "Statistics show you can lose your house and everything when you start too small."

"I worked in a restaurant once," Herman said, "back in high school. For the people who owned it, it was like coining money. Especially during the season."

"Does that mean you're interested?" Mitch asked. "Or are you just being your old late-fifties self?"

"I'm interested," Herman said, draining his glass, "and so is Terry the Numbers Man."

Terry worked in his company's accounting department. He knew the ins and outs of pro forma statements and cash flow management. "I think there's room in this town for an innovative pizza parlor," Terry said. "My brother-in-law's into one in Duluth, and I've seen the books for his second year. He's making a profit just on the write-off."

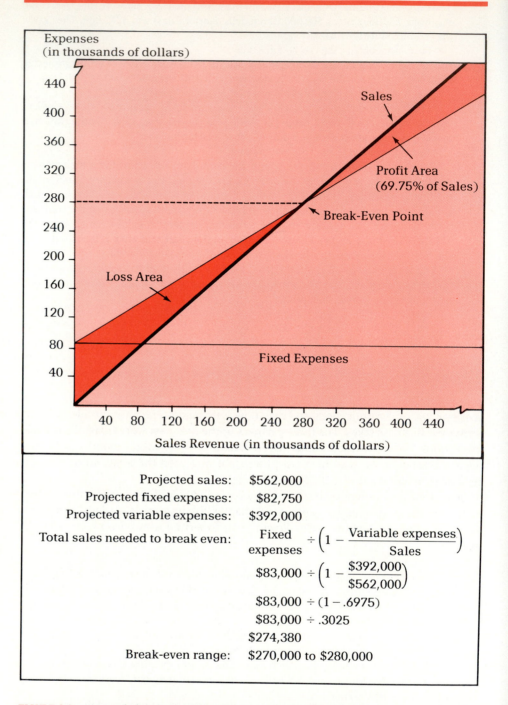

Projected sales: $562,000
Projected fixed expenses: $82,750
Projected variable expenses: $392,000

Total sales needed to break even:

$$\frac{\text{Fixed}}{\text{expenses}} \div \left(1 - \frac{\text{Variable expenses}}{\text{Sales}}\right)$$

$$\$83,000 \div \left(1 - \frac{\$392,000}{\$562,000}\right)$$

$$\$83,000 \div (1 - .6975)$$

$$\$83,000 \div .3025$$

$$\$274,380$$

Break-even range: $270,000 to $280,000

FIGURE 9.3   A simple break-even chart like this may be all it takes to convince your banker that a small loan now means big profits later.

"I like it," Herman said. "I like the sound of being my own boss."

"Herman Smith," Mitch said, "the Great Entrepreneur."

"My advice," Terry said, "is to hang on to your jobs while I pull some numbers together. They'll tell us a lot."

"Well, hurry it up," Herman said. "My boss is on my nerves."

Terry worked four weeks on the numbers. Herman and Mitch couldn't believe it took so long. Both of them had drawn up personal financial statements, and each was ready to put $20,000 into Three-Way Pizza—the name they'd settled on.

Then Terry came back with the bad news. He showed them the computer printouts. All Herman and Mitch could understand were the totals.

Three partners putting in $20,000 apiece would give them a total of $60,000 to start a business. Just the sound made them feel rich.

In addition, they would borrow $30,000 from family and friends, to give them $90,000 total start-up capital. A king's ransom.

"Expenses will eat us alive the first year," Terry explained, "even with the leased equipment. As you can see, the big expenses are salaries and supplies. We've got to have a first-rate hostess, and they don't come cheap. And if we go into the pizza delivery business—where the money is—we won't reach the break-even point for at least eight months."

"Lucky for me I didn't kiss off my boss," Herman said. He felt depressed.

"Ninety grand," Mitch said, "is just a drop in the bucket."

"There is a way," Terry said. "Let me talk to my buddy, John. He's a tax lawyer who specializes in small businesses."

"All lawyers are crooks," Herman said. "Why, I remember, back in Oshkosh, there was this lawyer who. . . ."

Terry and Mitch met with John, the tax lawyer, while Herman went bowling alone. The lawyer told them that Three-Way Pizza should be chartered as a **subchapter S corporation**. (The *S* stands for *small*.) All three partners were in a top tax bracket, and except for their families, they had few deductions. As founders of a subchapter S corporation, they could deduct early business losses on their personal income tax returns.

subchapter S corporation
a small, closely held corporation that is taxed like a sole proprietorship

"Hey," Herman said when he heard the good news, "this is better than my crummy tax shelter plan at work. Why didn't you guys think of this in the first place?"

Three-Way Pizza opened in February, three months before the start of the summer season. It lost money for seven and a half months, but then began making a small profit. The partners were better off at tax time, and by the second year, they were realizing a nice profit.

SHOEBOX ACCOUNTING: LEAVING A PAPER TRAIL

If you're the typical entrepreneur, you're not real big on details and you're very busy; nonetheless, you know it's important to keep good records. One solution for you is shoebox accounting—a simple procedure that will give your accountant or bookkeeper a chance to put together financial statements and prepare your tax returns. The idea of the system is to leave a paper trail.

How to Implement the System

Open a business checking account—even if you are just doing business under your own name. Deposit all business income into this account, making a note in the checkbook (or check register) as to the source of the deposit: for example, "Sat., 10/21, Swap Meet Sales." Write a check for each business expenditure, even if it's only one dollar. Enter in the checkbook what the check was for. Get a receipt and write the check number on the receipt. During the first few weeks, toss everything into a shoebox. When the shoebox begins to fill up, purchase an alphabetical file folder—one of those brown accordion jobs—and file all receipts there according to some system. (Ask your accountant or bookkeeper.)

If you must pay for items with cash, use a petty cash box or a bank bag. Get a receipt for every cash purchase, also, and clip all of the receipts for cash purchases together. When you have made enough cash purchases that it makes sense to write a business check to yourself—perhaps $10–$20 or so—write yourself a check, being careful to record the check number on each cash receipt.

Together, the business checkbook and the file folder are the paper trail you leave for your accountant or bookkeeper—and for the IRS. This trail could save your neck in an IRS audit. The system is a step up from the "pocket" system—that is, in one pocket and out the other—and only a stopgap until you move into a one-write bookkeeping system, which is explained in Appendix A.

SUMMARY

Not surprisingly, many entrepreneurs find to difficult to project numbers for their business. There are several explanations for this:

> They're action people who are in a hurry; they don't think they have time to sit down and *think*.
>
> They're creative; their strengths are greater in the innovation area than in the justification area.
>
> They tend to think in visual terms, rather than in terms of numbers or words.

Nonetheless, business is a numbers game, and in spite of the entrepreneur's feelings about numbers and projections, survival in the marketplace depends upon having the right numbers in the right color of ink. This chapter helps you get that kind of numbers down on paper.

The idea in projecting numbers is to make them as realistic as possible. You need to relate each projection to your specific business and to industry standards, and then to *document* them (tell where they came from) in your Business Plan. The case studies and the examples in this chapter will help you make your projections believable to your banker as well as to yourself.

That is the key. Your numbers may seem reasonable to you, but you must make them seem reasonable to others as well. You make them believable by keeping them realistic and by documenting them properly.

THINK POINTS FOR SUCCESS

◀ It's cheaper to make mistakes on a spreadsheet before you go into business.

◀ When you work out numbers for your Business Plan, hit the return-on-investment section with underlines.

◀ When you visit your banker to ask for money, make sure you know how much you're going to need for the long run.

◀ Projecting will help you control the variables of your business—numbers, employees, promotion mix, product mix, and the peaks and valleys of seasonality.

◀ At the very *least,* leave a "shoebox" paper trail of your business dealings so that a professional accountant or bookkeeper can bail you out.

REFERENCES

Bank of America Marketing Publications Department. *Bookstores.* Small Business Reporter Series. San Francisco: Bank of America, 1979. [The B of A SBR series has several excellent booklets that contain information on ratios and other hard-to-find items. Most B of A branches have booklets on hand, or you can write SBR Series, Bank of America, Department 3120, P.O. Box 37000, San Francisco, CA 94137.]

Business Plan for Retailers. Washington, D.C.: Small Business Administration, 1981.

Business Plan for Small Manufacturers. Washington, D.C.: Small Business Administration, 1981.

Milling, Bryan E. *Cash-Flow Problem-Solver.* Radnor, Pa.: Chilton Book Co., 1981.

Purcell, W. R. *Understanding a Company's Finances: A Graphic Approach.* Boston: Houghton Mifflin, Co., 1981.

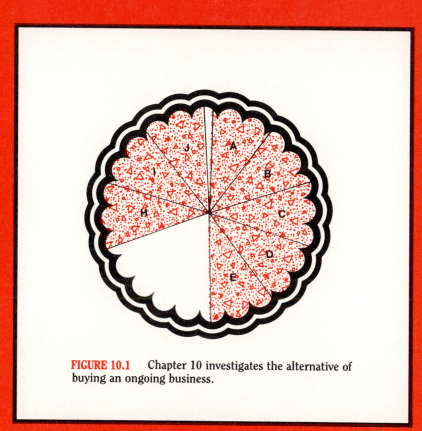

FIGURE 10.1 Chapter 10 investigates the alternative of buying an ongoing business.

10

Buying a Business

LEARNING OBJECTIVES

■ To grow in your understanding of the big world of small business. ■ To recognize a dishonest seller. ■ To discover the secrets of business-opportunity brokers. ■ To evaluate objectively businesses that are for sale. ■ To understand the pros and cons of purchasing an ongoing business. ■ To assess the market value of an ongoing business. ■ To sense when you need professional help. ■ To assess the market value of goodwill. ■ To decide whether it is better for you to buy an ongoing business or to begin from scratch.

In this chapter, you'll learn some ways to evaluate businesses that are up for sale. Although we focus on ongoing, independent operations, many of the tactics are the same for evaluating franchise opportunities. We'll discuss franchising more specifically in chapter 15.

When you buy an ongoing business you're buying an income stream. You may also be buying inventory, a location, goodwill, and an agreement that the seller will not compete with you. When you buy a franchise, you're primarily buying the right to use a name. In addition, you may also be buying a training program, a Business Plan, advertising assistance, lease negotiation assistance, and purchasing advantages.

You should explore businesses for sale whether you're serious about buying or not. By now, you're far enough along on your quest to sense the atmosphere of the marketplace. Talking to sellers is just one more step in your education in entrepreneurship.

So have fun, but leave your checkbook at home.

WHY BUY AN ONGOING BUSINESS

The overwhelming reason for buying an ongoing business is *money*, primarily the income stream. If you do your research and strike a good deal, you can start making money the day you take over an ongoing business. Since most start-ups must plug along for months (even years) before showing a profit, it's smart to consider this doorway to business ownership.

If you find a "hungry seller," you should be able to negotiate good terms. You might get into the business for very little cash up front, and you might also get a good deal on the fixtures and equipment. (See Figure 10.2.)

How to Buy and How Not to Buy

Smart buyers scrutinize everything about a business with microscope, geiger counter, computer analysis, clipboard, and sage advice from business gurus. They do not plunge into a business for emotional reasons. For example, you may have eaten lunch around the corner at Millie's Cafeteria with your pals for years, and when the place goes up for sale, nostalgia may make you want to write out a check for it on the spot. That would be a wrong reason to buy. *Don't* buy a business that way.

Every business in the country is for sale sometime. Deals are like planes. If you miss one, another one will be along soon.

Good buys are always available to the informed and careful buyer, but they may be difficult to discover. Seeking the right business to buy is much like an employment search: the best deals are seldom advertised. In contrast, the worst business opportunities are advertised widely, usually in the classified sections of newspapers. When you see several ads for a particular type of business, you know where the unhappy businesspeople are.

Running your own ad can be a good idea, however. A man ran this ad in the business section (not the classifieds) of a large-circulation Midwestern newspaper:

> Sold out at 30. Now I'm tired of retirement and ready to start again. Want to buy business with over 1 million dollars in annual sales. Write me at Box XXXX. H. G.

H. G. received more than one hundred replies and he says that reading the proposals was one of the most educational and entertaining experiences he's ever had. Five of them looked like good deals, but only one fit his talents and interests. After three

FIGURE 10.2   Four reasons to consider buying an ongoing business.

months of investigation, he decided he would rather start his next venture from scratch. (The firm he almost bought was a beer distributorship whose supplier went out of business the following year. Perhaps the seller knew something.)

Getting the Word Out

Once you're ready to look for a business to buy, you'll need to learn what's for sale. These tips will help you do that:

1. Spread the word that you are a potential buyer.
2. Contact everyone you can in your chosen industry—manufacturers, resellers, agents, dealers, trade associations, and so on; let them know you are looking.
3. Ask your network of bankers, attorneys, CPAs, and community leaders to help you in your search.
4. Advertise your needs in trade journals.
5. Send letters of inquiry to potential sellers. (See Action Step 47.)
6. Knock on doors.
7. Check with business-opportunities brokers.
8. Talk with firms that deal in mergers and acquisitions.
9. Don't allow yourself to be rushed; time is your ally, and the deals will get better.

Action Step 47 will help you get the word out. It should be real interesting to read the letters you receive in response to your form letter.

INVESTIGATE THE BUSINESS FROM THE OUTSIDE

Once you've found a business that looks promising, check it out by playing marketplace detective. This section will suggest some techniques that will make you feel like a super spy. After checking it out from the outside, you'll be ready to move inside, to check the books and talk to the owner and attempt to learn the real reasons he or she is selling. But the first step is to get your telescope and your telephoto camera and gather as much information as you can from the exterior. Unfortunately, Ben and Sally Raymundo didn't do this, and they learned about fraud the hard way.

A Horror Story from the Suburbs

Ben and Sally Raymundo bought a women's sportswear store in a thriving community about two miles from a regional shopping mall. They learned too late that the seller had a more profitable store in another part of the county and that she had used that store's records to misrepresent the store they bought. Here are the particulars:

1. The seller moved the cash registers from the higher-volume store to the store she wanted to sell so that the store's sales were greatly inflated.
2. The price was fixed at inventory plus $10,000 for goodwill. This seemed a bargain for a store whose cash register records showed it was grossing $300,000 per year at a 40% average gross margin.

ACTION STEP 47

Prepare a letter of inquiry.

Write a form letter of inquiry and send it to three to five firms that you may be interested in buying. Keep it open-ended; let them make the disclosures.

It's best to learn of businesses being for sale by networking, but you can find some of the most eager sellers by their advertising in the newspaper classified section.

Leave your checkbook right where it is for now. This action step will cost you practically nothing. The goal is to learn what's out there and how sellers talk about their businesses.

3. Ben and Sally paid full wholesale value ($60,000) for goods that had been shipped there from the other store. The goods were already shop-worn and out of date and eventually had to be marked down to less than $20,000.

4. Ben and Sally assumed the remainder of an iron-clad lease at $5,000 per month, and the landlord made them sign a personal guarantee that pledged their home as security on the lease.

5. The location proved to be dead foot-traffic location in a marginally successful center.

Fortunately Ben had kept his regular job. Sally worked at selling off the unwanted inventory and replaced it with more salable stock. They spent another $50,000 for advertising during the twelve months they stayed in business. It was another year before the landlord found a new tenant and Ben and Sally could get out of the lease.

Learn from Others' Mistakes

What could Ben and Sally have done to avoid this fiasco? Many things. They could have asked the mall merchants how well the shopping center was doing. They could have spent some time observing the store and the shopping mall before they committed. They could have insisted that Sally be allowed to work in the store prior to or during the escrow period, with a clause that would have allowed them to bail out.

Ben and Sally were honest, hard-working people who took the seller at face value. This was a huge mistake. A talk with suppliers might have uncovered the seller's fraud. They are now suing, and the CPA and attorney they have hired could have helped them before they purchased the business. It's only going to get more expensive for them, and their chance of recovery is slim.

Some sellers don't count the value of their own time as a cost of doing business. This makes the firm show an inflated return on investment (ROI). Let's say such a firm earns $60,000 per year and has an inventory of $100,000. This could be a bad buy if the seller, his spouse, and their two children work a total of 200 hours per week and if a $100,000 investment could earn 10% or more per year in high-yield bonds.

Look at each deal from the viewpoint of what it would cost to hire a competent manager and help at market wage rates. In this case, let's suppose you had to pay $30,000 a year for a manager, $20,000 a year for an assistant, and $20,000 a year for two hourly employees. You would have spent $70,000 and lost the opportunity to earn another $10,000 on your investment. Yes, this would be a "no-brainer," but a lot of businesses are bought with even less going for them.

It's time now to go out and investigate a business on your own. Remember what you've learned from Ben and Sally's bad experience, and take along your new eyes and your camera. You'll be surprised how much there is to see. Action Step 48 tells you how to do it.

Know when You Need Outside Help

We've already discussed the need for a team of small business gurus to help you realize your dream of small business ownership. When you evaluate a small business for purchase, however, you may need a special kind of outside help. If you have any lingering doubts about the business you are researching, you may need the perspective of someone who is more objective than one of your team players. If you're not

---

ACTION STEP 48

Study a business from the outside.

Let's say you've got your eye on a business you think is a real money machine. What can you do to find out more about it without tipping your hand and driving up the asking price?

1. Make sure the business fits into the framework of your industry overview. You want a business that's in the sunrise phase, not the sunset phase, of the life cycle.

2. Diagram the area. What's the location and how does the area fit into the city/county planning for the future? What is the life-cycle stage of the community? Where is the traffic flow? Is there good access? How far will your TC have to walk? Is parking adequate? Is the parking lot a drop-off point for car poolers?

3. Take some photographs of the exterior. Analyze them carefully. Is the building in good repair? What are the customers wearing, driving, and buying? What can you deduce about their lifestyle? Take photographs on different days and at different times of day.

4. Ask around. Interview the neighbors and the customers. What do the neighbors know about the business? Will the neighbors help draw target customers to your business?

Be up front with the seller's customers, since they may soon be your customers. What do they like about the store? Is the service good? What changes would they recommend? What services or products would they like to see added? Where else do they go for similar products or services?

5. Check out future competition. Do you want to be close to competitors (like Restaurant Row, Mile of Cars, and other such successful business areas), or do you want to be miles away? Could a competitor move in next door the day after you move in?

Studying the business from the outside will tell you if you should go inside and probe more deeply.

the Sherlock Holmes type yourself, hire someone who is. Your dream may be shattered by this kind of investigation, but you'll save money in the long run.

Georgia Webster had some doubts about the business she and her husband were considering. See what you can learn from her experiences.

I'd worked for a large ad agency in New York for twelve years before I gave it up and moved west, to the Bay Area. I couldn't believe it—no snow, no grey-black winter slush, no icicles in April—and I soon became a sports freak, to make up for all the years I'd spent indoors, I guess. I took up tennis, then racquetball, then biking, then volleyball, then hiking.

I met Fred on the tennis court. It was love at first sight, for both of us, and we were married six months later. Fred is real creative, and he'd always wanted to have a business of his own. Since we both loved sports, we decided to look around for a sporting goods store to buy.

We found the perfect store by networking our sports-minded friends. It was called The Sports Factory, and it was located a block from a complex of tennis courts, three blocks from a new racquetball club, and a quarter-mile from a park where volleyball tournaments are held every other month.

A friend of ours who's an accountant checked over the books. He said they looked perfect. "Great P and L," he said, "and accounting ratios you wouldn't believe for this business. If you get the right terms, you could clear fifty G's every quarter, and *that's* only the beginning. This guy doesn't even advertise."

We learned that the owner wanted to sell the store because he was tired of it—the long hours, being tied down, and so on. He'd been doing that for a dozen years and he wanted to start enjoying life.

But I'm from New York, and I wasn't so sure. I sensed we needed help—some sort of Sam Spade of the business world—but Fred was in a hurry to close the deal.

"This is our golden opportunity, Georgie," he kept saying, "a real opportunity. We'd never find such a good deal again."

I knew Fred was unhappy in his job, but half the money we were going to invest was mine, and I felt something was not quite right. Frankly, the owner of The Sports Factory didn't look all that tired to me.

So I asked around—networking again—and I located a community college professor who knows a lot about small business. His name is Harry Henkel, and he's written a book about going into small business. I called him, and he listened real patiently when I told him our story. Then we made an appointment to talk some more. After fifteen minutes he told me he'd be glad to check things out for us for a small fee. I told him to go ahead, but I didn't tell Fred about it.

Two days later, my marketplace detective called and said he had some news.

"Oh?" I said. "So soon?"

"Yes. Do you remember seeing a bulldozer working across the street from The Sports Factory?"

"No, I don't. *What* bulldozer?"

"It started grading last week. Right across the street."

"We were just there Sunday," I told him, "and we didn't notice anything like that."

"Well," he said, "I talked to the driver on his lunch break. It seems a developer is putting in a seven-store complex, and one of the stores is going to be a discount sporting goods store." He paused.

"Oh, no," I said. "Are you sure?"

| **chain**
| two or more stores operating
| under the same name

He explained that the store going in was part of a monster chain. I could see that we would have a hard time competing with them. I asked him if the owner knew, and if maybe that's why he's so "tired."

"Yes," Harry said, "I double-checked at the city planning office, where building permits are issued," and he paused again.

I was having trouble catching my breath. "Could I get this in writing," I asked, "so that I can show my husband? He likes everything documented."

Harry chuckled. "No problem," he said. "I'll get it in the mail tomorrow. Let me know what you decide, okay?"

"Don't worry," I said. "And thank you. Thank you very much."

This marketplace detective work cost us $475, but it saved us thousands of dollars and years of heartache. Armed with what we learned through that experience, we examined almost a hundred businesses before we found the right one for us. It pays to investigate.

Georgia and Fred Webster came very close to buying the wrong business. The outsider's perspective helped them avoid making a very terrible mistake. Now it's time to get some inside perspectives.

INVESTIGATE THE BUSINESS FROM THE INSIDE

Once you've learned all you can from the outside, it's time to cross the threshold for a look at the interior. This is an important, time-consuming process, and it's an important milestone in your quest.

There are two ways to get inside the business: you can either contact the owner yourself, or you can get assistance from a business-opportunity broker. We recommend that you use a broker, because brokers have access to a lot of listings. You can locate them in the yellow pages under *Real Estate* or *Business Brokers* and in the newspaper classifieds.

Call some brokers to learn if they have any listings in your area of interest. If so, check out the ones that appear interesting. Be prepared for disappointment. You will probably look at a great many businesses before you find anything close to your requirements. Nevertheless, you will learn a lot from the experience.

Dealing with Brokers

Business-opportunity brokers are active in most communities and they often play an important role in matching up sellers with buyers. Their level of competency ranges from specialists who know as much about fast-food franchises as McDonald's, Inc., to part-timers who know so little about business that they will only waste your time. A good broker can save you time and be very helpful in playing a third-party role in negotiations.

A broker has a fiduciary responsibility to represent the seller and is not paid unless he or she sells something. Typically, the broker's commission is around 10%, but it's less on bigger deals, and everything is open to negotiation.

Some sellers list with brokers because they do not want it generally known (to their customers, employees, competitors) that they want to sell their business. Most sellers who list with brokers, however, do so out of desperation because they've already tried to sell their business to everyone they know. Probably nine out of ten fall into this category.

Spending time with a skilled broker can be a fascinating educational experience. If you want a particular type of business and are able to examine a half-dozen that are on the market, you will probably end up with a better grasp of the business than the owners. Network your business contacts to locate a competent broker. Ask brokers for referrals from their former clients. Quiz their business knowledge. (Can they explain a cash-flow forecast, an earn-out, the bulk sales law?) And as we've said so many times before, leave your checkbook at home. Don't let anyone rush you.

business-opportunity broker
a real estate broker who specializes in representing people who want to sell businesses

How to Look at the Inside of a Business

Once you have gotten your foot in the door and established yourself as a potential buyer, you will be able to study the inner workings of the business. Take full advantage of this opportunity.

Study the Financial History.   What you need to learn from the financial history is where the money comes from and where it goes. Ask to see all financial records, for at least five years back if they're available, and take your time studying them. If you don't understand financial records, hire someone who does. Your aim in buying an ongoing business is to step into an income stream. The financial records give a picture of that stream.

Look at the history of cash flow, profit and loss, and accounts receivable. If the seller has a stack of accounts receivable a foot high, remember that:

> After three months, the value of a current accounts dollar will have shrunk to 90 cents;
>
> after six months, it will be worth 50 cents;
>
> after a year, it will be worth 30 cents.

Review every receipt you can find. If a tavern owner tells you he sells 30–40 kegs of beer per week, ask to see the receipts from the suppliers. If none is offered, ask permission to contact the suppliers for records of shipment. Make him prove to you what he has bought from suppliers. You can then accurately measure sales. If the seller won't cooperate, run—don't walk—away; he's hiding something. You can use this technique with any firm that is buying and marking up material or merchandise.

Evaluate closely any personal expenses that are being charged to the business. (Your CPA will help you determine a course of action that will keep you out of trouble.) This allows you to get a clearer picture of the firm's true profits.

It's also a good idea to look at canceled checks, income tax returns (probably for the last five years), and the amount of salary the seller has been paying himself. If your seller was stingy with his own salary, decide whether you could live on that amount.

Tip: You can use the seller's accounts receivable as a point for negotiation, but don't take over the job of collecting them.

Compare What Your Money Could Do Elsewhere.   How much money would you be putting into the business? How long would it take you to make it back? Have you figured in your time?

Let's say you would need to put $50,000 into this business, and that the business will give you a 33.3% return, which is full payback in three years. Are there other investments you could make that would yield the same amount on your $50,000?

If you will be working in the business, you need to add in the cost of your time; that's $25,000 per year (your present salary) over the three-year period, or $75,000 (assuming no raises). In three years, the business would need to return $125,000 after expenses and taxes in order to cover the risks involved with your $50,000 investment and to compensate you for the loss of $25,000 in annual salary.

tangible assets
things you can see and touch

Evaluate the Tangible Assets.   If the numbers look good, move on to assess the value of everything you can touch, specifically the real estate, the equipment and fixtures, and the inventory.

1. **Real Estate**   Get an outside, professional appraisal of the building and the land.

2. **Equipment and Fixtures**   Remember, this stuff is used. You can get a good idea of current market values by asking equipment dealers and reading the want ads. Scour your area for the best deals, because you don't want to tie up too much capital in equipment that's outmoded or about to come apart. Suppliers have lots of leads on used equipment, so check with them. If you're not an expert in the equipment field, get help from someone who is.

3. **Inventory**   Count the inventory yourself, and make sure the boxes are packed with what you think they are. Make certain you specify the exact contents of shelves and cabinets in the purchase agreement. Don't get careless and write in something vague like "All shelves are to be filled"; specify what goes on the shelves.

   Once you've made your count, contact suppliers to learn the current prices.

   If you find merchandise that is damaged, out-of-date, out-of-style, soiled, worn, or not ready to sell as is, don't pay full price for it. *Negotiate.* This is sacrifice merchandise and it should have a sacrifice price tag.

inventory
items carried in stock

Talk to Insiders.   There's no substitute for inside information. Every detective takes it seriously.

Suppliers   Will suppliers agree to keep supplying you? Are there past difficulties between seller and supplier that you would inherit as the new owner? Remember, you're dependent on your suppliers.

Employees   Identify the key employees early, and talk to the credit manager. In small business, success can rest on the shoulders of one or two persons, and you don't want them to walk out the day you sign the papers and present the seller with a fat check.

Competitors   Identify the major competitors and interview them to learn what goes on from their perspective. Expect some bias, but watch for a pattern to develop. (Chapter 5 tells how to identify the competitors; refer to that discussion if you need to.)

Get a Noncompetition Covenant.   Once you buy a business, you don't want the seller to set up the same kind of business across the street. Customers are hard to come by, and you don't want to pay for them and have them spirited away by a cagey seller. So get an agreement, in writing, that the seller will not set up in competition with you—or work for a competitor, or help a friend or relative set up a competitive business—for the next five years. You may need a lawyer to help you.

Whether you get a lawyer or do it yourself, be sure to specify the exact amount you're paying for the noncompetition covenant. That way, the IRS will allow you to deduct it against ordinary income over the life of the covenant.

Analyze the Seller's Motives.   People have all kinds of reasons for selling their business. Some of these reasons favor the buyer, and others favor the seller. Here are some reasons for selling that can favor the buyer:

1. retirement, ill health
2. too busy to manage—seller has other investments
3. divorce, family problems
4. disgruntled partners
5. expanded too fast—out of cash
6. poor management
7. burned out, lost interest

These reasons for selling will favor the seller (Buyer beware.):

1. local economy in a decline
2. specific industry declining
3. intense competition
4. high insurance costs
5. increasing litigation
6. skyrocketing rents
7. technological obsolescence
8. problems with suppliers
9. high-crime-rate location
10. lease not being renewed
11. location in a decline

Examine the Asking Price.   Many sellers view selling their firms as they would view selling their children; that is, they are emotionally attached to the business and they overvalue its worth. Pride also plays a role; they might want to tell their friends that they started from scratch and sold out for a million. If you run into irrational and emotional obstacles, walk away or counter with unreasonable terms—such as $100 down and 10% of the net profits for the next four years, limit one million dollars.

Some industries have rule-of-thumb bench marks for pricing. For example, a service firm might be priced at 6–12 months its total revenue. Such pricing formulas are often unwise. The only formula that makes sense is the return on your investment minus the value of your management time.

$$\text{R.O.I.} - (\text{Hours spent} \times \text{Value of your time per hour})$$

If you can earn 10% without sweating on high-grade bonds, you should earn at least a 30% return on a business that will make you sweat.

price/earnings ratio
a measure of the value of a share of common stock; the ratio of its market price to its earnings per share

It can be useful to consult the newspaper financial pages to learn the **price to earnings ratios** of publicly traded firms. Firms whose P/E ratios are low (the stock price is less than 10 times its earnings) are not regarded as growth opportunities by sophisticated investors. Firms with above-average P/E ratios (price is more than 25 times its earnings) are regarded as having above-average growth potential. Thus, you should be willing to pay a higher price for a firm with above-average growth potential than for one that is declining. In fact, you should not buy a declining business unless you think you can either purchase it very inexpensively and turn it around or dispose of its assets at a profit.

goodwill
an invisible commodity used by sellers to increase the asking price for a business

ill will
all the negative feelings about a business; the opposite of goodwill

Negotiate the Value of Goodwill.   If the firm has a strong customer base with deeply ingrained purchasing habits, this has value. It takes a while for any start-up to build a client base, and the wait for profitability can be costly.

Some firms have built up a great deal of ill will—customers who have vowed never to trade with them again. A large proportion of the businesses on the market have this problem. If the amount of ill will is great, the business will have little value; it may be that *any* price would be too high.

A smart seller will ask you to pay something for goodwill. Thus you'll need to play detective and find out *how much* goodwill there is and *where* it is. For example, consider the seller who has extended credit loosely. Customers are responding, but there's no cash in the bank. If you were to continue that policy and keep granting easy credit, you could be in the red in a couple of months. Or maybe the seller is one of those very special people who is loved by everyone and will take the goodwill with him—like a halo—when he walks out the door.

So negotiate.

Let's say the asking price for the business you'd like to buy is $100,000 and that its tangible assets (equipment, inventory, and so on) are worth $50,000. In other words, the seller is trying to charge you $50,000 for goodwill. Before you negotiate, do these things:

1. Compare the goodwill you're being asked to buy to the goodwill of a similar business on the market.
2. Figure out how long it would take you to pay that amount. Remember, goodwill is intangible; you'll be unhappy if it takes you years to pay for it. Even the smilingest goodwill comes out of profit.
3. Estimate how much you could make if you invested that $50,000 in T-bills.

This gives you a context in which to judge the seller's assessment of the value of goodwill, and you can use the hard data you have generated to negotiate a realistic— and no doubt, more favorable—price.

Learn if Bulk Sales Escrow Is Needed.   You need to know if any inventory you would buy is tied up by creditors. If it is, the instrument you'll use to cut those strings is a bulk sales transfer, a process that will transfer the goods from the seller to you through a qualified third party. In most states, bulk sales transfer is specified under a series of regulations known as the Uniform Commercial Code.

If there are no claims by creditors, the transfer of inventory should go smoothly. If there are claims, you'll want to be protected by law. Either consult an attorney who has experience in making bulk sales transfers, or get an **escrow** company to act as the neutral party in the transfer. The quickest way to find an escrow company is to look in the yellow pages under *escrow*. A *better* way is to ask your banker or CPA to recommend one. Try to find one that specializes in bulk sales escrows.

(*Escrow* comes from *escroe*, Old French for "parchment," "deed," or "scroll." The distant Indo-European root is *skeru-*, which means "to cut"—and you'll need an expert to help you cut off creditors who have strings attached. For a look at the jungle of documents you can encounter in buying a business, read pages 169–221 of *Buying and Selling Business Opportunities* by Wilfred E. Tetreault.)

bulk sales escrow
an examination process intended to protect buyers from unknown liabilities

escrow company
a neutral third party that holds deposits and deeds until all agreed upon conditions are met

An Earn-Out Success Story

Sam Wilson had held several key executive positions in large manufacturing firms after receiving his MBA in the 1950s. His last position was as president of a medium-size U.S. firm with branch offices throughout the Free World. Sam got squeezed out when a large conglomerate purchased the firm and moved the headquarters to London.

After doing some free-lance management consulting, Sam arranged to purchase an executive search firm that specialized in finding engineering talent in the aerospace industry. Buying the business seemed like a good idea to Sam because the business had been profitable for more than twenty years. The key personnel agreed to stay with the firm. It had loyal customers, a solid reputation, and Sam knew it would take him years to build a similar business from scratch, even though he understood the business.

He purchased the business for no cash down and agreed to pay off the entire purchase price from the earnings over the next five years. [This is called an **earn out**.] The seller was an older man who had known of Sam's reputation as a winner. Sam was one of the few prospective buyers who were willing to pay full price for the business and seemed qualified to continue the growth of the firm. The business did prosper, but its growth was somewhat limited to what could be achieved while keeping a watchful eye on cash flow. Sam had to pay the salaries long before he received payment from clients.

earn out
the seller agrees to accept (a portion of) his payment for the business from the business's future earnings

Sam worked in the firm one to two days a week, and monitored activities by daily reports. He had plenty of time to run another business, but it would have to be a type of business whose cash flow is "front-loaded," rather than "back-loaded" like the search firm. Front-loaded businesses are those whose customers pay cash up front before the product or service is delivered. They include such businesses as hotels, bed and breakfast inns, bridal shops, custom printers, magazine publishers, and so on.

Sam chose to purchase a travel agency. He found a medium-size firm that had five excellent travel agents but was only slightly profitable. He purchased it for a low six-digit figure on a no-money-down, earn-out basis.

The travel agency cash flow was positive, and Sam saw some opportunities to make the firm more profitable. Observing that many travel agencies are run by "hobbyists" who know little about marketing and management, he refocused the agency efforts on exotic cruises and up-scale vacation adventures. The agency was located in a very affluent area, and yet none of the competitors were specializing like this. He also knew that volume is the key to profit; some of the large chain agencies were earning 17% commissions on trips that paid small firms only 10%. Sam is now in the process of purchasing four more good agencies on an earn-out basis so that he can take advantage of the larger commissions.

Buying a business on an earn-out basis is an option only if the seller has great confidence in the buyer's skills and knowledge of the business. Thus the burden of convincing the seller to agree to such terms is on the buyer. It's necessary to show the seller that the business will continue to show a profit.

Sam conducted both transactions described in the case study by developing a detailed Business Plan that demonstrated to the sellers that he was an expert—and his track record and references backed him up.

Few people are able to manage more than one business at a time. Sam can, however, because he knows how to set up controls. He stays in daily contact with his key people, and perhaps most importantly, he spends a lot of time talking to customers—which ensures him of the highest level of feedback.

Too many people purchase businesses emotionally. They buy a business as if it were a home, a car, or a suit. They are drawn to businesses that they think will enhance their image—that will impress their friends and relatives. Physically attractive businesses are often the worst investments, because "image-conscious" buyers have bid the price up to an unreasonable figure. The "ugly" business or the "invisible business" often provides the best return on time and investment.

Many people view buying a business as buying a *job;* they look at it as providing them with "employment." (Sam's experience demonstrates that this is a narrow view.) Such people lack the experience to make a good choice, and they often invest their life savings in ventures that demand 70–100 hours per week to run and pay them less than their forty-hour-week jobs did.

Does the thought of walking into someone's business for the purpose of "snooping" around, looking at the books, and asking the owner probing questions fill you with anxiety and make you nervous? It shouldn't. Sellers expect prospective buyers to do those things, and you are seriously looking for a business to buy. What's more, you are now *prepared* to investigate a business close up—and to enjoy it. You are ready for Action Step 49.

THE DECISION TO BUY

Even if you think you're ready to make your decision, don't do it—not yet. Read the checklist in Box 10.1 first. It reminds you of thirty-three important details you might have overlooked. Even if you *know* you've found your dream business, complete this checklist before you sign the papers.

BOX 10.1   Final Checklist

_____ How long do you plan to own this business?
_____ How old is this business? Can you sketch its history?
_____ Is this business in the embryonic stage, the growth stage, the mature stage, or the decline stage?
_____ Has your accountant reviewed the books and made a sales projection for you?
_____ How long will it take for this business to show a *complete* recovery on your investment?
_____ What reasons does the owner give for selling?
_____ Will the owner let you see bank deposit records? (If not, why not?)
_____ Have you calculated utility costs for the first 3–5 years?
_____ What does a review of tax records tell you?
_____ How complete is the insurance coverage?
_____ How old are receivables? (Remember, age decreases their value.)
_____ What is the seller paying himself? Is it low, or high?
_____ Have you interviewed your prospective landlord?
_____ What happens when a new tenant takes over the lease?
_____ Have you made spot checks on the currency of the customer list?
_____ Who are your top 20 customers? Your top 50?
_____ Is the seller locked into 1–3 major customers who control the business?
_____ Are you buying inventory? What is seller asking?
_____ Have you checked the value of the inventory with vendors?
_____ Have you checked the value of the equipment against the price of used equipment from another source?
_____ Who does your seller owe money to?
_____ Has your attorney checked for liens on the seller's equipment?
_____ Do you have maintenance contracts on the equipment you're buying?
_____ Has your attorney or escrow company gone through bulk sales escrow?
_____ Have you made certain that:
      _____ you're getting all brand names, logos, trademarks, etc., that you need?
      _____ the seller has signed a noncompetition covenant?
      _____ the key lines of supply will stay intact when you take over?
      _____ the key employees will stay?
      _____ the seller isn't leaving because of stiff competition?
      _____ you aren't paying for goodwill but taking delivery on ill will?
      _____ you're getting the best terms possible?
      _____ you're buying an income stream?

ACTION STEP 49

Study a business inside out.

Looking at a business from the inside enables you to determine its real worth and to see what it would be like to own it. Make an appointment—or have a business-opportunity broker arrange it—to take a serious inside look at the business you think you want to buy. Before you go, review everything we've explained in this section and write down a list of things you hope to learn while you're there. Don't allow anyone to rush you. Leave the checkbook at home; this fun is free.

Prepare for the Negotiations

Let's say you know you're ready to buy. You've raised the money, and the numbers say you can't lose, so you're ready to start negotiating. (If you're an experienced entrepreneur, you already know how to negotiate. If not, some good books on the fine art of haggling are listed in the Reference section at the end of the chapter.)

We suggest two things about negotiations. First, when it comes time to talk meaningful numbers, the most important area to concentrate on is *terms*—not asking price. Favorable terms will give you the cash flow you need to survive the first year and then move from survival into success. Unfavorable terms can torpedo your chances for success, even when the total asking price is well below market value.

Second, when the seller brings up the subject of goodwill, be ready for it. Goodwill is a "slippery" commodity; it can make the asking price soar. It's only natural for the seller to attempt to get as much as possible for goodwill. Because you know this ahead of time, you can do your homework and go in primed to deal. Action Step 50 will help you do your homework. When the seller starts talking about goodwill, you can flip the coin over and discuss ill will—which hangs on longer, like a cloud above the business.

Only you can negotiate out a high price for goodwill, the intangible commodity. You're going to be on your own. Action Step 50 will help you. Go for it!

Protect Yourself

Evaluate each business opportunity by the criteria we present in this chapter. When you find one you think is right for you, start negotiating. Your goal is the lowest possible *price* with the best possible *terms*. Start low; you can then negotiate up if necessary.

If you are asked to put down a deposit, handle it this way:

> Deposit the money in an escrow account, and
>
> include a stipulation in your offer that says the offer is *subject to your inspection and approval* of all financial records and all aspects of the business.

Doing this gives you an escape hatch so that you can get your deposit back—and back out of the deal—if things don't look good. Also, consider working in the business for a few weeks with the option to back out if you have a change of heart.

Expect Some Pleasant Surprises

Well, you've come a long way and you've worked hard on your research. You may be wondering if the digging was worth it. Only you can answer that. There *are* bargains to be found out there—businesses like Woolett's Hardware. For hunter–buyers with vision and persistence, beautiful opportunities are waiting behind ugly facades.

> I heard about Woolett's being up for sale more than a year ago. I'd just opened up my second store at the time—it's also in the hardware line—and it took me just about a year—April to April—to streamline the paperwork. Thanks to a computer and a good manager, my sanity remained intact.
>
> So when I finally got over there to check things out, Woolett's had been on the market a year and a half or so. One look from the street, and I could see why.

ACTION STEP 50

Probe the depths of ill will.

How many products have you vowed never to use again? How many places of business have you vowed never to patronize again? Why?

Make a list of the products and services you won't buy or use again. Next to each item, write the reason. Does it make you sick? Does it offend your sensibilities? Was the service awful?

After you've completed your list, ask your friends what their negative feelings about particular businesses are. Take notes.

Study the two lists you've made. What are the common components of ill will? How long does ill will last? Is there a remedy for it, or is a business plagued by ill will cursed forever?

Now turn your attention to the business you want to buy. Survey your target customers. How do you feel about the business? You need to learn as much as you can about the ill will that exists toward the business.

Have fun with this step, but take it seriously—and think about the nature of ill will when your seller starts asking you to pay for goodwill.

The store was a mess. The building was pre–World War II, and so was the paint. Out front, the sign was sagging. The parking lot needed lots of work; there were potholes six inches deep. The entryway was littered with scraps of paper, and the front door was boarded up.

Inside, things weren't much better. The floor needed a good sweeping. The merchandise was covered with dust. And all around there was this feeling of mildew, age, and disuse. It was dark—like a *cave.* It was tough finding a salesperson, and when you did, you couldn't get much help. Yet there were customers all over the place.

After you've been in business a while, you develop a sort of sixth sense about things. And the minute I stepped into the store, I knew there was something special about it— something hidden, something the eye couldn't see right off. I knew I had to dig deeper.

A visit to the listing real estate broker didn't help much. "Make us an offer," he said. "We just dropped the price yesterday. To $400,000."

"What do the numbers look like?" I asked.

He dug into a slim manila folder. "Last year," he said, "they grossed just under $600,000. The net was around $200,000."

"What about inventory?" I asked. "What about loans and liens and accounts receivable? When can I interview the manager? And why is the owner selling?"

"Are you just asking that," he said, "or is this for real?"

"This is for my son," I said. "He's new to the business, and we don't want a lot of surprises."

"Like I said, make us an offer."

"Let me check the books," I said. I deposited five hundred dollars with an escrow company, making sure I got my usual escape clause—a deposit receipt saying my offer for the business is contingent upon my inspection of all assets and my approval of all financial records. Doing this has saved me tons of heartburn over the years.

The minute they got wind of a buyer, the manager and two of the employees up and quit. The back office was a mess, and it took me three days of searching to find something that would tell me I was on the right track. I found a supply of rolled steel. It was on the books at $12,000, but I knew it was worth $150,000. I took that as a buy signal.

The next day, I made an offer—twelve thousand down, with the balance to be paid out of profits over the next five years. The owner accepted, and we cleared escrow in thirty days.

The first thing we did was clean the place up. We surfaced the parking lot with asphalt, added a coat of paint, fixed the door, added lighting.

Business picked up right away. My son, newly married, was settling down and learning the business. He seemed to have managerial talents.

Then we found another set of records that had been hidden away in a safe. They showed us that the Woolett Corporation owned a bank account containing $180,000 and five acres of land, mostly along the road leading to town, right in the path of future growth! We had bought the *whole corporation.*

The first year we did just over a million dollars in sales. And there was every indication that we would do better from then on.

People who come into the store now hardly recognize the place. We've spent some more money on new lighting fixtures and we've added a large kitchen section—to appeal to the yuppies. And in the summer we're staying open until eight.

If you're in the area, stop by.

> **lien**
> a legal obligation filed against a piece of property

SUMMARY

There are two good reasons to explore businesses for sale: you'll learn a lot by exploring the marketplace, and you might find a gem like Woolett's Hardware—a business that will make money right from the start.

If the seller is "hungry," you may be able to obtain terrific terms. For example, let's say you find a business for sale with an asking price of a million dollars. Its profit last year was $50,000. You and the seller agree on

$20,000 down

a no-interest loan of $980,000

payments of 20% of net profits each year until the loan is paid off

Result: each year you'd have an ROI of 200%. Your loan payment would be 20% of $50,000, or $10,000 a year. You'd have a profit of $40,000 left each year. After ten years, you'd have paid the owner $100,000, and your profit would have been $400,000. With such good terms, you wouldn't need to think about paying off the loan for a long, long time.

THINK POINTS FOR SUCCESS

◄ Stick to what you know. Don't buy a business you know nothing about.

◄ Don't let a seller or a broker rush you. A business is not a used car.

◄ If your seller looks absolutely honest, check him out anyway.

◄ Worry less about price; work harder on terms.

◄ Most good businesses are sold behind the scenes, before they reach the open market.

◄ Make sure you're there when the physical inventory takes place. Look in those boxes yourself.

◄ Get everything in writing. Be specific.

◄ Always go through bulk sales escrow.

◄ Buying a corporation is tricky. Have an experienced attorney help you.

REFERENCES

Bank of America. *How to Buy or Sell a Business,* SBR Series. [When we were going to press this publication was out of print, but many B of A branches have some on hand. Write to Bank of America, Department 3120, P.O. Box 37000, San Francisco, CA 94137.]

Burstiner, Irving. *The Small Business Handbook.* Englewood Cliffs, N.J.: Prentice-Hall, 1979.

Buying and Selling a Small Business. Washington, D.C.: Superintendent of Documents. Stock #045-000-00003-6, page 122.

Choosing a Retail Location. Washington, D.C.: U.S. Small Business Administration, Office of Business Development. Management Aid No. 2.021, 1988.

Cohen, Herb. *You Can Negotiate Anything: How to Get What You Want.* Secaucus, N.J.: Lyle Stuart, 1980. [An intriguing look at the tactics of wheeling and dealing, with case studies and scenarios for working the marketplace.]

Franchise Opportunities Handbook. Washington, D.C.: U.S. Department of Commerce, Industry and Trade Administration, Office of Minority Business Enterprise, 1979.

Frost, Ted. *Where Have All the Woolly Mammoths Gone?* West Nyack, N.Y.: Parker Publishing, 1976.

Jurek, Walter. *A Reference Manual on Buying and Selling a Business.* Quality Services, Inc., 3887 State Street, Santa Barbara, CA 93105.

Sullivan, Daniel, and Joseph Lane. *Small Business Management: A Practical Approach.* Dubuque, Ia.: Wm. C. Brown Publishers, 1983.

Tetreault, Wilfred E. *Buying and Selling Business Opportunities: A Sales Transaction Handbook.* Reading, Mass.: Addison-Wesley Publishing Company, 1981. [Explains the overwhelming number of documents needed to buy a business. One look at this book may convince you to handle your own start-up.]

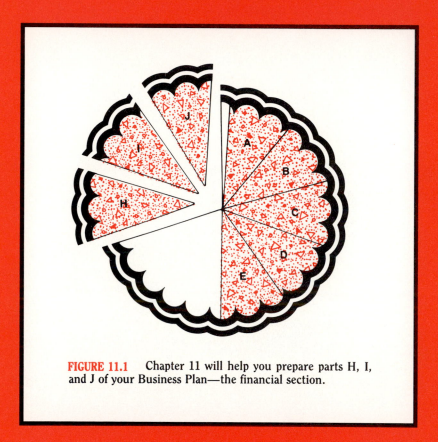

FIGURE 11.1   Chapter 11 will help you prepare parts H, I, and J of your Business Plan—the financial section.

Shaking the Money Tree

LEARNING OBJECTIVES

■ To understand that you need to establish connections in the world of money. ■ To understand that your banker is a gatekeeper to the world of money. ■ To develop strategies for working with your banker. ■ To develop a more sophisticated concept of money and its power. ■ To develop confidence and street survival skills in the worlds of high and low finance. ■ To learn how to seek out potential lenders. ■ To learn how to generate cash from customers. ■ To develop a vendor statement that will allow you to make intelligent purchasing decisions quickly. ■ To scour the lending arena for money to fund your new business.

Would it sound too easy if we told you to go out and simply shake a money tree to get financing for your business? Yes, of course. You know it will not be that easy. First you must become familiar with the world of money. Then you must learn to tell the forest from the trees. And then you must find the right tree. Once you've accomplished these things, you might be surprised how money turns up.

LOOKING FOR MONEY

Before we get to specifics, let's see how Alexander Adams learned some things about the world of money.

Alexander Adams worked for a giant telecommunications conglomerate as "Assistant to the Associate Vice-President for Region X, Subsection C, Department of Marketing and Market Research." His forte was product development. His territory was the East Coast, from New England to South Carolina. He worked 50–70 hours a week and traveled two weeks out of three. Alex was valuable to his company because his innovative ideas allowed his employer to change the competitive arena.

Down deep, however, Alex felt that the computer was a toy and that international electronic networking was just so much gossip at light-speed. But money was money, so he kept cranking out new ideas for his employer.

One day after he had presented yet another terrific idea to his superiors and they had once again failed to see the value of it, Alex made a decision. He told his wife, Jayne, about it at dinner. "I'm getting out," he said. "I've had enough. Remember the idea I had last night? The one about the double mini-disks in one slot and the Winchester in the other?"

"Of course," Jayne lied.

"Well, they shot it down. Bang-bang. Just like that. This is the fifth time in two months. I feel strangled. I feel caged. If I don't get out, I'll go crazy."

"It scares me to hear you talk that way, Alex."

"It scares me *not* to," he said, and he left the table.

Alex got most of his good ideas in dreams. That night he dreamed about a man on a shady park bench. The man wore a Palm Beach suit. A straw boater rested on the bench beside him, on top of a folded copy of the *Wall Street Journal*. The man was feeding the pigeons, and he—Alex—was one of the pigeons. When he recognized his own face above the plump body of a pigeon eating corn nuts, he woke up.

On his next business trip, Alex found himself in New York. He had twenty minutes between meetings, so he went to Central Park for a walk. As he came around a bend in the walk, he saw the man in the Palm Beach suit feeding pigeons. As Alex walked toward him, the man smiled, said hello, and held out his hand. Alex took it. For some reason the man reminded Alex of his grandfather. They talked. The man seemed to know a lot about finance. He hinted that he had been an unofficial adviser to three U.S. Presidents. Alex told the man about his job, his feeling of being caged, and his desire to escape. The man offered Alex some advice.

"I felt that way once," he said, "when they wanted me to go into the family business. I was afraid to go out on my own, and yet I heard the call of adventure. If I'd worked in the family business, I'd have gone crazy early. It should be easier now, because the financial market is so splintered, and there are a lot of opportunities. Here's what I'd do if I were your age—first, hang onto your job while you build up some personal credit. Do you get those offers in the mail—just sign your name here for credit?"

"Sure. I throw them away."

"Well, start gathering them together. You can probably get a hundred thousand in credit just by signing your John Henry. You own your house?" the man continued.

"Yes," Alex smiled, "and so does the bank."

"Use your house as collateral to open another line of personal credit. Where do you bank?"

"One of the big interstates."

"All right. Find out if they lend money to small operators. If they don't, find a smaller bank—one where you can shake hands with the president. What's your cash position?"

"Eleven thousand," Alex said. "In CDs. It's our emergency fund."

"How much can you borrow, short term?"

"I don't know. Why should I?"

"Because you want to open your new account with a big bankroll. Try to open with a minimum of $10,000. Then when potential creditors ask your bank about your credit, the bank will only say that you opened with a five-figure amount. You want to make their eyes pop. Get ahold of your friends and relatives. Offer them a half-percent over what they're making, for just long enough to open the account. Pay them back as soon as you get the account opened."

"That's a great idea!" Alex said.

The man talked for several more minutes, giving Alex more good ideas. Then he asked: "How will you make money once you've quit your job?"

"I'm good at marketing," Alex said. "I won't have any problem finding something else."

"That's just another cage, isn't it?"

"No," Alex said. But he knew it was, and the idea made him sad.

A pigeon waddled up. The man reached for a handful of corn nuts. As he dropped them one at a time, he said something to Alex that struck home: "Life's pretty simple. There are the pigeons waiting to be fed, and there are the feeders. It's all in deciding what end of the corn nut you want to be on."

Alex said nothing. He just thought about his dream, when his face had been attached to the body of a feeding pigeon.

Well, by this time he was late for his appointment so had to run. As the men shook hands, the older man handed Alex a package. Alex hurried off. When he opened the package later, he found two books, a clipping from the *Wall Street Journal*, and the stranger's business card. One book was *Megatrends*; the other, *Nine American Lifestyles*.

The two books blew Alex's mind. The information was so relevant, so timely, so easy to absorb. The *Journal* clipping was about the aging population. Today, it said, there are 27 million people 65 years or older, and by the year 2030—when Alex would be 81 and retired in Florida—there would be 64 million Americans over 65. *Megatrends* said Florida was a bellwether state, a forecaster of patterns to come, with lots of young people, lots of old people, and a huge age gap in between. *Nine American Lifestyles* said households would increase from 89 million in 1985 to 97 million by 1990, and household size would decrease from 2.59 persons to 2.50.

Alex put the facts together: Florida, elderly population increasing, household size decreasing. He linked them to some personal considerations—his need for escape, his plan to retire in Florida, his need for a job, his creativity. Then he thought of people he knew. His father had just been mugged two blocks from his home in a St. Louis suburb. His mother hated the Midwest cold. Some of their friends had retired to Orlando.

His excitement kept him awake that night. He called his parents early in the morning. He explained his idea: "Emerson Landing," condo complex for seniors. It would contain medium-priced living quarters, social areas, easy access to markets, an infirmary, and a wellness clinic.

Alex's parents weren't wealthy, but they offered to loan him $47,000 up front and $90,000 more when their house was sold. Furthermore, they volunteered to help him raise funds among their friends, in return for a small percentage off the top.

Alex's escape machine was in motion.

He returned home and went to see his banker, who liked the idea and offered to help him develop a Business Plan. His bank was interested in Florida developments, he said, and they loved real estate projects created by innovative people who had their numbers together.

Jayne liked the idea, too.

Alex made a phone call before going to bed. He called the man he'd met on the park bench to thank him."

"Is there room for another investor?" the man asked him. "This city's too cold, and I've been wanting to get my teeth into a project."

"You don't mean—?" Alex cried.

"Why don't we have lunch and talk about it. I can free up some capital. How does twenty-two million sound?"

"Ulp," Alex said. "I mean, it sounds terrific."

"Let's get rolling," the man said. "These old fires have been banked too long."

"Yes, sir," Alex said.

That night, Alex's dreams were in technicolor.

What Can You Learn from Alex?

When Alex needed to escape from the golden handcuffs of the large corporation, what did he do? Did he insult his boss? No. Did he march into his bank and demand $100,000 in seed capital? No. What Alex did was *plan*:

1. He located someone who knew more about money than he did and learned from him.
2. He kept abreast of trends in the marketplace. He read and he used his new eyes to analyze and sense what was going on around him.
3. He lined up banking connections and lines of credit before quitting his job.
4. He started looking for money close to home—his parents, friends of his parents. People who knew him were eager to invest in his good idea.
5. He opened his business bank account with an impressive dollar figure. Later, when he went to the bank for a credit line, it was smooth sailing.

Learn How Much Money You Need Each Month

Lenders will want to know as much as possible about your money management skills, so it's a good idea to concentrate first on your personal, household budget. After all, personal money management and business money management involve the same skills. You need to determine how much money you need each month and what you have coming in each month. Table 11.1 will help you do this. Notice that the table asks you to give a high figure and a low figure for each item. Budgeting this way will give you two budgets: a fat budget and a bare-bones budget. Try not to overlook anything, because surprises are dangerous to your financial health.

The time to think about your personal financial status is right now. Down the road a ways you're going to need to show lenders that you will have enough money to live on when you open the doors of your new cash-hungry business.

Learn How Much Credit You Have

Now it is time to have a little fun. Let's find out how much unsecured credit you have. This will give you a very general picture of how the financial world rates you at this time. On the business side, once you've done this, you can determine if there are any untapped sources of funds for your start-up, or fall-backs and emergency sources for your business or personal expenses. Use Table 11.2 or a sheet of blank paper. To learn your credit limits on your charge accounts, look at your most recent statements. You may need to call or write to some businesses for this information. When you've filled in the amounts for each account you have, add them up.

Surprised? Few people are aware of how much credit they have. However, before you tell your boss what he can do with his job, there are some things you may want to do while you still have a job, a steady income, and a benefits package. For example,

TABLE 11.1 Your Monthly Income and Outgo

ITEM	HIGH	LOW
Expenses, monthly		
Food		
Clothing		
Shelter: mortgage/rent		
utilities		
maintenance, cleaning, etc.		
Car payments		
Insurance		
Dependents' expenses		
Contributions, dues		
Credit card bills		
Other		
Expenses, periodic *(Convert these to monthly amounts.)*		
Taxes		
Auto registration, maintenance		
Holidays, gifts, vacations		
Other		
TOTAL monthly expenses		
Income *(Convert these to monthly amounts if necessary.)*		
Your income (if it will continue)		
Your spouse's income		
Interest on savings		
Stock/bond dividends		
Retirement		
Insurance payments		
Trust fund		
Other		
TOTAL monthly income		

1. Get complete medical checkups for the entire family—whatever is covered by your current insurance—eyes, dental, general medical.

2. Check on the cost of continuing the insurance coverage provided by your employer—life, dental, eye, disability, medical, retirement, other.

3. Apply for two (additional) credit cards—one VISA and one MasterCard. Set them aside to use only for business expenses when you start. Pay the bills when they come due with a company check. The banks don't care who writes the check, as long as it clears. In addition, it will give you good documentation for your bookkeeper and the IRS. Plus you will have some additional credit for your business.

4. Consider applying for a personal line of credit. Usually, depending on the four C's of credit (your capital, character, capacity, and collateral), you can obtain anywhere from $5,000 to $50,000 of unsecured credit at very attractive rates. If you have a personal line of credit, you are in a much more flexible position with your new business. If you need it to finance the new business, it's available. If not, it can be your security blanket, to be there for you if unexpected expenses should pop up.

TABLE 11.2   Your Current Unsecured Financial Sources

SOURCE	AMOUNT/LIMIT
Department Stores	
Sears	
J. C. Penney	
Others	
Oil Companies	
Exxon	
Standard Oil	
Mobil	
Texaco	
Shell	
Others	
Bank Credit Cards	
American Express	
Diner's Club	
VISA	
MasterCard	
Discover Card	
Others	
Personal Lines of Credit	
Bank	
Savings & Loan	
Credit Union	
Others	
Any Other Unsecured Credit	
TOTAL Credit Available	

With regard to points 3 and 4 above, bankers are much more relaxed about extending credit to a "steady citizen": a person with steady employment income. Also, you would be making arrangements for the money when you don't need it. Bankers tend to like lending money to people who don't really need it.

One reason we suggest that you obtain two bank cards is that your business will have at least limited sources of credit for which payments can be delayed up to 45 or even 60 days without interest. This can be a big help with cash flow. See Table 11.3. Notice that the two cards in the example complement each other in that they allow the holder to get 45 to 60 days of free credit on charge purchases made any day of the month, provided the proper card is used. As you can see, the technique provides the maximum credit when purchases are charged early in the billing cycle. Warning: payments must be in the bank's hand on or by the payment due dates. This technique will also work with suppliers who offer credit terms.

Collin Smith financed his business with $8,500 in cash and some bank credit cards. His history may inspire you.

TABLE 11.3   How to Get 45 to 60 Days' Free Credit with Two Credit Cards

CARD	CLOSING DATE OF BILLING CYCLE	WHEN TO USE		TIME FROM PURCHASE TO PAYMENT (EXAMPLE)
		START	STOP	
VISA	4th of the month	5th	19th	Charge July 5th, pay September 3rd (60 days)
MasterCard	19th of the month	20th	4th	Charge July 20th, pay September 18th (60 days)

Collin was twenty-one years old when he had the idea to start his own limousine service. He had been working for Big Orange Lincoln/Mercury for five years. For the last six months, he had been the assistant manager in the parts department.

After being turned down by his bank for a start-up loan for his limo business, he sat down to review his finances. When he completed his credit list he found that he had had two car loans, one for a stereo, three department store charge cards and both a VISA and MasterCard. He also noted that he had never been late with a payment. A pretty good credit history, he thought.

He had been talking with Chuck Miller, the owner of Custom Limo Mortgage, and knew that he could get an 85% loan on a good used limo. Collin has $8,500 in savings and would have $4,000 left after a $4,500 down payment on a good $30,000 used limo.

Because of the limo industry's track record, the insurance company wanted the full year's premium of $2,500 up front. That would leave only $1,500 for all the other start-up expenses, permits, phones, and so on, but Collin believed the $1,500 would just about do it. That would be cutting it pretty close.

His VISA and MasterCard accounts had credit limits of $1,000 and $1,500, respectively, and he owed only $200. If he could get both cards to raise their limits by $500 and get cards from two other banks, he might have up to $5,500 or $6,000 of credit. He figured that if he applied while he still had $8,500 in the bank and his good job, he shouldn't have any trouble.

Things worked out even better than he'd thought they would. The current credit cards raised his limits to $2,000 and $3,000, and the new card companies came through with $1,500 each. This gave him a total of $8,000 of credit! That was more than enough to cover the first few months' operating expenses plus some unfortunate surprises if they should occur.

So with $8,500 in cash and $8,000 in bank card credit, Collin bought a used limo and launched Royal Class Limo Service.

Seven years later, Royal Class Limo has twelve limos (four of them brand new), over a million dollars a year in sales, and ten credit cards with a little over $50,000 in loans. "I don't like paying 18% interest on those credit-card loans," said Collin, "but even with my seven profitable years, the banks aren't interested in lending money to my limo business. Without credit cards, I wouldn't be drawing a high five-figure salary from a business that's worth somewhere between $500,000 and $750,000. Plus, I just bought a condo a block from the beach. Not bad for a 28-year-old former assistant parts manager who had $8,500 to invest!"

When you own a business, your financial return comes from two sources. One source is some type of steady income/benefits stream. This may be in the form of a salary, owner's draw, a company car, insurance, and a retirement plan. The second source is what you realize from the sale of the business, a merger, or taking it public.

In Collin's case, the two sources total approximately $200,000 more than his salary would have been the past seven years, even with raises and promotions—a difference of about $30,000 per year. Plus, if he sold out today, he could walk away with at least a half-million dollars. This would bring his total to $700,000, or $100,000 per year. Not bad for an $8,500 investment!

There's no dollar figure for the fun and excitement Collin has had building his business. He says he wouldn't trade the past seven years for anything. "What I have done and how I feel can only be compared to being the winning quarterback in the Super Bowl."

It's time to look at your personal financial situation and your lifestyle. Figure out how you can go into business *and* keep a roof over your head. Do Action Step 51 now.

BEFORE YOU SHAKE THAT TREE

What action do you take when you need money to start a business? Do you ask the bank? Do you ask Aunt Alice, or your co-workers? Do you write to your congressman? Do you refinance your home?

Most new ventures begin with the entrepreneur's own capital. Funds can usually be borrowed if you have other sources of income and collateral—such as good equity in a home.

bank
a place where some people park their money

bankers
gateways to the world of money

Although **banks** are in the business of lending money, they also have a responsibility to their depositors. Thus **bankers** tend to choose the safest deals. They want to help businesses expand, but they have to be picky. Banks can help you in many areas, but they are not investors, so don't expect them to take risks.

Piggy Bank Blues

Suppose you worked ten years for a well-known firm and are now out on your own working as a consultant. Last year, your first year in business, you made three times your former salary. You can now afford a nicer house, but lenders say you don't qualify. The reason: you're self-employed. You now have an erratic income stream, and you can't provide two years of self-employed income tax returns.

Welcome to the world of the independent contractor! A lender may treat you like a pal while you're employed by XIT, the megacorporation up the freeway, and then when you go to work for yourself, give you the cold shoulder.

So how can this be avoided? By building lender relationships. Take a banker to lunch. Get to know the officers of your bank. Ask your banker for advice on pulling together your Business Plan. If you build a relationship before you need cash or credit, you'll save yourself much aggravation.

Also, think about what kind of bank you want to do business with. In large banks, for example, loan officers move around from branch to branch. In a small bank, the chief loan officer may be a part-owner. You're hunting for a permanent relationship, not merely a place to park your money. Bear in mind that your business could outgrow a small bank and that some firms need support services that only a large business bank can offer, such as import–export assistance.

Few bankers are thrilled about lending to start-ups. Nonetheless, bankers are *people*, so start seeking a banker who understands you and your needs. Network your attorney, your tax person, the Chamber of Commerce, civic clubs, lead clubs, and people in your trade association for recommendations. Ask your accountant to accompany you on your introductory visit to the bank, especially if you are fuzzy about the details of your financial statement. Be prepared to spend a lot of time on this search. Nurture the relationship, and keep your banker informed of changes and updates. But also, find a backup banker.

ACTION STEP 51

Make a money list.

Before starting to look for outside money, review the personal financial statement you developed in Action Step 41. Figure out how much money you will need to cover your personal expenses each month. (If there's more than one owner, each owner should do this.)

Once you have this worked out, determine where you will get money to live on for at least six months—in some cases 12 or 18 months. The longer you can go without drawing money out of your business for your living expenses, the higher the probability of success.

Preparing for the Search

Before hunting the money tree, prepare, prepare, prepare.

Research the World of Money.   Money creates its own world, with its own customs, myths, and rules. Before you go around with your hand out asking for money, spend three or four months studying the **world of money**. If you are new at this, a good place to start is *Money* magazine. Then go on to books like those listed in the reference section at the end of this chapter.

world of money
a strange and mysterious place where the signposts are written in $ signs

Sit at the Feet of a Money Guru.   Think of three people who know more about money than you do. Seek out one of those persons. Begin to build a money network.

Buy Some Stock.   Invest a small amount of money in a few shares of **common stock** of a business you want to know about. When you read its financial reports, monitor your emotions. Write down how you feel as you open up the *Wall Street Journal* to check the roller-coaster of your ups and downs. When it comes time to ask people to invest in *your* business, read over what you wrote.

common stock
a certificate of equity ownership representing a certain number of shares

Watch Your Four C's.   Continually ask yourself these questions:

1. *Capital.* How much liquid cash (savings and checking accounts) do I have?
2. *Character.* Do I pay my bills on time?
3. *Capacity.* Do I have the ability to repay the loan out of the profits of the business?
4. *Collateral.* Which of my tangible assets—such as my car, securities, condo, life insurance—can I use to secure a loan?

the four C's
a classical series of questions lenders use to screen potential borrowers

Check Out Your Personal Credit.   Ask the credit bureau for a copy of your credit report. The cost is minimal, and they are required by law to make it available to you. You may find some surprises, such as black marks that were posted in error. Make sure your credit report is clean or explainable before you go to the bank.

Sketch Out Your Business Plan Now.   The Business Plan is your showcase for displaying all the ideas and information you've gathered in your venture adventure. A suggested format for the plan appears in Chapter 16. Start thinking about your plan now and test it on family, friends, and bankers.

Befriend a Banker, and a Backup Banker.   Banks are conservative, and they probably will not want to lend you start-up money unless you pledge real property or security. However, bankers can lead you to money sources you hadn't considered. Seek your banker's advice on pulling your Business Plan together. If you get your banker's input, he will have a hard time refusing help later on. Your banker is one gateway to the world of money, but you should know more than one banker.

YOUR BANKER

Bring your banker into your **information loop** and involve him or her in your business idea. People lend money to people, and bankers are people. They get excited about good ideas. Stop thinking about a banker as someone who will lend you an umbrella only on a sunny day. *You* would not lend money to a stranger, so make sure your banker knows what you are up to.

information loop
a network of people who need to be kept informed about your business successes

How to Deal with a Banker

Here are some strategies for dealing with bankers.

1. Never ask a banker for money; ask for *advice* and *information*. Ideally, a banker will *tell you* when it is the right time to seek money.

2. A bank may seem like a formidable medieval fortress or a modern cathedral. Cut through this symbolism and mythology with new eyes. If you choose to see a banker on his or her own turf, always: 1) make an appointment (it's polite; it also makes the banker feel worthwhile); 2) dress conservatively (nothing impresses a banker like order and neatness); 3) act as if you don't need any money.

your turf
a place where you invite your banker when you want advice and information

3. Lure a banker to **your turf**. Say: "It's difficult to explain to you exactly what my shop is like. Why not come out for a look-see? We could have lunch. How's Thursday around noon?" On your own turf, you will be in a stronger position. You should feel more at ease, and communication will probably flow more easily for both parties.

4. Once you have your loan or line of credit, stay in touch with your banker. Keep your Business Plan up to date and keep your banker friend informed about how things are going in your business. Keep positioning yourself on the ladder in your banker's mind.

5. While you're negotiating with one bank, get yourself a backup bank. You can use information from one bank to cross-check the other bank. Shop for money like you would shop for any major purchase. The deals could surprise you.

6. Negotiate for your line of credit or loan while you are still employed. A personal line of credit is often reviewed annually. You may have to prove that you are still a good credit risk after you are in your own business. If you keep up a good credit rating, however, the chances are good that you will be able to keep the personal lines of credit.

Keep a running list of questions to ask prospective bankers. These will get you started:

What are your lending limits?

Who makes the decisions on loans?

What are your views on my industry?

What experience do you have in working with businesses like mine?

Could you recommend a highly qualified lawyer? Bookkeeper? Accountant? Computer consultant?

equipment lease
long-term arrangement with a bank or leasing company for renting capital equipment

Are you interested in writing **equipment leases**?

accounts receivable
what is owed to a firm

What kind of terms do you give on **accounts receivable** financing?

Does your bank offer businesses VISA and MasterCard accounts? What credit limit could I expect for my business credit cards?

What handling charge would I have to pay on credit card receipts?

What interest can I earn on my business checking account?

Do you have a merchants' or commercial window?

Do you have a night depository?

If you can't lend me money, can you direct me to people who might be interested in doing it?

SBA-guaranteed loans
loans where up to 90% of loaned funds are insured by the federal government

Do you make **SBA-guaranteed loans**?

If I open up a business checking account here, what else can you do for me?

Make Your Banker a Member of Your Team

A helpful banker can be an entrepreneur's best friend and a member of his or her auxiliary management team or "taxi squad." Business growth demands money from external sources. The more successful you become, the more likely you will need a close bank relationship to help you finance prosperity. If you grow more than 25% a year, you'll need lots of financing help. Manufacturers get into trouble fast, but even service firms have to wait for their customers to make payments. Your creditors and employees will want their money when it's due them. So keep your banker in your information loop. Bankers are more willing to help if they understand your needs and know you are trying to anticipate your needs.

Now read about how Steve McWhorter handled his cash flow problems by helping a banker to understand the business he was in.

> Things went really well our first year. My third invention—a battery-operated fuel monitor for the new diesel turbos being made in Germany—was selling like hotcakes, and I'd found a great production manager to keep things going down on the line.
>
> Then cash flow troubles developed.
>
> It happened in February of our second year when a couple of the big car makers—customers that purchased at least half of our product—slowed down on their payments. Some payments were more than ninety days past due.
>
> I stay pretty much in the lab and the shop, because that's the fun part of the business for me, so I didn't find out about the cash problems for almost three weeks. When I did find out, we invoiced the customers again. Still no money. The first week in March, I had trouble meeting the payroll. The second week I had to pay a couple of crucial supplier accounts. The third week, except for petty cash, the company was almost out of money.
>
> I gave my banker a call. We were on good terms, and I had four accounts at her bank. When I told her my problem, she simply asked me how much I needed and for how long. Instant **line of credit**. What a relief.
>
> Well, we got that squared away, and when things were rolling smoothly again, my banker sat down with me and the company books, and we worked out a strategy for bridging the gap between billing and customer payment.
>
> Those sessions really bored me, so I started looking around for someone to help out on the numbers. My banker helped here, too, with advice and recommendations about what kind of person would be best at keeping track of money.
>
> When I worked for someone else, I never thought of a banker at all. Since I've been in business, I've come to realize a banker can be a businessperson's best friend.

Action Step 52 will get you started in your developing relationship with a banker.

SECRETS OF SMALL BUSINESS SURVIVAL

Make Your Dollars Work Overtime

Steve McWhorter discovered the art of managing money in the eleventh hour. It's no secret that start-ups are expensive, and those first few months can be a make-or-break time for the entrepreneur. You want to make your dollars work efficiently. Here are some tips:

1. Find out who you have to pay right now.
2. Find out who can wait awhile.
3. Keep asking what you're getting for your money.

line of credit
an unsecured lending limit

ACTION STEP 52

Befriend a banker.

Money creates its own world. There are several doorways into that world. Your banker sits at the threshold of one of those doors. (In a sense, your banker is the guardian of the gate.)

Start with a familiar place, the bank where you have your checking account. Make an appointment to talk to the chief officer (president, vice-president, or branch manager). Here are some questions to ask:

1. Do you lend money to new small businesses?

2. Do you make SBA-guaranteed loans?

3. What are your criteria for loans?

4. Would you describe the loan approval process?

5. What do you think of my Business Plan?

If you are happy with your banker's answers, talk over the possibility of opening an account for your business. If you have money tucked away in life insurance or a money market fund somewhere, ask about the bank's money market accounts.

How to Save Money

If you work the dollars you do have, you won't have to shake the money tree so hard. Here are some tips that could save you money. Read through the list. How many of these ideas have you thought of? How many are new to you?

cash deposits
funds paid in advance of delivery

trade credit or dating
a vendor's extension of the payment term into the near future

on-site improvements
modifications to real estate to accommodate the special needs of the business

dead goods
merchandise no longer in demand

liquid cash
funds that can be used immediately, usually held in checking or other accounts

nonbank lenders
institutional lenders other than banks

1. Ask your customers for **cash deposits** when they place orders.
2. Persuade your vendors to give you more **trade credit** or **dating** and more time to pay.
3. Lease your equipment.
4. Run a lean operation; do not waste anything.
5. Work out of your home if you can.
6. Get your landlord to make **on-site improvements** and finance the cost over the term of the lease.
7. Stay on top of your receivables. Be aggressive.
8. Keep track of everything. Try to resell whatever waste or by-products you have in your business.
9. Return goods that aren't selling.
10. Take markdowns quickly on **dead goods**.
11. Use as little commercial space as you can.
12. If your customers do not visit your business facility, it does not have to be highly visible or attractive.
13. When you have to borrow money, shop around.
14. Make sure your **liquid cash** is earning interest.
15. Shop **nonbank lenders** like commercial credit firms.
16. Do not collateralize your loans unless you have no other alternative.
17. Survey your friends and relatives for loans. They might lend you money at rates higher than they would get in the money markets but lower than you would have to pay institutional lenders.
18. Befriend a venture capitalist who funds your type of firm.
19. Consider selling limited partnerships. You could become the general partner with little or none of your own capital invested.
20. Consider selling stock. (Consult an attorney.)

The Vendor Statement Form

An often overlooked technique for reducing your capital requirement is to probe your vendors (major suppliers) for the best prices and terms available. Professional buyers and purchasing agents ask their vendors to fill out an information sheet that forces them to write down the terms and conditions of their sales plans. This is a good idea for you as well.

vendor statement
a personally designed form that allows you to negotiate with each vendor from a position of informed strength

A small business must buy professionally, and a **vendor statement** will help you do just that. With this form, your vendors' verbal promises become written promises. How well you buy is as important as how well you sell, because every dollar you save by "buying right" drops directly to the bottom line. To compete in your arena, you need the best terms and prices you can get. The statement will help you get the best.

Personalize your form by putting your business name at the top. Then list the information you need and provide blanks for them to write on. This list provides some of the basics for you:

1. Vendor's name
2. Vendor's address and phone number
3. Sales rep's name
4. Business phone (Will vendor accept collect calls?)
5. Home phone (for emergencies)
6. Amount of minimum purchase
7. Quantity discounts? How much? What must you do to earn?
8. Are dating or extended payments terms available?
9. Advertising/promotion allowances
10. Policies on returns for defective goods (Who pays the freight?)
11. Delivery times
12. Assistance (technical, sales, and so on)
13. Product literature available
14. Point-of-purchase material provided
15. Support for grand opening (Will supplier donate prize or other support?)
16. Nearest other dealer handling this particular line
17. Special services the sales rep can provide
18. Vendor's signature, the date, and some kind of agreement that you will be notified of any changes

Remember, the information the vendor writes on this statement is the starting point for negotiations. You should be able to negotiate more favorable terms with some vendors, because these people want your business. Revise your application form as you learn from experience how vendors can help you.

A Success Story

You met Rich Cameron in an earlier chapter. He was in marketing, working for a large firm, when he decided to go into business for himself. He attended seminars, interviewed owners, walked neighborhoods, and read trade journals for quite awhile before opening his toy store.

The store opened in May, but Rich knew from doing industry research that he would have to start placing orders for the Christmas season right away. The problem was that his store would hold $100,000 worth of toys, but Rich had only $30,000 to use for his inventory. He knew he would have to be well-stocked by Thanksgiving or miss out on the profitable holiday business.

The unwritten rule in a new business is that suppliers want you to pay cash up front—for everything. You are a new account, unproven in the grand arena of trade and commerce. They want to wait and see how well you do before they extend credit.

Rich found a way to get around this. He showed his Business Plan to his suppliers' credit managers.

What happened?

"They were amazed," Rich says. "They'd been dealing with toy store owners for years, and mine was the first Business Plan they'd seen from a toy store owner. I showed them everything in black and white—industry trends, projections, marketing plan, management-team statistics, promotion strategy, everything—and when they had read it, they gave me extended dating terms."

The Business Plan didn't do all Rich's work for him. He also bought merchandise for his store very carefully (See Box 11.1.) and he developed his own personalized vendor statement to use when he spoke to sales reps.

"A vendor statement really helps," Rich says, "because the survival items are written down. It puts sales reps on the spot. If they want your business to succeed, they have to deal with the questions.

ACTION STEP 53

Design a vendor statement form.

One of the best ways to save money is to get help from your vendor/supplier. To do that, you will need to create your own special form that specifies, in writing, the terms to be negotiated.

Be tough. Be firm. Be pleasant.

Personalize this form by putting the name of your business at the top. Prepare your list of needed information using the list of eighteen suggestions we've given you.

The vendor form will give you talking points. Most vendors hold something back; design your form to help you learn what those things are and get the best deal for your business.

When negotiating, use a lot of open-ended questions like "What else can you do for me?"

BOX 11.1   Merchandise Buying Tips for the First-Time Buyer

1. Attend seasonal merchandise shows at your local fashion market center. Here, you can review merchandise from competing manufacturers. You can compare price points and delivery availability. You can see what you are buying.
2. Start small. You want to test items while minimizing your risk. Manufacturers will try to sell you more by offering large-lot discounts. Beware.
3. Do not allow any vendor to ship an assorted selection. If you choose the widgets, you know what you're buying; if they choose the widgets, they'll send you the stuff that's just passed into the decline stage.
4. Don't pay for merchandise until it's delivered. C.O.D. is a good way to go. Check the packing slip before you pay to ensure that you got what you ordered.
5. One of your protections when you place an order is a cancellation date. Set a date beyond which you will not accept merchandise.
6. As you are buying, think of your target customers. Buy for them, not for the world. Don't try to please everyone.
7. Watch what is moving; this will tell you what your customers want.

"I got some strong resistance when I brought out my vendor statement form. One guy spent thirty minutes on long distance, telling me why he wouldn't sign it. He wanted all cash up front for the first sale, 75% cash for the second, 50% for the third, and 30% of net after that. But using the statement, backed by my Business Plan, I was able to negotiate him into dating, which means I bought toys in early summer and didn't have to pay for them until December 10. Dating saved my business."

Rich smiles as he recalls those early days. "The interesting thing about negotiating is that it gets you in close enough so you can ask for other assistance. A lot of my advertising and promotion comes free through the vendors because they want my store to be a success. If I hadn't gone in to deal, they wouldn't have known I was going to be a major customer for the long run. And I couldn't have moved confidently without that vendor form."

If you're a new account, flash 'em your Business Plan. Then flash 'em your vendor form. Tell them you're going to be a very important customer very soon.

Now it's time to prepare your own vendor statement form. Action Step 53 will help you.

SCOUTING THE FOREST

lender
person or firm who advances money

inducement to a lender
an extra benefit offered to a lender—can be a stock warrant, discount, or control of company

By now you've befriended a banker, you've increased your money savvy, and you have prepared a vendor statement form. Now is time to zero in on your **lenders**. Action Step 54 asks you to prepare on paper by listing potential lenders and investors and by developing your persuasive tactics ahead of time. Without persuasive **inducements to lenders**, they have no reason to invest in your business. If you need help in listing your reasons, you might begin by profiling your target customer, the one who's out there waiting for your product or service. You might list industry trends, and dovetail them with a scenario of where your product or service fits. Move from there to marketing strategy, selling, the profit picture, and return on investment.

In the final part of Action Step 54 you test your tactics on friends. Ask your friends to respond as though they were potential investors. You *want* to hear their objections so that you can answer their objections on paper. When you have completed this action step, you will be truly prepared to meet your lender.

SHAKING THE MONEY TREE

In Action Step 41 you prepared a personal financial statement that gave you an idea of your net worth. You will use that information as you shake the money tree.

Face it. It is your business, and you are going to have to use some money of your own. That's only fair. But you might be surprised at how money turns up when you start looking around with new eyes.

Sources of Capital

Make a list of potential sources of capital for your business, and add to it when you think of a new source. Here's a list to get you started.

1. Savings.
2. Borrow on your life insurance.
3. Refinance your car, boat, camper.
4. Take out a **second mortgage**. A third? A fourth?
5. Get a line of unsecured personal credit from your bank, credit union, or other financial institution.
6. Research your assets (coin collections, old baseball cards, or whatever).
7. Sell that crummy stock you have been holding and write off the loss. Or get a loan on the securities you want to retain.
8. Get a part-time job; moonlight your way to more money.
9. Network your friends and family. You may be surprised at the nest eggs lying there.
10. Look at nonbank sources (Figure 11.2):
    a. savings and loan associations
    b. credit unions
    c. insurance companies (They prefer to make big loans—starting at a million dollars.)
    d. commercial credit corporations. (The Money Store, for example, makes SBA-guaranteed loans.)
    e. cooperative venture with customers
    f. stock brokerage houses
    g. the SBA
    h. SBICs
    i. venture capitalists
    j. BDCs

Let's look at several of these potential money trees.

Small Business Administration

The Small Business Administration (SBA) of the U.S. government has two major categories of loans, guaranteed and direct. The guaranteed loans are made by banks and nonbank lenders. The direct loans are made directly to businesspeople by the federal government. Direct loans are scarce. Guaranteed loans are changing.

The guarantee is between the SBA, an arm of Congress, and the bank. If the business goes under, up to 90% of the loan is repaid by the government. (This figure is dropping, perhaps to 75%. Get the latest information at your nearest SBA office.)

second mortgage
a second lien or note on real property that is subordinate to the first mortgage

cooperative venture with a customer
a lucky break where you find a major user who will finance your business

SBA
federal agency whose mission is to help small business

FIGURE 11.2 When seeking out institutional lenders, don't stop with just one bank. Lenders come in many shapes and forms.

Small Business Investment Companies

Small Business Investment Companies (SBICs) are privately operated companies that are licensed by the SBA to provide money to small firms. Most SBICs are owned by banks or groups of individuals. The money for loans comes from the SBA, which gets it from the U.S. Treasury, which gets it from you.

SBICs
nonbank lending institutions licensed by the SBA to provide money to small business

Venture Capital Firms

With venture capital firms we enter an area of myth, the world of high rollers and higher flyers. Unlike banks, which lend money that is secured, usually by real estate, venture capitalists don't lend money; they buy a piece of the business. They gamble on the business's rapid growth, hoping to reap a 300%–500% return on their investment. The payoff for most venture capital firms occurs when the company interests enough investors for a public issue of common stock or when it is purchased by a larger business. When the business "goes public," the venture capital people take their money out.

Venture capital people prefer to enter the financial picture at the second stage of a firm's development—when the business has proven its potential and needs a large infusion of cash to support growth. They tend to like high-tech concepts in embryonic industries with high growth potential. As we move toward the year 2000, venture capital companies will grow in number and become more significant in financing entrepreneurial America.

Venture capitalists come in lots of shapes. For example, there are family firms (Rockefeller), industrial firms (GE), bank firms (Bank of America), and other firms (insurance companies, finance companies). The names smack of adventure—Bay Venture Group (San Francisco), Zero Stage Capital Equity (Cambridge), Nautilus (Boston). These people will let you run the show if you give them a healthy ROI.

There's a good list of names and addresses of venture capital firms in *The Guide to Venture Capital Sources*, listed in the reference section at the end of this chapter. Names of local and regional venture capital firms are sometimes compiled by business editors of newspapers. *Inc.* magazine publishes an updated list in December, and *Venture* magazine publishes a yearly list called "The Venture Capital 100" in its June issue.

Business Development Corporations

Business Development Corporations (BDCs) are private concerns that operate at the state level. Their goal is to increase employment within their specific state. New York has the largest BDC in the country.

You can locate your state's BDC by contacting your state economic development agency. Try the government information number in the phone book white pages.

SUMMARY

Money creates its own world. It has its own customs, rituals, and rules. Before you start asking people for money for your business, spend three to four months researching the world of money. Here are some things you can do to streamline your research:

1. Read back issues of *Money* magazine.

2. Read books like *The Small Business Guide to Borrowing Money, Up Front Financing,* and *The Seven Laws of Money.*

3. Find someone who knows more about money than you do, and ask questions.

4. Invest a little money in a few shares of stock in a business you want to know about. Read the stockholders' reports.

5. Know that loans are made on the basis of the four C's—Capital, Character, Capacity (to repay), and Collateral.

6. Start to outline your Business Plan. You will need the plan to show to bankers, vendors, and lenders. For now, an outline is good enough. (See chapter 16 for a model plan.)

7. Begin thinking of a banker as your gateway to the world of money.

THINK POINTS FOR SUCCESS

◄ Your banker can be a doorway to the world of money. Use that door.

◄ How well you buy is as important as how well you sell.

◄ Business is a game. Vendors enjoy having secrets. Try to learn those secrets so that you can get the best deal.

◄ In dealing with bankers and vendors, use lots of open-ended questions like "What else can you do for me?"

REFERENCES

Bank of America. *Business Financing,* Small Business Reporter series. San Francisco: Bank of America, 1988. [The Bank of America *Small Business Reporter* series has sixteen excellent booklets that focus on the area of entrepreneurship: management, computers, franchising, financing, marketing, personnel and accounting. They may be ordered (order forms/prices at any Bank of America branch) from: Small Business Reporter, Bank of America, Dept. 3631, P.O. Box 37000, San Francisco, CA 94137.]

Burlingham, Bo. "Let Them Make Mudpies." *Inc.* July 1983, 65–74. [Inside look at the way one loan application was turned down by the SBA.]

"Clubs with Capital Ideas." *Changing Times,* January 1986, p. 77. [Highlights venture capital clubs.]

Fenn, Donna. "Raising Money—Lots of Money: How One Entrepreneur Got the Venture Capital She Needed to Grow." *Working Woman,* January 1988, p. 35.

Fenn, Donna. "What to Do before You Even Think about Venture Capital—and Where to Find It when You're Really Ready." *Working Woman,* January 1988, p. 40.

Finegan, Jay. "Are Bigger Banks Bad for Small Business?" *Inc.,* December 1987, p. 16.

Gladstone, David. *Venture Capital Investing: The Complete Handbook for Investing in Small Private Businesses for Outstanding Profits.* Englewood Cliffs, N.J.: Prentice-Hall, 1988.

Goldberg, Philip, and Richard Rubin. *The Small Business Guide to Borrowing Money.* New York: McGraw-Hill, 1980.

Gumpert, David E., and Jeffrey Timmons. *The Encyclopedia of Small Business Resources: Everything You Need to Know to Help Your Business Prosper.* New York: Harper & Row, 1984.

Gumpert, David E., and Jeffrey Timmons. *The Insider's Guide to Small Business Resources.* New York: Doubleday & Co., 1982.

Hicks, Tyler G. *Business Capital Sources*, third edition. Rockville Centre, N.Y.: International Wealth, 1987.

Klugman, Ellen. "How to Attract Money." *Working Woman*, October 1980, 83–86, p. 112.

Larkin, Marilyn. "How I Financed My Business: Five Entrepreneurs Tell how They Got Their Start-Ups Started." *Sylvia Porter's Personal Finance Magazine*, November 1986, p. 52.

McKeever, Mike P. *Start-Up Money: How to Finance Your New Small Business.* Berkeley, Ca.: Nolo Press, 1984.

Mangelsdorf, Marthe E. "Matchmaker." *Inc.*, February 1988, p. 12.

Martin, Thomas J. *Financing the Growing Business.* New York: Holt, Rinehart & Winston, 1980.

Nelson, Wayne E. *How to Buy Money: Investing Wisely for Maximum Return.* New York: McGraw-Hill, 1981.

Posner, Bruce. "Laughing All the Way from the Bank: How a Few Clever Companies Finance Their Growth without Relying on Those Undependable Lenders." *Inc.*, December 1987, p. 56.

Posner, Bruce G. "A Rare Case of Bourgeois Values." *Inc.*, June 1983, p. 71–76. [Interesting piece about Bourgeois Fils, an investment banking firm in New Hampshire that puts together money packages for venturers.]

Pratt, Stanley E., ed. *Pratt's Guide to Venture Capital Success*, eleventh edition. Phoenix, Arizona: Oryx Press, 1987. [This guide is very expensive, so try your library first.]

Rennhoff, Harley A. *Get That Business Loan: Convince Your Banker to Say Yes.* Gretna, Louisiana: Pelican, 1987.

Rich, Stanley R., and David E. Gumpert. "Business Plans: What Turns Investors On, What Turns Them Off: Eight Key Do's and Don'ts to Make Your Business Plan a Winner." *Working Woman*, January 1986, p. 38.

Richardson, Clinton. *The Venture Magazine: Complete Guide to Venture Capital.* New York: NAL, 1987.

Roha, Ronaleen R. "Start-Up Help for Your Business." *Changing Times*, June 1987, p. 73.

Schilit, W. Keith. "How to Obtain Venture Capital." *Business Horizons*, May–June 1987, p. 76.

Stevens, Mark. "Boost Your Borrowing Power: When the Banks Balk, Here's where to Go." *Sylvia Porter's Personal Finance Magazine*, December 1987, p. 88.

Stevens, Mark. "Negotiating a Loan: How to Bargain with Your Banker for Better Terms." *Sylvia Porter's Personal Finance Magazine,* July–August 1987, p. 20.

Zonana, Victor F. "Despite Greater Risks, More Banks Turn to Venture Capital Business." *Wall Street Journal*, November 28, 1983. [Seventy banks now have venture-capital subsidiaries, and they include Bank of America, Continental Illinois, and First Chicago. Ask your banker about it.]

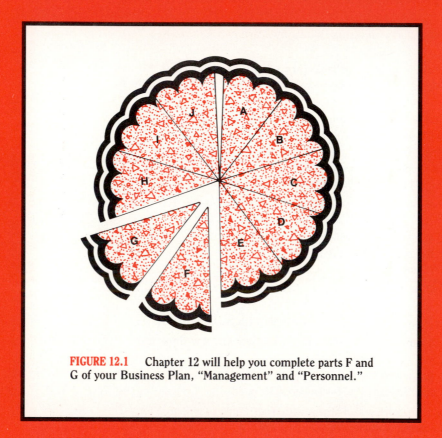

FIGURE 12.1   Chapter 12 will help you complete parts F and
G of your Business Plan, "Management" and "Personnel."

Legal Concerns

LEARNING OBJECTIVES

■ To decide which legal form (sole proprietorship, partnership, corporation) is best for your business. ■ To understand the importance of getting everything in writing. ■ To anticipate potential surprises of your going into business with someone else. ■ To understand the power of psychological forces and the need for appropriate escape routes for yourself. ■ To understand legal escape routes. ■ To develop tactics for finding the right attorney. ■ To develop questions for probing the mind of an attorney. ■ To explore the reasons for incorporating. ■ To recognize signals that you should incorporate. ■ To explore the pitfalls of "offshore" incorporation. ■ To get assistance in writing leases, contracts, labor policies, and other legal documents. ■ To conduct secondary research into corporations and incorporating.

ACTION STEP PREVIEW

55   Take a lawyer to lunch.

56   Do some secondary research on corporations.

In your interviews of successful entrepreneurs, you've probably run across the three main legal forms for small business: sole proprietorship, partnership, and corporation. It's common for a small business to start out as a sole proprietorship or a partnership and then become a corporation later. The Tax Reform Act of 1986 is making the shift to a corporation tricky. A lawyer is needed for that. This chapter is about the care and feeding of your attorney. By now your new eyes should be pretty sharp. Use them now to look ahead.

IT PAYS TO LOOK AHEAD

incorporate
form an artificial, immortal business entity

Imagine that you are in a great business with a partner you trust and respect. When should you **incorporate**? Perhaps sooner than you think. That's what Phil Johnson would tell you now.

The power sailer was my idea. My partner, Steve Savitch, said it would break us, and I should have listened to him. Steve's an engineer and inventor. He's great with numbers and computers, but he doesn't know much about people, which is my department. We'd been friends for a dozen years, at least, and we'd been partners—Savitch and Johnson, Business Consultants—for the last three. We were each going to clear over eighty thousand dollars this year.

money market fund
a pool of managed money secured by short-term corporate IOUs

Steve's tight with a nickel. I knew he'd sock his money away in a **money market fund** at a conservative rate. But I had this idea that we could buy a boat for the partnership, write off the down payment as an expense, and do our company image a world of good.

Selling is 50% sweat, 40% image, and 10% product. I've been in sales all my life. I know.

"I don't know, Phil," Steve said when he saw the boat. Her name was *The Ninja*. She was forty-six feet long, with polished brass fittings and wood that gleamed back at you when you smiled. "What does a fancy rig like that have to do with anything?"

"Image, Steve," I said. "Image."

"Uh-oh," Steve said. "Here we go with the unmeasurable intangibles."

"It's not intangible when you think about those prospects coming from Chicago next week," I said. "A cruise to Catalina should soften them up, don't you think?"

"Maybe," Steve sighed. He gave me his engineer's thin smile. "I trust you, Phil. You're the people person."

Steve's reluctance faded some when he saw the numbers. The power sailer was listed at 25% below market, and the owner was eager to carry back some paper. We took our banker for a sail that weekend, and by Monday noon, we had a check for the difference. The first payment wasn't due for a month, and when Steve and I took it out with our wives, I tell you, I felt like a prince of the sea. We'd pulled off a smooth deal, and I patted myself on the back every time I thought about the **write-offs**.

write-offs
legitimate business deductions you can report to the IRS

The Ninja boosted business, just like I'd thought it would. We closed the Chicago deal and we were busy on a couple of others that looked promising. We made the first payment with no trouble, and when Steve **counter-signed** the check, he admitted he was beginning to like the boat.

countersigning
a situation in which two or more signatures are required before action can occur

"If it's okay with you, Phil, I'm going to sleep there a couple nights this week. My house is full of in-laws, and I've got to get my projections done for those guys from St. Louis.

"Be my guest," I said.

So for a couple of weeks, Steve took his portable computer and slept on *The Ninja*. We took her out that weekend, with four prospects from St. Louis, and Steve seemed a little preoccupied. I closed the deal with them Sunday, fifteen minutes before putting them on the plane for home, but when I called Steve's house to tell him the good news, his wife, Mary, told me he was still at the boat.

Thinking back later, I remembered hearing something funny in Mary's voice. But at the time, I was so excited I didn't think anything about it.

Monday, Steve didn't come to work until almost noon. He looked hung over, but he handed me his projections and we got on with planning our strategy for the next couple of weeks.

"Anything wrong, partner?" I asked. "You seem a little far-off today."

"Sorry," Steve said. He was never one to admit to having emotions. "My mind wandered a bit there. Where were we?"

I should have gotten suspicious right then. But I'm not one to pry, so I didn't. We all like our privacy.

On Tuesday and Wednesday, Steve was at the office when I got there, working away at his computer. On Thursday, the first thing I saw when I got to work was a stack of computer printouts two inches high. It was Steve's half of the next three jobs.

By noon, Steve still hadn't made it to work. I called his house. No answer. I thought of driving down to the dock to check the boat, but I had to pick up a couple of clients at the airport. They were flying in from Minneapolis. We were scheduled for an evening aboard *The Ninja*. When we arrived at our dock, around 4:30 that afternoon, there was no sign of *The Ninja*. Someone on the next boat said Steve had taken off early this morning with a woman on board.

I was in shock. There I stood, with two clients in deck shoes and Bermuda shorts.

Then Joey, the guy who pumps gas, came up waving a gas bill for eight hundred dollars—one I'd thought Steve had paid. And the bad news didn't end there. The next day, a fellow who sells radar equipment called me. Seems Steve had bought two thousand dollars' worth of radar, and this fellow was wondering when he would be paid.

As I hung up the phone, my secretary buzzed me. It was Mary, Steve's wife, wanting to know where Steve was.

Now my stomach was really hurting. My partner Steve was gone—no one knew where—and I was liable for all his business debts, including the payments on *The Ninja*. Terrific.

The problem was that Steve and I had never seen the need for having anything in writing. We were both men of good faith. We had each pulled our weight in the business, and we had balanced each other's skills.

Now that Steve was gone, I felt lost, angry, and betrayed. For the first time in twenty-two years of business, I made an appointment to talk to a lawyer. He just shook his head.

"You should have come to me sooner, Phil," he said. "A lot sooner."

Last week when I was closing the place down and getting ready to go back to work for my old boss, I got a postcard from Steve, from Tahiti. "Sorry, Phil," it read. "Didn't mean to run out on you. It was the only way I could handle it. These things happen. Wanda says hi. Your pal, Steve."

The Good and Bad of Partnerships

A **partnership**, as lots of people find out too late, is only an accounting entity. It does not shield you from trouble. It won't make your business immortal or continuous, and it's taxed at the same rate you are.

The great thing about partnerships is that they're warm, easy to form, and feel good right from the start. You can form a partnership with a handshake, and **dissolve** it without one. A partnership is dissolved when one of the partners dies or when some easy legal steps are taken. The best thing about a partnership is that it allows the financial and moral support of a teammate.

A partnership is somewhat of a paradox. In a legal sense the partnership doesn't do much for you, but as many partners admit, there are sound psychological reasons for going into business with someone else.

What are some of those reasons? Let's say you've analyzed your personal skills and you realize you need balance in a couple of critical areas. For example, you may be an engineer who can come up with twenty original ideas a day but couldn't sell canned heat in an Arctic snowstorm. Or maybe you don't have much money so you need a partner who can supply your new business with capital. Or maybe you get

partnership
an enterprise in which two or more people are engaged as owners or owner/operators

dissolution of a partnership
the separation of partners; an eventuality that needs to be prepared for with intricate planning and much thought

along with people and love to sell and you need to team up with an inventor/producer who can supply you with products to sell. Many successful business owners would never have started a business without a partner.

Before you commit yourself to a partnership, read the rest of this chapter. Then project your cash flow and your P and L to get a ballpark look at your first couple of years. Then, on the basis of a careful business analysis, decide which legal form is best for your business.

The legal form of your business is just that—a form, a shape. To your customers, the particular form you choose will make no difference, but to you, the right shape is absolutely essential. You want your business to be rock-solid, stable, and protected—and you want to be able to change the form if it doesn't work.

THE THREE LEGAL FORMS FOR SMALL BUSINESS

Your small business can exist in one of three legal forms: a sole proprietorship, a partnership, or a corporation. Beyond the mental images we have of these forms of ownership (Figure 12.2), there are business realities—and various amounts of paperwork—that you should know about. Table 12.1 summarizes the differences.

The Sole Proprietorship

Most small businesses start as sole proprietorships. If you start a business on your own—without partners—you will be a sole proprietor. If this form is your choice, the paperwork will be relatively easy. You might get by with a city business license,

TABLE 12.1   Comparison of Business Legal Forms

FORM	WHO'S IN CONTROL	PAPERWORK REQUIRED	SOURCES OF CAPITAL	TAX BURDEN	OWNERS' PERSONAL LIABILITY	CONTINUITY
Sole proprietorship	The owner	None	Limited	Personal rate	Total	Uncertain
Partnership, general	The general partner(s)	None, but written agreement is advised	Greater	Shared by all partners; personal rate	Unlimited	Depends on buy–sell agreement
Partnership, limited	The general partner(s)	Agreement should be drawn up by attorney and filed with the State	Greater	Shared by all partners; personal rate	Limited to the amount invested	Terminated by death
Corporation	Stockholders, board of directors	Much (need attorney and CPA)	Can sell stock; relatively unlimited	Corporate rate, may be higher than personal rate	None unless owners sign a personal guarantee	Potential for immortality
S corporation	Stockholders, board of directors	Much (need attorney and CPA)	Can have no more than 35 stockholders	Gains or losses passed on to stockholders	None unless owners sign a personal guarantee	Potential for immortality

FIGURE 12.2   Common mental images of the three legal forms of business ownership. Beyond these images there are business realities that you should investigate before you decide which form is right for you.

a resale license, and a "doing-business-as" or fictitious business statement (a "DBA"). If you use your own name, you won't need the DBA. But you may discover that your business is sending you signals that another form would better suit your needs.

The Partnership

Many small businesses start as partnerships and it works out great. The start-up paperwork may be as easy as for a small proprietorship. Although *you* would want a good lawyer to put together the partnership agreement for you, it is possible to form a valid partnership with a handshake. If you decide to enter a partnership, get a partnership agreement; you'll be glad you did in the long run. Figure 12.3 presents a sample partnership agreement.

A partnership is made up of at least two parties. There can be more—six, ten, a baker's dozen—but the more partners a business has, the more tricky are the decisions. Think of a ship with a dozen captains. Who makes the decisions?

There are two types of partnerships: limited and general. In a general partnership, each partner has a hand in managing the business and assumes unlimited personal liability for any debts.

In a limited partnership—composed of two or more limited partners and one general partner—the general partner assumes both management duties and the downside risk. A limited partners' liability is limited to the *amount* of his or her original investment as long as he or she has had no role in management decisions.

On the surface, partnerships make a lot of sense. Two or more entrepreneurs face the unknown together and pool their skills. They can raise more capital than one person could alone. But forming a good partnership is more difficult than forming a good marriage.

The Corporation

A corporation is a legal entity created by the state. It stands legally separate from the owners and it does business in the name of the corporation. It can sue and be sued.

Because a corporation is an artificial entity, a creation on paper, it needs more paperwork to justify its existence. There are fees required, and meetings of the Board of Directors. The secretary of the corporation must keep accurate, complete records of what transpires at meetings. Nonetheless, for many businesses, it's worth going to the trouble to form a corporation because a shield is created between the creditors and the owners' personal wealth. To keep the shield in place, active owners become *employees* of the corporation; their business cards have the corporate name and logo and specify their job title. Owners sign contracts as *officers* of the corporation.

GET A LAWYER

Businesses are built on people, of course, and this is why you need a business structure that will gives you flexibility when the people in your business want to make a change. Don't underestimate the power of psychological forces. This chapter is designed to help you anticipate those internal forces that can make you wish you had planned escape routes ahead of time.

small business attorney
an attorney who specializes in small business

A good **small business attorney** can help you create the right business structure for a partnership or a corporation—a structure that gives you the flexibility you'll

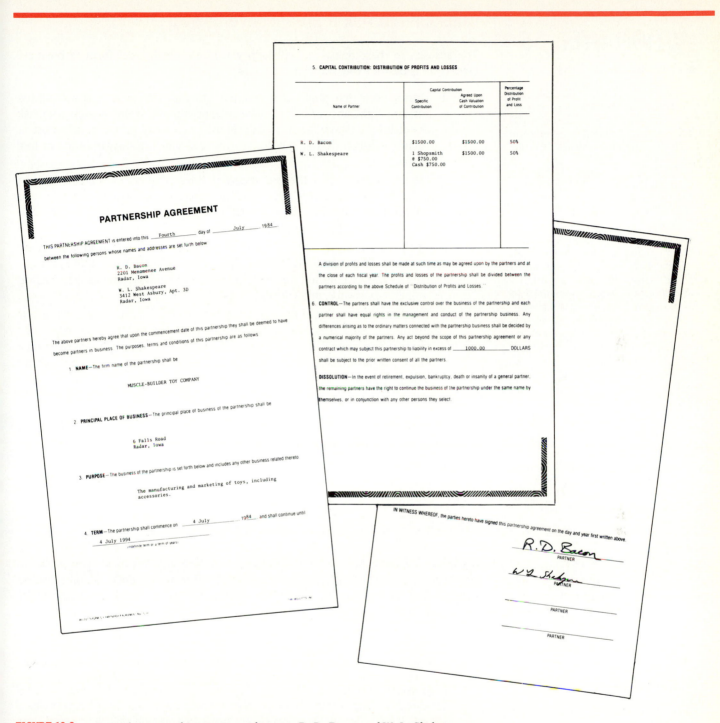

FIGURE 12.3   A sample partnership agreement between R. D. Bacon and W. L. Shakespeare, both of Radar, Iowa.

need. Network your contacts for a lawyer with experience in your industry. You need to have a lawyer on your **taxi squad**. Once you've found one you think might be right for you, make an appointment with him or her.

taxi squad

human resources outside your business that you can call upon as needed

ACTION STEP 55

Take a lawyer to lunch.

Network your business contacts for the names of 3–5 attorneys with experience in forming small business corporations and partnerships. Concentrate on those who have worked in your industry.

Check them out on the phone and then take the most promising candidates to lunch. (Lunch is optional—but your inquiries are vital.)

The first thing you're looking for is someone you can get along with. Then look for experience in the world of small business. A hot trial lawyer may have a lot of charisma, but you want a nuts-and-bolts small business specialist who can save you time, pain, and money.

During lunch, find out about fees and costs. Compare the cost, for example, of having your lawyer write up a complex partnership buy-out agreement with the cost of setting up a corporation. This section of this book lists some questions to start you off in your discussions with your prospective attorney.

A good lawyer will offer perspectives that will be helpful in the formation of your business. You may have to look awhile, and it may cost you some dollars up front, but there's no substitute for good legal help.

Questions to Ask a Prospective Lawyer

The answers to these questions will help you know which legal form of business ownership is best for you and your business.

1. During your first phone conversation: Do you offer a free get-acquainted session? If the answer is yes, make an appointment. If the answer is no, ask about lunch. (Many lawyers can't afford to give free sessions, but most of them eat lunch. If you buy lunch, you can get forty-five minutes of free advice.)

2. On the phone, before the first meeting: What information do you need in order to help me decide what legal form of business will be best? Do you have a list of questions for prospective business owners that you can mail me? Where can I get sample partnership agreements?

3. At the first meeting, after the lawyer knows exactly what kind of business you're in: What would be the pros and cons of sole proprietorship, partnership, and incorporation for me with regard to liability, tax burden, raising money, paperwork, and control.

4. If there will be more than one owner: What are the pros and cons of our forming a general partnership/a limited partnership/a corporation/a subchapter S corporation? What are the setup costs? What does it cost to change from one form to another? Are there time restrictions on when I could change forms?

Be sure to prepare your own agenda for each conversation with the lawyer. If you're organized you will save money on your fee.

Now you're ready to do Action Step 55.

Provide for Contingencies: Look Ahead

contingencies
unforeseen events in the future that alert you to prepare Plan B

If you don't use a good lawyer to help you structure your business, you probably won't have a plan to handle **contingencies**, and unforeseen events can take you by surprise. If Paul Webber had used his imagination to look ahead, his story might have turned out differently.

Paul was a computer programmer when he met Jerry Dominic. Jerry was a likable guy and a dynamite salesman—and after reading *Megatrends* he knew there was money to be made in the information business—so he got together with Paul and formed a software consulting business. They specialized in microcomputers, because that's where the action was. Their first year was okay—they netted over $40,000 apiece—but their second year was looking even better.

By May of their second year, their projections told them they could make a hundred thousand each before the end of summer. They thought it felt great to be rich.

To celebrate, they went to a neighborhood bar for a couple of drinks. Jerry got into an argument with a bald-headed guy about politics. There was a fistfight and Jerry ended up on the floor. As Paul stooped down to help Jerry up, he noticed his partner felt heavy, like dead weight.

At forty-nine years old, Jerry Dominic was dead of a heart attack.

Two days after the funeral, Paul was on the phone with a customer when Jerry's widow walked in. Mildred had just inherited Jerry's half of the business.

Paul didn't like Mildred being his partner, but there was nothing he could do. He knew he would have to break his back to teach her the business. Computer software was fast-track and competitive—it changed before you could take a breath—and Mildred would have to learn an awful lot in a short time.

Paul was a good guy, so he tried. The first week, he was extra tired because he was handling his own customers while he spent long hours trying to teach Mildred the business. The second week, two of Paul's customers on hold defected to a competitor. Paul heard about it on the grapevine. The third week, the company almost ran out of cash, and Paul had to dump in $5,000 from his personal account to keep suppliers happy.

The other problem was that Mildred wasn't learning the business. She was getting in Paul's hair, and she was spending money. But she wasn't able to hold up her end, and there was no improvement in sight.

Paul hung on for a couple more weeks. Then he did the only thing he could do for his own survival: he took what customers he had left and rented an office six blocks away and tried to keep going. He figured he had paid his dues to Jerry. He hoped Jerry understood, wherever he was.

Sometimes, Paul wishes he and Jerry had had something in writing to cover *contingencies*. In business, you always need a Plan B.

If you still want to form a partnership, get a lawyer to draw up a **partnership agreement** and consult your insurance agent about getting some protective insurance. If you're able to look ahead, you'll avoid problems regardless of the legal form of your business.

partnership agreement
a written agreement between two or more partners that should specify profit sharing, capital gains distribution, and tactics for painless dissolution

CORPORATIONS AND SMALL BUSINESS

There are at least seven good reasons for incorporating. In general, we think most owners of small businesses fail to incorporate because they don't see the signals their businesses are giving. If you don't see the signals, don't incorporate. If you do, check it out with an attorney. (See Box 12.1.)

Seven Reasons for Incorporating

1. You Limit Your Liability. A corporation acts like a shield between you and the world. If your business fails, your creditors can't come after your house, your condo, your Porsche, your first-born, and your hard-won collectibles—provided you've done it right. Fortunately for Harry Bemis, he'd done it right.

BOX 12.1   **Two Clear Signals that You Should Incorporate**

If you are in business now and are thinking about incorporation, answer these two questions. Your business may be giving you signals that you should incorporate.

1. Could you be sued? If you are vulnerable to litigation, then incorporate or buy lots of protective insurance.

2. Do you want a different, more prestigious image? Again, if the answer is yes, incorporate.

Henry Bemis was going great guns with his coffee service when a piece of his equipment spewed boiling water all over the hands of Jody Dawn, a professional model.

Miss Dawn's hands earned her over $200,000 a year. The day her hands were burnt, she was at a branch of a major bank, doing a DeBeers-sponsored commercial for diamond rings and safety-deposit boxes.

Her hands were her living and her future. On the advice of her attorney, Miss Dawn sued Henry Bemis and his Easy-Cup Coffee Service.

Henry had insurance, of course. But it stopped at $350,000, and the courts were about to award Miss Dawn two million dollars. Here's the way they figured it:

She had been earning $200,000 a year.

She could figure on an active career of at least ten years.

Ten years × $200,000 = $2,000,000.

Luckily, Henry had had the good sense to incorporate when he went into business. So while the courts went after Easy-Cup Coffee Service, Inc., Henry's house and car and personal properties were safe.

Also, because he'd gotten into a couple of networks, Henry was able to start another business right away.

This time, he didn't go into coffee.

To keep your corporate shield up, make sure you: (1) hold scheduled board of directors meetings, (2) keep up the minutes book, and (3) act as if you are an employee of the corporation.

Here's an example that illustrates the corporate shield: your secretary gets into a fender-bender while driving on company business. If you're a corporation, the injured parties will come after your corporation, not you. (If your employees use their own cars on company business, make sure they're insured for a minimum of one million dollars.)

2. You Change Your Tax Picture.   Consult the current IRS schedule or ask a CPA for advice.

3. You Upgrade Your Image.   What does the word *corporation* mean to you? IBM? Exxon? TRW? Texaco? TWA? GM?

Heavy hitters, right?

Let's look at that word. It comes from the Latin *corpus,* which means "body." *To incorporate* means to make or form or shape into a body. Looked at from that angle, *incorporating* starts to sound creative.

It will sound that way to lots of your target customers, too. As a corporation, you may:

have more clout and solidity in the world,

attract better employees, and

enjoy more prestige.

4. You Have the Opportunity to Channel Some Heavy Expenses.   With some legal help, you can write a medical assistance clause into your by-laws. Here's the way it works:

insurance premium
a rated payment on insurance coverage

1. Your corporation pays your health insurance **premiums**.
2. Your corporation reimburses you for the deductible.
   a. Your corporation writes off the money paid to you as a business expense.
   b. You aren't liable for taxes on the reimbursement.

F.I.C.A.
contribution to federal government
for Social Security

3. You can deduct **F.I.C.A.** payments as a business expense.

5. You Simplify the Division of Multiple Ownership.   For example, say you're going into the printing and graphics business with two good friends. The business needs $100,000 to get started.

> You can put your hands on $60,000.
> Friend A delivers $25,000.
> Friend B delivers $5,000.

The way to handle the ownership is with stock. You get 60%, Friend A gets 25%, and Friend B gets 5%.

6. You Guarantee Continuity.   If one of the owners skips town, the corporation keeps on chugging. That's because you've gone through a lot of red tape and planning to set it up that way. It's one of the few justifications for red tape we know of.

7. You Can Offer Internal Incentives.   When you want to reward a special employee, you can offer some stock or a promotion (for example, a vice presidency) in addition to (or in place of) pay raises. Becoming a corporate officer carries its own special excitement, and this gives you flexibility.

What a Corporation Will Not Do

Becoming a corporation won't solve all your problems. For example, a corporation will not:

> immunize you against all creditors (The bankers and creditors will still want a personal guarantee—which could mean your collateral.)
>
> make *you* immortal
>
> protect you if you fail to hold meetings, keep minutes, and keep your state corporate records current

Subchapter S Corporations

Subchapter S corporations are semicorporate bodies that limit the owner's liability while still allowing a pass-through of business losses to the personal income statements of the owners, founders, and others. *Subchapter S* refers to the section of the 1958 IRS code that describes it.

The number of stockholders is limited to thirty-five, and corporate income (or loss) is allowed to be passed directly to the stockholders. There is no corporate tax. The IRS has specific time requirements for filing, and some states do not recognize the tax aspects of the Sub S category. Check out these things for your state. Your attorney can help you.

Do Research Now

We've told you a lot of what you need to know about corporations, but it's not enough. You need to start reading widely on the subject. Action Step 56 will get you started. It takes time to incorporate properly, so it pays to get started early.

ACTION STEP 56

Do some secondary research on corporations.

Before you take any action about legal forms you need a lot of information. Go to the library and the bookstore, and start reading books like *Inc. Yourself* by Judith McQuown, *How to Form Your Own Corporation without a Lawyer for Under $50* by Ted Nicholas, and *Incorporating Your Business* by John Kirk. See the reference section at the end of the chapter.

When you have become familiar with the broad concepts, do some research on specific corporations in your industry. (Start with your incorporated competitors.) You can get information from the library, from a stock broker, or by writing to the corporations.

While you're doing this research, keep looking around with new eyes.

SUMMARY

There are three basic legal forms for a small business: sole proprietorship, partnership, corporation.

You can start doing business as a sole proprietorship with a minimum of hassle. You might need only a city license, a resale license, and perhaps a DBA (fictitious name) statement.

The legal paperwork for a partnership is almost as simple. You can form a partnership with a handshake and dissolve it without one. There are good psychological reasons for forming a partnership. Only eight percent of the small businesses in the U.S. are partnerships. If you decide a partnership is right for you, get a lawyer to prepare a partnership agreement to protect you against trouble.

Forming a corporation takes the most paperwork, but it gives you more flexibility, as well as a shield to protect you in case your business hurts someone. With a corporation, you:

1. limit your liability
2. change your tax picture
3. upgrade your company image
4. can rechannel some expenses (like medical)
5. can simplify multiple ownership by apportioning company stock
6. can guarantee continuity
7. can offer internal incentives to key employees

THINK POINTS FOR SUCCESS

◄ We only remember what we want to. Get everything in writing.

◄ If your business is small and you like it that way, keep it simple—like your hobby.

◄ Most growth businesses need outside infusions of cash. Don't pay Uncle Sam more than you have to.

◄ When you create corporate stock in your by-laws, think about creating at least ten times more than you intend to sell at start-up.

◄ Even if you incorporate, a banker may still want a personal guarantee for loans.

◄ Forget about incorporating in Nevada or Delaware (unless you live there), or in exotic offshore locations. You'll be a foreign corporation (out-of-state) and you'll have to pay extra to do business at home.

ACTION STEP REVIEW

Two action steps teach you more about legal forms.

55 Take a lawyer to lunch. Use the time to determine the lawyer's personality and his or her ability to help you.

56 Read some books about corporations and the art of incorporating. Learn all you can now.

REFERENCES

Ames, Michael D., and Norval L. Wellsfry. *Small Business Management.* St. Paul, Minn.: West Publishing Co., 1983.

Cook, Wade B. *Incorporation Handbook for Small Business Owners.* Scottsdale, Arizona: Regency Books, 1986.

Diamond, Michael. *How to Incorporate: A Manual for Entrepreneurs and Professionals.* New York: Wiley, 1987.

McQuown, Judith H. *How to Profit after You Inc. Yourself.* New York: Warner Books, 1986.

McQuown, Judith H. *Inc. Yourself: How to Profit by Setting Up Your Own Corporation.* New York: Warner Books, 1984.

Mancuso, Anthony. *How to Form Your Own California Corporation,* sixth edition. Berkeley, Calif.: Nolo Press, 1985. [Now also available for Texas and Florida.]

Mancuso, Anthony, and Peter Jan Honigsberg. *The California Professional Handbook,* third revised edition. Berkeley, Calif.: Nolo Press, 1987.

Professional Report Editors and John Kirk. *Incorporating Your Business.* Chicago: Contemporary Books, 1986.

FIGURE 13.1 Chapter 13 will help you prepare the Management and Personnel parts of your Business Plan, parts F and G.

Building a Winning Team

LEARNING OBJECTIVES

■ To accept that you probably can't do everything well. ■ To understand the importance of balance to the survival of your business. ■ To take another look at yourself and identify your weaknesses. ■ To explore new ways of putting together a team. ■ To look back, and see if there's anyone you wish could work with you in this venture. ■ To use brainstorming techniques to assemble a team. ■ To use the DISC Performax personality profile (and other systems) to identify who you are and the types of people you need for balance. ■ To survey your competitors and network your vendors for potential team members. ■ To brainstorm with your new team *before* you open the doors, so you can take advantage of your people resource.

ACTION STEP PREVIEW

57 Categorize your friends and acquaintances.

58 Brainstorm your ideal team.

59 Network your competitors and vendors to build a winning team.

60 Tap your people resources by brainstorming with your team.

DISC
a system for profiling prospective or existing team members

Building a winning team can be one of the most enjoyable tasks you face. To do this, you must first look at yourself objectively, and then build your team around your business and psychological needs. That's what the successful entrepreneur does. This chapter will show you how to build to win.

BUILDING BALANCE INTO YOUR TEAM

Balance is essential to a team. You're maybe thinking you already understand everything you need to know about balance. If you're a person who tries to solve every problem yourself, it may be awhile before you admit you need help. Fortunately, tools are available to give you perspective.

One such tool is the **DISC** system developed by John Geier in the 1970s. We'll explain the system later in the chapter, but for now we want you to start thinking about the four categories the DISC system uses to describe people. *DISC* is an acronym for the names of Geier's four personality types:

D = Dominant
I = Influencing
S = Steady
C = Compliant

Think about these personality types as you read the following case study. Try to categorize Bob, Carol, Ted, and Alice.

Friends as Team Members

Four friends decided to spend vacation at Bufadora, a small fishing village on the coast of Baja California. They drove down in two vehicles. Carol and Bob drove Carol's Mercedes, and Ted and Alice drove their Chevy Blazer with four-wheel drive.

The house they rented overlooked the ocean. Carol, an expressive person, kept exclaiming how beautiful it was. "Have you ever seen anything," Carol said, "as lovely, as beautiful, as gorgeous as that blue?"

The thirteenth time she said it, Ted became irritated and began to snipe. "How about the desert outside Las Vegas?" he said. "You've just won a million dollars, and the world is your oyster."

"Las Vegas is ugly," Carol said, "but I did enjoy hearing Frank Sinatra. He was wonderful!"

"That guy," Ted said.

They went on arguing until Alice got them organized on lunch. She sent Ted off to the market for some matches. She assigned Carol the job of assembling a platter of fruit. She asked Bob to figure out how to light the gas-fired barbecue. He had to take it apart and clean the feeder lines to make it work. Thus lunch was delayed.

When the barbecue was working again, Ted cooked the meat to perfection. Everyone enjoyed the meal. Carol ate mostly fruit. Bob and Ted ate mostly meat. Alice ate a balanced meal of meat, fruit, and vegetables.

After lunch, the four went for a drive in the Mercedes. Carol drove with a lot of flair, tooting at people in the street. Ted didn't think she drove very well and told her so. Bob frowned at him for badgering Carol, while Alice did her best to smooth things over for everyone's sake.

Six miles outside town, Carol saw a sign pointing to a church she was sure would be charming and turned off the main highway. Dust boiled up around the car. A mud hole soon appeared in the road. Carol decided to drive through it, disregarding Ted's warning to slow down. The Mercedes ground to a halt.

"What on earth happened?" Carol said.

"You got us stuck!" Ted said.

"I'm sure it's not a big problem," Alice said.

Ted and Bob worked for an hour but could not free the rear wheel of the car. During this time Carol sat in the shade, and Alice cheered the men on and tried to be helpful.

"Okay," Ted said, "enough! We're going to have to hike back to town."

"In these shoes?" Carol said, pointing to her new pumps from Saks Fifth Avenue.

"It does seem a little far," Alice said.

"Six point two miles to be exact," Bob said.

"The road curved around," Ted said. "The town is just over this hill about a mile as the crow flies."

"Let's wait for someone to come along," Carol suggested.

"You can wait if you want," Ted said, "but I'm hiking over that hill."

An argument ensued. While Bob studied a map of the area, Alice, the perpetual peacemaker, attempted to come up with some compromise that would please everyone.

In the end, Ted and Alice hiked up the hill. At the top, they saw the ragged string of Bufadora rooftops. They waved to Carol and Bob back at the car, but Carol was listening to the car stereo and Bob was studying alternate routes on the map.

Ted and Alice walked to the village and got help, and the Mercedes was towed out by sunset.

That evening they went out to dinner. Carol was glitteringly beautiful—the belle of the cafe. She ordered a bottle of champagne for Ted and Alice and toasted them as the world's greatest explorers. Bob spent dinnertime analyzing why the car had gotten stuck.

Let's Analyze This Team

Ted is pushy. He knows he's right, and he's ready for adventure—or an argument; he doesn't mind confrontation. Under stress, he must take action, whether it's right or not; he cannot sit still and wait for a plan. On the DISC scale, Ted is a Dominant.

Carol is glib, pretty, and glittery. She enjoys the spotlight, speaks in superlatives, and dresses to impress. Under stress, she needs lots of people around her. She likes to persuade people to her point of view. On the DISC scale, she's an Influencer.

Alice is sweet. Her main goal is to keep things moving, and pleasant. She hates confrontation and spends her energy negotiating the energies of others. Alice is a Compliant.

Bob is precise. He likes numbers and measurements. He has the best mind of the four and he keeps it in shape by analyzing things. Bob loves to tinker with machinery. Under stress, he probes the situation with careful analysis before taking any action. Of course, Bob is a Steady.

D's need other people, other types. Ted, a flaming D, is married to Alice, a cool C. They make a good team because their personalities balance each other. Carol, a flamboyant I, is married to Bob, a precise fellow who keeps things under control.

How Does This Relate to Your Small Business?

If you're an entrepreneur, there's a good chance you're a Dominant. You probably like adventure, and thrive on challenges. Management, however, may bore you. You may be able to motivate people when you're in the mood, but when you're not in the mood, forget it. You're maybe not so great at sales, either. (After all, why should you have to sell anyone on a product that is obviously superior?) If you're a D, you probably think people who don't see things your way are dumb, or stupid. If you're a D, you most likely lack the patience to repair broken equipment; instead, you have someone else repair it or you replace it. D's, like so many entrepreneurs, must get on with it.

But to do that, you need a balanced team. Here's how it works:

For management, negotiations, smoothing over, you need a Compliant.

For sales, advertising, promotion, anything flashy, you need an Influencer. You need someone with pizzazz and spark.

For the precise tasks like accounting, engineering, computer work, operating a switchboard, you need a Steady.

DISC is not the only quadrant-oriented profiling program. There are others, and large organizations use them to help people connect in more fruitful ways. If you're coming out of a large organization into small business, you've probably had experience with one or more of these profiling systems. You're bringing a lot of skills and experience with you to the world of small business. You might not have the time for elaborate testing when you're building a team for your own business, but you can still use the insights gained from the research that has gone into shaping these systems.

This is a good time for you to practice profiling some personalities you know well by doing Action Step 57. The system we want you to use is similar to the DISC system.

An Example

balanced team
a group of individuals with complementary skills, aptitudes, and strengths

Harry Marquez needed a **balanced team** and didn't know it.

Harry was a terrible student in high school. His grades in English were rotten and he couldn't spell. To him, history was a laugh, government a lie, and science an unimaginative way of looking at the world.

Harry did all right in three courses: art, physics (he liked electricity), and Latin. But you can't graduate with three strong subjects and ten weak ones, so Harry joined the Army. The Army sent him to Germany, and he quickly became invaluable as a tank repair specialist. He fixed tanks, and the Army gave him weekend passes.

At the end of his tour, Harry married Liliane, a young model he'd met in Germany, and they moved to Harry's home town. Harry looked up his old physics teacher. After a lot of scrambling and maneuvering, Harry made it into a good university.

There, he could choose courses he could handle, and he met an English teacher who taught him how to write. Harry finished his electrical engineering degree in three years. In two more, he had his doctorate. And along the way, he had discovered a field that looked hot: industrial robots.

Harry landed a job with a *Fortune* 500 firm. The pay was good, but he hated the lack of freedom. When he couldn't create, his mind slowed down and he felt dead. Working at night, he developed an idea to make a two-armed robot. When he presented the idea to a vice-president, he was told that the company wasn't interested. So Harry formed his own company.

He didn't know the first thing about business, but he hired a man who did. Fred Winslow had a sales background, a sincere smile, a warm handshake, and a way with words that could have made him a preacher or politician. Winslow told him the only place for this kind of firm was the Silicon Valley, so that's where they went.

balance sheet
a financial tool that gives you a picture of your business at one point in time

Harry and Liliane owned all the stock of Marquez Robotics. Their first year, they grossed just under a million. Harry loved it. He didn't understand a **balance sheet**, and talk about cash flow put him right to sleep, but he loved having money to spend.

They bought a Turbo Porsche and an Eldorado. Harry had worked hard, and now that they could afford it, he wanted all the creature comforts. He also wanted stimulation, and that meant people like himself, who were loaded with ideas, people who could work through the night on a project and cap it off with a party. So Harry hired a lot of people like himself, and lots of times the phones would ring like crazy and no one would answer them.

The second year, Winslow wanted a piece of the company, but Harry didn't want to let go. He felt it was *his* company—built with his Army money plus the money he and Liliane had saved while he was breaking his back in big business—and it was *his* two-armed robot. So Harry said no.

Then two things happened. Liliane decided she wanted a divorce, and Winslow left the company. Liliane went to San Francisco, and Winslow went down the road a half-mile and founded Winslow Electromagnetic. With him went two of Harry's key employees—both inventor–engineers, and seventeen of Harry's largest customer accounts.

One by one, the wild-and-crazy engineer–inventors left when Harry didn't have enough cash to meet his payroll. Meanwhile, Harry was busy in his lab, working night and day on an electric motor that would take the place of the hydraulic engines used in most robots.

There was no one in the front office, no one to answer the phones. The books went from bad to worse. Harry was in a race with his creditors, who would ship only with a C.O.D., but he was so involved with his new invention that he hardly noticed.

What Can Harry Marquez Teach Us?

Harry's business failed for at least two reasons. Number one, he could design great equipment, but he could not design a winning team. True, he did hire Winslow, who in many ways was his perfect complement, but Harry couldn't read the man's drives for power and control.

Number two, Harry didn't take time to listen to his employees. The people he hired did not fill real business needs. In business, that's fatal. It's important to hire good people and then listen to them. A company is no more than its people. Successful businesses of all sizes view their employees as resources.

Let's go back and try a **personality analysis** of Harry. We can say that he:

was bright, creative

was impatient with day-to-day operations

was a dreamer

was a quick learner, but a terrible student

was able to fix almost anything mechanical or electrical

liked to be surrounded by attractive people (his model wife, the people he hired)

needed a certain amount of flash in the world (the cars he bought)

didn't want to give up even a very small piece of his company (He felt like a proud parent.)

didn't understand the power drives of Fred Winslow

went back to his lab (womb, retreat from the world) when the going got tough, to perfect yet another dazzling invention

It's probably obvious to you that Harry's team needed balancing, but it wasn't obvious to him. He needed the DISC system.

THE DISC SYSTEM

Yes, Harry needed something like the DISC system to help him understand people and how people can balance each other. The DISC system, developed by John Geier, is owned by Performax Systems International. It's inexpensive and thorough, and it

---

ACTION STEP 57

Categorize your friends and acquaintances.

Make a list of your friends, acquaintances, and people you've met in the previous action steps. Classify these people into four groups:

Adventurers are pushy, always looking for the next horizon. Adventurers must lead and be in control, even when they're wrong. They question procedures and are always creating new procedures.

Spotlighters love to talk, tell stories, amuse. They hog the spotlight. They need people and more people. They have lots of charm and are often physically attractive.

Negotiators smooth things over, make groups cohesive. They smile a lot while they are introducing Adventurers to Spotlighters. They feel best in situations where everything is nailed down by rules and regulations.

Handlers get their kicks from handling details. To a Handler there is no such thing as too much detail. They take their time assessing, studying, examining, and probing. They also take a long time to reach a decision.

Now, from each category, select one person who could help you in your small business. List three skills the person has that could help balance your entrepreneurial team. Transfer the list of skills to a separate sheet of paper. Keep your list in pencil and prepare to make adjustments as you learn more about your potential team members. The decisions you make in building your founding team are among the most important decisions you will make.

---

personality analysis
an enlightening way of looking at yourself and at the people around you

can give the busy entrepreneur insight and quick perspective on people. DISC takes about twenty-five minutes, and it's easy to analyze. Reminder:

D = dominance
I = influencing
S = steadiness
C = compliance

Look at the grid in Figure 13.2. Where would you put Harry? Where would you put Fred Winslow? See Figure 13.3.

The Right Kind of Help

top-heavy team
a team composed mostly of chiefs

The DISC grid can show at a glance where you are. Harry's was a top-heavy team. He didn't have anyone to handle day-to-day operations. He didn't have anyone to answer the phones. In fact, when it came to phones, Harry was the caller, not the answerer. Harry needed help, but he didn't know it. What sort of help did he need?

Janet Ames is a capable woman in her mid thirties who has two well-behaved children. When her youngest reached the age of ten, Janet went back to work.

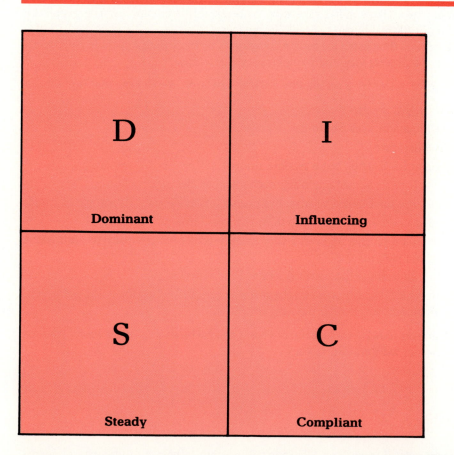

D	I
Dominant	**Influencing**
S	C
Steady	**Compliant**

FIGURE 13.2   The DISC grid allows you to classify an individual's personality as one of four types.

FIGURE 13.3   Harry's team was top-heavy.

Janet began working for Marquez Robotics three weeks after the previous vice-president for marketing, a Mr. Winslow, went off with several key employees and some very influential customers.

Janet went right to work as the new vice-president for marketing. It took her just two full working days to shape up the front office. The first thing she did was to hire Rudy to handle the telephones. He was a fussy young man who kept a very tidy desk. Before noon on his first day, Rudy had established his own territory in one corner of the front office. He had his own desk, his own nameplate, and a wastepaper basket with his initials monogrammed on it in large letters. Janet liked that. It bespoke order.

Once she got the phone question settled, she began networking her contacts for someone to straighten out the books. Janet was a good bookkeeper, but she knew a mess when she saw one, and off in the distance she could smell tax problems for her new boss. In this instance, an expert was definitely called for.

Janet saw Dr. Marquez, the president and CEO, the day she was hired, and then she didn't see him again for eleven days. Although that might have bothered someone else, it suited the very stable Mrs. Ames just fine. One of her philosophies was that it takes all kinds.

To her, Dr. Marquez and the men in the lab seemed like playful children; they needed freedom to create. If they had been real children, of course, she would have applied some well-needed discipline. But they were adults, and you don't tell adults when it's time to scrub behind their ears, especially if you are employed by them. So Janet worked hard at being diplomatic, at smoothing over rifts in the company surface, at helping and counseling and controlling.

Nine months after Janet came to work, the company was again in the black. She celebrated by hiring a young woman to help out in the front office. Her name was Sandra Star, and she wanted to be an actress. Her smile made the customers happy, and she took the office PR load off Rudy, who was promoted to Communications Chief.

Rudy spent three entire weekends personalizing his new office. With his name on the door lettered in gold, he was delighted with his new title, and he felt a renewed loyalty and devotion to Janet and the company.

Portrait of a Balanced Team

Dominant
a person who shapes the environment by overcoming the opposition

Turn back to the DISC grid (Figure 13.2). We have already placed Harry as a **Dominant**. Where would you put Janet Ames? Rudy? Sandra, the secretary–receptionist?

Let's do a quick DISC analysis of Janet Ames. She:

> understands the need for control
>
> is diplomatic with everyone
>
> checks for accuracy
>
> is good at analysis, critical thinking, and sizing up situations
>
> complies with authority
>
> gets the job done
>
> likes standard operating procedures (If there aren't any, she can establish them.)
>
> enjoys being part of a group

Compliant
a person who works with existing circumstances to promote quality in products or services

You can see that Janet is probably a **Compliant**. Such people make good managers, and that's what Marquez Robotics needed.

Rudy Bowman, a classic **Steady**, is no slouch as a team member, either. Steadies love to sit in one place and control a very small turf. They are invaluable for specialized skills, listening, doing the books, security tasks. They get to work on time; they leave on time. Treat a Steady right and you'll be rewarded with tons of loyalty and fidelity.

Steady
a person who cooperates with others to carry out the task

And finally, Sandra Star, the secretary–receptionist, is an **Influencer**. She's the neon entertainment—great for the front office as long as the working conditions are favorable. A ripple or two and she'll be off to another adventure. Figure 13.4 shows the completed team picture.

Influencer
a person who shapes the environment by bringing others into alliance

FIGURE 13.4   Janet Ames instinctively hired people who balanced Harry's team.

ACTION STEP 58

Brainstorm your ideal team.

What do you need to win at the game of small business? Money, of course. And energy, tremendous energy. (You've got that or you wouldn't have read this far.) You also need footwork, a terrific idea, intensity, the ability to concentrate, a sense of industry and thrift, and the curiosity of a Sherlock Holmes.

And you need people. People to support your effort. People to balance your skills. People to take up the slack. People to help you with tasks you find distasteful or don't understand.

So analyze yourself first. What do you like? What are you good at? What do you hate? What does your business need that you cannot provide yourself? Who can fill that need for you?

This one idea alone will get you started on building your ideal team.

self-analysis
an introspective look at your strengths and weaknesses

joy in life
where you get your main reason for being

marketing
all the activities that take place between identification of the need for a product or service and its delivery

team building
the orderly procurement of a group of people who together can achieve maximum results for the firm

winning team
what you must build to succeed in business

Action Step 58 asks you to do some **self-analysis** and to think about the types of people that could complement your personality and skills. Think about what kinds of help you need.

Another Look at the Team's Founder

Take a minute to think about the personality of Harry Marquez. Do any of his traits remind you of your own?

We can't reproduce all the DISC profiles here, but we can summarize Harry's personality briefly. Harry is a creative achiever who likes to dominate and control. In many ways, he is the typical entrepreneur:

1. *He operates from internal motivation and deeply felt goals.* Harry's main **joy in life** was to invent. He set and met his own goals and was surprised when others in the organization didn't do the same. He was unaware that some people need goals set for them. He did his work and expected everyone else to do theirs.

2. *He is bored with routine work.* Harry couldn't believe that some people actually thrive on routine tasks. People like Harry are so busy setting their own pace that they seldom look back. Under pressure, they become aggressive and competitive. They like the limelight, and when they don't get it they can get sulky.

3. *He judges others by concrete results.* Harry couldn't believe Fred Winslow wanted a piece of the company because he couldn't see that Fred had accomplished anything. To an inventor, sales is invisible and insubstantial. Money exists, but the sales and **marketing** functions of a business seem like mumbo jumbo and double-talk. From Harry's point of view, Fred Winslow never really did anything except smile and glad-hand and take customers to lunch on company time. This shows Harry's limited point of view.

4. *He is a super-quick thinker.* When he was on his own turf, Harry had the fastest feet in the business. He was inventive, and if led along the right path, he could have invented a system to handle the problems of his organization. But business matters bored Harry, so the best thing for him to do was to hire someone to manage the day-to-day affairs, negotiate, and smooth over the rough spots.

Without a balanced team, Harry Marquez would have been out of business fast. Since he didn't want to work for someone else, he would have been in trouble. Remember this: the smaller an organization is, the more important is the team. **Team building** is important.

SCOUTING AND HIRING

If you need help balancing your team, Appendix 13.1 lists addresses for three kinds of personality profiles. DISC is among those listed. In Action Step 59 you use the idea of balance to scout potential team members. If you're able to imagine how each candidate would work out in your new business, you'll be well on your way to building a **winning team**. Do Action Step 59 now.

Later, when you're hiring, try to hire the best-quality people you can find. There's wisdom in this old adage:

If you're first rate, you hire first-rate people.
If you're second rate, you hire third-rate people.
If you're third rate, you hire fourth-rate people.

How long can you make it with anything but a first-rate team? With what kind of materials do you want to build your business?

In a large firm, a poorly placed employee or one who's not pulling his or her weight can be transferred to a different job. There are lots of jobs, lots of slots. If you've got a "Driver" answering phones, you can move her to R&D. If you've got a "Steady" going crazy in a leadership position, you can move him to a job that requires attention to detail. On the other hand, in a firm with only three employees, for example, one weak employee makes you 25% less effective. Two weak employees will cut your effectiveness in half. Choosing the right team is one of the most important decisions you will make.

A Team of Part-Timers

Charlene Webb has built a winning team of part-time employees.

> After Charlene Webb sold her gourmet cookware shop, she opened a women's specialty store. The shop is small—about 3,000 square feet—and is located in a neighborhood center in an upscale community of about 10,000 people.
>
> Charlene discovered that her ideal employees were local women who are active in the community life and who prefer to work only one day a week. Monday's help is a golfer whose country-club friends come in to visit and buy from her on her day of work. Tuesday the tennis player is on, and her friends have followed her to the store. Wednesday is the yacht club member; Thursday, a leader of hospital volunteers; Friday, a well-known club woman; and Saturday, an attorney's wife. All of them are friendly women who know a lot about fashion and have a lot of energy, because they never have a chance to tire from the routine.
>
> Charlene, who writes a society column (as free PR) in the community newspaper, has positioned herself as a social force, and many women have come to view her shop as *the one* to buy from for formal events at the country club and the nearby Ritz Carlton Hotel.
>
> Her part-time helpers are not only an effective marketing tool; they also serve as local fashion consultants. They help Charlene make wise purchasing decisions. They are valuable members of her team, and her friends as well.

Get a Mentor

If you're starting up a business for the first time, there's a good chance you need a mentor—a person who can give you advice and encouragement. Perhaps you have a mentor already. If not, how can you find such help? First, network your friends, co-workers, and business associates. Tell them what you're looking for—that is, a successful business owner with a good track record. The perfect mentor would be one with experience in your particular segment. Second, join the Chamber of Commerce and one or more civic clubs. Third, keep your new eyes peeled for a mentor appearing on that horizon. If your community has a chapter of SCORE (Service Corps of Retired Executives), contact them to see if you can find a match.

Once you've located some candidates, develop a set of questions and set up a meeting. You want to pick the brains of all the candidates. Here are some things to consider in selecting a mentor:

> Do you feel comfortable with this person?
>
> Can you trust him or her?
>
> Is he (she) easy to communicate with?
>
> Does he (she) have experience and contacts that can help your new business?

Once you've made your choice and the person has agreed to help you, keep in close contact. See the person at least once a month, and use phone calls to smooth out rough spots. Your mentor may be able to help you establish banking connections

ACTION STEP 59

Network your competitors and vendors to build a winning team.

After you've taken the time to do some research into your own personality (your strengths and weaknesses), you'll begin to get the feel for what kind of help you need in your venture.

Start with the list you made in Action Step 57. Is there anyone there who can balance some of your skills?

Now make a list of the people you know. Beside each name, make a note about where that person fits on the DISC grid.

If you're a D-intensive entrepreneur, how many more D's can you take on and still have a winning team?

Now that you have the idea of balance firmly in mind, network your vendors and your competitors for potential team members. Whenever you meet someone new, try to apply DISC (or one of the other balancing systems). Keep asking yourself: "How would this person work out in my new business?"

Keep looking for your future team with new eyes.

and vendor–supplier relationships. A good mentor can be invaluable for checking your leases and contracts.

Here's a story that illustrates the kinds of assistance mentors can provide.

> Dick Knox is the proud owner of a seven-year-old, three-million-dollar company, Personal Computers, Inc. Dick started selling from his garage and moved to a warehouse facility. Filling a gap left by IBM, he sells personal computers in an office environment, with full-service follow-up to every customer. Dick's training was in computer programming. He had the energy but not the knowledge to start up a small business, so he kept his eyes open for a mentor.
>
> Enter Bob Redman. Bob's computer programming firm had just been purchased by a *Fortune* 500 company. The deal required that Bob stay on for two years as president. He wasn't happy in this role, so when Dick approached him with the mentor offer, he jumped at it. He loved being associated with a start-up, and the day he left his president's chair he was ready to step into his own business—a five-person computer consulting firm. [Mentoring works both ways, you see. Dick gave Bob a new angle on a tired life; Bob gave Dick almost a million dollars in sales leads.]
>
> Dick's second mentor was Mickey McCarthy, a wild and crazy entrepreneur who had sold his last venture for forty million dollars. Mickey was tired. Starting businesses took energy and he was ready to retire to a cottage in the mountains. Before he packed his bags, however, he agreed to be a mentor to Dick.
>
> A month later, Dick was having cash-flow problems. He was meeting payroll but had not taken a salary himself for three months. The cupboard was bare, and Dick had lost eight pounds.
>
> Over the next couple months, Mickey worked with Dick on a complete Business Plan/bank package with projections for the next five years. These projections in hand, Dick met with Mickey's banker. Three weeks later, he had a credit line of $100,000 and the provision that he could expand it to $300,000 when he needed it.

With mentors like Bob and Mickey, how could Dick lose?

INTERNAL UNDERSTANDING MAKES A STRONGER TEAM

Many bright, intelligent, energetic entrepreneurs lack self-knowledge. One such entrepreneur was E. G. Bogard, a world-beater, CEO, and adventurer whose business was growing beyond the world of small business. Bogard had come up the hard way—a one-man shop, a disastrous partnership, a small corporation. As we arrive on the scene, the growth of Bogard's company threatens to undermine his spectacular success. He has no idea how to handle it. He can barely admit there's a problem, and the problem is with himself.

> E. G. Bogard's corporate family didn't understand him. If they had, they would have known better than to waste his valuable time.
>
> Bogard was a self-made man. He'd started fourteen years earlier in his garage workshop in Skokie, and this year his Chicago manufacturing firm, which employed 200 people, was about to gross $17 million.
>
> In his industry, Bogard had a reputation for running a **lean operation**. Three of his toughest competitors had gone down during the last recession, but Bogard had not only stayed afloat, he'd managed to make a profit by trimming fat. By laying off employees and giving minimal raises, Bogard trimmed selling costs by 7% in one year.
>
> *Inc.* magazine wrote him up as "Jack Sprat Bogard: The CEO with the Seven per Cent Solution," but the article hadn't done much to help internal understanding. Just yesterday, the **executive committee** had come in with a recommendation about company cars, company blazers, and all-expenses-paid trips to Hawaii—and it had taken them six pages, single-spaced, to get their message across.
>
> Bogard hated waste.
>
> Bogard was thinking about firing the lot when he went off for his regular Thursday game of handball. That was one ritual he never missed. His opponent was Maury Apple-

lean operation
using the talents of a very few hard-working people to achieve business objectives

executive committee
advisers to the chief executive

baum. Maury was in advertising, a dozen years younger than Bogard, and the only fellow around who could give Bogard a game. Bogard was ferocious that day. He took three straight games. After the match, Maury asked him what was going on.

"It's nothing," Bogard snapped.

"Hey. Come on, E. G. This is Maury, remember? You were crazy out there today. You were wild."

"It's nothing," Bogard said.

But finally, over his one beer for the day, Bogard admitted what was going on. "It's my gang at the plant," he said. "They don't understand me. Maybe it's time to cash out and spend my days on the beach in Miami."

"You wouldn't last a week," Maury said.

"Probably not," Bogard said. "But lately I just can't seem to communicate to my people."

"I may have an answer for you," Maury said. "Can you give me half an hour tomorrow morning?"

"Where would I find a half-hour?"

"Fifteen minutes, then."

Reluctantly, Bogard agreed.

The next morning, Maury Applebaum arrived, accompanied by a woman named Mary White, an intelligent, no-nonsense person. Mary took one look at E. G. Bogard's desk—the high D's **paper jungle**—and went right to work.

"Mr. Bogard, I realize you're a busy man, so we'll get right to it. This is a **measurement tool** that can increase communication inside your company." Mary held out a light-blue folder. Bogard eyed it with suspicion.

"How long?" he asked. "And how much?"

"Fifteen minutes," she answered. "Eight dollars."

Bogard gave her a flinty smile. "Time me, Maury," he said, and dove into the folder.

The pale-blue folder contained a personality measuring tool called DISC. Bogard turned out to be high in D (Dominance), low on I (Influencing others), medium high on S (Steady) and very low on C (Compliance).

His personality was categorized as "Developer." A breakdown of the Developer traits showed:

Strong individuality

Self-reliance

Bypasses convention, comes up with innovative solutions

Forceful behavior

Can be shrewd at manipulating people and situations

Hates boredom most of all

Lacks empathy

Wants to get things done

"Hey," Bogard said, "that's *me!*"

Mary smiled at Maury, who pointed at his watch. More than thirty minutes had passed since Bogard had begun his profile, but the CEO, intent on the DISC instrument, hadn't noticed.

He looked up. "How soon can we get a couple hundred of these?" he asked. "I want to shoot them down to my people."

"How about Monday?" she said.

"How about this afternoon. I'll have the comptroller issue a check now." Bogard reached for the phone.

Almost all Bogard's employees were delighted with the **profiling system**. At first, a few people felt threatened, but taking the test proved to be fun, and when the employees began to compare notes, they reached insights about themselves and others.

The best thing to come out of the experience was a new understanding of the boss. All memos were now triple-spaced, short, and easy to read. The memos actually felt lean.

Bogard was happy. He was no longer misunderstood. He knew his family, and they knew him. There were still differences among people—nothing can do away with that—but somehow, everyone was working together with a lot more efficiency.

paper jungle
the mark of a Dominant person on the DISC scale

measurement tool
any device that allows management to assess productivity

profiling system
a system that measures differences between people

ACTION STEP 60

Tap your people resources by brainstorming with your team.

Before you sign a lease, go into the hole for $50,000 worth of equipment, hire a lot of people, or spend $2,000 for six-line telephone service, get your new team together and brainstorm the organization and objectives of your new business. A blackboard is a handy tool here, so that everyone can follow the track of the session. One way to begin is to ask every member of your team to write down what they believe would be good objectives for the business.

You've found some good people, and it's taken some hard work. Make that work pay off by tapping your human resources. Brainstorming will get you going. You'll be surprised at what develops.

If you have trouble narrowing down after the ideas start flowing, go back and review the seven-step procedure in chapter 3.

Now it's your turn. Action Step 60 is to be completed once you have built your team. It's your chance to brainstorm for ways to win. Make the most of all the creative human resources you've just brought on board! We think this action step is a great way to end this chapter on team building, and a great way to start your new business.

SUMMARY

It's fun being an entrepreneur. You're on your own, doing your own thing, running your own show. And one of the toughest things you have to admit is that you can't perform all business tasks with the same success. This chapter helps you focus on what you can do and where you need help.

This chapter provides tools to help you learn more about yourself and how you relate to people. One tool is the DISC Personality Profile. We like DISC because it is relatively inexpensive and quick to take. Once you've spent 20–30 minutes with it, insights begin to flow, and there's enough explanatory material to guide you through your own interpretation. If you don't like the DISC system, others are available; two of them are listed in the appendix to this chapter.

Another tool is the concept of balance. You want to construct a team in which people's skills and personalities are complementary. The case studies of Harry Marquez and Janet Ames illustrate the way different personality types can balance each other. Harry, a typical entrepreneur, is energetic, creative, forceful, single-minded, and impatient with detail. Janet, an excellent manager, is calm, organized, supportive, and patient. She plans well and will see to it that the bills are paid and the phones answered.

We touch on how to scout and hire the members of your team and stress the importance of internal understanding for a stronger team.

Balance, proportion, the right materials, and the structural forces of personality—all of these are important in building a winning team.

THINK POINTS FOR SUCCESS

◄ People tend to "hire themselves." How many more like you can the business take?

◄ A winning team is lurking in your network.

◄ Look to your competitors and vendors for team members.

◄ Your company is *people.*

◄ Balance the people on your team.

MBO
establishing measurable objectives for a specified time period

◄ Have each team member write objectives for his or her responsibilities within the business. Set up your own internal **MBO** (management by objectives) system.

◄ You can't grow until you have the right people.

◄ How much of your team can be built of part-timers and moonlighters?

REFERENCES

Alessandra, Anthony, Philip S. Wesler, and Jerry D. Dean. *Non-Manipulative Selling,* second edition. Englewood Cliffs, N.J.: Prentice-Hall, 1987.

Baty, Gordon B. *Entrepreneurship for the Eighties.* Reston, Va.: Reston Publishing Co., 1981.

David, Harry R. "Building a Winning Business Team." *Nation's Business,* August 1981.

Eisenberg, Richard. "Getting Rich in America." *Money,* July 1986, p. 49.

Feingold, S. N*orman,* and Leonard G. Perlman. "A Quiz for Would-Be Entrepreneurs." *Nation's Business,* March 1986, p. 26.

Goleman, Daniel. "The Psyche of the Entrepreneur." *New York Times Magazine,* February 2, 1986, p. 30.

Horn, Jack C. "Making Quality Circles Work Better." *Psychology Today,* August 1986, p. 10.

Ouchi, William G. *Theory Z: How American Business Can Meet the Japanese Challenge.* New York: Addison–Wesley, 1981.

Peters, Thomas J. *A Passion for Excellence: The Leadership Difference.* New York: Random House, 1985.

Peters, Thomas J., and Robert H. Waterman, Jr. *In Search of Excellence: Lessons from America's Best-Run Companies.* New York: Harper & Row, 1982. [Not really in the area of small business, but has good advice for every business on action, autonomy, the customer, running lean, and so on.]

"Quality Control Circles," Part 1. *Small Business Report,* July 1986, p. 44.

"Quality Control Circles," Part 2. *Small Business Report,* August 1986, p. 30.

Steck, Robert N. "Why New Businesses Fail: A Conversation with Peter Drucker." *D&B Reports,* November–December 1985, p. 35.

Zimmerman, Mark. *How to Do Business with the Japanese: A Strategy for Success.* New York: Random House, 1985.

ACTION STEP REVIEW

No matter what personality type you are, four action steps get you into the spirit of creative team building:

57 Look at the people you know and categorize them by their personalities.

58 Brainstorm your ideal team. What kind of help do you need to win at the game of small business?

59 Network your competitors and vendors for team members. It's time to try to make that ideal team reality.

60 After you've assembled a winning team, set aside a couple of hours to brainstorm ways you're going to win.

FIGURE 14.1   Chapter 14 will acquaint you with ways the computer can help you plan and manage your small business.

The Entrepreneur's Toolkit

LEARNING OBJECTIVES

■ To determine how badly you need a computer for your small business. ■ To identify tasks in your business that can be done better with the aid of a computer. ■ To become aware of what is going on in the computer industry and how it affects your selection of a small-business system. ■ To know what questions to ask, and to distinquish between who wants to help you and who is out to take your money and run. ■ To learn reliable sources of information about what is happening in information processing. ■ To resolve to keep learning about computers, even if the speed at which they change makes you dizzy.

This chapter will help you investigate the tools you will need for operating and controlling your new and growing business. The entrepreneur's toolkit must also be adequate to accommodate changing customer needs. For example, to prosper in the Information Age, businesses are using the telephone for more than conversation; many customers want to send orders on fax machines, leave messages on answering machines, and send data via computer modem.

Your toolkit may need to include a calculator, a cash register, a "one-write" bookkeeping system (see Appendix A), and special equipment unique to your type of business. The most important item in your toolkit, however, will probably be a computer.

INVENTORY YOUR TOOLKIT

computer
a machine that processes information

Throughout this book, we have encouraged you to use your head. "Think," we say. "Plan, plan, plan. Make a list. Get out a pencil and paper and do a mind map. Before you plunge into the marketplace, use your new eyes. Before you design the machine to build your product, profile your target customer. Before you sign a lease, play marketplace detective and check out the neighborhood. Brainstorm. Do interviews. Ask questions. Make a list. Make a chart. Make another list."

The reason for this advice is simple: the road to success is in your mind, so to reach success, you need to use your mind. Your most basic tools are pencils and lots of paper, of course, but a computer also is helpful. Later in this chapter we'll lead you through the process of selecting a computer for your small business. For right now, however, take stock of the tools you have already used in exploring small business by doing Action Step 61. Figure 14.2 may help you.

COMPUTERS AND SMALL BUSINESS

The Computer as a Symbol

In his book *The Third Wave,* futurist Alvin Toffler writes about the shift we're making, as a nation and as a people, from the Industrial Age to the Information Age.

The First Wave, Toffler says, was Agriculture: farms, livestock, harvest. The Second Wave was Industry: machinery, smokestacks, factories, robber barons. The Third Wave is electronic; that is, the Age of Information is based on the pulsing beat of the computer. The Third Wave has come about relatively quickly; whereas the shift from Agriculture to Industry took at least one hundred years, the shift from Industry to the Information Society has taken place in a few lightning-fast years.

The Third Wave is symbolized by the **computer,** a machine that has already reorganized our lives and our minds. If you have a digital watch, you're computerized. If you use a pocket calculator, you're computerized. When you receive a phone bill, a light bill, or a personalized letter you know went to a million other folks, you've been computerized.

The computer is quiet, unidirectional, unemotional, tireless, error-free. And it's here to stay.

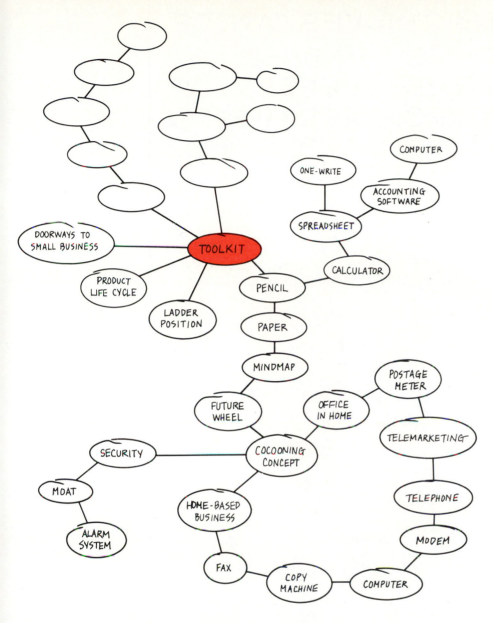

FIGURE 14.2 Mind map of small business tools. See Action Step 61.

The Computer as a Tool

The **microcomputer** seems to have been created especially for the entrepreneur. The right micro, with the right software, can make all the difference in the world in your small business. It can become an electronic extension of your mind and personality. It will take orders, handle details, print while you're doing something else, do your filing, cross-check files, probe the future of profit and cash flow, print payroll checks, and put you in touch with business information that will help you survive (Figure 14.3).

microcomputer
a desk-top information processor that has created an entire industry

FIGURE 14.3 The microcomputer seems to have been created especially for the entrepreneur.

The micro is amazing. It sits on a table or desk. It doesn't cost an arm and a leg. If it needs moving, you can move it. It can handle any repetitious detail in your business and thus leave your hands and your head free for entrepreneurial creativity. It will do accounting, word-processing, **general ledger**, mailing lists, customer (patient, client, student) files, flyers, inventory control, newsletters, memos, and so on.

The mark of an entrepreneur is fast footwork. The reason you can succeed is not because your advertising budget can compete with the hefty purses of Madison Avenue. The reason is because you can spot an opportunity and get tooled up to deliver faster than the big guys can. And with a micro on your desk, you can be even quicker.

general ledger
a master collection of all accounting transactions

Where to Begin

The computer selection process consists of three steps:

1. First, identify problems that need solving and tasks you want done.
2. Then, locate software programs that will solve the problems and do the tasks.
3. Finally, find hardware that will:
   a. accommodate the software,
   b. keep you happy punching keys and studying the screen, and
   c. not shatter your pocketbook.

Before and After

If you talk to successful entrepreneurs who have computerized their small businesses, you soon learn that a business itself may tell the entrepreneur why the business needs a computer. The information is after the fact. Business owners often kick themselves for not acting sooner—and with more strategic planning. You may be able to learn from the entrepreneurs in the following case studies and avert the marketplace crises that forced them to rush into computerization.

ARLENE JAMESON—PROPERTY MANAGEMENT

"The reason we finally decided to computerize was because the business was exploding. We'd started it four years earlier—just my husband and myself, doing property management—working out of our home. As we expanded, we bought a trailer that we'd park at construction sites. Then we hired someone and bought another trailer, and by the fourth year we knew we'd either have to find a way to control the business or stop writing management contracts. We could tell we were at a decision crossroads in our business.

"So we consulted a **computer consultant**. He told us what kind of software we needed, and what kind of hardware would go best with the software, and we got our system.

"For two weeks, I almost went crazy learning it. Converting our books was the hardest part. It took me three months, and all that time I was still doing books manually, with a pencil and a calculator.

"Now that I understand the electronic spreadsheet method, I'll never go back to the old way. Computers saved our business."

PAUL TAKAHASHI—CONSULTANT

"I had $500 in the bank when I was laid off. Like a lot of guys in that position, I went into the consulting business. After I'd been in business about a year, I knew I wasn't going to survive if I didn't get some help, especially with the repetitive parts of my business. That means numbers, of course, keeping the records straight. But it also means newsletters, flyers, printed invoices, and such things as that all-important letter that I'd been meaning to revise that was sitting there, in the typewriter, waiting.

computer consultant
a specialist who can help you solve problems with the computer

cross-filing
a reference system in which information is listed by two or more categories

"Well, the computer did all that, and more. I couldn't have survived without it. It gives my one-man show the capabilities of a much larger outfit."

RON TERKEL—INSURANCE AGENT

"The thing that sold me on computers was a file program called the Data Factory.

"I'm an independent insurance agent, and one of the problems we have is **cross-filing**. We've got at least twenty different categories of claims and an incredible variety of possible adjustments. Sometimes it takes hours for my staff to locate vital information.

"Well, with this computer system, backed up by the Data Factory, we can search from one file to another. It's great. It's like having X-ray vision and being able to see through a hundred manila folders all at once. Now that we're on the system, I don't know how we ever did without it."

JIM WINNER—TOY CROSSROADS

The toy business had been flat for three years, and new competition had come into town. Through a lot of hustle Jim was able to keep his sales about level, but because of increasing costs, his profits slipped.

Finally, Jim computerized last year, and it made a big difference. The smile on Jim's face after the winter holiday season was ear-to-ear. When asked why, Jim explained, "Our sales were down for the year but profits were the highest in our history. We ran out of inventory on several popular items the day before Christmas. With the new computer system, my buying skills improved 110%. The system tells me quickly how a new toy is doing, and I just increase, decrease, or cancel orders accordingly. End result: less inventory to sell at reduced prices, and fewer dollars tied up in inventory. It was a great year. You know, it's still fun to be in the toy business."

Action Step 62 will help you take the first step toward computerization. It asks you to list problems and tasks in your business. The list of questions will help you focus on your business's needs.

ACTION STEP 62

Identify your problems and tasks.

Take a minute to list some problems and tasks in your small business. Think first about *repetition*. What things do you do over and over? Think next about *detail*. What do you do that has to be precise? Think next about monitoring *time*. Where are the time lags in your business, and how can they be tracked? Accuracy and efficiency are the computer's main contributions, you see.

Use these questions to trigger your thoughts:

1. What are the demographic characteristics of your ten top customers? The top twenty? The top one hundred?

2. Is there a time lag between a sale and when you bill the customer?

3. Do you pay overtime? Do you pay hourly overtime to salaried employees?

4. Do you have a list of your most active customers and another list of customers who make fewer purchases but who are still important to your business?

5. Would you like to update your profit and loss statement without having to consult your accountant?

6. Do you have trouble managing inventory?

7. Do you have 100 or more vendors? Does your buying produce more than 100 purchase orders per month?

8. Do you write more than 100 checks per month?

9. Would you like to do your own spreadsheet analysis so that you can get your financial picture on your own?

10. When you update your Business Plan, would you like to be able to change a few numbers and have the new version printed while you're doing something else?

11. Do you write the same business letter to several customers?

12. Would you like to be able to coordinate your customer mailing list with a program that corrects your typos and spelling errors?

HOW TO SHOP FOR A MICROCOMPUTER

Gather Information

Once you have identified the tasks you need help with and the problems you want to solve, you are ready to learn more about available **computer systems**. A computer system is composed of hardware and the software to make it go. Think back to the three steps. Remember that you need to focus on software first. This may seem strange to you. Just remember, every machine in the marketplace is limited in the kinds of software it can use. If you go out shopping for hardware before you have identified what software will be best for you, you're putting the cart before the horse.

To make the best decision, you must have information, and one of the best places to get it is the very marketplace where salespeople are pushing computer systems. (See Box 14.1.)

Mentally Prepare Yourself

We're going to help you prepare for your first visit to a computer systems store by having you imagine yourself in a scenario. The action takes place in a large computer emporium, and you are just beginning to investigate computer systems.

SALESPERSON: How can I help you?
YOU: I'm looking for a computer system.

SALES: You've come to the right place! What capabilities do you want?

YOU: Well, I'm in business for myself. Some of those ads in the *Journal* caught my eye, and I'd be interested in seeing the new Compaq portable. [*Reading from your list*] I'm also interested in A.S.T., IBM, and Apple Macintosh. I need help with accounting, mailing lists, data-base management, general ledger, and payroll.

SALES: Let me ask you something. If we can put you on a system today—a system that will do everything you've ever dreamed of—could you take delivery this afternoon?

YOU: Hey! I just started looking!

SALES: Just asking. You look like a person who'd be interested in getting 27% off list.

YOU [*Looking around. Can this be true?*]: This is the first store I've been in. I'm not sure what I want.

SALES: No problem. Take your time. But let me tell you, this is the deal of a lifetime.

YOU: What kind of system is it?

SALES: My friend, we've got factory authorization from the head office of Micro-Batics—it's in Silicon Valley—to discount their micro 17%. Our distributor is discounting another 10% on top of that. It's a *super* buy. The sale's been going on for two weeks, and today's the last day. You've seen our ads in the paper, in the Business section?

YOU: Sorry. Who makes this system?

SALES: Like I said, it's a Micro-Batics 9000, the top of their line. It'll do everything but chew gum.

YOU: Micro-Batics? Never heard of it.

SALES: You *will*. Why not try it out? It's right over here.

[*You sit down and stare at screen. You feel nervous, edgy.*]

YOU: The screen is purple.

SALES: Compu-Mauve is the latest development for protecting **VDT** users against eyestrain. You haven't heard of Compu-Mauve?

YOU: There seem to be a lot of buttons.

SALES: We call this the keyboard. Those are function keys. Incidentally, this is an 8-bit machine; market research showed us that 16-bit was overpowered. This particular unit is CP/M-based, with an optional add-on card that gives it modem capability. It comes, standard, with 640K of RAM and can be configured to any printer with a parallel port interface. The word-processing program is built right into the hardware here, so there's none of that changing disks when you want to do something simple like type a memo. All you do is hit a button, here, like this. [*Hits button. Words appear on screen.*]

YOU: How much does all of this cost, anyway?

SALES: Okay. I thought you'd never ask. The CPU goes for $1,500. The *VDT*—with the new Easy-Eye Compu-Mauve screen—is $400. The monitor interface runs $500. You've got to have it anyway to interface with your printer. One drive or two?

YOU: I . . . uh . . . what's a drive?

SALES: We recommend two. Of course, if you'd like to go hard disk, I can get you a real deal on a Davong. I'd have to double-check that with my sales manager, but since I was the top salesman for the last two months, he'll probably see it my way. That hard disk retails for $1,995, but I can save you some bucks today, because of the sale. This system comes with a complimentary carton of paper, but diskettes are extra. Shall we write this up now?

YOU: I have to go. I'll come back some other time. Have you got any brochures on this stuff?

SALES [*Miffed*]: Sorry. We're fresh out.

This salesperson is just off the used-car lot; he's trapped back in the Industrial Age, where **pushing hardware** was the name of the game. You're making a purchase to hook you into the Information Society. There's someone out there to help. You may have to pay a consultant's fee, but a consultant will help you make a better decision. Be careful in selecting a consultant. Ask for references, and check out three to five of them.

By the way, you did pretty well in the scenario. You didn't let yourself be intimidated. Although many people shop for computers the same way they shop for cars, stereos, and refrigerators, you remembered to shop for solutions. A computer may

---

computer system
computer hardware plus the software that tells it what to do

Silicon Valley
area southeast of San Francisco, California; the heart of the microcomputer industry

VDT
video display terminal

BOX 14.1 **Free Help and Information**

You can find lots of free offers of help and small business information in the ads in your local newspaper and the *Wall Street Journal*. The ads are placed by firms that have something to sell, but almost all companies are willing to give help and advice to gain customers. Hunt through the ads for the information you need.

---

pushing the hardware
emphasizing the hardware over all other considerations

Industrial Age hardware
cars, stereos, refrigerators, boilers, and so on

look like one more chunk of **Industrial Age hardware**, but it's not. It's your access to the Age of Information.

One problem people face in computer-system selection is that the field changes fast. In 1982 Apple was the micro leader. By 1983 the IBM PC had taken the lead, and lots of companies were copying it. In 1987 Compaq was the leader; its sales exceeded a billion dollars. It's important to keep aware of such things. One way to keep up is to read computer magazines. Keep in mind that the future of the computer age is software.

With these things in mind, you're now ready to go out into the market to shop for solutions to your business problems. You don't need to become an expert on computers; you just want to get one foot on the information treadmill. Action Step 63 shows you how.

Before You Buy a Microcomputer

If you have found a computer system (software and hardware) that seems right for you, no doubt you're eager to test-drive your micro. Before you close the sale, however, we want to give you a little advice.

1. Think problem first, software second, hardware third. Invest a lot of time listing your problems and tasks. Invest a lot more locating software that will do the job. Work those computer salespeople. Read the trade magazine evaluations.

2. Don't buy for forever. Once you've identified your immediate needs, buy a system for the next 18 months or so. This is the Age of Information, and the computer will change your life; a fancier system with more bells, more whistles, and more power is already on its way from some new Silicon Valley somewhere.

3. Expand, expand, expand. Buy a system you can expand. Research the components you might need at some future date (things like printer and modem), and then check each system for the ports you plug into and the possibilities for upgrading when you need more power.

4. Buy locally, from a reputable dealer; you get what you pay for. If it's your first computer system, buy from a local dealer who will throw in training, support, service, and hand-holding. During the first 200 hours of initiation into the World of Computers, the hand-holding is essential. (It's true—you can get some good deals out there, price-wise. But a dealer who's pulling in business with loss leaders is not going to help out when your computer says SYNTAX ERROR CAN'T READ DRIVE ONE NO FILE OPEN. Because you're in business, you don't want to be asking your computer for favors. Remember the movie *2001*? "Open the pod door, Hal.")

5. Hire a consultant. If this is your first system, you can save yourself lots of grief by hiring a computer consultant. A good consultant will help you identify what your problems are and how to solve them. Get references.

software cost
ideally, at least 50% of the total system budget

6. Budget for software. Budget at least 50% of your total system cost for **software cost.** The right software means the difference between happiness and despair.

7. Experience pays; innocence hurts. After you've learned thoroughly what your system can do, then you can start shopping around for discount software in the mail-order market. But remember, with mail-order shopping you are on your own and without dealer support, so be careful.

ACTION STEP 63

Check out a computer system.

Now that you have identified some of your business problems, it's time to check out computer systems.

Get your problem list together and make some phone calls. Ask to speak to a salesperson who has knowledge about business systems. Play detective.

Say something like: "Hi. My name's _____ and I'm interested in locating software that will help me solve some problems in my business."

If the answer is "What kind of problems do you have?" you're off and running.

If they want to know what kind of system you have, it's "carrot-and-horse" time; they want to sell you hardware. Explain that you are researching software and that when you find that, you'll decide on the hardware to go with it. This should get their attention.

What you are hunting for is a salesperson with some business knowledge—and a heart. Once you find the human vibrations you like, visit the store and test-drive a micro.

While you're exploring this new world, keep repeating to yourself: solutions through software. . . . solutions through software. . . .

8. Educate yourself. Keep taking computer classes. Knowledge will keep you on the leading edge.

Learning from Others' Mistakes

Fortunately, we learn things from our mistakes. Nonetheless, what's even better than learning from our mistakes is learning from the mistakes *others* make. That's why we think you'll appreciate this true story about a *Fortune* 500 company. Remember, you as a small business operator have the opportunity to be more astute than many of the big guys. Big does not mean smart.

In the early seventies, just before the great computer boom, the management of a well-known *Fortune* 500 company decided to make the transformation from caveman bookkeeping to computer bookkeeping. They bought a mainframe plus terminals for all of their telephone order clerks.

The caveman method was characterized by primitive tools: pencils, paper, carboned order forms, typewriters, and an intricate network of grey tunnels (or chutes). The tunnels were about three inches in diameter, and they connected departments with other departments in the corporate headquarters building. The order clerks would place the order forms inside message cylinders, snap the little metal doors shut, and then insert the cylinders into an entry port, from where they would be whisked away by air pressure.

Exciting.

Because of **bureaucratic lag**, it took several months of negotiation and research before management could agree on the best replacement for the system of grey tunnels. The system that was finally chosen, a combination in-house mainframe computer with peripherals from other *Fortune* 500 giants, was magnificent.

bureaucratic lag
the span of time in the corporate world when things should get done (but often do not, which drives entrepreneurs crazy)

"This system, without a doubt, will serve our firm until at least 1990," said one of the top managers.

"Yes," said another manager, "and perhaps beyond."

"Agreed," intoned a third. "The system has great capacity. We'll interface with markets everywhere. For us, it's perfect."

At the end of the first week, everyone was delighted with the system. Furthermore, everyone was using it like crazy because it was so useful, and so fast.

During the second week, the system was showing signs of overload. People were having to stand in line to use it. They had discovered the computer could save them time, which they could use for phone calls, conferences, and thinking.

By the end of the third week, the system was overloaded beyond its capacity.

Moral: Even if you're a big hitter, the computer will change your life in ways you never imagined. Buy a system you can expand.

Some Final Thoughts

The microcomputer can help you complete your Business Plan in two ways. (1) If you create your Plan on a word processor, you'll be able to make changes easily, and (2) if you use an electronic spreadsheet, you will be able to speed up your financial projections. The sample Business Plan in chapter 16 contains several financial statements generated using an electronic spreadsheet.

As we end this chapter on microcomputers, we want to refer you to one of the best places to learn the latest trends in the fast-moving microcomputer field: the yearly Comdex trade show. Comdex shows are announced in the *Wall Street Journal* and other national business and computer publications.

SUMMARY

Computers are here to stay. If you are going into small business, you need to consider getting one. Two questions will arise:

1. How badly do I need a computer?
2. What model do I need, and where should I buy it?

This chapter discusses the computer as a business tool and as a symbol of the future. Here's some advice to think about before you start searching for your computer with new eyes:

1. Think of computer acquisition as a three-step process—define your tasks and problems; locate software to do the job; locate hardware to run the software.
2. Buy a good computer, but do not lock yourself in with overpriced hardware. The computer industry changes fast, and fancier, more powerful products will be coming along soon.
3. Buy a system you can expand.
4. Buy your first system locally, from a reputable dealer. You'll spend more money up front, but you're going to need dealer support during your first days, weeks, and months of operation.
5. Think about hiring a consultant.
6. Budget at least 50% of your total system cost for software.
7. Wait until you're familiar with your machine and with software programs before you start buying discounted programs through the mail.
8. Keep taking computer courses, and keep reading.

THINK POINTS FOR SUCCESS

◀ A computer can be an extension of your creative, entrepreneurial personality.

◀ The hardware for your computer system will be relatively easy to select—if you work from problems to solutions to software. Software needs determine hardware needs.

◀ Take a computer course. Educate yourself about the Information Society.

◀ If you find yourself balking at computers because you don't know how they work, analyze your feelings about driving a car. You probably don't know how the internal combustion engine works, but that didn't keep you from learning to drive.

◀ You've got to compute to compete.

REFERENCES

Badgett, Tom. "Revitalizing the Small Business." *Personal Computing,* October 1986, p. 135. [Focuses on personal computer use in small businesses.]

Farmanfarmaian, Roxane. "Does Computerizing Really Help?" *Working Woman,* March 1988, p. 42.

ACTION STEP REVIEW

The three action steps in this chapter help you inventory your entrepreneurial toolkit.

61 List the tools that have been helpful to you as you've been examining the world of small business. Move from simple to complex, starting with *pencils* and *paper.*

62 Identify problems and tasks in your small business that might better be handled by a computer. Look for tasks that are *repetitive,* that demand attention to *detail,* and that relate to monitoring *time* (schedules).

63 Once you've identified tasks the computer might help you accomplish, hit the streets and check out systems—software first, and then hardware. Find software that will solve your problems and be easy to use. Find a computer that's compatible with other computers.

Harvey, Greg. *Mastering SuperCalc 4.* Berkeley, Calif.: Sybex, 1987. [Sybex publishes a large number of computer-related business manuals. You can contact them by writing to: Sybex, Inc., 2021 Challenger Drive, No. 100, Alameda, CA 94501; phone 1-800-227-2346.]

Korngold, Bob. "Building a Check Register into a General Ledger." *Small Business Computers,* March/April 1983, 50–53. [Takes the beginner through a simple program in Visicalc.]

McWilliams, Peter. *The Personal Computer Book.* New York: Doubleday (Quantum Press), 1984.

McWilliams, Peter. *The Word Processing Book.* New York: Doubleday (Quantum Press), 1984.

Micro-Computers for Use in Small Business. Small Business Management Training Instructors' Guide No. 108. Washington, D.C.: U.S. Small Business Administration, Office of Management Assistance, 1984. [Produced by the American Association of Community and Junior Colleges under contract to the U.S. Small Business Administration, Contract No. 4873-MA 80.]

Naiman, Arthur. *Word Processing Buyer's Guide.* New York: McGraw-Hill, 1983. [Naiman developed a 100-point checklist, which he uses to evaluate fourteen programs exhaustively and another 104 programs briefly. Naiman gives prices, addresses, and sharp advice on word processors. He can't keep up with the industry, but who can?]

Stevens, Mark. "Six Small Business Problems Computers Can Solve." *Working Woman,* September 1987, p. 33.

Stewart, Michael M., and Alan C. Shulman. *How to Get Started with a Small Business Computer,* Management Aid No. 2.027. Washington, D.C.: U.S. Small Business Administration, Office of Business Development, 1987.

Venture: The Entrepreneur's Handbook. Torrance, Calif.: Star Software Systems, 1989. [A pull-down, menu-driven, IBM PC/PS-2 software package that allows you to develop a fully integrated Business Plan. It includes specific programs for manufacturing, wholesale, retail, and service businesses. Write to Star Software Systems at 363 Van Ness Way, Torrance, CA 90501-1420, or call them at 800-242-STAR.]

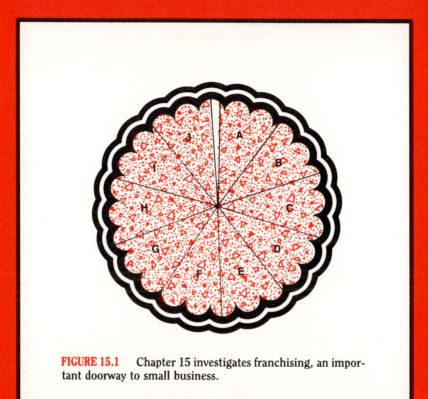

FIGURE 15.1 Chapter 15 investigates franchising, an important doorway to small business.

Buying a Franchise

LEARNING OBJECTIVES

■ To explore the vast world of franchising. ■ To develop techniques for examining franchises. ■ To understand the relationship between franchisor and franchisee. ■ To learn the benefits and liabilities of owning and operating a franchise. ■ To understand the risk–reward relationship of a ground-floor opportunity. ■ To learn why the stronger franchises tend to operate an "insiders only" game. ■ To learn why some people should consider *only* franchises. ■ To understand why the true entrepreneur is always the *franchisor*. ■ To decide if buying a franchise is the right step for you.

ACTION STEP PREVIEW

64 Investigate the franchise system by interviewing franchisors and franchisees.

65 Visit a franchise exposition.

Our walk-through of opportunities in small business is almost finished. Decision time approaches. If you've followed the action steps, you've spent several months gathering data and talking to people in small business. You have spent some time exploring businesses that are up for sale and talking to sellers. If you wanted to write a Business Plan now, you could sit down and do it. Before you do that, however, there is one other doorway to explore, the doorway to a franchised business.

The franchise industry is enormous. If you were to buy or rent a car tomorrow morning, put gas in it, and then drive it to a fast-food restaurant for lunch, you might be supporting a franchise at every turn.

WHY BUY A FRANCHISE?

The overwhelming reason for buying a franchise is to benefit from name recognition. Consumers grow to trust brand-name products and services. Look at the places where you do business. Do you drink Coca-Cola? The Coca-Cola headquarters are in Atlanta, but the beverage is bottled by regional franchisees. Do you buy gas at a Mobil, Texaco, Exxon, or Shell station? They're franchises, too. If you buy milk at 7-Eleven, buy hamburgers at Burger King, purchase books at Little Professor, or use a Century 21 realtor, you're into the franchise system. Franchised products and services are predictable and reliable. Many consumers go out of their way to do business with franchisors. This customer loyalty is worth paying for.

What the Franchisee Gets

franchisor
the firm that sells the rights to do business under its name and continues to control the business

franchise
authorization granted by a manufacturer or distributor to sell its products/services

franchisee
the individual operator who is licensed to operate under the franchisor's rules and directives

Let's examine what you can get when you pay money to a **franchisor** for a **franchise**—that is, when you become a **franchisee**. A franchise can provide:

1. Brand-name recognition. If you ask the right questions and pick the right franchise, the marketing boost you get from the name of your franchise might be worth what it will cost you.
2. Support from corporate. Corporate services can include help with selecting a site, employee training, inventory control, vendor connections, a corporate-produced Business Plan, and more.
3. Training. The franchisor will teach you the business.
4. Money. Lenders prefer to lend to new franchisees over new start-ups.
5. Planning. You are buying a proven Business Plan.
6. Bargains. You may share in economies of scale in purchasing goods, services, and promotion.
7. Continuous training.
8. Psychological hand-holding and field visits from the franchisor.
9. Assistance in layout and design.
10. Location and leasing assistance.
11. Reduced odds of failure.
12. Pretested products and promotion.
13. The opportunity to buy another franchise in your area.
14. Assistance of a store-opening specialist. This person can help get you off to a running start.

Figure 15.2 illustrates some of these benefits of franchising as well as a couple of its drawbacks.

FIGURE 15.2   A franchise can provide you with a number of things.

When you buy a franchise, you're really buying a license. If you wanted to bottle Coca-Cola—the best-known franchise in the world—you'd have to negotiate for a license from the Coca-Cola Bottling Company. You might find a bottler who wanted to sell you his license, but you'd still have to negotiate with Coke. In some cases, buying a franchise is like buying a supplier for eternity. Nonetheless, many people have been happy to do that, because approximately 20% of the small businesses in the country are franchises.

Franchisors often sell the rights to a region, state, or county to a master franchisor, who in turn sells and manages franchise sales to individuals.

What the Franchisor Gets

Franchisors earn money in several ways:

1. They collect a **franchise fee** for the rights to use their name and system. This ranges from $3,000 for a small service firm to over $100,000 for a well-established name such as that of a hotel, auto dealership, or major restaurant.
2. They collect a **royalty fee,** which ranges from 2% to 15% of gross sales.
3. They may make a profit on items they sell to franchisees.

In addition, franchisees commonly pay franchisors advertising and promotion fees. These generally range from 2% to 5% of a franchise's gross sales.

Some of the fees may be open to negotiation—especially with a new franchisor. For example, it might be possible to delay the royalty fee for six months or until the franchise is profitable. It's always a good idea to ask for concessions.

franchise fee
fee paid by a franchisee for the rights to represent the franchisor in a given geographic area for a specified length of time. commonly 5–10 years

royalty fee
ongoing obligation to pay the franchisor a percentage of the gross sales; may or may not include advertising fee

Franchising Growth and Trends

Table 15.1 documents the phenomenal growth of franchising from 1970 to 1987. In 1987, 499,000 franchise outlets provided a whopping $591 billion in revenues. Comparing that with 396,000 outlets (generating $120 billion) in 1970, you can see how franchising has mushroomed.

In Table 15.2, figures for individual industries help you add to your knowledge of trends, which you began thinking about in chapter 2. If you're interested in becoming an auto or truck dealer, your window of opportunity has grown smaller (from 37,200 franchises down to 27,800). But if you're in business aids and services, the window has grown in size (from 10,500 to 61,300).

It's certainly not necessary to memorize these tables. They are included here to show you the vast range of opportunity in franchising, which seems to be moving from smokestacks and manufacturing to information and services. Franchises in the service sector are enjoying a lot of growth now. Real estate, for example, is a natural. Others that share a network of technology or body of information include Century 21 and Dale Carnegie.

TABLE 15.1 Franchising in the United States, 1970–1987

ITEM	UNIT	1970	1975	1980	1981	1982	1983	1984	1985[1]	1986[1]	1987[1]
DOMESTIC[2]											
Number of franchised establishments	**1,000**	**396**	**435**	**442**	**442**	**439**	**442**	**444**	**455**	**467**	**499**
Company-owned[3]	1,000	72	81	85	86	87	86	87	86	87	91
Franchisee-owned	1,000	324	354	357	356	352	355	357	369	380	406
Sales of products and services	**bill. dol.**	**120**	**191**	**336**	**365**	**376**	**423**	**492**	**543**	**556**	**591**
Company-owned[3]	bill. dol.	23	29	47	51	55	59	64	68	70	76
Franchisee-owned	bill. dol.	96	162	289	314	321	364	428	475	486	515
Average sales per establishment	$1,000	302	439	760	824	856	958	1,108	1,193	1,192	1,186
Employment	1,000	(NA)	3,511	4,668	4,878	4,927	5,165	5,671	6,283	(NA)	(NA)
INTERNATIONAL											
U.S. companies operating foreign outlets	number	[4]156	222	279	288	295	305	328	342	(NA)	(NA)
Foreign outlets	1,000	[4]3.4	11.0	20.4	21.4	23.5	25.7	27.0	30.2	(NA)	(NA)

Source: *Statistical Abstract of the United States,* 108th ed. (Washington, D.C.: U.S. Department of Commerce, 1988), p. 742; based on data in U.S. Dept. of Commerce, International Trade Administration, *Franchising in the Economy, 1985–87.*

NA Not available.   [1]Estimated by respondents to annual survey of franchisors.   [2]Excludes foreign outlets of U.S. companies.   [3]Represents establishments owned by the parent company.   [4]1971 data.

TABLE 15.2 Number of Establishments and Sales by Kind of Franchised Business, 1970–1987

KIND OF FRANCHISED BUSINESS	NUMBER OF ESTABLISHMENTS (1,000)						SALES (Millions of dollars)					
	1970	1975	1980	1985	1986[1]	1987[1]	1970	1975	1980	1985	1986[1]	1987[1]
All franchising, total	**396.3**	**434.5**	**442.4**	**455.2**	**466.8**	**498.5**	**119,758**	**190,931**	**336,220**	**542,969**	**556,231**	**591,332**
Auto and truck dealers[2]	37.2	31.8	29.4	27.5	27.6	27.8	58,812	94,497	143,861	282,560	293,592	305,617
Percent	9.4	7.3	6.6	6.0	5.9	5.6	49.1	49.5	42.8	52.0	52.8	51.7
Restaurants (all types)	32.6	43.0	60.0	73.9	78.3	86.4	4,602	12,262	27,867	47,678	51,488	57,951
Percent	8.2	9.9	13.6	16.2	16.8	17.3	3.8	6.4	8.3	8.8	9.3	9.8
Gasoline service stations[2]	222.0	189.5	158.5	124.6	120.2	117.0	29,340	47,387	94,470	100,767	90,388	94,907
Percent	56.0	43.6	35.8	27.4	25.7	23.5	24.5	24.8	28.1	18.6	16.3	16.0
Retailing (nonfood)	30.7	37.2	35.2	45.1	46.1	50.7	13,133	9,031	10,517	20,571	22,110	25,179
Percent	7.7	8.6	8.0	9.9	9.9	10.2	11.0	4.7	3.1	3.8	4.0	4.2
Auto, truck rental services	[3]10.7	6.5	7.3	11.2	11.4	11.5	[3]1,177	1,475	3,146	5,686	6,101	6,538
Automotive products and services[4]	20.4	47.5	40.2	36.5	37.4	40.4	1,936	5,006	7,084	10,659	11,676	12,910
Business aids and services	10.5	22.2	40.7	49.8	53.8	61.3	723	1,397	6,749	11,970	13,486	15,545
Employment services	2.9	2.7	4.4	4.8	5.2	6.0	516	553	1,594	2,732	3,067	3,565
Tax preparation services	4.7	7.5	9.2	8.1	8.1	8.3	85	161	289	427	458	485
Accounting, credit, collection, and general	1.1	3.5	2.4	2.1	2.2	2.6	20	165	121	169	171	212
Other	1.7	8.3	24.7	34.8	38.3	44.4	101	518	4,745	8,642	9,790	11,283
Construction, home improvement, maintenance, and cleaning	.7	10.8	14.3	17.5	18.4	22.2	63	639	1,475	4,067	4,466	4,937
Convenience stores	8.8	13.5	15.6	15.1	15.7	16.6	1,727	3,906	7,821	10,839	11,706	12,803
Educational products and services	4.9	1.3	3.2	8.2	8.2	9.1	86	173	339	768	746	851
Equipment rental services	(3)	1.4	2.2	2.5	2.7	2.9	(3)	157	356	669	720	816
Food retailing[5]	(NA)	11.8	15.5	18.7	20.8	23.6	(NA)	1,445	7,430	10,081	10,755	11,643
Hotels and motels[6]	3.4	6.4	6.4	7.5	8.0	8.6	3,540	4,601	9,506	14,771	15,694	16,729
Laundry, dry cleaning services	4.1	3.2	3.4	2.3	2.7	3.2	144	214	286	303	346	425
Recreation, entertainment, travel	2.7	3.4	4.6	7.8	8.3	8.9	77	162	516	2,318	2,659	3,191
Soft drink bottlers[2,7]	2.7	2.4	1.9	1.4	1.3	1.3	4,102	8,165	14,352	18,321	19,249	20,032
Miscellaneous	4.8	2.7	3.6	5.5	6.1	7.2	295	414	447	942	1,050	1,257

Source: *Statistical Abstract of the United States*, 108th ed. (Washington, D.C.: U.S. Department of Commerce, 1988), p. 742; based on data in U.S. Dept. of Commerce, International Trade Administration, *Franchising in the Economy, 1985–87.*

NA Not available. [1]Estimated by respondents. [2]Estimated by source on basis on Bureau of the Census and trade association data. [3]Equipment rental services included with auto, truck rental services. [4]Includes some establishments with significant sales of nonautomotive products such as household appliances, garden supplies, etc. [5]Excludes convenience stores. [6]Beginning 1975, includes campgrounds. [7]Includes soft drinks, fruit drinks and ades, syrups, flavoring agents and bases. Excludes independent private-label and contract-filler bottling companies, which accounted for 22 percent of the value of shipments of the total industry in recent years.

ACTION STEP 64

Investigate the franchise system by interviewing franchisors and franchisees.

Franchises are everywhere—McDonald's, Roto-Rooter, Dale Carnegie, RE/MAX, Holiday Inn, Exxon, Midas, Hertz, and many, many others. To learn more about the system, interview people on both sides of the franchise agreement.

Part A. Franchisors. Leave your checkbook at home and interview at least three franchisors. Here are some questions to start you off:

What's included in the franchise fee?

What's the duration of the agreement?

How can the agreement be bought back or canceled?

What are the royalty fees and other assessments?

What level of training and service could I expect?

Is the territory well-defined?

What are the minimum volume requirements?

How much help could I expect with advertising and promotion?

Part B. Franchisees. Now interview several franchisees. Ask them the same questions.

A handy reference is the *Franchise Opportunities Handbook* published by the U.S. Department of Commerce.

· **voluntary chain**
wholesaling organization established by wholesalers or retailers to gain purchasing power and other economies of scale

INVESTIGATING FRANCHISE OPPORTUNITIES

As you can see from tables 15.1 and 15.2, franchising is a major force in the U.S. economy. You can learn a lot about small business by investigating franchises. We recommend that you talk with franchisors and franchisees to get a feel for the world of franchising.

It may be that you would not be comfortable operating by the rules and regulations set down by franchisors—many entrepreneur-types are not. Nonetheless, it makes good sense to check out franchise opportunities (especially those in your industry), because it will give you a better picture of the marketplace. Action Step 64 will get you started on this.

Franchise Problems

Some notable pitfalls plague franchising in general:

1. Competition is becoming intense among competitive franchisors. Franchisers of fast-food outlets, quick-printing shops, and specialty retailers often oversaturate markets, which causes many failures.
2. Many of the training programs are poor or nonexistent.
3. Multilevel distributorships and pyramid sales schemes may benefit only the promoters.
4. The best opportunities are seldom offered to outsiders.

Beware of "ground-floor" franchise opportunities; it's pretty risky to be an early franchisee. A franchisor offering such an "opportunity" would be experimenting with *your money.* You want to buy a recognized brand name, a proven Business Plan, excellent field support, and experience that demonstrates the particular franchise will work in your location.

Voluntary chains—such as True Value and Ace Hardware stores, for example—are often a more desirable option. Members of those chains remain independent and pay no royalty or franchise fee. Look for more such organizations in the near future.

A Franchising Success Story

Susan Moore and her husband were lucky when it came time to investigate franchises; they had a source of inside information right in the family. They were also lucky because the franchisor they chose provided excellent support. Note that corporate support was more important than name-brand recognition to Susan and her husband.

Three years ago my husband was having to travel a lot in his job and I was working very hard for a large company. While we were both drawing good salaries, we felt we had what it took to succeed in small business. We decided to go the franchising route.

We were both interested in the printing industry, and we chose a medium-sized national chain that seemed to have a franchise package we could live with. We did have some inside information on this particular franchisor. My brother had been with them for three years, in the Pacific Northwest area, and he was making a good living.

While we were interested in the quick-print industry, we weren't experts, so the two weeks of training was incredibly valuable. In addition, the people from **corporate** helped us with site selection, market analysis, negotiating the lease, and the layout and design of our shop. There are so many details to think of when you're starting a business; it's very helpful to have experts take over some of the tasks.

Another good feature of this franchise is that corporate will allow you to finance up to 80% of your start-up costs. This particular franchise can run as high as $100,000 up front, so that helped us.

We opened a second shop last January, and both stores are doing nicely. We print stationery, business cards, flyers, invitations—and we're developing a reputation for being on time in an industry known for being perpetually late.

corporate
the franchisor

A good way to learn a lot about franchising in a short time is to attend a franchise exposition. You can learn when and where they are to be held in your area by watching for announcements in major newspapers. Go and enjoy yourself (leaving your checkbook at home), and complete Action Step 65.

As you look for a good franchise opportunity, bear in mind that the best opportunity may lie with a young franchise that has proven its concept, has twenty to thirty winners, and is looking for growth in an area with which you are familiar.

EVALUATING A FRANCHISE

Evaluating a franchise opportunity is much like evaluating any other business that's up for sale, but because of the nature of franchisors, you need to ask some additional questions. For example:

How long has this franchise been in business?

Who are the officers? What is their track record?

How many franchise outlets are operating right now?

How well does this franchise compete with similar franchises?

Where is this franchise in its life cycle?

What will this franchise do for me?

In chapter 10 we presented a checklist to use in evaluating an ongoing business you are considering buying. That checklist applies to franchises as well. To supplement it, we're giving you a checklist prepared specifically for evaluating franchise opportunities; see Box 15.1. The questions will help you generate a profile of the franchise and make a wise decision.

Typically, current franchisees are offered new locations before they are offered to outsiders. Rarely is a new player offered a sure thing. New players are offered those that have already been passed over. This was Myron Bailey's introduction to franchising.

By the time Myron was twenty-nine years old he'd made a lot of money in the stock market, but he felt he was too young to retire. After making several attempts to purchase one of the better-known fast-food franchises and waiting almost a year, he was offered a location in another state.

The store had been open for three years and not yet turned a profit. Other franchise owners had already turned down the opportunity to take over the operation. Myron liked what he saw and made an offer. The unsuccessful franchisee welcomed his offer as a graceful exit, and the franchisor could hardly wait to see if a new franchisee could turn the loser around.

Myron is a "people person" and a strong manager. His employees followed his enthusiastic leadership, and new customers came in droves. In less than a year the store

ACTION STEP 65

Visit a franchise exposition.

Most major cities have at least one franchise show a year. Attend one and visit with the exhibitors. Learn what you can from their sales presentations.

Collect their literature and select one that seems worth a second look. Write up a brief summary of your findings to present as an oral report to your class. Have your classmates evaluate the franchise.

Remember, it's usually the small and new franchisors that exhibit at the shows, and their salespeople work on commission. Don't allow yourself to be pursued; you are there to observe and evaluate. You are probably not yet ready to buy.

BOX 15.1 Franchise Evaluation Checklist

GENERAL

	yes	no
1. Is the product or service:		
a. considered reputable?	_____	_____
b. part of a growing market?	_____	_____
c. needed in your area?	_____	_____
d. of interest to you?	_____	_____
e. safe,	_____	_____
protected,	_____	_____
covered by guarantee?	_____	_____
2. Is the franchise:		
a. local?	_____	_____
regional?	_____	_____
national?	_____	_____
international?	_____	_____
b. full-time?	_____	_____
part-time?	_____	_____
possible full-time in the future?	_____	_____

3. Existing franchises
   a. Date the company was founded _____
     Date the first franchise was awarded _____
   b. Number of franchises currently in operation or under construction _____
   c. References
   Franchise 1: owner _____
           address _____
           telephone _____ date started _____
   Franchise 2: owner _____
           address _____
           telephone _____ date started _____
   Franchise 3: owner _____
           address _____
           telephone _____ date started _____
   Franchise 4: owner _____
           address _____
           telephone _____ date started _____
   d. Additional franchises planned for the next twelve months _____
4. Failed franchises
   a. How many franchises have failed? _____ How many in the last two years? _____
   b. Why have they failed?
   Franchisor reasons: _____

   _____

   Better Business Bureau reasons: _____

   _____

   Franchisee reasons: _____

   _____

continued

Box 15.1, *continued*

5. Franchise in local market area
   a. Has a franchise ever been awarded in this area? _____
   b. If so, and if it is still in operation:
      owner _____
      address _____
      telephone _____ date started _____
   c. If so, and if it is no longer in operation:
      person involved _____
      address _____
      date started _____ date ended _____
      reasons for failure _____
      _____
   d. How many inquiries have there been for the franchise from the area in the past six months? _____
6. What product or service will be added to the franchise package:
   a. within twelve months? _____
      _____
   b. within two years? _____
      _____
   c. within two to five years? _____
      _____
7. Competition
   a. What is the competition? _____
      _____
      _____
8. Are all franchises independently owned?
   a. Of the total outlets, _____ are franchised, and _____ are company-owned.
   b. If some outlets are company owned did they start out this way, _____ or were they purchased from a franchisee? _____
   c. Date of most recent company acquisition _____
9. Franchise operations
   a. What facilities are required, and do I lease or build?

	build	lease
office	_____	_____
building	_____	_____
manufacturing facility	_____	_____
warehouse	_____	_____
_____	_____	_____
_____	_____	_____

   b. Getting started—Who is responsible for:

	franchisor	franchisee
feasibility study?	_____	_____
design?	_____	_____
construction?	_____	_____
furnishings and equipment?	_____	_____
financing?	_____	_____
employee training?	_____	_____
lease negotiation?	_____	_____

continued

Box 15.1, *continued*

FRANCHISE COMPANY

1. The company
   a. Name and address of the parent company, if different from the franchise company:
      name _____
      address _____
   b. Is the parent company public, ___ or private? ___
   c. If the company is public, where is the stock traded?
      New York Stock Exchange ___
      American Stock Exchange ___
      over-the-counter   ___

      _____   ___

2. Forecast of income and expenses
   a. Is a forecast of income and expenses provided? _____
   b. Is it:
      based on actual franchisee operations? ___
      based on a franchisor outlet? ___
      purely estimated? ___
   c. Does it:

	yes	no
relate to your market area?	___	___
meet your personal goals?	___	___
provide adequate return on investment?	___	___
provide for adequate promotion and personnel?	___	___

3. What is the best legal structure for my company?
   proprietorship ___
   partnership ___
   corporation ___

4. The franchise contract
   a. Is there a written contract? _____ (Get a copy for lawyer and accountant to review.)
   b. Does it specify:

	yes	no
franchise fee?	___	___
termination?	___	___
selling and renewal?	___	___
advertising and promotion?	___	___
patent and liability protection?	___	___
home office services?	___	___
commissions and royalties?	___	___
training?	___	___
financing?	___	___
territory?	___	___
exclusivity?	___	___

Source: Adapted from C. R. Stigelman, *Franchise Index/Profile*, Small Business Management Series, No. 35 (Washington, D.C.: Small Business Administration, 1973), pp. 31–41.

became very profitable, and the franchisor offered Myron three new locations, all of which he accepted.

Myron's touch was magic; two of the three new stores also became very successful. But try as he would, he couldn't make money on the third one. After three more years,

Myron decided that too much of his time was being drained by the one loser. He called the franchisor and asked them to assist him in selling it. They found several prospective buyers and chose the one they thought was the best operator. He wasn't able to turn it around either. Myron now devotes all his time to working with his winners.

Reasons for Not Buying a Franchise

Many entrepreneurs have decided against buying franchises. Here are some of the reasons they have given:

1. I know the business as well as they do.
2. My name is as well-known as theirs.
3. Why pay a franchise fee?
4. Why pay a royalty fee and advertising fee?
5. My individuality would have been stifled.
6. I don't want others to tell me how to run my business.
7. I didn't want a ground-floor opportunity where I'd be the guinea pig.
8. I'd have been committed for the rest of my life.
9. There were restrictions on selling out.
10. If I didn't do as I was told, I would lose my franchise.
11. The specified hours of business did not suit my location.
12. The franchisor's promotions and products did not fit my customers' needs or tastes.
13. They offered no territory protection.
14. I would not be in control of my business.

If you can develop a winning formula, you can become a franchisor yourself. Many entrepreneurs have done this. This is another reason to learn all you can about franchising now.

A Final Word about Franchises

If you have few business skills, or perhaps little business experience, then your chances of succeeding are far greater as a franchisee. A franchisor with a well-developed Business Plan will keep you on track. Ask to see that Business Plan.

The key here is gut feeling. If you should decide to buy a franchise and then feel like an employee of the franchisor, strike out on your own. Develop your own Plan, and go for it. Look at franchising as an option—an example to learn from—and then blend that knowledge into a unique business that explores the gaps exposed back in chapter 3, "Power Marketing."

If you're not ready to be on your own yet, franchising may be the way for you to start.

SUMMARY

There are two good reasons to consider buying a franchise: first, if the brand name is respected you'll already be positioned in the marketplace; second, if the franchisor is sharp, you'll inherit a Business Plan that works. Examine the franchise's appeal with consumers carefully; you want to get a marketing boost from the name.

ACTION STEP REVIEW

We suggest you examine franchising in two steps.

64 Investigate the franchise system by interviewing franchisors and franchisees. Ask a lot of questions.

65 Visit a franchise exposition. Talk to franchisors and see how they operate.

Depending on the franchise, you may also get other services for your money (for example, help on site selection, help on interior layout, and vendor connections), but the main thing you're buying is brand-name recognition.

Just as if you were investigating an ongoing, independent business, study the opportunity thoroughly. Examine the financial history, and compare what you'd make if you bought the business to what you'd make if you invested the same money elsewhere.

THINK POINTS FOR SUCCESS

◀ Avoid ground-floor opportunities. "Grow with us" can mean *caveat emptor* ("Let the buyer beware").

◀ Talk to franchisees.

◀ The franchisor gets a percentage of gross sales for advertising and royalty fees whether the franchisee is profitable or not.

◀ Do you really need the security blanket of a franchise?

◀ Read the proposed agreements carefully.

◀ Would you be comfortable relinquishing your independence?

REFERENCES

Areddy, James T. *Buyer's Guide: Wall Street Journal Reports on Small Business.* July 10, 1988. [This supplement appears every six months. In 1988, with 509,000 outlets in the U.S., goods and services pushed through franchises were expected to total over $600 billion in 1988. Hot segments: oil-change centers, detailing, maid-service, cleaning, child-care, and temporary help. In the mature phase, heading toward decline: printing, copying, yogurt, ice cream, cookies, restaurants, and video stores. There are 26,000 video rental outlets, and that does not count the 15,000 other outlets where tapes can be rented. Newest competition to video franchises is the video vending machine. In other words, the future is now.]

Bank of America. *How to Buy and Sell a Business or Franchise. Small Business Reporter* series. (See chapter 9 References for information on the Bank of America *Small Business Reporter* series.)

Battle, Donald L. "The Great American Franchise Extravaganza." *U.S. News and World Report,* 28 July 1986, p. 36.

Brown, Buck. "Small Business: Testing Psyches of Future Franchisees." *Wall Street Journal,* May 20, 1988. [If you're independent and creative, the chances are good that you'll be screened out by this two-and-a-half-hour test. Developed by Franchise Developments, Inc., of Pittsburgh, the test selects people who will work well within the system. Entrepreneurs, pass by.]

Bunn, Verne A. *Buying and Selling a Small Business.* New York: Arno Press, 1979.

Burstiner, Irving. *The Small-Business Handbook.* Englewood Cliffs, N.J.: Prentice-Hall, 1979.

Business Planning: Road Map to Success. Small Business Management Training Instructors' Guide, No. 102. Washington, D.C.: U.S. Small Business Administration, Office of Management Assistance, 1984. [Produced by the American Association of Community and Junior Colleges under contract to the U.S. SBA, Contract No. SBA 4873-MA 80.]

Cohen, Herb. *You Can Negotiate Anything: How to Get What You Want.* Secaucus, N.J.: Lyle Stuart, 1980. [An intriguing look at the tactics of wheeling and dealing, with case studies and scenarios.]

Evaluating Franchise Opportunities. Management Aid No. 7.007. Washington, D.C.: U.S. Small Business Administration, Office of Business Development, 1987.

Kostecka, Andrew. *Franchising in the Economy, 1986–1988.* U.S. Department of Commerce. [Send $4.75 to the Superintendant of Documents, U.S. Government Printing Office, Washington, DC 20402.]

Small Business Incubator Handbook: A Guide for Start-Up and Management. Washington, D.C.: U.S. Small Business Administration, Office of Private-Sector Initiatives, 1986.

Star Software Systems. *Venture: The Entrepreneur's Handbook.* [A pull-down-menu-driven IBM PC PS/2 software package that allows the development of a fully integrated Business Plan. It includes specific programs for manufacturing, wholesale, retail, and service business. Contact Star Software Systems at 363 Van Ness Way, Torrance, CA 90501-1420, or by calling 1-800-242-STAR.]

Sullivan, Daniel, and Joseph Lane. *Small Business Management, a Practical Approach,* second ed. Dubuque, Ia.: Wm. C. Brown, 1983.

Tetreault, Wilfred E. *Buying and Selling Business Opportunities: A Sales Transaction Handbook.* Reading, Mass.: Addison-Wesley, 1981. [Contains an overwhelming set of documents needed when buying a business. One look at this book, and you'll decide to handle your own start-up.]

United States Department of Commerce. *Franchise Opportunities Handbook.* Washington, D.C., 1979.

The following books and magazines are available through the International Franchise Association, 1350 New York Avenue, NW, Suite 900, Washington, DC 20005:

The Franchise Advantage [by Donald D. and Patrick Borolan, franchise consultants; $18.95]

The Franchise Option: How to Expand Your Business through Franchising [by William Ginalski and DeBanks M. Henward III and revised by Kathryn L. Boe, Assistant Dean, Creighton University School of Law; $18.95 paperback, $25.95 hard cover]

Franchising: The How-To Book [by Lloyd Tarbutton, cofounder of EconoLodges of America; $17.95]

Franchising World [bimonthly magazine of the I.F.A.; $12 a year]

How to Be a Franchisor [by Robert E. Kushell, franchising attorney, $5]

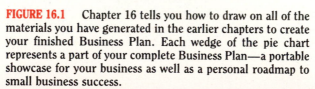

FIGURE 16.1   Chapter 16 tells you how to draw on all of the materials you have generated in the earlier chapters to create your finished Business Plan. Each wedge of the pie chart represents a part of your complete Business Plan—a portable showcase for your business as well as a personal roadmap to small business success.

Pulling the Plan Together

LEARNING OBJECTIVES

■ To pull all the information together into one coherent unit, which becomes a portable showcase for your business. ■ To study a sample Business Plan to see how one group of entrepreneurs defined and showed off their business. ■ To match or surpass the sample Business Plan in power and effectiveness. ■ To put your finished Business Plan to work.

Business Plan
a portable document that becomes the blueprint for your business

Your Business Plan could be the most important document you've ever pulled together. It will help keep you focused while you're out there doing the work on your start-up, researching, finding the gaps, interviewing small business owners, profiling your target customers, and so on. Staying focused is important because you're going to get a lot of distracting ideas for more new businesses while you're out there hunting.

A **Business Plan** will keep your creativity on track and your power grooved. How? By being a constant reminder of who you are and where you are going.

When you've finished your Plan, you've got something in writing to show to the people who are important to your business: your banker, lenders, relatives, venture capitalists, vendors, suppliers, key employees, friends, the SBA, and others. The Plan is portable, and you can make as many copies as you need to show to the people who can help you succeed. You can even mail it to contacts clear across the country.

Planning is hard work. You'll stay up nights over this, maybe lose some sleep, but you'll save time in the end. Just as a pilot would not consider a long flight without a plan, neither should you consider a business venture without a Business Plan.

HOW TO WRITE YOUR BUSINESS PLAN

Two-Part Structure: Words and Numbers

Your Business Plan tells the world what kind of business you're in. For ease of handling, divide your plan into two sections, and provide the needed documentation in appendixes at the end. In Section I use *words* to briefly introduce your strategies for marketing and management. Try to "hook" your reader with the excitement of creating a business, assessing the competition, designing a marketing plan, targeting customers, finding the right location, and building a team—all those human things that most people can relate to, even if they're not in business.

In Section II present *numbers:* income statement, cash flow projection, and projected balance sheet. This section is aimed primarily at bankers, credit managers, venture capitalists, vendors, SBICs, commercial credit lenders. At the same time, you've got to make it accessible to the casual reader who searches for the bottom line.

Support the two sections with *appendixes*. This is where you put resumes, maps, diagrams, photographs, tables, reprints from industry journals, letters from customers, letters from vendors, credit reports, personal financial statements, bids from contractors, and other documentation that demonstrates the viability of your plan. Note that in most cases, material in the appendixes comes from existing sources. You're not stating anything new here; you're just supporting what you've already said. (Appendixes vary according to each business; for that reason sample appendixes are not included in this book.)

By following the action steps in this chapter, you will complete all the components you need to make a winning Business Plan. If you want to jump ahead for a quick overview of your Plan, take a look at our sample table of contents in Figure 16.3.

The Relationship of Your Plan to This Book

You may be closer to your Business Plan than you think. If you have completed the action steps in the preceding chapters, you already have the major components of your Plan. The earlier chapters gave you the materials, and this chapter gives you the structure.

Section I, the description of your business, draws its parts directly from chapters 2–7 and 12 and 13. For example, chapter 2 helps you prepare Part A, "The Product or Service."

Section II draws from chapters 8, 9, and 11. Those chapters give you the background and the skills to crunch numbers for the three financial statements that compose this section. The same chapters prepare you for writing good explanatory notes to accompany each financial statement. These notes will make the statements meaningful to readers who don't relate to the numbers so easily.

How to Start Writing

If you're a creative thinker, chances are your thought processes don't always follow a linear sequence. That's great—it will help you as an entrepreneur! Nonetheless, the action steps in this chapter *do* follow a linear sequence, the sequence of the parts of a finished Business Plan. This is a matter of convenience—you get to see an example of each part as it would appear in the finished product. Bear in mind, however, that we don't expect you to write each part directly in sequence.

The best way to start writing a Business Plan is to begin with the material with which you feel most comfortable. For example, if you really enjoyed interviewing target customers, you might begin with Part B, "The Market and the target customers," referring to chapters 3 and 4 for boosts. Once you have a foothold, the other parts will seem easier to reach.

In this chapter the action steps can serve as a checklist for keeping track of which parts of the Plan you have written. For example, in practice you would probably write the cover letter last of all, although that is the first action step we present. Think of the writing of this first cover letter as a valuable exercise. The more cover letters you write, the easier it becomes to write them effectively.

cover letter
a tailored introduction to your Business Plan

THE COVER LETTER

To aim your Plan so that it will achieve the most good, you use a cover letter. Each time you send the Plan to someone, you write a special cover letter addressed to that specific reader. The cover letter introduces the excitement of your Plan, and it tells the person why you are sending it to him or her.

Read the sample cover letter in Figure 16.2 now.

Let's summarize what's good about our sample cover letter. We can see that:

1. The writer is making use of a previous contact.
2. The writer tells his reader—the manager of a bank—that he is in the market for a loan. He does not put her on the spot by asking for money.
3. Instead, he asks for advice on where to find sources of capital.
4. The writer struck the right tone. (To do that, he rewrote the letter several times.)

You can do as well or better—and it's worth the effort! As you draft your cover letter, remember that the reader will pass judgment on your Business Plan (and on your business ability) on the basis of the letter. Do you want your small business to look bright, attractive, and welcoming? Your cover letter needs to give the same impression. A good cover letter will make its readers want to become involved in your venture.

Action Step 66 will help you write your cover letter.

ACTION STEP 66

Write a cover letter for your plan.

Address your letter to a specific person who can help your business. Be brief; aim for about two hundred words.

State the reason you are sending the plan. If you are asking for money, tell the person what you want it for and how much you need. One well-written paragraph should be all you need to do this.

Your purpose in writing the cover letter is to open the door gently and prepare the way for further negotiations. The cover letter is bait on your hook.

If you are putting money into the business, or if you have already donated, indicate how much.

The tone you are after in this opening move is confident and slightly formal. You want to appear neat, bright, organized, and in control of your venture.

Be certain to explain briefly how you will repay the money.

Refer to the sample letter in Figure 16.2.

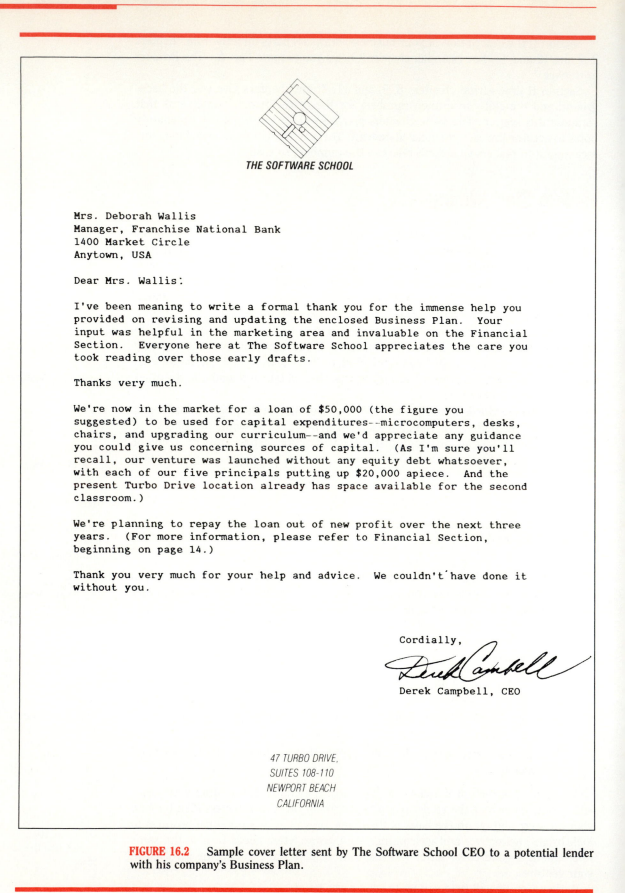

FIGURE 16.2   Sample cover letter sent by The Software School CEO to a potential lender with his company's Business Plan.

PRELIMINARIES

The Table of Contents

Figure 16.3 provides a sample table of contents to give you a quick overview of a finished Business Plan; it appears on page 294. In practice, the table of contents is prepared last.

The Executive Summary

The executive summary serves as an introduction to the Business Plan. In function, it is similar to the preface of this book: it is written to acquaint the reader with the subject of the material that follows, to direct the reader's attention to whatever strengths the author (entrepreneur) wants to emphasize, and to make the reader want to turn the page and read, read, read. Because the executive summary gives perspective to the entire Business Plan, it needs to be written last—after Parts A through J are written.

As you write your executive summary, remember that lenders prefer "hard," numerical data and facts; they cannot take speculations about things real seriously. Therefore, such phrases as "50% return on the original investment" and "secured agreements from 17 area businesses" make the following example a strong executive summary. They help to paint a picture of good management and solid growth for The Software School.

Executive Summary

The Software School is a user-friendly, state-of-the-art microcomputer training center. In our first six months of operation, we demonstrated our unique and profitable way of exploiting a strong and growing market within a fast-growing industry. The Software School's sophisticated electronic classroom provides "hands-on" education that teaches computer users how to use new software programs. By January 2, 19XX we were operating at 92% capacity (50% is break-even) and had a waiting list of 168 students.

We plan to add a second classroom in order to double our capacity. This expansion will allow us to attain $400,000 in sales by the end of our 18th month. At that time, our pretax profits will have reached almost $50,000, representing a 50% return on our original $100,000 investment.

Our target customers seem to have insatiable appetites for software application knowledge, and The Software School anticipates an annual compound growth rate of 50% over the next five years. We have secured training agreements from 17 retail computer stores in the area and firm contracts for more than 700 employees from 84 industrial users.

Our competitors continue to train in the traditional classroom style and currently show no sign of copying our unique instructional approach. Occasional price-cutting by competitors has had no effect on our enrollment.

Management, led by Derek Campbell, has demonstrated how to offer superior training at competitive prices. Our plans for the future include developing additional profit centers by providing on-site counseling and training for firms throughout Southern California. Research and customer surveys indicate that we have just begun to satisfy the ever-increasing need for software education.

TABLE OF CONTENTS

*The need for specific appendixes varies greatly from Business Plan to Business Plan. For that reason, this chapter does not include sample appendixes. As you draft your Plan, you will see needs to document and substantiate your business strategies; this kind of documentation is best included as appendixes.

FIGURE 16.3   The table of contents page of The Software School's Business Plan.

ACTION STEP 67

Write an executive summary.

Imagine you had two minutes to explain your business venture to a complete stranger. . . . This gives you an idea of what information you need to put into writing for your executive summary.

Practice explaining your venture to friends and strangers, limiting yourself to two minutes. Ask them to raise questions, and use their questions to guide you as you revise, and hone, your presentation.

When you are satisfied with your oral summary, write it down and type it up. It should not exceed three typed pages. (The Software School's executive summary that serves as our example was less than one page, single-spaced.) This may constitute a very small portion of your Business Plan, but it could be the most important part of it.

You, too, can write an effective executive summary. Action Step 67 will help you to decide which facts and numbers will portray you and your business venture as credible and promising and then to summarize them on paper.

SECTION I: DESCRIPTION OF THE BUSINESS

Do you know your business? You need to prove it with words and numbers. By the time your reader finishes your Business Plan, you should have a convert to your side. To give you examples to follow, we reprint key sections from the Business Plan (newly revised and updated) for The Software School, an ongoing business that is seeking financing for acquiring more equipment. Regardless of whether your business is ongoing or just starting up, the goals of Section I are the same—to demonstrate that you know your business and that you're a winner.

Part A: The Product or Service

Here's how The Software School tackled this part of Section I.

The Service We Provide

The Software School, a California Corporation, is a microcomputer training facility located in Newport Beach, between John Wayne Airport and a high-density executive business complex. It's the heart of Orange County's microcomputer users. Now in its seventh month of operation, the school has a waiting list of 168 students (67% of whom have put down deposits).

We train people in computer software systems from the Top Ten List of best-selling microcomputer software packages. Because of their power, these systems are complex. They provide a learning hurdle, especially at first.

Students are drawn to our teaching method because it gives them **hands-on experience** and because it's fast. Working people are busy, and a student can upgrade a given software skill by 80% in eight hours. (Slower learners are guaranteed a second try, and a third, at no cost.) Most of our courses can be completed in one day or two evenings. In contrast, the average college course (which emphasizes concepts, rather than hands-on software systems) takes 12 to 18 weeks. Our price is $100 for most courses, and so far no one has complained about the cost.

The Software School achieves this space-age learning speed with a sophisticated electronic teaching system adapted from flight-simulation techniques used by airlines for training pilots. We are constantly streamlining and upgrading the system, using funds already allocated in our start-up budget.

One especially bright note: We have done far better than we had hoped. Our actual income figures average 24% above our original projections. Projected income for the first six months, with an assumed **occupancy rate** of 50%, was just over $10,000 a month. The actual occupancy has not peaked, and for the past two months we have operated at 92% capacity.

As a service business, we sell seats as well as skills and information, and as Appendix 1 shows, our promotion has generated a heavy demand for present courses like Computer Fundamentals, Wordstar, and Visicalc. At the same time, customers are asking for courses to meet their needs—for example, a course in Lotus 1-2-3, a second-generation data handler tailored for the IBM PC.

Until the end of our fifth month, we were open six days a week from 8 A.M. to 10 P.M. To meet demand with our current classroom facilities, we are now open on Sundays from 9 A.M. to 6 P.M., and the Sunday classes are full.

The demand increased dramatically when we contracted with some of Southern California's large computer retailers to develop a training program. (See Appendix 2 for letters from specific sales managers.) These retailers sent us their salespeople for training; the salespeople, in turn, have referred their customers to us. Computer retailers quickly discovered they can sell better systems to buyers who are not afraid of computers, and they are in the business of selling, not training. We combat customers' fears in a logical way, with knowledge.

Our equipment (IBM PCs) is top-quality. Our staff combines excellent training skills with attention to people and their needs. We have launched a solid start-up in a heated growth industry, and we plan to continue our growth and success.

hands-on experience
nonacademic exposure to real life

occupancy rate
the percentage of a commercial property or development that is occupied

ACTION STEP 68

Describe your product or service.

Excite your reader about your business. Excitement is contagious. If you can get your reader going, there's a good chance you'll be offered money. Investors love hot ideas.

If this is a start-up, explain your product or service fully. What makes it unique? What industry is it in? Where does the industry fit in the big picture?

Mention numbers wherever you can. Percentages and dollar amounts are more meaningful than words like *lots* and *many*.

If this is a going business, your records of sales, costs, and profit and loss will substantiate your need for money.

Keep the words going and the typewriter smoking. You need to convince the reader to keep reading.

The Software School will get its funding because the writer of the Plan proves that his business is a winning concern. The writer has:

1. let the facts speak for themselves,
2. supported all claims with numbers,
3. avoided hard-sell tactics, and
4. refused to puff the product.

The writer does a terrific selling job without appearing to be selling at all. Now it's your turn. Do Action Step 68.

Part B: The Market and the Target Customer

Knowledge is power, especially in the Information Age. The Software School—an information business—capitalized on expert knowledge to define the marketplace. In the same way, if your research is sound, it will show up in your writing.

As you continue to read The Software School's Business Plan, remember:

1. This is a revised Business Plan, so the writing is smooth. You will need to do several revisions in order to smooth out your writing. (How many revisions are you planning?)
2. The reader of your Business Plan is a special kind of target customer. (How can you use your marketing abilities to look at this reader with new eyes? Have you developed a profile of this very special target customer?)

The Market and Our Target Customer

INDUSTRY OVERVIEW

Fifteen years ago, the personal computer did not exist in the U.S. marketplace. There were **mainframes**, of course, and terminals linked to invisible data banks—but nothing you could carry home in a suitcase.

mainframes
massive hardware for processing data

Things are different today. Approximately 200 firms are making personal computers. The lion's share of the market goes to Apple, IBM, Radio Shack, Compaq, and so forth, and yet someone brings out a new PC (personal computer) almost every day of the year. The microcomputer industry is moving so fast that statistics can't keep pace. In 1981, the one-millionth computer was sold. The next year, 1982, a million computers were sold. It's projected that two million computers will be sold in 1990, and three million in the year 2000.

With all this sales flurry and emphasis on space-aged speed, some people are being left behind because they don't know how to use computers. A computer can be your best friend, but only if you learn how to use it. This makes training people to use computers a booming industry, and The Software School is on the **leading edge** of a major growth segment.

leading edge
the latest state of the art

TARGET MARKET

Our potential **total market** is Southern California, with a logical concentration in Orange County—which will increase in population from 1,970,000 in 1988 to 2,800,000 in the year 2000.

total market
every person or business that might need a product or service

Geographically, our target market encompasses Long Beach, La Habra, and Brea on the north; San Clemente on the south; Huntington and Newport Beaches on the west; and Orange, Fullerton, and Mission Viejo on the east. We are looking ahead to possible future expansion through the Southwestern United States.

continued

For now, our focus is Orange County. Within this highly concentrated population area, our target customer is the small business person. Latest statistics show 76,000 small businesses in Orange County.

OUR TARGET CUSTOMER
Our primary target customer is the small business, profiled here:
> Size: 1–30 employees
> Annual sales: $250,000 to $5,000,000
> Type of business: service industry
> Major output: paper (reports, letters, documents, etc.)

Our secondary target customer is the home user:
> Sex: 50% male, 50% female
> Age: 18–45
> Education: some college
> Owns PC: 22%
> Access to computer at work: 52%
> Lives near computer store: 73%
> Household income: $55,000 plus
> Occupation: professional, managerial, executive, entrepreneurial

Action Step 69 gives you a chance to show what you know about your market and your target customer. If you need help getting started, review your work in chapters 3 and 4. You can also review what the Business Plan for The Software School says about its market and TCs. Be sure to use secondary sources (like documents, tables, and quotes) to lend this portion credibility.

Part C: The Competition

Obviously if you know who your competitors are and how they fail to meet market needs, you are well on your way to strategic competition. You need to persuade your reader how great your competitive tactics are. (If you need a reminder, reread chapters 4 and 5. Competition changes according to the life-cycle stage of the industry, so a good way to begin your section on competition is to place your industry in the proper life-cycle phase.)

How tough do your competitors look? As you read The Software School's assessment of its competition, note that the writer takes a cool, objective look at the competition. He does not belittle them, and he certainly doesn't underestimate them.

> ### ACTION STEP 69
>
> Describe the market and the target customer.
>
> Bring all of your marketing research into this section and wow your reader with a picture of your target customer just sitting there waiting for your product or service.
>
> Use data from secondary sources to give credibility to the picture you are painting.

The Competition

The competition for computer training in Orange County is minimal at this time. The Software School has four main competitors:

Traherne Schools. Our oldest, most entrenched competitor. Three locations in Orange County: Brea, Garden Grove, and South Coast Plaza. Traherne's conducts a 6-hour course on Introduction to Microprocessors for $95. They currently run a course on desktop publishing for the Mac, and they have been planning to introduce a word-processing course for some time.

Traherne's target market is on the north rim of ours. Their South Coast Plaza operation is closed on Saturdays.

Big Micro Computer Instruction. Excellent classroom facilities, located in El Toro,

continued

near the San Diego Freeway. All instruction is tied to MacIntosh machines, and is free if you buy your hardware from Big Micro. Otherwise, courses usually cost around $95, and take 6–8 hours.

The instructors try hard, but Big Micro is really in the business of pushing hardware.

Micro Hut Computer Center. Friendly salespeople with teaching skills double as teachers. Courses at Micro Hut are divided between Compaq and Apple. Costs: Visicalc, $89; Word Processing, $149. The Word-Processing course takes about 12 hours of classroom time and is available only on Apple computers.

Micro Hut is not in the education business. They offer courses only to help sell systems.

Your Micro and You. Local facility developed by professional educators. The atmosphere of YMAY is excellent. They offer a normal range of programs and a course in using the computer in a small business, each course costing about $125. All instruction is tied to the Apple. Their market seems to be divided between adults with a casual interest in computers and children aged 10 to 15.

These people have done it right.

MEETING THE COMPETITION
The Software School is in the computer education business. We do not sell hardware or software.

Our program of instruction is geared to the times. We teach popular software, and we are constantly on the lookout for trends that will lead us to new markets. Furthermore, our prices are competitive, and we teach classes seven days a week.

ACTION STEP 70

Describe your major competitors.

Briefly profile the businesses that compete with you directly. Try to be objective as you assess their operations.

What are their strengths? What are their weaknesses? What can you learn from them?

After you've described your competitors, indicate how you're going to ace them out of the picture.

The Software School's Business Plan leaves no doubt that management is exploiting a market gap that is ignored by the competition—training people how to use popular software on the emerging industry leader, the IBM PC and IBM PS/2. This is more than a matter of writing skill. Early on, the entrepreneurs who founded The Software School did the right research so they could make decisions ahead of time—just as you were asked to do in the earlier chapters.

How will you handle the competition in your Business Plan? Your readers will expect you to be cool and objective. Now you're ready to complete Action Step 70.

Part D: Marketing Strategy

Now it's time to describe your marketing strategy. Need a reminder? Look back at your work in chapter 6.

The Marketing Strategy excerpt from The Software School's Business Plan demonstrates a carefully reasoned approach. The excerpt describes conscious marketing policies that will help this small business be competitive. If you read a Business Plan in which the writer did not demonstrate this care and deliberation, how much faith would you have in the writer's business abilities?

Note that The Software School uses a three-pronged approach to reaching the public. This business understands the importance of finding a good promotional mix.

Marketing Strategy

An analysis of our competitors indicates that our price—$99 for a one-day course, $198 for a two-day course—is between two extremes. These prices are competitive but still maintain our image of quality.

continued

We use a wide range of strategies to let our customers know where we are: mass-media advertising (newspapers, television, and radio), special promotions (press releases, brochures, newsletter, etc.), and personal selling (commissioned salespeople, networking, corporate contracts, trade shows, etc.)

MASS-MEDIA ADVERTISING

The Software School has been placing ads in the *L.A. Times* and smaller, area newspapers to keep a continuous presence in front of our target customers. In the beginning, we used inducements (two-for-one offers, 15% reductions, etc.), but that is no longer necessary as our waiting lists grow.

As we continue to expand, we will develop advertising on radio and TV.

CREATIVE PROMOTIONS / INK / FREE INK

In our first month of operation, we sponsored a scholarship contest in the local high schools, which resulted in some very positive press. In addition, the school has been featured in several local newspapers and in *Venture* magazine.

We are in the Information business, and toward that end we are presently developing three different publications—a computer handbook, a newsletter, and a brief history of the founding of The Software School. In time, we hope that this history (a how-to for computer educators) will become a guide for the industry.

Our mailing list grows daily. We log all incoming phone calls with information on the callers and how they found out about us. This information helps us define our target market.

PERSONAL SELLING

Personal contact has gained us our largest accounts so far. (Please refer to letters from computer retailers in Appendix 2.) We intend to intensify our efforts along these lines. Fortunately, our directors have experience and talent in the area of personal selling.

We maintain a booth at the major computer trade shows in the area. Approximately 17% of our hobbyist/home-user business has been generated this way.

mass-media advertising
reaching unselected hordes of people through print, sound, or visuals

The entrepreneurs who run The Software School stay on top of the changing market picture. They have demonstrated this by:

1. dropping discount inducements from their continuous print campaign,
2. looking ahead to radio and TV exposure,
3. logging calls and gathering information on the callers to maintain a base of up-to-date information on their target market, and
4. determining how they have gained their largest accounts and planning to intensify their efforts in that area.

Action Step 71 will help you to refine your marketing strategy. Note that you must continue to focus on the target customer.

Part E: Location

The next part of your Business Plan is the one on location. You may want to review your work in chapter 7 now.

Read how The Software School shows off its location to advantage.

ACTION STEP 71

Describe your marketing strategy.

Now that you've profiled your target customer and assessed your competition, take some time to develop the thrust of your market strategy. Which techniques will get the best and most cost-effective response?

Because pricing is such an important consideration, you might start with what your TC sees as a good value, and then develop your marketing mix.

business zoning
legal designation of property for business use

Our Location

The Software School is currently in the first year of a three-year lease at 47 Turbo Drive, Newport Beach, California. The facility is all on the ground floor and occupies 2,100 square feet. The area, which is **zoned for business use**, is a hotbed of high-technology activity. Within the immediate area, there are two computer stores, one computer furniture store, one software dealer, an electronics store, and two printers, one of which does typesetting work directly from software diskettes. Within a four-mile radius are 27 computer dealers.

During our lease negotiations, we persuaded the landlord to make extensive improvements in the interior, and to spread the cost out over the three-year term of the lease. The decor—blue carpet, white walls, orange furniture—gives the effect of a solid, logical, somewhat plush business environment in which our target customer will be comfortable and learn fast.

The building is divided into five areas: a reception area (300 square feet), a director's office (100 square feet), a classroom (700 square feet), a lounge (200 square feet), and a storage area (800 square feet).

The principals envision the storage area as a second classroom. See diagram in Appendix 9.

You need to paint an attractive picture of your business site and at the same time, keep your reader interested by inspiring confidence in your choice. Location takes a tremendous amount of analysis. The Software School writer gives himself a subtle pat on the back by describing the lease arrangements and by identifying the need for a second classroom. If the reader needs more, he or she is referred to the appendix. This is smart writing.

Your Plan will become very real when you showcase your physical facility. Complete Action Step 72.

ACTION STEP 72

Show off your location.

The great thing about a location is that it's so *tangible*. A potential lender can visit your site and get a feel for what's going on.

A banker will often visit your business site. That's good news for you because now the banker is on your turf.

Clean up the place before your banker arrives.

In this section, you want to persuade potential lenders to visit your site. Describe what goes on here. Use photographs and diagrams and illustrations to make it feel almost like home.

Part F: Management

Management will make or break your small business. You are a member of the management team, and you want this Business Plan to inspire confidence in your team. Writing this section will help you focus more closely on your management team members. (If you need a refresher, review your work in chapters 12 and 13.)

Now let's see how The Software School introduces *its* management.

Management

Derek Campbell. Mr. Campbell was born in Shaker Heights, Ohio, in 19—. He took a B.S. degree in Industrial Engineering at Purdue University and then spent five years in the Marine Corps, where he was a flight instructor, a check pilot, and a maintenance officer. While in the service, Mr. Campbell completed an M.A. degree in Marketing, Management, and Human Relations.

Following military service, Mr. Campbell was employed as a pilot for United Airlines. He is currently the CEO of EuroSource, a software importing company. He is the author of several articles on computers and the Information Age and is listed in *Who's Who in California.*

continued

Robert Jericho. Mr. Jericho was born in Dallas, Texas, in 19—. He has a B.S. degree in Geology and Physical Sciences at the University of Oklahoma and served six years in the Marine Corps, where he was a flight instructor, flight operations officer, and schedules officer.

Following military service, Mr. Jericho was a pilot for Trans World Airlines. He has completed training in the Nestar system managers' course, the Apple computer maintenance course, and has been working as an accountant and comptroller for EuroSource for the last two years.

DIRECTORS

C. Hughes Smith. Mr. Smith was born in Corpus Christi, Texas, in 19—. He has a B.A. degree from Tulane University in Political Science and Philosophy, a M.A. degree in Business Administration from Stanford, and a Law degree from the University of Texas at Austin.

Mr. Smith is a senior vice-president of Lowes and Lockwood, a residential homebuilding firm, and a partner in Graebner and Ashe, a Houston law firm. He is the author of numerous articles in the field of corporate planning and taxes. (Please see Personal Resumes in Appendix 4.)

Phil Carpenter. Mr. Carpenter was born in Duluth, Minnesota, in 19—. His B.A. degree is from the University of Kansas and his M.B.A., with a marketing specialty, is from the University of Wisconsin.

Mr. Carpenter spent 20 years in the corporate world (IBM, TRW, Inter-Comp, etc.), where he worked in marketing and industrial sales. Currently a professor of Business at Huntington Beach Community College, Mr. Carpenter is the general partner in two businesses and a small business consultant. He has written and lectured widely in the area of small business.

Dan Masters. Mr. Masters was born in Palo Alto, California, in 19—. His degrees (B.A., M.B.A.) are from Stanford, where he specialized in marketing and finance. Mr. Masters served his Army duty in Korea, where he worked on the United Nations Korean Civil Assistance Program, a long-term plan for making Korea economically independent. Following his military service, Mr. Masters worked for Kodak and then for Sylvania (senior account sales executive, sales manager, etc.) for a total of 25 years.

Mr. Masters is currently an associate professor of Business at San Juan Capistrano Institute of Business Science. He is active in several small businesses, lectures widely, and has published numerous articles in the field of small business.

OTHER AVAILABLE RESOURCES

The Software School has retained the legal firm of Farney and Shields and the accounting firm of Hancock, Hancock, and Craig. Our insurance broker is Sharon Mandel of Fireman's Fund. Our advertising agency is George Friend and Associates.

This management team shows balance, diversity, experience (some interesting track records), the will to succeed, and above all, a love of adventure. Robert Jericho and Derek Campbell were both flight instructors. Now they're using space-age industrial training techniques in the computer classroom. In addition, pilots must plan and must take responsibility—good experience for running their own show.

Balance is important too, and this shows up in the short resumes. Jericho is the technician who handles systems management. Campbell is the marketeer and manager. Both have good people skills. Who do you suppose is the idea man?

The Software School is a corporation, and the authors of the Business Plan were wise to include resumes of the directors. In this case, the background of the directors enhances the balance of the team. All three directors have admirable depth in their business careers, with two of them sharing a combined 45 years of experience in the corporate world. Campbell very wisely uses his directors to assist him in the sales function.

The listing of the legal counsel, accounting firm, an insurance broker, and advertising agency also adds to the impression of solid business practices. We sometimes refer to these people as the "taxi-squad," but in a Business Plan, the language is more formal.

Nothing is more important than the people who will make your business work. Present their pedigrees, and focus on their track records and accomplishments as you complete Action Step 73.

Part G: Personnel

Part G of your Plan shows off your personnel. For a start-up business, you're peering into the future with confidence—doing informal job analyses for key employees who will help you to succeed. For an ongoing business, you need to list your present employees and anticipate your future personnel needs. If you have five employees now and you want to indicate growth, try to project how many jobs you'll be creating in the next five years.

When you start thinking about tasks and people to do them, review your work in chapters 12 and 13. Preparing this part of your Plan is important because it gives you one more chance to analyze job functions before you start interviewing, hiring, and paying benefits—all of which are expensive.

You'll notice that The Software School gives a very brief rundown of its personnel situation.

Personnel

At the end of six months of operation, The Software School has three full-time employees and 14 part-time employees. The full-time employees include:

1. Manager, salaried at $3,000 per month
2. Receptionist, salaried at $8 per hour
3. Training Director, salaried at $1,500 per month

The part-time employees include three directors, who assist in the marketing function, three outside commissioned salespeople, and eight part-time instructors. According to our plan, one salesperson will become full-time at the end of the seventh month.

We will continue to hold down overhead with part-time employees as long as it is feasible. We believe that running a lean operation is important to our success.

In describing their lean operation, the entrepreneurs who run The Software School keep their description lean as well. They show good sense when they express a commitment to hold down operating costs. Their decision reflects business discipline and foresight. If you were a potential investor in this business, wouldn't you appreciate some tight purse strings?

Every person on your team is important. Action Step 74 will help you describe the kinds of people you will need and how you will help them to become productive.

SECTION II: FINANCIAL SECTION

Good Numbers

The financial section is the heart of your Business Plan. It is aimed at lenders—bankers, credit managers, venture capitalists, vendors, SBICs, commercial credit lenders—people who think in numbers. Lenders are professional skeptics by trade; they will not be swayed by the enthusiasm of your writing in Section I. Your job, therefore, is to make your numbers do the talking. This is easier than you may think.

You started jotting down numbers in chapter 8, when you began thinking about money. You projected cash flow and income in chapter 9. In chapter 10, you tested your numbers on real lenders in the real world. Now you're ready to organize your numbers into three standard instruments:

1. the projected income statement,
2. the cash flow projection (also called a "pro forma"), and
3. the projected balance sheet.

Examples from The Software School will serve as models for you. You can adapt them to fit your business.

The idea is to know where every nickel is going. You need to show when you'll make a profit and appear neat, orderly, in control, and conservative. You'll know you've succeeded when a skeptical lender looks up from your Business Plan and says, "You know, these numbers look good."

Good Notes

One way to spot a professional lender is to hand over your Business Plan and watch to see which section he or she reads first. Most lenders study the notes that accompany income and cash flow projections first. Knowing this allows you to be forewarned. Use these notes to tell potential lenders how you generated your numbers (for example, "Advertising is projected at 5% of sales") and to explain specific entries (for example, "Leased Equipment—monthly lease costs on IBM microcomputers").

Make these notes easy to read, with headings that start your readers off in the upper left-hand corner and march them down the page, step-by-step, to the bottom line. (Some sample projection charts use tiny footnotes, on the same page. We prefer *large* notes on a separate page. Notes are important, so they should be big.

Creating your Business Plan takes a lot of time. It's only natural for you to hope that lenders will read it, get excited, and ask questions. These notes can help you accomplish that, even if you haven't started up and the numbers are projections into the future.

Part H: Projected Income Statement

Your next task is to put together your projected income statement (sometimes called a "profit and loss" statement). With the information you've gathered so far, it shouldn't be too hard. In fact, it will be enjoyable—if the numbers look good.

The Software School's projected income statement is shown in Table 16.1, and the careful documentation of each item is reprinted here. For instance, if a lender wanted to know how the figures for commissions were generated, Note 6 explains that they are estimated as 10% of sales.

TABLE 16.1 The Software School's projected income statement

INCOME STATEMENT/SOFTWARE SCHOOL

	7th Month	8th Month	9th Month	10th Month	11th Month	12th Month
SALES						
Instruction	23285	24950	26630	28215	29900	31580
Books	215	250	270	285	300	320
TOTAL SALES	23500	25200	26900	28500	30200	31900
Cost of Instr/						
Clssrm Matrls	1765	1890	2020	2140	2265	2395
Inst/Personnel	2500	2500	2600	2600	2700	2700
Books	150	175	190	200	210	225
TOTAL COST/						
INSTR/BOOKS	4415	4565	4810	4940	5175	5320
GROSS PROFIT	19085	20635	22090	23560	25025	26580
EXPENSES						
SALES:						
Commissions	2330	2495	2665	2820	2990	3160
Advertising	1175	1250	1335	1410	1495	1580
Credit Cards	295	315	335	355	380	400
ADMINISTRATIVE:						
Salaries	3300	3300	3300	4500	4500	4500
Payroll taxes	570	580	600	695	715	725
Leased Equip	1270	1270	1270	1270	1270	1270
Licenses/fees	2330	2495	2665	2820	2990	3160
Accounting	500	500	500	500	500	500
Rent	3890	3890	3890	3890	3890	3890
Office Suppl	60	65	65	70	75	80
Dues/Subscrip	20	20	20	20	20	20
Repair/Maint	235	250	265	285	300	320
Insurance	80	80	80	80	80	80
Telephone	355	380	405	430	455	480
Utilities	470	505	540	570	605	640
Depreciation	1170	1170	1170	1335	1335	1335
Interest				650	650	650
Miscellaneous	705	755	805	855	905	955
TOTAL EXPENSES	18755	19320	19910	22555	23155	23745
NET PROFIT	330	1315	2180	1005	1870	2835
Reserve for taxes	65	265	435	200	375	565
NET PROFIT AFTER TAXES	265	1050	1745	805	1495	2270

TABLE 16.1   *Continued*

INCOME STATEMENT/SOFTWARE SCHOOL

	13th Month	14th Month	15th Month	16th Month	17th Month	18th Month	TOTAL
SALES							
Instruction	33265	34945	37915	39600	42770	42770	395825
Books	335	355	435	500	530	530	4325
TOTAL SALES	33600	35300	38350	40100	43300	43300	400150
Cost of Instr/							
Clssrm Matrls	2520	2650	2875	3000	3240	3240	30000
Inst/Personnel	2800	2800	2900	2900	3000	3000	33000
Books	235	250	305	350	370	370	3030
TOTAL COST/							
INSTR/BOOKS	5555	5700	6080	6250	6610	6610	66030
GROSS PROFIT	28045	29600	32270	33850	36690	36690	334120
EXPENSES							
SALES:							
Commissions	3325	3495	3790	3960	4275	4275	39580
Advertising	1660	1750	1895	1980	2135	2135	19800
Credit Cards	420	440	480	500	540	540	5000
ADMINISTRATIVE:							
Salaries	4500	4500	4500	4500	4500	4500	50400
Payroll taxes	745	755	785	795	825	825	8165
Leased Equip	1270	1270	1270	1270	1270	1270	15240
Licenses/fees	3325	3495	3790	3960	4275	4275	39580
Accounting	500	500	500	500	500	500	6000
Rent	3890	3890	3890	3890	3890	3890	46680
Office Suppl	85	90	95	100	110	110	1005
Dues/Subscrip	200	20	20	20	20	20	420
Repair/Maint	335	355	385	395	435	435	3995
Insurance	80	80	80	80	80	80	960
Telephone	505	530	575	600	650	650	6015
Utilities	670	705	765	800	865	865	8000
Depreciation	1335	1335	1335	1335	1335	1335	15525
Interest	650	650	650	595	595	595	5685
Miscellaneous	1010	1060	1150	1205	1300	1300	12005
TOTAL EXPENSES	24505	24920	25955	26485	27600	27600	284505
NET PROFIT	3540	4680	6315	7365	9090	9090	49615
Reserve for taxes	710	935	1265	1475	1820	1820	9930
NET PROFIT AFTER TAXES	2830	3745	5050	5890	7270	7270	39685

Notes for Projected Income Statement

1. **Instruction.** Based on 2.5% occupancy growth per month, starting at 35% (235 students) and growing to 60%. Students pay $99 per course.
2. **Books.** Revenue from books sold averages approximately 1% of instructional sales, rounded to bring total sales to an even $100 figure.
3. **Classroom Materials.** $7.50 per student.
4. **Instruction Personnel.** Instructor cost is $100 per 8-hour class, starting with 25 classes and growing to 30 classes by the end of the year.
5. **Books.** Cost of books is 70% of selling price.
6. **Commissions.** Average 10% of instructional sales.
7. **Advertising.** Projected at 5% of sales.
8. **Credit Cards.** Approximately 50% of sales are paid with credit cards. The cost is 2.5% of the sale.
9. **Salaries.** Start with 3 full-time employees. Bring on one additional person beginning the 10th month.
10. **Payroll Taxes.** The company's share of employee taxes averages 7% of commissions and salaries.
11. **Leased Equipment.** Monthly lease costs on IBM microcomputers.
12. **Licenses and Fees.** 10% of instruction sales paid for license (right to use copyrighted material).
13. **Accounting.** Average accounting and bookkeeping costs for the area and size of the business.
14. **Rent.** Based on 3-year lease.
15. **Office Supplies.** Estimated at 0.25% of sales.
16. **Dues and Subscriptions.** Estimated costs for magazines, newspapers, and membership in organizations.
17. **Repair and Maintenance.** Projected to be 1% of sales.
18. **Insurance.** Based on current insurance contract for next 12 months, payable every 6 months.
19. **Telephone.** Figured at 1.5% of sales.
20. **Utilities.** Figured at 2% of sales.
21. **Depreciation.** Schedule established by accounting firm.
22. **Interest.** Loan at 13% with $5,000 payments due every 6 months until paid off.
23. **Miscellaneous.** Figured at 3% of sales.
24. **Reserve for Taxes.** State and federal taxes estimated at 20% of net profit.

ACTION STEP 75

Project your income statement.

What you're driving at here is *net profit*—what's left in the kitty after expenses—for each month and for the year.

First, you figure your *sales*. The first big bite out of that figure is the *cost of goods sold*. (In a service business, the big cost is labor.) Subtracting that gives you a figure called *gross margin*.

Now add up all your *expenses* (rent, utilities, insurance, etc.), and subtract them from gross margin. This gives you your *net profit before taxes*. (Businesses pay quarterly installments.)

Subtract taxes. There's your net profit.

Action Step 75 will help you project your own monthly profits and losses for 12 months. Refer to Table 16.1 as you predict your income.

Part I: Projected Cash Flow

Next focus your attention on the projected cash flow— the lifeblood of your business. By projecting cash flow figures out across the year, you get a month-by-month picture of how healthy your business will be.

The Software School's cash flow projection is set out in Table 16.2. The notes for these numbers are reprinted here. If you compare the projected income statement (Table 16.1) with the cash flow projection, you will see that some items are treated differently in the tables. For example, expenses in the projected income statement are divided into monthly installments, whereas the same expenses in the cash flow projection are shown as bulk payments when due. Now look at insurance expense. In the projected income statement we find a total expense of $960 shown as twelve monthly debits of $80 each. The same expense in the cash flow projection is shown as two payments of $480 each, falling due in the seventh and thirteenth months. If the entrepreneurs running the business had only $80 available to pay for insurance in the seventh month—that is what is shown in the income statement—they would be in trouble.

Notes for Cash Flow Projection

1. **Beginning of the Month.** Cash available as the month begins.
2. **Sales.** Includes all sales paid by cash, check, or credit card at the time the class is taken. Does not include accounts receivable.
3. **Credit Card Expense.** Fees of 2.5% paid to credit card companies. Approximately 50% of customers use charge cards.
4. **Loans.** Loan for new course development and audiovisual equipment.
5. **Total Cash Available.** Sum of all money available during the month.
6. **Books.** Books for sale are ordered and paid for one month in advance of projected sale.
7. **Instructional Materials.** Covers course materials purchased from licenser.
8. **Salaries.** Net salaries paid employees approximate 80% of gross salaries paid.
9. **Payroll Taxes.** Total of amount withhold from employees, plus Income Statement payroll tax item.
10. **Advertising.** Established as 30-day accounts with all media companies.
11. **Leased Equipment.** Lease payments are due the first of each month.
12. **Licenses and Fees.** License fees are due the 15th of the following month.
13. **Legal and Accounting.** Due 30 days after bill is received.
14. **Rent.** Due the first of each month.
15. **Office Supplies.** Paid at time of purchase or with subscription. No credit.
16. **Insurance.** Paid every 6 months in advance.
17. **Telephone and Utilities.** Paid within 30 days of receipt of bill.
18. **Interest.** Interest only, paid each month.
19. **Loan Payback.** $5,000 loan payment due every 6 months.
20. **Miscellaneous.** Paid in month expense occurs.
21. **Income Tax Reserve.** Paid into a special tax account at the bank.
22. **Total Disbursements.** Total cash expended during the month.
23. **Net Cash before Capital Investment.** Cash balance before capital investment payments.
24. **Capital Equipment.** Purchase of additional audiovisual equipment.
25. **Contracted Course Development.** Contract payments due for new course development.
26. **Monthly Cash Flow.** Cash balance after all payments at the end of the month.

ACTION STEP 76

Project your cash flow.

Get used to doing cash flow. Once a month is not too often to do it. If you prepared a cash flow for your business back in chapter 9, bring those numbers forward. If you skipped that step do it now. Here's how it's done:

1. Write down all the cash you will have for one year.

2. Add net profit.

3. Add any loans.

4. Figure your total cash needs for the year.

5. Spread these numbers out across the year. You may have a lot of cash at the start of the year; you want to make sure you have enough to get all the way through.

6. Now list all disbursements. Spread these out, too.

7. Now examine the figures. Is there any time during the year when you will run short of cash? It's better to know the truth now, when you're still working on paper.

8. If your cash picture looks good, drop in a couple of what-ifs. (Let's say you've budgeted $300 for utilities, and the air-conditioner goes out. It will cost $200 to repair it, and the lease says it is your expense. Or let's say you see an opportunity for a sale, but you would have to hire someone to handle it for you. Can your cash flow handle such surprises?)

Profits don't pay the bills and the payroll; cash flow does. Potential lenders look at cash flow projections first, so Action Step 76 can make or break you.

TABLE 16.2   The Software School's cash flow projection

CASH FLOW/SOFTWARE SCHOOL

	7th Month	8th Month	9th Month	10th Month	11th Month	12th Month
CASH-RECEIPTS						
Beginning of month	3970	7365	6015	51575	47060	35275
Sales	23500	25200	26900	28500	30200	31900
Less: credit card expense	(295)	(315)	(335)	(355)	(380)	(400)
Loan			60000			
TOTAL CASH AVAIL	27175	32250	92580	79720	76880	66775
DISBURSEMENTS						
Books	175	190	200	210	225	235
Instr/Materials		6000			7500	
Salaries:						
Instruction	2000	2000	2040	2080	2120	2160
Admnstrtn	2640	2640	2640	3120	3600	3600
Commissions	1730	1865	1995	2130	2255	2390
Payroll taxes	2045	2195	2250	2435	2690	2755
Advertising	1080	1175	1250	1335	1410	1495
Leased Equip	1270	1270	1270	1270	1270	1270
Licenses/fees	2160	2330	2495	2665	2820	2990
Legal/Accntng	500	500	500	500	500	500
Rent	3890	3890	3890	3890	3890	3890
Office Suppl	60	65	65	70	75	80
Dues/Subscrip	20	20	20	20	20	20
Repair/Maint	235	250	265	285	300	320
Insurance	480					
Telephone	325	355	380	405	430	455
Utilities	430	470	505	540	570	605
Interest				650	650	650
Loan Payback						
Miscellaneous	705	755	805	855	905	955
Income Tax Rsrv	65	265	435	200	375	565
TOTAL DISRSMNTS	19810	26235	21005	22660	31605	24935
Net Cash Before Capital Investment	7365	6015	71575	57060	45275	41840
Capital Equip			10000			
Contracted Crs Development			10000	10000	10000	10000
MONTHLY CASH FLOW	7365	6015	51575	47060	35275	31840

Part J: Projected Balance Sheet

liquidity
convertibility to cash

The professionals will look at your balance sheet (sometimes called a "statement of financial position") to analyze the state of your finances at a given point in time. They are looking at things like **liquidity** (how easily your assets can be converted into

TABLE 16.2   *Continued*

CASH FLOW/SOFTWARE SCHOOL

	13th Month	14th Month	15th Month	16th Month	17th Month	18th Month	TOTAL
CASH-RECEIPTS							
Beginning of month	31840	28645	27900	33115	43895	47800	364455
Sales	33600	35300	38350	40100	43300	43300	400150
Less: credit card expense	(420)	(440)	(480)	(500)	(540)	(540)	(5000)
Loan							60000
TOTAL CASH AVAIL	65020	63505	65770	72715	86655	90560	819605
DISBURSEMENTS							
Books	250	305	350	370	370	385	3265
Instr/Materials		9000			9000		31500
Salaries:							
Instruction	2200	2240	2280	2320	2360	2360	26160
Admnstrtn	3600	3600	3600	3600	3600	3600	39840
Commissions	2530	2660	2795	3030	3170	3420	29970
Payroll taxes	2805	2870	2925	3025	3075	3170	32240
Advertising	1580	1660	1750	1895	1980	2135	18745
Leased Equip	1270	1270	1270	1270	1270	1270	15240
Licenses/fees	3160	3325	3495	3790	3960	4275	37465
Legal/Accntng	500	500	500	500	500	500	6000
Rent	3890	3890	3890	3890	3890	3890	46680
Office Suppl	85	90	95	100	110	110	1005
Dues/Subscrip	200	20	20	20	20	20	420
Repair/Maint	335	355	385	395	435	435	3995
Insurance	480						960
Telephone	480	505	530	575	600	650	5690
Utilities	640	670	705	765	800	865	7565
Interest	650	650	650	595	595	595	5685
Loan Payback			5000				5000
Miscellaneous	1010	1060	1150	1205	1300	1300	12005
Income Tax Rsrv	710	935	1265	1475	1820	1820	9930
TOTAL DISRSMNTS	26375	35605	32655	28820	38855	30800	339360
Net Cash Before Capital Investment	38645	27900	33115	43895	47800	59760	480245
Capital Equip							10000
Contracted Crs Development	10000						50000
MONTHLY CASH FLOW	28645	27900	33115	43895	47800	59760	420245

cash) and capital structure (what sources of financing have been used, how much was borrowed, and so on). Professional lenders will use such factors to evaluate your ability to manage your business.

Table 16.3 shows two balance sheets for The Software School. Note that the first one shows its actual position at the end of its first 6 months and the second is a

capital structure
source of funds; debt vs. equity capital

TABLE 16.3   The Software School's balance sheet

	ACTUAL BALANCE SHEET/ SOFTWARE SCHOOL AS OF SEPTEMBER 30, 19XX (AFTER FIRST 6 MONTHS)			PROJECTED BALANCE SHEET/ SOFTWARE SCHOOL AS OF SEPTEMBER 30, 19XX (AFTER FIRST 18 MONTHS)		
ASSETS						
Cash	3970			59670		
Inst Mat & Bks	2500			**4495**		
TOTAL CORRECT			6470			64165
Lshld Imprvmnts	41000			41000		
Furniture	15100			15100		
Audio/Visual	10600			20600		
Office Equip	3600	70300		3600	80300	
Less Dep		7020	63280		22545	57755
License Agrmnt			25000	25000		
New Courses				50000		75000
TOTAL ASSETS			94750			196920
LIABILITIES						
Inst Salaries	1250			1500		
Admin "	1650			2250		
Commissions	2165			4275		
Accnts Payable	4495			9020		
Crrnt Lbltls		9560			17045	
Long Term Debt		-0-			55000	
Total Liabilities			9560			72045
NET WORTH						
Capital Stock	100000			100000		
Retained Earnings	(14810)		85190	24875		124875
TOTAL LIAB & NET WORTH			94750			196920

projection of where it will be at the end of its first 18 months. If you're just starting up, *all* figures will be projections.

Let's talk for a minute about ROI, return on investment. **ROI** is a bottom-line figure that shows how much is earned on the total dollars invested in the business. You have this kind of information up front if you invest money in bonds. The interest tells you your return on investment. Imagine that you had two funds, Bond A and Bond B, and Bond A paid you a 4% return and Bond B paid you 25%. Which bond would have the better ROI?

You compute ROI for a business by dividing the net profit by investment dollars. For The Software School, the profit after taxes is $39,685 (from Table 16.1). Divide that by the owner's investment of $100,000 (from Table 16.3):

$$\frac{\$39,685}{\$100,000} = 39.7\%$$

Could you get 39.7% from a savings account or a bond fund? It's not a bad ROI. It would dazzle lenders and probably draw the attention of a venture capitalist.

ROI

$$\frac{\text{net profit}}{\text{owner's investment}}$$

The Software School did not provide notes to its balance sheets, because in this case no notes are needed. In conjunction with the income statement and the cash flow projection, all the entries in the balance sheet will make sense to your professional readers. Under some circumstances, you would want to note unusual features of a balance sheet for an actual fiscal year, but in most cases—and in most projections—this won't be necessary.

Now project a balance sheet for your business. Action Step 77 will help you.

EPILOGUE: It's Time to Act on What You Know

Well, do you feel like you're ready? You are. You have thoroughly researched your product or your service, your market and your target customer, your competition, your marketing strategy, and your location. You've discovered how to prepare for surprises you can't afford, how to handle numbers, how to pursue financing, when and why you should incorporate, how to build a winning team, and whether you should buy, franchise, or start on your own. You've surveyed the vistas that a small business computer can open up for you. And you've written it all up in a beautiful showcase: your winning Business Plan.

Before you take off running, we want to give you one more tool that we think every entrepreneur should have—a tool to help you put your Business Plan to work. It's called **PERT**—an acronym for *Program Evaluation and Review Technique*—and it's often used to establish schedules for large projects. It was pioneered in military research and development as an aid for identifying activities and their optimal sequence, and then monitoring progress. The aerospace industry, the construction industry, and other big businesses that must plan complicated projects use PERT charts, and so can you.

A PERT chart is just the thing if you feel overwhelmed by the tasks of starting up and don't know where to begin. If you're a person who sometimes tries to do everything at once, PERT is also recommended. It will help you focus your energy on the right job at the right time. A sample PERT chart is provided in Table 16.4. Yours will need to be bigger and more detailed. You can use days, weeks, or months to plot the tasks ahead. (If you think you should use years, reassess your industry.)

Action Step 78 is the last one we give you in this book, and it symbolizes the first one you take on your own as an entrepreneur. It's the end, yes, but also the beginning. All our best wishes go with you as you embark on your great adventure. We hope that this book and its action steps have convinced you that you can achieve success—whatever it means to *you*—and have fun at the same time. Good luck! Work smart, and enjoy your adventure!

SUMMARY

It's been a long haul, and you're now ready to create your Business Plan. The Business Plan is a portable showcase for your business. When you visit vendors, bankers, and potential lenders, you can take along a copy of your Business Plan to speak for you, to show them you've got a blueprint for success.

Begin writing by starting with the material you feel most comfortable with. Once you have finished one part of the Plan, the other parts will fall into place more easily. Fortunately, your work in earlier chapters has prepared you for each section.

You'll need to write a cover letter for each copy of the Plan you send out. The cover letter will personalize the Plan and aim it so that it does the most good.

What I hear, I forget.
What I see, I remember.
What I do, I understand.
—Old Entrepreneur

PERT
Program Evaluation and Review Technique

ACTION STEP 77

Project your balance sheet.

A projected balance sheet is simply a prediction, on paper, of what your business will be worth at the end of a certain period of time. This prediction allows you to figure your actual and projected ROI, which is the real bottom line.

1. Add up your assets. For convenience, divide these into *Current* (cash, notes receivables, etc.), *Fixed* (land, equipment, buildings, etc.), and *Other* (intangibles like patents, royalty deals, copyrights, goodwill, contracts for exclusive use, etc.). You'll need to depreciate fixed assets that wear out. As value, you show the net of cost minus the accumulated depreciation.

2. Add up your liabilities. For convenience, divide these into *Current* (accounts payable, notes payable, accrued expenses, interest on loans, etc.), and *Long-Term* (trust deeds, bank loans, equipment loans, balloons, etc.)

3. Subtract the smaller figure from the larger one.

You now have a prediction of your net worth. Will you be in the red or in the black?

ACTION STEP 78

Construct a PERT chart and go for it.

Rehearsal is over. Now it's time to step onto the stage and get the drama under way. One way to shift from planning into action is to develop your own personal PERT chart. A PERT chart will serve as a script for you. It also will tell you and the other members of your team how long certain jobs should take.

List the tasks you need to accomplish—befriending a banker, filing a fictitious name statement, taking a lawyer to lunch, ordering business letterhead, selecting a site, contacting vendors, and so on—and set your deadlines.

As you already know, a successful package is made up of many, many details. If you take the details one at a time, you'll get there without being overwhelmed. The sample PERT chart in Table 16.4 can guide you.

TABLE 16.4   A Sample PERT Chart

TASK	WEEK					
	1	2	3	4	5	6
Befriend banker	x	x	x	x	x	x
Order letterhead		x				
Select site	x					
Get fictional name statement	x					
Bulk mail permit			x			
Ad agency	x					
Lunch, lawyer			x			
Appointment, accountant				x		
Vendor statement					x	
Utilities deposits					x	
Review promotional material					x	
Survey phone system			x	x	x	
Order phone system						x
Open House						x

THINK POINTS FOR SUCCESS

◄ Section I should generate excitement for your business. Section II should substantiate the excitement with numbers.

◄ Be sure to use sufficient footnotes to explain the numbers in your financial statements—Parts H, I, and J.

◄ The Executive Summary should read like ad copy. Hone it till it's tight and convincing.

◄ Now that you have Plan A, have you thought about Plan B?

REFERENCES

Bangs, David H., Jr., and William R. Osgood. *Business Planning Guide,* rev. ed. Portsmouth, New Hampshire: Upstart Publishing Co., 1987. [An excellent handbook for structuring a Business Plan. Clear writing, humorous examples. Their model business is Finestkind, a retail fish market located in York, Maine. Copies of the book can be ordered from Upstart Publishing Co., P.O. Box 323, Portsmouth, NH   13801; 603-749-5071.]

Business Plan for Retailers. Management Aid, No. 2.020. Washington, D.C.: U.S. Small Business Administration, Office of Business Development, 1987.

Business Plan for Small Manufacturers. Management Aid No. 2.007. Washington, D.C.: U.S. Small Business Administration, Office of Business Development, 1987.

Eliason, Carol. *The Business Plan for Home-based Business.* Management Aid No. 2.028. Washington, D.C.: U.S. Small Business Administration, Office of Business Development, 1986.

Milling, Bryan E. *Cash-Flow Problem-Solver: Procedures and Rationale for the Independent Businessman.* Radnor, Pa.: Chilton, 1984.

Policastro, Michael L. *Developing a Strategic Business Plan.* Management Aid No. 2.035. Washington, D.C.: U.S. Small Business Administration, Office of Business Development, 1987.

Purcell, W. R. *Understanding a Company's Finances: A Graphic Approach.* New York: Harper & Row, 1983.

Rich, Stanley R., and David E. Gumpert. "How to Write a Winning Business Plan." *Harvard Business Review,* May–June 1985, p. 158.

Rosenberg, Nathan. *Technology and American Economic Growth.* New York: Harper & Row, 1972.

Scheiber, Harry. "Federalism and the American Economic Order, 1789–1910." *Law and Society,* vol. 10, no. 1, Fall 1975.

Scheiber, Harry. "The Road to Munn: Eminent Domain and the Concept of Public Purpose in the State Courts." *Perspectives in History,* 1971.

Scherer, F. M. *Industrial Market Structure and Economic Performance.* Chicago: Rand McNally, 1979.

Schilit, W. Keith. "How to Write a Winning Business Plan." *Business Horizons,* September–October 1987, p. 13.

Sears, Marion, and Thomas Navin. "The Rise of a Market for Industrial Securities, 1887–1902." *Business History Review* (1955), pp. 112–16.

Siegel, Eric, et al. *The Arthur Young Business Plan Guide.* New York: John Wiley and Sons, 1987.

Small Business Reporter series. San Francisco: Bank of America, 1988. [The series consists of sixteen excellent booklets on entrepreneurship, management, computers, franchising, financing, marketing, personnel, and accounting. They may be ordered (obtain an order form and prices at any B of A branch) from Small Business Reporter, Bank of America, Dept. 3631, P.O. Box 37000, San Francisco, CA 94137.]

Sobel, Robert. *The Age of Giant Corporations: A Microeconomic History of American Business 1914–1970.* Westport, Conn.: Greenwood Press, 1972.

Spencer, Austin H. "Relative Downward Industrial Price Flexibility, 1870–1921." *Explorations in Economic History,* vol. 14, no. 1, January 1977.

Tarbell, Ida. *The History of the Standard Oil Company.* New York: McClure, Phillips & Co., 1904.

Temin, Peter. *Iron and Steel in Nineteenth-Century America: An Economic Inquiry.* Cambridge, Mass.: MIT Press, 1964.

Temin, Peter. "Manufacturing." In L. E. Davis et al., *American Economic Growth.* New York: Harper & Row, 1972.

Thorelli, Hans B. *The Federal Antitrust Policy: Origination of an American Tradition.* Stockholm: Akademisk Avhandling, 1954.

Thorp, Willard L., and Grace W. Knott. "The History of Concentration in Seven Industries." *The Structure of Industry.* Temporary National Economic Committee, Monograph No. 23. Washington, D.C.: United States Government Printing Office, 1941.

Uselding, Paul, and Bruce Juba. "Biased Technical Progress in American Manufacturing." *Explorations in Economic History,* vol. 11, no. 1, Fall 1973.

Uselding, Paul, and Bruce Juba. "Measuring Techniques and Manufacturing Practice." In *The American System of Manufacturing,* edited by Otto Mayr. Washington, D.C.: The Smithsonian Institution, 1981.

Wilcox, Clair, and William G. Shepherd. *Public Policies toward Business.* Homewood, Ill.: Irwin, 1975.

Woolf, Arthur G., "Electricity, Productivity, and Labor Savings: American Manufacturing, 1900–1929." *Explorations in Economic History,* vol. 21, no. 2, April 1984.

Williamson, Harold, et al. *The American Petroleum Industry.* 2 vols. Evanston, Ill.: Northwestern University Press, 1959.

ACTION STEP REVIEW

66 Write a cover letter that will open the door for future business transactions.

67 Grab attention with your executive summary.

68 Describe your product or service against the backdrop of industry. You want to excite your reader without being flamboyant.

69 Discuss your target market and profile your target customer.

70 List your major competitors and tell how you will disarm them.

71 Describe your marketing strategies. What techniques will best serve your small business?

72 Discuss your site and explain how it will contribute to your success.

73 Introduce your management team. Depict a great management track record in your industry.

74 Describe the kinds of employees you will need. Emphasize that you'll run lean.

75 Project an income statement to give an idea about net profit for your first year—and then for the next three, if possible.

76 Project your cash flow to learn when you're going to need money.

77 Show your potential investors and lenders what they can expect for an ROI by projecting balance sheets.

78 Construct a PERT chart and go for it.

APPENDIX A
One-Write Bookkeeping

NECESSITY'S GIFT TO THE SMALL BUSINESS PERSON

Though the one-write bookkeeping system may have been patented in Europe in 1916, it took World War II to explode its popularity.

When the war effort drastically curtailed the manufacture of bookkeeping machines, the "poster" or "writing board" came into common use as a temporary replacement. These were familiarly referred to as "pegboard" systems, because some form of pegs was used to align the multiple forms involved. No longer a stop-gap innovation, pegboard bookkeeping has been shaped and reshaped through the years until it has become a basic tool in thousands of today's small businesses and branch offices of large corporations.

The present-day version, usually referred to as *one-write,* is the simplest of all bookkeeping methods and has proven more than adequate in meeting the record-keeping requirements of most small firms—quite inexpensively. This is not surprising, because it's the one bookkeeping system designed specifically for small businesses and professional offices.

SAVES TIME AND ELIMINATES MISTAKE-PRONE REPETITIVE STEPS

Since a check or receipt, a journal, an earnings record or a ledger all require the same information, instead of completing each record individually, this system allows them to be completed in one writing. See Figure A.1.

The poster holds two or more forms in alignment so that one writing simultaneously produces multiple records. Through precision forms design and the use of Waxspot® carbon or sensitized paper, the desired information—and only that—transfers through from the form being written. The forms, themselves, overlap like shingles on a roof and can be inserted or removed with ease. The design of the poster or "pegboard" facilitates their alignment.

One-write eliminates the need for multiple postings.

One-write eliminates the errors inherent in reposting numbers.

Because only a single posting is required, there's just one record to balance. One proof reconciles all records, and these are both accurate and up-to-date.

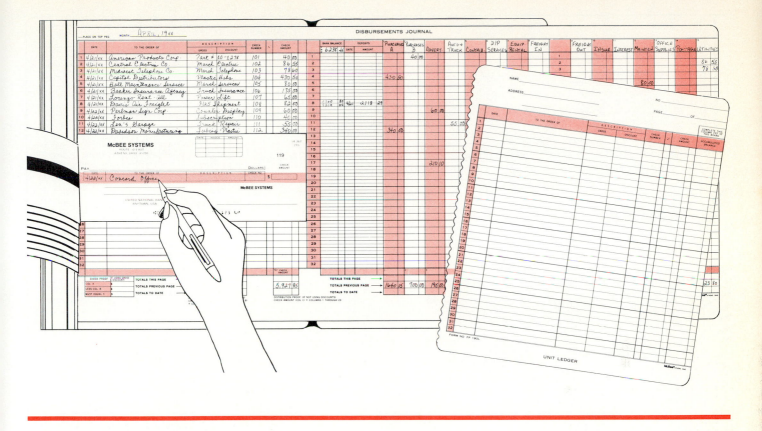

The system makes balancing the books a simple affair. After completing entries, you only need to run adding machine totals to check the balance. Yet such a set of books provides ongoing positive control in both check-writing and receipting functions.

Far simpler than a purely manual set of spread sheets, a three-up checkbook and separate ledgers, a one-write system costs just about the same. More important, it's so simple that anyone can use it proficiently with only a few minutes of instruction.

A one-write system likewise helps you gain greater use of your accountant's time and expertise. It gives your accountant organized journals to work with instead of having to ride herd on loose vouchers and check stubs. Knowing that the subsidiary books balance and that possible transcription errors are eliminated speeds and simplifies the preparation of your financial statements. With less time needed to straighten out the books, one-write frees more time for your accountant to spend analyzing them and advising you.

FIGURE A.1 Though just two pieces of paper, a check and a journal, this disbursements system, the simplest of all one-writes, provides all the benefits of sound bookkeeping: known distribution, sequential check control, an audit trail, balanced totals, a running bank balance, instant review. In a word, *accountability*.

CASH DISBURSEMENTS SYSTEM FOR USE WITH COMPUTERS

This system provides a well-organized, preproven document—namely, the journal—precisely for data processing purposes. See Figure A.2. The sequencing of "Check Number," "Account," and "Check Amount" makes it an ideal source of client input. The journal is coated to allow for a duplicate copy. Because both you and your accountant have a copy, the time constraints of having to return data and respond to questions, phone calls, and mailings are eliminated.

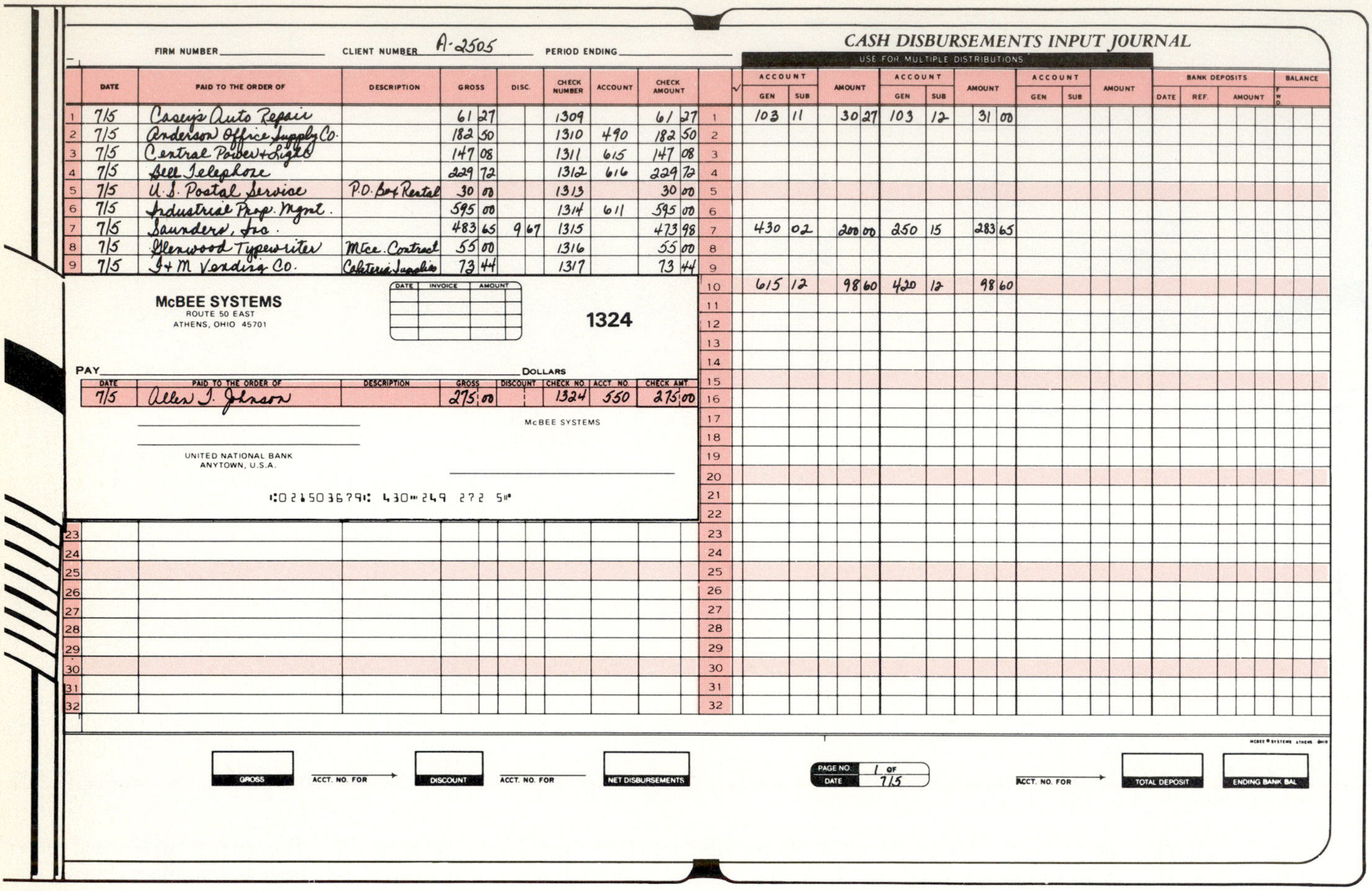

CASH DISBURSEMENTS INPUT JOURNAL

FIRM NUMBER ______ CLIENT NUMBER A-2505 PERIOD ENDING ______

	DATE	PAID TO THE ORDER OF	DESCRIPTION	GROSS	DISC.	CHECK NUMBER	ACCOUNT	CHECK AMOUNT		ACCOUNT GEN	ACCOUNT SUB	AMOUNT	ACCOUNT GEN	ACCOUNT SUB	AMOUNT	ACCOUNT GEN	ACCOUNT SUB	AMOUNT	BANK DEPOSITS DATE	REF.	AMOUNT	BALANCE
1	7/5	Casey's Auto Repair		61 27		1309		61 27	1	103	11	30 27	103	12	31 00							
2	7/5	Anderson Office Supply Co.		182 50		1310	490	182 50	2													
3	7/5	Central Power + Light		147 08		1311	615	147 08	3													
4	7/5	Bell Telephone		229 72		1312	616	229 72	4													
5	7/5	U.S. Postal Service	P.O. Box Rental	30 00		1313		30 00	5													
6	7/5	Industrial Prop. Mgmt.		595 00		1314	611	595 00	6													
7	7/5	Saunders, Inc.		483 65	9 67	1315		473 98	7	430	02	200 00	250	15	283 65							
8	7/5	Glenwood Typewriter	Mtce. Contract	55 00		1316		55 00	8													
9	7/5	J+M Vending Co.	Cafeteria Supplies	73 44		1317		73 44	9													
10									10	615	12	98 60	420	12	98 60							

McBEE SYSTEMS
ROUTE 50 EAST
ATHENS, OHIO 45701

1324

PAY ______ DOLLARS

DATE	PAID TO THE ORDER OF	DESCRIPTION	GROSS	DISCOUNT	CHECK NO.	ACCT. NO.	CHECK AMT.
7/5	Allen J. Johnson		275 00		1324	550	275 00

McBEE SYSTEMS

UNITED NATIONAL BANK
ANYTOWN, U.S.A.

GROSS — ACCT. NO. FOR — DISCOUNT — ACCT. NO. FOR — NET DISBURSEMENTS — PAGE NO. 1 OF — DATE 7/5 — ACCT. NO. FOR — TOTAL DEPOSIT — ENDING BANK BAL.

FIGURE A.2 Three sets of columns have been provided to accommodate multiple expense distributions when the amount cannot be expensed properly to a single G/L account.

The Account Number column is divided into "General" and "Sub" accounts for departmental or branch accounting.

When posting is finished, you simply down-add and balance the journal and update the bank balance. Two proofing checks are printed on the journal as reminders.

PAYROLL SYSTEM

Accurate and auditable payroll accounting records are a must for all businesses. The one-write version is well suited for the small- to medium-size company or for the executive payroll of a corporation. The Employee Earnings Record is simply slipped between the check and the journal. In this case, a top-write check is used with a detachable stub serving as the employee's record of earnings. See Figure A.3.

Because the Earnings Record, the Statement of Earnings, and the Journal are all automatically posted in a single writing, they can be balanced in a single proofing, saving additional time and eliminating possible transcription errors.

CASH DISBURSEMENTS/PAYROLL COMBINATION SYSTEM

Here you can switch from writing disbursements to writing payroll simply by inserting the employee earnings record between the check and the journal: the same check is used, the same journal is used, the same writing board is used. See Figure A.4. With either application, one-write completes all records simultaneously. It's the ideal system for the small business that does not need to maintain separate bank accounts for general disbursements and payroll.

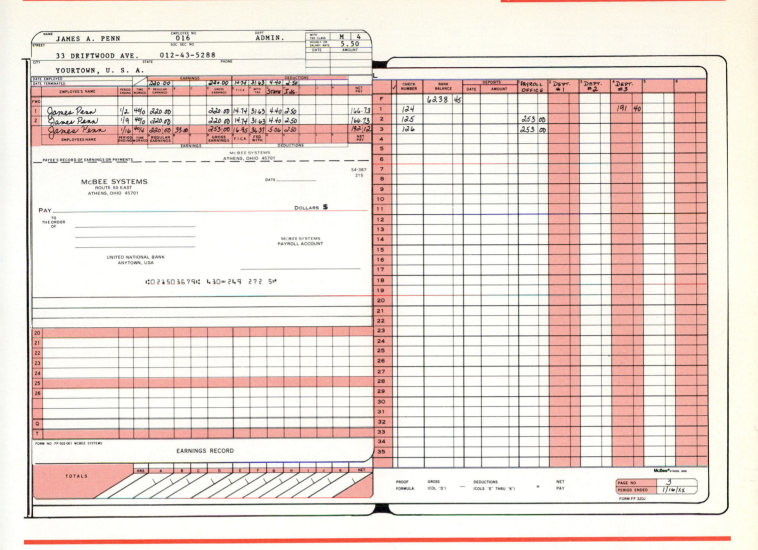

A journal featuring Sales and Cash Receipts information on the back flap is an available option. It's perfect for the business that keeps daily register totals and/or totals from individual sales tickets.

ACCOUNTS PAYABLE

For a business to be able to sell on credit, it normally must buy on credit because of limited working capital. Therefore, accounts-payable (accrual) accounting is an almost universal business function. It gives you an up-to-date picture of your firm's liabilities.

However, its terminology and the variety of ways of handling payables often make this the most "mysterious" phase of accounting. The result is that many businesses neglect to have a systemized approach. One-write simplifies the mechanics. See Figure A.5.

ACCOUNTS RECEIVABLE

Needed cash won't flow in unless your firm's billing flows out—smoothly and regularly. This calls for a *system,* not just repetitive paperwork.

FIGURE A.3 The Earnings Record, divided into quarters, facilitates the preparation of federal, state and local required reports. In addition to "F.I.C.A." and "Fed. With.," two earnings and five deduction boxes can be overprinted with the headings of your choice, illustrative of the flexibility of one-write. The journal offers 20 or more columns of distribution for breaking down individual employee pay by job, product, department, etc.

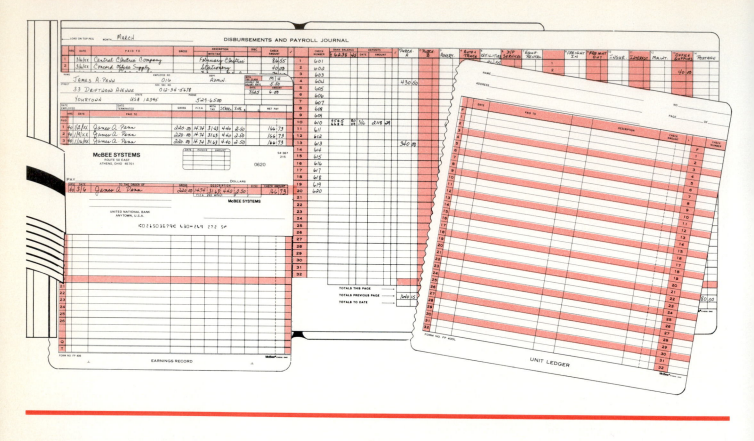

FIGURE A.4 The Center-Write Check is available in duplicate form. The duplicate serves as a handy proof of payment when attached to a paid invoice as well as providing an easy means of auditing the records. The duplicate copy plays an important role in payroll preparations because it serves as the employee's Statement of Earnings.

A one-write Accounts Receivable system can help smooth your cash flow. See Figure A.6. Customer Statements and A/R Ledgers are prepared as *by-products* of posting daily sales slips. Therefore, statements are ready to be mailed at any time, and overdue balances become easy to spot.

CASH RECEIPTS SYSTEM

It's easy for cash to fall through the cracks. That's why it's important to use some form of receipting system. Each transaction should be recorded. One-write takes this a step further—offering tighter control over your cash payments, and it's more efficient than the receipt book method. See Figure A.7.

HAS ONE-WRITE BEEN BURYING ITS LIGHT UNDER A BUSHEL BASKET?

If one-write bookkeeping is such a boon to small business, how come it's so little known?

It's not that one-write is one of America's best-kept secrets. It's more the case that its popularity cannot keep abreast of that eye-opening number of new business start-ups year after year. It's not the type of product that's nationally advertised or talked about on the computer platform.

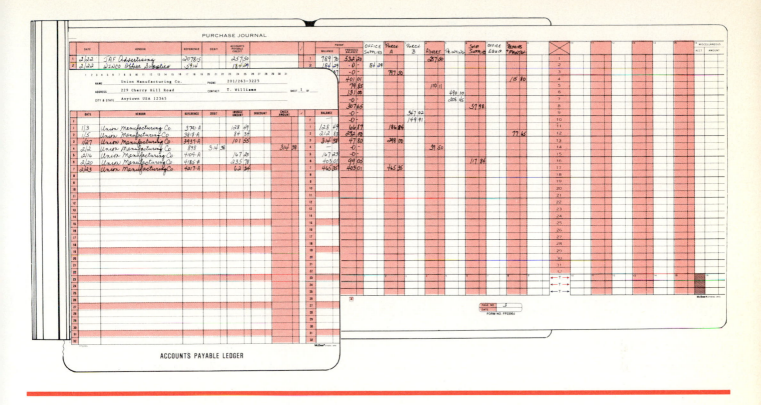

The rule of thumb is that any firm with less than 25 people on the payroll and/or that writes as few as 25 checks a month is a candidate for one-write bookkeeping. The estimate is that almost 80 percent of the small business market does not use a one-write system. Rather than having rejected it, most of these firms have yet to learn about it—for several reasons:

1. Old-line accountants have never used one-write and they are reluctant to change.

2. Though many accountants praise it, many new businesses exist for years before hiring an accountant.

3. Rarely is it found in the college curriculum, even for accounting majors.

4. Only recently have some banks started promoting one-write, and then only small, nonmetropolitan institutions.

This last point is worth amplifying. The new owner of a small business, upon opening a commercial account at a bank, invariably winds up ordering a three-up checkbook. Most of the time is spent discussing the desired color of the checks and whether or not a logo is to be printed on them. Little or no attention is given to the idea of check writing *as a system*.

Yet, that's exactly what the check with the "black strip on the back" is all about: a check-writing and recordkeeping system all in one. In fact, because of its flexibility, one-write offers the assurance that each entrepreneur can have the check writing system best suited to his or her firm's needs.

Regrettably, one-write is just one of dozens of products the bank's busy New Account Representative has to deal with. However, in today's heated competition for retail banking business, the accent falls heavily on *customer service,* which is where one-write belongs. Banks small enough to change without layers of committee meetings are beginning to think of one-write as a viable check alternative.

FIGURE A.5   *Incurring the Expense* (illustrated here): Invoices are posted to the Accounts Payable Ledger and to the Purchase Journal simultaneously.

Paying the Bills (not shown): As checks are written, entries are simultaneously posted to the Accounts Payable Ledger and to the Disbursements Journal.

This plan forces the bookkeeper to maintain accurate figures so that the status of your payables is always known. Peak work loads are avoided. Multiple postings are eliminated. And one balancing proves all records—journals, ledgers, and checks are posted correctly.

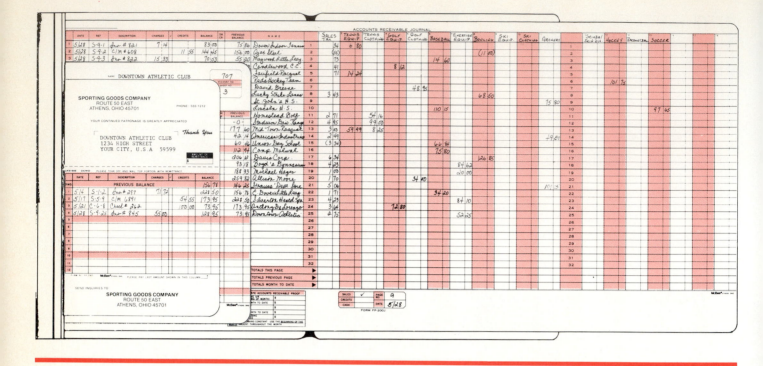

FIGURE A.6

FIGURE A.6 When posting charges, the Accounts Receivable Journal, the A/R Ledger, and the Customer Statement are put in position on the "pegboard."

For payments received, the Cash Receipts Journal is used along with the A/R Ledger and Statement.

You can get a fully custom designed sales ticket, invoice, or receipt as part of your A/R one-write system at surprisingly little cost.

HALLMARKS OF ONE-WRITE: SIMPLICITY AND FLEXIBILITY

The one-write systems described in this appendix are only a few basic accounting applications. Bear in mind, there are dozens of simple, flexible one-write systems or plans. Generally speaking, there are three categories of one-write systems:

1. Off-the-shelf or stock plans
2. Custom-designed systems
3. Between these ends of the spectrum, there are a whole range of individualized plans.

By design, one-write can handle four forms at the same time. The wide version of the poster board, for example, can accommodate two different ledgers simultaneously. You can have journals with preprinted column headings of your choice. There are duplicate journals and duplicate checks. The permutations are practically endless. The significant point is that a one-write system can be assembled to fit a need.

HOW AND WHERE TO FIND THE RIGHT ONE-WRITE FOR YOUR BUSINESS

Though they are still not available at your local stationery store, one-write bookkeeping systems are easily attainable through forms distributors and mail-order catalogs—provided you want a basic or "stock" system and you already know how to use it.

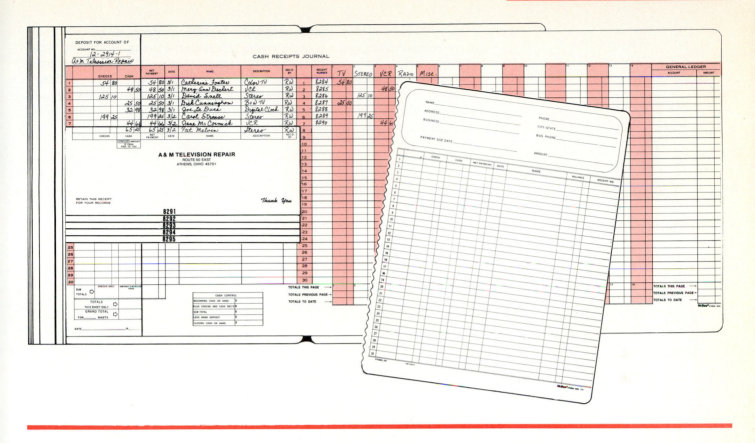

However, there are a few companies that specialize in one-writes. These are national concerns selling through a distributor or their own national sales force. Such companies offer a catalog of one-write systems covering all basic accounting functions and designed for a number of different businesses. Here's a partial list of such applications:

- Cash Disbursements
- Accounts Payable
- Payroll
- Accounts Receivable
- Combination PR/Disbursements
- Combination AP/Payroll
- AR/Aged Trial Balance
- Cash Receipts
- General Ledger
- Organized Computer Input
- Inventory Control
- Time Control
- Telephone Message

And specially designed plans for the particular needs of:

- Accountants
- Builders, Remodelers
- Franchise Operators
- Insurance Agents
- Lawyers
- Medical Offices and Labs
- Property Management Firms
- Real Estate Offices
- Restaurants
- Schools
- Self-Storage Facilities

There's also a Personal Income Control system for home use to help organize your personal finances.

Equally important, these companies are continuously developing new versions to meet the changing needs of the marketplace. In real estate, for example, there are now more than a dozen one-write systems ranging from property management to rent collection and from escrow/trust to commission settlement.

FIGURE A.7 *Cash Receipts Journal* provides a chronological listing of all cash receipts. You are given a choice of 5 or 23 columns, for example, for analysis purposes and a General Ledger column for miscellaneous income.

Cash Receipts are offered in single or duplicate format. The duplicate copy can be retained for auditing reference.

Bank Deposit Slip, created as a by-product of posting the receipts, assures all payments are deposited in the bank.

One-write likewise offers unique advantages to national franchise chains by unifying the recordkeeping in a way that's compatible with the needs of corporate headquarters. Whether it's hamburgers or health clinics, whether you're building homes or selling them, it doesn't matter. That's why household names like Burger King®, Century 21®, the U.S. Department of Health and Human Services, and the National Association of Home Builders all offer and encourage their branches or franchisees to employ one-write bookkeeping.

APPENDIX B
Small Business
Start-Up Forms

INFORMATION NEEDED FOR SELLER'S PERMIT AND/OR USE FUEL PERMIT*

When applying for a Use Fuel Permit, you will need to show the registrations for all diesel vehicles. If you have just recently purchased the vehicle, also take along a copy of the bill of sale signed by the seller.

Sole Ownership or Partnership

You must apply for a permit in person. At least one partner is required to apply.

1. Business address and phone number
2. Owner or owners' Social Security number(s) and drivers license number(s)
3. Residence address(es) and phone number(s) of owner(s)
4. Estimated monthly expenses and sales (Seller's Permit only)
5. Three personal references with names, complete addresses, and phone numbers
6. Names and addresses of banks—both personal and business

Corporation

At least one corporate officer is required to apply for the permit. If one is not available, a notarized power of attorney is required.

1. Articles of incorporation
2. Business address
3. Estimated monthly sales and expense figures (Seller's Permit only)
4. Federal Identification Number
5. Corporate Number
6. Names, residence addresses, phone numbers, drivers license numbers, and Social Security numbers of all corporate officers
7. Bank name, location and corporate account number
8. Names of corporate stockholders and percentages held

---

*Authors' Note: If your business requires the collection of sales tax, contact the closest state tax office and be prepared to offer the same information.

A MAIL CERTIFIED COPIES TO:

NAME _____

ADDRESS _____

_____

☐ First Filing   Renewal Filing

Current Registration No. _____

B PUBLISH IN NEWSPAPER: _____

COUNTY CLERK'S FILING STAMP

FICTITIOUS BUSINESS NAME STATEMENT
THE FOLLOWING PERSON(S) IS (ARE) DOING BUSINESS AS:

1. Fictitious Business Name(s)

2. Street Address, City & State of Principal place of Business in California   Zip Code

3. Full name of Registrant   (if corporation - show state of incorporation)

Residence Address	City	State	Zip Code

Full name of Registrant   (if corporation - show state of incorporation)

Residence Address	City	State	Zip Code

Full name of Registrant   (if corporation - show state of incorporation)

Residence Address	City	State	Zip Code

Full name of Registrant   (if corporation - show state of incorporation)

Residence Address	City	State	Zip Code

4. This Business is conducted by: (CHECK ONE ONLY)
( ) an individual   ( ) a general partnership   ( ) joint venture   ( ) a business trust
( ) co-partners   ( ) husband and wife   ( ) a corporation   ( ) a limited partnership
( ) an unincorporated association other than a partnership   ( ) other—*please specify* _____

5. The registrant commenced to transact business under the fictitious business name or names listed above on _____

6A.
Signed _____

Typed or Printed _____

6B. If Registrant a corporation sign below:

Corporation Name _____

Signature & Title _____

Type or Print
Officer's Name & Title _____

This statement was filed with the County Clerk of _____ County on date indicated by file stamp above.

NOTICE

THIS FICTITIOUS NAME STATEMENT EXPIRES ON DECEMBER 31, 19_____. A NEW FICTITIOUS BUSINESS NAME STATEMENT MUST BE FILED PRIOR TO DECEMBER 31, 19_____.

I HEREBY CERTIFY THAT THIS COPY IS A CORRECT COPY OF THE ORIGINAL STATEMENT ON FILE IN MY OFFICE.

_____
COUNTY CLERK

BY _____ DEPUTY

File No.___ _____

Fictitious Business Name Statement

MEMBER FDIC

DANA NIGUEL BANK N A

34180 PACIFIC COAST HIGHWAY • DANA POINT, CA 92629 • 714/661-4100

Bank use only

Sic.#_____

Officer_____

Initial_____

BUSINESS LOAN APPLICATION INSTRUCTIONS

Date _____

Please fill in all blanks, and answer all questions. Please print or type. All information requested is needed to properly process this application and only for this purpose. Failure to complete all items, particularly full names and address, may result in delay and inconvenience to you. Please be assured that all information will be held in strictest confidence.

Firm Name: _____ Phone: (   ) _____

Address: _____ City: _____ State: _____ Zip: _____

Equipment Located at: _____ City: _____ State: _____ Zip: _____

Type of Business: _____ Fed. Tax No: _____

No. of years in Business: _____   Corporation ☐   Insurance Carrier: _____ Agent: _____

Sole Owner ☐ Partnership ☐   Address: _____

OWNERSHIP

Principal: (1) _____ Title: _____   Own ☐ Rent ☐

Home Address: _____
CITY   STATE   ZIP

1st ☐ Mortgage
Lender _____ Indicate 2nd ☐ Mortgage   Cost _____ Present Market Value _____

Loan No. _____ Year acquired _____ Total Balance owed _____

S.S. # _____ D.L.# _____ Exp. Date _____ State _____ Phone # (   ) _____

Principal: (2) _____ Title: _____   Own ☐ Rent ☐

Home Address: _____
CITY   STATE   ZIP

1st ☐ Mortgage
Lender _____ Indicate 2nd ☐ Mortgage   Cost _____ Present Market Value _____

Loan No. _____ Year acquired _____ Total Balance owed _____

S.S. # _____ D.L.# _____ Exp. Date _____ State _____ Phone # (   ) _____

BANK

Name of Bank (1): _____   ☐ Checking Acct. # _____
                                                ☐ Savings Acct. # _____

Address: _____ City: _____   ☐ Loan # _____ Amt. _____

Phone: (   ) _____ Bank Officer: _____   Past Loan # _____ Amt. _____

Name of Bank (2): _____   ☐ Checking Acct. # _____
                                                ☐ Savings Acct. # _____

Address: _____ City: _____   ☐ Loan # _____ Amt. _____

Phone: (   ) _____ Bank Officer: _____   Past Loan # _____ Amt. _____

Name of Bank (3): _____   ☐ Checking Acct. # _____
                                                ☐ Savings Acct. # _____

Address: _____ City: _____   ☐ Loan # _____ Amt. _____

Phone: (   ) _____ Bank Officer: _____   Past Loan # _____ Amt. _____

TRADE

CREDIT REFERENCES

Name: (1) _____ Address: _____ Phone No.: _____

Name: (2) _____ Address: _____ Phone No.: _____

Name: (3) _____ Address: _____ Phone No.: _____

EQUIPMENT

EQUIPMENT

Vendor: _____ Contact: _____

Address: _____ Phone: (   ) _____

Type of Equip.: _____ Amount _____ Tax _____ Total _____

Terms: _____ MOS.@ _____ Deposit _____

Sample Business Loan Application   *continued*

Are there any unsatisfied judgments against the business or principal owner(s)? Yes ___ No ___
If "yes": Amount $ _____ to whom owed: _____

has the company or principal owner(s) declared bankruptcy in the last 10 years? Yes ___ No ___
If "yes" give details on a seperate form.

Banking Relationship

Are you willing to change your prime banking relationship if the subject loan is approved?
Yes___ No___If "no" why? _____

LIST FIVE MAJOR CUSTOMERS

Name	Address	Telephone	Account Officer
1.			
2.			
3.			
4.			
5.			

───────── REQUIRED FINANCIAL INFORMATION ─────────

Last Fiscal year-end Business Statement of Condition including Profit and Loss statement.

Last Interim Business Statement of Condition if fiscal year end is more than 90 days from date of this application; include Ageings of Accounts Receivable and Accounts Payable, Profit and Loss Statement.

Complete Copy of last two years Federal Tax returns on the Business.

Personal financial statement on each principal owner.

Complete Copy of last year's Federal Tax Return on each principal owner.

OWNERSHIP additional principal(s) not listed on the reverse side of this application with ownership of 20% or more; use a seperate Business loan application form.

The information contained in this statement is provided to induce you to extend or to continue the extension of credit to the undersigned or to others upon the guaranty of the undersigned. The undersigned acknowledge and understand that you are relying on the information provided herein in deciding to grant or continue credit or to accept a guaranty thereof. Each of the undersigned agrees to notify you immediately and in writing of any change in name, address, or employment and of any material adverse change (1) in any of the information contained in this statement or (2) in the financial condition of any of the undersigned or (3) in the ability of any of the undersigned to perform its (or their) obligations to you. In the absence of such notice or a new and full written statement, this should be considered as a continueing statement and substantially correct. You are authorized to make all inquiries you deem necessary to verify the accuracy of the information contained herein, and to determine the credit-worthiness of the undersigned. Each of the undersigned authorizes you to answer questions about your credit experience with the undersigned.

Business Name: _____

By: _____
           Name   Title

Date: _____

By: _____
           Name   Title

Sample Business Loan Application, page 2

PERSONAL FINANCIAL STATEMENT

Submitted to: **DANA NIGUEL BANK N.A.**

34180 Pacific Coast Hwy., Dana Point, CA. 92629

• **IMPORTANT: Read these directions before completing this Statement**

☐ If you are applying for individual credit in your own name and are relying on your own income, or assets and not the income or assets of another person as the basis for repayment of the credit requested, complete only Sections 1, 3 and 4

☐ If you are applying for joint credit with another person, complete all Sections and provide information in Section 2 about the joint applicant. If appropriate, the joint applicant may complete a separate personal financial statement (C-100), and the applications may be submitted together.

☐ If you are applying for individual credit but are relying on income from alimony, child support, or separate maintenance or on the income or assets of another person as a basis for repayment of the credit requested, complete all Sections. Provide information in Section 2 about the person whose alimony, support, or maintenance payments or income or assets you are relying on. Alimony, child support, or separate maintenance income, need not be revealed if you do not wish to have it considered as a basis for repaying this obligation.

☐ If this statement relates to your guaranty of the indebtedness of other person(s), firm(s), or corporation(s), complete Sections 1, 3 and 4.

Section 1 - Individual Information (type or print)	Section 2 - Other Party Information (type or print)
Name	Name
Address	Address
City, state & zip	City, state & zip
Position or occupation	Position or occupation
Business name	Business name
Business address	Business address
City, state & zip	City, state & zip
Length of employment	Length of employment
Res. phone Bus. phone	Res. phone Bus. phone

Section 3 - Statement of Financial Condition as of .... **19** ....

Assets (Do not include assets of doubtful value)	In dollars (omit cents)	Liabilities	In dollars (omit cents)
Cash on hand and in this bank		Notes payable to banks-see Schedule E	
Cash in other banks		Notes payable to other institutions-see Schedule E	
U S Gov't & marketable securities-see Schedule A		Due to brokers	
Non marketable securities-see Schedule B		Amounts payable to others-secured	
Securities held by broker in margin accounts		Amounts payable to others-unsecured	
Restricted, control, or margin account stocks		Accounts and bills due	
Real estate-see Schedule C		Unpaid income tax	
Accounts, loans, and notes receivable		Other unpaid taxes and interest	
Automobiles		Real estate mortgages payable-see Schedules C & E	
Other personal property		Other debts (car payments, credit cards, etc.)-itemize	
Cash surrender value-life insurance-see Schedule D			
Other assets-itemize-see Schedule F if applicable			
		Total Liabilities	
		Net Worth	
Total Assets		**Total Liabilities and Net Worth**	

Section 4 - Annual Income For Year Ended ____ 19 ____	Annual Expenditures	Contingent Liabilities			Estimated Amounts
Salary, bonuses & commissions $ _____	Mortgage rental payments $ _____	Do you have any	Yes	No	$ _____
Dividends & interest _____	Real estate taxes & assessments _____	Contingent liabilities (as endorser, co-maker or guarantor? On leases? on contracts?)	☐	☐	
Real estate income _____	Taxes federal state & local _____				
Other income (alimony, child support, or separate maintenance income need not be revealed if you do not wish to have it considered as a basis for repaying this obligation) _____	Insurance payments _____	Involvement in pending legal actions?	☐	☐	
	Other contract payments (car payments, charge cards, etc) _____	Other special debt or circumstances?	☐	☐	
		Contested income tax liens?	☐	☐	
	Alimony, child support, maintenance _____	If "yes" to any question(s) describe			
	Other expenses _____				
Total $ Income	**Total $** Expenditures	**Total $** Contingent Liabilities			

(COMPLETE SCHEDULES AND SIGN ON REVERSE SIDE)

Sample Personal Financial Statement   *continued*

SCHEDULE A - U.S. GOVERNMENT & MARKETABLE SECURITIES

Number of Shares or Face Value of Bonds	Description	In Name of	Are These Registered Pledged or Held by others?	Market Value

SCHEDULE B - NON-MARKETABLE SECURITIES

Number Of Shares	Description	In Name of	Are These Registered Pledged or Held by Others?	Value	Source Of Value

SCHEDULE C - RESIDENCES AND OTHER REAL ESTATE EQUITIES (PARTIALLY OR WHOLLY OWNED)

Address and Type of Property	Title in Name of	% of Ownership	Date Acquired	Cost	Market Value	Monthly Payment	Mortgage Amount	Mortgage Holder
Residence(s)								
Residence(s)								
Other								
Other								

SCHEDULE D - LIFE INSURANCE CARRIED, INCLUDING GROUP INSURANCE

Name of Insurance Company	Owner of Policy	Beneficiary and Relationship	Face Amount	Policy Loans	Cash Surrender Value

SCHEDULE E - BANK AND OTHER INSTITUTIONAL RELATIONSHIPS

Name and Address of Creditor	Original Loan Line Amount	Date of Loan	Maturity Date	Unsecured or Secured (List Collateral)	Monthly Payment	Amount Owed

SCHEDULE F - BUSINESS VENTURES

List Name and Address of Any Business Venture in Which You Are a Principal or Partner	Total Assets Listed In Section 3	Your % of Ownership	Your Position/Title In the Business	Total Assets Of Business	Line of Business	Years in Business

(USE ADDITIONAL SCHEDULES IF NECESSARY)

The information contained in this statement is provided to induce you to extend or to continue the extension of credit to the undersigned or to others upon the guaranty of the undersigned. The undersigned acknowledge and understand that you are relying on the information provided herein in deciding to grant or continue credit or to accept a guaranty thereof. Each of the undersigned represents, warrants and certifies that the information provided herein is true, correct and complete. Each of the undersigned agrees to notify you immediately and in writing of any change in name, address, or employment and of any material adverse change (1) in any of the information contained in this statement or (2) in the financial condition of any of the undersigned or (3) in the ability of any of the undersigned to perform its (or their) obligations to you. In the absence of such notice or a new and full written statement, this should be considered as a continuing statement and substantially correct. You are authorized to make all inquiries you deem necessary to verify the accuracy of the information contained herein, and to determine the credit-worthiness of the undersigned. Each of the undersigned authorizes you to answer questions about your credit experience with the undersigned.

Signature (individual) _____

Social Security Number _____

Date signed _____, 19_____ Date of Birth _____

Signature (other party) _____

Social Security Number _____

Date Signed _____, 19_____ Date of Birth _____

Sample Personal Financial Statement, page 2

OMB Approval No. 3245-0016

U.S. Small Business Administration

Application for Business Loan

Applicant	Full Address	

Name of Business		Tax I.D. No.

Full Street Address		Tel. No. (Inc. A/C)

City	County	State	Zip	Number of Employees (Including subsidiaries and affiliates)

Type of Business	Date Business Established	At Time of Application _____
Bank of Business Account and Address		If Loan is Approved _____
		Subsidiaries or Affiliates _____ (Separate from above)

Use of Proceeds: (Enter Gross Dollar Amounts Rounded to Nearest Hundreds)	Loan Requested	SBA USE ONLY
Land Acquisition		
New Construction/ Expansion/Repair		
Acquisition and/or Repair of Machinery and Equipment		
Inventory Purchase		
Working Capital (Including Accounts Payable)		
Acquisition of Existing Business		
Payoff SBA Loan		
Payoff Bank Loan (Non SBA Associated)		
Other Debt Payment (Non SBA Associated)		
All Other		
Total Loan Requested		
Term of Loan		

Collateral

If your collateral consists of (A) Land and Building, (D) Accounts Receivable and/or (E) Inventory, fill in the appropriate blanks. If you are pledging (B) Machinery and Equipment, (C) Furniture and Fixtures, and/or (F) Other, please provide an itemized list (labeled Exhibit A) that contains serial and identification numbers for all articles that had an original value greater than $500. Include a legal description of Real Estate offered as collateral.

	Present Market Value	Present Loan Balance	SBA Use Only Collateral Valuation
A. Land and Building	$	$	$
B. Machinery & Equipment			
C. Furniture & Fixtures			
D. Accounts Receivable			
E. Inventory			
F. Other			
Totals	$	$	$

PREVIOUS SBA OR OTHER GOVERNMENT FINANCING: If you or any principals or affiliates have ever requested Government Financing, complete the following:

Name of Agency	Original Amount of Loan	Date of Request	Approved or Declined	Balance	Current or Past Due
	$			$	
	$			$	

SBA Form 4 (2-85) Previous Editions Obsolete   GPO 919-454

Application for SBA Loan   *continued*

INDEBTEDNESS: Furnish the following information on all installment debts, contracts, notes, and mortgages payable. Indicate by an asterisk (*) items to be paid by loan proceeds and reason for paying same (present balance should agree with latest balance sheet submitted).

To Whom Payable	Original Amount	Original Date	Present Balance	Rate of Interest	Maturity Date	Monthly Payment	Security	Current or Past Due
	$		$			$		
	$		$			$		
	$		$			$		
	$		$			$		

MANAGEMENT (Proprietor, partners, officers, directors and all holders of outstanding stock — <u>100% of ownership must be shown</u>). Use separate sheet if necessary.

Name and Social Security Number	Complete Address	% Owned	*Military Service From	*Military Service To	*Race	*Sex

* This data is collected for statistical purposes only. It has no bearing on the credit decision to approve or decline this application.

ASSISTANCE   List the name(s) and occupation(s) of any who assisted in preparation of this form, other than applicant.

Name and Occupation	Address	Total Fees Paid	Fees Due
Name and Occupation	Address	Total Fees Paid	Fees Due

Signature of Preparers if Other Than Applicant

THE FOLLOWING EXHIBITS MUST BE COMPLETED WHERE APPLICABLE. ALL QUESTIONS ANSWERED ARE MADE A PART OF THE APPLICATION.

For Guaranty Loans please provide an original and one copy (Photocopy is Acceptable) of the Application Form, and all Exhibits to the participating lender. For Direct Loans submit one original copy of application and Exhibits to SBA.

Submit SBA Form 1261 (Statements Required by Laws and Executive Orders). This form must be signed and dated by each Proprietor, Partner, Principal or Guarantor.

1. Submit SBA Form 912 (Personal History Statement) for each person e.g. owners, partners, officers, directors, major stockholders, etc.; the instructions are on SBA Form 912.

2. Furnish a signed current personal balance sheet (SBA Form 413 may be used for this purpose) for each stockholder (with 20% or greater ownership), partner, officer, and owner. Social Security number should be included on personal financial statement. Label this Exhibit B.

3. Include the statements listed below: 1, 2, 3 for the last three years; also 1, 2, 3, 4 dated within 90 days of filing the application; and statement 5, if applicable. This is Exhibit C (SBA has Management Aids that help in the preparation of financial statements.) All information must be signed and dated.

1. Balance Sheet   2. Profit and Loss Statement
3. Reconciliation of Net Worth
4. Aging of Accounts Receivable and Payable
5. Earnings projections for at least one year where financial statements for the last three years are unavailable or where requested by District Office.
    (If Profit and Loss Statement is not available, explain why and substitute Federal Income Tax Forms.)

4. Provide a brief history of your company and a paragraph describing the expected benefits it will receive from the loan. Label it Exhibit D.

ALL EXHIBITS MUST BE SIGNED AND DATED BY PERSON SIGNING THIS FORM.

SBA Form 4 (2-85) Previous Editions Obsolete

Application for SBA Loan, page 2

5. Provide a brief description of the educational, technical and business background for all the people listed under Management. Please mark it Exhibit E.

6. Do you have any co-signers and/or guarantors for this loan? If so, please submit their names, addresses and personal balance sheet(s) as Exhibit F.

7. Are you buying machinery or equipment with your loan money? If so, you must include a list of the equipment and cost as quoted by the seller and his name and address. This is Exhibit G.

8. Have you or any officers of your company ever been involved in bankruptcy or insolvency proceedings? If so, please provide the details as Exhibit H. If none, check here: ☐ Yes ☐ No

9. Are you or your business involved in any pending lawsuits? If yes, provide the details as Exhibit I. If none, check here: ☐ Yes ☐ No

10. Do you or your spouse or any member of your household, or anyone who owns, manages, or directs your business or their spouses or members of their households work for the Small Business Administration, Small Business Advisory Council, SCORE or ACE, any Federal Agency, or the participating lender? If so, please provide the name and address of the person and the office where employed. label this Exhibit J. If none, check here: ☐ Yes ☐ No

11. Does your business, its owners or majority stockholders own or have a controlling interest in other businesses? If yes, please provide their names and the relationship with your company along with a current balance sheet and operating statement for each. This should be Exhibit K.

12. Do you buy from, sell to, or use the services of any concern in which someone in your company has a significant financial interest? If yes, provide details on a separate sheet of paper labeled Exhibit L.

13. If your business is a franchise, include a copy of the franchise agreement and a copy of the FTC disclosure statement supplied to you by the Franchisor. Please include it as Exhibit M.

CONSTRUCTION LOANS ONLY

14. Include a separate exhibit (Exhibit N) the estimated cost of the project and a statement of the source of any additional funds.

15. File the necessary compliance document (SBA Form 601).

16. Provide copies of preliminary construction plans and specifications. Include them as Exhibit O. Final plans will be required prior to disbursement.

DIRECT LOANS ONLY

17. Include two bank declination letters with your application. These letters should include the name and telephone number of the persons contacted at the banks, the amount and terms of the loan, the reason for decline and whether or not the bank will participate with SBA. In cities with 200,000 people or less, one letter will be sufficient.

EXPORT LOANS

18. Does your business presently engage in Export Trade?
Check here ☐ Yes ☐ No

19. Do you plan to begin exporting as a result of this loan?
Check here ☐ Yes ☐ No

20. Would you like information on Exporting?
Check here ☐ Yes ☐ No

AGREEMENTS AND CERTIFICATIONS

Agreements of Nonemployment of SBA Personnel: I/We agree that if SBA approves this loan application I/We will not, for at least two years, hire as an employee or consultant anyone that was employed by the SBA during the one year period prior to the disbursement of the loan.

Certification: I/We certify: (a) I/We have not paid anyone connected with the Federal Government for help in getting this loan. I/We also agree to report to the SBA office of the Inspector General, 1441 L Street N.W., Washington, D.C. 20416 any Federal Government employee who offers, in return for any type of compensation, to help get this loan approved.

(b) All information in this application and the Exhibits are true and complete to the best of my/our knowledge and are submitted to SBA so SBA can decide whether to grant a loan or participate with a lending institution in a loan to me/us. I/We agree to pay for or reimburse SBA for the cost of any surveys, title or mortgage examinations, appraisals etc., performed by non-SBA personnel provided I/We have given my/our consent.

I/We understand that I/We need not pay anybody to deal with SBA. I/We have read and understand Form 394 which explains SBA policy on representatives and their fees.

If you make a statement that you know to be false or if you over value a security in order to help obtain a loan under the provisions of the Small Business Act, you can be fined up to $5,000 or be put in jail for up to two years, or both.

If Applicant is a proprietor or general partner, sign below:

By: _____
                                        Date

If Applicant is a Corporation, sign below:

_____
Corporate Name and Seal   Date

_____

By: _____
            Signature of President

Attested by: _____
            Signature of Corporate Secretary

ALL EXHIBITS MUST BE SIGNED AND DATED BY PERSON SIGNING THIS FORM.

SBA Form 4 (2-85) Previous Editions Obsolete

Application for SBA Loan, page 3

INSTRUCTIONS ON REVERSE SIDE

MONTHLY CASH

NAME OF BUSINESS		ADDRESS				OWNER					

	Pre-Start-up Position		1		2		3		4		5	
YEAR MONTH	Estimate	Actual	Estimate	Actual	Estimate	Actual	Estimate	Actual	Estimate	Actual	Estimate	Actual
1. CASH ON HAND (Beginning of month)												
2. CASH RECEIPTS (a) Cash Sales												
(b) Collections from Credit Accounts												
(c) Loan or Other Cash injection (Specify)												
3. TOTAL CASH RECEIPTS (2a + 2b + 2c = 3)												
4. TOTAL CASH AVAILABLE (Before cash out) (1 + 3)												
5. CASH PAID OUT (a) Purchases (Merchandise)												
(b) Gross Wages (Excludes withdrawals)												
(c) Payroll Expenses (Taxes, etc.)												
(d) Outside Services												
(e) Supplies (Office and operating)												
(f) Repairs and Maintenance												
(g) Advertising												
(h) Car, Delivery, and Travel												
(i) Accounting and Legal												
(j) Rent												
(k) Telephone												
(l) Utilities												
(m) Insurance												
(n) Taxes (Real Estate, etc.)												
(o) Interest												
(p) Other Expenses (Specify each)												
(q) Miscellaneous (Unspecified)												
(r) Subtotal												
(s) Loan Principal Payment												
(t) Capital Purchases (Specify)												
(u) Other Start-up Costs												
(v) Reserve and/or Escrow (Specify)												
(w) Owner's Withdrawal												
6. TOTAL CASH PAID OUT (Total 5a thru 5w)												
7. CASH POSITION (End of month) (4 minus 6)												
ESSENTIAL OPERATING DATE (Non-cash flow information) A. Sales Volume (Dollars)												
B. Accounts Receivable (End of month)												
C. Bad Debt (End of month)												
D. Inventory on Hand (End of month)												
E. Accounts Payable (End of month)												
F. Depreciation												

SBA FORM 1100 (1-83) REF: SOP 60 10 Previous Editions Are Obsolete

SBA Cash Flow Projection Form

FLOW PROJECTION

Form Approval:
OMB No. 3245-0019

	TYPE OF BUSINESS			PREPARED BY			DATE	

6		7		8		9		10		11		12		TOTAL Columns 1—12		
Estimate	Actual	Estimate	Actual	Estimate	Actual	Estimate	Actual	Estimate	Actual	Estimate	Actual	Estimate	Actual	Estimate	Actual	
																1.
																2.
																(a)
																(b)
																(c)
																3.
																4.
																5.
																(a)
																(b)
																(c)
																(d)
																(e)
																(f)
																(g)
																(h)
																(i)
																(j)
																(k)
																(l)
																(m)
																(n)
																(o)
																(p)
																(q)
																(r)
																(s)
																(t)
																(u)
																(v)
																(w)
																6.
																7.
																A.
																B.
																C.
																D.
																E.
																F.

Form **SS-4**
(Rev. August 1988)
Department of the Treasury
Internal Revenue Service

Application for Employer Identification Number

(For use by employers and others. Please read the attached instructions before completing this form.) **Please type or print clearly.**

Offical Use Only

OMB No. 1545-0003
Expires 7-31-91

1 Name of applicant (True legal name. See instructions.)	
2 Trade name of business if different from item 1	3 Executor, trustee, "care of name".
4 Mailing address (street address) (room, apt., or suite no.)	5 Address of business, if different from item 4. (See instructions.)
4a City, state, and ZIP code	5a City, state, and ZIP code

6 County and State where principal business is located

7 Name of principal officer, grantor, or general partner. (See instructions.) ▶

8 Type of entity (Check only one.) (See instructions.)
- ☐ Individual SSN _____
- ☐ REMIC
- ☐ State/local government
- ☐ Other nonprofit organization (specify) _____
- ☐ Farmers' cooperative
- ☐ Estate
- ☐ Other (specify) ▶
- ☐ Personal service corp.
- ☐ National guard
- ☐ Trust
- ☐ Plan administrator SSN _____
- ☐ Other corporation (specify) _____
- ☐ Federal government/military
- ☐ Partnership
- ☐ Church or church controlled organization

If nonprofit organization enter GEN (if applicable)_____

8a If a corporation, give name of foreign country (if applicable) or state in the U.S. where incorporated ▶

Foreign country	State

9 Reason for applying (check only one.)
- ☐ Started new business
- ☐ Hired employees
- ☐ Created a pension plan (specify type) ▶
- ☐ Banking purpose (specify) ▶
- ☐ Changed type of organization (specify) ▶_____
- ☐ Purchased going business
- ☐ Created a trust (specify) ▶_____
- ☐ Other (specify) ▶

10 Business start date or acquisition date (Mo., day, year) (See instructions.)	11 Enter closing month of accounting year (See instructions.)

12 First date wages or annuities were paid or will be paid (Mo., day, year). **Note:** *If applicant is a withholding agent, enter date income will first be paid to nonresident alien. (Mo., day, year).* . . . . ▶

13 Enter highest number of employees expected in the next 12 months. **Note:** *If the applicant does not expect to have any employees during the period, enter "0."* . . . . ▶	Nonagricultural	Agricultural	Household

14 Does the applicant operate more than one place of business? . . . . ☐ Yes ☐ No
If "Yes," enter name of business. ▶

15 Principal activity or service (See instructions.) ▶

16 Is the principal business activity manufacturing?. . . . . ☐ Yes ☐ No
If "Yes," principal product and raw material used. ▶

17 To whom are most of the products or services sold? Please check the appropriate box. ☐ Business (wholesale)
☐ Public (retail) ☐ Other (specify) ▶ ☐ N/A

18 Has the applicant ever applied for an identification number for this or any other business?. . . . . ☐ Yes ☐ No
Note: *If "Yes," please answer items 18a and 18b.*

18a If the answer to item 18 is "Yes," give applicant's true name and trade name, if different when applicant applied.

True name ▶ | Trade name ▶

18b Enter approximate date, city, and state where the application was filed and the previous employer identification number if known.

Approximate date when filed (Mo., day, year)	City, and state where filed	Previous EIN

Under penalties of perjury, I declare that I have examined this application, and to the best of my knowledge and belief, it is true, correct, and complete.

Telephone number (include area code)

Name and title (please type or print clearly) ▶

Signature ▶ | Date ▶

Note: *Do not write below this line. For official use only.*

Please leave blank ▶	Geo.	Ind.	Class	Reason for applying

For Paperwork Reduction Act Notice, see instructions. ☆U.S. Government Printing Office: 1988-523-133/00332 Form **SS-4** (Rev. 8-88)

Application for Employer Identification Number (IRS Form SS-4)

List of
Action Steps

14 THE ENTREPRENEUR'S TOOLKIT

15 BUYING A FRANCHISE

16 PULLING THE PLAN TOGETHER

Index

Study Guide

CONTENTS

1
Doorways to Small Business

Matching

Match each numbered item with the lettered statement that best describes it.

1. target customer
2. mind workers
3. gap
4. Megashifts

5. Faith Popcorn
6. Business Plan
7. high growth industry

8. primary research
9. segment
10. buying an ongoing business

_____ A. founder of BrainReserve
_____ B. gathering real information in the field
_____ C. the customer with the highest probability of buying your product or service
_____ D. doorway one
_____ E. a slice of the total market
_____ F. from a national economy to a world economy
_____ G. a blueprint for your business
_____ H. denizens of the Information Society
_____ I. an area in which emerging market demand exceeds supply
_____ J. where market needs are not being met

True/False

Determine whether each statement is true or false and enter a T (True) or F (False) in the space.

_____ 1. The vast majority of new jobs in the seventies were created by *Fortune* 500 companies.
_____ 2. One reason you can succeed in small business is because you can move faster than the giants of big business.
_____ 3. Because big business takes a long time to get into position, "cracks" of opportunity open in the market floor.
_____ 4. If you learn to see with new eyes, you should be able to deduce a life-style from the contents of a shopping cart in the supermarket.
_____ 5. Psychographics means a study of population data.
_____ 6. According to job expert Tom Jackson, you'll change jobs only once during your lifetime.
_____ 7. Most new jobs in the private sector of our economy are created by firms with less than 200 employees.
_____ 8. The metaphor *smokestack society* refers to businesses located in California's Silicon Valley.
_____ 9. Secondary research means you're gathering predigested information that's been printed or otherwise assembled for you.

_____ 10. One reason for focusing on an achievement-oriented skills picture is to boost your confidence so that you can excel in your great adventure.

_____ 11. For the purposes of this book, a small business is any venture with spirit.

_____ 12. A dreamer cannot be a successful entrepreneur.

_____ 13. Brainstorming is an exacting analytical task, bolstered by logic, which is carefully based on numerical data gathered from stock quotations and demographics.

_____ 14. The father of brainstorming was Attila the Hun.

_____ 15. *Megatrends* was written from data assembled by information engineer Derek Campbell.

_____ 16. There are four doorways to small business ownership.

_____ 17. No matter which doorway you choose, you should develop a Business Plan.

_____ 18. If you buy a franchise, you'll be buying a Business Plan from the franchisor.

_____ 19. Labor unions are growing, both in size and in power.

_____ 20. According to Naisbitt, we are moving from an industrial society to an information society.

_____ 21. In the eighties, big business again began to grow. The business media called it "upsizing."

_____ 22. There are now more than 16 million small businesses in the United States.

_____ 23. The "enchanted fortress" is where an imaginary family of the future lives, works, and plays.

Multiple-Choice

Select the best response for each item and enter the corresponding letter in the space.

_____ 1. To do new-eyes research, you:
   a. research books and periodicals about information processing.
   b. see an optician.
   c. use your intuition to play marketplace detective.
   d. watch videotapes instead of reading texts.

_____ 2. Which one of the following job titles is not considered an "information" job title?
   a. teacher.
   b. bureaucrat.
   c. insurance broker.
   d. coal miner.

_____ 3. The book that will give entrepreneurs a quick overview of the movement of society in the next 10–15 years is:
   a. *Up the Organization!*
   b. *The One-Minute Manager.*
   c. *In Search of Excellence.*
   d. *Megatrends.*

_____ 4. Which one of the following entrepreneurs from the case studies in chapter 1 is the least enmeshed in the Information Society?
   a. Joseph Talmadge—liqueur expert.
   b. Derek Campbell—engineer.
   c. Judd O'Herlihy—branch manager.
   d. Marci Reid—travel agent.

_____ 5. Interviewing small business owners in the field is an example of:
   a. secondary research.
   b. your definition of success.
   c. how you remember the Industrial Age.
   d. primary research.

_____ 6. The document which stands between you and small business failure is your:
   a. SBA management leaflet 6602.03.
   b. first year's ROI.
   c. Business Plan.
   d. skills dossier.

_____ 7. You can generate a secret profit profile of a business if you know only certain key figures because:
  a. you can estimate some expenses with reasonable accuracy.
  b. net profit always equals about 10% of cost of goods sold.
  c. the IRS makes all business income tax returns available for public scrutiny.
  d. all small businesses have about the same return on investment.

_____ 8. One of the best sources of up-to-date business information is:
  a. *Life* magazine.
  b. *Redbook.*
  c. *Ellery Queen's Mystery Magazine.*
  d. the *Wall Street Journal.*

_____ 9. Businesses are classified by a coding system known as the:
  a. American Business Code.
  b. Standard Industrial Classification.
  c. Business Classification Standard.
  d. Retail/Service/Manufacture Code.

_____ 10. There are three types of research:
  a. main, secondary and private.
  b. retail, service, manufacturing.
  c. primary, secondary, and private.
  d. primary, secondary, and new eyes.

_____ 11. Faith Popcorn:
  a. popularized the concept of cocooning.
  b. is noted for her "New Age" forecast.
  c. demonstrated the potential of microwave cooking.
  d. is consumed in great quantities by certain religious groups.

Short-Answer

1. What are your career plans? What industry do you want to be working in five years from now?

_____

Why? _____

10 years from now? _____

2. What would you do if you had one year off, with no money worries?

1st priority _____

2nd priority _____

3rd priority _____

3. Name three small businesses in your immediate area that you think meet your criteria for success.

  a. _____

  b. _____

  c. _____

4. List four criteria for success in small business.

  a. _____

  b. _____

  c. _____

  d. _____

5. What skills do you have that will help you succeed in small business? (see Action Step 8)

   a. _____   d. _____

   b. _____   e. _____

   c. _____   f. _____

6. What do you need to learn to supplement the skills that you already have?

   a. _____

   b. _____

   c. _____

7. Review your field interviews from Action Step 9 and summarize what you learned about the most outstanding of the businesses interviewed.

   Name of business _____

   Type of business _____

   Industry _____

   Location _____

   Owner's name _____

   Owner's personality _____

   _____

   Target market:

   Sex _____

   Age _____

   Income _____

   Education _____

   Residence _____

   Occupation _____

   Lifestyle summary _____

   _____

   Owner's promotional strategy _____

   _____

   Gross sales (if available) _____

   Profits (if available) _____

   Marketing budget _____

   Rent _____

   Salaries _____

   Anything that could be improved _____

   _____

   Mistakes owner will admit to _____

   _____

Any recommendations on banker, attorney, accountant, etc.?

_____

Capsule summary [In what way is this a helpful model for your business?]:

_____

_____

_____

8. Profit profile. After you have interviewed three or four business owners, use your numbers to develop a profit profile. List what you know. Then try to figure out what each business was making.

a. Gross sales _____

    Cost of goods sold _____

    Rent _____

    Salaries _____

    Marketing _____

    FICA/benefits (est. 20%–30% of salaries) _____

    Other expenses (est. 8%–12% of gross sales) _____

b. Gross sales _____

    Cost of goods sold _____

    Rent _____

    Salaries _____

    Marketing _____

    FICA/benefits (est. 20%–30% of salaries) _____

    Other expenses (est. 8%–12% of gross sales) _____

c. Gross sales _____

    Cost of goods sold _____

    Rent _____

    Salaries _____

    Marketing _____

    FICA/benefits (est. 20%–30% of salaries) _____

    Other expenses (est. 8%–12% of gross sales) _____

d. Gross sales _____

    Cost of goods sold _____

    Rent _____

    Salaries _____

    Marketing _____

    FICA/benefits (est. 20%–30% of salaries) _____

    Other expenses (est. 8%–12% of gross sales) _____

2

The Big Picture: Charting Trends for Your Small Business

Matching

Match each numbered item with the lettered statement that best describes it. (Statements P–T on p. 8.)

1. trend
2. life cycle
3. one-color stationery
4. shelf velocity
5. new-eyes research
6. deep discount
7. market signal

8. high touch
9. target neighborhood
10. workaholic
11. heavy user
12. target customer
13. fad
14. information

15. *Wall Street Journal*
16. trade journal
17. bank
18. gap analysis
19. Faith Popcorn
20. *Sales and Marketing Management* magazine

_____ A. the habitat of your target customer
_____ B. a person whose chief joy in life comes from achievements at work
_____ C. a trend that doesn't last
_____ D. reading this gives you a big picture update
_____ E. a publication written and distributed for the members of a particular industry or business
_____ F. a procedure for identifying unmet needs in the marketplace
_____ G. an institution that rents money
_____ H. as you consume it, it grows
_____ I. a large moving tendency that can be intuited and used to advantage by the entrepreneur who can see the handwriting on the wall
_____ J. a smart purchasing move that helps save entrepreneurs money at start-up time
_____ K. speed at which merchandise sells
_____ L. a creative view of the marketplace that can be correlated with secondary sources
_____ M. when the marketplace is flooded, this is what products sell at
_____ N. society's attempt at balancing the electronic technology of the Information Age with human softness
_____ O. they are everywhere, and they tell you where a product is on the life cycle

_____ P. a four-stage pathway of inevitability for virtually all industries, products, and services
_____ Q. a target customers who buys the lion's share of a particular product or service
_____ R. the person most likely to buy your goods and/or services
_____ S. "mom foods"
_____ T. *Survey of Buying Power*

True/False

Determine whether each statement is true or false and enter a T (True) or F (False) in the space.

_____ 1. The life-cycle yardstick is important because it will give you a quick sense of what's happening in the world of business.

_____ 2. Because of the positioning of designer jeans in the marketplace and also because of the HMUF (high mark-up factor), manufacturing designer jeans would be a lucrative venture for the creative entrepreneur.

_____ 3. You really don't need to decide what business you're really in until the doors of your business have been open for at least a year.

_____ 4. Mary Clarke was really in the business of stabling horses.

_____ 5. The automobile industry has been in a high-growth phase since the early 1980s.

_____ 6. One reason the railroads went into decline was because they forgot what business they were really in.

_____ 7. Hula hoops, designer jeans, Rubik's cube, and spidery wall-walker toys are all examples of marketplace fads.

_____ 8. *Megatrends* was based on research from 6,000 local papers over a period of a dozen years.

_____ 9. Once you succeed in defining your business, you can sit tight and watch those dollars roll in because a definition is the final word.

_____ 10. If you think you're in one kind of business, and your target customers think you're in something else, the obvious strategy is to show those customers the door, fast.

_____ 11. Letterhead stationery is helpful to your information-gathering activities because it tells the world you're serious about going into business.

_____ 12. Another way of talking about being in software sales is by saying you're in the problem-solving business.

_____ 13. When you play marketplace detective, you can learn more about trends in small business by studying the national chains than by wasting time studying locally owned or regionally owned businesses.

_____ 14. Market signals can be helpful indicators for workers in large industries as well as for small business owners.

_____ 15. One reason a business like Private Screenings can exist is because certain segments of the marketplace are adopting a more relaxed attitude about sex.

_____ 16. There is no need to "walk the neighborhood" and spy on strangers when you can find out everything you need to know by writing the appropriate U.S. government agency for the needed data.

_____ 17. If you see a shopping cart loaded with baby food, disposable diapers, dog food, boxed cereal, large cartons of milk, you can assume that the shopper has a senior citizen life style, loves fishing, hunting, knitting, billiards, bingo, and dry martinis on the weekend.

_____ 18. A full parking lot is absolute proof of a booming shopping center.

_____ 19. If you're eager to try your wings in small business, there's no need to waste time taking a lot of personality tests.

_____ 20. If you're in the baby bedding business, a child's nursery can be your marketplace.

Multiple-Choice

Select the best response for each item and enter the corresponding letter in the space.

_____ 1. The life-cycle yardstick is an important tool because:
     a. it is an absolute mathematical instrument.
     b. it always correlates with the Dow–Jones averages.
     c. it can help you target a growth segment of a growth industry.
     d. it will prevent you from making foolish mistakes with your time and money.

_____ 2. A good example of a hot growth industry would be:
  a. sedan-sized autos.
  b. robotics.
  c. tobacco.
  d. railroads.

_____ 3. If you get into a business like toy retailing, your survival will depend on how well you can:
  a. keep one eye on the future.
  b. handle a 30-hour work week.
  c. forget you used to be a kid and concentrate on accounting controls.
  d. understand computer programming language.

_____ 4. Gap analysis and segmentation:
  a. depend for their success on how close you are to getting your MBA in marketing.
  b. are deeply mathematical in nature.
  c. are fun because they allow you to be imaginative.
  d. always correlate precisely with high-level entrepreneurial theory from the major universities.

_____ 5. Knowing what business you're in is important because:
  a. it will guarantee you an income of six figures in your first year.
  b. it means you'll never have to waste time redefining your business goals.
  c. it cuts down customer confusion.
  d. it can be ascertained by amassing statistics from the files of the U.S. Census Bureau.

_____ 6. Railroads in the United States went into a decline for all the reasons below except which of the following?
  a. The RRs forgot what business they were in.
  b. The new plastic tracks became portable and flexible.
  c. Jumbo jets carried people and goods faster.
  d. The interstate highway system connected the country and made travel and shipping more flexible.

_____ 7. Which of the trends below was not much of a consideration in the intimate apparel business?
  a. Specialized consumer tastes.
  b. A geographic shift from Frost Belt to Sunbelt.
  c. High-tech/high-touch.
  d. Relaxing attitudes about sex.

_____ 8. You are out walking your target neighborhood. You see baby strollers, people walking dogs, four-year-old station wagons, bikes, newly planted lawns. The trees are small and supported with sticks. Some of the streets are still being put in. You can make the following marketplace assumption:
  a. adult condo complex, restricted to retirees over 60.
  b. singles condo complex catering to people of both sexes between 22 and 33 years old.
  c. family residential area, perhaps for first-time buyers.
  d. old established residential area, heart of town.

_____ 9. One of the newest hot-growth industries may well be:
  a. automobile manufacturing.
  b. book publishing.
  c. steel mills.
  d. bio-genetics.

_____ 10. One of the many signals that a giant industry is in trouble would be:
  a. layoffs, shrinking back orders, slow payment of bills, deferred maintenance.
  b. sponsorship of rock concerts in the desert.
  c. bringing in consultants on creativity, right hemisphere problem-solving, and the arts of Japanese management.
  d. deciding what business they're in.

Short-Answer

1. Where is your industry on the four-stage life-cycle yardstick? If you're in the decline stage, can you think of a related business that's in a different stage? Do any of your skills qualify you to move to a business venture in another stage?

_____

_____

_____

_____

2. Write down what business you're really in.

_____

Now write down what *other* business you're in. (For example, if you want to open a camera shop where your major activity will be the memory business, you'll have several minibusinesses to be aware of: processing, camera rental, your photographer's school, retailing. List all your possible minibusinesses here.) _____

_____

3. How old is your industry? How old is your particular segment? Below, list five to seven turning points in your industry. (For example, if you're thinking of going in the printing business, you should know that one major breakthrough came with Gutenberg, back in the 1400s. If you're in the computer service business, you know that your industry was born in the summer of 1969, when IBM let go of its profitable computer packages.)

   Date   **Turning Point/Trend**

1.

2.

3.

4.

5.

4. **Model for a Shopping Cart Survey. Part I.** Your venture will be more fun if you train your mind to look for marketplace data. The following is a composite study, drawn from the marketplace. To prepare for Action Step 15, use this case as a model. Imagine you observe the following:

A. Contents of cart:
   1. Imported beer, 2 cases
   2. Mixed nuts, 4 cans
   3. 16 steaks, porterhouse
   4. Greens, tomatoes, imported olives

   5. French bread
   6. 17 Idaho potatoes, carefully selected
   7. Cheese, imported Camembert
   8. Cognac, 2 bottles

B. Shopper description:
   Clothes—Bermuda shorts, expensive shirt
   Shoes—tennis, no socks
   Jewelry—gold I.D. bracelet, gold watch, wedding band
   Hair style—razor cut, medium
   Eyeglasses—dark, prescription
   General appearance—neat, careful dresser, excellent tan

The next step is to briefly summarize your observations. You should emerge with a pretty solid profile, as follows:

   Marketplace Observations: This upscale TC was observed on a Sunday afternoon at a food store located in an upper-middle-class residential area. Census data for the area suggested a median household income of $65,000. The total bill came to $129.97, and was paid with cash from a large sheaf of bills. The TC was preparing for a party. Based on observation only, the following demographic profile can be assumed:
   Sex: male
   Age: early 50s
   Education: high probability for college degree
   Occupation: executive

Income: $50,000 +
Residence: $170,000 +

Part 2. When you move out into the arena to do your shopping cart survey, use the case as a guide. First, list the contents of the cart. Second, describe the shopper. Third, summarize your observations.

A. Contents of cart:

1.

2.

3.

4.

   5.

   6.

   7.

   8

B. Shopper description
  Clothes—
  Shoes—
  Jewelry—
  Hair-style—
  General appearance—
    Marketplace Observations:

Part 3. To develop your marketplace probe further, consider these questions:
Where is the location of the life-cycle yardstick?
Leaving the food store, how far would you have to drive to feel you're in a different economic customer base?
    Did you make your study at rush hour? Lazy weekend afternoon? Early morning?
If you saw our upscale TC buying the same $129 worth of groceries at 2:30 P.M. on a weekday, what would you conclude about his occupation?
If a store is open 24 hours a day, what does it suggest about the target customers?
Is there any way you can sell your goods or services to any of the customers profiled?

5. Write down five business names that would tell your TC what business you're in. When you get your list, check with friends and fellow students. What do they think the names mean? (*Hint:* Quick Copy, Hamburger Hamlet, One-Hour Foto, $1 Cleaners.)

1.

2.

3.

   4.

   5.

6. List your three most important information sources; on a separate sheet of paper write a brief paragraph about what you learned from each that will help you shape your Business Plan.

1. _____

2. _____

3. _____

3 Power Marketing

Matching

Match each numbered item with the lettered statement that best describes it.

1. power marketing
2. business objectives
3. psychological rewards
4. no competition
5. life cycle
6. positioning
7. industry breakthrough

8. component parts
9. forecasting
10. segment
11. demographics
12. psychographics
13. problems
14. support services

15. brainstorm
16. matrix grid
17. software
18. product
19. power pricing
20. clone

_____ A. one of the four P's
_____ B. screen or filter through which ideas are passed in order to form solutions
_____ C. a new development in a particular product that changes the arena of competition
_____ D. a four-stage yardstick that helps you look more carefully at business opportunities
_____ E. the program that runs the computer
_____ F. a free-for-all idea session that calls on creativity and flights of imagination for help in coping with problems
_____ G. an activity that is usually trimmed with a product's price
_____ H. a study of life-style—buying habits, dreams, attitudes, ambitions, and so on
_____ I. a slice of the marketplace pie
_____ J. a procedure practiced by market researchers that attempts to predict the future
_____ K. a tool that helps you exploit gaps in the marketplace and connect your skills to your research
_____ L. a feeling of satisfaction, hard to express, but quite real and powerful
_____ M. an organized set of dreams that you are trying to translate into reality through hard work, tenacity, and information
_____ N. means you're alone in your segment, like the first hunter arriving at the still and silent pond
_____ O. one example of an industry breakthrough in the microcomputer industry
_____ P. a strategy for establishing yourself on a ladder in the mind of the prospect
_____ Q. can be turned into opportunities by the streetwise entrepreneur
_____ R. a study of population involving measurable observables like sex, age, income, and education
_____ S. is determined the value to the customer
_____ T. an NCR "copycat" computer with a lower price

True/False

Determine whether each statement is true or false and enter a T (True) or F (False) in the space.

_____ 1. Power marketing is a tool that helps you aim your mind at a particular segment of the marketplace.
_____ 2. All five members of the Info Team case study had technical or engineering backgrounds.

_____ 3. Listing business objectives helps you focus and plan.

_____ 4. The father of brainstorming was Alexander the Great of Persia.

_____ 5. People get together in teams to balance their strengths and weaknesses.

_____ 6. The average small business can get up and running in seven days.

_____ 7. If you can locate an industry that really has magnetic pull for you, you'll be more interested and have more fun.

_____ 8. When researching, you can do a much better job if you forget organization and just dive in.

_____ 9. In the computer industry, the life cycle of a piece of hardware can be as short as 18 months.

_____ 10. After the "shakeout" in the microcomputer industry in late 1983, there was no more competition in the hardware segment.

_____ 11. Apple introduced the micro in the midseventies.

_____ 12. Before 1982, most programmers had aimed their software at the Apple. In late 1982, the new "wrinkle" in the microcomputer industry was that more people were developing software for the IBM PC.

_____ 13. The Info Team in the case study finally decided the best business to be in was retailing hot computer hardware.

_____ 14. Once you begin to profile your target customer, you're on your way to finding your segment.

_____ 15. An eager entrepreneur can transform a problem into a business opportunity.

_____ 16. In the early micro days, when manufacturers were trying to market software, one of the obvious problems was user frustration.

_____ 17. In marketing circles, "support" means there are services to backstop and expand the value of the sale.

_____ 18. The obvious target customer for a school that teaches computer software techniques is an unhappy micro user who cannot understand the complicated documentation.

_____ 19. Armonk is GHQ for IBM.

_____ 20. One of the key moves in power marketing occurs when you use a little entrepreneurial alchemy to translate problems into solutions.

Multiple-Choice

Select the best response for each item and enter the corresponding letter in the space.

_____ 1. Power marketing convinced the Info Team to go into which of the following segments:
  a. hardware repair.
  b. software production.
  c. computer education.
  d. none of the above.

_____ 2. Which of the following are reasonable business objectives?
  a. safety of investment.
  b. psychological rewards.
  c. fun and adventure.
  d. all of the above.

_____ 3. The name of the grid used to sift data and correlate objectives is:
  a. Bernoulli's Sieve.
  b. matrix.
  c. Alchemist's Urn.
  d. Iacocca's Ladle.

_____ 4. Which of the following was not a problem that could be transformed into an opportunity by the Info Team?
  a. unhappy, frustrated users.
  b. IBM had declared bankruptcy.
  c. minimal support from manufacturers.
  d. confusion in the marketplace.

_____ 5. Which of the following best describes the primary target customer discovered by the Info Team?
  a. female, 45–57, college degree plus, income $55,000, suburban/rural, owns stable, rides six days a week.
  b. female, 18–34, some college, metro residence, $17,500, clerical/supervisory, reads _Cosmo_, _Glamour_.

      c. male, 18–34, some college, rural residence, $19,500, construction/crafts/artist/artisan.

      d. male, 18–35, some college, might own PC, access to computer at work, urban/suburban, $35,000, lives near computer store.

_____ 6. What year did Apple introduce the micro?

      a. 1485.

      b. 1977.

      c. 1945.

      d. 1984.

_____ 7. The phrase that best describes what was happening in the computer hardware marketplace in the early 1980s is:

      a. gentlemen's agreement not to compete.

      b. Bernoulli Effect.

      c. hot competition.

      d. Apple took over IBM HQ at Armonk.

_____ 8. In 1983 the life cycle of a piece of computer hardware could be as short as:

      a. 9 months.

      b. 36 months.

      c. 3 months.

      d. 18 months.

_____ 9. Which of the following is not an accurate description of power marketing?

      a. a tool that helps you exploit gaps in the marketplace.

      b. a highly quantified system, firmly based in statistics.

      c. a technique that aims the power of your mind at a particular segment of the marketplace.

      d. a way to connect skills to a body of research.

_____ 10. One reason you need to be alert to industry breakthroughs:

      a. they give you the ammunition to jeer at your competitors.

      b. they prevent your key employees from selling company secrets.

      c. they give you the chance to change the competitive arena.

      d. they guarantee you a nonturbulent, debt-free start-up.

Short-Answer

1. Briefly describe your total market. (This is easier than it sounds. *Example:* The total market for the computer school would be everyone who owns, uses, or plans to own a micro.)

_____

_____

_____

2. Segment your market, using logic combined with associative leaps. For help in starting segmentation, think of a large industry that's highly visible, like the auto industry. You can segment according to *size* (Pinto, Cadillac limo), *price* (Mercedes, Chevette), *age* (Model T, Stutz Bearcat), *rarity* (Royale—there were only six) *versus mass-market* (Toyota), *county of origin* (Japan, Sweden, Germany, France, United States), *geographic distribution* (front-wheel drive Saabs in New England, Pacific Northwest; four-wheel drive Subarus in New Mexico; large sedans in the Midwest). Sometimes, it helps to create your own mind map. Use this space for your map.

3. Profile your target customer.

Person   Business

   Sex: Size:

   Age: Industry:

   Income: Number of employees:

   Occupation: Type of employees:

   Residence: Branch offices:

   Education: Location:

   Marital status: Product/Service:

   Geographic region   SIC code:

   Cultural origin: Public/Private:

   Religion:

   Leap into psychographics.

   Buying habits:

   Dreams:

   Ambitions:

   Attitudes:

  For help on your psychographic leap, see Box 4.3.

4. List major problems faced by the segments you discovered.

   1. _____

   2. _____

   3. _____

   4. _____

5. Brainstorm mad solutions for each major problem in this space. Use a mind map, a list, or whatever else is useful to you.

6. Use this matrix grid to squeeze some conclusions out of your data. Along the left-hand side, list your business objectives. Along the top, list your solutions. In the boxes, place a +, 0, or — each time an objective clicks with a solution. Key: + = 3, 0 = 2, — = 1. Then find your total and see where you stand in your adventure.

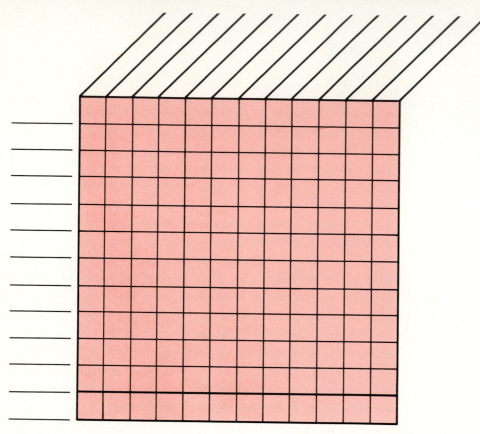

7. What has been the most fun so far in your adventure? _____

   Why was it fun? _____

   _____

4

Profiling the Target Customer

Matching

Match each numbered item with the lettered statement that best describes it.

1. target market magazines
2. heavy user
3. Hugh Hefner
4. *Playboy* empire
5. demographic data
6. newspaper
7. *McCall's* reader

8. magazine rack
9. display ad department
10. competition
11. baby boom
12. primary target customer
13. invisible target customer
14. interview

15. psychographics
16. profiling
17. Business Plan
18. SIC codes
19. VALS onion
20. segmenting

_____ A. a sudden increase in the number of births during a given period that results in a marketing phenomenon some 20 years later
_____ B. what develops when two or more hungry combatants decide they want the same slice of the marketplace pie
_____ C. drawing a magic circle around your customer
_____ D. a study of life-styles
_____ E. a customer who emerges, like magic, after you have been in business for awhile
_____ F. the most visible segment of your target market
_____ G. *McCall's, Cosmo, Playboy, Time*
_____ H. a blueprint for your business
_____ I. a target customer who accounts for a high percentage of sales of a certain product or service
_____ J. an entrepreneur with a clear picture of his target customer
_____ K. the place you write to when asking for demographic information from magazines and newspapers
_____ L. a kingdom built on images and information
_____ M. an often overlooked guide to interest areas in a specific community
_____ N. female, 19–55, $27,000, metro-suburban, a high percentage are married, with children under 18; a high percentage are employed
_____ O. facts and numbers relating to the study of population
_____ P. one good local source of marketing data
_____ Q. an excellent technique for getting to know your target customer face-to-face
_____ R. federally sponsored standardized classification system of major industries and elements
_____ S. includes purchasing habits of survivors and sustainers.
_____ T. is like slicing a pie.

True/False

Determine whether each statement is true or false and enter a T (True) or F (False) in the space.

_____ 1. It is impossible for an entrepreneur to acquire new skills.
_____ 2. *Psychographics* refers to crazy people who write on walls with spray paint.
_____ 3. One of the best sources of customer profiles is the display ad departments of magazines.
_____ 4. If you can find out what your TC reads, watches, or listens to, you'll make your promotion task simpler.
_____ 5. When you go out for interviews, there's no real advantage to making up questions in advance if you just hit the street and wing it.
_____ 6. Interviewing target customers is a very useful technique when you're gathering information about the marketplace.
_____ 7. Once they heard about Fred's soccer shop, invisible customers began to appear.
_____ 8. If you've been in business before, there's no real need to waste time profiling your customers again and again. Just get to work and tell them how sharp you are.
_____ 9. A car driven by your target customer can be an indicator of income, self-image, and lifestyle.
_____ 10. Sarah Routledge is an example of a cagey entrepreneur because she learned how to survive by studying the needs and wants of the marketplace.
_____ 11. A habitual reader of romance fiction is one example of a heavy user.
_____ 12. The target market for *Cosmopolitan* magazine is predominantly male, 35–45, Master's degree or higher, $42,000 income, living in three metro areas: Los Angeles/San Diego; Seattle/Tacoma; Dallas/Fort Worth.
_____ 13. In the 1990s, we are surrounded by special-interest magazines advertising a host of special-interest products.
_____ 14. If a magazine goes under, one cause might be that, like the railroads, it forgot what business it was in.
_____ 15. *McCall's* is *Playboy's* biggest competition for readers.
_____ 16. One reason to observe people at magazine racks is so you can begin to correlate life-style with reading behavior.
_____ 17. Advertising money is important for a magazine because it pays the bills.
_____ 18. A magazine cover is an important sales tool.
_____ 19. Hugh Hefner created his target customer out of thin air and imagination.
_____ 20. One way to begin market research is to start with what you read, listen to, watch, or buy—and then contrast your habits with habits of people from another life-style.

Multiple-Choice

Select the best response for each item and enter the corresponding letter in the space.

_____ 1. The visionary entrepreneur who built the Playboy Empire from a small business that started on a kitchen table in Chicago was:
     a. Mayor Richard Daley.
     b. Lee Iacocca.
     c. Hugh Hefner.
     d. Ray Kroc.
_____ 2. Which of the following pieces of data doesn't fit the *Playboy* reader profile?
     a. male, 18–34.
     b. urban/suburban residence.
     c. housewife, five children, heavy user of romances.
     d. consumer of alcoholic spirits.
_____ 3. Which of the following magazines is probably not vying for the same reader as *McCall's?*
     a. *Redbook.*
     b. *EasyRider.*
     c. *Ladies' Home Journal.*
     d. *Good Housekeeping.*

____ 4. A terrific book that profiles target customers is:
   a. *Subliminal Seduction.*
   b. *The Great Gatsby.*
   c. *Writing the Natural Way.*
   d. *Guerilla Tactics in the Job Market.*

____ 5. Which of the following magazines is more special-interest than general-interest?
   a. *Colliers.*   c. *Coronet.*
   b. *Look.*   d. *Runner's World*

____ 6. The letter from the romance publisher to Sarah Routledge:
   a. was a pink rejection slip.
   b. described a possible target reader.
   c. was an agreement to write a dictionary for gourmet cooks.
   d. contained several grammatical errors and misspelled words.

____ 7. Competition in business can be defined as a situation that arises:
   a. when the world was young and green.
   b. in the Garden of Eden.
   c. when two hungry contestants go after the same slice of marketplace pie.
   d. when everyone leaves the arena.

____ 8. Which of the following places should you avoid for help in launching a new business?
   a. the SBA.   c. banks.
   b. SCORE.   d. get-rich-quick magazine ads.

____ 9. Which of the following was not a factor in the success of Fred Bowers's soccer shop?
   a. Investors liked his Business Plan.
   b. He knew soccer, had coached it.
   c. After he'd been open awhile, invisible customers began to appear.
   d. The tennis boom bubble burst, and a lot of people became overnight soccer players.

____ 10. Which of the following questions would give you the least help when you interview potential target customers?
   a. How did you like the store?
   b. When I open up a similar (and far superior) place next door, can I count on you to switch your business?
   c. Do you shop here often?
   d. How far did you drive to get here?

Short-Answer

1. List five magazines or periodicals that you read regularly.

   1.   4.

   2.   5.

   3.

2. Ask two friends what magazines they read regularly.

   Friend 1   **Friend 2**

   1.

   2.

   3.

   4.

   5.

How can you correlate what your friends read with their lifestyles and consumption patterns?

_____

_____

_____

3. Select one magazine from your list for a quick market analysis.
   a. The cover is a sales tool. Describe the photo/art/layout and the words:

   What dominates?
   What attracts?

   To what market does the cover or front page appeal? _____

   _____

   b. Ads pay for the magazine. Using chapter 4 of your text as a guide, analyze the ads.
      Age-range of models:
      Dress/clothing:
      Major activity:

   c. Editorial content usually supports or extends the message of the advertisers. Describe the editorial content. Range of topics covered:

      1.

      2.

      3.

      4.

      How does the copy relate to the ads? _____

      _____

      _____

      _____

4. In a list or brief paragraph, describe the lifestyle of your primary target customer. (Questions to get you started: What are your TC's ambitions? Attitudes? Activities? Dreams? Buying habits?) Remember you are trying to get under the skin of your TC.

   _____

   _____

   _____

   _____

   _____

5. List five publications probably read by your target customer. (Use one of the directories available in your library like _Ulrich's, Gale's Directory, Standard Rate and Data._)

   1.

   2.

   3.

   4.

   5.

6. Pay a visit to the market research department of your local newspaper. Tell them you're starting a new business and you're developing your promotion mix. Describe the target market you're trying to reach, then ask their market researchers for assistance and advice. Summarize what you learn here.

_____

_____

_____

_____

7. Census Bureau Data. Visit the nearest Federal Depository to locate the following information: List 10 items you purchased in the last six months, and list the SIC Codes of at least five of them.

Product	SIC Code
1.	
2.	
3.	
4.	
5.	
6.	
7.	
8.	
9.	
10.	

8. Using the latest _Survey of Buying Power_ (published by _Sales and Marketing Management_ magazine), select an area that would be most likely to contain the target customers for your product or service.

Area: _____

9. Develop 10–15 questions to use when you interview target customers. For a start, see the questions from the Julia Gonzales case study in chapter 4.

1. _____

2. _____

3. _____

4. _____

5. _____

6. _____

7. _____

8. _____

9. _____

10. _____

11. _____

12. _____

13. _____

14. _____

15. _____

10. List the names of 3–5 target customers you interviewed, and in a brief sentence state your conclusions from each interview.

    1. _____   _____

    2. _____   _____

    3. _____   _____

    4. _____   _____

    5. _____   _____

5

Reading the Competition

Matching

Match each numbered item with the lettered statement that best describes it.

1. embryo
2. competition
3. target customer
4. arena
5. conglomerate
6. stealing customers
7. profit

8. product innovation
9. blind competition
10. decline stage
11. ladder
12. gasoline service station
13. mystery shopper
14. maintaining a presence

15. competing with yourself
16. competitor test matrix
17. changing the arena
18. product differentiation
19. core market
20. positioning

_____ A. a focus of design which attempts to set a product off from its competitors by price, service, or repairs

_____ B. a metaphor for how a target customer ranks similar businesses; it also represents your step-by-step journey to the top

_____ C. a tool which allows you to rank your competitors in a number of areas including image, location, innovation, and flexibility

_____ D. establishing a ladder inside the mind of the prospect, or target customer

_____ E. when transforming a product or service by adding a simple benefit also transforms the nature of competition

_____ F. first stage of a business life cycle

_____ G. a heated contest in which the combatants have lost their ability to see clearly while they seek to destroy the other

_____ H. a fancy way of saying you've kept your image in front of the customer

_____ I. involves two steps: 1) you develop a first-class quality product; 2) when competitors smell money and try to penetrate your market with a cheapie, you've got one ready to ship

_____ J. an example of a service business in the mature stage of the life cycle

_____ K. a disguise adopted by cagey entrepreneurs as they study their competitors

_____ L. a form of technical breakthrough

_____ M. time to leave the arena

_____ N. one of your main reasons for being in business

_____ O. the person most likely to buy your product or service

_____ P. what ensues when two or more hungry combatants go after the same narrow slice of the marketplace pie

_____ Q. consumers whose perceived needs best fit the characteristics of a product

_____ R. a giant company composed of many diverse businesses

_____ S. a strategy for surviving in the mature stage of the life cycle

_____ T. a metaphorical battleground where business contests occur

True/False

Determine whether each statement is true or false and enter a T (True) or F (False) in the space.

_____   1. Competition is not affected in any way by the four-stage life cycle.

_____   2. Product innovation is not important enough for top management to worry about.

_____   3. If you choose a business in the mature stage, you're going to have to steal more customers than you would have to steal in the growth stage.

_____   4. There is more competition in the embryonic stage than in all of the other stages put together.

_____   5. There has never been a business venture started over alcoholic beverages at lunchtime.

_____   6. The team which developed skates for ducks was unbalanced by having too many technical people and engineers.

_____   7. Pricing is very easy to establish in the embryonic stage.

_____   8. The reason production runs get longer in the mature stage is because business owners want to take full advantage of capital equipment and experienced management.

_____   9. If you spend dollars on advertising in the growth stage, and then can't follow up with distribution (getting the product to the consumer), you're going to lose sales and credibility.

_____   10. In the embryonic stage, resellers and distributors clamor for your products.

_____   11. One good way to promote is through contests.

_____   12. Smaller firms rarely win price wars.

_____   13. One signal that a product is in the mature stage occurs when manufacturers bring out several variations.

_____   14. A faddish product can reach the decline stage in 90 days.

_____   15. When a product such as rocking chairs enters the decline stage, there still might be opportunities for small entrepreneurs who sell to the core market.

_____   16. A helpful definition for positioning is "establishing a ladder in the mind of the customer."

_____   17. One good way of dealing with your competitors is to study their operations while you probe for strengths you can neutralize and weaknesses you can exploit.

_____   18. If you're going into an industry in which you don't have much experience, your best strategy for disarming the competition is to dive in and scare them with the force of your splash.

_____   19. When researching your competition, helpful tools include a camera and a map of the area.

_____   20. Competing with your own products by developing cheap product B is dishonest.

Multiple-Choice

Select the best response for each item and enter the corresponding letter in the space.

_____   1. The book that goes into detail about ladders in the mind of the customer or prospect is:
   a. *Guerilla Tactics in the Job Market.*
   b. *Nine American Lifestyles.*
   c. *Positioning: The Battle for Your Mind.*
   d. *The Third Wave.*

_____   2. Which of the following is not a smart competitive strategy?
   a. packing expensive lenses in popcorn.
   b. being ready with cheap product B to follow quality product A.
   c. changing the arena by product innovation.
   d. fighting to the bitter end, to the final gasp of the decline stage.

_____   3. A competitor test-matrix will help you to get a fix on:
   a. image.
   b. location.
   c. flexibility.
   d. all of the above.

_____   4. Which of the following is not a sound strategy for disarming the competition?
   a. Do it better.

    b. Treat your TCs like people.

    c. Do it faster.

    d. Start a price war the day you throw open your doors.

5. The arena that shifts a huge market can be the size of a:

    a. quarter.

    b. TV screen.

    c. microchip.

    d. all of the above.

6. Competing with yourself in business means:

    a. you've got cheap product B ready to throw into the arena.

    b. you wait for the decline stage before you advertise.

    c. you argue with yourself about the 4 P's.

    d. you enjoy playing both sides of the chessboard at once.

7. If you're planning on opening a gasoline service station, you'll be in which stage of the life cycle?

    a. embryo.

    b. growth.

    c. maturity.

    d. decline.

8. Which of the following is not likely to occur in the embryo stage?

    a. not much competition.

    b. complete product acceptance.

    c. limited distribution.

    d. experimental pricing.

9. If you advertise your product, and get the TCs panting for it, and your distribution channels are not ready, what's likely to happen?

    a. The competition will hold off shipping until you're ready.

    b. Potential customers will keep clippings and videotapes of your ads and keep calling the retailers to check on availability.

    c. You're going to lose sales and credibility.

    d. Chase Manhattan will offer you an interest-free line of credit until you get your machinery rolling.

10. In what two stages of the life cycle is your core market likely to be most visible?

    a. embryo, growth.

    b. growth, maturity.

    c. embryo, decline.

    d. maturity, decline.

Short-Answer

1. Now you've got a good idea where your business will be on the life-cycle chart. Some segments of your business may be in different stages. For example, if you were to open a record store, you'd have LPs in decline, cassettes in late maturity, CDs in high growth, and video holograms on floating laser-driven bubble chips in the embryo stage. Use the life-cycle chart here. Segment the various phases of your business, and position each in its proper slot.

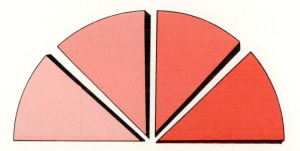

2. List three competitors you think will be tough for you to handle.

   1. _____

   2. _____

   3. _____

3. Develop an analytical stance on each competitor. View them first from the outside and then move inside. (In the next step, these notes will be transferred to a competitor test matrix.)

   Competitor A—from the outside
      Name:
      Location:
      Geographic proximity to market:
      Parking:
      Image
         perceived by you:
         perceived by TC:
         perceived by neighbors:
      Advertising:

   If this were your business and you had unlimited funds, what changes would you make? _____

   _____

   _____

   _____

   From the inside
      Layout:
      Service:
      Atmosphere:
      Quality of merchandise:
      Cleanliness:
      Perceived sales volume:
      Pricing:

   What changes would you make? _____

   _____

   _____

   Competitor B—from the outside
      Name:
      Location:
      Geographic proximity to market:
      Parking:
      Image
         perceived by you:
         perceived by TC:
         perceived by neighbors:
      Advertising:

If this were your business and you had unlimited funds, what changes would you make? _____
_____
_____
_____

From the inside
   Layout:
   Service:
   Atmosphere:
   Quality of merchandise:
   Cleanliness:
   Perceived sales volume:
   Pricing:

What changes would you make? _____
_____
_____

Competitor C—from the outside
   Name:
   Location:
   Geographic proximity to market:
   Parking:
   Image
      perceived by you:
      perceived by TC:
      perceived by neighbors:
   Advertising:

If this were your business and you had unlimited funds, what changes would you make? _____
_____
_____
_____

From the inside
   Layout:
   Atmosphere:
   Quality of merchandise:
   Cleanliness:
   Perceived sales volume:
   Pricing:

What changes would you make? _____
_____
_____

4. Use this competitor test matrix to compare the data you gathered in question 3.

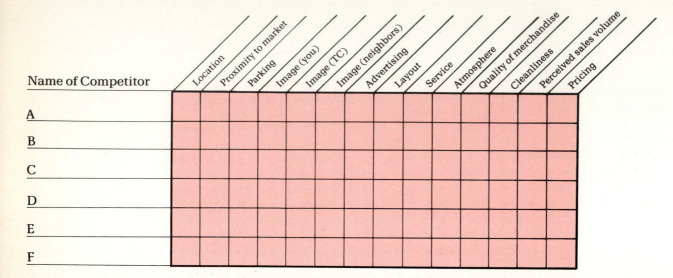

Name of Competitor

A _____

B _____

C _____

D _____

E _____

F _____

5. Networking your way in. Who do you know who knows someone who can give you inside information on your competition? Banker? Stock-broker? Librarian? Vendor salesperson? List possibilities here.

   1.

   2.

   3.

6. Changing the arena. Once you study your competitors, you may have to make only one improvement to change the arena, thereby disarming your competition. *Example 1:* A manufacturer of baby bedding discovered that his competitors were slow on deliveries. By speeding up his own deliveries, he won the admiration of his customers. *Example 2:* An entrepreneur saw an increase in the number of two-wage-earner households so he developed a door-to-door cleaning service. Again, delivery was the key. How will you change your arena? _____

_____

_____

_____

7. Pretend you had unlimited funds. What's the wildest idea you can think of for disarming your competition? Mind map your thought processes here.

6

Promotion: Connecting with the Customer

Matching

Match each numbered item with the lettered statement that best describes it.

1. P-O-P display
2. trade show
3. personal selling
4. promotional mix
5. freebies

6. piggy back
7. co-op advertising
8. direct mail
9. free ink
10. news conference

11. grand opening
12. mailing list broker
13. big spender list
14. leads club
15. Chamber of Commerce

_____ A. all the elements that you blend to maximize the most effective communication to your TC
_____ B. they can grab your customer's attention, create interest in a new product, or allow you to gather market research
_____ C. should act as a silent sales clerk
_____ D. ties local promotional activities to national or regional advertising efforts
_____ E. can be a very expensive way of selling
_____ F. a place where denizens of the same industry gather to present their products and services to one another
_____ G. advertising costs are subsidized by participating vendors
_____ H. promotes local businesses and statewide and national business legislation
_____ I. a group of business and professional people who meet regularly to exchange sales clues
_____ J. a good way to keep track of those few customers that give you a big share of your business
_____ K. using the mail to attract individual customers
_____ L. print media attention—usually in response to effective news releases and personal cultivation
_____ M. firms who will sell you names of potential customers who fit your target market profile
_____ N. the big bang event to herald your arrival in the marketplace
_____ O. calling in members of the media to communicate a newsworthy event

True/False

Determine whether each statement is true or false and enter a T (True) or F (False) in the space.

_____ 1. A contest drawing is a really easy way to build your mailing list.

_____ 2. Magazines will often rent you their subscriber lists.

_____ 3. Trade shows display your product or service in a high-intensity way.

_____ 4. The owner of a small firm is often its most effective salesperson.

_____ 5. If you listen, your target customers will tell you what it takes to induce them to buy.

_____ 6. The first step to gaining free ink (free publicity) is to probe your business and find something newsworthy.

_____ 7. Success in direct mail depends upon how well you have defined your target market.

_____ 8. P-O-P displays are usually very expensive.

_____ 9. Promotion is a pure science, and may be handled with numbers and rules.

_____ 10. A good ad will gain both the attention and interest of the target customer.

_____ 11. A smaller ad is likely to get lost on a page.

_____ 12. Newspapers often offer special supplements at reduced cost. The offer often includes free editorial copy.

_____ 13. A highly visible owner is often the best form of promotion.

_____ 14. Effective advertising is expensive, but you always get what you pay for.

_____ 15. Vendors often furnish tear sheets free of charge.

_____ 16. Leads clubs are made up of people from the same profession, business, or industry.

Multiple-Choice

Select the best response for each item and enter the corresponding letter in the space.

_____ 1. Market research is:
   a. asking your customers what they think.
   b. analyzing census data in the library.
   c. reviewing and analyzing appropriate secondary information.
   d. all of the above.

_____ 2. Promotion is:
   a. clawing your way up the corporate ladder.
   b. advancing one idea over another.
   c. all the things that you do to communicate your business message to your potential customers.
   d. limited to personal selling and paid advertising.

_____ 3. Display advertising is easy to spot because it is:
   a. usually sold by the column inch or fraction of a page.
   b. something that is put in your shop window.
   c. less graphic than classified advertising.
   d. most effective for products that require that they be in motion for demonstration purposes.

_____ 4. Point-of-purchase displays:
   a. always match your merchandising scheme.
   b. are silent salespeople.
   c. are never free.
   d. are primarily available to customers in the industrial and government markets.

_____ 5. Cooperative advertising:
   a. is usually more expensive than other forms of advertising.
   b. is always based on the national ad rate.
   c. rarely is subsidized by the vendor.
   d. none of the above.

_____ 6. A winning promotional mix:
   a. is the most effective blend of all elements to reach the target customer.
   b. consists of product development, distribution channels, and the four P's.
   c. is the same as the product mix, only with more flair.
   d. should be blended carefully to nullify the impact of random consumer perception.

_____ 7. A press kit should:
   a. include photographs of principals, the facility, and the product or service in use.
   b. relate newsworthy facts about the firm.

    c. be presented in an attractive folder to influential representatives of the media.

    d. all of the above.

_____ 8. Coupons:

    a. give you positive feedback on your promotion.

    b. should have an expiration date and multiple use disclaimers.

    c. should be coded to identify the source and tested in small quantities before major use.

    d. all of the above.

_____ 9. Direct mail:

    a. is most effective when the potential customers are few in number and can be accurately located.

    b. must have twelve-digit zip code addresses.

    c. needs a response of at least 50% to justify its use.

    d. is the least sophisticated form of communication with your customers.

_____ 10. Commission sales representatives:

    a. are a fixed business cost.

    b. require no training or field assistance.

    c. should always be avoided because they lack motivation.

    d. none of the above.

Short-Answer

1. Study the list in chapter 6 on "The Right Promotional Mix," and then list three to six components of your promotional strategy.

    _____   _____

    _____   _____

    _____   _____

2. Clip or copy three to five examples of free ink for a small business in your area. Describe them.

    1.

    2.

    3.

    4.

    5.

3. Free ink/free air (publicity) can save you a lot of advertising dollars. On a separate sheet of paper, use a mind map or list to brainstorm ways you can get free ink for your business.

4. A trade show can be important to your business. List the upcoming trade shows in your area. (*Hint:* you can get information from trade associations and local convention centers; from *Exhibit Schedule,* published by Successful Meetings, 1422 Chestnut Street, Philadelphia, PA 19102; and from *Trade Show Convention Guide,* Budd Publications, Box 7, New York, NY 10004.)_____

    _____

    _____

5. At the Show. What devices are people using to gather primary data on their potential customers?

    _____

    _____

6. At the Show. Look around. What surprised you?

    _____

    _____

7. At the Show. On a separate sheet of paper, draw a rough diagram of the main floor. Enter the names of exhibitors. Label eating areas, restrooms, entrances, exits. Then use arrows to indicate traffic flow. Where is the most traffic?

8. List three trade associations that deal with firms in your industry and in your market area that might be helpful to you:

_____

_____

_____

9. Develop two techniques for building a mailing list for your business:

1. _____

_____

2. _____

_____

10. List three sources that will help you do secondary market research:

1. _____

_____

2. _____

_____

3. _____

_____

11. Finish this sentence: Proprietors of small firms are usually effective in the selling function because

_____

_____

12. List three actions you can take to enhance your personal profile and call attention to your business:

1. _____

2. _____

3. _____

13. List three media kit sources that contain information on at least one segment of your market:

1. _____

2. _____

3. _____

14. What three ways can a map help you conduct market research?

1. _____

2. _____

3. _____

15. List three government agencies and/or public utilities that might have information on the projected growth of an area:

1. _____

2. _____

3. _____

16. Describe how a sales leads club works: _____
_____
_____

17. Brainstorm a novel promotion that would be appropriate for your business:
_____
_____

18. Rough out a promotional budget. Try to list your promotional tools (advertising, free ink, contest, direct mail, etc.) in priority order and then estimate what each would cost.

    Tool   **Cost**

    1.

    2.

    3.

    4.

    5.

19. After you rough out your promotional budget, write down the first step you need to take to get things rolling:
_____
_____

7

Location

Matching

Match each numbered item with the lettered statement that best describes it.

1. anchor tenant
2. food store
3. gross lease
4. 100% location
5. master plan
6. security factors

7. triple net lease
8. signage
9. census tracts
10. lease with option to purchase
11. cost per square foot
12. zoning

13. CC & Rs
14. traffic counts
15. labor pool
16. footprint
17. local newspapers
18. retail lease

_____ A. one type of destination location
_____ B. major foot traffic draw for customers
_____ C. usually provided by police departments and insurance companies
_____ D. sign requirements and where sign may be placed
_____ E. useful to ensure rights of occupancy at the discretion of the tenant
_____ F. how monthly rent is often quoted on commercial or industrial buildings
_____ G. U.S. government data on demographics of a specific area
_____ H. a projected plan for growth or redevelopment of specific land use
_____ I. fixed rent without additional assessments
_____ J. mythical perfect site—a useful benchmark
_____ K. tenant can be charged for taxes, insurance, improvements in addition to base rental
_____ L. often a source of recent market data in specific areas
_____ M. covers conditions and restrictions that are a part of the deed
_____ N. how much space a building takes up on the lot
_____ O. provided by the department of highways or independent research firms
_____ P. regulation for use, policed by city or county government
_____ Q. available workers often listed by occupation
_____ R. a lease that may be long and have many restrictions

True/False

Determine whether each statement is true or false and enter a T (True) or F (False) in the space.

_____ 1. A 100% location is mythical and probably doesn't exist.
_____ 2. A good location is more important for a brand new business than for an existing one.
_____ 3. A plumbing service business does not require a high traffic location.
_____ 4. A manufacturing business might play it smarter to locate near raw materials and a labor pool than near its customers.
_____ 5. A small retail merchant does not need to worry about drawing traffic generated by nearby stores.

_____ 6. Part of your location consideration should be to check on the level of municipal services.

_____ 7. If you have a great business, your customers will always find you.

_____ 8. High visibility can save you some advertising dollars.

_____ 9. Business locations have life cycles.

_____ 10. Real estate leasing agents are expensive, and you should do your best to avoid them.

_____ 11. An anchor tenant is found most commonly in boatyards.

_____ 12. Highway departments frequently do traffic-flow studies.

_____ 13. Most local planning agencies will let you view their master plan for an area.

_____ 14. Public utility companies have no need to do long-range planning activities on population growth and energy needs.

_____ 15. Once you settle on your location, there is no need for you to double-check with municipal authorities on restrictions and land use.

_____ 16. Leases are drawn by landlords and their lawyers and there is little in a lease to protect the tenant.

_____ 17. The smartest way to break a lease is to throw a gigantic and obnoxious lease-breaking party.

_____ 18. Net and gross leases are exactly the same except that a gross lease is much less expensive.

_____ 19. A good lease, like a good contract, is fair to both parties and tells each what to expect from the other.

_____ 20. Newspapers and chambers of commerce have useful information on local markets.

Multiple-Choice

Select the best response for each item and enter the corresponding letter in the space.

_____ 1. A good example of a destination location is:
   a. a food store or doctor's office.
   b. a gift shop specializing in china.
   c. a flower shop.
   d. usually marked in red on your city map.

_____ 2. Gross leases are:
   a. usually based on cost per square yard.
   b. agreements that include everything in the monthly rate.
   c. less common today than in the 1970s.
   d. to make rent a variable cost for the tenant.

_____ 3. Generally speaking, a 100% location:
   a. has no competition within a ten-mile radius.
   b. costs twice as much as a 50% location.
   c. is the perfect place for your business.
   d. must be visible from the street.

_____ 4. A mall location:
   a. has more foot traffic.
   b. has the most restrictions.
   c. usually comes with a fixed plus percentage of sales rate.
   d. all of the above.

_____ 5. The best location:
   a. is away from all competition.
   b. is always the least expensive place for your business.
   c. makes you accessible to customers, suppliers, workers, transportation, and so on.
   d. demands a sharp building, expensively maintained and well-lighted for security reasons.

_____ 6. A gift shop, to be successful:
   a. needs to be close to high-traffic anchor retailers.
   b. is a destination location.
   c. will do well near hardware stores.
   d. will usually be leased on an industrial net basis.

_____   7. A labor pool:
     a. is a place for workers to relax during inclement weather.
     b. is termed illegal under the Taft–Hartley Act.
     c. will affect the location of a manufacturing firm more than a service firm.
     d. is seldom a concern in a high-income area.

_____   8. A cost of living cap or ceiling on the rent:
     a. will be of little help if hyperinflation occurs.
     b. will limit your annual rent increase.
     c. is standard on most commercial leases.
     d. tends to favor the landlord.

_____   9. Restrictive covenants:
     a. are discriminatory and illegal.
     b. dictate what you cannot do to a tenant.
     c. should be read and understood before you sign your lease.
     d. both a and b.

_____   10. The commercial lease:
     a. is a standard legal form and, by statute cannot be modified.
     b. is designed by the building owner to protect the owner's interest.
     c. need not be shown to a prospective tenant's legal counsel because it has already been drawn up by a competent attorney and all lawyers are members of the same bar.
     d. is usually no more binding than the lease signed by apartment dwellers.

Short-Answer

1. List the elements of a 100% location for your business:

    _____

    _____

    _____

2. List five kinds of businesses that are destination locations. Then list five that are not:

Destination Locations	Not Destination Locations
1. _____	1. _____
2. _____	2. _____
3. _____	3. _____
4. _____	4. _____
5. _____	5. _____

3. On a separate sheet of paper, make a rough drawing of your ideal site location in a commercial or industrial center. In your drawing, label the anchor tenant, your potential neighbors if there's a vacant building you're looking at, competitors (if any), parking (count the slots available to you), access, traffic, peak hours. If you're looking at a specific building, focus on suitability. For example, would you want a hearing aid store next to a record store? A book shop next to an auto body shop? Will your customers need a map to find you?

4. Develop a ranking of commercial or industrial centers in your area and arrange in order of priority (which is best for your firm?).

    1. _____

    2. _____

3. _____

4. _____

5. Information on local crime rates can be obtained from:

_____

6. Information on local labor pools can be obtained from:

_____

7. List variables that need to be weighed when you're considering certain types of leases:

_____   _____   _____

_____   _____   _____

8. A high-visibility location could save you money that would normally be spent on:

_____

9. List three ways you can determine the going market rate of a square foot of space in your area:

1. _____

2. _____

3. _____

10. How much parking space will you need? _____ At what times of day can you anticipate

peak parking needs? _____

11. Locations, like people and products and industries, go through life cycles. Where is your location on the life-cycle yardstick?

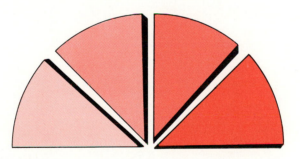

12. In what ways does the location affect a firm's image?

_____

_____

13. For your type of business, list some advantages of being

1. Close to competitors: _____

_____

_____

2. Away from competitors: _____

_____

_____

14. A mature business might have less need for a 100% location. Explain.

_____

_____

15. A lease that allows the landlord to charge tenants for taxes, insurance, and improvements is called a _____ lease.

16. A lease that calls for a fixed rate of rent per month is called a _____ lease.

17. An anchor tenant adds value to your location because:

_____

_____

18. A CPI cap in a lease accomplishes the following:

_____

_____

19. Only the following will legally release you from the obligations of a lease:

_____

_____

_____

8

Surprises You Can't Afford

Matching

Match each numbered item with the lettered statement that best describes it.

1. fringe benefits
2. partnerships
3. CC & Rs
4. workers' disability insurance
5. opportunity cost
6. specific business experience
7. energy audit
8. fidelity bond
9. licenses, police permit
10. building inspector
11. flood, fire, earthquake, and so on
12. misuse of product
13. shrinkage
14. huge increases in the prime rate
15. major supplier going out of business
16. penalty clause
17. owner only can sign checks

_____ A. have a high dissolution rate
_____ B. other payroll costs, like health plans, vacations, sick days, FICA
_____ C. covenants and restrictions contained in the deed that limit the use of real estate
_____ D. additional business cost, required in most states
_____ E. specific investment costs in terms of time and capital
_____ F. what creditors look for first in an entrepreneur
_____ G. insurance to protect you from dishonest employees
_____ H. supplied by most power companies
_____ I. although a nuisance, are there to protect you and the community
_____ J. may be required by city, county, and state agencies before you open your doors
_____ K. will force contractors to finish the job on schedule
_____ L. is a strong argument for secondary sources of supply
_____ M. should be factored into costs
_____ N. can become the problem of the manufacturer
_____ O. can eat your profit with high debt cost
_____ P. can be insured against
_____ Q. will give you more control over the firm's cash

True/False

Determine whether each statement is true or false and enter a T (True) or F (False) in the space.

_____ 1. It is better not to seek permission from building inspectors, because they'll just get in your hair and cause you tons of grief.
_____ 2. State and local controls are always in the best interests of small business.

_____ 3. Start-up costs for most small businesses usually run 47% below owner estimates.

_____ 4. A personal financial statement is a balance sheet.

_____ 5. Assets minus liabilities equal net worth.

_____ 6. People who keep a personal budget usually have less trouble understanding cash management.

_____ 7. Timing is a key planning ingredient.

_____ 8. Good planning includes a long list of what-ifs and optional strategies for dealing with changing circumstances.

_____ 9. An entrepreneur is as likely to underestimate the amount of time required to set up a small business as he is the amount of capital required.

_____ 10. Most entrepreneurs fail to calculate the true value of the time they invest in their firms.

_____ 11. Job benefits for employees rarely exceed 10% of salary.

_____ 12. Any new business is automatically exempted from Social Security (FICA) payments during its first 12 months of operation.

_____ 13. Small businesses are more likely to be embezzled by dishonest employees than larger firms.

_____ 14. It is much safer to have one giant customer than it is to nickel and dime yourself to death with a lot of smaller customers.

_____ 15. Planning is a day-to-day matter because even the near term is impossible to anticipate.

_____ 16. Every business should provide the owner with two sources of financial return.

Multiple-Choice

Select the best response for each item and enter the corresponding letter in the space.

_____ 1. A personal financial statement:
   a. is a balance sheet.
   b. is totally unlike the financial statement of a business.
   c. often includes goodwill.
   d. is seldom required if the owner is guaranteeing the debts of the firm.

_____ 2. Public utility companies:
   a. usually request advance deposits.
   b. can help you estimate your bills.
   c. will tell you how to save energy.
   d. all of the above.

_____ 3. City hall:
   a. has no enforcement power if you violate city codes.
   b. will tell you what special permits are required for your business.
   c. is full of fools who have an interest only in stopping you from making a living.
   d. will never be influenced by other established businesses who don't want to see you open.

_____ 4. Your first estimate of monthly expenses:
   a. will probably be lower than the real amount spent.
   b. will not be necessary, because estimating is a foolish waste of time. (Future profits are guaranteed to protect any overspending that occurs.)
   c. will probably be higher than the real amount spent.
   d. need not include minor details like office equipment and supplies.

_____ 5. Advertising expenses:
   a. will be most needed in your early months of operation.
   b. should be divided equally among all available media.
   c. should be placed under the firm control of a major advertising agency.
   d. should be adjusted downward if sales lag.

_____ 6. An insurance agent can provide you with the following types of protection:
   a. employee fidelity bond.
   b. partnership insurance.
   c. fire, theft, and liability.
   d. all of the above.

_____ 7. Your competitors:
    a. will always treat you fairly.
    b. will do all they can to keep you from getting their customers.
    c. will shop you for weaknesses.
    d. b and c.

_____ 8. The best way to minimize surprises is to:
    a. have lots of business experience.
    b. stay on top of your accounting reports.
    c. read trade journals, newspapers; attend trade shows.
    d. all of the above.

_____ 9. Which of the following will help you identify missing inventory?
    a. color coding.
    b. weekly lie detector test for employees.
    c. regular body search; regular inspection of employee homes.
    d. frequent and random counting of inventory.

_____ 10. Most inventory shrinkage is caused by:
    a. sophisticated embezzlers.
    b. employees.
    c. organized crime figures.
    d. customers who pilfer.

Short-Answer

1. List the agencies (if any) that will need to inspect or approve your business facility.

    1. _____   4. _____
    2. _____   5. _____
    3. _____   6. _____

2. Contact your local planning and zoning departments to learn what ordinances you will have to follow. Briefly note what you learn here: _____

_____

_____

_____

3. What unforeseen surprises did the small business owners you interviewed (in Action Step 9) encounter? _____

_____

4. Contact your local public utility for a forecast of increased energy costs for the next five to ten years. Request energy-saving guidelines for your small business. Summarize the guidelines here.

_____

_____

_____

5. List other investment options you could pursue with your money if you did not begin your own business. _____

6. Since you're thinking about starting your own business, devise an audit of your time for a realistic idea of how much time and energy you have to invest. Here's how. Use a two-week period. In a separate notebook, divide each day into 15-minute slots. For two weeks, write down what you did every 15 minutes. Start with the past two hours. What did you do?

Hour One	Hour Two

1st quarter:
2nd quarter:
3rd quarter:
4th quarter:
When you finish your time audit, sit down and study it. Ask yourself what percentage of your time did you have to rest? Do you have the tenacity to do sustained work? Where were you most excited? Where did insights occur?

7. If you're thinking about forming a partnership, list special provisions you need to include in your partnership agreement. (See chapter 12.)

_____

_____

_____

8. List in priority the possible circumstances that could adversely affect your business.

   1. _____

   2. _____

   3. _____

   4. _____

9. List at least two reasons you should think about bonding your employees. (What circumstances could arise that would make you wish you *had* bonded them?)

   1. _____

   _____

   2. _____

   _____

10. Contact a security alarm company to discuss your security needs. List the systems they recommend for small

    businesses like yours. _____

    _____

    _____

11. Identify a backup banker or capital source: _____

12. What techniques can be employed to evaluate the character and resources of a potential partner? (Helpful hint: to

    find out if you and your partner are really meshing, see chapter 13.) _____

    _____

13. Contact an insurance agent who specializes in small business. On a separate sheet of paper, list the types of coverage you'll need, along with prices for premiums.

14. Contact some vendors and find out what percentage of your sales will be offset by returns of defective goods. Write the percentage down:

    Vendor 1:

    Vendor 2:

    Vendor 3:

15. List areas in which your business might be liable: _____

    _____

    _____

    _____

9

Numbers and Shoebox Accounting

Matching

Match each numbered item with the lettered statement that best describes it.

1. turnover
2. projected profit and loss
3. cash-flow projection
4. projected sales forecast

5. return on investment
6. break-even point
7. cost of goods sold
8. fixed expenses

9. extended dating
10. net profit
11. gross profit

_____ A. sales minus cost of goods sold
_____ B. payment terms usually beyond 30 days
_____ C. that point where you make no profit and have no loss
_____ D. gross profit minus expenses
_____ E. anticipated sales for future time periods
_____ F. annual sales divided by average inventory investment
_____ G. how much profit you estimate you will earn
_____ H. the percentage rate of return on the capital invested in the business
_____ I. a projected analysis of working capital needs
_____ J. cost of inventory, including freight
_____ K. type of expenses required just to look like you're in business

True/False

Determine whether each statement is true or false and enter a T (True) or F (False) in the space.

_____ 1. High markup is usually needed for high-fashion items and items with a slow stock turn rate.
_____ 2. For the small business owner, most seasonal purchasing is done 6–11 months ahead.
_____ 3. Many seasonal vendors will extend credit well into the season.
_____ 4. In the travel and printing businesses, it's common practice to collect money before the product or service is delivered.
_____ 5. Because of slow receivables, the bed and breakfast business has slow cash flow problems.
_____ 6. The quicker you can resupply inventory, the more stock you need to carry.

_____ 7. Every business that extends credit should set aside a reserve for bad debt.

_____ 8. The manufacturing business has much less need for working capital than a service business of the same magnitude.

_____ 9. Writing checks on your business checking account will help you track expenses.

_____ 10. Most trade associations publish information on monthly sales percentages for their members.

_____ 11. Cash management means knowing where your cash is, and making sure you use it for maximum efficiency.

_____ 12. An accurate sales forecast is one key to developing a winning Business Plan.

_____ 13. A projected profit and loss statement will tell you when you're going to start making a profit.

_____ 14. When you do project profit and loss, you may also find out what legal form you should choose for your business.

_____ 15. One year of sales divided by the average inventory gives you the stock turnover rate.

_____ 16. As a general rule, the higher the stock turn, the higher your anticipated mark-up.

_____ 17. Gross profit minus expenses equals net profit.

_____ 18. No problems in a business are so serious that they can't be solved by giant increases in sales.

_____ 19. If a corporation anticipates a first-year loss, then the founders should consider starting out as a Subchapter S corporation.

_____ 20. Extended dating means a long courtship with your main vendor.

Multiple-Choice

Select the best response for each item and enter the corresponding letter in the space.

_____ 1. The term *break-even point* signifies:
   a. piercing the corporate veil.
   b. that period in business which is prior to making a hefty profit.
   c. a theoretical point between profit and loss.
   d. a time when cash flow is equalized.

_____ 2. Extended dating means:
   a. a long courtship between the entrepreneur and one of the target customers.
   b. extended payment terms.
   c. a process used to develop plums for the fresh fruit industry.
   d. none of the above.

_____ 3. Return on investment means:
   a. the percentage of earnings based on amount of investment.
   b. finding lost capital.
   c. dividends paid by a *Fortune* 500 corporation.
   d. retained earnings.

_____ 4. an income statement projected over months:
   a. traces the flow of cash through the business cycle.
   b. is a snapshot taken at an exact time in a business.
   c. requires an attorney to process it through the court system.
   d. is a moving picture of your business.

_____ 5. A balance sheet:
   a. consists of assets and liabilities.
   b. is very much unlike a personal financial statement.
   c. is no longer required by bankers when you apply for a loan.
   d. develops a finely tuned balance between profit and loss.

_____ 6. Turnover rate refers to:
   a. the timely rotation of dated stock.
   b. a figure you get when you divide annual sales by average inventory.
   c. rolling over bank assets worth more than $50,000.
   d. a ratio that, if reduced, will increase profitability by a specified percentage over the term specified.

_____ 7. Cost of goods sold:
   a. when deducted from sales will yield gross profit.
   b. shows cost less allowances of goods and materials.
   c. minus total expenses equals net profit before taxes.
   d. all of the above.

_____ 8. A cash flow statement:
   a. may include bank loans.
   b. shows total cash available for each month.
   c. allows you to identify cash needs.
   d. all of the above.

_____ 9. The income statement:
   a. tells you when you will make a profit.
   b. is a financial snap shot.
   c. gives you the net profit before taxes.
   d. both B and C.

_____ 10. A manufacturing business:
   a. is not capital intensive.
   b. will probably need cash for a long period of time.
   c. will have fewer cash flow problems than a bed and breakfast operation.
   d. none of the above.

Short-Answer

1. Project your sales percentages by the month for a 12-month period for a model business in your industry. For example, if the model business does 3% in January, you write 3% in the box. What's the percentage in February? In March?

   Jan. _____ %   Apr. _____ %   July _____ %   Oct. _____ %

   Feb. _____ %   May _____ %   Aug. _____ %   Nov. _____ %

   Mar. _____ %   June _____ %   Sept. _____ %   Dec. _____ %

2. Which financial projection is the most important and becomes the basis for all other financial projections: _____
   _____

3. When do you expect to become profitable? _____
   When would you change the legal form of your business? _____

4. What is your industry standard for a stock-turn ratio? _____
   What is your source? _____

5. What will your average mark-up cost be? _____

6. Depending on the business, customers pay _before_ delivery, _at time of_ delivery, or _after_ delivery. Learn the payment standards, lags, and so on in your business. When are your customers most likely to pay for services? _____
   _____

7. If you offer credit, what percentage might be uncollectible? _____

8. List the reasons for using written, numbered purchase orders:
   _____
   _____
   _____

9. Describe accounts receivable. _____

_____

10. Describe accounts payable. _____

_____

11. Briefly discuss the reasons for using a cash-flow projection. _____

_____

_____

12. What is a break-even point? How do you determine it? Let's follow one example.
    Your fixed expenses are $120,000.
    Your variable expenses are $1.07 per unit.
    You're selling the gizmo at $3.98 per unit.

$$\text{Break-even point (units)} = \frac{\$120,000}{\$2.91} = 41,237 \text{ (rounded)}$$

To figure break-even sales volume, multiply break-even units needed by selling price per unit.

$$41,237 \times \$3.98 = \$ \text{_____}$$

13. List three to six ways you can use your income statement.

_____   _____

_____   _____

_____   _____

14. What is an electronic spreadsheet? _____

_____

15. How are subchapter S corporations taxed? _____

_____

10

Buying a Business

Matching

Match each numbered item with the lettered statement that best describes it.

1. income stream
2. the deal
3. magic threshold
4. business brokers
5. escape hatch
6. covenant not to compete

7. financial records
8. accounts receivable
9. tangible assets
10. goodwill
11. ill will

12. sacrificed goods
13. earnout
14. decision to buy a business
15. apparently honest seller
16. bulk sales escrow

_____ A. a must when buying a business; among other things it helps you make sure inventory is not tied up by creditors
_____ B. seller must do something else for awhile
_____ C. intangible asset that seller will use to raise asking price
_____ D. point for tough negotiation because they keep losing value
_____ E. everything you can touch
_____ F. picture of an income stream
_____ G. means unhappy customers
_____ H. paying off the seller with future earnings
_____ I. distressed goods, usually sold at any price
_____ J. should be handled with logic, not emotion
_____ K. a signal for you to be suspicious; check out motives anyway
_____ L. one good reason for buying an ongoing business
_____ M. a shorthand way of talking about negotiating terms
_____ N. what you cross to get inside a business
_____ O. agents who sell businesses
_____ P. a device that allows you to back out of the purchase of a business painlessly

True/False

Determine whether each statement is true or false and enter a T (True) or F (False) in the space.

_____ 1. The overwhelming reason for buying a business that's already going instead of building one with your own hands is money.
_____ 2. The smart buyer will plunge into a business because of a sudden surge of raw emotion.

_____ 3. Every business in the country is for sale sometime.

_____ 4. Deals are like buses. If you miss one, another one will be along soon.

_____ 5. The investigative and information-gathering tactics for buying a business or for buying a franchise are very different.

_____ 6. Your best bet for finding a business to buy is to search the classified section of your local paper under Business Opportunities.

_____ 7. An earnest money deposit is to show the seller you are an interested buyer and not a lookie-loo.

_____ 8. The main function of an offer with an escape hatch is to cheat the IRS.

_____ 9. Goodwill is an example of a tangible asset.

_____ 10. The covenant not to compete is to keep the seller from opening a similar business in your market area.

_____ 11. A buyer should study the financial records for at least five years back if they are available.

_____ 12. Examples of tangible assets include real estate, equipment, fixtures, goodwill, and inventory.

_____ 13. In small business, success can rest on the shoulders of one or two key employees.

_____ 14. If you get it in writing, the IRS will allow you to deduct the cost of a covenant not to compete over the life of the covenant.

_____ 15. A smart seller is going to ask you to pay him for building up an invisible wealth of Goodwill.

_____ 16. Franchise means you're buying a license.

_____ 17. When you're evaluating a franchise, you go through most of the same steps you would use to evaluate a business for sale.

_____ 18. In the overall business-buying strategy, the terms for the deal are more important than the purchase price.

Multiple-Choice

Select the best response for each item and enter the corresponding letter in the space.

_____ 1. The overwhelming reason for buying a business that's already going instead of building one with your own hands is:
   a. attractive inventory.
   b. goodwill.
   c. income stream.
   d. employees who need the work.

_____ 2. An advantage of buying an ongoing business is:
   a. less cash up front.
   b. a good deal on fixtures and equipment.
   c. a possible bargain in hidden inventory.
   d. all of the above.

_____ 3. The last place to look for a business to buy is:
   a. your own network of associates.
   b. classified ads in the newspaper.
   c. local bankers.
   d. business brokers.

_____ 4. If you are asked to make an "earnest-money" deposit, you should handle it with:
   a. a cashier's check, made out to seller.
   b. an offer with an escape hatch.
   c. a lawyer.
   d. a CPA.

_____ 5. When you explore the inner intricacies of a business, check the following:
   a. financial history.
   b. your suppliers.
   c. the seller's motives.
   d. all of the above.

_____ 6. Accounts receivable that are six months old are worth approximately:
   a. 90 cents on the dollar.

b. 70 cents on the dollar.
c. 50 cents on the dollar.
d. 30 cents on the dollar.

_____   7. When checking out all the tangible assets, your job is to evaluate all of the following except:
a. real estate.
b. goodwill.
c. equipment/fixtures.
d. inventory.

_____   8. All of the following contribute to ill will except:
a. delivery.
b. cash.
c. advertising.
d. service.

_____   9. When evaluating a franchisor, check out all the following except:
a. blood types of franchisors.
b. how long this franchise has been in business.
c. who are the officers.
d. number of franchised operations like this one in existence.

_____   10. All of the questions below except for one are good to ask franchisors:
a. What's included in the franchise fee?
b. What's the duration of the agreement?
c. What level of training and service can you offer?
d. Say I get tired of this business—can I relocate any time I wish?

Short-Answer

1. Identify a business that you think is a real money machine.

   Type of business: _____

   Name: _____

   Address: _____

2. Where is it on the life cycle? _____

3. Once you've found the business and checked its position on the life cycle, gather more data about it. Visit your city or county planning office. What are the plans for the area for the next 5–10 years?

   Five years: _____

   _____

   Ten years: _____

   _____

4. Go to the site. On a separate sheet of paper, diagram everything you can.

   Traffic flow
   Major arterials
   Access
   Parking (Is parking lot a drop-off point for car-poolers?)
   Is building in good repair? (If not, what will it need before you move in?)

5. Take a good look at the customers. Describe what they're wearing: _____

   _____

   Describe what they're driving: _____

   _____

What can you deduce about their life-style? _____

_____

How far do they travel to get here?

   Longest distance: _____

   Shortest distance: _____

   Average distance: _____

Interview some customers. What do they say about the business? _____

_____

_____

_____

About the trading area? _____

_____

_____

Is there mostly goodwill? _____

Is there mostly ill will? _____

6. Investigate your neighbors. Which neighbors will help you draw customers?

_____

_____

_____

Which neighbors won't help?

_____

_____

_____

Where is your major competition? How strong is the competition? Can competitors move in to this trading area?

Location of competitors: _____

Strength: _____

Assault probabilities: _____

7. Move inside the business. Either contact the owner directly or get the assistance of a business opportunity broker. Study the sales figures. Check profit percentages. Evaluate the tangible assets. Of special importance are:

  a. Sales. List the percentage of change for last five years.

     1.

     2.

     3.

     4.

     5.

  b. Profit. List the profit figures for the last five years.

     1.

     2.

     3.

     4.

     5.

  c. Tangible assets. Using the format that follows, list all assets. Look at the books and write down the accounting value. Then go out into the marketplace and get the current value.

Asset	Accounting Value	Current Value
1. _____	_____	_____
2. _____	_____	_____
3. _____	_____	_____
4. _____	_____	_____

d. Terms. What kind of terms can you negotiate with the seller? (Try to get the seller to let you pay for the business out of profits you make after you take possession.)

_____

_____

_____

8. You'll want to know if the vendors who have been supplying the seller will continue to supply you, as the new owner. Interview them. Will vendors continue to supply you?

_____

_____

_____

What suggestions do they have for improving the business?

_____

_____

_____

Can you get credit terms? (What are they?)

_____

_____

_____

9. Rethink your moves. Does it look as if you could do better by starting your own business from scratch instead of buying this business?

_____

_____

_____

_____

11

Shaking the Money Tree

Matching

Match each numbered item with the lettered statement that best describes it.

1. capital
2. banker
3. bank
4. guaranteed loan
5. money guru
6. possible source of money
7. accounts receivable financing

8. BDCs
9. character
10. plastic
11. capacity
12. collateral
13. SBICs
14. Business Plan

15. vendor form
16. unsecured credit
17. venture capital firms
18. limited partner
19. private placement
20. going public

_____ A. shows you pay your bills on time
_____ B. one gateway to the world of money
_____ C. showcase for displaying all the ideas and information you've gathered in your venture adventure
_____ D. detailed information on each supplier
_____ E. life insurance
_____ F. provided by some banks and factoring firms
_____ G. knows more about money than you do
_____ H. goal is to increase employment within their specific state
_____ I. licensed by the SBA to provide money to small firms
_____ J. one type of SBA loan
_____ K. lenders who want equity participation
_____ L. regarded by some people as a formidable fortress or great modern cathedral
_____ M. tangible assets that can secure a loan
_____ N. your liquid cash
_____ O. earning power; ability to repay a loan
_____ P. street name for credit cards
_____ Q. guaranteeing loans and payments with your signature
_____ R. selling your securities in the open financial market
_____ S. investors who are not stockholders, have no liability
_____ T. capital stock sale to a limited group of investors

True/False

Determine whether each statement is true or false and enter a T (True) or F (False) in the space.

_____ 1. Money creates its own world, with its own customs, rules, myths.

_____ 2. "Collateral" indicates that you have a visible money stream for lenders to dip into.

_____ 3. Banks are conservative, and they probably won't want to lend you start-up money unless you sign over your house.

_____ 4. People lend money to people.

_____ 5. One good way to conserve cash is to persuade your customers to give you cash deposits when they place orders.

_____ 6. When goods are moving slowly, the best strategy is to shelve them in the back room or warehouse and hold until next season.

_____ 7. It is best to avoid collateralizing your loans, unless you have no choice.

_____ 8. When you have to borrow money, you should shop around.

_____ 9. Buying smart is not nearly as important as raising money or selling.

_____ 10. When negotiating, you should use a lot of open-ended questions like: "what else can you do for me?"

_____ 11. When you're ready, it's a good idea to shake the money trees close to home first.

_____ 12. Borrowing on your life insurance can be a good source of money for your new business.

_____ 13. An unsecured personal line of credit from your bank is not a good source of money for a brand-new business.

_____ 14. Credit unions are considered nonbank lending sources.

_____ 15. The SBA has only one kind of loan program: "guaranteed."

_____ 16. The SBA makes fewer guaranteed loans than any other type.

_____ 17. SBICs (Small Business Investment Corporations) are privately operated companies that are licensed by the state within which they operate.

_____ 18. Venture capitalists come in lots of shapes—family firms (Rockefeller), industrial arms (GE), bank arms (B of A), and other arms (private groups of investors).

_____ 19. Venture capitalists will usually let you run the show if you give them a healthy ROI.

_____ 20. How well you buy is not nearly as important as how well you sell.

Multiple-Choice

Select the best response for each item and enter the corresponding letter in the space.

_____ 1. Before hunting the great money tree, you should:
  a. sit at the feet of a money guru.
  b. sketch out your Business Plan.
  c. befriend a banker, and befriend a backup banker.
  d. All of the above.

_____ 2. All of the following questions are good to ask your prospective banker except:
  a. What do you think of my Business Plan?
  b. Do you lend money to large businesses?
  c. Do you make SBA-guaranteed loans?
  d. What are your criteria for loans?

_____ 3. Which of the following is not a good strategy for dealing with bankers?
  a. asking for money before you ask for advice and information.
  b. luring a banker to your own turf.
  c. negotiating for your line of credit or your loan while you're still working.
  d. getting yourself a backup bank while you're negotiating with another bank.

_____ 4. Which of the following is not a good tip on saving?
  a. work out of your home.
  b. lease your equipment.

c. borrow money on goods (inventory) that aren't selling.

d. get your landlord to make onsite improvements and finance the cost over the term of the lease.

_____ 5. Which of the following items do you want to ask for on your Vendor Form?

a. amount of minimum purchase.

b. terms of dating or extended payment.

c. nearest competitor handling the same line.

d. all of the above.

_____ 6. All of the following are reasons why lenders would want to lend you money for your business except:

a. no competition.

b. good marketing strategy.

c. good profit picture.

d. good ROI (return on investment).

_____ 7. Which of the following is not a good tip on saving?

a. use as little commercial space as you can.

b. keep your liquid cash in a safe place (like a lock box).

c. shop nonbank lenders.

d. look into R & D partnerships for product development funds.

_____ 8. The following are good sources of money for your new business, except:

a. refinancing your car, boat, camper, or airplane.

b. researching your assets (coin collections, old baseball cards, and so on).

c. selling that crummy stock you've been holding.

d. finding a competitor that's doing a good deal of business and borrowing from him.

_____ 9. Which of the following is not a good source of money for your small business?

a. venture capital firm.

b. stock brokerage house.

c. Goodwill Industries.

d. credit union.

_____ 10. It's best to line up personal credit:

a. after you begin your new venture.

b. when you are in a cash bind.

c. before you leave your salaried job.

d. Personal credit is useless for a business.

Short-Answer

1. Visit your local bank. Find out the following:

A. Name of chief officer:

_____

B. Do they lend money to small businesses? _____

C. Do they make SBA-guaranteed loans? _____

   1. If yes, do they lend money to start-ups? _____

   2. If yes, do they have a minimum and maximum loan amount? _____

   3. If yes, what are the time-periods for repayment?

   _____

   4. If yes, what's the percentage rate? _____

D. What are their criteria for loan approval?

_____

_____

E. Ask them to describe the loan approval process.

F. Do they offer lines of credit? If so, under what conditions and what terms?

_____

_____

G. Ask this question: "Would you review my Business Plan?"

Answer: _____

2. When you have found one bank that makes small business loans, phone some more until you locate two or three that make loans to start-ups.

Backup Bank 1

A. Name of bank: _____

B. Lending rate: _____

C. SBA-guaranteed loans: _____

D. Contact person: _____

Backup Bank 2

A. Name of bank: _____

B. Lending rate: _____

C. SBA-guaranteed loans: _____

D. Contact person: _____

Backup Bank 3

A. Name of bank: _____

B. Lending rate: _____

C. SBA-guaranteed loans: _____

D. Contact person: _____

3. When talking to bankers, try to get insight into how they evaluate small business loans. Try these questions for probes:

A. What types of businesses are they most interested in?

_____

_____

B. Are there any they won't lend money to?

_____

_____

C. Ask your banker to rate each of the items below in relation to the loan-decision process. What's important? What's not important? Try to get your banker to use a 1–10 scale.
   1. target customer
   2. amount and type of competition
   3. industry trends
   4. product or service
   5. marketing strategy
   6. method of selling
   7. profit picture, both gross and net
   8. return on investment
   9. founders' team
   10. personal assets or net worth

4. List friends or relatives who might be willing to invest in your business (or lend you money for the business):

_____

_____

_____

5. Explore your list in question 4, above. Select two or three people from that list to talk to. Let them see your Business Plan. Talk over the possibilities of getting them on board as investors.
   A. On a separate sheet of paper, list all their objections.
   B. Then list their positive comments.
   C. For each objection, come up with a solution. There's a good chance you'll get the same objections from bankers and venture capital people. On your sheet of paper, summarize your findings as shown:

Objection	Solution
1.	1.
2.	2.
3.	3.
etc.	etc.

6. Let's have some fun. If you're in a class, form several teams. If you're not in a class, get together some friends and relatives. Develop two lists. The first list contains the areas you believe the federal government should get out of. The second list contains areas where you think the government could be of more help. Compile your findings, vote on the major suggestions, and compose a letter to your congressman, state senator, legislator, assemblyman, alderman, senator, or other representative.
   A. Areas where the government could be more helpful:

   1. _____

   2. _____

   3. _____

   4. _____

   5. _____

   6. _____

   7. _____

   8. _____

   B. Areas the government should get out of:

   1. _____

   2. _____

   3. _____

   4. _____

   5. _____

   6. _____

   7. _____

   8. _____

12

Legal Concerns

Matching

Match each numbered item with the lettered statement that best describes it.

1. corporate shield
2. partnership agreement
3. lawyer
4. partnerships
5. corporation
6. limited partnership

7. sole proprietor
8. general partner
9. personal guarantee
10. corporate reports
11. form a subchapter S corporation
12. corporate president

13. shareholders
14. offshore corporations
15. a corporate charter
16. minute book
17. do-it-yourself corporation

_____ A. unlimited liability
_____ B. a legal form which gives the owner absolute control
_____ C. limits liability of noncorporate investors
_____ D. a way of organizing your business so that you get the lowest tax rate
_____ E. taxed as an individual
_____ F. member of the taxi squad; not needed to form sole proprietorship
_____ G. a written contract between two or more people that describes duties, sharing of profits, and dissolution
_____ H. stands between you and your creditors
_____ I. are tricky and may not save you money
_____ J. another name for corporate owners
_____ K. must be an employee of the business
_____ L. if you are losing money
_____ M. a good source of secondary research material when you are studying legal forms of business
_____ N. often required by bankers to secure a corporate loan
_____ O. must be kept current
_____ P. may not provide the benefits you need
_____ Q. tells the state what your corporation will be doing

True/False

Determine whether each statement is true or false and enter a T (True) or F (False) in the space.

_____ 1. A company which is incorporated in Delaware can only do business in California as a foreign corporation.
_____ 2. Most growth businesses do not need outside infusions of cash.
_____ 3. A Sub S corporation is limited to 75 owners.
_____ 4. Sub S corporate owners have unlimited liability.
_____ 5. A sole proprietor is limited to setting aside only $500 per year for retirement.
_____ 6. All corporate fiscal tax years must end on December 31.

_____ 7. Active owners of a corporation are known as employees.

_____ 8. A partnership agreement, drawn up by a lawyer, is required in order to establish a general partnership.

_____ 9. When setting up a corporation, you should secure the services of a "hot" trial attorney.

_____ 10. A corporation usually has more money-raising ability than other legal forms of business ownership.

_____ 11. In a limited partnership, one of the partners must be a general partner.

_____ 12. A corporation is said to have snob appeal.

_____ 13. To the consumer, the legal form of business ownership is often invisible.

_____ 14. You can form a partnership with a handshake.

_____ 15. In 1982, Congress changed the laws to discourage incorporation by professionals like lawyers and doctors.

_____ 16. Once you are incorporated lenders are less likely to seek a personal guarantee.

Multiple-Choice

Select the best response for each item and enter the corresponding letter in the space.

_____ 1. A partnership:
   a. is a shield between you and trouble.
   b. will make you immortal.
   c. is taxed at the same rate as an individual.
   d. is very difficult to establish.

_____ 2. A sole proprietor has:
   a. absolute control; no need for written agreements; lots of money-raising ability; limited liability.
   b. divided control; no need for written agreements; limited money-raising ability; limited liability.
   c. absolute control; need for written agreements; limited money-raising ability; unlimited liability.
   d. absolute control; no need for written agreements; limited money-raising ability; unlimited liability.

_____ 3. A corporation has:
   a. shared control; a need for a lawyer to form; snob appeal; cancellation by death.
   b. shared control; lots of good reasons for a lawyer to form; snob appeal; an adjustable tax year.
   c. divided control; no need for written agreements; unlimited liability; adjustable tax year.
   d. absolute control; limited liability; adjustable tax year; no need for written agreements.

_____ 4. A limited partnership has:
   a. at least two partners; an overwhelming need for written agreements; moderate capital-raising ability.
   b. absolute control; no need for written agreements; a tax tier divided into four stages.
   c. shared control with limited partner; no need for written agreements; personal tax rate.
   d. control by general partner; no need for written agreements; a four-stage tax tier, graduated by increments of $25,000.

_____ 5. Which of the following questions is not helpful when you're dealing with a prospective lawyer?
   a. What kind of signals suggest that I should designate my company stock as IRS Section 1244?
   b. Can you give me a concrete example of how IRS Section 368 (a) (b) works?
   c. How does my corporation handle the "depreciation recapture" rule?
   d. Can you give me a concrete example of how the Bernoulli effect relates to cash flow?

_____ 6. Whom would be least helpful when using your network to search for a good lawyer?
   a. your friends
   b. local business associations.
   c. local bar association.
   d. local bankers.

_____ 7. All of the following are true about programmer/entrepreneur Paul Webber except:
   a. Paul was a computer programmer.
   b. Paul sold out to Jerry.
   c. Mildred became Paul's new partner.
   d. Mildred didn't know the business.

_____ 8. You limit your personal liability when you:
- a. form a corporation.
- b. form a sole proprietorship.
- c. become a general partner.
- d. sign a personal guarantee.

_____ 9. As a sole proprietor, you:
- a. upgrade your image.
- b. control your fiscal year.
- c. guarantee continuity.
- d. none of the above.

_____ 10. What a corporation won't do:
- a. limit your liability.
- b. eliminate taxes altogether.
- c. let you upgrade your image.
- d. let you set aside more dollars for retirement.

Short-Answer

Note: Items 1 to 4 can be completed as either an individual or class project.

1. Find a lawyer who has worked with several small businesses. Ask small business owners whom they have worked with and whom they would recommend to help you with your start-up.
   - a. Find the owners through:
     1. Chamber of commerce (See if you can attend a meeting as a guest.)
     2. Local bankers
     3. Local accountants
     4. Leads clubs
     5. Local shopping centers or business parks (entrepreneurs love to talk about business).
   - b. On a separate sheet of paper, list the names you come up with. Use the following headings:

Name of Lawyer	Source	Recommend?

   - c. Continue the list until at least one lawyer has been recommended three or four times.
2. Select a name from C, above. Give the lawyer a call. Say you're starting a new business and you're in the process of selecting an attorney and that he or she has been recommended by several owners. You'd like to arrange a get-acquainted meeting. If there is no charge, set up a meeting. If there is a charge, go to the next name on the list.
3. Once you get a meeting set up, ask the following questions:
   - a. Does working with small businesses provide the bulk of revenue for your practice?
   - b. Can you give me the names of small businesses you've worked with? Preferably one sole proprietor, one partnership, and one corporation?
   - c. Could you give me a breakdown of different types of fees? What fee basis do you suggest for working with a new start-up like mine?
   - d. What's the extent of your experience with real estate leases? What's a normal charge for reviewing a lease?
   - e. Are there other small business professionals you would recommend who might help me?

     1. Accountant: _____

     2. Banker: _____

     3. Insurance agent: _____

     4. Tax person: _____
   - f. Have you ever worked with a client who bought or sold a business?

Name: _____

Name: _____

g. If yes, what are the major items to watch for in a buy-out? In a sale?

_____

_____

_____

4. After your meeting, write down your reactions to the meeting. Do it ASAP so that you won't forget.

a. Comfort-level—Did you feel comfortable with this person?

b. Confusion quotient—Could you understand what he or she was saying?

c. Expertise—Did you feel he or she knew the ins and outs of the world of small business?

d. Other—Write your reactions here.

5. Team Project. If possible, divide your group into three teams—sole proprietors, partners, and corporate types. Each team will then do in-depth research on the pros and cons of one type of legal form of business ownership. Select a spokesperson from each team to present findings. Develop a matrix grid (see chapter 3 for a model), and rate all three forms.
   a. Suggested sources:
      1. Books
         Inc. Yourself, McQuown
         How to Form Your Own Corporation without a Lawyer for Under $50, Nicholas
         Incorporating Your Business, Kirk
      2. Recent articles
         Inc. magazine
         Venture magazine
         Wall Street Journal
      3. Interviews with local business owners (Ask them the pros and cons of their type of ownership.)
      4. Attorneys, accountants, and other professionals
   b. Categories for organizing your research:
      1. Ease of starting
      2. Ability to raise capital
      3. Liability
      4. Costs
      5. Lifespan
      6. Government regulation or control
      7. Personal interest
      8. Decision-making process
      9. Power to attract key employees
      10. Strengths and weaknesses of management team
      11. Taxes
      12. Divided authority
      13. Possible disagreements
      14. General partnership
      15. Limited partnership
      16. General corporation
      17. Sub S corporation

13
Building a Winning Team

Matching

Match each numbered item with the lettered statement that best describes it.

1. entrepreneur
2. enterprise
3. DISC
4. D
5. I

6. S
7. C
8. top-heavy team
9. brainstorming
10. Harry R. Marquez

11. successful team building
12. Janet Ames
13. balance
14. one-to-one interviews
15. secret ballot

_____ A. the last step in a large team-building process, when team members select teammates
_____ B. diplomatic, accurate, understands need for control, gets job done, can establish standard operating procedures
_____ C. a French word that means master architect, master builder
_____ D. industry, money, initiative
_____ E. the secret is to analyze yourself first
_____ F. DISC scale—stands for Influencing
_____ G. everybody interviews everybody else
_____ H. Dominance and Influence types all over the shop, competing like crazy, not answering the phones
_____ I. personality profile, useful for team-building
_____ J. DISC scale—stands for Dominance
_____ K. DISC scale—stands for Steadiness
_____ L. case study entrepreneur who was bright, quick, impatient, a dreamer
_____ M. one way to utilize your precious people-resources
_____ N. DISC scale—stands for Compliant
_____ O. the essential ingredient of a successful team

True/False

Determine whether each statement is true or false and enter a T (True) or F (False) in the space.

_____ 1. The word *entrepreneur* comes from the Latin *il miglior fabbro,* which means "the little craftsman."
_____ 2. Harry R. Marquez was a poor student.
_____ 3. A company is no better than its people.
_____ 4. A small business management team doesn't need balance so much as it needs salespeople to clear out the inventory.
_____ 5. The DISC system was developed in the late seventies by Jacob Bernoulli, a psychologist working in a lab with rats. The copyright is owned by Bernoulli Effect, Inc.

_____ 6. The beauty of the DISC grid is that it shows at a glance where you are and what DISC types will help you get a balanced team together.

_____ 7. On the DISC grid, Harry R. Marquez is an I, or Influencing type of person.

_____ 8. Frederick R. Winslow, on the other hand, is a definite S, which stands for Steadiness.

_____ 9. Janet Ames, the woman who came to work at Marquez Robotics as manager, was a C.

_____ 10. The smaller the organization, the more important the team.

_____ 11. Networking your competitors and vendors is a good way to build a winning team with people who know the business.

_____ 12. If you're first-rate, you'll hire first-rate people.

_____ 13. If you're second-rate, you'll also hire first-rate people because you'll realize you need them.

_____ 14. Happiness is knowing who you are—and being able to exploit it.

_____ 15. Given the chance, people will hire themselves.

_____ 16. Your business can't grow until it has the right people.

_____ 17. Charlene Webb built a team of part-time workers who did more to help the store than full-time employees.

Multiple-Choice

Select the best response for each item and enter the corresponding letter in the space.

_____ 1. The work *entrepreneur* comes from the Latin verb:
  a. *bigetan.*
  b. *pre-hendere.*
  c. *prise.*
  d. *Star Trek.*

_____ 2. Mind movies include:
  a. slides of your trip.
  b. sights.
  c. fun people you met along the way.
  d. all of the above.

_____ 3. Harry R. Marquez started a company that built:
  a. hot sports cars.
  b. computers.
  c. robots.
  d. lasers.

_____ 4. Frederick S. Winslow was a good member of the Marquez Team because he had a solid background in:
  a. sales.
  b. inventing.
  c. designing.
  d. finance.

_____ 5. In team building it is important to:
  a. build your team before it's too late.
  b. test them out before it starts costing you money.
  c. hire good people, then listen to them.
  d. all of the above.

_____ 6. The Harry R. Marquez personality analysis concluded that Harry:
  a. understands need for procedures and controls.
  b. is a dreamer.
  c. is diplomatic with everyone.
  d. all of the above.

_____ 7. Which of the following personality styles does *not* form part of the DISC acronym?
  a. Dominance.
  b. Sado-masochism.

　　　　c. Influencing of others.
　　　　d. Compliance.
_____　　8. Rudy Bowman, a classic S, is no slouch as a team member. Steadies are important to the team because they:
　　　　a. are extremely creative.
　　　　b. make good managers.
　　　　c. love to control a very small turf.
　　　　d. hog the spotlight and are good at entertaining the clients.
_____　　9. Richard White developed a step-by-step method of teambuilding, which involved all of these except:
　　　　a. Carl Rogers encounter groups.
　　　　b. ice-breaker.
　　　　c. one-to-one interviews.
　　　　d. secret balloting.
_____　10. E. G. Bogard turned out to be a Developer. Which does not fit Mr. Bogard?
　　　　a. prefers innovative solutions.
　　　　b. displays lots of self-reliance.
　　　　c. loves to operate the telephone switchboard.
　　　　d. fears boredom.

Short-Answer

1. Take a breather and think about your trip so far.
   a. What have you learned?

   _____

   _____

   _____

   b. Has it been fun?

   _____

   _____

   c. Whom have you met that you found interesting, exciting, or especially helpful?

Name	Personality Type
1. _____	_____
	_____
2. _____	_____
	_____
3. _____	_____
	_____

2. Brainstorm your ideal team.
   a. Sit down with a few friends, relatives, or classmates who have a good feel for the type of business you plan to start. Ask everyone to list your strengths and weaknesses. (You can tell them briefly about the DISC scale and ask them whether you're a D, I, S, or C.) Compile their analyses here. Then thank them and go on to part B alone.

Strengths	Weaknesses	DISC Type
_____	_____	_____
_____	_____	_____
_____	_____	_____

b. Once you discover how people perceive you, it's time to brainstorm the other members of your ideal team—people who will balance your strengths and weaknesses. What kind of people do you need for balance? Use the spaces provided to list your ideal team members.

Job Strengths	Personal Qualities	DISC Type
1. _____	_____	_____
2. _____	_____	_____
3. _____	_____	_____
4. _____	_____	_____
5. _____	_____	_____

Do any of the people who are helping you fit the ideal team? Who? _____

_____

_____

Why? _____

_____

What would it take to get them on your team? _____

_____

_____

3. Now that you have an idea what kind of team you need, take your thoughts out into the business arena and see how many players you can find.

Name	Team Position	Now Employed	DISC Type
a. _____	_____	_____	_____
b. _____	_____	_____	_____
c. _____	_____	_____	_____
d. _____	_____	_____	_____
e. _____	_____	_____	_____

4. Bring your new team together (or form a team with your classmates) and learn what they think of your organization. What should it look like? What image should it project? How can they help? Brainstorm some company objectives and organizational ideas. Keep track of your team's ideas on a separate sheet of paper.

14

The Entrepreneur's Toolkit

Matching

Match each numbered item with the lettered statement that best describes it.

1. defining problems and tasks
2. applications software
3. micro
4. fax machine

5. electronic spreadsheet
6. word processing
7. computer hardware
8. memory

9. operating system
10. modem

_____ A. will fit on a desk; often called a personal computer
_____ B. will allow a document to be transferred over telephone lines
_____ C. the portion of the computer that you can see and touch
_____ D. the program that drives the computer
_____ E. capacity to store information
_____ F. program designed to perform a specific function
_____ G. a generic term for computerized accounting software
_____ H. the first step toward considering the purchase of a computer
_____ I. required in order to have a telephone connection between computers
_____ J. a highly efficient and flexible capacity for creating letters, documents, etc.

True/False

Determine whether each statement is true or false and enter a T (True) or F (False) in the space.

_____ 1. It is a violation of copyright law to copy and sell proprietary software.
_____ 2. Computer hardware is the program that drives the computer.
_____ 3. A computer system is both hardware and software.
_____ 4. A modem will let your computer talk to another computer.
_____ 5. The most important consideration in buying your first computer system is dealing until you squeeze the price down to a respectable level.
_____ 6. A hard disk or Winchester drive is far less expensive than a floppy disk drive.
_____ 7. A floppy disk is a defective hard disk.

_____ 8. When a disk becomes "floppier" through exposure to humidity, and also through extended use, it is now in the "mature stage" and will allow hardware to interface with programs from any operating system whatsoever.

_____ 9. A new microcomputer should go through its burn-in period in a very warm office situation.

_____ 10. Fifty percent or more of your computer budget should be allocated to software.

_____ 11. Computerphobia is a disease that occurs when a user-friendly program is debugged and the result is electric shock and information sickness.

_____ 12. The first step before purchasing a computer should be to define the problems that need solving in your business.

_____ 13. More and more, you need to understand programming languages (BASIC, Pascal, FORTRAN, COBOL) before purchasing a computer for business use.

_____ 14. Computers are useful in the performance of repetitive tasks.

_____ 15. There are good reasons for purchasing a small home computer before you need one in your business.

_____ 16. The experts say that when you're buying a computer, you should select the hardware on the basis of a well-known logo, then find software to fit, then begin developing applications to your particular type of business.

_____ 17. Microcomputers are of small value in spreadsheet analysis.

_____ 18. It can take 30–90 days to switch from a manual accounting system to a computerized system.

_____ 19. When shopping for a computer system, you should find a microcomputer store that has salespeople who understand small business problems and how to solve them.

_____ 20. There is a strong chance that word-processing software will make business use of the typewriter obsolete.

Multiple-Choice

Select the best response for each item and enter the corresponding letter in the space.

_____ 1. The first step in purchasing a computer should be:
   a. evaluating your physical space availability.
   b. learning a programming language.
   c. looking for a well-known company logo so you'll be assured of service and support.
   d. evaluating your needs.

_____ 2. Computers are most useful:
   a. in performing repetitive tasks.
   b. in digesting the inertial flow produced by AT&T's UNIX.
   c. in performing one-time functions.
   d. in developing antidotes to the Bernoulli Effect as it relates to corporate time management.

_____ 3. Powerful word processing programs can:
   a. speed up letter composition.
   b. personalize form letters.
   c. merge names and addresses from a mailing list.
   d. all of the above.

_____ 4. Some word processors have the capacity to:
   a. correct spelling.
   b. sign your name to letters.
   c. work without electrical power.
   d. both A and B.

_____ 5. A floppy disk:
   a. is warm and soft.
   b. contains instructions for the hardware.
   c. can be played at different rpms.
   d. is not subject to copyright laws.

_____ 6. Software:
   a. is open copyrighted.
   b. gives instructions to the hardware.

    c. is often for sale in retail stores.

    d. all of the above.

_____   7. A microcomputer:

    a. is different from a personal computer.

    b. usually weighs over 200 pounds.

    c. costs more than a minicomputer.

    d. none of the above.

_____   8. A good way to learn about the micro for small business is to:

    a. read computer magazines.

    b. talk to people in similar businesses who are using computers.

    c. enroll in a course in microcomputer fundamentals.

    d. all of the above.

_____   9. A computer system:

    a. consists of software and hardware.

    b. is software alone.

    c. requires a CPU and a hard disk drive before it will operate.

    d. is required by the IRS for all retail firms incorporated after 1979, as result of the Berkman-Sterns Act.

_____   10. A video display terminal:

    a. can be almost any color.

    b. is like a TV screen.

    c. can cause eye fatigue.

    d. all of the above.

Short-Answer

1. What's the first step when you're thinking about buying a computer?

_____

2. The 2nd step? _____

3. The 3rd? _____

4. Describe the routine functions of your business that might be handled by a computer. (Hint: invoicing, accounting, mailing list, form letters, etc.)

_____

_____

_____

_____

_____

5. What are the components of a computer system? _____

_____

6. What three computer magazines would be most helpful for your type of business?

    1. _____

    2. _____

    3. _____

7. Name two more ways to keep up with computer developments:

    1. _____

    2. _____

8. Visit a computer store. Tell the salesperson what your business problems are. Ask for suggestions about solutions. What advice are you given?

_____

_____

_____

9. Network your way to several computer consultants. What do they suggest in the way of a system? What is the value of using a consultant? Can they save you money on your system? Summarize their advice. _____

_____

_____

_____

_____

10. List your purchase options.

	Software	Hardware
Costs: Outright Purchase	_____	_____
Lease	_____	_____

11. On a separate sheet of paper, develop a time-line chart for installation or conversion to a micro system that will handle your business tasks. Events might include:
    Education
    Purchase evaluation/shopping
    Testing
    Consulting
    Info/file conversion
    Operator training
    Decision day

12. For comparative purposes, contact two accounting services in your area and find out what they would charge to handle some of your routine tasks. (If you check the *Wall Street Journal,* you'll see ads for free seminars for small business owners by large computerized companies like ADP.)

    Firm 1: _____

    Firm 2: _____

13. List sources in your area for computer education. Start with the yellow pages, under "Computer." You'll find courses at public schools, private colleges, specialized computer training centers, dealer-operated schools, weekend seminars, and so on.

    _____

    _____

    _____

    _____

14. Using your five-year growth plan, describe four or five functions that you would like a computer to perform after you've been in business awhile.

    1. _____

    2. _____

    3. _____

    4. _____

    5. _____

15

Buying a Franchise

Matching

Match each numbered item with the lettered statement that best describes it.

1. franchisee	8. brand name recognition	15. equipment and tenant improvements
2. franchise exposition	9. advertising fee	16. lender's preference
3. franchisor	10. license agreement	17. right of first refusal
4. corporate franchise	11. economies of scale	18. Hallmark Cards
5. royalty	12. uniform quality standard	19. Century 21
6. operating manual	13. voluntary chain	20. Dale Carnegie
7. franchise fee	14. lease and location assistance	

_____ A. owned by franchisor
_____ B. percentage of sales to cover administrative costs and franchisor's profits
_____ C. similar to a Business Plan
_____ D. presold customers
_____ E. percentage of sales to cover promotions
_____ F. the owner of a franchise
_____ G. an international real estate franchise
_____ H. generally less restrictive than a state-approved franchise
_____ I. the organization that is selling franchises
_____ J. a show organized to present franchisors to the public
_____ K. mass purchasing power—sometimes passed on to franchisee
_____ L. a personal development service franchise
_____ M. not a franchise, but a distribution plan
_____ N. usually required of all franchisees
_____ O. Ace Hardware
_____ P. usually supplied to retail franchisees by franchisor
_____ Q. often offered to existing franchise owner on new locations
_____ R. an extra expense usually not included in franchise fee
_____ S. bankers often view franchisee more favorably than they do independent business owners

True/False

Determine whether each statement is true or false and enter a T (True) or F (False) in the space.

_____ 1. Franchisors are independent owners of franchise operations.

_____ 2. Ground-floor opportunities are always ideal for the prospective franchise owner.
_____ 3. Most lenders prefer to lend money to a franchise operator than to a new start up.
_____ 4. Coca-Cola bottlers own franchises.
_____ 5. Service-sector franchises are enjoying a lot of growth.
_____ 6. Auto dealerships are seldom franchises.
_____ 7. Despite their high visibility, franchises play only a minor role in the U.S. economy.
_____ 8. A franchise fee is the same as a royalty fee.
_____ 9. Voluntary chains and franchise operations are identical.
_____ 10. A franchise contract cannot be cancelled except in case of fraud.
_____ 11. The franchisor is more of an entrepreneur than the franchisee.
_____ 12. A franchise generally is a safer venture for a person with few business skills.
_____ 13. Most states have strict laws governing franchises.
_____ 14. Existing franchise owners often have an inside track for purchasing a new franchise near their area.
_____ 15. Franchise owners often feel that they are employees more than independent owners.
_____ 16. All franchise offerings are approved by the Federal Trade Commission before they are offered to the public.
_____ 17. Big firms as well as small independent firms can be franchisees.
_____ 18. It's illegal for the franchisor to buy back a failing franchise.
_____ 19. It's always wise to investigate the track record of the principles behind the franchisor.
_____ 20. A franchise agreement will protect your territory from other franchise owners as well as from owners of similar franchises.

Multiple-Choice

Select the best response for each item and enter the corresponding letter in the space.

_____ 1. The right of first refusal for a new location:
   a. is usually offered to existing franchisees.
   b. is illegal under antitrust laws.
   c. is discouraged because the franchisor usually wants the operators to focus all their time on just one single location.
   d. gives potential new operators an equal opportunity to purchase a new franchise.
_____ 2. Many franchisors:
   a. own some of their outlets themselves.
   b. are true entrepreneurs.
   c. expand with little capital by selling franchises.
   d. all of the above.
_____ 3. A good reason for purchasing a franchise is that:
   a. they have a lower failure rate than most new start-up firms.
   b. they have a recognized name and have cloned their tested ideas.
   c. they offer ongoing supervision and advice to franchisees.
   d. all of the above.
_____ 4. Most franchisees:
   a. have few restrictions on their operations.
   b. do not have to pay a royalty fee.
   c. pay both a royalty fee and an advertising fee.
   d. pay a percentage of net profits to the franchisor.
_____ 5. A franchise and a distributorship differ in that:
   a. a distributor does not pay a royalty fee.
   b. a distributor agreement is usually more complex.
   c. it's more difficult for a distributor to terminate the agreement.
   d. in most states there is no difference.

_____ 6. An example of a voluntary chain is:
  a. Avis Rent A Car.
  b. Holiday Inn.
  c. True Value Hardware.
  d. Volunteers of America.

_____ 7. In the 1980s, the franchise industry demonstrated growth in:
  a. bowling establishments.
  b. fast-food, printing, and service industries.
  c. Mrs. Field's Cookies.
  d. nuclear energy.

_____ 8. A reason for electing not to buy a franchise is that:
  a. a franchise is not a truly independent business.
  b. you might be as successful as an independent and avoid the franchise fee and the royalty payment.
  c. the franchisor guarantees the franchisee profitability.
  d. both a and b.

_____ 9. A successful franchise owner:
  a. is likely to be offered opportunities to purchase additional locations before others are.
  b. can substitute his name in place of the franchisor.
  c. need not heed the instructions of the franchisor.
  d. is exempt from state and federal regulations.

_____ 10. When considering the purchase of a franchise you should:
  a. interview other franchise owners.
  b. review the financial strength of the franchisor.
  c. consult an attorney to examine the contract.
  d. all of the above.

Short-Answer

1. Identify a franchise that you believe is earning a high income on investment:

Type of business _____

Name _____ Address _____

What percentage of maximum capacity do you estimate they are realizing? _____

Estimate of total sales _____

Franchise fee _____

Your estimate of all expenses _____

Your estimate of profits _____
A. List the advantages of owning the franchise.

_____

_____

_____

B. List the disadvantages of owning the franchise.

_____

_____

_____

2. List 5–10 service franchises that are operating in your area.

_____   _____

_____   _____

_____   _____

_____   _____

3. Contrast a franchise, a distributorship, and a voluntary chain.

_____

_____

4. Identify a franchise that has failed and list the reasons it failed.

_____

_____

_____

5. List franchises that you believe are well-suited to absentee ownership.

_____   _____

_____   _____

6. Identify an independently owned business that operates near and competes against a franchise.

Business _____ Address _____

How well is it doing? _____

How could it do better? _____

7. Examine the annual report (10-K) of a franchisor whose stock is publicly traded. What observations can you make?

_____

_____

8. List some types of business that you believe are well-suited for franchising.

_____   _____

_____   _____

_____   _____

16

Pulling the Plan Together

Matching

Match each numbered item with the lettered statement that best describes it.

1. Business Plan
2. executive summary
3. "magic numbers"
4. appendixes
5. cover letter
6. excitement

7. net profit
8. cash-flow section
9. entrepreneur
10. demand
11. selling seats
12. industry overview

13. competitors
14. information business
15. projected balance sheet
16. bad management
17. leasing equipment

_____ A. the reason cited by experts for the failure of most small businesses
_____ B. a fast-growing industry that offers many opportunities for eager entrepreneurs
_____ C. a numerical tool that shows what your business will be worth after a certain period of time if your forecasts are accurate.
_____ D. hungry combatants who are eyeing the same slice of the marketplace pie
_____ E. a smart way to save money at start-up time
_____ F. a long look at an industry, compiled from important dates, breakthroughs, failures, and opportunities
_____ G. a portable blueprint of your business
_____ H. a way of talking about how many units will be sold
_____ I. a brief introduction to your Business Plan that summarizes what your business is and why it will succeed
_____ J. a major source of revenue for airlines, movie theatres, and industrial schools
_____ K. income, cash flow, balance sheet
_____ L. a person who has lots of ideas
_____ M. where you put resumes, photographs, location diagrams, product descriptions, or articles from industry journals
_____ N. allows you to aim the Plan at a specific reader
_____ O. what's left in the kitty after you subtract expenses
_____ P. your banker will probably look here first
_____ Q. your reader's response to your Business Plan

True/False

Determine whether each statement is true or false and enter a T (True) or F (False) in the space.

_____ 1. A Business Plan is your roadmap to riches.
_____ 2. Your Business Plan could be the most important document you've ever prepared.

——— 3. A Business Plan has nothing to do with keeping your entrepreneurial creativity on track.

——— 4. The Business Plan is portable.

——— 5. Good business planning is not hard work.

——— 6. Section I of the business plan is the numbers section.

——— 7. The numbers section includes the income statement, cash flow projections, and projected balance sheet.

——— 8. Sections I and II of the Plan are followed by various appendixes.

——— 9. To aim the Plan to a specific reader, you write a special cover letter.

——— 10. Each time you send the plan to a different reader, all you need to do is pull out your old cover letter and address it to the new reader.

——— 11. The cover letter should be 5,000 words long, minimum.

——— 12. The purpose of writing the cover letter is to open the door gently, to make way for future discussion.

——— 13. The cover letter should not offend the reader by explaining how the money will be repaid. Save money talk for the appendixes.

——— 14. Investors love hot ideas.

——— 15. Percentages and dollar amounts speak more loudly than words; mention numbers whenever you can.

——— 16. You should briefly profile the businesses that compete directly with you.

——— 17. Save your ideas on how you're going to ace the competition for the appendixes.

——— 18. Since a lot of consideration should be given to pricing, you might start with what your TC sees as a good value.

——— 19. The great thing about a location is that it's so tangible.

——— 20. Almost every study you read on small business failure puts the blame on bad management.

——— 21. Job descriptions will help you control the people who work for you.

——— 22. With the income statement, the main figure you are seeking is gross sales.

——— 23. Doing a cash flow projection once a year, with a casual six-month update, is all that's required for most small firms.

——— 24. With a projected balance sheet, you're trying to predict, on paper, what your business will be worth at the end of a certain period of time.

——— 25. Section I gets readers interested in the Plan; Section II is where you hook them.

Multiple-Choice

Select the best response for each item and enter the corresponding letter in the space.

——— 1. When you are in business, a Business Plan can:
   a. keep your creativity on track.
   b. keep your power grooved.
   c. both a and b.
   d. none of the above.

——— 2. When doing your Plan, you will probably:
   a. work hard.
   b. stay up late and lose some sleep.
   c. save time in the end.
   d. all of the above.

——— 3. Section I includes all but which of the following?
   a. assessments of the competition.
   b. bids from contractors.
   c. profiles of target customers.
   d. a look at your team.

——— 4. Section II should include all but which of the following?
   a. management resumes.
   b. balance sheet.
   c. cash flow projection.
   d. income statements.

_____ 5. Appendixes to your Plan could include all but which of the following?
  a. detailed resumes.
  b. personal financial statements.
  c. a design of your marketing plan.
  d. bids from contractors.

_____ 6. The cover letter should:
  a. glorify your management team.
  b. tell your reader why you're sending the Plan.
  c. describe your TC with demographics and psychographics.
  d. explain, in a minimum of 5,000 words, how you're going to disarm the competition.

_____ 7. In describing your business, you:
  a. need to excite your reader about the business.
  b. could include photographs of equipment and location in an appendix.
  c. could refer to another appendix providing diagrams that show traffic flow, parking, access, transportation lines, and so on.
  d. all of the above.

_____ 8. The target market for the Software School was:
  a. the world.
  b. bounded on the south by San Clemente, on the north by Long Beach, La Habra, and Brea.
  c. too soft to profile.
  d. diagrammed in detail by several movie studios who paid the school $2 million for rights to film a $40 million Compu-Kids movie in late 1983.

_____ 9. The primary target customer for the Software School was:
  a. female, age 13–17, subscriber to _Seventeen_ magazine.
  b. male, 55–67, poker player, resident of Leisure World.
  c. female, 22–54, $27,000 income, metro-suburban residence, married 73%, two children under 18 living at home, subscriber to _McCall's_ magazine.
  d. small business, 1–30 employees, sales from $250,000 to $5 million, with a major output of paper.

_____ 10. When assessing your competition, you should look into all but which of the following?
  a. strengths.
  b. weaknesses.
  c. key employees.
  d. their private company books.

Short-Answer

1. Write two cover letters for your Business Plan. Letter A should be addressed to your banker or another prospective lender. Letter B should be addressed to a person you'd like to have on your team—one of your key members. Use the following to prepare your letters.

Letter A

Name: _____

Position: _____

Address: _____

Goal for writing: _____

Some items you must include: 1. _____

2. _____

3. _____

Letter B

Name: _____

Position: _____

Address: _____

Goal for writing: _____

Some items you must include: 1. _____

2. _____

3. _____

2. Now turn loose your creativity. In this space, develop an outline or mind map that you can turn into a paragraph or two describing your business. You want to excite your reader. Cover the following: What business you're in; description of product/service; what's unique about your business; what industry you're in. Whenever you can, use dollars or percentages to base your dream on reality.

3. Now put your marketing data into a free-flow description of your market and your target customer. Use the following categories to organize your thoughts.

Industry Overview. _____

_____

_____

_____

Target Market. _____

_____

_____

Target Customer (Primary). _____

_____

Target Customer (Secondary). _____

_____

4. List your major competitors and describe their strengths and weaknesses.

Competitor A

Strengths: _____

Weaknesses: _____

Competitor B

Strengths: _____

Weaknesses: _____

Competitor C

Strengths: _____

Weaknesses: _____

Competitor D

Strengths: _____

Weaknesses: _____

Competitor E

Strengths: _____

Weaknesses: _____

5. Develop your "attack plan" here. What techniques will you use to get the best, most cost-effective response from your market? How do you plan to disarm your competitors?

_____

_____

_____

_____

_____

_____

6. Write a brief summary of why you picked your location. In your reader's mind, build the picture of the perfect location, the site that cannot fail.

_____

_____

_____

_____

_____

Now list all the benefits of this location to target customers.

_____

_____

_____

7. Let's hear it for your management team! List the members in order of their importance to the business. For each member, note experience, accomplishments, education, training, flexibility, imagination, tenacity, and finally, what they can do to help make your business a winner.

Team Member A: _____

_____

_____

_____

Team Member B: _____

_____

_____

_____

Team Member C: _____

_____

_____

_____

Team Member D: _____

_____

_____

_____

8. Now that your management team is in place, list the other types of personnel you'll need. Cover the topics listed here.

Skills: _____

_____

_____

Pay: _____

_____

_____

Training

    Kind: _____

    Length: _____

Fringe Benefits: _____

_____

_____

_____

Overtime: _____

_____

_____

Answers

1 Doorways to Small Business

Matching

A. 5	D. 10	G. 6	J. 3
B. 8	E. 9	H. 2	
C. 1	F. 4	I. 7	

True/False

1. F	7. T	13. F	19. F
2. T	8. F	14. F	20. T
3. T	9. T	15. F	21. F
4. T	10. T	16. F	22. T
5. F	11. T	17. T	23. T
6. F	12. F	18. T	

Multiple-Choice

1. C	4. A	7. A	10. D
2. D	5. D	8. D	11. A
3. D	6. C	9. B	

2 The Big Picture — Charting Trends for Your Small Business

Matching

A. 9	F. 18	K. 4	P. 9
B. 10	G. 17	L. 5	Q. 2
C. 13	H. 14	M. 6	R. 11
D. 15	I. 1	N. 8	S. 19
E. 16	J. 3	O. 7	T. 20

True/False

1. T	6. T	11. T	16. F
2. F	7. T	12. T	17. F
3. F	8. T	13. F	18. F
4. F	9. F	14. T	19. F
5. F	10. F	15. T	20. T

Multiple-Choice

1. C	4. C	7. B	9. D
2. B	5. C	8. C	10. A
3. A	6. B		

3 Power Marketing

Matching

A. 18	F. 15	K. 1	P. 6
B. 16	G. 14	L. 3	Q. 13
C. 7	H. 12	M. 2	R. 11
D. 5	I. 10	N. 4	S. 19
E. 17	J. 9	O. 8	T. 20

True/False

1. T	6. F	11. T	16. T
2. F	7. T	12. T	17. T
3. T	8. F	13. F	18. T
4. F	9. T	14. T	19. T
5. T	10. F	15. T	20. T

Multiple-Choice

1. C	4. B	7. C	9. B
2. D	5. D	8. D	10. C
3. B	6. B		

4 Profiling the Target Customer

Matching

A. 11	F. 12	K. 9	P. 8
B. 10	G. 1	L. 4	Q. 14
C. 16	H. 17	M. 6	R. 18
D. 15	I. 2	N. 7	S. 19
E. 13	J. 3	O. 5	T. 20

True/False

1. F	6. T	11. T	16. T
2. F	7. T	12. F	17. T
3. T	8. F	13. T	18. T
4. T	9. T	14. T	19. F
5. F	10. T	15. F	20. T

Multiple-Choice

1. C	4. A	7. C	9. D
2. C	5. D	8. D	10. B
3. B	6. B		

5 Reading the Competition

Matching

A. 18	F. 1	K. 13	P. 2
B. 11	G. 9	L. 8	Q. 19
C. 16	H. 14	M. 10	R. 5
D. 20	I. 15	N. 7	S. 6
E. 17	J. 12	O. 3	T. 4

True/False

1. F	6. F	11. T	16. T
2. F	7. F	12. T	17. T
3. T	8. T	13. T	18. F
4. F	9. T	14. T	19. T
5. F	10. F	15. T	20. F

Multiple-Choice

1. C	4. D	7. C	9. C
2. D	5. D	8. B	10. C
3. D	6. A		

6 Promotion: Connecting with the Customer

Matching

A. 4	E. 3	I. 14	M. 12
B. 5	F. 2	J. 13	N. 11
C. 1	G. 7	K. 8	O. 10
D. 6	H. 15	L. 9	

True/False

1. T	5. T	9. F	13. T
2. T	6. T	10. T	14. F
3. T	7. T	11. T	15. T
4. T	8. F	12. T	16. F

Multiple-Choice

1. D	4. B	7. D	9. A
2. C	5. D	8. D	10. D
3. A	6. A		

7 Location

Matching

A. 2	F. 11	K. 7	O. 14
B. 1	G. 9	L. 17	P. 12
C. 6	H. 5	M. 13	Q. 15
D. 8	I. 3	N. 16	R. 18
E. 10	J. 4		

True/False

1. T	6. T	11. F	16. T
2. T	7. F	12. T	17. F
3. T	8. T	13. T	18. F
4. T	9. T	14. F	19. T
5. F	10. F	15. F	20. T

Multiple-Choice

1. A	4. D	7. C	9. C
2. B	5. C	8. B	10. B
3. C	6. A		

8 Surprises You Can't Afford

Matching

A. 2	F. 6	J. 9	N. 12
B. 1	G. 8	K. 16	O. 14
C. 3	H. 7	L. 15	P. 11
D. 4	I. 10	M. 13	Q. 17
E. 5			

True/False

1. F	5. T	9. T	13. T
2. F	6. T	10. T	14. F
3. F	7. T	11. F	15. F
4. T	8. T	12. F	16. T

Multiple-Choice

1. A	4. C	7. D	9. D
2. D	5. A	8. D	10. B
3. B	6. D		

9 Numbers and Shoebox Accounting

Matching

A. 11	D. 10	G. 2	J. 7
B. 9	E. 4	H. 5	K. 8
C. 6	F. 1	I. 3	

True/False

1. T	6. F	11. T	16. F
2. T	7. T	12. T	17. T
3. T	8. F	13. T	18. F
4. T	9. T	14. T	19. T
5. F	10. T	15. T	20. F

Multiple-Choice

1. C	4. D	7. A	9. D
2. B	5. A	8. D	10. B
3. A	6. B		

10 Buying a Business

Matching

A. 16	E. 9	I. 12	M. 2
B. 6	F. 7	J. 14	N. 3
C. 10	G. 11	K. 15	O. 4
D. 8	H. 13	L. 1	P. 5

True/False

1. T	6. F	11. T	15. T
2. F	7. T	12. F	16. T
3. T	8. F	13. T	17. T
4. T	9. F	14. T	18. T
5. F	10. T		

Multiple-Choice

1. C	4. B	7. B	9. A
2. D	5. D	8. B	10. D
3. B	6. C		

11 Shaking the Money Tree

Matching

A. 9	F. 7	K. 17	P. 10
B. 2	G. 5	L. 3	Q. 16
C. 14	H. 8	M. 12	R. 20
D. 15	I. 13	N. 1	S. 18
E. 6	J. 4	O. 11	T. 19

True/False

1. T	6. F	11. T	16. F
2. F	7. T	12. T	17. T
3. T	8. T	13. F	18. T
4. T	9. F	14. T	19. T
5. T	10. T	15. F	20. F

Multiple-Choice

1. D	4. C	7. B	9. C
2. B	5. D	8. D	10. C
3. A	6. A		

12 Legal Concerns

Matching

A. 8	F. 3	J. 13	N. 9
B. 7	G. 2	K. 12	O. 16
C. 6	H. 1	L. 11	P. 17
D. 5	I. 14	M. 10	Q. 15
E. 4			

True/False

1. T	5. F	9. F	13. T
2. F	6. F	10. T	14. T
3. F	7. T	11. T	15. T
4. F	8. F	12. T	16. F

Multiple-Choice

1. C	4. A	7. B	9. D
2. D	5. D	8. A	10. B
3. B	6. C		

13 Building a Winning Team

Matching

A. 15	E. 11	I. 3	M. 9
B. 12	F. 5	J. 4	N. 7
C. 1	G. 14	K. 6	O. 13
D. 2	H. 8	L. 10	

True/False

1. F	6. T	10. T	14. T
2. T	7. F	11. T	15. T
3. T	8. F	12. T	16. T
4. F	9. T	13. F	17. T
5. F			

Multiple-Choice

1. B	4. A	7. B	9. A
2. D	5. D	8. C	10. C
3. C	6. B		

14 The Entrepreneur's Toolkit

Matching

A. 3	D. 9	G. 5	I. 10
B. 4	E. 8	H. 1	J. 6
C. 7	F. 2		

True/False

1. T	6. F	11. F	16. F
2. F	7. F	12. T	17. F
3. T	8. F	13. F	18. T
4. T	9. F	14. T	19. T
5. F	10. T	15. T	20. T

Multiple-Choice

1. D	4. A	7. D	9. A
2. A	5. B	8. D	10. D
3. D	6. D		

15 Buying a Franchise

Matching

A. 4	F. 1	K. 11	P. 14
B. 7	G. 19	L. 20	Q. 17
C. 6	H. 10	M. 18	R. 15
D. 8	I. 3	N. 12	S. 16
E. 9	J. 2	O. 13	

True/False

1. F	6. F	11. T	16. F
2. F	7. F	12. T	17. T
3. T	8. F	13. T	18. F
4. T	9. F	14. T	19. T
5. T	10. F	15. T	20. F

Multiple-Choice

1. A	4. C	7. B	9. A
2. D	5. A	8. D	10. D
3. D	6. C		

16 Pulling the Plan Together

Matching

A. 16	F. 12	K. 3	P. 8
B. 14	G. 1	L. 9	Q. 6
C. 15	H. 10	M. 4	
D. 13	I. 2	N. 5	
E. 17	J. 11	O. 7	

True/False

1. T	8. T	15. T	22. F
2. T	9. T	16. T	23. F
3. T	10. F	17. F	24. T
4. T	11. F	18. T	25. T
5. F	12. T	19. T	
6. F	13. F	20. T	
7. T	14. T	21. T	

Multiple-Choice

1. C	4. A	7. D	9. D
2. D	5. C	8. B	10. D
3. B	6. B		